The Great
Ormond Street
Book of
Baby and
Child Care

The Great Ormond Street

Book of

Baby and Child Care

TESSA HILTON
with Maire Messenger

THE BODLEY HEAD
LONDON

First published 1991
Reprinted 1991
© Institute of Child Health, London, 1991
The Bodley Head, 20 Vauxhall Bridge Road, London, SW1V 2SA

A CIP catalogue record for this book is
available from the British Library

ISBN 0-370-30604-X

Printed and bound in
The United States of America for
The Bodley Head

Designed by Judy Linard

CONTENTS

Note to parents x
Foreword xi
Acknowledgments xiii

1 BEFORE PREGNANCY BEGINS 1

Why does preconceptual care matter? 2   Environmental factors 3
Genetic factors 10   Genetic counselling 18

2 PREGNANCY 23

A new life begins 23   Fertility 27
How can you tell if you are pregnant? 29   Decisions, decisions 31
The novice's guide to antenatal care 37
Other tests during pregnancy 40   Eating sensibly and weight gain 45
Avoid X-rays in early pregnancy 46   Minor physical problems 47
More serious problems in pregnancy 52
Pregnancies needing the five-star treatment 59
Mixed emotions – how you feel during pregnancy 65
Shopping for the baby 71   Towards the end of pregnancy 78

3 LABOUR AND DELIVERY 81

The start of labour 81   What happens in labour? 84
Birth – what will it be like? 87   The role of the father 89
The question of pain relief 90
A checklist that will help you to a better birth 98
Checking on you and your baby during labour 100
The first moments of life 103
Medical interventions – and why they may be needed 105
Problems in labour and delivery 113   Stillbirth 120

4   YOUR NEW BABY 125

First reactions 125   Fathers 133   Initial impressions 134
What is the world like for your baby? 135
Minor problems after delivery 137
More serious problems after delivery 138
Your baby's first check-up 140   Tests and immunisations 150
Looking after your new baby 150
After the birth – you and your new baby 165

5   BABIES NEEDING SPECIAL CARE 175

How much special care? 175   Babies needing surgery 177
Small babies 177
Babies in special care – what it means for the family 181
The problems of babies in special care 184
The future for special care babies 196
Parents' reactions to premature births 197
Babies who may not live 199
Cot death (Sudden Infant Death Syndrome) 200

6   FEEDING YOUR BABY 203

The big decision – breast or bottle? 203
Home truths about breast and bottle-feeding 207
Women who are not able to breastfeed 208
Women who do not want to breastfeed 210
Breasts and breastfeeding 211   Expressing and storing milk 219
Going back to work 222   Breastfeeding problems for mothers 223
Giving up breastfeeding 227   Breastfeeding problems for babies 227
Bottles and bottle-feeding 229   Vitamin supplements 239
Feeding second and subsequent babies 241
Problems with early feeding 242   Weaning 245   Eating out 252
Food intolerance 252

7   FEEDING THE UNDER-FIVES 257

What is a balanced diet? 257   Good eating habits – lessons for life 261
Tips for feeding a young family 262
Good meals don't have to be a chore 263   Drinks 265   Sweets 265

Family eating habits 266   Eating problems 268   Fat children 272
Behaviour problems and food intolerance 275

8   SLEEP, WAKEFULNESS AND CRYING 279

'Is he a good baby?' 279   What is sleep and why do we need it? 280
A bed for a baby 284   A book at bedtime 289
Sleep problems 291   Crying in young babies 299
Babies who won't stop crying 300   Nearing the end of your tether 306

9   GROWING AND MOVING 309

How your baby grows 309   Measuring growth 312
Growth in the toddler and pre-school child 315
Feeding and growth 317   Movement 318
How your child learns to move 320   Boys and girls 327

10   THE SENSES 331

Your baby's eyesight 331   Hearing 339   Touch 345
Taste and smell 350

11   LANGUAGE 353

What is language? 354   How language develops 354
Stages of development 355   First communications 358
First words 361   Talking with your child 364
Stories, books and television 367   Reading and writing 371
Early language problems 374

12   PLAY AND EARLY EDUCATION 379

Different types of play 379
How parents can help children have richer play experiences 380
Play stages 383   Organising play 391
The importance of messy play 393   More than one child 398
Routine 399   Making friends 400
Play for sick children 400   Playgroups and nurseries 403   Schools 410

13   TOILET TRAINING 415

Body waste 415
How do you know when your child is ready to start
toilet training? 416   Early setbacks in toilet training 419
Potty or lavatory? 419   Common problems with toilet training 420
Illness and infection 424

14   RELATIONSHIPS 429

Your baby 429   How your baby learns 430
You and your baby 435   Separation 437
Leaving your baby 438   Your baby and other people 441
Social problems 453   Aggression 454   Sharing 456
Good behaviour 457   Fears 461
Going back to work – who minds the baby? 462
Communicating with children 469 – marriage difficulties, separation and
divorce, death, illness and handicap, religion, sex

15   PROTECTING YOUR CHILD 477

Safety 477
Parents' check-list – how to protect your child
from accidents 480
Emergency first aid 496   Hygiene 504

16   DOCTORS AND MEDICINES 511

Doctors 511 – choosing a GP, changing GPs, how to get the best from
your GP, referrals, when to call the doctor
Medicines 522 – your attitude to drugs, giving medicines, taking the
medicine, antibiotics, allergic reactions, the pharmacist, over-the-counter
medicines, immunisation   Health visitors and health clinics 531 –
developmental check-ups
Your child's teeth 534 – teething, looking after teeth, food for healthy
teeth, going to the dentist

17   COMMON HEALTH PROBLEMS 541

Raised temperature and fever 542
Infectious diseases causing fever 547 – chicken-pox, *rubella*, measles,
mumps, scarlet fever, whooping cough
Colds, coughs and sore throats 550
Tonsils, tonsillitis and adenoids 554   Croup 555
Skin problems 557   Stings and bites 562   Parasites 563
Mouth problems 567   Ear problems 568   Eye problems 573

Urinary and kidney infections 578
The gut and its problems 580   Minor orthopaedic problems 583
The clumsy child 585

18   SERIOUS ILLNESS AND TREATABLE CONGENITAL DEFECTS 589

Asthma 589   Eczema 595   Epilepsy 600
Serious infectious illnesses 605 – tetanus, poliomyelitis, diphtheria,
meningitis and encephalitis   Kidney (renal) problems 607
Jaundice 608   Haemophilia 609
Childhood cancer including leukaemia 610
Sickle cell disease 612   Thalassaemia 614   Short stature 614
Diabetes 615   Cystic fibrosis 619   Coeliac disease 621
Heart problems 621   AIDS 626   Cleft lip and palate 627
Genital problems 629

19   HANDICAP 631

Handicap 631 – why do handicaps happen?, types of handicap,
how are handicaps discovered?, living with handicap
Deafness and other severe hearing problems 635
Visual impairment 638   Cerebral palsy 639
Spina bifida 641   Muscular dystrophy 643
Severe learning difficulties 645 – mental handicap,
Down's syndrome, autism

20   CHILDREN IN HOSPITAL 653

Preparing children for a hospital stay 654   Operations 658
Who's who in hospital 661   Common hospital procedures 663
Staying or visiting? 663   Breastfed babies 667
How parents can help 667   Looking after yourself 671
Coming home 672

Addresses 673
Index 677

NOTE TO PARENTS

We have used the masculine form throughout the book rather than the feminine as the latter seemed just as discriminatory and to be a rather superficial way of making a point about a subject which is in fact profoundly important. The equal solution – a fifty-fifty split between 'he' and 'she' – is only confusing and we hope readers will agree that the big issues about sexual equality will not be resolved by hair-splitting over conventions.

FOREWORD

This is a book for the parents of babies and young children under five. It aims to help them bring up their children to be as happy, as intelligent and as healthy as possible.

There are many books about child upbringing already available for parents. Why is this book different? The explanation lies in where the book comes from and how it is written.

Great Ormond Street Children's Hospital is one of the most famous children's hospitals in the world. The Institute of Child Health, which is linked to the hospital, carries out more research into children's health and illness within its walls than anywhere else in the United Kingdom. Its staff are experts on the causes and treatment of all the problems encountered by young children, and on how to encourage normal healthy growth, both physical and mental. The hospital itself mainly sees children with unusual conditions, but many of its staff also work at the linked Queen Elizabeth Hospital, Hackney Road, where children are seen with a whole range of common illnesses and difficulties in development.

Parents want guidance on how they can best care for their children in day-to-day life during their first five years. All this the book provides. However, they are also naturally worried by common problems such as early feeding difficulties, slowness in speech, bed-wetting, skin rashes and a host of others besides, and sometimes by more serious illness. They want, and deserve, the very best advice on how to prevent these happening, and how to deal with them if they do occur, as sometimes, even with the best of parents, they inevitably do. The senior doctors at Great Ormond Street are all experts with international reputations, as are many of the non-medical staff. This book draws on their expertise and has the backing of their authority. If they don't know the answer to a question (and sometimes in this book there is an honest admission that this is the case), then probably there is no one in the world who knows the answer either.

How was the book written? Hospital and Institute staff worked with two journalists, both experienced in writing for parents of young children, first to produce an outline and then a detailed text. Doctors, nurses, psychologists, speech therapists, dieticians, playleaders and many others discussed their particular field of interest with the authors, and then carefully checked, commented on or rewrote the drafts that were produced. This method of working has resulted in a book which is both authoritative and readable.

Hospital staff working with sick children like to think they can also be helpful in the prevention of disease as well as encouraging normal growth. It may not be possible yet to create a world in which all the children's hospitals are empty and the child guidance clinics are closed for lack of customers, but this book represents at least a small step in this direction.

CAROLINE BOND
Chairman,
Hospital for Sick Children,
Great Ormond Street

ACKNOWLEDGMENTS

The publishers would like to thank the following for permission to reproduce illustrations and photographs: Jane Bottomley, pp. 418, 440, 478, 494, 544, 556, 559, 562, 604; British Deaf Association, p. 637; Bubbles, pp. 308, 381, 422, 448, 467; Lupe Cunha, pp. xiv, 7, 35, 42, 72, 77, 169, 249, 251, 260, 267, 287, 290, 298, 328, 352, 369, 376, 394, 401, 406, 409, 428, 436, 464, 476, 493, 506, 510, 514, 528, 532, 535, 540, 592, 648, 656; Department of Medical Illustration, Institute of Child Health, 569, 576, 588, 640, 652, 660, 664, 670; Format Partners Photo Library, p. 390; Greg Holmes, p. 111; Linda Jeffrey, pp. 91, 320, 321, 322, 323, 324, 325, 335, 337, 361, 365, 372, 373, 383, 384, 385, 386, 387, 388, 389, 392, 503, 525, 565, 594; Camilla Jessel, pp. 22, 80, 124, 149, 202, 231; Sandra Lousada/Susan Griggs Agency Limited, pp. 129, 174, 256, 278, 341, 348, 414, 433; Danny McKenzie, pp. 270, 283, 334, 420, 441, 452, 455, 496, 586, 597, 618; Coral Mula, pp. 12 (below), 14, 15, 16, 17, 24 (above and below), 25, 26, 27, 28, 47, 48, 50, 54, 55, 61, 64, 85, 86, 102, 109, 112, 116, 117, 118 (above and below), 119, 140, 144, 152, 153, 157, 158, 159, 160, 161, 162, 163, 185, 211, 214, 219, 220, 221, 224, 225, 226, 233, 235, 236, 237, 238, 264, 302, 304, 482, 486, 487, 500, 551, 573; Gillian Oliver, pp. 93, 190, 191, 192, 194, 281, 554, 570, 572, 584, 607, 620, 623, 624; ASBAH, 630; Professor Marcus E. Pembrey, pp. 11, 12 (above) both reproduced first in J. A. Fraser Roberts and Marcus E. Pembrey, *An Introduction to Medical Genetics* (Oxford University Press, 1940); Anthea Sieveking/Collections, pp. 104, 132, 139, 240, 313, 330, 333, 378, 485, 488.

They would also like to thank Dr Karen E. Morton, MA, MRCP, MRCOG, for advice on chapters 2 and 3; Egnell Ameda Limited for permission to reproduce the breast pump on p. 221; and Tesco and Brent Cross Shopping Centre for permission to use their premises for the photographs on pp. 260 and 648.

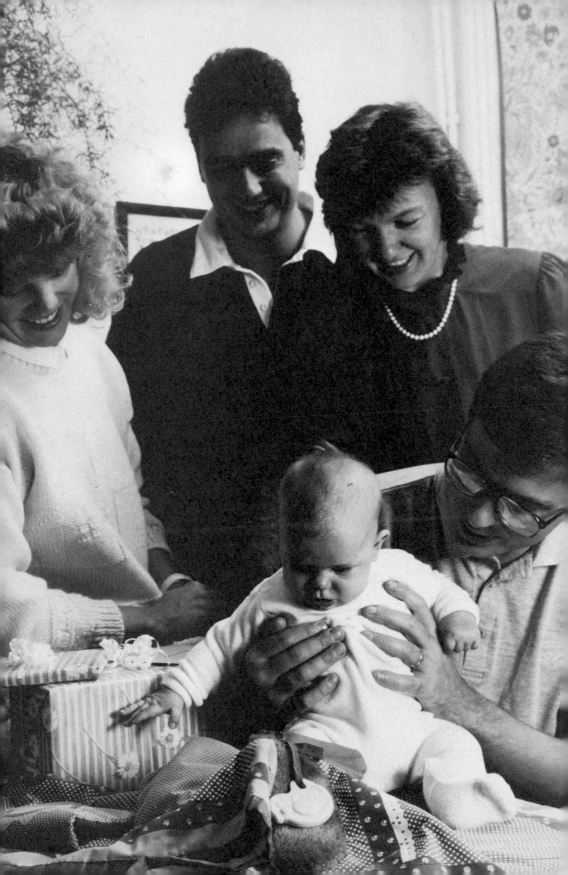

Chapter 1

BEFORE PREGNANCY BEGINS

Why does preconceptual care matter? **Environmental factors**
Genetic factors **Genetic counselling**

Health is the best birthday present any parent could ask for their new baby. No wonder from time immemorial the first question at the moment of birth, asked in a look, a touch, or in words, has always been: 'Is my baby all right?' Most people know that good health begins before birth and that looking after mothers and their unborn babies during pregnancy is very important. But did you know that good health care can begin even before conception? It may seem strange to think that both men and women can help to give their baby a healthier start in life, even before life begins for their baby, but it is true.

A couple planning and looking forward to starting a family slowly begin to see the world around them in a different way. Pregnant women, babies in pushchairs and even advertisements for products like nappies and prams, which have been a hitherto unnoticed backdrop to a child-free life, suddenly come sharply into focus. But while the reality of a baby is still a day-dream, a young couple's thoughts tend to turn inwards and dwell most on how life will change for them. Women think about how pregnancy will change their bodies, and what the birth will be like. Both men and women wonder how becoming parents may change their relationships and way of life. It takes an effort of mind as well as the right supply of information to realise that how you live and look after your body now can matter to this child who exists only in your imagination. If you are reading this book before pregnancy has begun, you have an extra opportunity to try to stack the odds in favour of a head start in health for your future family.

Preconceptual care means both partners cutting known risks before trying to conceive, to make it as likely as possible that the egg and sperm which will grow into an embryo are healthy and normal, and also to create the best environment for that embryo to grow and develop into a fit baby.

WHY DOES PRECONCEPTUAL
CARE MATTER?

Your baby's first twelve weeks of life in the uterus, or womb, are the most critical in many respects. During this time all the essential organs are being formed and by three months most are beginning to work. However, the majority of women do not even suspect they are pregnant until they miss a period, and even if they are very prompt in going to their GP and having their pregnancy confirmed they are unlikely to have their first antenatal appointment much before they are eight or nine weeks pregnant – and often much later than that.

If this seems a worrying thought take comfort in the fact that the vast majority of babies develop and grow safely and healthily. But what doctors have now discovered is that there are easy measures every couple can take which will reduce risks even further. The idea of trying to minimise risks to a baby even before he is conceived is relatively new, but it makes sense to avoid environmental factors which we now know can pose a hazard to the unborn baby and to follow simple guidelines which we know to be beneficial.

That is not to say that every unborn baby who is exposed to such factors will be damaged in some way. Like adults, some unborn babies are more susceptible or more vulnerable at certain times and in certain ways than others. There are babies who seem to have incurred only slight risks before birth yet, for reasons which may not be fully known, have sadly suffered some degree of damage. And there are babies who have been exposed to very many risks, sometimes considered serious, who have been born perfectly normal and healthy. In between babies born with a specific abnormality and babies born free of such damage there is a wide spectrum of varying shades of grey in terms of fitness and health. A baby who weighs less than 2,500 grams (5½ lbs) at birth is classified as having a low birth-weight. These small babies are more vulnerable in the early weeks and months of life and can take time to catch up with larger babies. We know that some environmental factors can often combine to prevent babies growing properly in the uterus, and that some of these factors can be avoided.

Because there is no way of telling in advance which babies are likely to be vulnerable, it makes sense for all prospective parents to try to avoid risks within their control. Preconceptual care means weighting the odds in favour of a baby who is able to realise his full mental and physical genetic potential. If you plan to have a baby here are some simple steps you can take towards helping your child, even before you try to conceive. Six months ahead of conception is not too soon to start thinking about your health, but certainly try to consider these points three months before you hope to get pregnant.

ENVIRONMENTAL FACTORS

USE BARRIER METHODS OF CONTRACEPTION FOR THREE MONTHS BEFORE

There has never been any suggestion that taking the Pill increases the risk of miscarriage or the possibility of any birth defects in later pregnancies. However, because it takes time for the effects of the Pill to disappear fully from a woman's system and for her normal hormonal pattern to re-establish itself, most doctors advise coming off the Pill three months before trying for a baby and using a barrier method of contraception instead – that is, a sheath or diaphragm.

What is the risk to a baby if the woman accidentally becomes pregnant and continues taking the Pill during pregnancy? The good news is that most recent studies – and several of them have been large – have not found any link between taking the Pill during pregnancy and birth defects in general or heart defects in particular.

Women who become pregnant accidentally when they have an intra-uterine device (IUD) fitted are 40% more likely to miscarry, but such pregnancies as do continue appear to have just as good a chance of a normal outcome as any other. Pregnancy when an IUD is in place, however, carries a greater risk that it may be ectopic – that is to say the fertilised egg implants in some place other than the uterus, usually a Fallopian tube. However, as long as the pregnancy is in the right place, it is generally thought better to remove the coil early in pregnancy and risk miscarriage, rather than leave it in the uterus.

The effect of taking the morning-after Pill if the pregnancy subsequently continues is not yet fully known because most women who try this go on to have a termination anyway if the Pill does not work. Most studies suggest that the baby has a good chance of remaining unharmed, however.

Women who become pregnant accidentally may naturally worry more about risks they have unknowingly incurred and feel guilty, and they may also feel very ambivalent about changing their lifestyle for the sake of their unplanned baby's health. They need extra support and an opportunity to talk about their feelings. Their GP is well placed to offer this, although much depends on his or her relationship with the woman, and community midwives, antenatal clinic staff or friends can also be helpful. For more on mixed feelings during pregnancy see page 65.

STOP SMOKING

'I tried many times to give up smoking and actually stopped once or twice, but I felt it was really a positive reason to give up when we decided to have a baby. I carried a mental picture of a tiny foetus shrivelling up in a smoke-filled womb – I know that sounds a bit morbid but it did the trick.'

It is now well documented that smoking can stop babies growing properly in the uterus, so that they are likely to be smaller and more vulnerable when they are born. Because it cuts the amount of oxygen that is being supplied to the baby through the placenta, it also puts the baby at risk before birth.

Giving up smoking, however, is very difficult because nicotine is highly addictive and if you are a confirmed smoker you will need a lot of help and support. It is important that your partner gives up as well: partly because it is unreasonable to expect you to try to give up alone, which will make it twice as hard for you, and partly because you can inhale a lot of nicotine just by sitting in a smoky atmosphere. Even women who do not smoke should avoid spending much time in places where people are smoking. Smoking may also make some men less fertile by affecting the numbers and mobility of their sperm.

Do not wait until you know you are pregnant before trying to give up smoking – your baby will already have spent his most vulnerable weeks suffering the effects. It also takes a few weeks, depending on how heavily you smoke, for the effect to clear from your system. If you or your partner feel unsure about making such an effort for a baby who does not exist yet, it may help to remember you are doing something which will be for your own benefit as well. Much literature is available on the subject from the Health Education Council or Action on Smoking and Health (ASH, see address section, pages 673–6) or your GP may be interested in trying to help you. Some people have found hypnosis or acupuncture helpful.

CUT DOWN ON DRINKING

It used to be thought that only heavy drinking could harm unborn babies, but research has now shown that even moderate drinking makes women more likely to miscarry and give birth to smaller, more vulnerable babies. These low birthweight babies can continue to be disadvantaged for some time. One study of babies born to moderate drinkers showed that when eight months old the babies were still smaller and less developmentally and physically advanced than a similar age group whose mothers did not drink at all.

What is moderate drinking? Research has talked of two drinks a day, meaning two glasses of wine or two pub measures of spirits. Six or more drinks a day puts the baby at risk of 'foetal alcohol syndrome'. These children are seriously damaged before birth and have abnormal and distinctive facial characteristics. They fail to thrive and can be delayed in their development. In addition, they have abnormal nails and can have heart defects. The best advice is to stop drinking alcohol, altogether if you can, before you try to become pregnant. As with all hazards, the baby is most vulnerable in the early days and weeks of life before you even know you are pregnant. If you find this hard, your partner should support you and give up too. If he drinks heavily this could make him infertile – one estimate was that three to four pints of beer a day could be enough to reduce the sperm count of some men to infertility level. Fertility should return after a few weeks of not drinking.

Women sometimes worry if they have been on a binge and drunk very heavily when they did not know they were pregnant. Unfortunately, as with many risks, there is no way of knowing if the unborn baby has been affected, although the great majority of babies will not have been.

EAT WELL

Eating a good, balanced diet with fresh food and not too much junk is probably even more important before conceiving than during pregnancy. This is because the unborn baby is most vulnerable in the first three months while the organs are still being formed. It is in these first fragile days and weeks of life, when many women do not even know they are pregnant, that nutritional reserves of vitamins and minerals probably matter most. Later, in the middle and last months of pregnancy, the unborn baby is able to become a far more effective parasite: the foetus will take what he needs from the mother, even if it is at her expense. So although, of course, a woman is better off if she is not on a poor diet or ill, the baby will usually still take what he needs to grow and thrive. Exceptions may be babies who are already vulnerable because of other factors, so all women should try to eat well during pregnancy.

What does eating well mean? In recent years we have been bombarded with theories about the best possible diet, but the basic rules are really very simple:

* Balance your diet by eating something from the five main food groups every day. These groups are milk and milk products; meat and high-protein foods; fruit and vegetables; cereal and grain products; and fats and oils.

* Eat fresh foods where possible, rather than prepackaged or convenience foods, and cut down on sugary foods.

* Follow your appetite and do not eat more than you need. For more discussion about weight gain see page 45.

With the exception of iron and possibly folic acid (see page 46), it is not usually necessary to take any extra vitamins or mineral supplements unless supervised by your doctor. It is sensible to avoid certain foods because of the risk of salmonella or listeria (see page 46).

Vegetarian and vegan diets Growing a baby takes a lot of protein. If you eat eggs, fish and cheese, you can easily take in as much as you need. But vegans, who avoid these foods as well as cutting out meat, need to take special care. If you do not take milk or milk products, then substitute soya milk and foods. Eat a good supply of nuts, pulses and seeds daily to supply protein. Vitamin B12 is found almost entirely in animal foods so take the advice of your doctor and nutritionist or specialist society (see address section, pages 673–6) about supplements.

DO NOT DIET BEFORE PREGNANCY

Do not go on any kind of diet in the three months before trying to become pregnant or during pregnancy, unless on medical advice. Fertility declines as women lose weight and it has been found that some women become infertile at weights we used to think ideal. Studies also suggest that the babies of women who are very underweight before conception are possibly more at risk. With any kind of restrictive diet there is a danger of missing out on some nutrients because such diets are not balanced, but rely on excluding complete food groups entirely. At the other end of the scale, obesity can also lead to infertility – so if you have a weight problem, see your doctor to try to sort it out well before you begin to think about having children. For more on weight gain and pregnancy see page 45.

THINK ABOUT POLLUTANTS

If you work with any kind of chemicals find out what they are before getting pregnant – you can ask your doctor's or possibly your trade union representative's advice. We still do not know a great deal about the unborn baby's vulnerability to many environmental factors, though studies suggest that people working with anaesthetic gases, or indeed the wives of men working with them, may run a higher risk of miscarriage and possibly even some birth defect. There has also been concern about the safety of working with VDUs (visual display units) during pregnancy, but there is no good research showing a higher risk of miscarriage exists from such exposure. More studies obviously need to be done in this field.

SAUNA BATHS AND HOT TUBS

It is possible that prolonged very high body temperatures can affect the early development of the unborn baby, especially the brain. So if regular sauna baths are your habit, give them a miss when you start trying to get pregnant and during the pregnancy. However, there is no suggestion that ordinary hot baths, warm atmosphere, hot weather, low fever or short spikes of high fever can be damaging.

DO NOT TAKE ANY DRUGS WITHOUT MEDICAL SUPERVISION

The safest rule is not to take any drugs at all, whether over the counter, prescribed, or illicit drugs such as cannabis or heroin, either while trying to conceive or during pregnancy. Always tell a doctor who is prescribing drugs for you if there is a chance you may be pregnant. Having said that, there will be some women who need to take drugs to control illness during pregnancy. Those with an existing condition, such as epilepsy, heart disease or diabetes, should always see their doctor before becoming pregnant to discuss how their condition can best be controlled and what drugs to take. It may be a good idea to ask the specialist or GP who normally supervises the control of your illness for a referral to an obstetrician for a consultation before becoming pregnant. Women who

become ill during pregnancy should always make sure whoever is treating them knows they are pregnant or, just as important, that they might be pregnant.

X-RAYS

X-rays are best avoided in the first three months of pregnancy, and radiologists usually ask if there is any possibility of pregnancy. For this reason, many operators avoid giving X-rays in the latter half of a woman's menstrual cycle (see also page 46).

STAY HEALTHY

Of course, we cannot always avoid illness and there is no need to get neurotic about catching the odd cold or cough, but in general it makes sense to avoid contact with infectious disease as far as possible.

German measles is the most dangerous of these, and is dealt with in the following section. However, apart from German measles there are a few other diseases which are known to pose possible risks – cytomegalovirus infection (CMV) is one such. The only symptoms of this virus may be vague aches and pains and possibly fever. It is thought that this virus may infect as many as 1% of unborn babies and of these infected babies about 10% may suffer permanent damage. As with German measles, the effect is likely to be most serious when a pregnant woman catches the disease in the first three months of pregnancy. It can cause various degrees of mental deficiency, blindness and possibly deafness. At the moment there is no preventive vaccine, but research is still under way and there may be one in the future.

A less common risk to the unborn baby is toxoplasmosis – a parasitic infection which causes fever and swollen glands. In this country it is thought that thirty to fifty babies a year are born seriously damaged as a result of their mothers being infected by toxoplasmosis, but in France the problem was serious enough for the government to introduce a compulsory screening programme for all pregnant women. It is thought that this is because the French eat far more undercooked or raw meat, the source of infection. Another source of infection is cats because there is a particularly resistant form of toxoplasma which is peculiar to members of the cat family. Do not throw out the family cat, but it makes sense for a pregnant woman to avoid cleaning out a cat's litter tray; to wear gloves when handling raw meat or gardening; not to eat raw or undercooked meat; to wash fruits well; and to see her doctor if she has enlarged glands, especially those in the neck.

Check you are immune to German measles

'I had two perfectly normal children, but during my third pregnancy I had what my doctor thought was scarlet fever in the early weeks. My daughter was born deaf and has only partial sight in one eye. I was never

8

tested to see if I was immune to German measles in my first pregnancies, and the third time I had a test later in pregnancy, which of course showed, by then, that I had had it.'

If a woman has German measles (*rubella*) in the first three months of pregnancy it can cause devastating damage to her baby. This is easily preventable because a simple blood test can show if a woman has immunity from the disease, and if not she can have a vaccination to protect her. Girls have been routinely vaccinated in schools since 1970, but sadly many women still slip through the net for various reasons, with the result that hundreds of babies are still born deaf, blind and mentally and physically crippled because the mothers were never protected. It is not enough to rely on the fact that you think you had German measles because there are at least twelve other viruses with similar symptoms. It is also possible to get German measles and not to be immune afterwards, and even, in rare cases, to be vaccinated and still not have immunity. It is therefore prudent, if you are considering pregnancy, to ask your GP to arrange a blood test to check your immunity and for you to have a vaccination if this proves necessary. You must not get pregnant for three months following the vaccination.

SEXUALLY TRANSMITTED DISEASES SHOULD BE TREATED

Syphilis, gonorrhoea, genital herpes and AIDS all represent serious risks to the unborn baby. If there is any chance you may be suffering from one of these diseases, or have had one in the past, you can easily be tested and get help by going to your doctor or one of the venereal disease clinics (usually called 'special clinics') attached to major hospitals.

Syphilis can cause miscarriage and stillbirth or, if the baby lives, it may be growth-retarded and suffer from bone and brain disease. Because it is possible to have syphilis and not know, all pregnant women are routinely screened during antenatal blood tests. Symptoms are a painless ulcer, called a 'chancre', which appears between ten and ninety days at the site of the infection. As it does not hurt and can sometimes occur under the foreskin in men or on the cervix in women, it can go unnoticed. The secondary stage can show six to twelve months later as a non-itchy rash, sore throat, slight fever, swollen glands and patchy hair loss. Again, symptoms can be so vague and transitory as to be ignored. During the primary and secondary stages, syphilis is highly infectious and a pregnant woman can infect her unborn baby, but after two years the disease is rarely passed on through sexual intercourse, and after four years it is usually not infectious. In the early stages, a pregnant woman can be treated with antibiotics which will cure the baby too.

Gonorrhoea is more common than syphilis and, again, can go undetected. Nine out of ten women have no symptoms, but if they do occur they can manifest as pain when urinating, a bad-smelling vaginal discharge and sometimes abdominal pain if it has spread to cause internal pelvic infection. Gonorrhoea increases the risk of miscarriage and prematurity and the baby may be ill and not grow properly after the birth. There is also a serious risk that the baby's eyes may be infected during delivery, leading to inflammation and possibly scarring and blindness if untreated. During pregnancy a woman who has gonorrhoea can usually be effectively treated with antibiotics.

Genital herpes usually only represents a risk to the baby if the virus is active during a vaginal delivery, though, like any virus during pregnancy, an initial attack can cause miscarriage. If the virus is active, the baby can become infected as it passes through the vagina at delivery, and though it is not known how many babies do get herpes this way, of those that do, more than half do not survive. After delivery the baby may develop a rash and be sick and of those who live half are likely to suffer serious damage to the eyes and nervous system. Unfortunately, there is still no cure for genital herpes, which usually shows as a first attack by fever and painful blisters around the entrance to the vagina and over the pubic area. Subsequent attacks are usually less severe and it can only be passed to a partner by having sex while the blisters are present. The same applies to the risk of infecting a baby, but women who have had an attack in the last few weeks of pregnancy will usually have their babies delivered by Caesarean. Symptoms can be controlled, though the disease cannot be cured, by taking a drug called Acyclovir or applying a solution called Herpid directly to the blisters. Sufferers need careful counselling and advice to help them cope, and the support of self-help groups (see address section, pages 673–6) can be very valuable.

GENETIC FACTORS

Many people are understandably confused about the exact meaning of words describing handicap. 'Congenital' simply means 'born with' so a congenital handicap is one which a child is born with. This can be due to genetic or environmental factors, or a combination of both. It is estimated that 25% of all congenital abnormalities are genetic, 10% are due to environmental causes (including drugs), and the remaining 65% are due to a combination of factors. As a general rule, the earlier the fault or error in development occurs (whether because of genetic or environmental factors), the more serious the damage. If that seems a terribly gloomy thought, you might consider the reverse, that once an organ has been properly formed, it rarely comes to harm, whatever happens to the mother. If there is thought to be a genetic risk, couples can be referred to a geneticist for genetic counselling (see page 18).

HOW SOME GENETIC MISTAKES HAPPEN

Genetic abnormalities can be either inherited from one or both parents so they are passed on in the chromosomes carried by the egg from the mother or the sperm from the father, or they may happen for the first time in just the particular egg or sperm involved in the conception of the unborn baby and are then called a 'fresh mutation'. Why do such mistakes happen in the first place? Although some contributory factors are known (like the mother's age in certain chromosomal abnormalities), a mutation is essentially an unlucky accident when, instead of genes being perfectly reproduced each time, there has been a copying error, so that an egg or sperm or one set of cells in the early embryo carries a small mistake which goes on to be multiplied with each cell division.

We may not always know *why* a genetic mistake happens, but we do know *how* it happens. Every individual is made up of billions of cells, each derived originally from the fertilised egg, and each cell has a centre called a 'nucleus'. Inside the nucleus is the genetic material divided up into 23 pairs of chromosomes. Along each chromosome are arranged thousands of genes – these are the chemical instructions and are made up of something called 'deoxyribonucleic acid', or DNA for short. Just before a cell divides the chromosomes can be seen under a microscope – they look rather like irregular sausage shapes, but the genes are too small to be seen.

To study a person's chromosomes, geneticists need to be able to grow cells in the laboratory from a sample of blood, or less commonly skin or bone marrow. Just at the point when the cells divide and the chromosomes can be seen most clearly, the process is halted so that a photograph can be taken of the preparation. The photographed chromosomes from a single

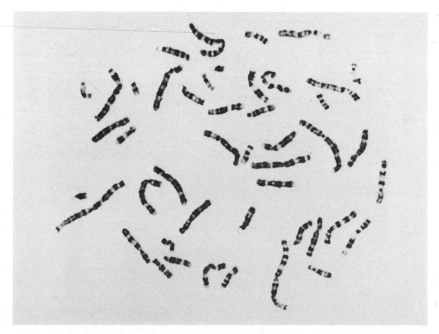

Human chromosomes visualised down the microscope as they appear in the nucleus of a cell

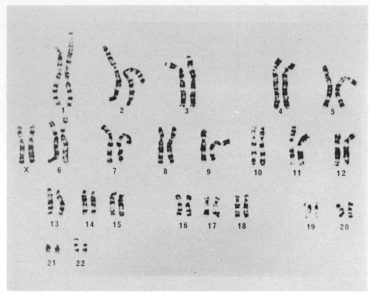

Chromosomes arranged in pairs to make what is called a karyotype. This person is female and has two X chromosomes

cell are cut out and arranged in their pairs in what is called a 'karyotype' (see above).

Every cell of the body has 46 chromosomes (23 pairs), except the eggs in a woman and sperm in a man. These are formed by a special cell division called 'meiosis' which results in each egg or sperm having only a single set of 23 chromosomes. When these two single sets come together at fertilisation, they become a complete set of 46 again and the beginning of a new individual.

THE SEX CHROMOSOMES

Of the 23 pairs of chromosomes in a cell nucleus, chromosome pairs 1 to 22 are common to both males and females, but the 23rd pair determines the sex of that individual. In a woman there is a matching XX pair, but a man has one X and one Y chromosome. As we explained, the special cell division called 'meiosis' results in eggs and sperms having only a single set of chromosomes, 23. Because a woman has only an XX pair, the egg always carries a single X chromosome, but the sperm from the man can carry

The twenty-third pair, or sex chromosomes

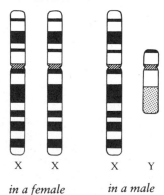

X   X   X   Y

in a female   *in a male*

either an X or a Y chromosome, and it is this which will decide the baby's sex. If an X-carrying sperm gets to the egg first, then the 23rd set will be XX – a girl. If a Y-carrying sperm wins the race and fertilises the egg, then the 23rd set will be XY – a boy.

MISTAKES IN CHROMOSOMES

On examining chromosomes, the first check is to count them – there should be 46. Sometimes a baby has one too many chromosomes and where there should be a pair there are three – this happens in Down's syndrome babies who have an extra chromosome number 21. Mistakes involving a whole chromosome usually happen when the egg or sperm is being formed. If the chromosomes do not separate properly, the egg or the sperm may carry an extra one. This can also happen after fertilisation during a cell division when the cells begin to divide and multiply to form the embryo. In this case some of the cells are normal and have the right number of chromosomes, but some carry an extra chromosome – this will mean the individual will be less severely affected and the pattern is called a 'mosaic', a mixture of two different cell types. More rarely, there may be one too few chromosomes – an example of this is Turner's syndrome where girls are missing one of the female X pair of chromosomes and fail to develop at puberty, though much can be done with hormone therapy.

The second type of mistake in chromosomes occurs when a chromosome has a part missing or is rearranged. Sometimes the missing part has become attached to another chromosome. Most chromosomal abnormalities are 'one off' events that do not run in families, but parents or relatives may be checked if it is thought the problem may be due to the less common inherited forms that might mean future children would be affected.

MISTAKES IN INDIVIDUAL GENES

While mistakes in the chromosomes can be seen under a microscope, mistakes can also happen in individual genes which are too tiny to be studied in this way. What causes these mistakes? Again, often we do not know *why* things go wrong, but we do know *how*. Imagine trying to photocopy thousands of tiny pictures hundreds of times so that each reprint is exactly the same as the original. That is what has to happen when the cells which contain 100,000 genes each divide to form eggs or sperm that are the starting point for a new person. A small mistake in just one reprint, or one gene, goes on to be multiplied, and may cause something to go wrong with the development of that baby. The existence of a single gene defect in an unborn baby would not be suspected if this was the first in the family. However, the original mutation – the photocopying mistake – may have occurred further back in the family and a history of the other family members having the condition can alert one to the risk of the baby having inherited the abnormal gene too.

If a single faulty gene always showed its presence by causing something wrong in the person, then it would be easy to track its inheritance through the family. However, this is not always the case. Fortunately, geneticists are making great progress in detecting faulty genes by examining the genetic material, or DNA, directly.

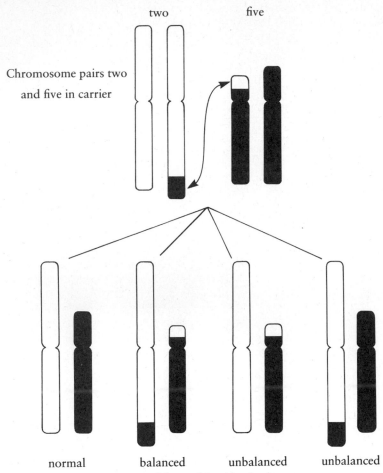

Four possible combinations in the gametes

One example of a person carrying a rearrangement of chromosome material between chromosomes two and five. While this person has no loss or gain of genetic material and is therefore healthy, his or her child has a high risk of ending up with genes missing from one of these chromosomes and extra copies of genes on the other. This causes the child to be born with brain and other malformations

PATTERNS OF INHERITANCE

Genetic diseases due to a single gene defect can be passed on through families in several ways. In normal individuals chromosomes exist in pairs, as do the genes they carry. Each pair of genes is made up of one that comes from the egg and one that comes from the sperm.

Recessive inheritance In some gene pairs a person can carry one faulty gene and the other normal gene will be able to cope on its own. A person will only have disease when both genes are faulty, i.e. he has no 'spare'. In this situation it means that both his parents must have passed on one copy of the faulty gene, although they themselves would have been healthy but called 'carriers'. If two carriers of the same faulty gene marry and have children they have a 25% chance of having an affected child. In this type of inheritance the genetic disease usually happens in one generation of a family only. An example of a recessively inherited disease is cystic fibrosis (CF) – an abnormally thick mucus clogs the lungs and digestive enzymes fail to flow from the pancreas into the intestine. It is thought that one in twenty people carry the CF gene, but it is only if two of these people marry that their child could inherit two CF genes and get the disease.

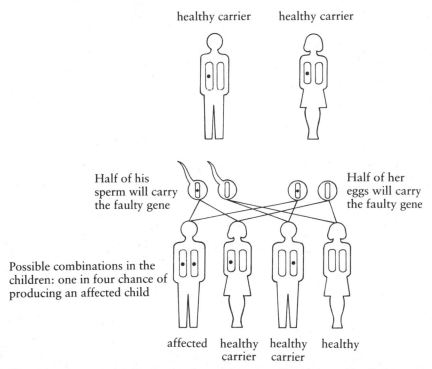

Recessive autosomal inheritance: those who are affected have the faulty gene present on both members of the chromosome pair. Those in whom the faulty gene affects only one chromosome are only carriers and are not affected

Dominant inheritance If a person inherits one faulty gene, the wrong programming in the faulty gene sometimes overrides the right programming in the healthy 'spare' and he or she has a disease. When that person comes to have children there is a 50% risk that the faulty gene will be passed on to any children. It is like flipping a coin: either the faulty gene or the normal gene is passed on purely by chance. This type of inheritance is called 'dominant inheritance' and can affect many generations of a family, both males and females. An example of such an inherited disease is Huntington's chorea. If a person inherits just one faulty gene of the pair that is responsible for this condition, he or she will have Huntington's chorea which comes on in middle life and causes characteristic jerky movements which slowly get worse. Unfortunately, a person may already have passed on the gene to children before symptoms appear in the parent confirming the presence of the faulty gene.

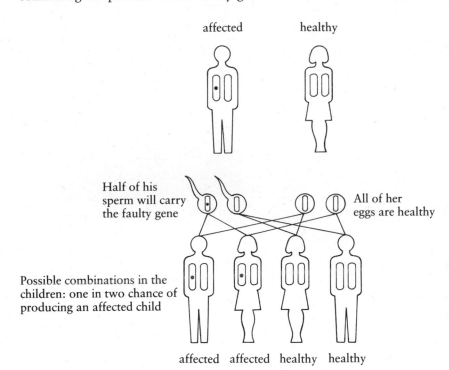

Dominant autosomal inheritance: only one chromosome has to have a faulty gene for a person to be affected

X-linked recessive inheritance A special type of inheritance happens when faulty genes occur on the X chromosome. Disease due to these faulty genes tends to occur in males. Females have two X chromosomes with two copies of all the genes on the X chromosome, so they have a back up. They will only have the disease if they inherit two X chromosomes which both carry the faulty gene, which is a very rare occurrence. If only one of their X chromosomes has a fault they will remain healthy but are called 'carriers'.

Men have only one X chromosome. The Y chromosome is much smaller and carries fewer and different genes. They therefore have no back up in the form of a spare, so if they inherit an X chromosome with a faulty gene they will get the disease. An example of this type of inheritance is seen with haemophilia, in which the blood does not clot in the normal way. If a woman with the faulty gene (a carrier) marries a normal man they can produce four types of children: a healthy daughter (normal X from mother and X from father); a healthy son (normal X from mother and Y from father); a daughter who is a carrier but is healthy herself (faulty X from mother but normal X from father); and a son who has the disease (faulty X from mother and Y from father). Other examples of X-linked diseases are Duchenne muscular dystrophy which is progressive muscle weakness, and a condition called 'fragile X syndrome' which is quite a common cause of mental retardation.

X-linked genes: a woman who is a carrier for an X-linked faulty gene has a one in two chance that any son will be affected and a one in two chance that any daughter will be a healthy carrier. However, if an affected male has children, all his daughters (who receive his X-chromosomes) will be carriers, but none of his sons (who receive his Y-chromosomes) will be affected

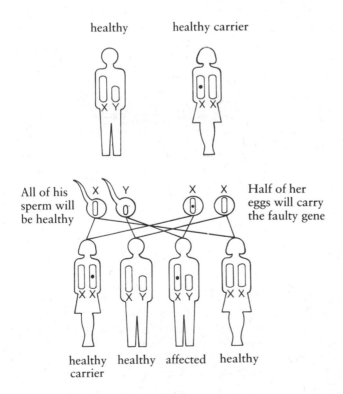

healthy   healthy carrier

All of his sperm will be healthy

Half of her eggs will carry the faulty gene

healthy   healthy   affected   healthy
carrier

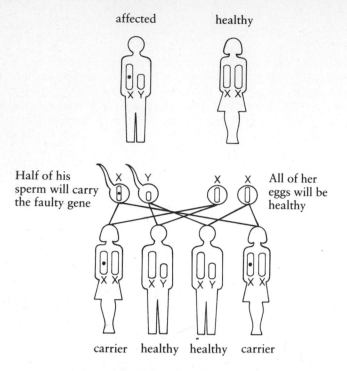

affected   healthy

Half of his sperm will carry the faulty gene

All of her eggs will be healthy

carrier   healthy   healthy   carrier

GENETIC COUNSELLING

As you have read, unborn babies can be damaged by outside or environmental influences during pregnancy – like disease, chemicals or alcohol. Sometimes a baby can be damaged by the process of birth itself, although antenatal care can often foresee and avoid or prevent that happening. Mistakes can also lie within.

When a baby is born with an abnormality, at some point the parents will ask: 'Why did it happen?' Unfortunately, there is not always a totally clear answer to this, but trying to discover the reason is sometimes part of the work of clinical geneticists.

WHY DO PEOPLE GO FOR GENETIC COUNSELLING?

Diagnosis A child with an abnormality may be referred to a geneticist who will try to find out what caused the problem. An accurate diagnosis will enable other doctors to treat that child and avoid unnecessary tests. It will enable the geneticist to tell the parent what chance there is of the same thing happening with other children. Many parents also find it helpful to have a name for their child's problem.

The risk of passing on a genetic abnormality A couple who already have an affected child, or have a genetic disease themselves, or a relative with a genetic disease or abnormality, will want to know the risk of the same thing being passed on to their children.

In X-linked diseases the answer to this question is often dependent on determining whether a female relative is a carrier of the faulty gene or not. If it can be shown that a woman is not a carrier then she can be reassured about her future sons. There are rapid developments in carrier detection tests for X-linked diseases.

Marriage of cousins We all carry at least one harmful recessive gene but, as explained in the section on recessive inheritance, as long as we have one healthy 'spare' it does us no harm. Only if we marry someone who carries the same harmful gene can we have a child with a double set of the same faulty gene and so an inherited disease.

Relatives share some genes in common. First cousins share an eighth of their genes in common and are therefore more likely to share the same faulty gene and are at higher risk of having a child with a recessive disease. In general marriage between first cousins or more distant relatives is not a major genetic risk for the couple concerned. A geneticist can put the genetic risks in perspective and sometimes help by telling if a fault is likely to exist in the family genes, making a marriage between cousins a concern.

Pre-natal diagnosis If there is a fairly high risk that a child may carry a genetic fault, a geneticist can sometimes make a diagnosis of the unborn child during pregnancy.

If the geneticist wants to study the baby's chromosomes, the most usual way is to take a sample of the amniotic fluid containing some of the foetal cells by amniocentesis (as described on page 43). The drawback is that this usually cannot be done until 16 weeks and, if the parents decide on a termination, it will mean inducing an abortion at 20 weeks or later which is a traumatic and distressing experience.

A newer way of obtaining a sample of the baby's cells is chorion villus biopsy (see page 43). This has the advantage of being able to be performed earlier, at 8 to 10 weeks, but carries a slightly higher risk of miscarriage.

The biopsy contains foetal cells with the same genes as those in the developing baby. Tests can be done to show up gene defects for some genetic disorders like cystic fibrosis, Duchenne muscular dystrophy, and haemophilia if it is known that the disease is in the family.

Many congenital abnormalities can be shown up by an ultrasound scan of the baby during pregnancy. In experienced hands a scan at 17 weeks of the pregnancy can pick up problems like *spina bifida*, brain problems like hydrocephalus when the head is swollen by fluid, some heart defects and even smaller details like a cleft lip (hare lip).

In a few cases, when other tests raise the suspicion of damage, a foetoscopy (see page 44) may allow a direct inspection of the baby inside the womb and can be used to take samples of foetal blood, skin and even, in a very few cases so far, of the liver. Foetal blood can be taken from the umbilical cord under ultrasound scan guidance.

No medical procedure is without its risks — in doing such tests to try to make a pre-natal diagnosis, the geneticist must weigh up the possible risks involved against the likelihood of the baby proving to have some abnormality, and he will explain these very carefully to the couple when he gives his advice. But, as with all medical decisions, the final choice of whether or not to have the test rests with the couple. As part of his counselling the geneticist will also explain, as far as he is able, what the possible effects of the suspected abnormalities may be because these will weigh with the couple in making a decision to have the test. If, sadly, the baby does prove to be damaged, then the geneticist will give the couple all the information he can about the nature and extent of the damage, the baby's chance of survival and life expectations. Most couples will want to know what sort of mental and physical capability their child could have, what sort of special care would be needed and how much of the damage could be corrected. Unfortunately, these are often difficult questions to answer. Even when a geneticist is sure of the diagnosis and knows the baby is suffering from a recognised syndrome, it may be impossible to say whether he will be severely or mildly affected. Such couples need all the information, support and counselling available to help them decide whether to continue with the pregnancy or to have a termination. Naturally the medical staff will give them full backing whatever their decision.

HOW DO YOU ARRANGE TO HAVE GENETIC COUNSELLING?

Your own GP or a specialist, for example an obstetrician, will give you a referral. They may be able to offer you some genetic advice themselves, but a proper diagnosis, assessment and advice on the probability of genetic risks is the job of a clinical geneticist working in a genetic clinic, usually to be found in large hospitals. This may mean travelling some distance, but usually only one or a very few visits will be necessary. Genetic clinics do not usually supervise treatment but rather pass the information on to your GP and any relevant specialists.

WHAT HAPPENS WHEN YOU GO FOR GENETIC COUNSELLING?

Before you go for your first appointment at the clinic, sit down with your partner and make a rough note of the details of your family tree. You do not need to draw it out in any way, just list the names, ages and relation to yourself. Each time ask yourself if there is anything relating to the health and condition of that relative which is out of the ordinary. If there is, then try to find out if they have ever been for treatment; the list should include relatives who have since died, and, if applicable, at which hospital and under which consultant. If the geneticist thinks their condition may be relevant this information will be very helpful because he will be able to write to the consultant to ask for confirmation or a diagnosis if one was made, and any other information. Start with your immediate brothers and sisters and their children, if any. Details about stillbirths or miscarriages will also be needed. Then go on to your parents, aunts, uncles and cousins. If you know there are members of the family who were affected by some abnormality and a diagnosis was never made, then a photograph may sometimes help the geneticist. If this is the case he will ask at your first visit when he will be making enquiries to find out what sort of information needs to be gathered together – for example, notes from other hospitals, results of post mortems or tests to be arranged. Sometimes the geneticist may want to have a karyotype done of both your chromosomes – this means taking a sample of blood which will be sent to the laboratory for analysis.

THE ASSESSMENT

Before he gives you his assessment the geneticist will have made it his business to find out everything he can relating to your problem. He will have set aside enough time, half an hour or even a full hour, to explain exactly what he thinks and on what he bases his assessment. Don't be afraid to ask him any questions – it sometimes helps to note down anything you want to ask in advance.

Understandably, there is often a great deal of anxiety and guilt about genetic abnormalities. One partner may feel it is their fault a child was born handicapped or that the problem stems from their side of the family. It is also very common to feel angry at the way things have worked out – 'Why us?' is a very usual reaction.

In the majority of cases couples want to know what their chances are of having a healthy or an affected child in the future. The geneticist will assess the risk in terms of probabilities and give you as accurate a figure as possible. For example, if a couple were given a one in two chance, it means that out of every two children born to that couple, one is likely to be affected, although of course both might be affected or both unaffected. The risk is the same every time for every pregnancy – chance has no memory. The probability of having an affected child can vary through lesser and lesser degrees of risk until you are talking about one in a hundred or smaller risks. Even if a geneticist cannot make a precise diagnosis, he will try to give the couple some idea of what he thinks the risks may be, what is a bad risk and what is a good risk.

He will also set the risk in some kind of context to help the couple assess what it means. Some geneticists estimate that any pregnancy has a one in thirty chance of producing a baby who will either be born with a serious abnormality, or will develop one in the early years. In broad terms it seems that genetic risks tend to fall into the risk category of either a one in ten chance or worse, or a one in twenty chance or better. Of course, in deciding whether to go ahead and have children, the couple will need to know as much as possible about the disease or abnormality they risk passing on, just as couples who go for a pre-natal diagnosis need to know. But again, the geneticist will never try to influence a couple's decision whether to have children or not. Indeed, in one study of couples attending a genetic clinic, it turned out that just over a third of those given a one in ten or worse risk decided to go ahead and have children. If that is the couple's decision they can arrange to go back to the geneticist when the time comes for a pre-natal diagnosis if they wish.

Chapter 2

PREGNANCY

A new life begins   Fertility
How can you tell if you are pregnant?   Decisions, decisions
The novice's guide to antenatal care
Other tests during pregnancy   Eating sensibly and weight gain
Avoid X-rays in early pregnancy   Minor physical problems
More serious problems in pregnancy
Pregnancies needing the five-star treatment
Mixed emotions – how you feel during pregnancy
Shopping for the baby   Towards the end of pregnancy

A NEW LIFE BEGINS

FERTILISATION

From puberty onwards a complex series of hormone signals and reactions stimulate one or other ovary to produce one egg a month until the menopause. A woman's cycle runs from the first day of one period to the first day of the next and is about twenty-eight days. When the egg breaks free from the ovary, usually around the fourteenth day of the cycle, this is called 'ovulation'. Filaments around the entrance to the Fallopian tube draw the egg into the tube and the rhythmic contractions of the tube waft it along towards the uterus. It takes four to five days for the fertilised egg to travel from the ovary to the uterus. If it is not fertilised it dies after one to two days and disappears, after which the lining of the womb, with its rich supply of blood vessels in preparation for a fertilised egg, begins to break down and is shed as a period at the end of the cycle.

Sperm have a longer life than eggs: it is usually thought to be about three to four days, and it takes them about an hour to swim the seven inches from the cervix (neck of the womb) through the uterus to meet the egg in the Fallopian tube. Usually the tiny canal through the cervix (the os) is blocked with a plug of mucus and sperm cannot pass through. But when ovulation approaches, hormone changes make the mucus thin, opening the door to sperm. Some women can recognise this change in vaginal fluid so that they know when they are approaching a fertile period, while a few women actually experience some kind of pain at the time of ovulation itself. The egg is most easily fertilised twelve to twenty-four hours after ovulation because changes in its structure make it easier for the sperm to penetrate. Although every ejaculation contains several hundred million sperm, only one can fertilise the egg. When the egg and the sperm merge at fertilisation,

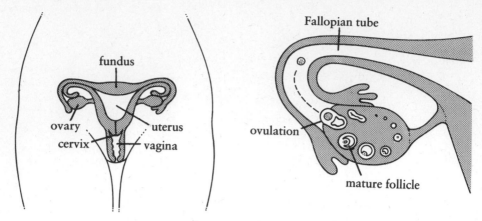

Female reproductive organs

the two halves of the chromosome set come together to form a complete set of forty-six again – one half from the mother and one half from the father (see page 12).

EARLY DAYS OF LIFE

Within about thirty hours of fertilisation the egg divides into two cells – the beginning of the complicated and amazing process of building a new person. By five days it has usually reached the sixteen-cell stage and has arrived in the uterus. It is now called a 'blastocyst' and, if all goes well, it will implant itself in the wall of the uterus. Sometimes mistakes happen and it implants in the wrong place, such as in the Fallopian tube. When this happens it is called an 'ectopic pregnancy' (see page 52). By about ten days the blastocyst has completely embedded itself in the lining of the uterus, but furious activity is going on within. The majority of the cells go on to form the placenta (called 'chorionic villi' during early development) and the membranes, whilst an inner cell mass becomes the embryo proper. The embryonic cells are divided into two layers. The first layer is the ectoderm, which makes the outer layer of the baby, skin, hair and nails, and will soon fold inwards to make the nervous system as well. The second layer is the endoderm, which makes all the organs inside the baby. In week three a third layer of cells, the mesoderm, starts to make the beginnings of muscles, blood, heart and bones.

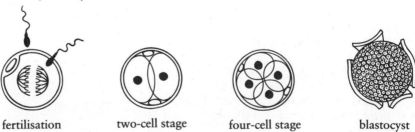

| fertilisation | two-cell stage | four-cell stage | blastocyst |

24

Weeks 4–5 The unborn baby is technically known as the embryo now. Although only the size of a pea it has a primitive heart which begins to beat. Finger-shaped projections, the chorionic villi, have grown into the tissue of the uterine wall to anchor the embryo and a string of blood vessels connecting mother and baby will form the umbilical cord.

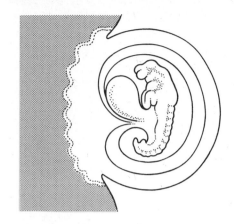

Weeks 6–7 Now about 6 mm. ($\frac{1}{4}$ in.) long from crown to bottom, the unborn baby has limb buds which can move and will soon grow into arms and legs. The head is much larger than the body with a bump where the brain is forming and dents which will soon become ears. The eyes are still covered with skin which will be eyelids, and stay closed until about the 26th week.

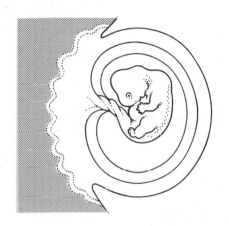

Weeks 8–9 From 9 weeks the unborn baby is called a 'foetus' and, although you may not have had your first antenatal check yet, all the internal organs are forming fast. He has tripled his size to measure about 2 cm. ($\frac{3}{4}$ in.). Although the head is still much larger than the body, he is beginning to look more like a baby, and toes and fingers are starting to form.

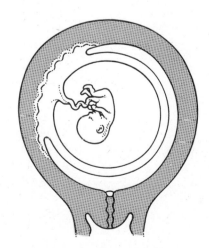

Weeks 10–14 By 12 weeks your unborn baby is fully formed. All the organs are complete and he needs only to grow and develop. Finger and toe-nails have begun to grow. He is about 7 cm. (2¾ in.) from head to bottom and the top of the uterus, the fundus, can usually be felt beginning to rise out of the pelvis.

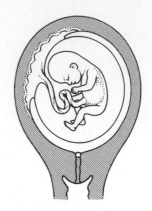

Weeks 15–22 Although your unborn baby will have been moving spontaneously from about week 12, he is usually not big enough for you to feel his movements until now. However, second-time mothers who recognise the fluttery sensations may notice them earlier. At 22 weeks the unborn baby is covered with a fine, downy hair called 'lanugo', which has usually been mostly shed before birth. A substance called 'vernix', a greasy, white protective film which is often still covering the baby born prematurely, has begun to form. Sometimes the baby's sex can be detected at this stage with ultrasound scans.

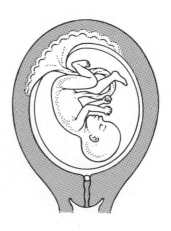

Weeks 23–30 From 28 weeks the baby is said to be viable – that is, if born now he has a good chance of living, although babies have survived from as young as 23 weeks. Its chances of survival at this stage are usually thought to be 75% in a special care baby unit. The downy lanugo has usually disappeared and the baby is covered in vernix. His movements are very clear and he still has plenty of room to manoeuvre, often turning complete somersaults. He may have regular patterns of activity and sleep, and some babies get hiccups which their mothers can

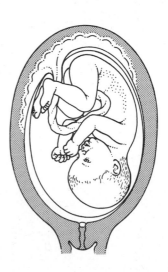

feel. The baby may respond to sudden or loud noises by jumping or starting, and experiments seem to suggest babies can respond to soothing sounds like singing or music. He probably begins to learn the rhythm and pitch of his mother's voice. At 30 weeks the unborn baby usually measures about 24 cm. (9½ in.).

Weeks 31–40 With every extra week that passes, your baby has a greater chance of surviving if it is born early. Most obstetric units have a special care baby unit which can look after a baby born from about 34 weeks if he is a good size. The baby begins to fill out and become plumper and both the downy lanugo and vernix disappear. By about 32 weeks the baby has usually settled into the head-down position ready to be born. If his head moves down into the pelvis it is said to be 'engaged', but sometimes this does not happen until labour begins.

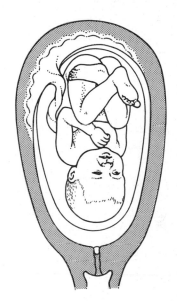

FERTILITY

BECOMING PREGNANT

Pinpointing ovulation – that is, the time when an egg is released from the ovaries – has always been very difficult. Ovulation is most commonly thought to occur fourteen days before the next period, but there can be very many variations, so even if you have a regular twenty-eight-day cycle it is not enough just to count the days.

A better, but still very imprecise way of pinpointing ovulation is to take your temperature. To do this you need a fertility chart, available from most chemists, and either an ordinary thermometer or a special fertility thermometer which makes things easier because the scale is bigger and it does not have such a wide range. First thing in the morning your body is at its lowest temperature – called the 'basal body temperature' – which is usually between 36.2°C and 36.3°C (97.2°F and 97.4°F). Leave the thermometer in for five minutes and record the temperature each morning on the chart before you get out of bed. When an egg has been released from the ovaries there is a sharp rise in the level of the hormone progesterone which causes the body temperature to increase – usually to a level of about 36.7°C (98°F) or above. Sometimes there is a drop in temperature a few hours before this rise. But remember, the increase in temperature does not mark the time of ovulation itself — it only shows that ovulation has taken place. It is thought that the day before this rise in temperature must be the time of ovulation, but obviously exact timing will vary with individuals and in many women the rise in temperature itself is not easy to pinpoint. After ovulation the temperature stays raised until the start of the next period.

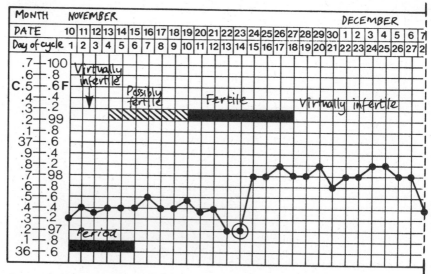

O Probable time of egg cell release

Another method is to test the urine for an increase in the level of a substance called 'luteinising hormone' (LH), which rises sharply and triggers ovulation about twenty-four hours later. There are a number of ovulation kits on the market which use dipsticks to test the LH levels in urine as a means of predicting the most fertile time in a woman's cycle, but they are expensive and it is possible to have an increased LH level without ovulating, perhaps because the ovary is not functioning properly.

FERTILITY PROBLEMS

Problems relating to fertility are not uncommon — it is estimated that as many as one in eight couples in this country have trouble trying to conceive. An average, fertile couple have a 15% chance of conceiving each month, which means that half the fertile population will take about four to five months to become pregnant and most normal couples will conceive within a year. Those who have not become pregnant after eighteen months of regular intercourse probably have some problem, but in many cases this may be minor and easily treated. How soon you seek medical help depends slightly on individual circumstances, but there are some known indications of possible fertility problems, so women to whom any of the following apply should see their GP if they have had no luck after six months of trying to conceive:

You are more than 36 years old Fertility declines in women as they near 40 and a quarter of all normal women are subfertile by this age. Unfortunately there is no way of knowing in advance which women are likely to belong to this group so it is a good idea for women over 36 hoping for a baby to get tests done if they do not conceive within about six months.

Infrequent periods Usually this can be easily treated.

Increasingly painful periods or deep pain on intercourse This may indicate a pelvic infection or a condition called endometriosis requiring treatment.

Previous severe pelvic infection, a burst appendix or miscarriage All these can sometimes result in a problem with the Fallopian tubes or the inside of the womb requiring treatment.

In about 50% of all cases of infertility the problem lies with the woman, in about 30% of cases with the man, and in 20% both partners. By far the most common male problem is a low sperm count or sperm of poor quality.

It is most important in cases of infertility that proper tests and diagnosis are made without wasting too much time. Failure to have the correct tests done may mean that a problem which is quite simple to remedy is actually missed and couples find themselves contemplating far more complicated procedures such as *in vitro* fertilisation (test tube baby treatment) which are in fact neither appropriate nor necessary.

HOW CAN YOU TELL IF YOU ARE PREGNANT?

'With my second baby, I knew even before I missed a period. My breasts starting aching and I went off coffee immediately – couldn't even stand the smell. Some of these signs might have been there with my first pregnancy but I just didn't recognise them.'

Some women are so in tune with their bodies that they say they know within days when they are pregnant; but at the other end of the scale there have been reports of women who manage to ignore or suppress the signs of pregnancy so completely that they do not know they are expecting a baby until they actually go into labour. However, most people do suspect within a few weeks, because some or all of these signs are present:

Missed periods Light bleeding, like a period, can still happen during pregnancy if levels of progesterone are not high enough, usually once or twice, but rarely through the whole pregnancy. Apart from pregnancy, missed periods (amenorrhoea) can also be due to emotional upset, illness, severe weight loss, over-exercising, anxiety about getting pregnant, approaching the menopause and coming off the Pill.

Breasts They may feel different immediately or not for three months, but at some point they will begin to feel heavier, fuller, and to ache or tingle.

Sickness This is very common in the first three months of pregnancy, sometimes first thing in the morning, but it can also happen at other times in the day. Some very unlucky women feel sick all the way through pregnancy (see page 50).

Urinating It is very common to have to pass water more often in the first three months of pregnancy, which often means getting up in the night too. This usually wears off slightly in the middle months and returns at the end when the baby is bigger and physically squashing the bladder.

Tiredness This can be noticeable in the first three months, but usually lifts in the middle months to return again when you are large and the baby has become heavy towards the end of pregnancy. Very early on you can often feel heaviness in the lower abdomen.

PREGNANCY TESTS

> *'I have used do-it-yourself pregnancy testing kits twice – once when I didn't want to be pregnant, and once eight years later when I did. Both times I was really keyed up and nervous. Luckily I got the result I wanted. My excitement the second time on being pregnant was just about as great as the relief I felt all those years ago when I got the negative result I was praying for!'*

All pregnant women start to produce a special hormone called human chorionic gonadotrophin (HCG) within two days of the fertilised egg becoming embedded in the wall of the uterus. Pregnancy tests look for HCG in blood or urine. The most easily available and usual form of testing can be done one to two weeks after a missed period with a sample of urine collected first thing in the morning. Wrong results do happen – false negatives are commoner than false positives, usually the result of doing the test too early before levels of HCG are high enough. Traces of detergent or something else in the container you use can also cause a false negative. False positives are rare but can occur because if you test around ovulation or approaching the menopause, another hormone, luteinising hormone

(LH), may be present. A recent pregnancy or miscarriage you are unaware of might cause traces of HCG to be present. Fertility drugs, some tranquillisers and antihistamines can also affect the reading.

Although they work out as one of the most expensive ways of getting a pregnancy test, DIY kits remain one of the most popular because they offer privacy and speed with the minimum of fuss. You can also get a test done by your GP, although he may charge you the price of the test if he does it himself on the spot, or at a family planning clinic, pregnancy advice centre, and some chemists.

EARLIER TESTS

In rare cases a woman may need to know if she is pregnant even before a period is missed, perhaps because she has fertility problems and it is suspected she is having repeated early miscarriages, or in the case of a rape victim or someone with a suspected ectopic pregnancy. The earliest accurate test is radio-immunoassay, which can be done four days before a period is due, which looks for traces of HCG in the blood. However, this test is mainly used in research and is only done at teaching hospitals or very rarely through a pregnancy advice centre. Another early test not yet in widespread use is called the Beta test and identifies just one part of HCG and can be used on the first day of the missed period.

ULTRASOUND SCANS

Very skilled specialists can detect pregnancy by scanning when your period is only three days late, but such precision is not widely available. More commonly the foetus can be identified with ultrasound at six weeks by a skilled operator.

DECISIONS, DECISIONS

As soon as you know that you are pregnant, certain decisions have to be made. The first is where the birth will take place.

WHERE WILL YOU HAVE YOUR BABY?

Whether it is their first or a subsequent baby, most women have strong feelings about the circumstances they would like to give birth in, and some of the things they would or would not like to happen.

In deciding on a place of birth, you are also choosing a set of options about who looks after your antenatal care and about the style of management of the birth itself.

Home It is generally accepted that the back up of hospital facilities gives a much better chance of survival if anything goes wrong with a birth. This is why some doctors do not agree with home births in any circumstances, although others are quite prepared to go along with the idea if everything

31

seems normal and this is a second or subsequent baby, up to number four or five.

If your GP is not registered for obstetric care you can register temporarily with another doctor during the pregnancy. The same applies if you want a home birth and your own doctor does not agree.

Antenatal care will be between your community midwife, either visiting you at home or at a health centre, and your GP.

Hospital Find out about your local hospitals by asking other mothers, local birth centres and organisations such as the National Childbirth Trust and your GP. See our suggestions below for questions you may want to ask. A full stay in hospital usually means seven to eight days and gives first-time mothers a chance to learn about looking after their baby. The disadvantages are separation from your partner and other children if you have them, and the drawbacks of hospital life. Other options usually include 48-hour and 6-hour stays. Hospitals outside your area may accept you, but only if they have room and your GP has referred you. Hospitals some distance away may also accept you, provided you stay nearby towards the end of your pregnancy. Antenatal care is shared between the hospital and the GP or community midwife, except in higher risk cases when antenatal care may be covered by the hospital throughout the pregnancy.

GP units These are run by GPs and community midwives, either as beds within a consultant hospital or in a separate building near the hospital.

Domino scheme The community midwife and GP look after your ante-natal care and, when labour starts, the midwife comes into hospital or to the GP unit to deliver the baby. Back up may be from hospital doctors or your own GP. The word 'domino' comes from *dom*iciliary midwifery *in* and *out*.

Twenty questions about hospitals Women living in more rural areas may have only one maternity hospital within reach of their home, but if you do have a choice these are some of the questions you may wish to consider:

* What kind of atmosphere does the hospital have?

* How friendly and helpful are the staff when you make enquiries?

* Do they run parent education and antenatal classes?

* Can your partner and/or a relation or friend stay with you all the time during labour and birth?

* Will you be given a shave and enema before birth?

* Are all mothers monitored continuously in labour or only at intervals (called intermittent monitoring)?

* Is there a high induction rate?

* Does the hospital have a high Caesarean rate? (In both these cases remember some large hospitals get more problem cases referred to them which may push up the rates.)

* Will you be able to move around freely during labour?

* Will they help you adopt any position you want during labour and birth?

* Are there any extra facilities – birthing beds, birth chairs or stools or birthing rooms with mattresses on the floor?

* How freely available are epidurals? Is there an anaesthetist on hand twenty-four hours a day who can give an epidural anaesthetic?

* Can they offer epidurals for suitably planned Caesareans?

* Will you be able to make your own decision about what type and how much pain relief you want?

* Will they be happy for the second stage to continue as long as the mother or baby are not distressed?

* Will the doctor or midwife attending the birth help you avoid an episiotomy?

* Is it possible to arrange for a short stay or a domino delivery?

* Can your partner visit you and the baby as often as he likes after the birth?

* Will you be able to keep your baby with you all the time after the birth?

* Does the hospital run well-planned and interesting post-natal classes for mothers to attend with their babies for either socialising or exercise sessions?

CHOOSING AN ANTENATAL CLASS

Hospital classes These can vary enormously and in the past old-style 'parent craft classes' often left much to be desired, but many hospitals have updated their approach to offer a really good service. Classes may be held in the hospital or in the community, in the daytime or in the evening, be geared for mothers alone or for couples, or even provide facilities for mothers to go along with older children.

A good class tries to be flexible and meet the needs of the people attending, but in general they aim to tell couples about the physical process of birth, what happens at each stage, and most teach some kind of breathing and relaxation techniques. Good antenatal classes also discuss all the other options for pain relief, and specifically what is available at that particular hospital. Even if you opt for another form of antenatal class, it is useful to attend some of the hospital classes as well, because they can tell you about that particular hospital's policy and approach on points which are dealt with differently in different hospitals.

It is useful to remember that in any one hospital two consultants can have very different attitudes, so talking to the registrar or another senior doctor from your consultant's team at the antenatal clinic is useful.

As well as the physical side of birth, hospital classes, like all antenatal classes, can be valuable places for discussion with other parents-to-be about the emotional and psychological changes involved in becoming a parent. Other couples who are going through the same process can be an invaluable source of support to each other, and many longlasting friendships stem from meetings in antenatal classes, clinics and maternity wards.

National Childbirth Trust (NCT) classes The NCT was formed in 1956 with the aim of improving women's knowledge about birth and promoting the teaching of relaxation and breathing techniques. It has had a great influence in changing medical attitudes, so that now it is expected and accepted that women who want to prepare themselves for birth, to know as much as possible and to work together with those attending the birth, will usually receive help and encouragement.

National Childbirth Trust teachers have undergone thorough training, and classes are usually held on an informal tutorial basis with groups of a dozen or so women or couples attending, usually at the teacher's home, though sometimes in hired premises. The exact flavour of each course depends on the personality of the teacher, but as well as breathing and relaxation techniques other forms of pain relief will be discussed and also how to adapt to difficulties if they should arise, and how to appreciate when medical intervention is necessary. Like hospital classes, NCT classes can form valuable support networks or friendships and an opportunity to discuss all issues arising from birth and parenthood. After the birth, the NCT offers post-natal support on a parent-to-parent basis and holds regular get-togethers for mothers or couples with children.

Breastfeeding counselling is another very valuable after-birth service. These counsellors are women who have breastfed their own babies and are trained to help and support mothers. It is not necessary to have attended an NCT course of antenatal classes to ask for help from breastfeeding counsellors or post-natal supporters and all mothers are welcome at post-natal tea afternoons or other meetings.

The NCT is a registered charity. There is a charge for a course of antenatal classes but advice from breastfeeding counsellors or post-natal supporters is free. In many areas the NCT is also involved with schools in education for parenthood classes. To contact your regional organiser who can tell you about these services, write to or telephone the headquarters of the NCT (see address section, pages 673–6).

Active Birth classes At the beginning of the 1980s a number of birth educators formed the Active Birth Movement and began teaching women how they could be helped during labour by staying upright and mobile and also by using a variety of different positions, such as kneeling or squatting,

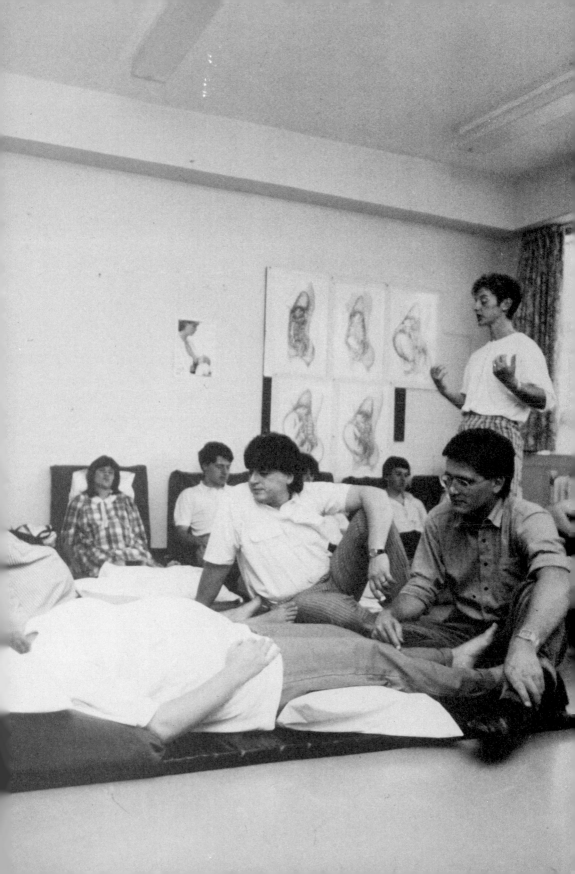

during delivery. Their ideas were based on women's experiences and backed by medical research which showed that women who stayed upright and mobile during the first stage of labour, instead of lying on their backs on a delivery bed, needed less pain relief and had shorter labours. The idea of using the force of gravity to make contractions in the first stage of labour more effective and to help with delivery has largely become accepted practice, and most hospital and NCT teachers have incorporated it in their antenatal teaching.

Yoga classes Such classes are not strictly an antenatal course in that they do not teach specifically about hospital practice and other areas associated with birth, but in some areas there are yoga classes designed for pregnant women. These may be run by individual teachers or local community associations. Try your nearest library or citizens advice bureau for contact addresses.

WORKING THROUGH PREGNANCY

After you have chosen where to have the baby and which antenatal class to attend, you may have to make a decision about your work. Most women expecting a first baby work through the early and middle months of their pregnancy, but many women are undecided about whether they will return to full- or part-time work after the birth.

From a purely practical point of view it is probably better not to announce your pregnancy at work too early as miscarriages in the first three months of pregnancy are quite common, and letting everybody know in the very first few weeks will make the pregnancy seem extra long. Around the fourth month is probably a reasonable time – miscarriage is less likely by now, and you and your employer both need enough time to make decisions and plans for the future. About this time you will also begin to look pregnant!

Your rights As far as your job goes, you have four basic rights:

* The right to take paid time off during working hours to attend antenatal appointments.

* The right not to be unfairly dismissed because you are pregnant.

* Depending on your job, the hours you work, the length of time you have been with the company and the size of the firm, you may have the right to return to work after the birth.

* The right to statutory maternity pay.

In addition to the rights listed above, some employers grant pregnant women extra rights. To find out if any special entitlements apply to your particular job you must talk to your boss or, in a larger firm, the personnel officer. To discover what you are entitled to, contact your local Department of Employment office which will be able to supply you with the necessary leaflet and information. If you have any problems your local citizens advice bureau or one of a number of maternity organisations (see address section, pages 673–6) may be able to help.

If you are not sure whether you want to return to work after the birth and the terms of your job allow for it to be kept open for you, it is probably wise to ask for this to be done, even if later you decide to stay at home.

Jobs which are dangerous in pregnancy If your job involves working with chemicals, toxic materials or radiation then obviously you need to think about this before becoming pregnant. Your own GP, consultant obstetrician or one of the preconceptual care clinics which exist in some large hospitals will be able to advise you if you think there may be some hazards attached to your work. In addition your trade union will be able to let you know about recent research developments and about your right to a change of job during pregnancy.

Work which is simply physically unsuitable during pregnancy is obviously less of a problem. In general, standing for long hours, lifting heavy goods or other manual labour only becomes more difficult during the middle to later months – unless you have a medical history of miscarriage or similar problems. However, depending on the individual circumstances of your employment, you could lose your job if being pregnant means you cannot do the work properly and no suitable alternative can be provided. Again, your trade union, citizens advice bureau, law centre, and many maternity organisations can give advice, but in the case of dispute, an industrial tribunal may have to be the final arbitrator.

For further discussion on working mothers see page 463.

THE NOVICE'S GUIDE TO ANTE-NATAL CARE

'The midwives were very good and took a real interest in how the pregnancy was going, but the doctors always made me feel like a lump of meat. After all those hours waiting to see them you expect to be told something about the baby – most of them just wrote notes and didn't speak.'

'The nurses and doctors couldn't have been better about discussing everything with me – the care was superb. My only criticism was the waiting involved – I had to take a complete morning off work for each visit.'

Antenatal clinics have come in for a lot of criticism but many are making great improvements with better appointment systems, facilities for children and various continuity care schemes which enable mothers to see the same midwives and doctors. However, long waits and impersonal attitudes still exist and can make antenatal appointments seem more of a chore. Women who have become pregnant accidentally or who, for various reasons, feel unsure about whether they want to be pregnant, may find antenatal appointments particularly irksome. Not understanding the point behind all those tests and questions can make antenatal care seem less important. If there is anything you are worried about or don't understand, always ask, but knowing something about the basics of antenatal care may help you to know *what* to ask.

Your first visit, called 'booking in', will probably take longer than most. The midwives will want to know about your own and your family's medical history, your normal state of health and menstrual cycle and any previous pregnancies. This is to help them plan your care during pregnancy.

CLINICAL TESTS

Height This is a guide to what your weight should be and can be an indication of frame size. Small women (under 5 ft) will be more carefully monitored in case their pelvis is too narrow for the baby's head to pass through. Shoe size used to be thought to be an indication of bone structure, but recent research reports do not confirm this.

Weight A record will be kept throughout pregnancy. Generally very slow gain or even weight loss is of more concern than gaining extra weight because it may be a sign that the baby is not growing steadily.

Blood pressure It is recorded like this: 120/80. The top figure is the pressure in the arteries while the heart is contracted and the bottom figure is the pressure when it is relaxed. The lower figure is the most important and anything higher than 80 needs watching to make sure it doesn't stay raised or get any higher.

Urine At your first hospital appointment you will be asked to perform a special trick well known to more experienced mothers – the collection of a mid-stream urine sample. This is not in fact as difficult as it sounds, though even second-time mothers might remember it is a lot easier without a curious toddler in tow! The purpose is to check for infection and it entails cleaning yourself with specially provided swabs and stopping mid-stream to pass some urine into a sterile specimen container. At subsequent antenatal checks, bring a small sample of urine collected first thing in the morning to be tested for:

* Sugar – pregnant women do have sugar in their urine occasionally but if it persists you should be tested for diabetes (see page 62).

* Protein – traces can mean an infection or be a feature of pre-eclamptic toxaemia, a special condition only associated with pregnancy where one of the main signs is high blood pressure (see page 53).

* Ketones – a by-product when fats are broken down. It can be a warning

that the kidneys are not working properly or may be present if a woman is suffering from a great deal of sickness.

Blood At your first visit a blood sample will be taken and screened for:

* Blood group – in case you ever need a transfusion. Everyone belongs to one of four groups – A, AB, B or O, and O is the commonest.

* Rhesus factor – positive or negative, for the significance of this see page 61.

* Syphilis – can damage the baby if left untreated.

* Viral hepatitis – a rare strain called 'Australian antigen' can be a risk to nursing and medical staff.

* *Rubella* immunity – if you are not immune you will be offered the vaccination after the birth to safeguard you in future pregnancies (see page 548).

* Other antibodies – previous illnesses may be shown up by the presence of antibodies in the blood.

* Sickle cell disease – a form of inherited anaemia only affecting people from Africa, the West Indies and Asia.

* Thalassaemia – a similar condition affecting especially people from Mediterranean countries.

* Haemoglobin levels – will be checked at the beginning and at subsequent intervals throughout the pregnancy. Haemoglobin is the oxygen-carrying substance in the red blood cells, which have to increase in number to meet the demands of the expanding uterus and growing placenta and baby. Ideally the level of haemoglobin should not fall below 12 grams per decilitre of blood. Below 10 grams per litre, the woman is anaemic. If a woman is verging on or has become anaemic at the end of pregnancy, even a small amount of blood lost in a normal birth can be enough to necessitate a blood transfusion.

Aids The current screening test for the virus causing AIDS (HIV) infection is called an 'ELISA test'. The situation is under debate but in the UK at the start of the 1990s this screening is only recommended for women who fall into a group likely to have been exposed to the AIDS virus.

MEDICAL EXAMINATION

A senior doctor – usually a registrar or consultant – will see you at your first appointment and want to find out if you are fit and in good health. For women having a home or domino delivery, this examination will be undertaken by the GP caring for them. The examination entails listening to heart and lungs, examining breasts for any abnormal lumps and to check for conditions such as inverted nipples which may need special care to enable you to breastfeed, noting varicose veins and any swelling of the legs or fingers. Later in pregnancy such swelling can be a feature of a condition called pre-eclampsia (see page 53). If you do have an internal examination it is usually for a cervical smear. Feeling the size of your uterus, using two fingers inside and pressing down on the outside of your stomach can enable the doctor to assess how pregnant you are. Such an examination may also be done to exclude abnormalities of the pelvis, vagina and cervix.

ANTENATAL CARE IN THE MIDDLE MONTHS

If all is normal the hospital will probably leave this period of care to your GP or community midwife whom you should see once a month to be weighed, have your urine tested and blood pressure checked. At each visit they will feel your abdomen, especially the height of the top of the uterus which is called the 'fundus', and which usually rises at a steady rate as the baby grows. They may listen to the baby's heart through a special ear trumpet. Although they will note the baby's position, this is not important until later months as the baby can move freely inside the uterus while he is still small.

ANTENATAL CARE AT THE END OF PREGNANCY

If this is a first baby, the hospital will probably see you again at 28 weeks, later for mothers who have had one or more straightforward pregnancies. In the last month, visits will be weekly. As the baby grows, there is less room for him to move and by 34 weeks it is hoped he will have settled into a head-down position ready to be born.

OTHER TESTS DURING PREGNANCY

SCREENING FOR ANENCEPHALY AND *SPINA BIFIDA*

Some hospitals perform this test. A blood sample taken in the 16th week is tested for a raised level of a protein called 'alpha-foetoprotein' (AFP) which may be an indication of anencephaly (a defect in the skull in which the brain does not form and the baby dies) or *spina bifida* (where the bones in the spine are not properly joined together so that some of the spinal cord protrudes). Other very common reasons for raised AFP levels are multiple pregnancy, the pregnancy being more advanced than was supposed, or threat of miscarriage. A positive test will be repeated and then followed up with a scan and amniocentesis (see page 43). Hospitals with good scanning facilities avoid the blood test by offering careful detailed scanning to all their patients. If the baby appears to be damaged, the parents will be counselled about the likely outcome of the pregnancy and asked if they want a termination. A very low level of AFP can sometimes be an indication of Down's syndrome (see page 647), but this is not always the case.

MATERNAL SERUM SCREENING TEST

This blood test was being developed in the late 1980s to identify women with an increased risk of carrying a baby with Down's syndrome to enable them to decide whether or not to go on and have an amniocentesis or chorion villus sampling. The test measures levels of three substances in the woman's blood: alpha-foetoprotein (AFP), unconjugated oestriol (uE3) and human chorionic gonadotrophin (HCG). The levels of the three substances are used in conjunction with the woman's age to estimate the risk of Down's syndrome. When the risk of Down's syndrome is 1 in 250 or more, the test result is said to be 'screen positive'. This result does not mean there *is* a birth defect, only that there is an increased risk and further tests are indicated. If the risk of Down's syndrome is found to be less than 1 in 250 then the result of the test will be 'screen negative'. More than nine out of ten women will have a screen negative result. It does not completely exclude the chance of Down's syndrome, but does detect two out of three cases of Down's. In the future this test will probably be incorporated in routine screening of all pregnant women to replace amniocentesis and chorion villus sampling on the basis of maternal age alone.

ULTRASOUND

This is often called 'scanning' or a 'scan'. Most hospitals do scans routinely around 16 to 18 weeks and some do one at the end of pregnancy. The mother's abdomen is covered with a film of oil so that the pick-up head or transducer can slide easily backwards and forwards. Very high-frequency sounds we cannot hear are directed into the uterus, the echoes bounce back off the tissue and bones of the unborn baby and are converted into a black and white picture which builds up on a television screen beside the couch. Real time scanners produce moving pictures, while static scanners give a single, still picture. A scan can sometimes answer these questions:

* Are you pregnant and is the baby alive? A skilled doctor can tell as early as 4 to 6 weeks.

* How many weeks pregnant are you? Before 12 weeks the baby's age is calculated by measuring from crown to bottom, and later by measuring the diameter of the head and comparing these to known average sizes of babies at particular stages in pregnancy.

* Are you expecting more than one baby? This can usually be answered after eight weeks.

* Is the pregnancy in the right place? Ectopic pregnancies where the

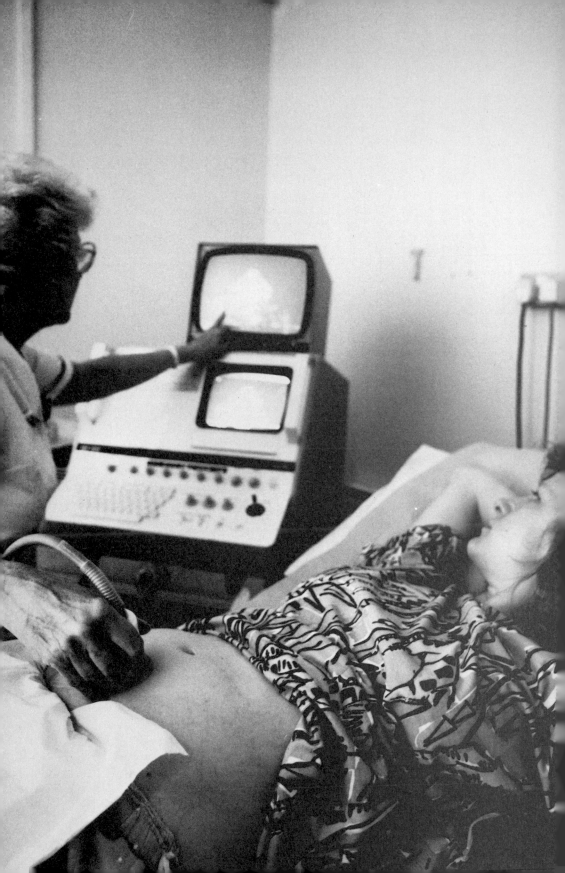

fertilised egg implants in the Fallopian tube or elsewhere outside the uterus can be diagnosed by ultrasound.

* Where is the placenta? A low-lying placenta can cause problems. This is not so significant in the early stages of pregnancy as the placenta may move upwards of its own accord. However, in later months of pregnancy it needs careful monitoring to make sure it does not overlap the outlet of the uterus – this is called *placenta praevia* (see page 53).

* Is the baby developing normally? Not all abnormalities can be ruled out by a scan, but neural tube defects making the head extra large or spine incomplete (hydrocephalus and *spina bifida*) can usually be detected. The 18-week scan is used to check the correct anatomy of the heart, the presence of kidneys, the normality of the gut and that there are no major skeletal abnormalities.

* Do you have fibroid cysts or tumours? These can be identified by ultrasound.

AMNIOCENTESIS

'I remember asking the nurse if it would hurt and she said "no" but held my hand. It's true it didn't hurt, but it was a very odd sensation feeling the needle going in so deep and I worried in case the baby moved.'

The baby's position is checked with a scan and then a fine, hollow needle is inserted through the abdomen to draw off a sample of amniotic fluid from inside the uterus. It cannot usually be done until 14 to 16 weeks when the uterus has risen out of the pelvis and there is enough amniotic fluid surrounding the baby. Some of the baby's cells present in the fluid can be examined under a microscope so the chromosomes are visible. This result takes about four weeks as the cells must be grown in cell culture so that there are enough for analysis. Down's syndrome shows as an extra chromosome, and other abnormalities may show as missing or damaged chromosomes. Amniocentesis is usually offered routinely to mothers aged thirty-seven or over or when a combination of the mother's age and a low AFP result indicates a risk of Down's syndrome (see page 647). Other reasons for the test may be a history of inherited abnormality, or to check the progress of a baby with rhesus disease. Later in pregnancy amniocentesis can tell us how mature the baby's lungs are – this is important if a baby has to be delivered prematurely. There is a very small chance of miscarriage (less than 0.5%) following this test.

CHORION BIOPSY

This is a new test, not yet widely available, which carries a slightly higher risk of miscarriage, but has the advantage that it can be done at about the 9th to 10th week. A hollow needle is inserted through the cervix or the

Having an ultrasound scan

abdominal wall to draw off some cells from the chorionic villi — they are the projections which anchor the embryo to the wall of the uterus initially and are then incorporated as part of the placenta or disintegrate. The test gives the same sort of information as an amniocentesis test, but in addition can be used to detect some genetic diseases such as cystic fibrosis, Duchenne muscular dystrophy, haemophilia and thalassaemia in families known to have those diseases.

CARDIFF COUNT-TO-TEN FOETAL ACTIVITY CHART

So called because it was a Cardiff hospital which first devised it. Mothers are given the chart at 28 weeks of pregnancy and are asked to note the first ten movements in a twelve-hour period starting from 9 a.m. and fill in the time at which they feel the baby's tenth movement of the day. If they have not counted ten movements by the evening, they are advised to ring the hospital and will often be asked to come in so that the baby's heart can be monitored on a machine.

MONITORING

Cardiotography (CTG) is the proper name. The mother wears a belt with a sensor round her middle. The baby's heartbeat is picked up and recorded on graph paper, and the strength of the mother's contractions, if in labour, can also be recorded. Babies' hearts usually beat between 120 and 160 times a minute and during a contraction, when the baby is under stress, the heartbeat speeds up a bit. It is also possible to monitor the baby's heart by connecting an electrode to its scalp during labour.

FOETAL BLOOD SAMPLING AND FOETOSCOPY

This is only available in a very few hospitals and may be done if other tests indicate a high risk of abnormality in the baby. As with amniocentesis, the baby's position is checked with a scan and a fine needle is introduced into the umbilical cord under ultrasound scan guidance. Sometimes a foetoscope — a fine tube containing a fibre optic telescope — is passed through the abdomen into the uterus. Samples of the baby's blood can be used to test for blood disease, such as haemophilia, sickle cell disease and thalassaemia, but these genetic diseases are now usually detected by chorion biopsy analysis. In cases of rhesus babies where their rhesus factor is incompatible with the mother's, blood transfusions can be given to the baby as early as 18 weeks of pregnancy to prevent him becoming fatally anaemic (see also page 62).

IN UTERO SURGERY

Although this is very rarely done, it can occasionally be used to save a life. Sometimes unborn babies have a blockage in the tube leading from the bladder so that urine cannot drain and the bladder swells up, eventually causing permanent damage to the kidneys due to back pressure. This can be detected by a scan, and under ultrasound control a shunt can be inserted which allows the urine to drain from the baby's bladder into the amniotic fluid and save the kidneys from permanent damage. In the future there will undoubtedly be many more ways of doctoring the unborn baby.

EATING SENSIBLY AND WEIGHT GAIN

Because being weighed is a regular part of every antenatal check, it is hard not to become very conscious of how much you are gaining. Advice about weight gain in pregnancy has ranged over the past years from 'eating for two' to trying to limit gain to a pound a week. Present-day expert advice is against specific limits and encourages you just to eat sensibly and let your weight look after itself. It is important to eat well during pregnancy and this means a balanced diet with something from each food group (see page 5). It does not always have to be fresh food, but cut down on cakes, biscuits and sugary foods and this will help take care of your weight.

Individuals vary tremendously in the amount they gain, but a very rough guide is that an average total gain tends to be between 10 and 12.5 kg. (22 and 28 lbs). Weight gain can also vary during pregnancy – you might put on a lot in a few weeks and then slow down.

Because doctors and midwives are ever vigilant for any signs which may mean the baby is not growing at the expected rate, they are likely to be more concerned about slow weight gain or weight loss. It may be worth pointing out, though, that one off-the-cuff remark at an antenatal check is not a reason for sleepless nights – one antenatal teacher reckoned that a half of all her pupils had been told at some stage that they did not appear to be gaining enough weight. What matters is gain over a prolonged period.

Women who are already very overweight would do well to consult their doctor about losing weight before they become pregnant, but it is not a good idea to go on a crash diet just before trying to conceive as gimmicky diets may leave your body low in essential minerals and vitamins. If you have a weight problem then pregnancy may be a time when it seems particularly hard to eat sensibly, but try not to use it as an excuse for binges of foods high in calories but not high in nutritional value. While it is estimated that pregnancy requires about 400 extra calories a day, an average pregnant woman only actually takes in about 200 extra calories – the other 200 calories are 'saved' by going about her ordinary life in a way which expends less energy. Women usually feel hungrier, especially in early pregnancy, so easily take in an extra 200 calories in slightly larger portions at ordinary mealtimes. About half a pint of whole milk, or four apples, or a roast chicken leg weighing 4½ oz. without skin or bone, or one ladleful (about 6 oz.) of beef stew is roughly equivalent to 200 calories. Those on a vegetarian or vegan diet need to be particularly careful (see page 5).

Iron Iron is needed to make red blood cells, and more of these cells are required in pregnancy to supply the placenta, uterus and unborn baby. At first the baby's needs are small but they start to be more marked from about 30 weeks. It is rare for a baby to become anaemic through lack of iron because he will take what he needs from the mother at her expense, but most women need some extra iron towards the end of pregnancy. If they reach term with a barely adequate iron supply, even the moderate amount of blood lost in a normal delivery can be enough to necessitate a blood transfusion. This is why the levels of haemoglobin, the oxygen-carrying part of red blood cells, are measured in regular blood tests at antenatal visits. If the level of haemoglobin falls below ten grams per litre of blood, the woman is said to be anaemic. In some places iron and folic acid (see below) supplements are given routinely, while in other hospitals they are given according to results of blood tests. There can sometimes be side effects from taking extra iron – nausea, indigestion and constipation are the commonest – but they are rarely severe. Eating well before pregnancy will help to keep natural levels of iron high, and good natural sources of iron are liver and dark green leaf vegetables like spinach.

Folic acid Pregnant women also need more than usual of this vitamin because it is used to form the baby's cells. As with iron, too little can make them anaemic. Research is still going on to establish the possible significance of folic acid deficiency in neural tube defects, like *spina bifida*. Most hospitals give combined iron and folic acid supplements, but eating a lot of fresh vegetables before and during pregnancy can boost stores of folic acid. Unfortunately, it is easily destroyed by cooking, so try eating raw, lightly steamed or microwaved vegetables.

Listeria and salmonella Most bacteria are harmless, but some – especially those associated with food, such as listeria and salmonella – can be very harmful to the unborn baby. So general food safety and hygiene are very important. If you are pregnant or likely to be it is best to avoid the following: soft cheeses such as brie, camembert and similar varieties, or mould-ripened cheeses such as Danish blue and Stilton because of the risk of listeria; raw or lightly cooked eggs because of the risk of salmonella – this includes foods containing raw eggs, such as homemade mayonnaise, and homemade icecreams, cheesecakes and mousses; pâtés because of the risk of listeria unless they are marked as pasteurised; and raw or lightly cooked meat because of the risk of toxoplasmosis (see page 508) and other bacterial and parasitic infections.

AVOID X-RAYS IN EARLY PREGNANCY

Even though the level of radiation used in taking ordinary X-rays is very low indeed, radiologists always take care to protect the reproductive organs of men and women and try not to expose women inadvertently to radiation in early pregnancy. If you think you may be pregnant tell the radiologist, though if the X-ray is for a serious purpose the risk to the foetus is very slight indeed and doctors will exercise common sense in putting your general health first. If you had an X-ray without knowing you were pregnant, it is highly unlikely any harm could have resulted. In theory high levels of radiation could produce an abnormality in the genes of the mother's ova (eggs) which might be damaging to subsequent offspring—this has been shown to happen in experiments on animals. Secondly, it is possible that very high levels of radiation during early pregnancy could produce an abnormality in the baby — in the past high levels were used to treat pregnant women who had cancer, and this did cause defects in some of their children. It is very unlikely indeed that diagnostic X-rays would do this, and indeed before the development of ultrasound they were used routinely in early pregnancy.

MINOR PHYSICAL PROBLEMS

BACKACHE

The ligaments supporting your spine become softened. You have more weight to support, your centre of gravity changes and you may get into the habit of standing and sitting badly, which can all contribute to backache. Give high heels a miss and learn to sit and stand correctly. Always bend your knees when lifting something from the floor instead of bending down, and keep heavy things close into your body. Do not stoop over a low work

Correct posture   *Bad posture*

Make sure that the small of your back is supported   *Try not to slump or cross your legs*

surface, and try a firmer mattress or board under your mattress to see if this makes a difference. Massage and relaxation exercises designed for pregnancy often help. If you have real problems with backache ask the obstetric doctor looking after you at your hospital for advice.

BLEEDING GUMS

The amount of blood circulating in your body increases during pregnancy and this extra blood supply to the tissues makes gums more likely to bleed during pregnancy. Do not get into the habit of accepting it as normal – it is still caused by a build-up of plaque. Brush teeth extra carefully with a soft brush, use dental floss and take advantage of free dental treatment in pregnancy.

CONSTIPATION

Hormone changes, relaxed muscle tone, and pressure of the womb on the bowel often cause constipation. Do not use laxatives but instead drink plenty of water and eat wholegrain foods like wholemeal bread, rice and pasta, plus plenty of fruit and vegetables. Iron supplements are likely to make constipation worse, so don't take them unless your blood tests show they are strictly necessary. Avoiding constipation can help avoid piles and varicose veins, but if it is a particular problem ask your doctor.

CRAMP

The cause is not known though it is very common in pregnancy – one suggestion is that it may be due to lack of calcium. Rub the muscle very hard and, if it is in your leg, bend your foot upwards.

FAINTNESS AND PALPITATIONS

These are due to changes in the heart and circulation system. Although such attacks can be worrying and rather unpleasant, they are not usually symptomatic of anything abnormal, simply one of the side effects of pregnancy. Some people seem to be more prone than others and, if you are at all worried, do discuss this with your doctor, but generally the best tactics are to take avoiding action as far as possible. This may mean altering travelling arrangements so that standing journeys in the rush hour are no longer necessary, shopping out of peak times to avoid long waits at the checkout, and giving social events which entail hours of standing in hot or crowded situations a miss. If you do feel faint, immediately find somewhere to sit down, even if it means asking someone to give up their chair or seat on the train, and if the feeling persists, put your head down between your knees so that the blood will flow more easily to the brain. Some women, especially in late pregnancy, find simply lying on their back is enough to make them feel faint because of the weight of the baby pressing on the large veins carrying blood back to the heart. If this is the case simply turn on your side and make a point of explaining the problem to nurses at antenatal appointments to avoid having to lie on your back for longer than is absolutely necessary.

HEADACHES

The occasional paracetemol is all right, but aspirin should be avoided. See your doctor if you have continuous, bad headaches. In later pregnancy these just might be a warning of high blood pressure.

HEARTBURN AND INDIGESTION

A valve at the entrance to the stomach relaxes in pregnancy, allowing stomach acids to filter back up the tube, causing that burning sensation we call heartburn. Pressure on the stomach from the growing baby also makes indigestion more common. Eat little and often and eat sitting upright, not slumping or lying back. Drinking milk can help, or try antacid medication.

INCONTINENCE

Needing to pass water frequently is common in the first three months and also in the last three months because of the pressure of the growing baby squashing the bladder. Some women, especially if they have already had several children, can find themselves prone to stress incontinence, which means that laughing, coughing or attempts at jumping up and down need to be undertaken with care and great concentration, because the extra stress can cause them to lose control and leak a small amount of urine. Stress incontinence usually disappears soon after the birth, though all women need to do pelvic floor exercises during pregnancy and after the birth to prevent it becoming a problem later in life. Continuing incontinence may indicate that nerve endings or muscles have been damaged during the birth and you should see your doctor.

INSOMNIA

Difficulty in sleeping is common as the baby gets very large. Many women

Use pillows to make yourself comfortable

often have vivid dreams in pregnancy about the birth and the baby. Try lying on your side with a pillow to support your tummy and take naps in the day if you can to make up for missed sleep. However, do not attach significance to dreams or treat them as premonitions, even though for some months they may suggest some anxiety or mixed feelings about the baby.

NOSEBLEEDS

These can be particularly common in pregnancy and, like bleeding gums, are due to the fact that an extra amount of blood is circulating around your body. The blood vessels lining the nose are simply more likely to rupture at this stage. The best way of treating a nosebleed is to pinch your nostrils hard together to encourage clotting and if necessary splash your face with icy cold water or put a cloth soaked in icy water across the bridge of your nose. A blocked or stuffy nose is common and is due to increased production of nasal mucus.

SICKNESS AND NAUSEA

Usually this eases off after 12 weeks, but for some unlucky women it can be a real problem which continues for much longer. Although commonly referred to as 'morning' sickness, attacks of nausea or actual vomiting can occur at any time of the day. It is thought that sickness may be caused by raised levels of female hormones circulating in the body, but despite the extent of the problem there has been surprisingly little research.

Traditional advice is to try eating something dry like a plain biscuit or a piece of toast first thing in the morning, eat little and often and avoid anything which makes you feel specially bad. It seems that each person has to experiment to find the best methods or foods to alleviate the problem. Smells, such as fried food or even petrol, can be enough to trigger an attack, but some women say certain smells – for example, that of sulphur when a match is struck – can help. Bland starchy foods, like plain bread and cereals, are usually safest and it has been suggested that eliminating tea, coffee and alcohol helps.

One age-old remedy is supposed to be ginger, but results are not guaranteed. The suggestion is to sip ginger tea – made with powdered ginger in boiling water or by steeping a small piece of fresh root ginger – first thing in the morning and half an hour before meals. However, since it has been suggested that a trigger for sickness can be swings in blood sugar levels, it is best not to seek a cure in ginger products which contain sugar such as ginger biscuits or ginger ale. Some women crave sweet foods to relieve nausea temporarily, but eating sugary foods causes a sharp rise in blood sugar levels followed by a drop to an even lower level. Eating small but frequent snacks of wholesome foods rather than foods full of sugar and white flour can avoid this roller-coaster effect.

If you are being sick all the time or feel intolerably ill see your doctor, but hard-learned lessons like Thalidomide, the anti-nausea drug subsequently found to cause major birth defects, and more recently suspicions about Debendox, have understandably made doctors wary of prescribing for a condition which, although extremely unpleasant, is not dangerous.

Very rarely, vomiting may lead to de-hydration and starvation. This is called *hyperemesis gravidarum* and needs treatment with a fluid drip in hospital.

SKIN

Stretch marks are red lines which fade into thin, silvery white lines. They occur when the elastic fibre under the skin breaks. Whether you get them or not depends on your inherited skin type, but using cream or oil to stop your skin getting dry, eating well before and during pregnancy, and lightly pinching and massaging skin to stimulate circulation can sometimes help.

Some people suffer from itchy skin, especially late in pregnancy. This can affect just the abdomen or occur all over the body, and sometimes causes patches of red flaky rash. If it is very bad see your doctor, but otherwise loose clothing made from natural (not synthetic) fibres, oils and creams may help, and some people suggest oatmeal in the bath does too.

Pregnancy is also a time for changes in pigmentation – a dark line develops down the centre of the abdomen from the navel from about the third month, but has no significance and fades after the birth. Some people get patches of lighter or darker skin which will also disappear. Freckles, moles and scars can all become temporarily darker or more pronounced.

SWEATING

Body temperature is higher during pregnancy. This is useful in winter, but summer pregnancies may need cool showers and rest to avoid overheating.

SWELLING

Legs, ankles, feet and hands may all swell up during pregnancy because the body holds more water than usual. As long as your blood pressure stays normal, it does not matter, but this should be checked because swelling (medical name 'oedema') can sometimes be a forewarning of a condition called 'pre-eclampsia' (see page 53). Try to rest with your feet higher than your heart, wear flat, comfortable shoes, and take things easy.

VAGINAL DISCHARGE

This is usually heavier during pregnancy anyway, but itching, soreness or an offensive smell may mean an infection such as thrush, so see your doctor.

VARICOSE VEINS AND PILES

Hormone changes and the pressure of the uterus on veins make varicose veins in the legs and vulva more likely in pregnancy. Wearing support tights, putting your feet up, avoiding standing for long periods or sitting with crossed legs, and not getting constipated from the beginning of pregnancy can help to prevent or relieve them. Varicose veins around the rectum are called 'piles' and usually arise because of constipation. If they are troublesome and cause itching and soreness, see your doctor, but usually both piles and varicose veins disappear after the birth.

MORE SERIOUS PROBLEMS IN PREGNANCY

ECTOPIC PREGNANCY

This happens when the fertilised egg implants and begins to grow somewhere other than the womb, usually the Fallopian tube, but occasionally in the abdomen. The word 'ectopic' simply means displaced. It usually happens because a blockage or kink in the Fallopian tube prevents the fertilised egg from reaching the womb. Signs are one – rarely two – missed periods, pain low down and to one side in the abdomen, often pain in the shoulder, faintness, and losing a slight amount of darkish blood. It is important such pregnancies are diagnosed because they can cause internal bleeding and shock. Since most ectopic pregnancies are in one of the Fallopian tubes, this usually means an operation to remove the tube, but pregnancy is still possible provided the other tube is undamaged.

MOLAR PREGNANCY

This is a rare condition when the embryo usually fails to develop and the placenta grows abnormally and quickly. Signs are a large-for-dates uterus but no sign of a foetal heartbeat and sometimes heavy bleeding. Although it has nothing to do with the kind of moles that grow on your skin, this 'false embryo' is referred to as a mole and will be removed with a D&C (see page 58) which may be repeated three months later when the tissues are checked because in unusual cases the cells can show abnormalities which may lead to malignancy if untreated.

BLEEDING IN EARLY PREGNANCY

Spotting sometimes happens at the time of a first missed period as the embryo implants in the wall of the uterus, but bleeding can also be a warning of threatened miscarriage (see page 55).

BLEEDING IN MIDDLE AND LATE PREGNANCY

Incompetent cervix This usually occurs around weeks 20 to 24 when the neck of a womb which is not able to stay tightly closed may begin to open. This could be because of damage during earlier pregnancies or during a gynaecological operation. Treatment is a special stitch to draw the cervix tightly closed – rather like the neck of a purse. This is usually done around week 14 under general or epidural anaesthetic and can be taken out again without anaesthetic at week 38.

Placenta praevia Painless bleeding from week 28 is usually due to this. If the placenta attaches itself to the wall of the uterus low down it partially or completely blocks the baby's exit by covering the cervix. If bleeding begins before the baby is due then bed rest is needed so that the baby is given as much time as possible to mature and develop in the uterus. A Caesarean section is needed if the placenta covers the cervix, but sometimes vaginal delivery is possible with a placenta which only extends close to the cervix. Ultrasound can easily check the position of the placenta and sometimes a low-lying placenta may move upwards of its own accord as the pregnancy progresses. Rarely, *placenta praevia* may not be evident until labour begins with heavy bleeding, and then an emergency Caesarean and a blood transfusion are usually needed.

HIGH BLOOD PRESSURE AND PRE-ECLAMPSIA

Some women already have high blood pressure, and others develop it during pregnancy. A family history of high blood pressure, blood pressure problems while taking the Pill, smoking and being overweight all increase the chance of this happening. High blood pressure is often the first sign of a condition called pre-eclampsia or toxaemia, which occurs only in pregnancy, and although it may make the mother or the baby very unwell, always gets better after the baby is born. The other features of pre-eclampsia are swelling (oedema) of the legs, fingers and face, and protein in the urine. Swelling also occurs in the placenta which makes it less efficient at giving oxygen and nourishment to the baby. Treatment is with rest initially, and tablets may be needed to bring the blood pressure down. Early delivery by inducing labour or even by Caesarean section may be necessary, in order to prevent eclampsia (see below) or harm to the baby.

We do not know exactly why pre-eclampsia happens, but it is very much more likely in the first pregnancy and is also linked with a family history of the condition. Research suggests that an immune reaction in the mother may be involved.

Ten per cent of women will get pre-eclampsia in their first pregnancy, and the risk is three times this if a woman's blood pressure was high before getting pregnant.

ECLAMPSIA

If unchecked, pre-eclampsia can lead to eclampsia – convulsions or fits like epileptic fits. It can be dangerous but is fortunately very rare. The mother loses consciousness, may injure herself and have trouble breathing which puts the baby at serious risk because the fit drastically reduces his oxygen supply. Prevention is nearly always possible, but very unusually such a fit can happen without warning signs and, if it does, treatment is anticonvulsant drugs and usually emergency delivery of the baby by Caesarean.

UNUSUAL BIRTH POSITIONS

Most babies are born head first, with the back of the baby's head towards the mother's abdomen. They usually settle into this head-down position around the seventh month when they become too large to do those amazing somersaults and turns which make your stomach jump around. The reason that this is the preferred position for birth is that the head is the largest part of the baby, and is also a hard, rounded surface which works better to open up the birth canal slowly as the baby is born. It is also, conveniently, the end which takes in oxygen. The head is said to be engaged when it descends into the pelvis and you will experience a noticeable easing as the bulge drops lower in your abdomen.

Doctors and midwives will be concerned about the position of the baby as more unusual positions sometimes need more care and attention at the birth.

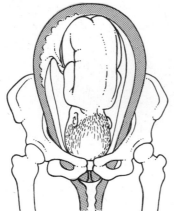 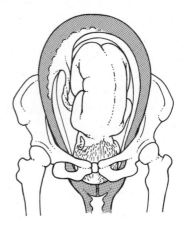

Unengaged   *Engaged*

Breech This means that the baby is lying bottom or feet first. It is very common in the middle months but only 6% of babies are still breech at 34 weeks and only 3% at term. Sometimes the doctor may try to turn the baby by gently manipulating him from the outside. Do not try to do this yourself though, because it can cause the placenta to separate if not done properly. Breech babies can be delivered vaginally, but will almost certainly need help with an episiotomy and perhaps forceps. Depending on

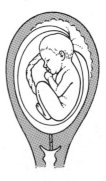

your circumstances a Caesarean may be suggested. Sometimes doctors suggest waiting for labour to begin naturally to see if a normal delivery looks possible.

Transverse This means the baby is lying crossways instead of vertically. This is more likely after several babies when the muscles of the uterus have already been stretched. Like breech babies, these positions can right themselves naturally and sometimes a transverse baby turns head down only when labour begins. If not, the presenting part, that is the part of the baby which is born first, will usually be the shoulder, in which case a Caesarean is needed.

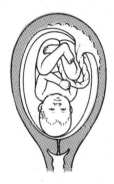

Posterior In this position the baby is head down, but instead of having the back of his head and backbone towards the mother's abdomen (anterior), he has his backbone to her backbone so face and limbs are all towards her abdomen. The most likely effect during labour is that you will experience backache rather than pains across your abdomen. It can help to use different positions during labour and even delivery to help things along if labour is not progressing swiftly enough (see page 90).

Unstable lie An unstable lie means simply that the baby is sometimes transverse and sometimes head down or breech and is not fixed in one position.

MISCARRIAGE

One in six of all pregnancies, it is estimated, end in miscarriage. The term applies to a foetus delivered dead before the 28th week of pregnancy – the stage at which, legally, a foetus is considered viable. In fact, the law lags behind medical skills in this respect because babies born as early as 23 weeks are now being saved in neonatal (newborn) intensive care units. If a baby is delivered alive after the 28th week, this is described not as a miscarriage, but as premature labour and delivery. A baby born dead after the 28th week is said to be stillborn. So the word 'miscarriage' actually has a very precise meaning. The medical term for miscarriage is 'spontaneous abortion', which can cause confusion because to many people the word 'abortion' means only the deliberate termination of a pregnancy.

Why do miscarriages happen? Inevitably, as couples try to come to terms with the shock of a pregnancy which ends in miscarriage, they search for a reason. Sadly, in the vast majority of cases of miscarriage no cause is readily apparent and because having even two miscarriages does not greatly alter the odds against success the third time around, doctors do not usually embark on major investigation until a woman has experienced three repeated miscarriages, known as 'recurrent miscarriage'. In the absence of any medical explanation, couples may worry that they could have caused the miscarriage – perhaps by making love, by working too hard, by being under stress, by moving house or having too many late nights. None of these factors have ever been shown to be linked with miscarriage, however, and when you consider the number of pregnancies which continue despite the most adverse conditions – war, famine and emotional upheaval of all kinds – it is unlikely that there would be a link.

There is still a great deal we do not know about why some pregnancies miscarry and why some others, especially when the baby has some kind of abnormal development, go on to term. However, there are some factors which are known. The largest cause of early miscarriage is thought to be some kind of genetic abnormality in the development of the baby. Studies of miscarriage where foetal tissue was examined – and this is only possible in 20% of miscarriages – show genetic mistakes in half of the cases. There appears to be some natural mechanism which operates to end such pregnancies, though it is obviously not infallible because of the numbers of handicapped children who are born. In cases of repeated miscarriage, couples can have genetic counselling (see page 18) to make sure they do not carry a chromosomal abnormality, but in most cases of single miscarriage the couple's chromosome pattern is normal and any genetic abnormality in the foetus is a one-off mistake. Some malformations may be genetic, but are not caused by chromosome abnormalities – for example *spina bifida* in which the spinal cord does not form properly.

Other causes of miscarriage include:

Physical abnormalities During pregnancy the mother's uterus must expand as the baby and its surrounding bag of water grows. Occasionally the womb may be misshapen due to abnormal development when the mother herself was a foetus. The womb develops from two tubes which fuse together, and failure to do this leads to a heart-shaped uterus or even two separate small uteruses, which may not expand so easily.

Another cause of expansion failure is fibroids (non-cancerous growths which are common particularly after the age of thirty) in the wall of the uterus. These rigid balls of fibrous tissue can misshape the womb and may need to be removed surgically before pregnancy.

Hormones These have long been blamed for miscarriage, and women thought to have a hormone deficiency can be treated with hormone therapy either by injection, pessaries or orally. In fact there is no clear evidence about the part hormone deficiencies play in miscarriage, and there is a good deal of disagreement about whether treatment with hormones has any effect. It is probably best to be cautious about taking hormones in early pregnancy. However, it is known that an over- or under-active thyroid can sometimes lead to repeated miscarriages. A blood test can be done to check that the thyroid is working normally.

Immunological This is a comparatively newly established cause of miscarriage and takes two forms. The first, which is thought to be responsible for a substantial number of all recurrent miscarriages (defined as women who have had three or more consecutive miscarriages) is when the mother's immune system reacts as though the cells of the foetus are foreign and rejects them – just as transplanted organs are often rejected. Of course, the baby's cells are made up of antigens (proteins) from both the mother and the father. Normally there is a mechanism which operates to prevent the mother's body reacting to the father's antigens – this is the production of antibodies by the mother which stop her immune system reacting to the baby's cells as foreign matter. Treatment is for the woman to be immunised with her husband's cells, by injecting blood lymphocytes, so that her body makes the required antibodies which will protect subsequent pregnancies from being rejected, but this procedure has had limited success. The problem is not caused by any abnormality in either husband or wife, rather it is a question of the choice of partner – with a different partner the woman would produce antibodies in the normal way.

In the second form it has now been recognised that certain women produce antibodies against fatty substances called phosopholipids which are found on the surface of all cells. This condition causes repeated miscarriage late in pregnancy, often after 20 weeks. Current treatment is with combinations of several drugs which may prevent miscarriage and allow the foetus to grow normally, but the risk of early labour still remains.

Infection German measles (*rubella*) is known to cause miscarriage as well as causing abnormalities in surviving babies, and so too may genital herpes during the initial infection. Uncertainty exists about the effect of other more common infections such as influenza which is hard to prove or disprove. Infections which can exist without causing any noticeable illness in the mother may cause miscarriage – toxoplasmosis and mycoplasma are two. In the case of repeated miscarriages a woman should be screened for such conditions which may show up in blood or cervical smear tests.

Age The risk of miscarriage does increase slightly with a woman's age, especially after thirty years, but, of course, most pregnancies in older women do not miscarry.

The coil (intra-uterine device, IUD) Pregnancies can happen with a coil inside the womb and if the coil is left in place there is a 50% chance of miscarriage and also a high risk of infection. For this reason, coils are always removed once a pregnancy is confirmed, if the coil string is accessible.

Signs of a miscarriage

'I started bleeding and went to see my doctor. He advised bed rest but after two days in bed I was still bleeding and I decided to get up. The miscarriage happened the next day. I had some tummy cramps and felt sweaty and shivery. I kept going to the loo and eventually passed what I recognised as a tiny embryo. I was twelve weeks pregnant but I was very shocked to find there was something there. I was terribly naïve. I thought it would just be blood clots.'

Bleeding of some description is usually the first sign of a threatened miscarriage. It can be a slight discharge of a brownish colour, a steady trickle of a bright red colour or blood clots. The good news is that about half of all pregnancies which have some bleeding in the first three months will actually settle down and continue normally with no harm at all to the foetus, any blood having come from the lining of the womb.

A woman should see her doctor as soon as she notices any bleeding during pregnancy. If the neck of the womb (cervix) is open and the bleeding heavy, she will be referred to hospital. An ultrasound scan can determine whether the pregnancy is still viable, that is able to continue. If not, then a D & C (dilatation and curettage) under general anaesthetic will be advised to remove any remaining clots or tissue. If the pregnancy is still viable, then the woman will usually be kept in hospital until the bleeding ceases. There is no evidence that staying in bed, either at hospital or at home, actually helps to prevent miscarriage, but it is still commonly prescribed because it is something which is obviously hard to subject to scientific measurement. There are clearly many cases where a pregnancy continues after a woman has stayed in bed, but we do not know whether that would have happened if the same woman had carried on normally. Certainly, it does no harm and seems to make sense. After the bleeding stops and the pregnancy settles down, doctors usually advise taking things easy at home for a further two weeks or so before slowly resuming a normal pace of life.

Sometimes a foetus may die in the womb without any sign of bleeding and this is usually detected on an ultrasound scan. To feel well and to be told out of the blue that the pregnancy is not viable can be a great shock. This can occur when the embryo and surrounding membranes appear to develop normally for a short time and then the embryo dies while the membranes continue to function for a little longer. An ultrasound scan will reveal an 'empty sac'. Some obstetricians refer to this as a blighted ovum, an archaic term wrongly implying that the error is always with the egg. A 'missed abortion' is the term used when the embryo dies but there is no bleeding nor signs of miscarriage. The causes are not clear, but are thought to be due to some defect in the egg or sperm. The tissue is removed by a D & C under anaesthetic, but this does not mean future pregnancies are more likely to run into problems.

Recurrent miscarriage After having one miscarriage, women are naturally fearful and want reassurance about the chances of future pregnancies ending this way. Happily, one miscarriage does not alter the odds of the next pregnancy being successful and, even if she has had two miscarriages, there is still more than a 75% chance of success. But, statistically, having three recurrent miscarriages does affect the odds, which is why doctors only investigate once a woman falls into this category. It is important that the couple are properly investigated, although they must still be prepared for disappointment as a cause is often impossible to pinpoint even after thorough investigation.

It is thought that probably the commonest cause of recurrent miscarriage is immunological. Genetic factors are common causes of a single miscarriage, but a much rarer cause of recurrent miscarriage. Women with a pattern of recurrent miscarriage also need to be screened to eliminate the possibility of infection, as well as any anatomical abnormality.

Coping with miscarriage As well as shock, guilt and a sense of loss, women often feel thoroughly disorientated. The birth of a baby requires many decisions and much planning. It is only when the event is suddenly removed that we realise just how much, subconsciously, it has begun to dominate the horizon. It is often hard to go back to ordinary life with enthusiasm. Some women feel an overwhelming desire to become pregnant again as soon as possible to replace the familiar horizon. Others may wish to make changes in their lives in order to take a new direction. It helps to be able to talk to others who have experienced this common disappointment and for couples to talk to each other. Breaking the news to family, friends and workmates is sometimes hard as their reactions can occasionally be unintentionally brisk – 'Never mind, you're young' – or, in the case of relatives, add to guilt by making misplaced suggestions as to possible causes.

It is a good idea to allow the hormonal balance to settle and wait several months before trying for another pregnancy and to discuss understandable worries with your GP or obstetrician first.

PREGNANCIES NEEDING THE FIVE-STAR TREATMENT

AGE AND OTHER RISKS

Probably the best age to have a baby from a purely physical point of view is between twenty and twenty-four. Of course, that is not always the best time socially or emotionally, but women who have existing illnesses such as diabetes can help to reduce the risks if they have their children during their twenties. Their pregnancies should be well spaced so that the body can recover in between and the mother is not too exhausted with the demands of several very young children.

Younger mothers Under the age of sixteen there is a higher risk of having a small or premature baby, of becoming anaemic and suffering from high blood pressure. Emotionally and socially such very young teenagers are likely to find pregnancy and motherhood much harder to cope with and need a great deal of support.

Older first-time mothers What is the greatest risk to the older mother? 'Her doctor's anxiety, I would say,' said an obstetrician at a London teaching hospital. Certainly, feeling that this may be a woman's last chance of having a baby, especially if she has had years of fertility treatment to enable her to conceive, may make her doctor more likely to intervene at the first hint of trouble. With careful monitoring, however, there is no reason why older first-time mothers of thirty-five or over should not be just as able to have a normal straightforward birth as a younger woman. The risk most associated with age is having a baby with some chromosomal abnormality, the most common being Down's syndrome (see page 647). A woman in her twenties has a chance of only one in several thousand of having such a baby, but by forty the risk is about 1 in every 110 births, and at forty-five the risk is about 1 in every 30. Amniocentesis can detect the extra chromosome which results in a Down's baby and is usually offered routinely to women who are thirty-seven or over. Fibroids, high blood pressure and prematurity are all slightly commoner amongst older first-time mothers.

NUMBER OF CHILDREN

A woman having her first baby is called a '*primigravida*' and a woman who has already had one baby is called a '*multiparous*' by doctors. First babies represent a slightly higher risk because the 'machinery' is untested and the mother inexperienced. Second and third pregnancies are more often straightforward, provided previous pregnancies have been free of complications. The risks begin to rise again with a fourth and successive pregnancies because the uterine muscles are slacker and less efficient and worn thinner, though this also depends to an extent on age and natural health.

HEART DISEASE

Pregnancy puts an added strain on the heart anyway – it has to pump about a third more blood round the body, and at a faster rate. It is quite common to feel your heart beating more rapidly or to feel breathless in pregnancy, but existing heart disease is a different matter and relatively unusual. Sometimes a heart condition can be discovered for the first time during pregnancy just because this may be the first time a woman has had a complete medical examination. If it is mild then taking things easy and staying calm may be enough. This could mean giving up work earlier in pregnancy, getting some help with housework or other children, calling on friends and relatives to lend a hand. If your heart condition is more serious, it could involve spending the middle and later months in hospital to ensure complete rest and more supervised care. Heart patients should not eat too much, should cut down on their salt intake to help keep their blood pressure down and their weight will be carefully monitored.

Unless there are other problems, they should be able to have a normal labour. An epidural may be suggested because it has the effect of lowering blood pressure and also reducing pain and therefore anxiety, and oxygen will be on hand to relieve breathlessness or chest pain. The effort of pushing as the baby moves down the birth canal is an extra strain on the heart and forceps are often used to avoid this stage. There is no reason why mothers with heart conditions should not breastfeed, but they must have a longer stay in hospital to make sure they are quite well. Again, pregnancies should be well spaced so that the body has time to recover.

THE RHESUS FACTOR

As well as belonging to one of four different blood groups, your blood can be either rhesus (Rh) positive or rhesus negative. It is Rh-positive if it contains a particular antigen – a substance which stimulates the formation of antibodies – which happens also to be found on the red blood cells of rhesus monkeys. Most people are Rh-positive. Your blood is Rh-negative if it does not have this antigen. Your baby is a mix of genetic information from both parents, and when an Rh-negative woman and an Rh-positive man have a baby, that baby could inherit the blood type of either parent. It is only a problem if he inherits his father's blood type and is Rh-positive – the opposite to his mother. During pregnancy, and particularly during the birth, some of the baby's blood cells may become mixed with the mother's and circulate in her body. This also happens with unsuccessful pregnancies which may be ectopic or end in miscarriage or termination. The mother's body reacts to these foreign blood cells by producing antibodies to fight them. These antibody molecules are small enough to cross the placenta and go back into the baby to start destroying the baby's red blood cells. If untreated, this could eventually make him so anaemic he will die.

Usually the level of antibodies is not high enough to do serious damage in a first pregnancy, but they will remain in the mother's blood and the problem becomes more serious with each successive pregnancy.

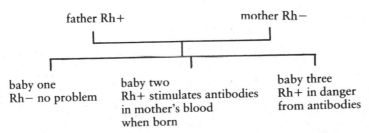

father Rh+   mother Rh−

baby one
Rh− no problem

baby two
Rh+ stimulates antibodies
in mother's blood
when born

baby three
Rh+ in danger
from antibodies

Fortunately, there is now a way of preventing this, and discovering a way to prevent rhesus babies has been one of the great success stories of obstetrics. If an injection of anti-D globulin is given to the mother within seventy-two hours of the first delivery (and this applies to miscarriages and terminations at whatever stage of pregnancy) it stops her becoming sensitised and making antibodies in future pregnancies.

However, if the woman has already become sensitised, perhaps because of an untreated earlier pregnancy or miscarriage, this injection cannot help. Instead, the level of antibodies in her blood will be monitored carefully through pregnancy, and the baby's condition may be checked by amniocentesis. The level of a yellowish pigment called 'bilirubin' in the amniotic fluid is a rough guide to the degree of anaemia in the baby and several tests may be needed. If the baby is in danger of becoming anaemic he can have a blood transfusion whilst still in the womb. This may be done either by injecting blood into the baby's abdomen from where it is absorbed into the bloodstream, or transfusing it directly into the umbilical cord blood vessels. Both these procedures are done using expert ultrasound pictures showing where to pass the fine needles. This may have to be done several times during pregnancy until the baby is mature enough to be delivered by Caesarean, and is a complicated procedure which can be done only at a few teaching hospitals. After birth the baby may need another transfusion, although this is a much simpler procedure.

DIABETES

Insulin is a hormone produced by the pancreas gland in the abdomen. Its job is to facilitate transfer of the glucose or sugar in the circulation into the cells where it can be used as a source of energy. Diabetics either do not produce any insulin or not enough. When the body cannot use glucose for fuel it begins to use fat instead and, in the process, substances called 'ketones' are produced. A build up of ketones in the blood upsets the body's chemistry, making a diabetic feel nauseous or even pass out. The glucose is unused and makes the blood glucose level very high. Because of the high blood level of glucose it begins to be passed out of the body in the urine and this is one of the first signs of diabetes. Diabetes carries a higher risk of miscarriage and some degree of foetal malformation – usually a single defect like a heart or lower spine abnormality – but provided the glucose levels are kept as normal as possible before and during pregnancy the risk is very small indeed. If the father is a diabetic his control before pregnancy does not make any difference to the risk.

Because the key factor in ensuring the successful outcome of a pregnancy for a diabetic woman is control of her diabetes, she should see her doctor or clinic well before she plans to become pregnant. Getting very good control of diabetes may mean two injections of insulin a day, possibly using a mixture of insulins. Once pregnancy is confirmed, this good control must continue, and because urine tests are not reliable enough, frequent blood testing is necessary. During pregnancy the amount of insulin needed changes rapidly and can double in the second half. Diabetic women need to eat especially carefully.

A careful check will also be kept on the baby's size, for babies of diabetics have a tendency to grow very large. It used to be the practice to deliver the babies of diabetic women early, but this in turn led to problems of prematurity in some cases. When diabetes has been carefully monitored and controlled, it is now often possible to leave such babies until term when they can usually be delivered vaginally. During labour a drip will be set up and insulin can either be added to the fluid which is being given through the drip or administered continuously with a special pump. Immediately after the birth the need for insulin will drop, and the day after the baby has been born the mother should go back to using the dosage and type of insulin she was on before she became pregnant.

Because the babies of diabetics are sometimes larger than average, they may lose a lot of weight in the first few days and seem sleepy, but after that they should develop normally. They will have tests in the first few days to check that their blood sugars are normal. Sometimes they may be immature if they have been delivered early and thus more likely to become hypo-glycaemic (very low blood sugar): for this reason they are sometimes nursed in a special care baby unit for a few days.

PREGNANCY DIABETES

Pregnancy predisposes the body chemistry towards diabetes which can occur solely as a condition of pregnancy, disappearing again after the birth. If it happens in one pregnancy, it is more likely to recur in later pregnancies and may occur mildly in later life. It happens more often in older women and the chance of it occurring increases slightly with the number of pregnancies. Treatment is just the same as for existing diabetes – diet and possibly insulin are needed to control the blood sugar levels.

TWINS, TRIPLETS AND MORE

Multiple pregnancies, where there is more than one baby, always need special care and monitoring.

Identical twins are the result of one fertilised egg splitting in two. The babies share one placenta and are always the same sex. Anyone has a 1 in 250 chance of having identical twins, though in unusual cases there may be a family history. Fraternal twins occur when two eggs are released and fertilised by two different sperm and have separate placentas which may, however, fuse together. The babies are no more alike than any brothers and sisters. Fraternal twins are about twice as likely as identical twins in Europe, but there is considerable racial variation in incidence. A family history through the maternal line makes fraternal twins more likely, and the chances are also slightly greater with taller women, older women,

women who conceive easily and with successive pregnancies. Triplets, quads, quins and sextuplets can occur spontaneously and are usually fraternal, but identical triplets have been known.

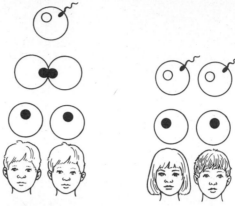

Identical twins   *Fraternal twins*

More usually nowadays these multiple births result from fertility treatment when drugs are used to stimulate ovulation and the ovary over-reacts and produces several eggs. The commonest such drug, Clomiphene, is mild, and rarely produces such a response. So-called test-tube treatments (IVF or *in vitro* fertilisation), when a fertilised egg is implanted back into the uterus, are also likely to produce more than one baby because doctors usually put several embryos back – with the couple's agreement – in the hope that one will survive. Sometimes more than one can develop, resulting in a multiple birth, and there have been cases of test-tube quads.

Wider use of ultrasound has made undiagnosed multiple pregnancies rare. The uterus grows more quickly in size, weight gain is faster and the mother often feels the side effects of pregnancy more strongly – sickness, tiredness, aching legs, varicose veins, plus a lot more movement and kicking inside. Now and again, one embryo does not survive and if this happens early in pregnancy it may be re-absorbed back into the body with no ill effects to the remaining embryo. If it happens later in pregnancy, the dead foetus will usually remain in the uterus and be delivered at the time of the birth of the live baby.

The main risk when there is more than one baby is that they will be born too early and be premature: this becomes a greater risk with the number of babies. Rest and drugs to relax the womb if contractions start can give babies more time to develop and a better chance at birth – and of course so can careful monitoring during pregnancy. Whether you stay at home or need to spend the last weeks in hospital depends on your circumstances and health, but usually women expecting three or more babies will be admitted to hospital. It is also most likely that in cases with three or more babies the delivery will be by Caesarean, but in the case of twins there is no reason – provided both twins are in the head down position and everything else is normal – why they should not be delivered vaginally. The risk of haemorrhage is greater with more than one baby, but medical staff will be well aware of this and take steps to prevent it.

There is no reason why mothers should not totally breastfeed twins and partly breastfeed any number of babies, though naturally this needs great motivation and extra help and support. The Twins Club (see address section, pages 673–6) is a national organisation which any mother of more than one baby will find helpful.

MIXED EMOTIONS – HOW YOU FEEL DURING PREGNANCY

During pregnancy most couples tend to think mainly of the birth ahead – it is hard to realise just how dramatically and permanently a baby alters your role in life for ever. Not only are you and your partner becoming a father and a mother, but your mother-in-law is becoming a granny, your sisters and brothers are becoming uncles and aunts. And so it goes on, in ever-widening circles. Having a baby and becoming a parent is one of the greatest changes in anyone's life, and mixed emotions, including some anxieties, are natural, but recognising some of the demands and problems which may arise makes it easier to cope.

ADJUSTING TO PARENTHOOD

'Involved' is the word of the moment to describe a modern father's role in parenting. Exactly what that means most fathers are still trying to work out. But it is true that very many marriage problems in later life can be traced back to the arrival of children. Why should this happen?

A first baby does tend to turn life upside down for a bit, and, however much you both wanted one, there will be times when you both also resent the loss of freedom and the tiredness that all new parents experience. It may seem distinctly old-fashioned in this age of equality and the 'new man' to talk about fathers being left out, but it would appear that very many men do feel excluded, and a parting of the ways at this early stage can sometimes lead to more serious problems later.

On the woman's side, she is often totally submerged in the demands of her children and this is especially so if she has two or more children very close together. On the man's side, it may seem that after a day at work all that is expected of him when he gets home is more work, and the arrival of a first baby may coincide with a time when his job is particularly demanding. He may unconsciously begin to spend more time at work which can lead to resentment when his wife feels she is being left to cope alone. She can feel under great pressure, not only with the practicalities of coping with a new baby (which can be very taxing) but also with coming to terms with a completely different role.

Most women work until a few weeks or months before the birth of their first baby. A woman may often know few people in the area where she lives and scarcely any other parents if this is her first child. In many cases, her relatives may live some distance away. Suddenly her day has no shape except the one she feels inclined to impose on it, and she may often be lonely and feel distinctly lost in her new world. Because most couples find it hard to look beyond the birth, this sort of situation can creep up and surprise them before either has realised exactly what the problem is. It really does help during pregnancy to talk to each other about exactly what the other one expects life will be like after the birth. Men need to understand just how displaced a woman who has given up a job may feel when she begins to adjust to motherhood and staying at home. Women need to understand how even the most involved father can sometimes feel a sense of loss when he sees his partner so completely submerged with the preoccupations and demands of parenthood.

The answer is to plan ways in which both of you can share each other's lives. Thinking about baby-sitting arrangements, which could work both in the day and evening to give you breaks to have time alone together and for the woman to have time away from her baby, is important – they need not be expensive, perhaps there are friends who would swap or relatives who might help out? A man who is willing to take over the baby for a complete day so that his wife can go out is much better able to understand the demands and problems of life with a small child. Most importantly, couples need to keep talking to each other as problems arise and as they feel difficulties are likely to crop up. Don't lose sight of the person in the parent – new fathers and mothers both need reassurance that they are still valued, loved and needed for themselves.

Friendships with other couples who have recently had children can be very supportive and helpful in understanding that most of the problems you will be experiencing are very common indeed. Antenatal classes which are designed for couples, or those which have several sessions for fathers to come along to, are good places to meet other parents.

More importantly, learning together about how pregnancy is changing your body, how the baby is growing and developing, and what will happen at the birth, means sharing the whole experience together. For men just to receive information secondhand from their wives who are attending antenatal classes on their own is not the same at all. Going to some classes together can often spark off the kind of discussions which lead to looking to the future and envisaging what sort of changes in both your lives the baby is going to mean. For example, how much will both of you be able to continue pursuing your interests, hobbies or sports? Normal life does not have to stop after a baby arrives – though it may sometimes feel like it! – but it is unrealistic to think you can continue just as before. Time is suddenly at a premium and if one partner expects or assumes that they will be able to continue all the things they enjoy without making any changes or discussing how it can best be worked out with their partner, it will naturally lead to some resentment.

Women who hope to return to work, either part-time or full-time, also need to discuss the future with their partner — neither parent would want to feel that making arrangements for the child's care during working hours is entirely and solely their responsibility. Looking at all the options together — child minders, nurseries, or paid help in the home — meeting potential child carers together so that you can both form a judgement, and discussing the whole question is very important. For couples who are losing half or a proportion of their joint income because the woman is giving up full-time work completely or moving to part-time work, managing on a much smaller income may also be a source of worry — like all problems it is better discussed.

Another source of stress in the future can be your changing relationship with your in-laws. Your relationship with them may have been quite distant in the past — inevitably with the arrival of a grandchild it will become much closer. If you get on together, sharing the excitement of the grandchild can be a great source of joy, but both husbands and wives who do not get on with their in-laws can feel distinctly put out when they realise that granny and granddad may be so much more on the scene. Again, it is not a problem to be ignored. Accept that all the grandparents will want to have far more contact with you after the arrival of the new grandchild. If relationships are difficult, work out how this can best be managed. This is another area where tension may gradually mount without either of you being aware of it until it explodes in an almighty row. Looking ahead can sometimes help to avoid that.

YOUR EMOTIONS IN PREGNANCY

All those hormones rushing around not only change your body, they also change the way that you feel emotionally. Very many women feel particularly sensitive, emotional and weepy during pregnancy and this can be especially marked in the first three months. It is very common to feel unusually sensitive as well as tired and possibly a bit nauseous at this time. It helps a great deal if your partner understands that this is something that happens to most pregnant women and is not just you being neurotic or emotional.

As well as excitement and joy about the pregnancy, most women have moments of feeling very uncertain and anxious as well. After all, you are saying goodbye to a certain stage of your life and a kind of lifestyle. For women who are on their own and without the support of a loving partner, or who have become pregnant by accident, these doubts and anxieties will probably be particularly powerful. It helps to voice your uncertainties to someone you trust who will understand that although you really want to go ahead with the pregnancy you need to talk about a lot of other conflicting emotions you are experiencing. Such a person may be a good friend, a relative or somebody you know less well personally such as your doctor, social worker, midwife, or even a marriage guidance counsellor.

During the middle months of pregnancy some of these uncertainties have usually been resolved and women tend to feel more confident about their bodies and also less emotional. But don't be surprised if you still find yourself inclined to cry easily.

During the last few weeks most women find the physical constraints of being so large very irritating – not being able to turn over easily at night, not being able to bend down to do up shoelaces easily, aching stomach muscles and legs if you have to stand too long. There is also a sensation of life suspended – it seems impossible to plan or to do anything that is not directly related to the pregnancy and the forthcoming birth. It is as though the birth is a wall which has to be climbed over, and until you can see the other side real life cannot go on.

MORBID FEELINGS

> '*I kept waking up at night and thinking about my parents dying. On several occasions I actually reduced myself to tears by thinking of my own mum dying. There was no reason why this should be because both of them are fit and healthy and only in their fifties. It worried me because I began to think I might make it come true by thinking about it.*'

Thinking about death – your own or more usually that of people very close to you – is also very common during pregnancy. It seems as though the heightened awareness of our bodies and the very fact of giving birth to a new life focuses our attention on ageing and on death. Try not to get too upset by these thoughts and recognise that they are an aspect of pregnancy that happens to many women. If you find yourself getting very morbid, seek out the company of other people and distract yourself in some way by watching television, ringing a friend, or just asking your partner to hug and cuddle you. It helps if partners can be sensitive and understanding about these morbid feelings without getting too desperately upset themselves. Nevertheless, if all this doesn't work and troubling thoughts, anxieties or depression persist you do need to consult your doctor.

DREAMS

> '*I dreamt I had had the baby and put it in a drawer somewhere. I suddenly remembered it and realised I hadn't fed it for weeks. I hunted everywhere but I couldn't find it.*'

Vivid dreams during pregnancy are very common and most people can recount some occasion when they woke up thinking they had had the baby and mislaid it, or that it disappeared, or even turned into an animal of some kind like the baby who turned into a pig in *Alice in Wonderland*! When this happens, it is probably just an expression of our subconscious worry about how we will cope as mothers or how the birth will go. Do not be tempted to treat such dreams as premonitions – just remember they happen to very many people and are nothing more than dreams.

SEX

Pregnancy can have different effects on the libido of different women. Some women may go off sex during pregnancy or for part of the time, while other women feel extra sexual. It is important to explain your feelings to your partner and continue to be loving and physically affectionate, even if you do not want to have intercourse, so that he does not mistake your lack of interest in sex as a lack of interest in him. How you regard your changing body during pregnancy will obviously have some effect on the way you feel sexually. The woman who hates being pregnant and hates the way her body is changing is unlikely to be a very loving or responsive partner. Feeling good about yourself and your body generally acts as a powerful aphrodisiac.

Of course, the way your man regards your changing body matters as well. If he openly admires your growing bulge you will obviously feel good. But if his reaction is more inclined to be undisguised horror when he catches a glimpse of you reclining in the bath it is likely to make you feel more like a beached whale than an alluring siren!

Many couples feel worried that sex during pregnancy will harm the baby or increase the risk of miscarriage. There is no evidence at all to suggest this is true, although if you have a history of premature labour or repeated miscarriages your doctor may suggest that it is best to avoid sex. During the later stages of pregnancy, as your stomach becomes much larger, you both need to experiment with different positions to find the one which is most comfortable for you both.

Throughout pregnancy, though, you should both remember that a change in the pattern of your sex lives is quite normal. As with all other aspects of your relationship, the important thing is to keep talking to each other, telling each other how you feel and what you are thinking.

SINGLE PARENTS

Women who have deliberately opted to have a baby without living with the father will feel very differently from women who become pregnant accidentally or who have separated or been widowed since becoming pregnant. Whatever your situation, it can be a lonely business looking forward to the birth of your first child without a partner to support and share the experience, and friends and relatives and the help and friendship they offer are even more vital to single parents.

Do not let your single status put you off joining in parent education and preparation classes — these are very likely places to meet new friends who are also expecting their first baby. It is especially important to choose someone who will come with you and stay with you during the birth. If you don't have a close friend or a relative you would like to ask, most antenatal teachers will be happy to stay with you. It helps to think ahead a little to after the birth, and see what arrangements or ideas you could have for leaving the baby with someone so that you can have time to yourself as well as an opportunity to enjoy adult company. It is essential that you plan your days so that you do not have a day alone followed by a lonely evening. While the baby is small and portable it is very easy to take him with you for weekends away or to visit friends. Don't be afraid to ask for help and let people know that you would like them to get in touch with you. Organisations like Gingerbread and the National Council for One-Parent Families can give help and advice on financial matters and put you in touch with other single parents (see address section, pages 673–6).

WORK

The conflict between work and full-time parenting is never easily resolved. If you do go back to work, through choice or necessity, you will very likely feel anxious about being separated from your baby and about who will take care of him. Conversely, if you decide to give up work completely, it is very common to suffer from temporary loss of status and identity as well as losing half the family income. Remember that guilt seems to plague non-working as well as working mothers, though for different reasons. The decision whether to continue working or not is essentially the woman's, but decisions about who looks after the baby should be shared by both parents. It is important during pregnancy that you both explore the avenues together.

The possibilities open to women who work part-time or full-time for alternative care for their baby are looked at on page 462.

FANTASY FEELINGS

However much you have wanted and are planning for a baby, most women find themselves feeling strangely unreal at some stages or for most of their pregnancy – it is so hard to imagine that at the end of this time you will actually be holding your own live baby. And that feeling is true even when the baby is large and kicking and turning somersaults inside you. Being pregnant for the first time makes you suddenly notice all the other pregnant women, all the babies in prams, and parents with their children. The thought that soon someone will be calling you 'Mummy' makes you laugh because the idea seems so ridiculous. Even going to the doctor's or the hospital and seriously discussing where you would like your baby to be born and what kind of pain relief you would hope to use seems unreal because it is all such a tremendous unknown to you.

This feeling of unreality holds true however many babies you have, but it is especially strong in a first pregnancy. The reality is the labour, and it leads to that moment of birth which everybody feels is truly a miracle. These feelings of fantasy are probably what give rise to some of the dreams which are so common in pregnancy and they can be especially strong at the time when you go to buy baby clothes and equipment because these are such tangible evidence of your expectations.

SHOPPING FOR THE BABY

This is definitely one of the fun parts of pregnancy — it is a strong woman who reaches the sixth month of pregnancy without having crossed the threshold of a shop that sells baby clothes. Picking up those tiny vests and minute socks for the first time is really quite exciting because they prompt the thought that very soon you will actually be putting these clothes on your new baby. In the beginning you may make one or two totally whimsical purchases — an adorable pair of silky bootees, a gorgeous little sunhat. But buying for a baby does not mean you have to spend a fortune by any means.

It is a fact that most first-time parents really want to buy almost everything new for their baby, regardless of their own financial position. It seems to be partly to do with wanting the very best for their first child and partly to do with their own excitement at the purchases. When it comes to first clothes this is especially understandable, but buying secondhand does not mean second best and there are some good bargains to be had in purchasing major items of equipment. Naturally you need to check items like prams, buggies, cots and playpens carefully for safety and make sure they are a reliable brand with a British Standards Institute number.

Here is what your new baby will need:

NAPPIES

The choice is between squares of terry towelling which will be used by more than one baby if you buy a good quality nappy, or disposable nappies. Debate goes on in the baby magazines about the relative costs of the two systems and those who say that disposables are not much more expensive or cost the same, take into account the cost of purchasing items like a washing machine and tumble drier, if you do not already have them, and electricity. However, apart from nappies, a new baby can get through an awful lot of clothes and a washing machine is an important asset to any family, regardless of whether you opt for terry nappies or disposables.

This is a very personal decision and one which is based on your own feelings and your lifestyle. But, if you opt for terries, buy the best quality because they will last through two or even more babies. Remember, though, in the beginning it is useful to have standby packets of disposables for outings and emergencies. If you decide to opt for disposable nappies, then the reverse is also true — it is useful to have a few towelling nappies as a standby in case you run out on some occasion. If you are going for terry nappies alone, the minimum number is thought to be two dozen, and you also need nappy liners — thick squares of papery woven material which enable you to separate and flush any solid matter down the lavatory before putting the terry nappy to soak in nappy solution in a bucket. Nappy safety-pins with the protective hood over the sharp point, not ordinary safety-pins, should be used for fastening nappies.

71

Plastic pants These are essential with terry nappies. There are many different varieties on the market, some that popper up the front, some that are simply strips of plastic which tie at each side and some with elastic legs. The best bet is to ask some experienced mums what they recommend and look at what is available in the shops – you will need about six pairs to begin with.

The design of disposable nappies has improved tremendously in the last few years, with elasticated legs and a much better fit, but plastic pants can be useful at night or when travelling to make extra sure there are no leaks.

CLOTHES

The main thing to remember is that new babies need changing far more often than you can ever imagine and they also hate being undressed. This means that all clothes should have easy access for nappy changes without having to take everything off, and should also be easy to get on and off. Choose stretchy neck openings which go over heads without a struggle and uncomplicated fastenings like poppers in preference to ribbons which have to be tied and which can easily become knotted or start to fray. Clothes also need to be machine washable and not hand wash only – an especially good point to remember when kind relatives or friends offer to knit clothes for you.

Vests New babies are not very good at keeping warm and also hate to be undressed completely. For this reason vests are an essential item of wear both in winter and summer. There are three types – all-in-one stretch body suits, front-fastening vests with ribbons which tie and the traditional style of vest with an envelope neck. Body suits give a nice smooth outline, but nappy leaks have a horrible habit of spreading upwards through the body suit which can mean a complete change of clothes every time. Envelope-neck styles are probably cheapest and best – you will need half a dozen and you can usually save money by buying them in bargain packs of three.

Stretch-suits These are the easiest garments to dress a new baby in and also very practical, with poppers around the crutch to allow for nappy changes without having to undress the baby completely, and they are also good at keeping him warm. You will need about half a dozen for a summer baby and a couple more for a winter one, but do not be tempted to get less than this because on a bad day you can get through an amazing number! Again, buying them in packs of three usually saves money.

Knitted clothes Many people get great pleasure out of knitting for a new baby, but do steer them clear of very open, lacy patterns which can easily get caught on a buggy or pram and which small fingers can often get tangled up in. Also avoid tie necks. A vest, stretch-suit and knitted cardigan or jersey will keep a baby warm in winter.

New babies usually like being wrapped up and held securely, but it is entirely up to you whether you fancy buying or knitting a shawl for your baby. If you want to avoid the expense you can just as easily use a cellular blanket which stretches well.

Other clothes Dresses for girls make nappy changing easier, but do hamper crawling babies. Easiest clothes for both sexes are track-suit-style tops and bottoms because you can remove the bottom half without interfering with the rest of the baby's clothes. Winter babies need pull-on woolly hats, but you do not need to dress them in an expensive all-in-one suit if you are taking them out in the pram because using a knitted cardigan and several layers of blankets and a quilt inside the pram will keep them just as warm. But an all-in-one suit *is* necessary if you intend to forgo the traditional pram and put them straight into a buggy – there are several on the market which are designed for newborn babies. Summer babies need cotton sunhats with a brim. Shoes are not at all necessary until babies actually begin to walk, and shop-bought socks or quilted bootees are fine to keep newborn babies' feet warm.

INCIDENTALS

A changing mat is a pretty essential piece of equipment, plus a good stock of the cheapest cotton wool (buy it in bulk) and baby lotion to clean your baby's bottom. Water will do just as well as lotion if you prefer, but tends to be more messy and involve more fuss. Baby wipes are an easy way of cleaning the baby, but are more expensive than other methods. Use a barrier cream at every nappy change to provide some protection from a wet terry nappy, though today's disposables, which incorporate special granules to absorb the moisture, have largely rendered this unnecessary. Cotton wool is also useful for cleaning your baby's face (see page 161). In addition you will need some baby soap or baby bath product and baby shampoo. Nail clippers are useful as using scissors to trim tiny nails can be tricky.

A good quality nappy bag which converts to a changing mat is also a very good investment, or perhaps an item which someone may like to give as a gift. Shop around and pick one which is large, hard-wearing and preferably designed so that using the mat does not mean emptying out the entire contents first. It will be useful for at least two years and longer if you have a second baby.

EQUIPMENT

Cribs and carry-cots Your baby will be fine sleeping in a carry-cot for the first few months, or you can put him in a special crib. Carry-cots can either be bought as a separate piece of equipment or, more practically, come with collapsible sets of wheels which can be adapted to form a buggy or pushchair when the carry-cot is removed. After about four or five months, a baby has usually grown out of a carry-cot or crib and needs to be moved into a cot. For this reason, you may wish to consider buying these items which have short-term use secondhand, but it is worth investing in a new mattress. A third alternative as a first bed is a Moses basket, which has the advantage of being easy to carry. Always buy equipment, including the mattress, which is approved to British safety standards. No baby should ever be given a pillow because there is a danger of suffocation. Instead, make sure the mattress is covered with a firmly stretched sheet – the stretchy towelling fitted variety are fine. A top sheet is not necessary but your baby needs to be kept warm and secure by being tucked in snugly with two or three layers of stretchy blankets or shawls. If your baby is prone to being sick after feeds, then covering the head end of the mattress with a muslin nappy saves changing the sheets every time. In cold weather it may help your baby to settle if you warm a blanket over a radiator before wrapping him in it, or warm the crib with a hot water bottle before you put him in, but never leave a baby in a crib with a hot water bottle at the same time.

Cot You can delay buying this until your baby has arrived, if you want to, because most babies are quite happy to spend the first three months in a carry-cot or crib. Again, cot and mattress must conform to British safety standards and it is important to check this if buying secondhand. You will need a good supply of cot-size sheets and blankets, but again no pillows. Duvets, baby nests and cot bumpers are not now recommended for babies under one year old. When using a cot bumper for an older baby, make sure the ties are not too long and that they are always done up securely with no trailing ends inside the cot. Most recent research on cot death shows that it is safest to place a baby on his back or side (and that becoming too hot is as much of a risk to a baby as being too cold; for more on this see page 164).

Car seat The first journey your baby makes in a car when you bring him home from the maternity hospital should be as safe as every subsequent trip. Rear-facing car seats are often hired or loaned by the maternity hospital itself, or by another agency acting through the hospital. They are very useful items of equipment in the first few months as your baby can be carried from the car to the house without being woken. They have largely replaced the older style bouncing chairs in the home, enabling your young baby to be supported and watch the life of the household.

Pram or buggy This is usually a major item of expenditure and one which you hope will do service for several years and for more than one child. The most important point when choosing this item is that it suits your lifestyle. Check how many functions you require from your pram or buggy: some are very versatile, with a lift-off carry-cot, and can double in function as a pram or pushchair.

If you have no car, and live where shops and other amenities are within walking distance, then the old-style carriage-built pram may be a good answer, especially if you are expecting a winter baby. The advantage of a traditional pram is that the baby can be put to sleep in it downstairs and wheeled out with very little disturbance just by adding a hat, extra layers of blankets and a cover. The big wheels of an old-style pram make them very easy to push and later, if you have a second baby, toddler seats can be fitted

75

across the top. The drawback of this type of pram is that they do take up a lot of space in the house, although it can be very handy to have the baby downstairs where you can easily rock him off to sleep. They are also difficult to negotiate down flights of stairs or steps and so are not suitable if you live in an upstairs flat without a lift. Most are pretty heavy and bulky to load in and out of cars. Bought new they also tend to be quite expensive. However, if you feel they may suit your needs, at least for the first three or four months while the baby is very tiny, a secondhand pram can usually be bought at small cost and, provided you look after it, you will be able to sell it again without much loss.

Car-bound mums or those who live in flats or those with older children who are continually having to pop out in the car may find that a buggy which is especially designed for a newborn baby with a tilting seat may suit their needs better. These generally cost less, take up very little space to store and will probably suit your baby right through until he is finished with the pushchair stage completely. The disadvantage in the early days, and especially if you have a winter baby, is that you have to dress him up very snugly in all-in-one suits as it is not so easy to tuck him underneath blankets, even in the most tilting seat. It also means a degree of disturbance having to get the baby in and out of the buggy. Buggies with small wheels and tyres tend to be difficult to push across rough country, so if you live in the countryside or plan a lot of walks, go for a variety which has larger wheels and thicker tyres.

There is such an enormous variety in the types of prams and buggies now available that a little shopping around should find the one to suit you. If you feel a little superstitious about investing in major items of baby equipment such as this before the baby is born, many big stores will deliver the pram or buggy after the baby's birth.

Playpen A playpen can be useful for putting a crawling baby in for a short period while you are cooking a meal, having to answer the phone or the door, but do not use a playpen to leave a baby unattended for long periods. In general, if you want to get your baby to accept being put into a playpen, it is best to start before he learns how to crawl by putting him in for two short sessions a day. Make sure it is stocked with a different variety of toys and change them frequently so that he does not get bored. Place the playpen in the room where you will be working so that he can still see you.

Baby walkers Many children do seem to enjoy baby walkers, but while parents may take care to watch them for 99% of the time, there is a higher chance of accidents in the remaining moments. Danger arises especially as the baby goes across any uneven surface or anywhere near a step. There is no evidence that putting a baby in a walker benefits walking at all, and there have even been cases where babies had to have physiotherapy to undo the imbalance in muscle development which can happen if walkers are used too soon, before about six months, or for a long time each day. However, if parents are aware of their limitations and dangers, they can be treated as aids to play, rather like a swing or slide.

TOWARDS THE END OF PREGNANCY

This is often quite a tedious time – most people have given up work and there is a distinct sense of waiting. Being so large can make it difficult to get comfortable in any position, whether you are sitting on a chair or lying down trying to get some rest. However, at the other end of the spectrum, many people have a tremendous burst of energy towards the end of pregnancy and are frantically decorating nurseries or whole houses, or even, against all advice, moving house. In theory this is not a good idea, but in practice there sometimes seems to be an unavoidable urge to get everything right and ready before the baby arrives.

YOUR BODY

During the last months of pregnancy breasts and nipples can be stimulated by expressing a few drops of colostrum. Midwives often recommend you do this if you are planning to breastfeed – if you doubt your ability to feed it can have the effect of giving you some confidence, but some women hate the feeling and do not like doing it, in which case don't bother. It makes very little difference, and you can just as successfully breastfeed a baby if you have never expressed any colostrum during pregnancy. Whether you plan to breastfeed or not, it is important to wear a well-fitting bra day and night during the end of pregnancy and also after the birth when the milk comes in. This has more effect on whether your breasts retain their original shape than whether you breastfeed or not.

Eating large meals towards the end of pregnancy is pretty well out because your stomach is so squashed by the size of the baby. Little and often is the rule when it comes to eating and the same sometimes applies to sleep unfortunately – your baby's movements and kicks can be enough to wake you in the night and getting comfortable is more difficult. If this is your first baby, take advantage of the chance to get plenty of rest and cat-naps during the day to make up for lost hours at night.

Life becomes more comfortable if the baby's head 'drops' during the last weeks of pregnancy – that is, the baby's head descends into the bony pelvic girdle ready for the birth. Sometimes, however, the baby's head does not engage until labour begins – in a first pregnancy where the head does not engage doctors will usually check with a scan to make sure there is nothing blocking the baby's path, for example, that the placenta is not low-lying or obstructing the baby's exit. It is more common that the head does not engage in second or subsequent pregnancies and this may be because uterine muscles have already been stretched and are not providing so much pressure.

During early and middle pregnancy the muscles of the womb have been contracting very slightly, but this is not enough to be felt. However, after about the twenty-fifth week you may feel this activity as a painless hardening of your abdomen as the muscles tense. It will go soft again as the muscles relax. This is the uterus limbering up for labour so that the muscles are in good trim: these contractions are called 'Braxton Hicks contractions', but are not the start of labour.

PACKING A BAG

Do not leave it to the last month to collect the things you need to take to the hospital – babies do sometimes come early. Cotton nightclothes are best, because hospitals are such very hot places. They should be front-opening if you plan to breastfeed. In addition you need sanitary pads, feeding bras or a good supporting bra, washing things, slippers and dressing gown. Check what your hospital requires you to bring in the way of clothes and equipment for the baby.

You may also have extra bits and pieces you want to take in to use during labour, and suggestions are extra pillows, foam wedges, hand-held fans, natural sponges, flasks to put ice in plus a piece of muslin to put the ice inside, cassette players and radios. Partners should think about taking some food supplies and money for the phone.

Leave your own and your baby's going-home clothes ready at home – putting together the bits and pieces your baby will wear is one of the nicest parts of pregnancy. You need vest, disposable nappies or towelling nappies plus plastic pants, a stretchy suit, a knitted cardigan plus a shawl or cellular blanket, and, depending on the weather, a hat.

TRAVEL ARRANGEMENTS AND PHONE NUMBERS

If you are having your baby in hospital, plan who is to drive you there and then make a second plan to fall back on in an emergency. If no transport is available, tell the hospital you will need an ambulance. More careful planning is needed if this is your second or subsequent baby because obviously other children will have to be taken care of. Keep a list with phone numbers of friends who can help out with a lift, plus the hospital number and have it on you when you go out or go away.

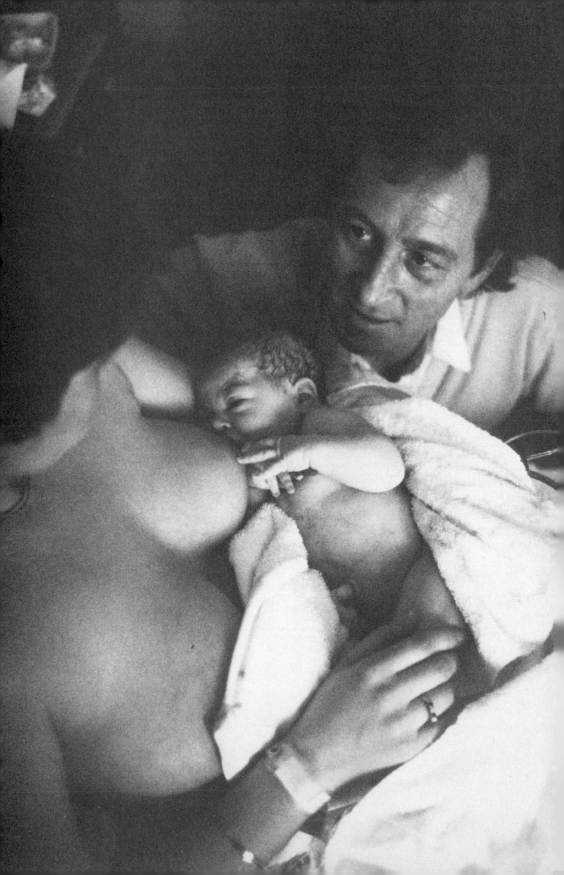

Chapter 3

LABOUR AND DELIVERY

The start of labour   What happens in labour?
Birth – what will it be like?   The role of the father
The question of pain relief
A checklist that will help you to a better birth
Checking on you and your baby during labour
The first moments of life
Medical interventions – and why they may be needed
Problems in labour and delivery
Stillbirth

THE START OF LABOUR

'I woke up early in the morning with a slight tummy ache and an attack of the runs and thought I must have a bug. It was only when the ache came back twice more that I realised that it was happening every half an hour. It went on like that all day, gradually getting more often and a bit stronger. We went to the hospital in the early evening and after five hours of strong contractions my baby was born at midnight.'

'I was bending down to pick up some washing when I felt this uncontrollable trickle of warm water down the inside of my leg. At first I thought I had suddenly become incontinent! Then I realised it must be the waters breaking. It didn't gush, just a steady trickle without any sensation of contractions. At the hospital they said I was three centimetres dilated, but I didn't begin to feel anything at all for another hour or so and then suddenly the contractions became very strong. My baby was born three hours later.'

'My labour stopped and started for two days. I went up to the hospital three times with contractions coming every ten minutes, only for everything to stop and I was sent home twice. But the third time when they examined me I was five centimetres dilated. I found walking round kept the contractions going, but lying or sitting stopped them. Only the last hour was difficult to cope with, but the actual birth was quite straightforward.'

The mechanism by which labour starts is not well understood, but it is thought that the baby triggers it off, possibly in response to the failing placenta. A chemical or hormone message passes from the baby across the placenta into the mother's blood stream, causing release of chemicals called 'prostaglandins', and a hormone called 'oxytocin' from the pituitary gland. These cause the cervix to soften ready for dilatation, and the uterus to contract.

In the days before labour begins, some women find they are unusually active and have a tremendous burst of energy: they start decorating, turning out cupboards and generally spring cleaning. It is a dangerous old wives' tale that babies may become less active as labour approaches, so always tell your doctor or midwife if you have reason to be worried by lack of movement over a period of twelve hours.

Some women find they have more frequent or loose bowel movements and increased hardening of the uterus in practice contractions.

Women often worry that they will not recognise when labour begins or that it will start with a dramatic flood as the waters break when they are queuing at the supermarket checkout. In fact both occurrences are rare. False alarms, with women arriving at hospital thinking they are in labour and being sent home, are much more common than missing the start of labour. Strong or regular Braxton Hicks contractions are usually to blame for this, but don't worry, hospital staff are happy to give advice and would rather you erred on the side of caution. Nor is it very common for a flood of amniotic fluid to be the first sign of labour – even if the waters do break while you are out it may just produce dampness or a slight trickle.

Labour can begin in a variety of ways, but there are three basic signs to look for and which your midwife or doctor will want to know about in order to determine if labour is about to begin or has already started:

A show This is the name given to a show of bloodstained jelly-like mucus which may be lost gradually over a day or so or in one go. During pregnancy the neck of the womb or cervix has remained tightly closed, sealed with this mucus plug. As muscle contractions begin to pull the sides of the uterus upward, dilating the cervix, so the plug is loosened and comes away.

Breaking or leaking of the amniotic waters Pressure of the baby's head downwards may cause the membrane sealing the amniotic fluid to rupture so that water either leaks in a slow trickle or gushes in a flood, although this is rarely the first sign of labour. It is not significant whether this happens at the start or much later in labour. Occasionally the waters may break without contractions commencing (see page 114).

Contractions These are usually felt as low tummy cramps or sometimes as backache. 'The kind of pains you have when you get an attack of the runs,' was one mother's graphic description. They usually begin as weak, erratic sensations, but begin to come with more regularity – once an hour, half an hour and so on – and also with increasing severity. In this very early stage of labour, if the waters are intact, it is best to stay active and carry on with ordinary life while alerting those who need to know, such as people who will look after other children or partners who have to get back from work.

Time how often the contractions are coming and how long they last. With a first baby, aim to get to the hospital when they are coming about ten minutes apart. Do not go in too early because it makes labour seem so much longer, but on the other hand do not be tempted to leave it too late because both car journeys and admissions procedures are harder to cope with in strong labour. It may help you to time your arrival in hospital if you remember that first babies are very rarely born in less than twelve hours. If labour is too slow or keeps starting and stopping then walking around and using various upright positions often helps. Timing when to call the hospital or midwife with a second baby is harder because things can speed up so much more unexpectedly.

When you ring the hospital, tell them your name, hospital number, which is on your co-operation card, the frequency and length of contractions and any other signs. If your waters have started to leak but you have no contractions, you should still ring the hospital. It is best to stay upright and active, provided your pregnancy has reached term, in the hope that this may stimulate contractions. The amniotic fluid was the baby's protection from infection and, once the waters have drained away, doctors usually like labour to begin within hours and will induce it if contractions do not begin naturally because of the risk of infection. For advice on premature labour see page 113.

YOUR ARRIVAL IN HOSPITAL

When you arrive at the hospital, the labour ward will have your notes ready and a midwife will go through the admissions procedure (lots of questions and form filling) and preparation for birth. Most of these medical procedures will also be done by a midwife if you have a baby at home. The routine usually consists of checking blood pressure, taking temperature and pulse and asking for a mid-stream urine sample to check for signs of protein, sugar or infection. The midwife will also examine your abdomen to find out in what position your baby is lying and how far down his head has descended into the pelvic girdle. Once the widest part of the head has moved down into the brim of the pelvis it is said to be 'engaged'. She will also examine you internally to find out how dilated the cervix has become. Some of these checks necessitate lying on your back, but some women find this very uncomfortable in labour – if this is so tell the midwife so that you do not need to spend more time in that position than is absolutely necessary. The midwife will usually listen to the baby's heart by pressing an ear trumpet to your abdomen, but this is usually followed later by electronic monitoring.

It used to be standard practice to give all women having a baby a full pubic shave as well as an enema in the belief that removing pubic hair cut the risk of infection and that a full bowel would make the baby's passage through the birth canal more difficult and the mother would be likely to defecate and soil the bed as she pushed the baby downwards and outwards. However, research has shown that leaving the pubic hair does not raise the incidence of infection and that most women empty their bowels naturally at the start of labour anyway. The majority of hospitals have stopped giving even a mini-shave and offer an enema or suppository only if the woman has not opened her bowels in the last twenty-four hours.

Lastly, the woman may be offered a warm bath or shower – the warmth of the water helps muscles relax. A few units have bathrooms adjoining the delivery room so that you can take another dip later in labour if you wish. You will either be given a hospital gown or be able to use one of your own nighties.

Some hospitals have a labour ward with several beds for women in early labour and then move them to a delivery room towards the end of the first stage, while others have individual labour and delivery rooms combined where you can stay until your baby is born. A few units offer extra facilities like birthing beds, which are usually beds able to convert to different positions, birth stools and chairs or mattresses on the floor to help mothers to adopt a more upright position by squatting or kneeling if they wish – you will need to have checked in advance what your hospital has to offer.

WHAT HAPPENS IN LABOUR?

FIRST STAGE

This is when the muscles of the uterus contract, pulling the cervix outwards and upwards so that it first thins and then begins to open out or dilate to let the baby out. The cervix is said to be fully open and the first stage complete when it is 10 cm. dilated. About half of this first stage is taken up with a quiet phase when contractions are mild and dilate the cervix to about 3 or 4 cm., and then an active phase when the contractions get more severe and dilate the cervix completely. The waters may break naturally at some point during this stage or be broken by the doctor or midwife as the colour of the water is a good guide to how the baby is coping with the contractions. Once the waters have broken, contractions usually get more intense as the baby's head presses directly on to the cervix with each contraction without the bag of waters to act as a buffer. To begin with, contractions usually last about 20 to 30 seconds and come every 30 minutes, but gradually increase until at the end of this stage they may last 1 to $1\frac{1}{2}$ minutes, and come every 2 or 3 minutes. With a first baby this stage usually takes 10 to 12 hours, but subsequent births may last half this time or less.

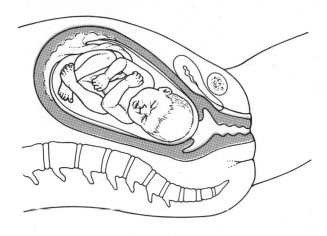

First stage

SECOND STAGE

This begins when the cervix is fully dilated and the baby starts to move down the birth canal and it ends when the baby is born. Instead of being used to draw the cervix up, the contractions of the uterus are now being used to push the baby out and down the birth canal. You need to help too by taking a deep breath, holding it, and pushing with your diaphragm and abdominal muscles. Usually there is an overwhelming natural urge to push, but if you do not feel such an urge, then moving into a more upright position usually helps.

At first the baby is moving directly downwards and, as his head presses on to the pelvic floor, the pressure on the bowel makes it feel something like trying to pass a grapefruit. Then the baby's head turns a corner and providing he is face down – the easiest birth position – the back of his head passes underneath the front arch of the pelvis. Now his head begins to push against the perineum, making it bulge outwards and producing a bursting, burning sensation, but with each push the entrance is slowly widened and the tissues gradually stretched to allow the baby's head through.

The increasing stretching and the pressure of the baby's head has a deadening effect on the nerve endings in this area and acts as a natural anaesthetic. The midwife will be watching the tissues of the perineum very carefully all the time for any signs that it may begin to tear – in fact research shows that a small tear probably mends more quickly and is less painful than an episiotomy may be, but this is still widely disputed. However, be reassured that you will not feel anything painful if an episiotomy does have to be made – this is a small cut at the entrance to the vagina in the tissues of the perineum to enable the baby's head to be born more easily (see page 107).

You can feel your baby's head yourself with your hands or use a mirror to see. Although it slips back a little in between each contraction, it gradually gains ground until it stays at the entrance to the vagina without disappearing – this is said to be when the baby's head is 'crowning'. The midwife will tell you not to push but to pant with the next contractions so that the head can be eased out very gently. A minute after the baby's head has been born it turns, with the help of the midwife, to the side: this is called 'restitution', and it enables the shoulders to turn sideways so that they can easily be slipped out of the vagina followed by the rest of the baby's body. Usually the body follows easily, though it may need a second contraction. If you want your baby delivered on to your abdomen ask the midwife early in labour – it is increasingly standard in many units. The warmth of your body will help to keep the baby warm, and you can enjoy the feel of your new baby against your skin as you feel and touch him for the first time. However, if you would rather your baby was cleaned up first, the midwife will be just as happy to do this and then hand him to you in a warm towel or blanket.

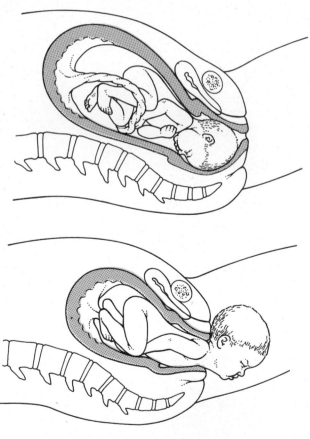

Second stage

86

THIRD STAGE

If there is no intervention, then the placenta, or afterbirth, should normally separate and come down into the vagina within twenty minutes after the birth. Once this happens, the midwife pulls gently on the cord to ease it out.

If your midwife follows the traditional approach, she will clamp the cord at a point about four inches away from the baby and place a second clamp about another two inches away from it. Using special scissors she cuts the cord at a point between the two clamps. There is no sensation in the cord and it does not hurt the baby, nor is there any loss of blood. See chapter 4 for more about your newborn baby's first seconds of life.

Some doctors, midwives and mothers believe in the natural delivery of the placenta, but in general medical opinion still supports the active management of the third stage of labour. This means that the midwife gives an injection of a drug called Syntocinon or a mixture of this and another drug called Ergometrine. These drugs make the uterus contract, causing the placenta to separate more quickly after the baby is born. The use of the injection makes the risk of bleeding after the birth far less likely because it causes the muscle fibres in the wall of the uterus to contract preventing blood loss.

Bleeding after the birth—the medical term is 'post-partum haemorrhage' — is rare, but it can be very serious, which is one of the main reasons in favour of active management. Timing of the injection is important. If the baby is born head first it is usually given into the mother's thigh once the baby's shoulders are born.

BIRTH – WHAT WILL IT BE LIKE?

'Contractions feel like that awful griping pain you get low down in your tummy if you have an attack of the runs.'

'Male doctors tell you contractions feel like bad period pains – how they should know what period pains feel like or be able to compare them with contractions I don't know. In fact my baby's backbone was pressing against mine and I just had continuous dull backache.'

'You tend to forget what labour feels like until you start to feel contractions again, and then it all comes back. At first it was just a hardening of the tummy muscles and a growing twinge that came and faded. But by the end of the first stage it was a really agonising pain all across the lower part of my stomach—the contractions were going very fast together. They keep telling you to relax but it is almost impossible. I had to concentrate and grit my teeth for all I was worth to cope with it.'

Everybody's experience of labour is entirely different. This is one of the reasons why it is so hard to prepare people for what to expect. The experience of childbirth varies not only from person to person, but with each baby born to the same person. It is one of the unfair facts of life that some women seem to sail through labour and childbirth without needing much, or indeed any, pain relief and report there was one 'uncomfortable' moment. There are also women who say that it was agony and who feel cheated that during antenatal classes people talked about 'discomfort' without really telling them that it could be so painful.

Obviously we all wonder about the first experience, but what makes one woman find labour and birth easy while another finds it so painful? There are very many factors involved and obviously a great many of them are outside our control. Our own personal attitude towards our bodies, towards pain, our pain 'threshold', obviously have a great deal to do with the way we cope with labour. Another factor which is often outside our control is the position of the baby, for there are some birth positions which are more likely to make labour difficult and painful. Even in cases where the baby is in the right position to start with, complications can arise during labour – for example, the baby's head may fail to rotate as it moves into the birth canal and this can mean that his backbone is pressing against yours. This may result in a slower descent, backache, and possibly a more difficult delivery.

However, there are some relatively simple things which all women can do to increase their chances of a good experience of labour and birth. The first is to find out as much as you can about the process: understanding what is happening makes it so much easier to cope with. The second is to stay upright, active and mobile for at least the early part of labour. This has definitely been shown to shorten length of labour and women who stay upright and walk around during most of their labours need less pain relief. The third point may seem contradictory but it is to follow your body's inclinations – if in your case you feel like curling up in a ball on your side on a bed and you find this helpful then do that. Finally, it helps to know what different types of pain relief are available and to stay open-minded about the type of labour and delivery you will have and about the type of pain relief you may or may not use.

Experienced midwives can all quote you examples of the woman who was very worried about the prospect of giving birth and determined that the only way she could cope was to have an epidural, and who then proceeded to have a short, easy labour which she found she could cope with perfectly well without help. They have also seen many examples of women who have set their hearts on a 'natural' birth without any pain relief at all, only to find it harder going than they thought and then felt very disappointed and let down because they did not achieve the goal they had set themselves.

Obviously, it is hard to prepare people for what is essentially always going to be a unique and individual experience, but some general points can be made. First, most women manage to cope in the early part of labour with breathing and relaxation exercises and by walking around – this is when contractions are well spaced and fairly mild. It is also true that at the other end of the first stage – the point where the cervix is very nearly dilated to its full extent but before pushing can commence – most women experience a time which is very painful. This can vary between one or two very sharp contractions to an extended period when contractions are very strong and also come very frequently with only short gaps in between. When you reach a point when you don't think you can cope any more it nearly always means that your baby is just about to be born. It will really help at the time if your partner can also understand what is happening and remind you that your baby will soon be there.

THE ROLE OF THE FATHER

Sharing the experience of labour and birth together can be a good start to parenthood for very many couples, and most fathers are pleased they were present at the birth of their child. It is also very common to feel some anxiety and apprehension beforehand: for the safety of their partner and the baby, about their own reactions to seeing their partner in labour and giving birth, and about the role they will actually play. Some women too may feel anxious about the effect that seeing the birth will have on their partners. Be honest with each other and talk about what you feel. Going to antenatal classes together and finding out about pregnancy and birth by reading and talking to other couples together will help you decide what to do.

Most antenatal classes discuss the ways in which partners can be of practical help during labour. Keeping a check on the passing of time and encouraging their wives that they are making progress is helpful, for it is very easy to become disorientated during labour. Reminding the mother-to-be to go to the lavatory at regular intervals, offering ice cubes, small drinks and glucose tablets to keep up her strength also helps, as does explaining her needs to hospital staff without being aggressive. Women vary a great deal in whether back massage is a comfort or not – don't be offended if she suddenly can't bear you to touch her or says you do it all wrong. It is very common to find she may suddenly only be able to tolerate the midwife touching her – whether that is really to do with the difference in technique or with confidence in a professional is uncertain. Certainly there is a special relationship which develops between midwife and mother which is different from that between the father and the midwife.

Most maternity units now welcome fathers who are calm and understand what is happening because it frees nursing staff for medical rather than purely supportive and supervisory work. But it would be wrong either for fathers to insist on staying or mothers to insist on the presence of their partners if there are serious worries on either side. Again, talking about things in advance helps.

THE QUESTION OF PAIN RELIEF

There are several ways of getting some relief from the discomfort and pain of labour, some of them very old methods indeed, but there are actually only two techniques which can completely take the pain away – a general or an epidural anaesthetic. Because no two labours are the same and no one can predict exactly how they will react in labour, it is best to know as much as possible about the kinds of pain relief available and think about what you feel will suit you best, though it is essential to go into labour with an open mind.

POSITION AND MOVEMENT

It is a natural reaction to ease pain of any kind by moving – rocking, rubbing or massaging the area or shifting to another position. If a child comes with a tummy-ache we automatically try to soothe it by stroking or gently rubbing where it hurts, and we ease aching muscles in our own bodies by stretching and bending. The idea of 'rubbing it better' is as old as the hills. To lie immobile during a contraction is to deny a natural source of pain relief, your own body. As well as shifting pressure, a rhythmic movement, like rocking or rubbing, acts as a way of distracting the brain from the sensation of pain. Breathing exercises work in the same way.

Lying down has a number of disadvantages – it means the weight of the uterus is pressing on central arteries and veins which reduces the blood flow both to your own heart and also through the placenta to the baby. It can also cause backache. In addition you are not making any use of a natural force which will make labour shorter and the baby's descent easier – gravity. Research has shown that more upright positions in labour make contractions more efficient and so shorten the time it takes for the cervix to dilate. Studies have also shown that women who stay active during labour need less pain relief.

The Active Birth Movement runs classes concentrating on position and movement, but most antenatal courses now teach something about alternative positions in labour. The simplest approach is to do what feels best. Walking around and pausing during contractions to lean against a wall or the back of a chair is often sufficient in early labour. As contractions get stronger you may find that kneeling, kneeling leaning forward on to a pile of pillows or against your partner, or sitting astride a back-to-front chair using the back as a support is helpful. During transition, a more upright posture or changing position can often help a baby in an unusual position shift into one that is easier for birth. In the second stage, the force of gravity can again help the baby's descent and some positions open the joints of the pelvis wider to allow more room for the baby to pass through.

Massage during labour is very much a question of personal choice – some women cannot bear to be touched during a contraction while others find that back rubbing helps, but only if their partner or birth attendant has the right technique. Some women want very firm, kneading massage, while others want a lighter touch.

Alternative positions which may give pain relief during labour

DIFFERENT BIRTH POSITIONS

We have talked about how staying upright and moving around during labour usually makes contractions more efficient and also easier to cope with – in general, research has shown that women seem to have shorter labours and need less pain relief if they stay upright and keep moving. However, towards the end of the first stage when contractions become very intense and often close together this does not suit everybody – if your inclination is to lie curled up on your side, then do so.

What about your position for the birth itself? Again, you do have a choice. Through the ages there have been different fashions in the most popular position to adopt for the birth of a baby – for example, birthing stools are not a new idea and were very popular in the Middle Ages. More recently, the most usual delivery position used to be for a woman to lie down, either on her back or on her side on a bed. Some midwives still favour the woman lying on her side today. Then the idea developed that a woman should be more propped up – although still basically lying on her back. It began to be usual for her to be supported by cushions or pillows, with her knees drawn up and open. This position is easy to adopt for the woman and it does make it easy for the midwife to deliver the baby. A drawback is that sometimes the pressure of the baby is on the base of the spine. As the baby's head moves down out of the uterus into the vagina and begins to turn the corner so that the head starts to press against the perineum it means you are effectively pushing uphill. However, difficult deliveries, and especially those needing forceps, usually require this position and often for a woman to be actually in the lithotomy position, which means lying back with your feet in stirrups.

What alternatives to the conventional positions are there, though, in the case of a normal delivery? Most midwives are increasingly willing to work with women to try to find the position which will be easiest for delivery. One alternative which is becoming more popular is kneeling on all fours. During contractions you either kneel on all fours or, more comfortably, lean forward against your partner, who can stand at the end of the bed, or against a large cushion for support. Between contractions you can rest back on your heels or kneel up. This has the advantage of taking the weight off the large blood vessels and you can vary how upright you are to control the effect of gravity. This means that if the baby is being pushed downwards too quickly and delivery looks like being too fast, then going forwards on to all fours or leaning down on to your forearms usually slows it down. If the second stage is very slow you can kneel in a more upright position. The position is not difficult to adopt for the woman, but it does need the co-operation of the midwife, who needs to feel confident about delivering in this position, so talk about it during early labour with her.

Squatting and supported squatting are other alternatives. Not many women are supple enough to be able to squat right down on their heels during labour or delivery and, even if you have practised this position, it

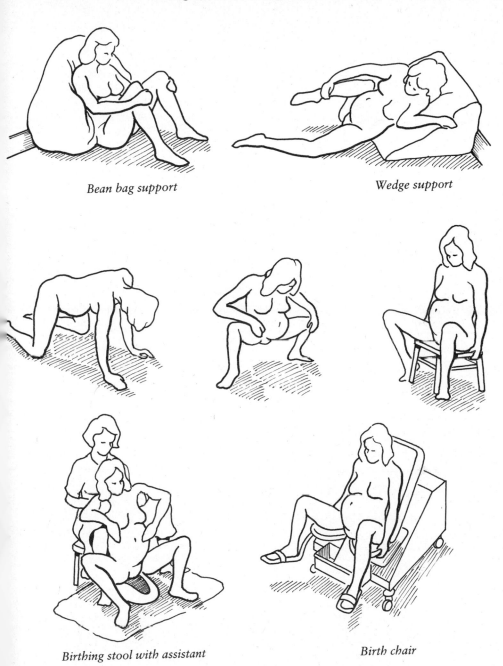

Bean bag support

Wedge support

Birthing stool with assistant

Birth chair

Different birth positions

93

can be more difficult for delivery. A supported semi-squatting position is much easier to adopt and also makes the delivery easier. For this you need your partner or helper to stand behind you with his arms supporting your weight under your armpits. As you push with a contraction, you can relax your whole weight on to his arms and collapse your knees outwards. This opens up the pelvic girdle as widely as possible and allows the full force of gravity to help the baby move downwards. Again, you need the co-operation of your midwife who needs to feel confident about this position. She will have to kneel, bend or crouch down to deliver the baby.

A supported squatting position can also be achieved with birth chairs, birth stools and some birthing beds. Birth chairs usually resemble a dentist's chair but with a semi-circular cut-out seat and foot-rests at either side. Birth stools are also semi-circular but your feet are flat on the floor and they are much lower, which again requires the midwife to kneel on the floor. At a pinch almost anything, for example an upturned bucket, can serve as a birth stool. Birthing beds, such as the Borning bed, can convert from flat delivery beds through various degrees of support into a chair which will support the mother in an upright squat. Because they are so expensive not very many hospitals have them yet. The advantage is that they can allow the mother to be upright while still making delivery easy for the midwife who does not have to crouch or kneel on the floor.

Birthing pools which allow a woman to stay in water during labour and even for the baby to be delivered underwater are still relatively rare now, but a few hospitals are beginning to be interested. Usually this is as a result of a consultant who is specially interested, so it is worth asking if that is the case at your local hospital. Alternatively some privately practising midwives and a few GPs will supervise home deliveries for couples who want an underwater delivery. There have been no studies yet as to whether labour is quicker or less painful, but women who have used pools during labour say that the freedom of movement and the support provided by the buoyancy of the water is very pleasant. The disadvantage from a midwife or doctor's point of view is that they cannot monitor the birth so easily. When the baby is born into the water it is still receiving oxygen through the blood supply reaching it via the placenta and the umbilical cord. It does not take its first breath through the air passages and lungs until it is lifted out of the water.

PSYCHOPROPHYLAXIS

This is a long word to describe a method usually summed up as natural childbirth. There are two parts to the theory behind this approach. The first is that fear causes pain because it makes women tense up and fight against what is happening to their bodies instead of relaxing with the contractions. To stop women being afraid, they need to understand what happens in labour and how they can help themselves. The second part of the theory is a way of distracting the brain from messages of pain by concentrating totally on another sensation — in this case a series of breathing exercises designed for all stages of labour and delivery. Nowadays both the Active Birth Movement and National Childbirth Trust teach this method combined with position, but most hospital antenatal classes include some kind of breathing techniques as well as explanation. All women will benefit from learning these breathing exercises, even if they intend to have an epidural or know in advance they need a Caesarean, because they can be used to distract your mind and to relax you during any kind of difficult procedure — for example, during an internal examination, while an epidural is being administered or for an epidural Caesarean.

PETHIDINE

This is a derivative of morphine given by injection, often together with a tranquilliser or antihistamine to counteract nausea. It produces a drowsy, detached state rather like a pre-med before an operation or feeling mildly drunk. Some people hate to feel they cannot concentrate totally on what is happening and prefer to have all their wits about them, while others say it made all the difference and just took the edge off the pain. Pethidine has a relaxing effect on muscles and sometimes labour progresses more quickly after it is given. However, it also crosses the placenta into the baby's bloodstream and can make him drowsy, so it should not be given within three hours of the expected delivery because it could interfere with the baby's reflexes and make it more difficult for him to start breathing. If the baby is born sooner than expected and is very drowsy an antidote can easily be given to counter the effect of the drug.

Pethidine tends to act as a mood enhancer in the same way that alcohol does — if you are feeling happy and confident it will accentuate that feeling, but if you are feeling unhappy or frightened it can sometimes increase that emotion too. It is usually given in doses of 50 to 100 mg.

GAS AND AIR

Entonox is a mixture of oxygen and an inhaled painkiller — also known as laughing gas because of the lightheaded, slightly high effect it produces. The mother holds a rubber mask over her mouth and nose and breathes in deeply — it is important that she hold the mask rather than anybody else, because if she takes enough to make her lose consciousness, she will automatically drop the mask. Because it takes twenty seconds to have an effect, she should start to use it as soon as a contraction begins so that the maximum effect is when a contraction is at its height. It does not affect the baby, and the mother can control just how much she uses. It is most useful at the difficult end of the first stage, during transition from first to second stage or for stitching.

EPIDURAL ANAESTHETIC

This is one of only two ways of giving total pain relief during birth (the other is a full anaesthetic) and is especially useful for deliveries which are likely to be difficult or require intervention – an unusual birth position, a premature baby or a multiple birth. Local anaesthetic is injected near to the spinal cord and blocks the sensations in the nerves from about the waist down so that the mother is awake and fully conscious but feels no pain. It works on the same principle the dentist uses when giving a local anaesthetic to block nerves in your mouth during a filling, but because having a baby takes rather longer than filling a tooth, more than one shot of anaesthetic is needed. It would be impractical to keep injecting, so the procedure is to insert a hollow needle between the bones of the spine (vertebrae) into a space which surrounds the spinal cord called the 'epidural space'. A fine tube (catheter) is fed down the needle into the space and the other end secured up your back to your shoulder with sticky tape. As the effect of the anaesthetic begins to wear off, it can be topped up by injecting more through the tube.

You are not free to move around with an epidural because although you can usually move your legs they feel numb and you would not be able to walk. An epidural also makes other intervention more likely. It lowers blood pressure and, although this can be useful when women suffer from high blood pressure, in ordinary circumstances care must be taken it does not fall too low, and a drip will be set up as a safety measure. Very occasionally an epidural has the effect of weakening contractions, in which case a hormone may need to be dripped into your arm to stimulate the uterus. The anaesthetic can be tailed off for the second stage, with careful management, so that you can feel enough to push your baby out, but this does not always happen and the rate of forceps deliveries is higher with epidurals. Because the mother cannot feel to empty her bladder this usually has to be done with a catheter.

Epidurals cannot be guaranteed to work perfectly, and sometimes one side is numbed while sensation can still be felt on the other. Women have also been known to complain of backache afterwards, but this is usually due to the position they were in rather than the epidural itself. Very rarely the needle can pierce the dura, which is the membrane surrounding the spinal cord, and this causes a bad headache afterwards.

TRANSCUTANEOUS NERVE STIMULATION (TNS OR TENS)

This is a relatively new method which is still being researched, but it can be used with the help of a midwife and is in operation in some maternity units. A small control box called a 'pulsar' has a nine-volt battery fitted and between four and six electrodes can be plugged into this power source. At the end of the wires leading from the box are flat rubber pads which are positioned either side of the mother's spine. They are usually taped in place. The mother holds a control button which she can press to send an electrical pulse as the contraction begins. She can make this stronger and more frequent during the contraction or switch it off altogether in between. At the lowest levels there is a faint tickle which is barely noticeable, but as the power is turned up the sensation is more like a fizz and then a definite buzz, although it is at no time painful.

TNS is said to work in two ways to help kill the pain of labour. The first is that it stimulates the body to produce more of its own natural painkillers which raise our pain tolerance threshold – these substances are called 'endogenous opiates' or 'endorphins'. The second effect is that it interrupts the pain pathways from the womb to the brain. As the muscles of the uterus tense in a contraction, the nerve endings send messages to the brain. The brain converts or interprets the messages into the sensation we call pain and sends them back so that we feel this pain in our backs or stomachs during a contraction. The electrical pulse of TNS blocks those messages. Imagine that the nerve pathways are telephone lines and the brain is the telephone exchange which converts the messages into pain and sends them back again. When TNS is in use, messages or calls cannot get through because the line is already engaged or occupied by TNS.

The technique has no side effects and mothers are free to move around during labour or adopt any position they want for delivery.

ACUPUNCTURE

This can be used quite successfully to ease pain during labour and delivery, but, unless you hit on a hospital doing research or where there is a member of staff with a special interest, it is normally a service you will have to arrange yourself. You either need a doctor who practises acupuncture or an acupuncture practitioner who is skilled in using it for childbirth, and you will also need the agreement of your consultant and the nursing officer for midwifery at the hospital. There are various forms of acupuncture, but this is one mother's experience:

'The acupuncturist met me at the hospital but he didn't put any needles in until contractions were quite strong and I needed help. I didn't feel them going in – one in my ear, one between my thumb and finger and three at the end of one leg. They were all down one side so if I had to move and they needed to be taken out he could put them in on the other side. He attached the end of the needles to a machine which vibrated them. That felt like a very slight electric shock but nothing painful. After a while he turned this off and although I couldn't see or feel anything the needles carried on vibrating. Within half an hour I began to find the contractions easier to cope with – I used breathing exercises as well. The whole labour lasted six hours and I pushed the baby out without any problems – this was my second baby. The needles stayed in place all the time and didn't bother me at all. I was very pleased with the result.'

HYPNOSIS

Again, this is only available in special circumstances if there are staff who practise it at the hospital, but you can find someone to teach you during pregnancy. It is not, as many people think, a matter of going into a trance so that you do not know what is happening, nor a way of becoming unconscious. In childbirth it is rather a question of teaching autohypnosis as a way of relaxation which mothers can use in labour. One mother recalls:

'I went to six classes in hypnosis as well as learning breathing techniques at the normal antenatal course. We learnt the theory of hypnosis – it is nothing to do with being under someone else's control and having to obey them. Instead we used to sit round and fix our gaze on a particular spot while the doctor talked us through until gradually we lost everything around us. He'd asked us to imagine we were on a beach, to hear the waves, feel the sun and sand. My blood pressure dropped and I felt totally relaxed after, although I'd been aware of what was going on all the time. During the birth I found I was able to practise the same technique, to relax totally and it helped during the first stage, although I also had some pethidine. But I couldn't use it in the second stage because too much was happening and I had to concentrate on breathing and pushing. I felt it was a help.'

A CHECKLIST THAT WILL HELP YOU TO A BETTER BIRTH

BEFORE THE BIRTH

* Find out, from classes, books and magazines, what will happen to your body during labour and delivery so that you understand what is going on at each stage.

* Prepare for birth by learning and practising breathing exercises, even if you intend to have an epidural.

* Stay supple and keep muscles toned with exercises designed for pregnancy. Antenatal classes, National Childbirth Trust, Active Birth Movement, or birth centres will give details or suggest books.

* Eat well and get plenty of rest at the end of pregnancy so that you avoid going into labour already tired.

* Talk to your partner about what will happen and how he can assist you. It really helps if you learn about the process together, and most antenatal courses include a fathers' session or are designed for couples together.

EARLY LABOUR

* If it is night-time or you are short of sleep, try to rest because you will need more energy later. Usually people cannot actually go to sleep because they are too excited!

* Eat something light and easily digestible which will give you energy. Do not eat anything heavy because digestion slows right down during labour and a full stomach makes nausea or sickness more likely. In an emergency which requires a full anaesthetic or a Caesarean, it also increases the risk of inhaling vomit.

* Most women feel excited and elated at the start of labour. Carrying on as normal and doing practical tasks is calming, while moving around and staying upright will encourage contractions.

* A warm bath, if the waters are intact, is often soothing and relaxing, or a shower if the waters have broken.

* Check everything is ready to take to the hospital — prepare last-minute things like sandwiches for your partner, a thermos of ice, drinks, etc. Having something practical to do is often helpful.

ESTABLISHED LABOUR

* Try to listen to your body and be guided by what seems best. Most women find contractions in early labour are easy to cope with in a vertical position, but do experiment — try walking, kneeling, sitting astride a chair or even squatting if you are agile and have been practising.

* Remember to go to the toilet at regular intervals throughout labour.

* Your partner can help by timing contractions and the gaps in between, by asking medical staff to wait if they want to do something and you are in the middle of a contraction, by massaging the small of your back or your stomach if you find this soothing and by reminding you to relax and breathe through contractions.

* It is very easy to become disorientated or feel overwhelmed towards the end of the first stage of labour, especially if it has gone on a long time. Usually contractions are at their most intense and you are at your most tired. It is important to take each contraction one at a time, and remember that each one is a step nearer to the birth of your baby. Try to relax as fully as possible in between and concentrate on the present moment.

* Remember that if you have one or two contractions that are very hard to cope with, this is usually the signal that you are near the end of the first stage.

* If any medical intervention is needed, make sure you understand what it is and why it has to happen – your partner can really help here by making your wishes known and also making sure you understand.

* You should not eat or drink anything during this stage, but many people find it helps to suck on ice cubes or a moist, natural sponge, and to use Vaseline or lipsalve on your lips to stop them and your mouth getting dry, something which often happens with breathing exercises.

SECOND STAGE

* Get into the easiest and most comfortable position for pushing the baby out – again, listen to what your body is telling you.

* Try to relax your pelvic floor – keep your mouth and jaw relaxed because the two go together and if you are clenching your teeth you are almost certainly contracting and tensing your pelvic floor muscles.

* Listen to what the midwife is telling you to do – if necessary your partner can often help by relaying information.

* Lots of people find it exciting or reassuring to realise that their baby is very nearly there – you can feel your baby's head crowning by reaching down with your hands, or use a mirror to watch.

* At the very moment of birth you do not need to push any more – the midwife will tell you to pant so that you stop pushing and the baby's head is eased out very slowly. It may take a second contraction for his body to be delivered. Don't worry because during this time he is still receiving oxygen via the umbilical cord – he does not need to get oxygen by breathing air in through his lungs until the cord is cut.

THIRD STAGE

* That marvellous moment – your baby is there and the birth is over. In your excitement at greeting him do not forget to help the midwife to deliver the placenta. She will probably ask you to push while she gently pulls on the umbilical cord to ease it out.

CHECKING ON YOU AND YOUR BABY DURING LABOUR

WHAT'S HAPPENING TO YOU

During labour the midwife will take your temperature and record your pulse and blood pressure at regular intervals, checking more frequently as labour progresses. She will also remind you to empty your bladder at intervals because a full bladder can block the baby's descent. If blood pressure is very high an epidural anaesthetic may be suggested because this always has the effect of reducing blood pressure. In women with normal blood pressure this can be a drawback because it may result in them having too low a blood pressure, but this is easily remedied.

What the midwife will be concerned with all the time is how far labour has progressed and how long it will be before the baby is born. The best guide to this is to time how often contractions are coming, how long they last and how strong they are — you will probably have learnt about this in antenatal classes. Apart from electronic monitoring, the midwife can also feel these things by putting her hand on your stomach and also by a vaginal examination to feel how far the cervix has dilated. Do remember that labour does not continue at the same even rate, so don't be depressed if you have been in labour for a long time but the cervix has only dilated a very small amount, because things can sometimes speed up very unexpectedly.

Early in labour the midwife will check for contractions every hour and then more frequently as labour progresses. Some hospitals do a vaginal examination every two to four hours routinely, while others may do only one when it is clear from the strength and frequency of contractions that the second stage is near. Again practice amongst individual midwives and doctors varies considerably.

WHAT'S HAPPENING TO YOUR BABY

There are various ways of checking on what is happening to the baby and one of these is for a midwife or doctor to feel (palpate) your abdomen to check what position the baby is in and how far down the head has moved. The commonest and easiest way for a baby to be born is head first, facing backwards, and with his head tucked tightly into his chest. However, the easiest way into the pelvic birth canal is looking sideways, so during the passage downwards, the baby's head must rotate so that his face is towards your backbone. The head should remain tightly tucked in or 'flexed' as it comes round the pelvic curve towards the perineum, so that the narrowest part of the head, the occiput, leads the way. The vast majority of babies — 98% — follow this pattern at birth.

Some babies are not head down but instead are bottom or feet down-wards. This is called 'breech presentation' (see page 54). A rarer variation is that a part of the head other than the occiput (back of the head), for example the face or the brow, is presenting first. If a baby is head down with the occiput leading the way but does not rotate so that his backbone is towards your stomach this is called an 'occipito-posterior position'.

Apart from checking what position the baby is in, the midwife will also listen very carefully to the baby's heartbeat — one of the most important indications of its condition. Normally a baby's heart beats 120 to 160 times a minute, and girls' hearts beat slightly faster than boys'. The baby's heart will usually speed up slightly in response to the extra stress of a contraction and then go back to its normal rate in between. If it begins to fall below 120 beats or rise above 160 this may be a sign that his condition

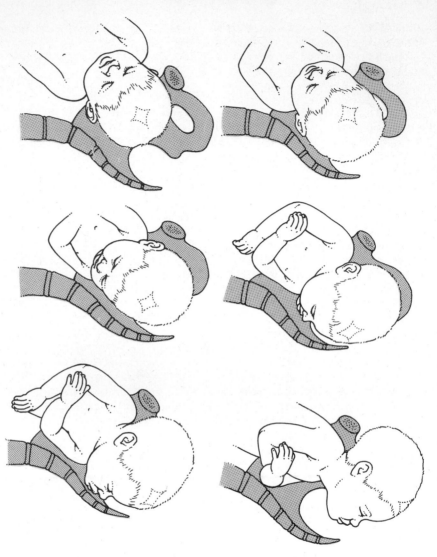

Rotation of the baby's head during a normal delivery

is not so healthy – the baby is said to be distressed. A midwife or doctor can listen to the baby's heart by putting a stethoscope or an ear trumpet against your stomach or by using an electronic monitor. There are portable monitors which can simply be held against the mother's abdomen or, alternatively, a receiver is strapped to your abdomen with a stretchy belt. This picks up signals from the baby's heart while a pressure gauge records the strength and length of contractions. The receiver in this belt is connected by a wire to a computer which gives a continuous printed record of the baby's heartbeat in relation to contractions.

After the waters are broken the baby's heart can also be monitored by fixing a clip through the cervix to the baby's scalp. In this case a wire leads from the clip out through the vagina to a computer. At the same time a catheter can be inserted into the uterus to measure contractions. Both these methods have the disadvantage of restricting movement in the mother so that she cannot get up and walk around, but in normal labour monitoring at intervals is usually sufficient. The monitoring can be done while you sit in a chair instead of lying in a bed if you prefer. Portable monitoring equipment is called 'telemetric equipment' and has the advantage that women can walk around. However it is quite expensive and not yet very widely available.

During a normal labour the midwife will want to listen to the baby's heartbeat at first every hour, then more frequently, and towards the end of labour probably after every contraction.

At some point before the baby is born the bag of membranes holding the amniotic fluid will either break naturally or be ruptured. When the fluid leaks out this is another opportunity for the midwife or doctor to make an important check on the condition of the baby because the amniotic fluid should be clear and colourless. If it is stained brown or green this may be a sign that the baby is becoming distressed and other checks will immediately be made on his condition. The discoloration of the waters will come from meconium which is the blackish, glue-like material inside the baby's bowel, normally expelled in the first few days of life. The intestines of a distressed baby may sometimes go into spasm causing him to pass a motion inside the uterus which discolours the amniotic fluid. However, discoloured amniotic fluid alone is not necessarily a reliable sign of distress in itself – simply a sign that other checks need to be made.

THE FIRST MOMENTS OF LIFE

While the baby is half in and half out of the vagina and when he is born he is usually a whitish, bluish colour which can be a shock if your partner or you expected the baby to come out looking pink immediately. Many babies are blue or purplish or pale as they have been squeezed through the final part of the birth canal and will go pink after their first few breaths of air. Some people believe that leaving the cord intact for a short period after the birth gives the baby a back-up supply of oxygen.

Some women feel very strongly about what they would like to happen after the birth – for example, they very much want the baby delivered on to their stomach or may feel that they would like the cord to stop pulsing before it is cut. Others may feel neutral or be quite happy to put their faith in the midwife's decisions. Depending on what you and your midwife agree beforehand, the baby can be either propped against your thigh until

the cord is cut, or the cord can be cut and the baby handed to you, or the baby can be placed on your stomach either before or after the cord has been cut. Many women simply need time to recover from the birth and are not ready to have the baby handed to them straight away. It very much depends on the individual. There is always a worry that the baby will get cold after the birth which is why the temperature in the delivery room should always be very high, but some hospitals also insist on the baby being wrapped in a clean warm cloth before being handed to the mother.

The placenta is delivered into a kidney dish and the midwife will examine it carefully to make sure it is complete and that no parts have been left behind. If the placenta is not complete, bleeding is likely to occur. Mothers are usually surprised by the size of the placenta – although flatter it is usually more than the width and length of the baby's head. Once the placenta is safely delivered, the midwife will examine the mother's vagina and vulva to see if any tissues have been torn. If any stitches are needed to repair a tear or an episiotomy, it is important that this is done as soon as possible after the birth while the tissues are still deadened. The areas will be carefully cleaned and anaesthetised with an injection of local anaesthetic. It is becoming more common for midwives in hospital to do their own stitching, as long as only a minor repair is necessary. Depending on the repair to be made, some doctors and midwives prefer women to lie back with their feet in stirrups for the stitching procedure. It can help to use gas and air if this is painful, although don't hesitate to ask for more local anaesthetic if you need it. The midwife will also check the mother's blood pressure, temperature and pulse.

MEDICAL INTERVENTIONS – AND WHY THEY MAY BE NEEDED

Sometimes some part of the pregnancy and labour is not entirely straightforward and a doctor or midwife may need to intervene, or to step in, and to do something to make sure the baby is born safely. In nearly all cases they will be at pains to consult you and explain what is happening and why, although in a real emergency this is more difficult. Nevertheless, you and your partner should never be afraid to ask if there is anything you are unsure about.

INDUCTION

This means inducing or starting labour artificially. The most common reason for inducing labour is that the baby has stayed in the uterus beyond the date when it should have been born – this is called 'post-maturity'. The worry is that it may begin to suffer from lack of oxygen because the placenta may start to fail and no longer be able to work properly. Some hospitals do not like to leave babies longer than 41 or 42 weeks, while others will leave them longer provided that checks show they are all right. Signs for concern may be fewer and weaker movements from the baby (although this is often hard to judge for mothers), any suggestion of an abnormal heartbeat and poor growth, together with an overall weight loss in the mother for two or three weeks. Post-mature babies will have begun to lose body fat and have saggy, wrinkly skin over their tummies, longer fingernails and often flaky, dry skin with very little vernix – that is the white creamy substance which protects their skin while they are in the womb. It is very important that the expected date of birth is calculated carefully so that a baby is not mistakenly induced and then proves to be premature. A scan at around 16 weeks can tell the baby's age and due date of birth most accurately.

Other reasons for inducing labour may be that a problem exists or develops during pregnancy so that there comes a point when the baby may be safer outside than inside the womb, even though this means he will be born early. Examples of this are mothers who develop pre-eclampsia, or those who have heart conditions, kidney disease or possibly diabetes. Babies who are not growing properly because the placenta is not working well enough to provide sufficient nutrients and vital oxygen supplies, babies showing signs of foetal distress or babies with rhesus disease may also fall into this group.

The oldest method of inducing or starting labour is castor oil, an enema and a warm bath and in fact if the cervix has begun to soften this can still be very effective, but do not try dosing yourself with anything unsupervised. Modern methods, however, include breaking the waters so that the baby's head begins to press directly on the cervix, helping to stimulate contractions, or administering hormones either in the form of pessaries or by means of a drip which will have the effect of stimulating labour. In deciding how to induce labour, midwives and doctors will try to determine how close the mother is to natural labour. An internal examination can tell how 'ripe' the cervix is: this closed ring of fibrous tissue begins to soften and relax as the time for the baby to be born draws near. If the cervix is quite ripe, if the baby is already due and if the mother has experienced erratic contractions, perhaps over a period of days, it may be sufficient simply to break the waters. This is done by passing an instrument through the cervix during a vaginal examination to break the membranes or 'bag' holding the fluid. It should not be more uncomfortable than an ordinary internal. After the first rush of water there will be more leaks with each contraction for a while. The condition of the water is an important guide to the baby's condition (see page 119).

If the cervix is unripe prostaglandin pessaries are used to induce labour. These can be inserted high in the vagina to make the cervix soften and start to dilate. They take several hours to work and usually contractions begin gently and follow a natural pattern of build up. Finally, a drip can be used to feed the hormone oxytocin directly into the bloodstream. This is the hormone produced naturally by the body to stimulate contractions.

Instead of a slow build up, contractions tend to start more strongly and to come more frequently, but labour is usually shorter. Care must be taken that contractions do not come so fast that the baby becomes distressed.

Induced labours will be monitored, but you can sit in a chair if that is more comfortable than a bed, and there is a certain amount of leeway in being able to move around, albeit anchored to a drip.

ACCELERATED LABOUR

There are various reasons for wanting to accelerate a labour. One of the commonest ones is if the labour progresses very slowly, in which case it could become dangerously long. When this happens, the risk of either you or the baby becoming distressed or getting an infection increases, and careful checks will be made to make sure this does not happen. A long labour may be caused by an abnormal pattern of contractions, an unusual birth position, disproportion (where the baby's head is too large to fit into the pelvis) or, very rarely, an undetected tumour in the pelvis blocking the baby's descent. Any or all of these reasons may make a Caesarean delivery advisable.

Sometimes other medical interventions can have the effect of making contractions diminish or become less effective – this can happen with an epidural anaesthetic or sedatives. Other reasons for wanting to accelerate labour, usually with a hormone drip, may be a stop-start pattern of contractions which never gets properly established, although the baby is due, or a long period of weak contractions after the waters have broken.

EPISIOTOMY

This is a small cut in the skin of the perineum to enlarge the vaginal entrance just before the baby is born. There is a good deal of controversy surrounding the practice, which used to be almost routine for first-time mothers in some hospitals. The traditional view is that an episiotomy prevents serious tearing which in a very few cases might even extend into the rectum. It is easier to repair and mends better than a ragged tear and helps prevent prolapse in later life. However, a more recent school of thought maintains that small tears mend and heal better and with less discomfort than an episiotomy, that many episiotomies extend into tears anyway, and that several episiotomies may actually make the risk of later prolapse greater. Most midwives take a great pride in trying to avoid an unnecessary episiotomy. The stretchability of the perineum, the skill of the midwife, coupled with the patience and perseverance of a mother, probably matter more than the size of the baby – very large babies have often been delivered without cuts or tears.

However, sometimes there may be special reasons for an episiotomy to deliver the baby quickly and without great pressure on the head. A baby showing signs of distress, or a premature or growth-retarded baby may need to be got out quickly, using forceps which form a protective cage round the baby's head so that it is not subjected to pressure during birth. Episiotomies and forceps generally go together, so an unusual position of the head, a multiple birth, or mothers who cannot push the baby out themselves – because they have had an epidural, lost their contractions or are too exhausted after a very long labour – are more likely to require an episiotomy. Women with high blood pressure or heart conditions who should not exert themselves by excessive pushing may also be delivered by an episiotomy and forceps.

An episiotomy is made as the baby's head begins to crown. The midwife will be watching carefully to see how the perineum is stretching. If it seems very rigid and likely to tear badly, or if there is a special reason for the baby to be delivered quickly, or the mother should not push, the midwife injects local anaesthetic and makes the cut with a pair of surgical scissors at the height of the next contraction. The skin is already deadened by stretching and the cut is usually painless. Although naturally this is a procedure which causes great concern in advance for first-time mothers, nearly all of them afterwards say they did not notice when it was happening.

The cut should be sewn up as soon as possible after the baby is born while the skin is still deadened – the longer it is left the more sensation returns to the area. Plenty of local anaesthetic should be used and given time to take effect, so ask for more if you are in pain. It is usually necessary to put a woman's feet in stirrups for the stitching – normally done by a doctor but in some units midwives are now beginning to stitch their own deliveries. The layers of the vagina, the muscles of the perineum and the skin all have to be closed separately, but usually with thread which dissolves rather than having to be taken out. For more about the care of the perineum after birth see page 166.

FORCEPS

These are really tongs which fit round the baby's head and can be used to help lift the baby out or turn him if the head is in an unusual position. If the baby is very small, premature or showing signs of distress and needs to be delivered quickly and without too much pressure on a delicate skull, forceps may be used. The blades of the forceps fit round the head like a cage, protecting it from pressure. They may also be used to protect the head in a breech delivery – that is when the bottom presents first. Other reasons for the use of forceps may be if the baby is very delayed in the second stage and the mother seems unlikely to be able to push him out herself, or if an epidural anaesthetic makes it more difficult for the mother to feel the contractions and push the baby out. Finally, forceps may be used when the mother has a condition such as heart disease or high blood pressure and should not over-exert herself.

If you have not had an epidural anaesthetic and there is no time to set one up, then a local anaesthetic will be injected into the vulva and around the vagina to numb this area. This is called a 'pudendal block'. An episiotomy is usually carried out with a forceps delivery to avoid both tears to you and extra pressure on the baby's head. You will probably be asked to lie back and put your feet up in stirrups (the lithotomy position) and your thighs will be covered with sterile drapes. Don't be alarmed by all this surgical-seeming preparation — most forceps deliveries really are painless and will ensure the safety of your baby. The majority are 'low forceps' when the baby has moved well down into the vagina and just needs help in the last stage. One blade of the forceps at a time is slid into the vagina and once they are both safely tucked around the baby's head the handles are locked into position. The doctor pulls very gently in time with the mother's contractions, stopping in between, until the head is low enough to be eased out.

Intervention is also required if the baby's head fails to rotate as it moves down into the birth canal, a condition known as 'transverse arrest'. Most babies' heads are turned to the side when they engage in the pelvis, known as 'occipito-lateral position'. Normally they rotate spontaneously so that the occiput, the bone at the back of the baby's head, is facing upwards towards the mother's stomach. This is the ideal birth position. However, the head may fail to rotate at all, or may rotate so that the baby's face points forwards — 'occipito-posterior' — and in both these situations the head is likely to get stuck and need to be turned with forceps. Once the baby's head has turned, it will usually move further down the birth canal to the entrance of the vagina quite easily. In general, difficult forceps deliveries with the head high up, which used to be common up until the mid-1970s, are simply no longer attempted, having been replaced by Caesarean section.

Marks left by the forceps on the baby's head can look worrying but nearly always disappear within twenty-four hours. Occasionally, a difficult delivery may leave longer-lasting bruises. As with all medical procedures, there is a slight risk of more permanent damage but the risk of the procedure has to be weighed against the risk of doing nothing.

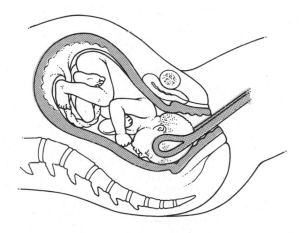

Forceps delivery

VACUUM DELIVERY

This is an alternative to forceps and is commoner in other European countries than it is in the UK. It entails using a piece of equipment called a 'vacuum extractor' or 'ventouse' which consists of a metal or rubber cup with a suction pump and chain attached.

The reasons for doing a vacuum delivery are similar to the need for forceps. In this country, the most common reason is probably when a baby becomes distressed, but the cervix is not yet quite fully dilated. In this case, using forceps would damage the rim of the cervix, but the ventouse or vacuum cup can be fixed to the head through the partially dilated cervix and, as the head is very gently drawn downwards, the rim of the cervix is eased back without any risk of tearing.

As with forceps, mothers usually have to lie back in the lithotomy position and be covered with sterile drapes. The cup is fitted over the back of the baby's head and a vacuum created with the suction pump so that the baby's scalp is sucked up into the cup. The doctor pulls gently on the chain in time with the contractions, in the same way as with forceps, to ease the head downwards. After the delivery, the baby will have a soft swelling on his head in the shape of a cup which, although it looks odd, always goes down in a couple of days and causes no lasting effects.

CAESAREAN SECTION

This is an operation done under general or epidural anaesthetic in which a cut is made through the abdomen and the wall of the uterus and the baby is then lifted out. The need for a Caesarean may be recognised during pregnancy, in which case it is called a 'planned' or 'elective' Caesarean, or it may arise because of an emergency either during labour or before.

A baby who is too large to pass through the mother's pelvis (disproportion), or when the placenta is covering the cervix (*placenta praevia*), or in cases when the baby is lying transversely, will have to be delivered by Caesarean. It may be thought a safer way of birth for very vulnerable babies as well – and these include babies who are premature, small or lying in an unusual position. A prolapsed cord (see page 119) will need a Caesarean delivery, and babies who become seriously distressed either during pregnancy or labour may also have to be delivered this way. Sometimes it may be done to protect the mother if she has a heart condition, very high blood pressure, pre-eclampsia, diabetes or a detached retina. Caesarean section may also be the answer if all attempts to induce labour fail, or the cervix does not dilate, or if there was a previous very difficult birth, perhaps requiring high forceps, though doctors will often allow a trial labour to see if there is a chance of a normal delivery. In many cases, a combination of reasons can lead to the decision to do a Caesarean. A previous Caesarean birth on its own is not a reason for a subsequent Caesar, unless the same complications exist, but

Delivery by Caesarean section – the mother is under epidural anaesthetic

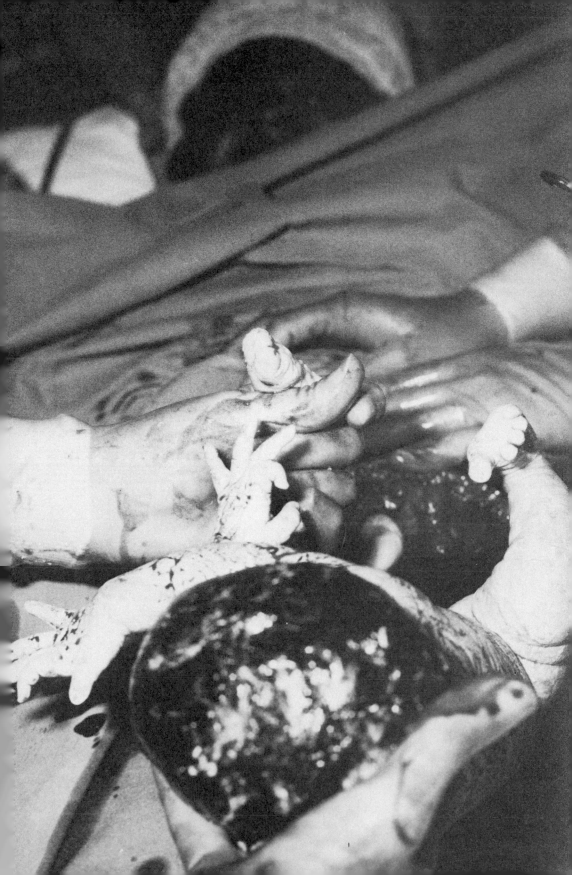

doctors will be monitoring the case more carefully to make sure the scarred uterus is working properly.

Like any operation, a Caesarean section requires pre-op procedures. This means not eating for a period beforehand, shaving pubic hair, possibly suppositories the night before, removal of false teeth, contact lenses and jewellery, but no pre-med injection as this would affect the baby. In an emergency, some or all of these procedures may have to go by the board. A drip will be set up and a catheter (hollow tube) inserted to drain the bladder, though if you are having a general anaesthetic this may be done after you go to sleep.

The whole operation takes about thirty to forty minutes from start to finish. Cutting through the wall of the abdomen and uterus and lifting the baby out is the quickest part and your baby will be born in about five minutes. Usually the cut is made horizontally very low down in the abdomen so it will not show above a bikini. Most surgeons do a horizontal rather than a vertical cut unless there are special circumstances, but ask beforehand. After the baby has been delivered you are given an injection of oxytocin, as in a normal labour, to help the placenta to separate, and this is also delivered through the cut. The longest part of the operation is stitching back the layers of tissue. A dressing will be put on the wound which will be inspected each day, and usually a tube to drain it will be in place for the first twelve to twenty-four hours. The stitches usually come out around the fifth day, depending on how the wound heals. The drip will be left in place until you are able to drink normally without feeling

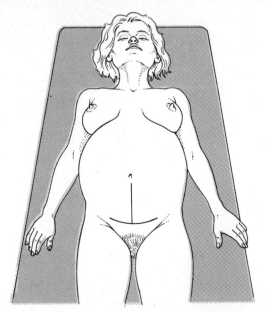

Alternative positions for Caesarean incision

sick – again this usually happens within the first twenty-four hours. For more on recovery after a Caesarean see page 166.

Under a general anaesthetic the gases do not affect the baby, but because there is a high risk of vomiting with a pregnant woman the anaesthetic will be given by a senior anaesthetist. Nowadays doctors prefer to do Caesareans under epidural anaesthetic when possible because the risks to the mother are less and because it is very enjoyable to see your baby immediately after he is born, but you will have the choice unless it is an emergency when there may only be time for a full anaesthetic. A general anaesthetic affects individuals differently, but it is common to feel nauseous afterwards and many women complain of a chesty feeling where mucus has gathered on their lungs and sometimes a sore throat caused by the tube which was passed down it.

An epidural is administered in the usual way (see page 96), but extra care is taken to make sure it is fully effective, which usually means lying in all sorts of different positions, and having several tests, such as testing pin-prick sensation before the operation. Although you can feel pressure there is no sensation of pain. Most consultants will be pleased for your husband to stay with you and a sterile green cloth will be pinned up across your chest as a screen so you do not have to watch what is happening. Your blood pressure and pulse rate will be monitored, as with any surgical operation.

As long as there are no complications, the baby will usually be given to you to hold while the wound is stitched and, once this is done, you can put him to the breast if you plan to feed him yourself. The epidural will usually be topped up once after the operation to give continuing pain relief.

PROBLEMS IN LABOUR AND DELIVERY

PREMATURE LABOUR

This is a labour which starts after 28 weeks but before 37 weeks – before 28 weeks it is, strictly speaking, said to be a miscarriage, but of course many babies survive having been born before this. It is often hard to say why labour has started early; it is usually a combination of factors. Illness in the mother can sometimes be a reason – for example, diabetes, high blood pressure, pre-eclampsia, uncontrolled heart disease, anaemia, urinary infection or an infectious fever. Accidental haemorrhage when the placenta begins to separate early and causes bleeding can also cause premature labour. Mothers under twenty or over thirty-five, smokers, and those suffering from poor nutrition and living standards may be more at risk, while an incompetent or damaged cervix, a failing placenta or a malformation in the baby can also cause labour to begin prematurely. The commonest foetal cause is a multiple pregnancy; the more babies, the earlier labour begins.

The baby's chance of survival in the case of a premature labour and delivery depends on how mature the lungs are. Maturity is not necessarily related to size and quite a large baby can be immature while a smaller one can have spent more time in the uterus and can be better developed to cope with life outside. As a rough guide, if the pregnancy is more than 34 weeks when labour begins then it will usually be allowed to continue because by this stage the baby should be mature enough, if there are no other complications, to be looked after in an ordinary hospital maternity unit.

Before 34 weeks doctors will take into account any known reasons for the start of labour – for example, illness in the mother or other complications which may make it more dangerous for the baby (or possibly for the mother) to stay in the uterus than to be born. If it is decided that labour should continue or if it is not possible to stop contractions and the pregnancy is less than 32 weeks then an injection of a cortisone-like drug may be given which will help the baby's lungs mature more quickly. Before 32 weeks the baby's lungs are likely to lack a substance called 'surfactant' which is secreted to line the mucous membrane inside the lungs and make them more flexible and less likely to stick together (see page 127). Cortisone injections boost surfactant production. If possible, labour will also be slowed down to allow time to move the mother to a hospital which has an intensive care unit which will give the baby a better chance of survival. A first step in stopping labour is bed rest, but if labour threatens to become established a drug can also be given, at first by drip into a vein in the arm and then as tablets – this sometimes works, but doctors vary in their opinion of this treatment. In delivering a very premature baby it is important to reduce the stress of the birth itself which may mean a Caesarean or the use of forceps or an episiotomy to reduce pressure on the baby's head as it is born. The baby's heart will be monitored electronically and mothers are nearly always offered an epidural. For more about the special care of premature and small babies see chapter 5.

WATERS BREAKING PREMATURELY

If the membrane containing the amniotic fluid ruptures, the water will either begin to leak slowly or to gush out. If it leaks slowly it can sometimes be mistaken for a vaginal discharge or urine and you need to see a doctor who can usually tell by an internal examination or tests whether it is amniotic fluid. Once the water has leaked out there is an increased risk of infection and, after 34 weeks of pregnancy, doctors will often decide to induce the labour if it does not follow naturally. Before 34 weeks doctors will normally try to give the baby extra valuable time in the womb, and resting in bed may be enough to delay labour. Swabs will be taken to check that there is no infection and antibiotics given to reduce its risk.

SMALL BABIES WHICH ARE NOT PREMATURE

Some babies may be born at the right time but still be very small because they have failed to grow properly in the uterus. They are usually known as small-for-dates babies which means that they are smaller than the average-sized baby would be at the same stage of pregnancy. Feeling the top of the uterus (the fundus) is a rough guide which enables the doctors to see if the baby is growing at the right rate, but ultrasound scans can give far more accurate and detailed information. A special scan looking at the pattern of blood flow through the placenta and in the baby's umbilical cord may be performed.

These small or low birthweight babies are more vulnerable than babies who have grown properly. Generally they are thought of as being babies which weigh less than 2,500 grams (5½ lbs). They are more likely to develop breathing or feeding problems and become ill, but given extra care in the early weeks they still stand a good chance of developing quite normally, although at first perhaps a little more slowly. They will eventually catch up with other children of the same age both in size and development.

The most common cause for a baby failing to grow is that the placenta is not working properly and the baby is therefore being starved before birth – he is not getting enough nourishment. This might be because the mother herself is ill (high blood pressure or kidney disease for example), is a heavy smoker or heavy drinker, or is suffering from poor nutrition herself. Women under eighteen or over thirty-five have also been shown to be slightly more at risk of having small babies.

Research is going on into the use of ultrasound scans to detect babies in the very early weeks of pregnancy who may be at risk – the scans can pick up which babies have a poor blood flow from the placenta. As yet these tests are in the research stage and not widely available. At the moment, therefore, doctors usually only pick up babies who are not growing properly later in pregnancy.

What can be done to help them? If tests show that the placenta is still working, then resting in bed, eating well and not drinking or smoking can give the baby a better chance. But if tests show that the placenta is beginning to fail altogether and the baby has stopped growing he may have to be delivered – despite the risks because of his immaturity – because the chances of his survival in the uterus are so much less. Even if they are not premature, small babies are also less able to withstand the extra stress of labour, and there is a higher chance that they may have to be delivered by Caesarean section or forceps, depending on their condition.

BLEEDING

The loss of bright red blood without any pain, either at the start of labour or during pregnancy, is likely to be a warning sign of a condition called *placenta praevia*. This means the placenta is lying low in the uterus, partially or completely covering the cervix and hence the baby's exit. A full *placenta praevia*, where the placenta is directly across the cervix, always calls for a Caesarean but there are degrees of the condition. Sometimes a scan may reveal that the placenta seems rather low, but as the baby grows and the uterus expands, so the position of the placenta may improve and move further away from the cervix.

Blood loss accompanied by pain, however, is usually a symptom of a different condition called *abruptio placentae*. In this case, the placenta is in the normal position in the upper third of the womb but begins to separate from the wall with bleeding which can be of varying amounts and from any part of the placenta. Sometimes there may be no visible bleeding from the vagina and diagnosis is often difficult. We do not yet know why this condition occurs – theories range from implicating high blood pressure, to abnormalities in the blood clotting factor, to accidental injury. The factors of each individual case need to be assessed to determine whether to deliver the baby by Caesarean – the baby's condition, the mother's blood loss, the maturity of the baby and whether the cervix has dilated or not, are some points which will be taken into account. It is rather more likely that the mother will need a blood transfusion following both these conditions.

ABNORMAL POSITIONS OF THE BABY

Breech In a normal birth the largest part of the baby, the head, slowly descends into the birth canal so the tissues are gently stretched. But with a breech birth the baby is lying head upwards and the head is born last and more quickly so there is an increased risk to the baby. Usually breech babies are born bottom first, but can also come out feet first. Doctors will assess the size of the pelvis to be certain there is plenty of room and try to make sure delivery is slow and controlled. Mothers are usually offered an epidural as the baby may need more manipulation or a forceps delivery. A Caesarean may be suggested, especially if the pelvis seems narrow or there are other complications, the baby is premature or very small, the baby becomes distressed at some point during labour, or the cervix does not dilate steadily during labour.

Transverse This means the baby is lying crossways and cannot be delivered either head or bottom first. Attempts may be made near the end of pregnancy to turn him but this should only be done by an obstetrician – do

| *Normal* | *Breech* | *Transverse* |

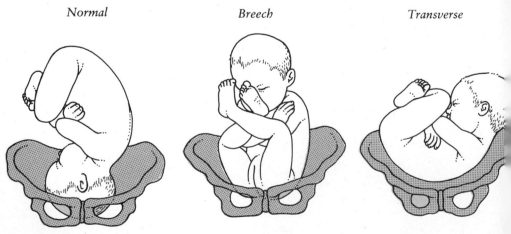

not try it yourself. If this fails a Caesarean will be needed. This position is more common in women who have had several babies.

Unstable lie A few babies keep changing from breech or head first to transverse, even in the last weeks of pregnancy, and this may be because a low placenta or even a tumour is blocking the cervix and their way out of the uterus. There is also a greater risk of a prolapsed cord (see page 119) when the waters break. Checks will be made to try to find the cause, which may mean a stay in hospital, and delivery is likely to be by Caesarean.

Different head presentations and positions Normally the narrowest part of the baby's head, the occiput, is born first and this is the part which is presenting – or leading the way. The baby flexes his neck so that his chin is tucked into his chest and his head turns from facing to one or other side so that his face is towards your backbone. His backbone lies uppermost towards your stomach. Sometimes the head turns the other way so that the baby's face is uppermost and then the back of the baby's head and his spine are towards your spine – this is called 'occipito-posterior position' and usually means a longer labour with backache. It is more likely to mean a forceps delivery and the use of a hormone drip to strengthen the contractions.

Deep transverse arrest occurs when the baby's head stays sideways and does not turn either towards your abdomen or towards your backbone. In this case, forceps are nearly always needed to turn the head and help the baby out.

If the baby's chin is not tucked tightly on to his chest, then a different part of the head will be born first which can make the second stage slower and mould the baby's head into an odd shape, although this will correct itself after a few days.

Rarely, the baby's head is not flexed at all and the face instead of the head is the presenting part – forceps can usually deliver these babies vaginally, but their faces are puffy and bruised for a few days from the pressure. Even more rarely, the brow can lead the way into the birth canal, leaving the head at such an angle that a Caesarean is sometimes the only way of delivery.

Shoulder presentation

Face presentation

Compound

Deep transverse arrest

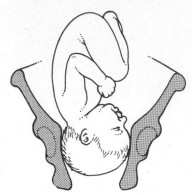

TWINS AND MORE

In nearly half of all twin pregnancies, both babies are lying head down by the end of the pregnancy, and in slightly fewer cases one baby is head down and the other is breech. It is rarer for both babies to be in the breech position and most uncommon of all for both babies to lie transversely. Identical twins develop from one large placenta and sometimes share one amniotic sac as well. Fraternal twins develop from two separate placentas and have two separate amniotic sacs.

Twins are more likely to be premature – about a quarter of all twins are born before the 36th week. This, coupled with an awkward position, can sometimes make a Caesarean more likely, but, if the pregnancy is quite well advanced, the babies are not very small, and one or both of them is lying in the head-first position, then an ordinary delivery is usually possible, though an epidural may be suggested in case extra help is needed. In the case of fraternal twins, who develop in separate amniotic sacs and have separate placentas, the cord of the first baby is cut after the birth and then the bag of water surrounding the second baby is broken – if it has not already done so. The second baby is usually born a few minutes later and much more easily as the tissues have already been stretched. In both cases, whether identical or fraternal twins, the placenta or placentas are delivered last as in a normal birth.

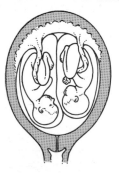

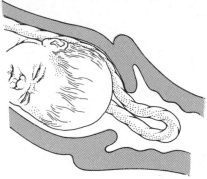

PROLAPSED CORD

This is when the umbilical cord drops through the cervix into the vagina ahead of the baby when the waters break. This can occur before or during labour. It is dangerous because the baby's head pressing on to the cord can cut off the oxygen supply to the baby. If the cervix has not fully dilated a Caesarean will be performed to get the baby out quickly but sometimes, if the cervix is fully opened, the baby can be delivered with forceps.

CORD ROUND THE NECK

It is very common for the cord to be wound once or several times round the baby's neck. It is usually easy for the midwife to slip the cord over the baby's head after the head has been born, but very rarely the cord has become so short that it begins to pull tight, restricting the baby's oxygen. If this happens, the cord can be clamped and cut after the head is born, allowing the body to be delivered easily and making the baby begin to breathe through his mouth and use his lungs.

FOETAL DISTRESS

This term means the baby is not getting enough oxygen. Warning signs that the baby is distressed are that his heart begins to beat at more than 160 beats a minute or less than 110, and the baby may pass meconium which will show as green or brownish staining of the amniotic fluid. Electronic monitoring will show how the baby is coping with the stress of contractions, and, once the cervix is partly opened, so will taking a blood sample from the baby's scalp in order to measure the level of acidity in the blood. To take the sample the mother usually lies back with her feet in stirrups and a thin metal tube is passed down the vagina and through the cervix so that the baby's head can be seen. Then a small prick is made in the baby's scalp and a tiny amount of blood collected in a capillary tube – if the cervix is not very dilated this can be painful for a moment and you need to use breathing techniques or gas and air if you have not already had any other pain relief. If labour is in the first stage and the cervix is only partly dilated, the baby may need to be delivered by Caesarean if he is in severe distress. But if the cervix is fully dilated, or the baby becomes distressed during the second stage when he is moving down the birth canal, then usually forceps or vacuum extraction can be used to get the baby out quickly.

DISPROPORTION

The baby's head may be either too large to fit into the pelvis or the pelvis too small to accommodate the head. An internal examination can help a doctor to estimate the size of the pelvis, but if there is any doubt an X-ray may be taken. Apart from being simply too narrow, the bones of the pelvis can be shaped in such a way as to make the passage of the baby's head very difficult. If there is doubt, a trial labour may be allowed to see if the head will descend into the brim of the pelvis, when it is said to be engaged. Rarely, an abnormally shaped pelvis is not discovered until labour begins and a Caesarean is necessary if the baby's head will not pass through easily.

BLEEDING AFTER THE BIRTH

A small amount of bleeding will come from an episiotomy or tear in the perineum, but if there is more blood the doctor will check whether there is a tear in the tissues of the vagina which may also need repairing. After the birth the uterus gradually decreases in size and as it does it sheds its lining. At first the discharge, called the lochia, is bright red but gradually turns reddish brown and finally a pale browny yellow. Breastfeeding stimulates the release of hormones which cause the uterus to contract so bleeding is usually heavier after feeding. This discharge should usually finish by about six weeks but if it suddenly gets much heavier or large blood clots appear consult your midwife or doctor. The commonest reason for heavier than normal bleeding or for bleeding not diminishing is that fragments of the placenta have broken off and are still attached to the wall of the uterus. Sometimes this is evident immediately after the birth because the midwife can see the placenta is not whole. A simple rule is that an empty, uninjured uterus does not bleed profusely so very heavy blood loss after the birth is unusual. When the complete placenta fails to separate from the uterus at all, then it is said to be 'retained'. The first resort, whether it is the whole placenta or only parts which have been left inside, is to give an injection of Ergometrine and to rub the mother's abdomen gently to produce a contraction while the midwife gently tugs on the cord. If this does not work a general anaesthetic is needed, either to do a D & C (scraping operation) if there are only fragments, or for the doctor to remove the placenta by hand.

STILLBIRTH

'Our first baby was stillborn. He died in labour and although they did an emergency Caesarean, it was too late to save him. At the time you think you'll never see the world again except in colours of grey. But

time does change things. I still think about our son, even though we have two school-age daughters now, but with regret and not the terrible misery.'

A stillbirth is a baby born without any sign of life after the 28th week of pregnancy. Both stillbirths and babies dying in the first week of life are included in perinatal deaths.

The main causes of stillbirth are congenital abnormalities, prematurity and lack of oxygen either before or during labour. A baby who has not been growing properly during pregnancy may have been suffering from a gradual lack of oxygen, and this, in turn, may make him more at risk in the case of prolonged or complicated labour. A few stillbirths will be the result of a sudden lack of oxygen. Prolapse of the cord (see page 119) can cause this and so can *abruptio placentae* (see page 116).

THE BIRTH

Even if it is known earlier in pregnancy that the baby has died, going into labour or continuing with labour will be a traumatic experience. Once it is known that a baby has died in the womb during a pregnancy, medical staff will arrange for the woman to come in and for labour to be induced — pessaries are usually tried first and, if not successful, a drip. Obviously, painkilling drugs can be given far more freely than in an ordinary labour.

A woman should always have someone with her — if not her husband or partner, then a close friend or relative. The experience of other couples shows that it usually helps for them to see and, if the mother wishes, to hold the baby in private. If the hospital staff do not offer to show parents their baby, they should never be afraid to ask. It is not a morbid request. It also helps to have a colour photo of the baby to take home. This can go some way towards making the baby's existence and death a reality which can be shared later with relatives and sympathetic friends. As with miscarriage, one of the isolating facts is that the couple are grieving for a child no one else but them knew.

Inevitably feelings of great shock, numbness, and often anger follow a stillbirth. Most women will want to be discharged from hospital as soon as possible, but while they are there they should be able to choose whether to stay in a room by themselves or in a ward with mothers who have babies. If there is anyone else who has suffered a stillbirth it helps to meet them. If a genetic or other abnormality is suspected the hospital will probably ask permission to do a post mortem to discover the cause of death. As with miscarriage, it is vitally important that the parents are given the opportunity to ask and to receive honest answers to all their questions, when they are ready. Most couples do want answers, perhaps not immediately, but more especially when they think of having another baby and want to know if there is a chance the same thing might happen again.

PRACTICALITIES

In a shocked, confused state parents can be bewildered by having to cope with registration of death and arrangements for the burial of their baby. Experience shows that having a proper funeral and burial helps considerably. Not having the baby buried in the way they would have wanted, because of misinformation or misunderstanding, can be a later source of pain and regret to parents.

One parent, usually the father, needs to go to the hospital administrative staff who will explain how and where to go to register the birth/death and also help with funeral arrangements. If parents want the hospital to arrange the funeral they may choose between cremation or burial. The hospital will provide a white coffin and burial can be in a public grave which is shared with other babies, or parents can pay for a private grave. Parents can ask any religious minister to hold a ceremony, or a service can be held in the hospital chapel. Of course, parents who wish to arrange a private funeral need only contact a funeral director – the hospital administration will help with telephone numbers if necessary, and provide the preliminary death certificate issued by the hospital.

The funeral is usually within ten days of the death. Although at the time going to the funeral may seem to be adding to misery, later most parents are glad that they did attend.

It is one of the cruel ironies of late miscarriage and stillbirth that the body continues to react as though a live, well baby had been born, so breasts will start to become engorged with milk two to three days after the delivery. Stitches, flabby tummies and other after effects of birth can be so much harder to cope with in these circumstances. Some women may dread returning for a post-natal to the hospital where their baby died, and if so their GP can usually do this for them. The hospital will automatically have informed him of the outcome of the pregnancy. Others may be reluctant to make this final signing off, the last acknowledgment of their baby's existence.

If the hospital doctor is sympathetic, the post-natal can be a helpful time for questions. In many cases a full explanation as to why the baby died will not be possible, despite an autopsy. If a couple feel disappointed by lack of information, it often helps for them to say so and to put into words what they feel, even though this is not going to produce the answers they want.

AFTERWARDS

'Everywhere I went I seemed to see nothing but pregnant women, tiny newborn babies in prams and couples with small children.'

This is a very common feeling and it helps to remember that a couple's view of the world is, at least temporarily, distorted. Talking to other couples with the same experience helps – not just immediately afterwards but months later, during a next pregnancy, and perhaps after the birth of a live baby too. SANDS, the Stillbirth and Neonatal Death Society, can help by putting couples in touch with such parents (see address section, pages 673–6).

Some couples react very differently and cannot accept comfort from each other or from other people. Sometimes there are difficulties in resuming sex after a stillbirth, even though both partners may be very loving towards each other. In all cases it helps to take things at one's own pace – not to try to force oneself to 'get over it' quickly or to rush at getting back to normal. If there are problems, couples should talk about them with each other and ask a doctor they trust for help or advice.

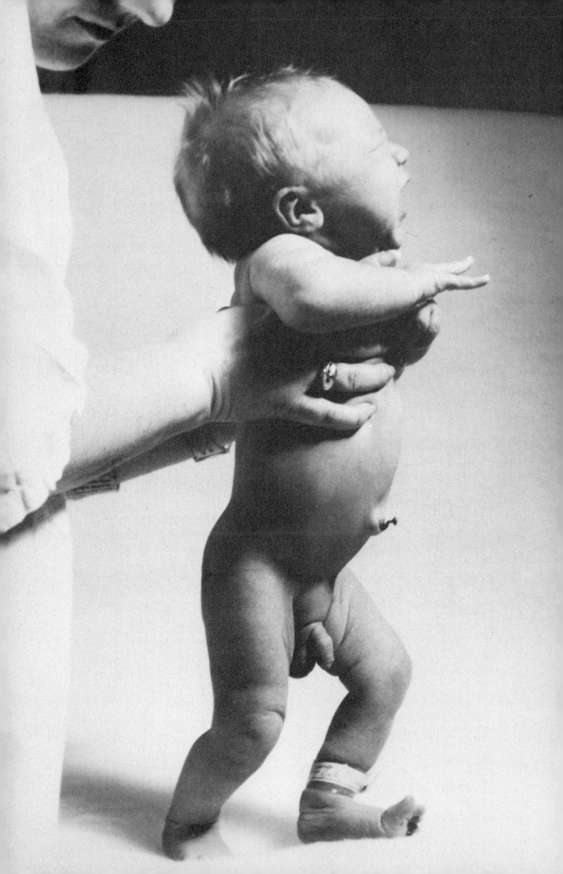

Chapter 4

YOUR NEW BABY

First reactions   Fathers   Initial impressions
What is the world like for your baby?
Minor problems after delivery
More serious problems after delivery
Your baby's first check-up
Tests and immunisations   Looking after your new baby
After the birth – you and your new baby

FIRST REACTIONS

'You can never really believe, all through pregnancy, and even during labour, that you are actually going to end up with a baby. I remember the shock of seeing what seemed like this huge, healthy baby, and thinking that just a second ago it had been inside me. It really is a miracle.'

'I must admit I didn't feel anything special towards the baby straight away. The birth had been so awful I was just thankful it was all over. I remember saying to my husband: "I suppose I've got to feed it now." It wasn't until about six hours later, when I'd been stitched up and moved to the ward, that I looked and saw him lying perfectly peacefully but awake, staring at me with little dark eyes. I began to feel something towards him.'

'I just felt a sense of wonder when I saw her for the first time. I still feel that often when I look at her now.'

That moment, after the birth, when you first see, touch and hold your new baby, is very special and highly personal. Everyone reacts differently and while many mothers feel an immediate rush of love and intense excitement, others can feel more detached and need time to adjust. Many women need time to recover from the labour and delivery, and this is especially true when they have had a difficult or painful birth. Ambivalent feelings can also be just as true of mothers who desperately wanted a baby as with those whose pregnancies may have been unplanned. Take your time. There is no 'right' or 'wrong' way to feel and such a major change in your life as becoming a parent will provoke very many different emotions in both of you at varying times.

BONDING

Much has been written and said about the importance of keeping mothers and babies together from birth and the way in which a sympathy, a bond, begins to develop between them as they learn about each other by looking and touching. The baby is already familiar with the pattern and pitch of his mother's voice from his months in her womb. He soon learns to put a face, a smell and a feel to the voice. A mother in turn begins to learn about her baby's needs from his cries and how to soothe and comfort him.

Suggesting there is a need for parents and their baby to be alone together after the birth makes it sound as though during those first few minutes a magical process should take place that a woman will immediately recognise and which will equip her to cope with the many and varied demands of motherhood. In fact, of course, a relationship between parents and children evolves gradually, in a different way and at a different pace for everyone. However, it does seem true that in many cases we are especially sensitive to our newborn in the period immediately after birth – a period which often coincides with a particular awareness and alertness in the baby. Often animals whose babies are taken away at birth reject them if they are returned some time later and, although our reactions and emotions are far more complex and sophisticated, it is the most natural desire for a mother to want to keep her new baby close by her side. That is why medical staff do all they can to keep them together as much as possible, even when the baby is ill and may need special care.

This idea of a sensitive period, when we are especially ready to learn something, seems to apply at other stages of development, too. Thus, there is a certain stage when learning language is easier, and children who miss out at this time – perhaps because they are temporarily deaf, or are not spoken to enough – will find it harder to learn to talk later, while babies who are not introduced to solid food at the right stage may be very resistant to eating it later. It does seem certain that the beginnings of a close relationship between parents and child are helped by time alone together after the birth, though it is also important to recognise that it is perfectly possible to form good relationships later on if the mother and the baby do have to be separated, for example because the baby has to be in intensive care, or because the mother is ill after a complicated delivery or a Caesarean section.

FIRST CONTACT WITH YOUR BABY

These days many midwives will ask if you want the baby delivered on to your stomach. This immediate skin-to-skin contact can be very soothing and reassuring for both you and your baby. Many mothers, however, want time to recover from the birth itself and will enjoy having their baby in close contact with them a few minutes later. Equally, some women may not like the idea of the baby being delivered directly on to their stomach because they are worried by the idea that the baby will be covered with mucus or blood. In fact there is not usually very much blood, although the baby will be wet from the amniotic fluid, but the midwife can easily wipe him clean and dry him and wrap him in a cloth before handing him to you or placing him on your stomach. The important thing is not to feel pressurised to behave in a certain way but to make your wishes known and do what comes naturally. In your own time you can enjoy a feeling of closeness by laying him on your stomach or between your breasts with a cloth over his back to help keep him warm. Keeping a newborn baby warm is important because even though the delivery room may feel very hot it is still about twenty degrees colder than the temperature the baby has been used to inside your womb. He will also lose heat more quickly at first because his skin will still be damp from the amniotic fluid.

TAKING A HOLD ON LIFE – YOUR BABY'S FIRST BREATH

Inside the womb your baby's lungs are filled with fluid, though he does practise breathing movements by moving amniotic fluid in and out in small amounts. After the birth the fluid is absorbed and the lungs can collapse inwards if they are not filled with air. Imagine the difference between a balloon filled with air and then shrivelled up after it is emptied. The sides of the shrivelled lungs are stopped from actually sticking together by important surface film called 'surfactant' which begins to cover them from about the 22nd week of pregnancy. This also makes the lungs more elastic and better able to expand. The biggest problem for babies born too soon is that they often do not have enough surfactant to help the lungs to work properly.

We do not know exactly what makes the baby take his first breath and draw air into his lungs – most probably it is a survival response as oxygen-carrying blood no longer flows through the umbilical cord. As explained in chapter 3, this normally happens at a point before the cord is actually cut – usually as the placenta begins to separate away from the uterus wall. Imagine the lungs like a bunch of grapes running off a central stem – the stems are the bronchial tubes and the grapes are the little air sacs, or alveoli. When your baby takes in his first breath, the air rushes down the tubes, filling out the alveoli. The remaining amniotic fluid which has not been squeezed out during the birth is absorbed into the bloodstream.

At the same moment as your baby begins to take in oxygen through his lungs, there is also a major change in the way his heart works. Inside the womb the two sides of the heart beat together, with oxygenated blood from the umbilical cord flowing into both sides, though the right side does most of the work. When the baby begins to breathe himself, then the pressure in the lungs decreases and the arteries which used to bring blood from the cord close down because there is no blood flowing through them any longer. These changes make ducts in the heart close so that the two sides are functioning separately as in normal life. One side receives blood-carrying oxygen from the lungs and sends it round the body, and the other side receives the 'used' blood which is coming back from the body without oxygen in it and sends it on to the lungs. This is the ordinary pattern for the rest of life. In the vast majority of babies, this seemingly complicated process happens without any problems and they begin to breathe as soon as they are born. But a few, for various reasons, may need help which can usually be given very easily.

CLEARING THE AIRWAYS

Your baby will still have some fluid in his nose and throat when he is born. Often it is enough to wipe his face gently and then lay him face down on your stomach or thigh so that it will drain naturally. If his airways seem blocked or he does not start breathing, any fluid can be sucked out of his nose and throat gently with a soft suction tube called a 'mucus extractor'. The midwife or doctor just inserts one end into the baby's nose and throat and gently sucks so that fluid is cleared and caught inside the tube. This takes only a few seconds and can either be done when the baby's head is born and while waiting for another contraction to deliver the body, or after the delivery itself.

CRYING

A cry is proof that the baby is breathing, and the traditional way to ensure that this happened used to be to hold him up by his heels and smack him on the bottom. This rather traumatic introduction to life has since been shown to be unnecessary, and gentle stimulation and drying of the skin alone is usually enough to ensure he has begun to breathe, with or without crying. If your baby doesn't cry, don't worry, because he is probably breathing perfectly well. Some babies come out crying right away and others begin to cry soon after the birth, which is entirely normal. Holding your baby close to your skin and stroking, cuddling and soothing him will calm him down.

IS MY BABY ALL RIGHT?

This is the question that floats in and out of all parents' thoughts at times during the long nine months of pregnancy. It is the question they want answered first with the proof of their own eyes at birth. A full, detailed examination of your new baby will wait until a little later, usually the following day, because newborn babies can easily get cold, but the doctor or midwife will automatically check for any obvious problems at birth. This is the point at which any mistakes in the development of the baby, such as extra fingers or toes, club foot, extra earlobes or hypospadias (a faulty position of the opening of the penis in boys), will be detected. Most of these can be corrected, some very simply by a small surgical operation. In addition they will also look at his overall condition, to see whether he is a vigorous, active baby with a good colour and able to suck well.

A method has been worked out so that the doctors and midwives all make the same checks in a standard way with every new baby and record

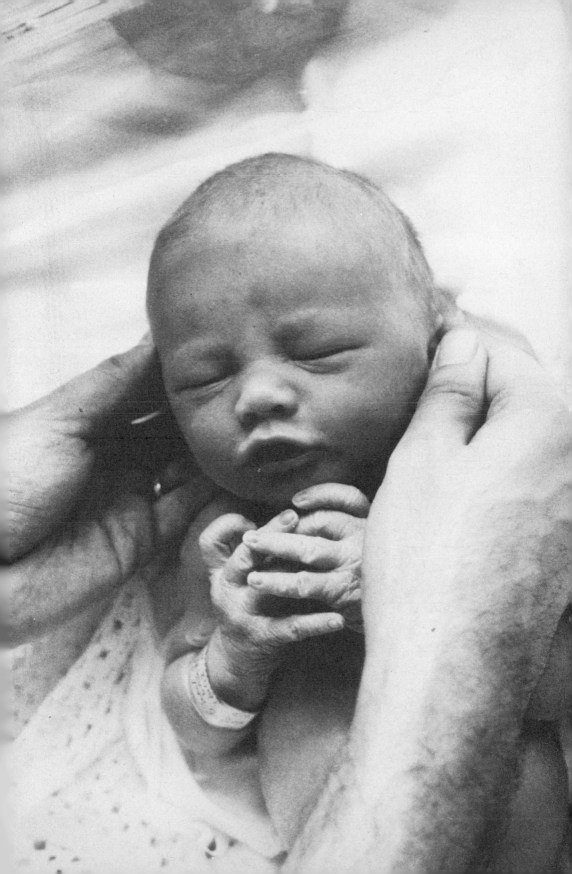

what they find. This is called the 'Apgar score' after an American paediatrician, Dr Virginia Apgar, who devised it as a method of assessing the condition of a new baby. At one minute after birth, and then again at five minutes, the midwife or doctor checks the baby's heartbeat, breathing, muscle tone, reflexes and colour and scores them 0, 1, or 2. A total score of 10 means a baby is in the best possible condition, but 7 and over is normal. Between 5 and 7 means the baby is all right, but will probably improve with some simple treatment like clearing his airways, or he may be slightly dozy from the effects of pethidine given late in labour. Babies with a score of less than 5 need extra oxygen to help establish better breathing (see page 137).

Heartbeat	Over 100	2
	Slow, below 100	1
	Absent	0
Breathing	Regular, crying	2
	Slow, irregular	1
	Absent	0
Muscle tone	Moving actively	2
	Moving extremities only	1
	Limp	0
Reflexes (usually response to catheter in nostril)	Cough or sneeze	2
	Grimace	1
	None	0
Colour	Pink	2
	Body pink, extremities blue	1
	Blue, pale	0

The two other important statistics to be recorded about your child's delivery will be his birthweight and the circumference of his head.

A low birthweight baby is classified as weighing less than 2,500 grams (5½ lbs) at birth, which is an important indication of the baby's health. Very small babies may need extra care and there are a number of ways of telling whether their size is because they are premature or have not grown enough in the uterus, or both. Obviously other factors influence the baby's size – not least the size of the parents and the mother's own birthweight which often corresponds with her baby's. Ill health during pregnancy and other environmental factors like smoking, drinking excessive alcohol or drugs can all retard the unborn baby's growth. At the other end of the scale, if a baby is very large, usually thought of as weighing 4,000 grams (10 lbs) or more, this may be an indication that his mother either has diabetes or has become temporarily diabetic during pregnancy (see page 62). Recording a baby's weight at birth also helps doctors to see how he is progressing later. Newborn babies usually lose between 5 to 10% of their weight during the first four days of life. This is mainly due to fluid loss until the mother's milk supply is established. Most babies have regained their birthweight by the tenth day and go on to gain around 150 to 200 grams (5 to 7 oz.) a week, or approximately one ounce per day.

Head circumference will obviously be related to your baby's overall size, thus large babies will have large heads and vice versa. An unusually small head, out of proportion to the rest of the baby's body, may be a sign of mental retardation and an unusually large head can be a symptom of hydrocephalus, a condition where fluid which normally bathes the brain collects in the head because the tubes that drain it are blocked. In some families head size may be larger than average, but intellectual function is entirely normal. An average head circumference for a baby weighing 3,300 grams (7½ lbs) would be around 35 cm. (14 in.). As with the baby's birthweight, one of the important aspects of this single statistic is to follow the way the baby develops so that subsequent measurements can show if the head is growing at the expected rate.

The actual shape of your baby's head will be influenced by the kind of birth as much as his inherited features at first — thus babies born by Caesarean section have perfectly formed heads, but babies who have had a long second stage or were a tight fit through the mother's pelvis will often have had their heads moulded into rather odd-looking shapes. This will correct itself fairly quickly. At the same time as measuring your baby's head, the midwife or doctor will feel the fontanelles, or 'soft spots' (see page 140).

Many hospitals also measure the baby's length, either at birth or on the second day of life. The average length for a normal weight baby is 50 cm. (20 in.).

SUCKING

In the period soon after birth your baby has a strong sucking reflex. If you touch his cheek with your nipple he will turn his head towards it — this is called 'rooting' for nipple. He will probably need help to latch on properly. Your partner can help you to get comfortable so that your arm is supporting the baby's head at the right level or he can support the baby's head himself. The baby's head needs to be very close to the breast to enable him to take the nipple fully into his mouth so that, as he sucks, the pressure of his mouth and gums is on the areola, not the nipple itself (see page 213). Some babies suck strongly straight away, others may just lick and nuzzle. If he does not seem interested at once this may be because he has either swallowed a lot of mucus or still has some mucus in his throat, or he may be sleepy because of pethidine given to you during labour. Try expressing a drop of colostrum — the extra-rich creamy substance which is present before the milk comes in — and putting it on to his lips to encourage him. At this first feeding session the baby will probably suck for only two or three minutes — if he does not release his hold on the nipple, or you want to transfer him to the other breast, break the suction by gently inserting your little finger into the corner of his mouth. Fixing the baby properly to the breast, and taking him off properly, are important safeguards against sore nipples (see pages 213–15).

Early sucking is important for three reasons. First, it stimulates your

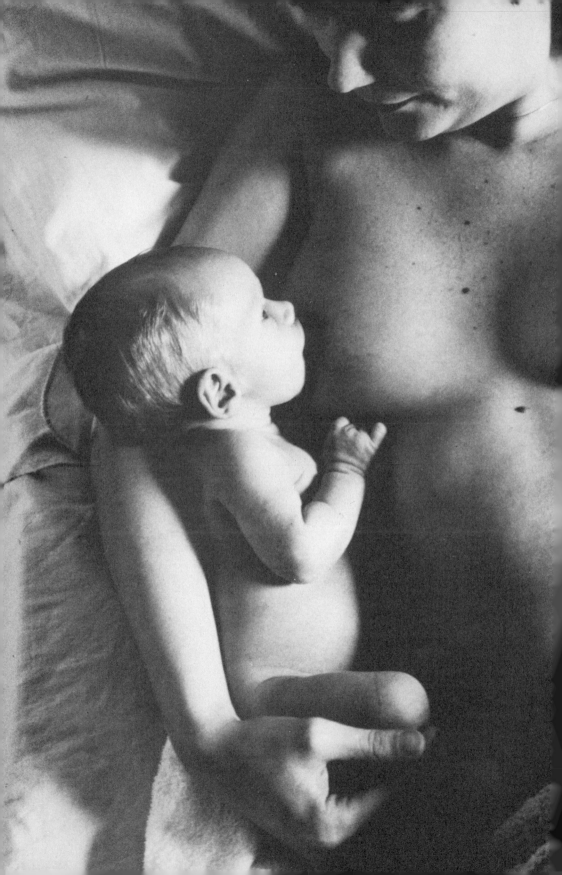

body to produce the hormone oxytocin, which helps the womb contract to the size it was before pregnancy and causes the placenta to separate. Second, it is a good start to establishing breastfeeding. Although the baby is getting protein-rich colostrum, not milk at this stage, the more he sucks, the sooner an ample supply of milk is established, and while he has a strong sucking reflex it is easier to get him to feed. Studies show that feeding within an hour of birth is an important stimulus to successful breastfeeding. Lastly, it helps to establish a closeness between you and your baby that you can both enjoy. (For a full discussion of breastfeeding see chapter 6.)

FATHERS

'I had agreed to stay for the first stage of labour but didn't want to stay for the birth. I am not good at coping with anything medical. But in the end it all happened much more quickly than anyone thought, and I ended up staying, even though I kept at the head end of the bed. I was surprised by how peaceful and unmessy it all was. In seconds the midwife was handing our daughter to us wrapped in green cloth. I was high for days afterwards.'

'At the very beginning of the pregnancy I felt a bit apprehensive when my wife said she wanted me to be at the birth. But we went together to a course of good antenatal classes and by the end of pregnancy it would have been unthinkable not to be there. I felt my presence was very necessary. I was able to massage her back, support her in different positions, and encourage her when she began to get very exhausted. After the birth the midwife, who we got to know really well, told me to unbutton my shirt, and I held our daughter, loosely wrapped in a cloth, against my chest.'

'It was terrifying, but amazing too. More so the second time because you know what to expect. There was this wrinkled skull, the colour of blue plasticine, emerging and then suddenly the rest of the baby sort of sprang out and it began to breathe and turn pink. The absolute miracle of the life force grips you. I must admit I had to wipe away the tears.'

Early contact with their newborn baby is just as important for fathers as for mothers. It is one of the drawbacks of hospital birth that although it may be safer, it does mean fathers do not have the same involvement in the early days. Many hospitals now encourage early discharge for mothers and babies and allow very free visiting by fathers. Certainly that time after the birth is one to be savoured together. Skin-to-skin contact is just as pleasant for fathers – if you feel a bit self-conscious about this, wait until the midwife has left you alone together, then unbutton your shirt so that you can hold your new baby against your chest. Warming young animals by holding them against our own bodies is a very natural reaction and by keeping a cloth or blanket loosely wrapped round the outside of your baby he will be well protected from getting cold. If the mother needs medical attention because of any complications or stitches, the midwife may hand the baby to the father first. Otherwise you can hold him after the cord has been cut, perhaps while your wife is being cleaned up and made comfortable. If your partner is going to breastfeed the baby, you can help her to get into a comfortable position and to latch the baby on to the nipple by supporting the baby's head very close to the breast – lots of babies do need help at first. Don't worry about doing the right or the wrong thing – at the time it will all come naturally.

SHARING CARING – LOOKING AHEAD

New parents take time to gain confidence in their abilities to look after their new baby. Remember, at the beginning neither of you know more than the other about looking after a new baby – it will help you both to adjust to parenthood more easily if you learn together. Of course, having a go at changing a nappy or wet baby clothes is more difficult at hospital visiting times than in the privacy of your own home, but it can be an important gesture. It can make couples feel closer, and it will also encourage your wife, who may be feeling slightly daunted at the enormous responsibility caring for a baby can represent. It is a responsibility which you are going to share together. If you feel self-conscious, remember that all the other couples in the ward will have eyes only for their own baby, and if any of the mothers do notice that you are doing more than just cuddling your baby, you can be sure they will soon be suggesting the same thing to their own mates!

INITIAL IMPRESSIONS

WHAT DO NEWBORN BABIES LOOK LIKE?

'New-born of course. She looked already a centenarian, tottering on the brink of an old crone's grave, exhausted, shrunken, bald as Voltaire, moping, mewing and twisting wrinkled claws in speechless spasms of querulous doom.'

Laurie Lee, from his essay 'The Firstborn'

It is true that babies look their least lovely in the moments after birth – except perhaps to their adoring parents. 'Purple and dented like a little bruised plum,' was writer Laurie Lee's graphic description of his daughter immediately after she was born. Strangely, newborn babies do often look old – they may have very wrinkled brows and their limbs may seem almost shrivelled. The skin may be relatively translucent so that veins can be seen underneath. Despite this apparently fragile appearance, though, your new baby is tougher than you think. Remember that the smooth-skinned, plump picture of babyhood that beams back from so many magazine and television pictures is usually weeks or months old. In just a few days your baby too will begin to look quite different and start to fill out and unfold. But, at the very beginning, expect a first encounter with a rather different sort of being – one whose limbs have yet to learn to adjust to the freedom of movement possible outside the womb, one who is used to existing in water and in darkness and who has just undergone the exhausting and terrifying process of birth.

Your baby will be wet from the amniotic fluid, which is colourless, and may have some blood picked up from the site of an episiotomy or tear as he passed through the lower end of the birth canal. There may also be quite a lot of vernix, especially in the folds of skin – this is the greasy, white substance which protects and lubricates the baby's skin inside the womb. Generally, babies born at term are more likely to have some vernix, whereas babies born after term may have rather drier, or even cracked or peeling skin. Sometimes patches of the fine, downy hair which covered him inside the womb – lanugo – may still be present. This is more noticeable in dark-haired babies and is seen most often on the shoulders, back and sometimes ears and forehead, but it will rub off in a couple of weeks and does not mean your baby will be hairy later in life.

Before the baby begins to breathe, he is a bluish colour, like the umbilical cord. As he takes his first breath, the colour changes to a normal flesh tone which can be reddish rather than pink.

The head is large in relation to the rest of the body, a quarter of the overall length, and is often oddly shaped at first because it has been moulded by the passage through the birth canal. It may be long and pointed, flattened, or even lop-sided, but this will disappear after about two weeks or even earlier. Your baby may have a fine head of hair or may be completely bald – colour and quantity at this stage are not necessarily an indication of future growth. The pressure of birth may make the baby's eyelids red and puffy. Purple or reddish marks on the eyelids (stork marks) are very common and will soon fade.

A new baby's genitals are often large in relation to the rest of his body – the effect of hormones from the mother which have crossed the placenta, and this can also make the breasts of both boys and girls swollen – something that will disappear in a week or two.

WHAT IS THE WORLD LIKE FOR YOUR BABY?

'She lay perfectly calmly in the cot beside me afterwards while I was being stitched, looking around so knowingly and intelligently with little dark eyes that seemed to have the wisdom of a hundred years, not just a few minutes, shining from them.'

The unborn baby becomes sensitive to sound, light, touch and pain quite early in pregnancy, so he is able to experience the sensations of birth in various ways. Pressure is the most obvious sensation he will experience, at first from the rhythmic squeezing of the uterus as it contracts to open the cervix, then he feels pressure from all sides, particularly on the head, as he is pushed down into the birth canal. Changes in the heartbeat and the amount of movement suggest that procedures such as blood transfusions done before birth are uncomfortable for the unborn baby. Having a scalp electrode implanted in the skin or a sample of blood taken from the scalp during birth, therefore, must be no less so. Some babies who have had difficult deliveries may act as though they have a significant headache afterwards.

YOUR BABY'S SENSES

Don't think your new baby is unable to take in much of his newfound world – his senses are already finely tuned to pick up the messages from all around.

Sight One of the commonest misapprehensions is that babies are born blind or see only very hazily. In fact the newborn baby can see very well and focus clearly on objects about 25 cm. (10 in.) away. This is about the distance between the mother's face and the baby during feeding, and parents often automatically position themselves at this distance when they talk to or do anything with their baby. New babies are sensitive to light and shut their eyes to avoid bright lights. They can tell the difference between shapes and patterns, and prefer patterns to solid colours, and stripes and angles to circular designs. They will follow their mother's face or an object that has caught their interest with their eyes, although in the early weeks they may have difficulty co-ordinating their eye movements. This can give them the appearance of a wandering eye or even of a squint: this, however, is not permanent and quickly improves as co-ordination increases.

Sound The new baby has already learnt to recognise his mother's voice from its pitch and speech patterns while inside the womb. Analysis of films has shown that newborn babies respond to the rhythm of the speaker addressing them by making movements with their own bodies or faces in response to a stressed word or pause. They very soon begin to copy the movements of the speaker's mouth – opening their own, putting their tongue forward, and so on. New babies are also startled by loud, sudden noises such as the bang of a door. Inside the womb they have been used to the rhythmic pulse of their mother's heart pumping blood around her body – mothers usually hold their babies to their left side and probably the sensation of heartbeat is reassuring in its familiarity. Recordings of 'womb music' – the sort of noises we think the baby heard inside the womb – sometimes have a calming effect on new babies.

Smell New babies also have a good sense of smell. They quickly learn to recognise the smell of their mother's body and her milk. At three days, studies have shown that babies can already tell the difference between their own mother's and another mother's milk on breast pads placed near to the nose.

Taste Three-day-old babies can also distinguish between tastes and prefer sweet to bitter flavours, although the taste of breast milk is the best of all.

MINOR PROBLEMS AFTER DELIVERY

Occasionally babies need extra medical attention or care after delivery for some particular reason. One of the most common reasons is that the baby does not start breathing spontaneously. Premature and small babies may have special problems, both immediately and for a longer period, but for more details see chapter 5.

BREATHING

It is very common for babies to need a little help to start breathing after the birth and does not necessarily mean they will need any further special care. A survey of 16,000 babies showed that nearly 5% had not breathed by three minutes after the birth. It may also be reassuring to know that newborn babies are better able to survive for a period without oxygen than adults because their metabolism is different. However, the midwife or doctor will be quick to give your baby some help if breathing does not begin naturally. Babies who have an abnormal delivery – for example, breech or Caesarean – are more likely to need help to begin breathing. If complications are known to exist a paediatrician may be on hand, or the mother may be delivered in a unit which has intensive care facilities for such babies if needed.

Often simply clearing the baby's airways more thoroughly using a mucus extractor is enough to stimulate him into drawing breath. If not, oxygen can be blown lightly over the face or the baby can be given oxygen by holding a rubber mask over the nose and mouth which is attached to a bag that is gently squeezed to pump air into the lungs. A more skilled procedure involves putting a fine tube down the baby's throat into the windpipe so that oxygen can be pumped directly into the lungs: this is called 'intubation'. This may be necessary if the baby has been deprived of oxygenated blood during the birth, perhaps because the cord became compressed, although again this does not necessarily mean the baby will need extra care or have other problems once breathing has been established.

BABIES AFFECTED BY PETHIDINE

Pethidine crosses the placenta and can therefore make the baby as well as the mother sleepy. If pethidine was given close to the time of delivery, and the baby still has breathing difficulties after oxygen has been given, then an antidote in the form of a drug called Naloxone may be injected into one of the baby's veins which reverses the effect of the pethidine very quickly.

MORE SERIOUS PROBLEMS AFTER DELIVERY

LACK OF OXYGEN

Babies who have been deprived of a supply of oxygenated blood for some time before birth and who do not breathe naturally after the birth may be at greater risk than those who simply fail to begin breathing by themselves. The baby will usually be intubated so that oxygen can be given directly into the lungs, and if the heartbeat is slow or stops (which is very unusual) then heart massage can be given. Babies who show signs of having been seriously deprived of oxygen before or after birth will need extra care in an intensive care unit (see pages 187–91). Permanent damage can result from this, but each case is different and the doctor will always explain what has happened and discuss with the parents how it may affect the individual baby.

MECONIUM INHALATION

Babies who have been stressed before birth may move their bowels in the womb. This substance, meconium, can mix with the amniotic fluid and may be taken into the baby's lungs if he tries to breathe before the birth itself. This can clog up the lungs and make it difficult for the baby to breathe; there is also a risk of developing a type of pneumonia caused by irritation from the meconium or from bacteria.

Babies who have passed meconium before birth need to be very carefully sucked out to stop any meconium in their throat or nose being drawn down into the lungs. If the paediatrician is on hand he may intubate the baby before he takes his first breath to stop this happening. A baby who does inhale meconium needs careful monitoring, possibly extra oxygen to make sure he continues to breathe properly, and antibiotics to stop him developing pneumonia. There is also a slight risk of inhaled meconium leading to a punctured lung.

Babies who develop symptoms related to meconium aspiration will require admission to special or intensive care units for close observation and possibly help, such as ventilation, for a few days until their breathing is established.

PNEUMONIA

In addition to meconium inhalation, the unborn baby can get pneumonia if the waters become infected and that infected fluid is drawn into their lungs. This is more likely to happen if the waters break more than twenty-four hours before delivery, and if this does happen the mother may be given antibiotics to prevent infection. For this reason it is now very rare for a baby to be born with pneumonia. Treatment after birth is with antibiotics, possibly oxygen to help breathing and careful monitoring.

An oxygen mask may help some babies to start breathing

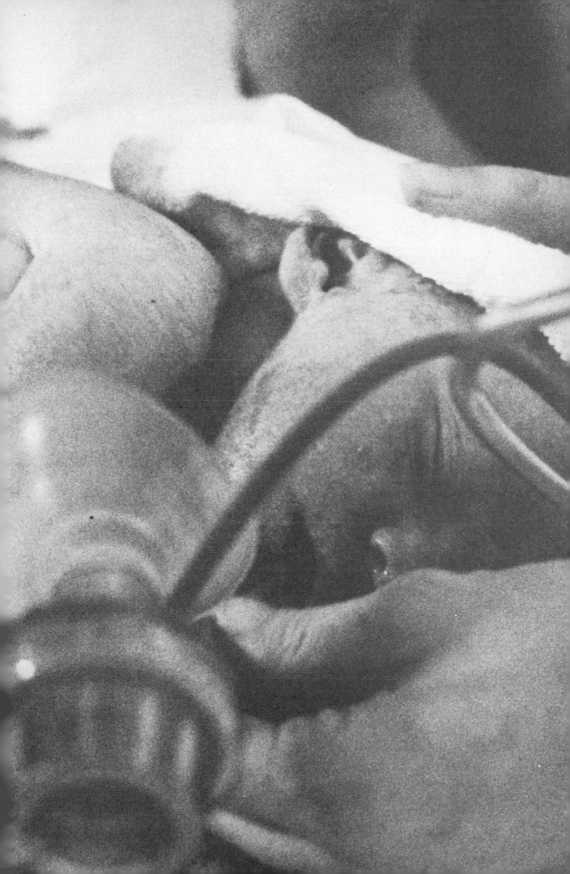

PUNCTURE OF THE LUNG (PNEUMOTHORAX)

A hole in one of the baby's lungs (pneumothorax) can result from too much pressure when the baby is given oxygen through a mask or tube, it can also occur when meconium is inhaled, or it can happen naturally when the baby is making strenuous efforts to breathe himself. If the hole is very small and just a little air leaks out, it will heal naturally without any further treatment, though the baby will need to be watched more carefully for a period. About 1% of babies have this condition.

A larger hole may cause the lung to collapse completely. This is fortunately quite rare but needs immediate emergency treatment under local anaesthetic. A tube is inserted through the baby's chest to draw off the air which now fills the chest cavity on the side where the lung has collapsed. As the air is drawn off, the pressure on the lung is relieved so it re-expands as the baby draws in breath. The tube will be left in for a few days and the baby nursed in an intensive care unit.

YOUR BABY'S FIRST CHECK-UP

At some point in your baby's first twenty-four hours of life he will be given a complete examination by a paediatrician. This usually happens the morning after the birth when you have both had time to rest and recover. The doctor will normally do the examination in your presence, near the bed if you are unable to get up yet. He will welcome any questions you may have so don't be shy about asking anything which may be bothering you, however trivial you may think it is.

HEAD

The four main bone plates of the skull have not yet fused together, thus allowing the head to mould to the shape of the birth canal. This can lead to odd-shaped heads and even ridges on the side of the head where the plates have overlapped at some point. This is only temporary and will readjust in a week or two. The doctor will be concerned about the size of the baby's head in relation to his body, about a quarter of his overall length, and will also feel the fontanelles or soft spots where the skull bones have not yet grown across. The two main ones are near the crown and above the brow. You can often see the baby's pulse beating under the skin, but in fact these areas are covered by very tough membrane and there is no danger of hurting the baby with normal hand-ling. If the fontanelles are sunken or

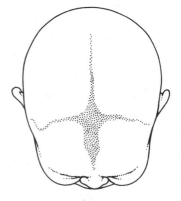

depressed it may be a sign that the baby is dehydrated. The doctor will usually also measure the circumference of the head for the baby's records.

EYES

Eyelids may be puffy and red from the pressure of birth. There can also be red or purple patches called 'stork marks'. A burst blood vessel in the eye, also caused by pressure, will show as a red spot which may enlarge in the white of the eye. This may look worrying but is actually quite harmless and does not hurt the baby. It will fade within ten days or so. Because new babies cannot focus both eyes together for very long, one may begin to wander. This does not mean they have a permanent squint – an inability to focus both eyes together. Often heavy folds of skin at the corner of the eye or close-set eyes can make new babies look as if they are squinting even more. Usually any apparent squinting has gone by four to six months but if you have any worries about this ask your doctor. If a squint persists beyond six months it should be seen by a doctor.

Sticky eye This is very common in new babies and is an infection of the eyes which shows as a yellowish discharge or crusting on the eye or lids. It is commonly associated with a blocked tear duct so that the fluid which normally lubricates the eye cannot drain. Treatment is to wipe the eyes with a saline solution or water and possibly drops or ointment. The eyes should be cleaned with separate swabs for each eye, wiping the eye inwards towards the nose as this is the way in which tears drain naturally into the tear duct. Wiping in the other direction could spread infection throughout the eye. Because eye infections spread easily, both eyes will probably be treated at the same time.

NOSE

A baby's nose is usually broad and flat at this stage which makes it easier for him to feed at the breast. Sneezing is very common and quite normal and does not mean the baby has a cold.

MOUTH

The doctor will feel inside the baby's mouth to make sure the palate is fully formed. Rarely, babies are born with one or more teeth present – these may have to be taken out because they can cause ulcers on the tongue. Tiny white cysts which may appear on the gums or palate are harmless and will disappear. Blisters may appear on the baby's upper and lower lips from sucking. Again, they do not need treatment and will fade.

EARS

A new baby's ears may produce wax, but a discharge is not normal and you should ask advice if this happens. It is difficult to test the hearing of a new baby, though parents can usually be sure within a few weeks that their child can hear by watching his reactions (see page 342). If there is any doubt, ask your health visitor or GP.

HEART

After the birth the baby's pattern of circulation changes (see page 127) and the heart has to work hard, which may mean that for the first few days it is slightly enlarged. It also has to beat faster than normal to meet the baby's needs which are greater as he adjusts to life outside the womb. Your baby's heartbeat will be above a hundred beats a minute. Because of the extra work, it is not uncommon for babies to have a heart murmur at the first examination. Nearly all these are innocent and are associated with normal eddies of blood. They will disappear as the heart settles down, although this will be checked at future examinations.

A baby born with something structurally or functionally wrong with his heart – congenital heart disease – is rarer. Just under one baby in a hundred has something significantly wrong with his heart but only a third of these need any treatment, the rest resolve naturally as the baby grows. Causes of heart disease are still largely unknown, although one known cause is German measles in the first three months of pregnancy, which can stop the heart developing properly. There is only a very slight tendency for heart disease to run in families and mostly it seems to be an unlucky fault in development. Conventional tests, such as X-rays and an electrocardiogram, when wires are attached to the chest to give a recording on paper, are routine in newborn babies and echocardiography is a new and fast-developing test. A probe about the size of a torch is run over the chest and the messages or echoes it picks up can be shown on a television screen in rather the same way as an ultrasound scan. It is quite painless and harmless.

The commonest heart problem is a small hole in the heart which means there is a communication between the two main chambers of the heart which should normally be kept separate. In more than 90% of babies who have this problem the hole closes, usually before they reach school age.

Other common problems include narrowing of a heart valve or the failure of foetal blood vessels to close at birth. A few babies with congenital heart disease will need an operation in the first year of life. Sometimes the fault will be corrected at the same time, but in others surgery can improve the condition so that the child can grow until he is big enough for a larger operation when the risk is much less. Some conditions do not need to be put right until the child is older.

Babies and children with heart conditions who are waiting for operations are very unlikely to have a sudden serious collapse, which is usually what parents fear. If their condition worsens it usually shows as a general slowing down, but parents will be advised by a heart specialist on what to look for and how to care for their child. Babies who have heart conditions are often more prone to chest infections and these need to be treated more seriously than in a normal baby.

LUNGS

During his routine examination the doctor will watch the baby's breathing pattern and listen to his lungs. These are filled with fluid before birth which is rapidly cleared in the first few minutes or hours of life. If the baby has any difficulty with his breathing, the doctor will discuss this with you. Many babies, especially those who are premature, do have rapid breathing after birth. This usually recovers quite quickly and the lungs are entirely normal afterwards.

ABDOMEN

The doctor will gently feel your baby's tummy to check the position and size of his liver, kidneys and spleen.

GENITALS

The genitals will also be checked. They may look rather large in proportion to the rest of the body at birth in both boys and girls, but this is quite normal, and readjusts after a short period. The breasts may also be slightly enlarged and in a few cases even produce drops of milk – known as witches' milk. All this is caused by hormones from the mother which have crossed the placenta and will soon disappear from the baby's system. For the same reason there may even be a very slight bleeding from a baby girl's vagina like a mini period. The doctor will check to see that a baby boy's testicles can be felt in the scrotum: they are usually easy to feel at birth but can be more difficult to feel later in childhood.

ANUS

He will also check that the anus is normal and enquire as to whether the baby has passed meconium. In a very few babies, the gut or gastro-intestinal tract is not properly formed, and there may be a narrowing (stenosis) or even a complete block (atresia), so that food cannot get through. This will show up by the baby's vomiting or not passing meconium or motions, but the problem may even be discovered before this during the doctor's initial examination. This can usually be put right by surgical operation shortly after it has been diagnosed.

UMBILICAL CORD

After the cord has been cut, a stump about one inch long is left with a clamp attached. This quickly begins to shrivel and dry up and within twenty-four hours usually turns almost black in colour. The midwife will show you how to care for it, keeping the nappy below the cord and not covering it as this will help it to stay dry. It should be cleaned daily with boiled salt water or chlorhexidine. The clamp will be removed on the third day and the rest of the cord will drop off around the seventh day and may leave a small raw or bloodstained spot which can be cleaned and kept dry in the same way; it will soon heal.

Infection of the cord is unusual in the first twenty-four hours of life, but quite common in the first week, and can usually be treated easily with antiseptic powder. Occasionally, the surrounding skin becomes inflamed and then antibiotics are given by injection or by mouth.

The shape of your baby's navel depends on the way the muscles lie around the base of the cord, not on the way the cord has been cut or clamped. Some children have flat navels very quickly while others protrude for some time. An umbilical hernia is present when there is a weakness or gap in the muscles around the base of the cord so that the abdominal contents bulge through under the skin making a soft lump. This may be present at birth or appear a day or so after and become larger when the baby coughs, cries or strains, though there is no need to stop him doing any of these things. Umbilical hernias usually get smaller as the baby grows and do not need to be operated on in infancy. An operation will only be considered if the gap in the muscles gets larger after the first year, or shows no signs of closing by about three years.

THE GROIN

The groin is another site where hernias are sometimes seen and are more common in boy than girl babies. In the case of a hernia in the groin, a paediatrician may consider operating quite promptly because there is a slight risk that some of the intestine can protrude and not go back in again easily.

HIPS

Congenital dislocation of the hips means that when the baby is born the head of the thigh bone (femur) does not fit properly into the socket of the pelvis so that it can easily come out or be dislocated. If this is untreated it means the child will walk with a limp and one leg will be shorter than the other. Fortunately, if it is detected, early treatment is both simple and successful, and this is why doctors always take great trouble examining the hips of all new babies.

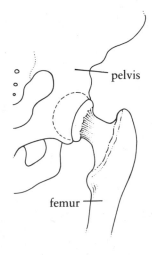

We do not know exactly what causes the problem, but it may be related to hormone changes before birth or to the position of the baby in the uterus. It is more common in breech babies, in girls, and when there is a family history of other babies having been affected. Between one and two babies per thousand are affected each year.

To test for hips which are dislocated or can easily come out of the socket, the doctor lays the baby on his back and gently bends both knees upwards. Then, holding the top part of the thigh bone between his thumb and finger, he gently pushes the baby's legs out to each side. Normally, the legs should fall away easily until the baby's knees are almost flat against the table on each side of his body. The 'ball' of the femur, if dislocated, will come into the socket of the pelvis and will not rotate smoothly. If the joint is dislocated, the doctor will feel a definite clunk or jerk as the ball slips in – this does not make a noise that can be heard and is different from normal clicking of hips with which it is often confused. Parents should never try this procedure themselves.

'Clicking hips' is a term to describe babies in whom the examination produces the normal clicking, grating or snapping noise; this can happen with any joint and is due to slight changes in the ligaments around it. The joint is normal and cannot be dislocated so no treatment is needed. About 10% of babies have clicking hips.

To treat dislocated hips, the baby's legs are placed in a froglike position with his legs going out at right angles to his body. The bones of the pelvis will then develop to form a well-moulded socket into which the head of the thigh bone will fit without coming out. This is best achieved by lying the baby on his tummy while sleeping. Eight out of ten babies will be back to normal after four weeks with this type of treatment. A few babies will need splints for their hips, and some babies may need to be kept in them for two to three months. There are a variety of splints, but all are padded and waterproofed, and cotton wool can be put underneath at any point which might rub. The splint stays in place all the time, going under, not over, the baby's clothes, and regular checks will be made to adjust it to allow for growth. It is perfectly possible to breastfeed a baby in a splint though obviously caring for such a baby does have its problems. All babies with dislocatable hips will need an X-ray at three to six months to check that the hips are normal.

SKIN

The skin of newborn babies may be quite mottled or reddish, and sometimes the hands and feet may be pale or bluish. This is because of his changing circulation which will quickly settle down. After a few days, the skin often becomes quite dry and flakes and peels slightly. Do not mistake flaky skin on the scalp for dandruff. Sometimes a thick circle of dead skin will form on the scalp. This is called 'cradle-cap' but it does not need any special treatment and will disappear by itself. You can soften these scales with baby oil.

Harmless spots Tiny white spots on the nose, often called 'milk spots' or 'milia', are just enlarged oily glands and will disappear by themselves. Also harmless, but often confused with septic spots, are red blotchy spots around a white or yellow weal. Called 'neonatal urticaria', these usually appear from around day two and go within forty-eight hours, often to be replaced by others elsewhere. They are quite common at any time in the first two or three weeks. They are harmless to the baby.

Septic spots These are the kind which need treatment because they are the result of infection. They are red and come to a white head filled with pus. Treatment is either a course of antibiotics or antiseptic solution or cream applied directly to the spots.

Birthmarks Stork marks are reddish or purple V-shaped marks on the back of the neck, so called because they look like the marks the legendary stork would leave when carrying the baby. They are a form of birthmark but are harmless and do not need treatment. These marks usually fade but if they stay they will be covered with hair.

Strawberry marks are raised red areas with white marks and are so called because they look like a strawberry. They are the result of blood vessel overgrowth and usually start as tiny red spots which then grow quickly for several weeks and, rarely, can become quite large. Most of these marks will disappear by themselves and usually begin to show white patches within the mark or round the edges and grow smaller between two and three years. Most are gone before the child's fifth birthday. If they still remain after this time and are on the face, plastic surgery may be a possibility. Treatment may be considered earlier if one occurs on an eyelid and stops the eye from opening.

Mongolian blue spot has nothing to do with mongolism, but refers to patches of darker pigment which sometimes occur in babies with dark skin. They can be mistaken for bruises and are mostly seen over the baby's bottom and lower back. They are harmless and will fade as the baby grows.

Port wine stains, as the name suggests, are marks which look like a wine stain, irregular patches of mulberry skin which are not raised and are of normal skin texture. These are rare, but unfortunately do not fade or diminish with time. They are most common on the face and very occasionally, if they are on the forehead or scalp, the brain underlying the stain may also be affected.

Most adults have thirty or more moles and occasionally babies are born with a few. They can be flat, smooth, raised or hairy. Babies with large or unsightly moles on the face can be referred to a plastic surgeon who may consider operating between the age of about eight years and puberty.

Jaundice A degree of jaundice is very common and one survey showed that about one in five newborn babies developed jaundice. The condition shows as a yellowish tinge to the skin, usually making the baby look as though he has a wonderful suntan, although in severe cases the skin has an obviously yellow colour. This change in skin colour is caused by the presence of too much bilirubin in the body, a yellow chemical which is produced in the process of breaking down the haemoglobin contained in red blood cells at the end of their life cycle. The most essential job of haemoglobin is to carry oxygen to the tissues of the body, but before birth the placenta is not as efficient at keeping the blood oxygenated as the lungs are after birth. This fact means the unborn baby has to have higher levels of red blood cells to provide more haemoglobin to give sufficient oxygen. After birth, when the baby begins to breathe, the lungs are much better at oxygenating the blood so the baby's liver has to work to break down a higher than normal number of red blood cells – a by-product of this process is a large amount of bilirubin. The new baby's liver is not very efficient at first in removing bilirubin from the blood so it often accumulates, making the skin yellowish. Usually this appears after the first twenty-four hours of life and is most marked between three and five days, disappearing after this time. In many babies the condition does not need any treatment.

However, a few babies will need treatment because blood cells are being broken down too rapidly, or because the liver cannot cope with the bilirubin. In general, jaundice which appears in the first twenty-four hours of life and continues after the seventh day, or which is producing a very high level of bilirubin in the blood or jaundice in a sick or premature baby, needs treatment. The colour of the baby's skin alone is not a guide to the degree of jaundice, but a simple blood test will be done to check bilirubin levels. Before effective treatments were devised, serious jaundice could lead to deafness or spasticity which is why it is always carefully checked and treated.

Apart from an immature liver, a different rhesus factor blood group from the mother can cause jaundice and so too can infection. Some mothers' milk contains a harmless substance which makes their babies jaundiced. This is not a reason for stopping breastfeeding and the jaundice usually resolves naturally. Rare cases of jaundice include abnormal thyroid gland activity and hepatitis. It is important that jaundice persisting for more than a week is investigated.

It was quite by chance that the nursery of an Essex hospital discovered that giving jaundiced babies a sun bath proved very successful in reducing the jaundice. They then found that jaundiced serum left in the sunlight was also paler. Bilirubin is broken down if it is exposed to bright light from several fluorescent tubes – this is called 'phototherapy' and is now a standard treatment. The baby is placed under the light wearing only a napkin so that the light can reach as much of the skin as possible; the baby is turned at intervals so that the light reaches both front and back. Pads are put over the baby's eyes to protect them from too much light. Side effects of phototherapy are transient skin rashes because the lights cause sweating, and also greenish, loose bowel motions because the substance formed by the breakdown of bilirubin is green. Phototherapy can be given alongside the mother's bed, and she should feed, cuddle and care for her baby as normal.

If phototherapy alone is not enough, then the baby's jaundiced blood has to be drawn off – usually by inserting a tiny tube into the vein in the baby's navel, and fresh blood of the same group and rhesus factor is injected. This will be repeated several times until his blood is exchanged, and is done in the special care unit.

YOUR BABY'S REFLEX ACTIONS

A reflex action is one we make automatically, without needing a conscious message from the brain, like swallowing, blinking or sneezing. At birth the baby has a number of primitive reflex actions which doctors can test to check that the skin is sensitive and that the central nervous system, muscles and nerves are all working properly. They can also be a guide to maturity. About seventy or more primitive reflexes have been described in the newborn, but for the purposes of checking your baby's health at his first general examination, doctors will probably only test a few. For your own understanding of some of your baby's behaviour, it may be interesting to know about the most obvious and best known reflexes.

Oral reflexes Newborn babies already have a very strong sucking reflex. If you put your little finger into his mouth you can feel the suction. The 'rooting' or search reflex means that when the baby's cheek comes into contact with something he turns his head to root for milk – you can make him root by touching your nipple against his cheek. If he does not do this he is probably not hungry – only the most premature babies lack these reflexes.

Eye reflexes Your new baby automatically blinks in response to light, sound or touch. In the first ten days of life you may notice that if his head turns to one side, there is a delay before the eyes follow the same movement, so they stay fixed for a second – this is called the 'doll's-eye response'.

The grasp reflex If you put your finger into your new baby's palm he will grasp it tightly, and if you pull away he will hold on and tense his arm muscles until his body begins to lift. Touching the sole of his foot behind the toes gets the same reaction, with the toes clenching to grasp the object. This usually disappears in about two or three months.

Moro reflex This is the most famous primitive response, but it is a frightened reaction, so when the doctor tests it he will do it gently. In response to the head or bottom being allowed to fall backwards towards the bed, or if the bed is slapped on either side of the baby, he flings his arms sideways with his fingers spread and stretches out his legs, and then brings his arms in again as if hugging or embracing something. He often cries and looks surprised. This reflex action is slightly different from another known as the startle reflex when the baby makes much the same movement in response to noise, or his chest being tapped, but keeps his arms bent and hands closed. Do not try to prompt your baby into these reflexes yourself,

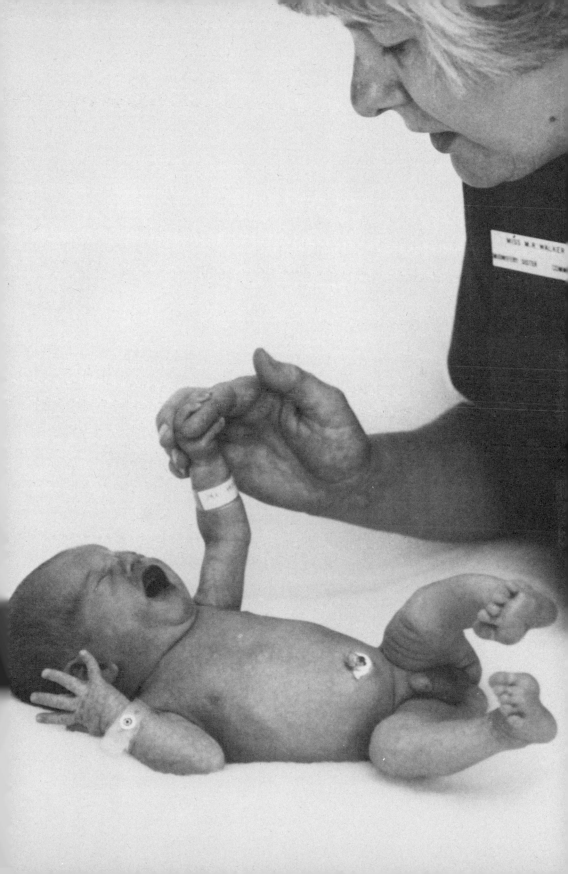

as it will upset and worry him. They usually disappear by about three to four months.

Walking reflex When a new baby is held upright so that the sole of his foot presses on to the table, he will automatically lift his leg and place the other down, as though walking. He also 'steps' up on to the table if the front of his lower leg is touched against it. This reflex disappears by about five to six weeks.

TESTS AND IMMUNISATIONS

VITAMIN K

Many hospitals routinely give all newborn babies vitamin K by injection or by mouth immediately after the birth. This increases the clotting ability of their blood and protects against a serious form of spontaneous bleeding which can occur in newborn babies.

GUTHRIE TEST

A simple blood test is done on about the sixth day when a small sample of blood is taken from the baby's heel and collected on absorbent paper to be analysed for high levels of an amino acid called phenylalanine. Babies with high levels may have an inherited condition called phenylketonuria (PKU) which is rare, affecting about one in 14,000 babies, but which causes brain damage if not treated. Treatment with a special diet results in normal brain function. The condition is inherited as a recessive gene and so parents of an affected baby have a one in four chance of another child having PKU.

The Guthrie test is also used to check the baby's thyroid function. Those who have a thyroid gland that is not working properly will also require treatment in order to ensure normal development.

BCG

Protection against tuberculosis may be given in the form of an injection of BCG before the baby leaves hospital in areas with many immigrants from outside Europe, North America or Australasia or if the baby is known to be in contact with tuberculosis.

LOOKING AFTER YOUR NEW BABY

'I'd never even held a baby until I had one of my own. I felt very strongly that I knew better than anyone what she needed, but I just didn't have the confidence to say so to all the people who offered advice. Relatives were harder to handle than midwives and nurses. The second time it was

so different. I was established as a mother and I didn't get the feeling everyone else was trying to take over.'

Trust your instincts and don't worry about following some mythical rule book. It often takes time to gain confidence in your own abilities as a mother, perhaps especially in hospital where you are surrounded by many people who seem possessed of great expertise and knowledge. But no one else will have studied your 'specialist subject' – your own baby – as closely as you, which gives you an expert knowledge of a particularly exclusive nature. You are an expert in your own baby's needs.

Whether at home or in hospital, be relaxed about those early days after the birth. Don't worry about routines. Looking after your baby at this stage is largely a matter of following his rhythms and supplying needs as they arise. Both of you need to get to know each other, to enjoy the comfort of each other's bodies and to rest. Mothers with other children will also need to balance this with their desire to be with them and to satisfy their needs for contact too.

FEEDING

All babies are born with a set of reflex actions (see page 148), and one of these is to suck. This instinct is very strong soon after birth and allowing your baby to suckle at the breast as soon as possible after delivery is one of the most important first steps in establishing successful breastfeeding. It also gives a new baby great pleasure and comfort as well as giving him the best nutritional start in life – the colostrum, which is the creamy substance present in the breasts before proper milk is made, is very high in protein and provides important antibodies which protect your baby's health. Suckling at the breast also stimulates the hormones in your body which are responsible for producing milk. A surge in the hormone oxytocin which occurs each time you feed your baby also helps the uterus to contract and shrink down to its pre-pregnant size – this is important both for your health and for your morale.

Your baby may sleep more in the few days following birth than he will later – a fact which often causes new mothers to feel they were doing it 'right' while in hospital, but that everything has gone all 'wrong' since they got home! In fact, it is just a question of the baby gradually becoming more aware and alert. If you are breastfeeding, milk will not usually appear until about the third day after the birth, but allowing your baby to suck at the breast when he wants to will stimulate milk production, comfort your baby and give him an all-important supply of colostrum.

Bottle-feeding mothers should follow just the same supply and demand pattern, offering a bottle whenever their baby seems hungry. Remember that hunger is the most common reason for crying. A new baby cannot usually go more than three to five hours without food and may often want feeding far more frequently. If you offer food, whether breast or bottle, whenever he seems hungry, and do not try to force food on him if he is not interested, nor regiment feeding to an every-four-hours routine, you will be doing fine. (For a discussion of breast versus bottle and details of both types of feeding see chapter 6.)

ASLEEP AND AWAKE

Even newborn babies can spend six to eight hours out of every twenty-four awake, so do not expect him to be either feeding or asleep all the time. Your baby may have periods when he is awake and calm, looking around and enjoying being talked to and played with. He may also have periods of wakefulness when he is less receptive and more inclined to be fretful. At the beginning, the new baby can only sleep for stretches of three to five hours and usually wakes from hunger. The length of time he can stay asleep increases as the brain matures, so by four months he will be sleeping between two to ten hours at a stretch and staying awake for two to four hours. Like adults, babies vary in the amount of sleep they need although their patterns can change. Place your baby on his back or side with the lower elbow slightly in front of him to prevent him from rolling on to his front. Keep his room at a constant temperature at night and do not allow him to become too hot or too cold – see page 164.

'Is he a good baby?' new parents are regularly asked, usually meaning does he sleep a lot at night. Most parents naturally long for the time when their baby sleeps through the night. Although in the early days it is very much a matter of following his natural rhythm of sleeping and waking, there are some things you can think about which may help your child to avoid sleep problems later (see chapter 8).

HANDLING YOUR BABY

Even if you have never held a new baby before, you will quickly become adept at this and able to handle your own. Nappy changes, which take ages at the beginning, soon become a matter of minutes and you will develop your own style of handling and holding your baby. This is one of the ways in which he recognises and distinguishes you from other people.

Parents instinctively support the baby's head, which is too heavy for the strength of his neck for several weeks. Don't be afraid to remind other people who want to hold him who may not realise this or have got out of the way of handling new babies. Nor should you be afraid to stop the proceedings tactfully if you think your baby has had

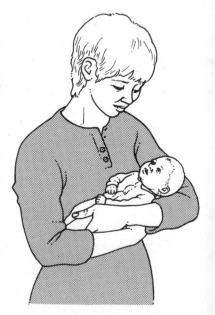

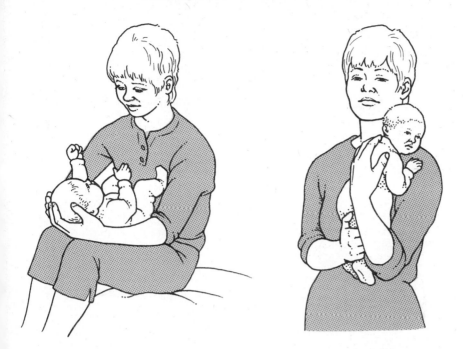

enough of being passed around among admiring friends and relatives, or is just unsettled and needs the reassurance of being held by you for the time being. The same goes for brothers and sisters. By all means let them hold the baby; the easiest way with little ones is sitting on a sofa or on the floor with the bulk of the baby's weight and head resting on a cushion, but even the youngest children can be told there are times when the baby is too tired, hungry or upset to be held by them. It is better to encourage them to think about how the baby feels than to view him as a dolly to be played with at any time.

New babies enjoy looking at mobiles and leaves waving in the wind when they are in the right mood, but the sight of a human face talking, smiling and responding to the imitative facial movements they begin to make is still their main amusement. Parents automatically look at their babies' faces as they feed them, and usually talk and play with them while they are changing, washing or dressing them. Talking and playing with your baby does not have to be confined to a special time.

With so much emphasis on the importance of a child's experiences in the first five years of life, it is easy to feel guilty if every spare minute is not spent stimulating, encouraging and educating your baby from day one! In fact, of course, new babies have a limited tolerance for attention, and the amount of time you spend in contact with your baby will depend on both your personalities and needs as well as other demands on your time. Just be natural, be yourself with him. Taking your baby into bed with you and carrying him around most of the time in a sling is only right if it is right for you. At the other end of the scale, of course, no baby will thrive on emotional neglect, even if his physical needs are catered for.

Don't worry if at first your love for your baby is mixed with many other reactions because adjusting to parenthood is often a longer, slower process and not just an immediate burst of unqualified devotion. For more about post-natal depression see page 167.

NAPPIES AND NAPPY CHANGING

Meconium is the greenish-black treacle-like substance which has filled your baby's bowels before birth and is usually passed in several bowel movements within twenty-four to forty-eight hours of birth. If this does not happen, your baby needs examining to make sure there is no blockage in his intestine. Just occasionally a baby may have passed meconium during delivery, but this has not been noted. Breastfed babies have fluid, yellow or mustard-coloured stools which do not smell unpleasant. They may be passed frequently, contain mucus or be green – all of which is normal. When your milk comes in around day two or three, your baby's bowel movements may be very frequent but later decrease. It is quite normal for a breastfed baby to have a dirty nappy at each feed or only once every two to three days, or even more infrequently. A bottle-fed baby will pass stools which are formed and may smell slightly. They do not contain mucus or fluid, but some milk formulas can make them dark green: this is also normal.

Even if your baby has not had a bowel movement, you will still find his nappy needs changing often: this is because new babies pass urine very frequently. A baby who does not pass urine within twenty-four hours of birth needs examining to make sure there is no blockage or other reason. If your baby subsequently stays dry for five or more hours mention this to your midwife for the same reason. Occasionally it can be a sign that a baby may be starting to run a fever.

Nappy changing, although a chore and not nearly as pleasurable as feeding a baby, does have a dual function. The first is the purely practical business of keeping your baby's bottom clean and as dry as possible, the second is that, just like feeding time, nappy changing is a time of intimacy and social interchange between the baby and the parent or carer. Obviously some nappy changes have to be much more hurried than others, but however quick the routine the adult inevitably leans over the baby, establishing eye contact and talking to him to distract and calm him while working.

Sometimes your baby will be in a wide-awake, playful mood and provided you are not in a hurry nappy-changing time will be a highly sociable opportunity allowing your baby to play and kick. At other times your baby will be tired, hungry or generally fretful and nappy changing needs to be carried out as swiftly as possible. Remember small babies are not good at maintaining body temperature so clothes which allow easy nappy-changing access with poppers around the crotch are preferable – if you do have to remove most of your baby's clothes a vest will help to prevent him getting too cold.

Equipment needed for nappy changing You will need a mat or towel, preferably with waterproof backing, to lay the baby on. There is no need to invest in specially designed changing trolleys or units unless you want to, but because nappies need changing about every four hours, usually when you feed your baby, it makes sense to allocate an area where all the gear can be set up instead of having to make a space and get everything out each time. As your baby grows and you become a more experienced mother you will discover that nappies can and do have to be changed in all sorts of unlikely and not tremendously convenient places, but you may as well make it easy for yourself in your own home. If you have a lot of stairs in your house or have another young toddler you do not want to take up and down stairs at every nappy change, it makes it easier if you can have a second nappy-changing station on the ground floor. In addition to a mat you also need cotton wool (bulk buy the cheapest variety); warm water or baby lotion or baby wipes; some kind of protective cream such as baby cream, zinc and castor oil or other form of barrier cream; clean nappy (plus liner, pins and clean waterproof pants if using towelling nappies); a nappy sack or bin for rubbish and a nappy bucket if using towelling nappies. Nappy liners are optional if using disposables made from material which is very absorbent and keeps moisture away from the skin but are convenient to allow solids to be flushed down the lavatory instead of being disposed of with the nappy in the household rubbish. If using re-usable fabric liners they need to be soaked, rinsed and washed in the same way as the towelling nappies themselves. The requirements of a 'nappy-changing station' are pretty basic – enough flat space to lay the baby on the changing mat with room to work and space for materials alongside, a convenient height that does not necessitate too much bending and somewhere which is warm and not too draughty. Never leave a baby unattended on a raised surface though, even if he has not yet learnt to roll over. You may find that the floor is the best place.

Towelling versus disposable Terry towelling nappies are either basic squares or else shaped to fit. The latter are easier for beginners to put on and give a neater fit, but the folding of the square gives a greater number of thicknesses at strategic points and consequently more absorbency. Squares come in different quality and thickness of towelling which is reflected in their price, but it is false economy to buy the thin, cheaper variety for a first baby if you plan to have more children as the better quality will easily do duty for two children and probably a third. You will need two dozen towelling nappies. Both types of towelling nappies also require pins, liners and plastic pants. Previous generations of mothers also invested in muslin nappies to use as liners, but nowadays their most useful function is as a bib or mouth wipe. Today's liners can be disposable or re-usable and have the primary purpose of helping to keep wetness away from the baby's skin, but they also make solid matter easier to dispose of down the toilet without rinsing the whole nappy and for this reason many parents use liners in disposable nappies as well. Plastic pants either button up the front, tie at the sides or are the pull-on variety and come in any assortment of different types of plastic. The important point is that they fit well without causing any red marks through tightness, but do an efficient job of encasing the nappy completely – stray folds poking through at leg or waist will mean changing damp clothes as well as nappies. In addition you will need two nappy buckets with lids on (one for the previous day's soaking nappies, one for the nappy just removed), sanitising powder and a washing machine. In winter a tumble drier is a boon to solve the problem of drying six plus nappies a day. When weighing up the cost of towelling nappies versus disposables, the ongoing laundry costs of electricity, wear and tear on the washing machine, soap powder, sanitising powder, plastic pants and liners all have to be considered along with the basic outlay for the nappies, but generally they work out rather cheaper than disposables over a long period.

The primary advantage of disposable nappies is that they are labour-saving, and a second consideration is that materials have improved so much that they now do keep a baby's skin drier than towelling. Disposables used to be less absorbent than towelling nappies, so requiring more frequent changes and being less likely to last the night, but better materials and designs have largely countered this. The disadvantage is cost and refuse disposal because despite their name they are anything but disposable and will quickly block the most efficient plumbing system if you try to flush them down the lavatory. Disposable nappies come in two basic varieties: all-in-ones which have waterproof backing, elasticated legs and sticky tape fasteners dispensing with the need for pants, pins and liners; the second type are rectangular pads which fit inside special plastic pants. The latter are cheaper but more fiddly and more inclined to leak.

Deciding whether to invest in towelling nappies or disposables depends on your lifestyle and personal preference as well as your finances and your concern for the environment: some mothers combine the two, using disposables when they are going to be out all day and once the baby becomes more active, as they tend to give greater freedom of movement than towelling.

Changing a nappy

* Check you have everything to hand before starting as it is dangerous to leave a baby unattended on a high surface even if he has not yet begun to roll over by himself. Remove the dirty nappy and use baby wipes, cotton wool and water or baby lotion carefully to clean the nappy area. Always wipe from front to back when cleaning a girl's bottom, i.e. towards and not away from her bottom, because bacteria from the bowel can very easily be transmitted to the vagina, causing an infection. Clean in between the folds of the groin and thighs of both sexes thoroughly.

* Pat dry using tissues or a towel if you have used water and if needed apply a protective layer of baby cream, zinc and castor oil cream or other barrier cream all around the nappy area to help protect the skin.

* Place the ready-folded towelling nappy (see page 159) plus liner or the disposable nappy underneath your baby's bottom, lifting him by his feet to do so. Secure the towelling nappy with one or two nappy pins placed horizontally, not vertically, so that if they do come undone there is less chance of the baby being hurt. Always use nappy pins with a safety catch rather than ordinary safety-pins and slide your hand down inside the nappy to form a protective layer between pin and skin as you fasten to avoid accidentally jabbing your baby. Disposable nappies simply need fastening securely with the sticky tabs, but make sure you have no baby cream or lotion on your fingers as this will prevent the tabs' adhesive from working.

* Put waterproof pants over the nappy, checking that no stray ends of nappy protrude and that the vest is not tucked into the top of the nappy at any point so that moisture spreads to the baby's clothing.

* Dispose of any solid contents of the nappy by flushing down the lavatory and place towelling nappies in a bucket of sanitising solution and used disposables in household rubbish sacks.

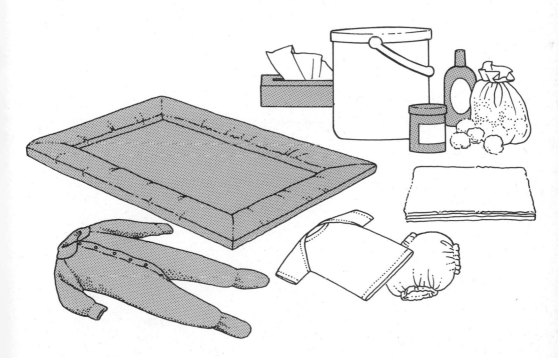

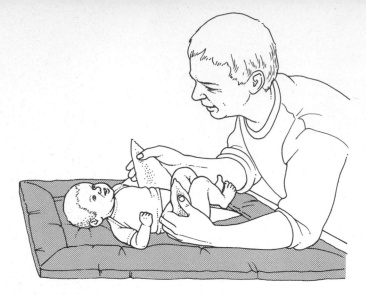

Remove the dirty nappy

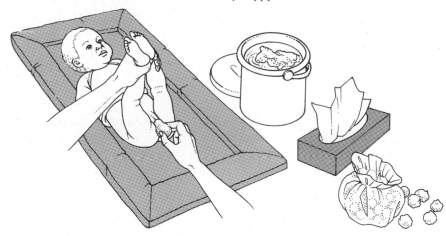

Clean the nappy area carefully

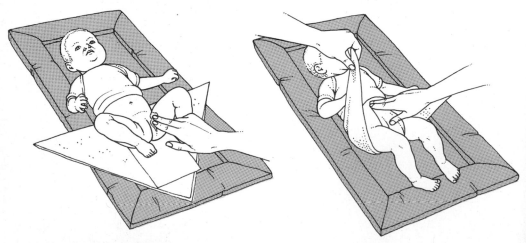

Apply barrier cream

Redress the baby in a clean nappy

Care of towelling nappies Washing alone is not enough to kill the bacteria and in the old days mothers actually used to boil up the nappies. Today sanitising solution is effective and is diluted according to the packet directions in a nappy bucket with a lid on. Every towelling nappy, whether wet or soiled, needs to be soaked in the solution and then rinsed thoroughly and washed on a hot wash if soiled.

Folding a towelling nappy

The kite method Place the nappy so that it lies in a diamond pattern in front of you and bring the two outer sides in to the centre to make a kite shape. Fold down the top corner and bring the bottom corner up towards the centre. This last fold can be adjusted to fit your baby – this shape is easy to fasten with two pins (see below).

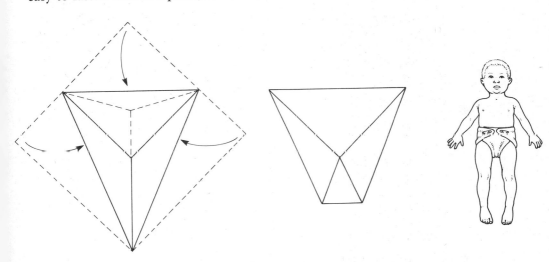

Traditional triangle Fold the nappy in two to make a triangle shape and place it before you with the centre point towards you. When putting it on the baby bring a single thickness from the lowest point of the triangle up between the baby's legs first, bring the two sides in and complete by bringing the lower thickness of the centre point up last. Be sure to secure all thicknesses with the pin (see below).

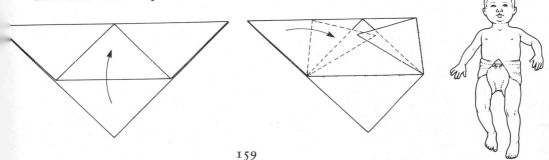

159

Triple fold Fold the nappy in four, by folding it in half and then in half again, giving four thicknesses. Place the square in front of you with the fold down the right-hand side and the unfolded edges at the top and left-hand side. Take the top left-hand corner of the first layer and open it out to the right. Keeping everything in place carefully turn the whole nappy over so the point now lies to the left. Take the two layers which still form a fold down the right-hand side and turn them over twice so you end up with a triangle shape with an extra thickness pleat down the centre. To fasten bring all three corners in, as for a triangular nappy, and secure through all thicknesses with the pin.

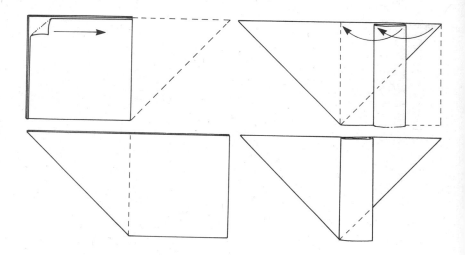

CLEANING YOUR BABY

A new baby often does not like being undressed or generally disturbed so keep such procedures to a minimum, doing everything very gently and soothingly and talking reassuringly to distract him from any unpleasant sensations. However, once undressed, many babies enjoy the freedom of movement lying naked on a towel gives, and often enjoy bathtime as well.

New mothers often worry about how frequently they should bath their baby – the answer is not at all in the first few days unless you want to. Certainly it is a good idea to wait until after the fifth day, because there is a real danger of the baby getting cold and most find it an upsetting experience. Young babies do not have to be bathed every day. A couple of times a week, or even once a week, is fine, as long as areas where the skin is soiled or where skin rubs against skin is cared for every day.

'Topping and tailing' This is the name midwives give to the routine of cleaning parts of your baby's body and it is usually taught to new mums in hospital or, if they have their baby at home, the community midwife will show them how. You need water which has been boiled and allowed to cool until it is body temperature or cooler, cotton wool and some kind of protective cream such as Vaseline.

Begin with the face. Use two separate pieces of cotton wool squeezed in the water to wipe the baby's eyes gently from the outer corner inwards. This is the natural way the eyes drain and prevents infection being wiped to the outer extremities of the eyes. The reason you should not do both eyes with the same cotton wool is that an infection in one eye will be transmitted to the other. Because of this risk of infection do not use cotton wool already used on any other part of the body.

Babies who are not yet eating solid food do not usually get dirty faces, but gently wipe all around the face and behind the ears. Lift his chin up or place him in a position where it is easy to reach the folds of skin under the chin and gently wipe here as well. Dry each area thoroughly by patting with a soft towel or dry cotton wool.

Raise each arm separately and wipe the armpit carefully as folds of skin rub together here and can become sore. Again, dry thoroughly and you can dust with baby powder if you like.

Until the cord has dropped off, it just needs to be kept as clean and dry as possible using antiseptic powder and making sure the nappy stays below and does not make the cord stump wet.

To avoid soreness, a baby's bottom needs to be kept as clean and dry as possible which means frequent nappy changes, cleaning the skin and applying a cream which will act as a barrier to protect the skin (for more on nappy rash see page 558).

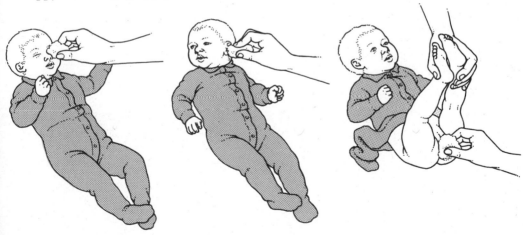

Bathing your baby Some babies take to water immediately and enjoy bathtime, others need a more gradual introduction. If yours is a baby who does not enjoy early bathing experiences and you find it difficult, a thorough top and tail routine each day is fine and you can limit baths to once or twice a week. Probably the secret to helping your baby enjoy bathing is to be relaxed and unhurried yourself.

Babies tend to get cold quickly, so make sure the room you choose to bath him in is warm. A portable baby bath means you can use the bedroom or living room if you wish, or put the baby bath inside the ordinary bath. Experienced mothers with older children may opt for dipping the baby in the bath before older children get in, but make sure the water is not too hot. If you are unsure about the temperature, test it with your elbow, not your hands which are often exposed to higher temperatures and are less sensitive. The water should feel warm but not hot.

* Collect everything you will need before you start undressing your baby. Two soft towels, clean nappy and clothes, soap or baby bath liquid and cotton wool. You do not have to bath your baby at the same time on each occasion, pick a time in the day when he is not too hungry or tired which will make him fretful, and when he has not just been fed which might make him be sick.

* Undress your baby except for his nappy and wrap him in a towel so that he does not get cold. Clean his face with cotton wool and water as you usually do in the topping and tailing routine.

* Wash his hair before putting him in the water so that you use clean water. Supporting his head and neck with one hand, hold him over the bath and wash his head with water – you do not need shampoo in the early days when he will have very little hair. Gently pat his head dry with the second towel.

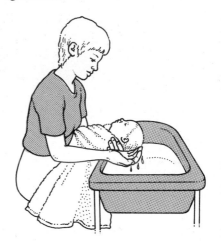

* Laying him in the crook of one arm, open the towel and gently soap his body front and back with baby soap. This is the part most new parents find hardest as it makes your baby slippery and hard to hold. Alternatively you can add baby bath liquid to the water beforehand.

* Lift your baby off the towel and gently lower him into the water, holding him with one arm around the back of his neck and shoulders and holding the far arm to stop him slipping. This leaves you with a hand free gently to swish the water around to remove the soap or to clean him if using bath liquid. Talk to your baby to reassure him and if he cries always check that the water is not too hot or cold. Generally, given time, most babies learn to enjoy the sensation of the water.

* Lift him out of the bath and wrap him in the towel, drying him thoroughly in all the areas where skin rubs on skin by gently dabbing rather than rubbing. If you use talcum powder, make absolutely sure he is completely dry first, otherwise it will clog into irritating lumps. Do not, of course, mix cream and powder and do not use powder on a little girl's bottom as it may cause irritation.

* Dress your baby in clean nappy and clothes. New babies often find all the sensations involved in bathtime quite exhausting and may be ready for a feed and sleep afterwards.

DRESSING A BABY

At first you may feel that dressing and undressing your baby is fiddly and difficult, but most baby clothes are designed to make this task as easy as possible and you will quickly become very adept at such tasks with the minimum of upset to your baby. When you have to undress your baby, for nappy changing, bathing or to change his clothes, choose a place where you can lay him down on a flat surface and which is warm. Before you begin make sure you have everything you need to hand, remembering you may find you need a fresh nappy.

In general, babies and young children do not like the fuss entailed in dressing and undressing so be very gentle as well as quick, and talk to distract him while you work. Taking clothes over his face and head is something he will specially dislike, so choose clothes that can be stretched wide and quickly popped over without having to drag things across his face. The same goes for cuffs and sleeves — stretch the cuff wide open and fold the rest of the arm down so that the whole thing can be easily fitted over the hand and fingers instead of trying to feed his hand and arm through the whole length of the sleeve. Most baby clothes are designed for easy nappy changing with crutch poppers or elastic waists, but if you always put a vest on your baby he will keep one layer of clothing to help him to stay warm even if you do have to change a whole outfit. Because a baby's circulation is not very efficient in the early days, his hands and feet can get cold – in winter you may need to put socks over the toes of baby suits. By the time your baby is about four months old he will almost certainly have grown out of first-size vests and suits – do not try to cram him into stretch-suits which are too short as the pressure on his feet can have the same effect as badly fitting shoes later, and can hinder the correct development of the still pliable bones in the foot.

CRYING AND COMFORTING

Crying is the only way a baby has of telling you he needs something, and it is a distress signal ingeniously designed by nature to be one which parents cannot ignore. Most mothers at some times experience the awful distress of having their baby crying when they cannot comfort him – perhaps because they are driving a car, trying to get through the checkout at the supermarket or seeing to another young child. The sound of crying will often stimulate the let-down reflex in breastfeeding mothers if it is near feeding time.

Finding out why your baby is crying is a process of elimination at which you will become increasingly skilled (see page 299). Like adults, babies have highly individual temperaments and personalities from the start, and therefore different things bother each baby to a different degree. Parents automatically stroke, rock, jiggle, pat or croon to their babies to find the best way to calm them. Some babies cry far more than others and may have set times of being fretful and crying when they are very hard to console, which can be extremely taxing (see also page 300). In general, do not think you will be spoiling your baby or encouraging bad habits if you pick him up when he is upset and crying – in fact by responding to his cries you are giving him a sense of confidence and security which will make him less fretful.

WARMTH

From birth babies have a working temperature control mechanism, like adults, which enables them to generate body warmth when they get cold. But unlike adults they cannot conserve that warmth and can become very cold very quickly if the surrounding air is at a lower temperature than normal. This risk increases when they are undressed for any reason because they have a relatively large surface area compared to body weight, which means they lose heat quickly. That is why maternity hospitals are always such hot places. A room temperature of 29°C (80°F) is about right for doing anything which means taking clothes off – changing, washing, and so on. For the first month babies need to be warmly dressed with a vest, stretch suit and cardigan or shawl, but after the first four weeks they do not need more clothes than their parents although they need protection from draughts, and outdoors they do need more clothes than adults. Most recent research on cot death shows that becoming too hot is as much of a risk to a baby as becoming too cold. The ideal room temperature is 18°C (65°F), and a simple wall thermometer will tell you if the room is the right temperature. You should never put your baby to sleep in front of a fire, by a radiator or heater, or by a very sunny window. Keep your baby's room at an even temperature so that you can put on the right number of blankets at the start of the night and know that your baby will not get cold later. It can be dangerous to put on extra blankets when the room is warm for fear that the temperature will drop later. A very rough guide to what is needed is a sheet plus three to four blankets when the room is at the right temperature. Do not use duvets, baby nests or bags for babies under a year. A nappy, vest and stretch suit are all that a baby needs to sleep in, and in hot weather he may need less. To check how warm your baby is, feel his tummy. Hands and feet can often feel cold or look blue but this is normal. If your baby's tummy feels hot though, or if he is sweating anywhere, he is too hot.

What are the signs that your baby may be too cold? If he is having to work hard to keep himself warm he may become fretful and cry, his breathing will be faster than normal and, though his body is still warm, his hands and feet are cold. As he becomes chilled he will not be able to spare the energy for crying and becomes very quiet and still and now his body, as well as his hands and feet, feel cold. In the most extreme stage, which is rare, the baby becomes very lethargic and almost unable to feed, and his hands and feet may become swollen and bright pink. Such babies need urgent medical attention and have to be carefully rewarmed to avoid fits. If you think your baby has begun to get cold do not just pile on extra coverings because this will keep the cold in — he does not have the energy to make more warmth himself. Instead, take him into a warm room and remove some of the layers so the warmth can reach him. Holding him next to your own body under a blanket helps, and so may a warm drink or feed.

AFTER THE BIRTH – YOU AND YOUR NEW BABY

YOUR BODY

'Two days after I had had the baby my stomach was flabby and hanging in positive folds of flesh, my stitches hurt like hell and my breasts were rock hard and engorged. Nobody warned me I would feel like this!'

A few women leave hospital with wonderfully flat stomachs and absolutely no problems from any of the unmentionable aspects of motherhood like leaky, engorged breasts, piles or painful episiotomy stitches. Very many more can be forgiven for wondering at some point after the birth if their body will ever be the same again. Perhaps it is because so much attention is focused on the birth and the baby that few antenatal teachers or even midwives give very much consideration to what women feel like after they have given birth.

Many women are rather unprepared and feel a bit depressed when they find that their stomach is saggy and flabby afterwards. However, flat stomachs are perfectly possible after having a baby and the skin does recover its elasticity, although you need to persevere at exercises. In general, the more weight you put on and possibly the older you are (because your skin is less elastic) the more perseverance is needed to get back into shape. All hospitals give mothers a series of post-natal exercises to do devised by a physiotherapist, and it is vital that you follow these carefully and do them every day to get maximum benefit. In addition, breastfeeding certainly helps the uterus shrink back to its pre-pregnancy size more quickly – this is because every time the baby suckles at the breast the hormone oxytocin is released, which stimulates the womb to contract. Breastfeeding also uses up a certain extra number of calories, but the way that it affects weight loss can be very variable. Some women find that weight just drops off while they are feeding, while others find they cannot lose weight at all until they actually stop feeding the baby. Stretch marks which may have occurred during pregnancy can also be distressing afterwards – but they really do shrink to thin, silvery lines, given time.

Bruising, stitches or small tears which do not need to be stitched cause discomfort to the perineum, and ice packs, cool baths and using a bidet can all help to relieve the pain. Sitting on a blow-up rubber ring of the type used to help children to swim is a practical step which can make hard chairs more bearable! Women often feel worried about emptying their bowels after they have had an episiotomy because they fear that the stitches will burst open, but in fact the pressure is not in this area and you have nothing to worry about. Drink plenty of liquids, and if you have trouble opening your bowels, ask your midwife about suppositories.

If you have had a Caesarean section, the wound will probably be quite painful for the first two or three days, but painkillers help considerably and are safe, even if you are breastfeeding. Moving as much as possible, and getting up once all the tubes and drips have been taken away is the best help in making a speedy recovery – staying absolutely still is the worst. Many women worry that their stitches will burst if they move too much, but there is no danger of this, though at first you need to support them to avoid pain when you sneeze, cough or laugh. The stitches will come out around the fifth day. Try circling your ankles and gently bending one knee at a time to help stiffness and circulation – the physiotherapist will give you a sheet of special exercises. Although your baby was delivered surgically, you will still have a vaginal discharge called 'lochia' which is normal after birth. At first it is red, then changes to brown. Waist-high pants and press-on sanitary towels avoid rubbing the stitches.

An unexpected, but very distressing complaint after having had a baby can be piles (haemorrhoids) or varicose veins in the rectum. These are likely to occur if a mother has become constipated during pregnancy and may be made much more painful during the second stage when the pressure of the baby's head may force them to 'come down' so that they protrude beyond the anus. Suppositories available on prescription can stop the itching, which can be very distressing, and so too can ice packs and cold baths – during a bath gently ease the piles back inside the rectum and they should gradually subside. If the problem persists, see your doctor because they can be treated fairly easily.

The increased levels of hormones during pregnancy predispose women to varicose veins because the walls of the veins become softer and the blood supply is increased. However, in very many cases such varicose veins disappear spontaneously without any treatment as the hormone levels subside.

When the milk appears around the third day after the birth, your breasts may become engorged: this may happen whether or not you are breast-feeding. There are many ways in which you can try to alleviate this (see page 216). However, it is very important to wear a good supporting bra day and night during this time so that the tissues and skin above the breasts are not stretched, and this will ensure that your breasts retain their same shape afterwards.

Because it is so hot in maternity units, many women find their skin becomes very dry after the birth, so it is a good idea to take plenty of moisturiser into hospital with you.

Be comforted by the fact that although in the first few days after the birth you may feel you don't recognise your own body, it really does possess tremendous powers of recovery. Eating a healthy, sensible diet, following post-natal exercises without trying to attempt anything too strenuous too quickly, and giving yourself plenty of time is the secret of getting back to normal physically. For most women it takes at least six months before they feel their bodies are back to some kind of normality, so don't be depressed if you can't zip back into your jeans by the time you go for your six-week check-up.

TIME IN HOSPITAL AFTER THE BABY

The majority of babies are born in hospital these days, although the time that you stay in afterwards can vary from six hours to eight days, or more if there are complications. It makes sense to try to get as much rest as possible during this time, and in the early days after the birth your baby is more likely to be sleepy. It has to be said, though, that many women find hospital wards, plastic-sheeted beds and the continual noise of hospital life hardly conducive to any kind of rest! Nevertheless, not having to think about meals and an unending supply of fresh linen for the baby is something to be enjoyed. It is also worth using the time to work out your post-natal exercises and get into the habit of doing them several times a day.

THE BLUES – OR POST-NATAL DEPRESSION

It is very common to feel emotional, weepy and even a bit down around the time between the third and seventh day after the birth. Generally known as 'the blues' this state of emotion is largely due to the sudden changes of hormone levels in the woman's bloodstream as the milk comes in. A feeling of being on a high of happiness and excitement one minute, and then plummeting to tears and feelings of depression or inadequacy the next is quite normal at this stage. So too are feelings of unreality or panic. Usually by the time the baby is around six to eight weeks old your emotions will be beginning to stabilise – although it is still common to feel more emotional and weepy than you did before.

You may be suffering from post-natal depression if these feelings do not go away but actually begin to get worse, with more low times finally developing into a continuously depressed state when everything seems too much effort. Symptoms vary, but continual tiredness, feeling totally inadequate, being overwhelmed with sadness, and being unable to see any hope for the future are common feelings. 'Everything in my life seemed to be painted in shades of grey – there was no colour in my life at all,' was how one new mother described her state of mind.

It is not known whether post-natal depression may be caused by the high levels of hormones circulating in the mother's body or by the actual mental upheaval which adjusting to parenthood entails, or both. However, there is general agreement that exhaustion is likely to make matters worse – new mothers need 'mothering' themselves, and having nobody who can help you with practical or emotional support in the early days can make the going harder. Getting to know a few other women who are expecting babies at the same time, avoiding major upheavals around the time of the birth or immediately afterwards, making arrangements to get as much assistance as you can in the first few weeks after the birth can all help to cut the risks. However, if you do start to feel very miserable or find that the blues develop into something that threatens to be more permanent, make sure that you talk to your GP or your health visitor, depending on whom you have the best relationship with, and explain exactly how you are feeling to your partner. Talking to other mothers can also be a help – you may be surprised just how many have experienced the same feelings. The Association for Postnatal Illness is also willing to put people in touch with members who have themselves suffered from depression (see address section, pages 673–6).

The most severe form of post-natal depression is termed puerperal psychosis. This has many of the same symptoms as post-natal depression, but in addition a woman may experience delusions, hallucinations and great agitation. Dramatic changes in mood to mania or severe depression, or swings between the two states, are also symptoms. Fortunately, such severe mental disturbance following birth is uncommon – about one in three thousand mothers may experience puerperal psychosis. The condition obviously requires medical treatment, usually hospitalisation, and there are units where mothers and their babies can be cared for together so that as the mother recovers she can gradually begin to resume more responsibility for her baby. Support and counselling are also important for fathers and in subsequent pregnancies.

COMING HOME

'I was terribly excited to dress the baby in her own clothes at last and to put my ordinary clothes on again. But there was also a slightly panicky

*feeling when we arrived home and I immediately realised it was time for
the baby's feed. In hospital you have absolutely nothing else to think
about and somehow when you are on your own all the time it all seems
so much more overwhelming. I remember asking my husband to fill up a
bucket with nappy solution because I had to change her nappy after
feeding her and he said rather incredulously, "It's all starting right away
then?"'*

It is the most colossal change in your life from being without children and
no special demands on your time to finding that you have someone who
demands attention twenty-four hours out of every twenty-four. Most
people feel thoroughly overwhelmed in the beginning and shocked by the
way that a baby completely consumes their time. Initially, it is hard to
come to terms with the fact that you can't pop to the shops easily or go to
sleep when you like. With a first baby it is also very hard to get any kind of
sense of perspective – it just seems that life has changed utterly and that
this state will go on for ever. In fact it actually lasts for a very short period
and once you get used to being with children all the time, it is just as hard,
at the other end of their pre-school years, to get used to the fact that there is
no one to take to the shops with you!

There is no doubt about it that life is very much easier for women who
have supportive relatives living nearby or even helpful neighbours who
will occasionally mind the baby for them. But friendships with other
mothers will be your greatest support – and this is something which is
open to all new mothers. Such friends can be helpful both in a practical and
emotional sense.

In the early days, it just helps to recognise that your baby is at his or her
most demanding and that things will only get easier. Don't try to force
some sort of routine on to your baby, but rather get a set of priorities and
don't get hung up about trying to live life as it was before you had him. If
you are somebody who gets very upset by an untidy disorganised house, it
can be harder for you to accept the fact that with a baby housework has to
come pretty low down your list of priorities. First place has to go to
keeping the baby fed, clean and happy. In second place come the needs of
you and your partner. If you are the kind of person whose happiness is at
least partially dependent on having an organised home and in being able to
serve up a proper cooked meal each evening, you will have to reach some
sort of compromise. Again, talking to your partner about what both of you
expect each other to do and about problems as they arise is very important
indeed.

It is also important to remember, if it is your first child, that life with a
baby is continually changing, because your child develops and changes so
very much in the first twelve months of life. This means that just when you
have got used to the fact that he has two naps, one in the morning and
another in the afternoon, he will suddenly go on to needing only one sleep
during the day and that probably at a very inconvenient time. And just
when you have rescheduled your life around that pattern, then your baby

suddenly goes into the awkward phase where he can almost manage to go a whole day without a nap at all, but not quite, and continually falls asleep around four to five o'clock which means that he will not sleep at all in the evening! The first year of your baby's life is hard work, but it is also unique, and trying to remember just how short a period it is may help you to feel less frustrated and to enjoy it to its maximum.

ORGANISING YOUR LIFE

The other great change that many women having their first baby have to get used to is the difference between working and staying at home, even if you are on maternity leave or plan to return to work eventually. When you work full-time you spend very little time in your own home and consequently rarely know many people in the area, unless it is an area that you have grown up in. Work also provides a structure and a framework, not only to each individual day, but to the weeks, to the months, to the years and ultimately to your expectation of life. When you are at home every day of the week there is no structure, and virtually no framework except the one that you care to impose upon it. Suddenly, the times that your partner leaves and comes back to the house have a greater significance because they put some kind of framework around an otherwise formless day and become landmarks which highlight weekdays from weekends and separate day from evening. Everything that happens requires initiative and energy from you to make it happen. All this can be very disconcerting at first, but it does help if you look rationally at exactly how many changes have happened in your life, and don't put everything down to the baby.

Getting out of the house and seeing other people can be very important to your morale and self-esteem, and this is also true when it comes to maintaining your self-confidence. It sometimes happens that being based at home looking after small children can make some women less confident about their abilities in situations and circumstances which they might not have given a second thought to when they were in full-time employment. Probably this is partly the result of doing what is, in effect, quite a solitary job, and partly also reflects the value and worth that society places on the job of parenting. Fortunately this last is changing, although very slowly, and there is more widespread recognition that the job of being a parent is extremely challenging and worthwhile. Certainly it helps not to minimise or undervalue the challenge involved in becoming a parent for the first time and to remind yourself just how many new skills you are learning at this stage in your life — from the practical aspects of child care right through to all the new emotional and psychological demands being made. After a couple of years, dealing with six different things at the same time comes automatically to most women, as does managing their time and energy with maximum efficiency. The organisational skills alone learnt during the years when you have pre-school children are ones which any management training scheme would be proud to be able to instil! And of course there are tremendous pluses in being able to free yourself from the nine to five routine.

While in the early days it may seem that your baby devours every single minute of your time, there will come a stage when you begin to see a little space which can be used for your own needs – an aerobics class with a crèche attached, a weekly adult education class in something which interests you while a friend or relative minds the baby, or even a chance to take up a new hobby or a sport. Of course, you have to plan carefully to make time for these activities – that is where the organisational skills come in – but the opportunity is there and it is well worth thinking about swapping schemes with friends if you do not have relatives nearby who can help out by minding the baby occasionally.

MAKING LOVE AGAIN

There is absolutely no 'right' time to begin having sex again after the birth of your baby. Some women – especially those who have had a very good sex life before, who have had an easy birth without any stitches, and whose babies sleep a great deal at night – may recover their libido very quickly. But for the majority, sheer exhaustion, coupled with discomfort from stitches, can make passion the last thing on their mind! However, it is important not to stop all forms of physical contact and all physical affection between you just because you don't actually want to have intercourse. It really is very important to talk to each other so that neither party feels rejected by the other. Women do need to feel loved and may often want to be cuddled, even if they don't actually want to have sex at that time. A common misconception is that the six-week post-natal check-up is the time when it is all right to begin having sex with your partner again – in fact the right time is simply when you feel like it.

What happens if weeks and then months go by and you still don't fancy your partner? The time after having had a baby is a key period for problems to begin between couples, so it is important to take action and not to allow yours to become a sexless marriage by habit. If there have been sex problems before which have been unacknowledged or not talked about, then the birth of a baby is often a convenient peg on which to hang old problems.

Talking to your GP is one step, and many doctors are willing to try to help. Alternatively, family planning clinics usually have some kind of psychosexual counselling service and so, often, do marriage guidance centres. There are a number of good books available and if you both read one of these it may make it easier for you to talk to each other.

Spending too much time alone in the house with the baby can often lead to lowered morale and less interest in sex. Too often couples end up seeing each other only against a continual backdrop of nappies and domestic life. Tiredness and the continual demands of a third party, as well as familiarity, prevent them from seeing each other clearly. The counter to this is to get out of the house as much as possible – both on your own during the day and as a couple in the evenings. In the early days, especially if you are breastfeeding, it is often easiest to take the baby along with you, but later it is worth making some effort to sort out baby-sitting arrangements so that you can get a break. Do not be tempted into thinking that it is all just too much trouble to arrange.

In order to be interested in sex, women need to feel that they are sexually interesting themselves — it is hard to feel this about yourself if you spend too much time alone, have no reason to dress up or bother about your appearance, and seldom have the chance to see yourself reflected in other people's eyes.

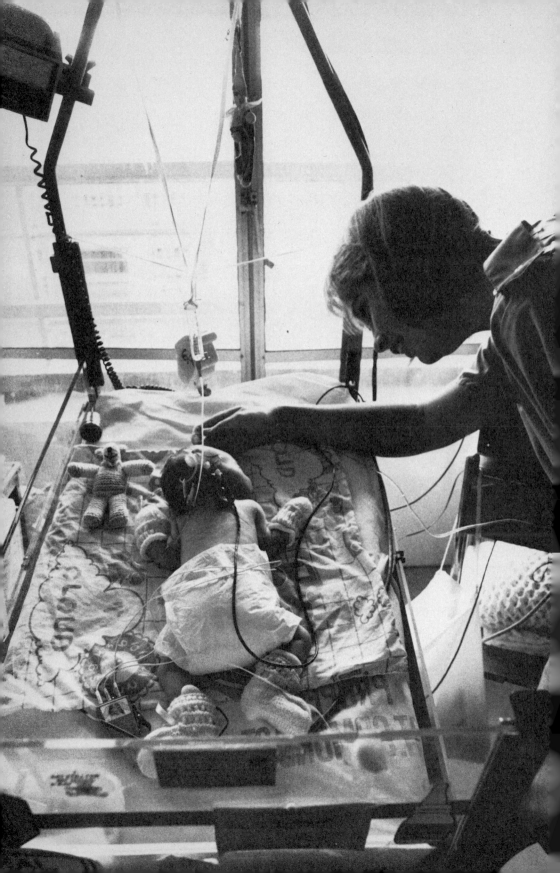

Chapter 5

BABIES NEEDING SPECIAL CARE

How much special care?   Babies needing surgery   Small babies
Babies in special care – what it means for the family
The problems of babies in special care
The future for special care babies
Parents' reactions to premature birth   Babies who may not live
Cot Death (Sudden Infant Death Syndrome)

The knowledge, skill and technology which can save tiny or ill babies is growing all the time. It means that many babies who would previously have died or been handicapped can now be helped to grow into normal healthy adults. Such increasing expertise may sometimes raise ethical questions which are not easy to answer, but it also brings hope to very many more parents for whom the answer to the question, 'Is my baby all right?' is not an unqualified 'Yes'.

HOW MUCH SPECIAL CARE?

Today many babies who used to be taken into special care can now be kept with their mothers and given any extra observation or care needed on an ordinary post-natal ward. These may include babies who needed help to start breathing but are otherwise well, babies born by Caesarean or forceps, breech babies, mildly jaundiced babies needing phototherapy, babies who need screening for low blood sugar or extra feeding, and babies with conditions which are not life-threatening, like cleft palate, hare lip, dislocated hip and Down's syndrome. Even some babies who are too premature to be breast or bottle-fed, but who are otherwise well and a reasonable weight, can sometimes be tube-fed on a post-natal ward. Different hospitals will vary slightly in their criteria for admittance to a special care unit.

Another form of intermediate care which may exist can be a ward acting as a half-way house between the post-natal ward and the special care baby unit. This ward is usually next to the SCBU and mothers and babies can stay together while the baby's care is shared between mothers and the special care unit's staff.

175

THE SPECIAL CARE BABY UNIT (SCBU)

About five babies out of every hundred born will need caring for in an SCBU. A first visit to such a unit can be both shocking and overwhelming for parents because of all the equipment and the fragile appearance of the very small babies. However, modern technology can now help babies to breathe before their lungs can work properly on their own, keep them nourished before they are able to suck, to swallow, or to digest food in their stomachs, and can also measure their temperature, heartbeat, breathing and the level of oxygen in their blood. The most sophisticated procedures are only carried out in a neonatal intensive care unit, which is discussed below, or an SCBU with facilities for intensive care. Each hospital has its own criteria for admitting babies to special care, but generally those born before 32 weeks or weighing less than 1,800 grams (4 lbs), or ill babies with persistent breathing difficulty, fits or blood disorders, will fall into this category – very seriously ill babies will need intensive care (see below). The basic principles of special care are, however, still the same as they were when the first nursery for newborns was opened over a hundred years ago by a French doctor in Paris – that is, to keep tiny or ill babies warm and free from infection.

THE NEONATAL INTENSIVE CARE UNIT

> *'The whole place was buzzing and clicking and humming with machinery and it was very hot – like a tropical electronic aviary. In the midst of it all were these pathetic scraps of humanity wired up to machines inside incubators. They showed us our son and my wife began to cry. He looked so helpless and we felt so helpless as well, not wanting him to be fixed to all that machinery and yet knowing he couldn't live without it.'*

Neonatal intensive care units in large hospitals, generally regional centres, are where the smallest and sickest babies are cared for with the most sophisticated technology and the highest degree of skill. The broad dividing line between special and intensive care is the baby's ability to breathe unaided. While SCBUs can give extra oxygen (by holding a mask to the baby's face or pumping oxygen into the incubator), putting a baby on a ventilator is intensive rather than just special care. Babies needing this kind of intensive care will be transferred from other hospitals in the area. Amazingly, babies born as early as 23 weeks are now regularly being saved to grow into healthy adults, although for such very premature babies the path to health is seldom straightforward. Having a very small or sick baby that has to be cared for during many weeks in an intensive or special care unit places tremendous strains on parents, and there is more discussion about ways for them to deal with this on page 181.

BABIES NEEDING SURGERY

Babies born with conditions needing an urgent operation, such as a heart defect or abnormalities of the nervous system like *spina bifida*, may be transferred to specialist centres such as our own Hospital for Sick Children in Great Ormond Street. This is because the doctors in charge of intensive and special care units are paediatricians rather than surgeons and these babies need to be moved to a hospital where there is a paediatric surgeon. Afterwards, babies that are also premature or small may be moved back to their original special or intensive care unit for continuing care until well enough to leave hospital altogether.

SMALL BABIES

'The nurses told me my son was very small but I was still shocked when I saw just how minute he was. He weighed one pound fifteen ounces and he was born at twenty-six weeks. Later, when I could hold him, he fitted easily into my hand with his legs dangling over my palm. I couldn't believe anything so small could survive.'

One of the first things that strikes visitors to intensive and special care units is that most of the babies are so very tiny. Any baby weighing less than 2,500 grams (5½ lbs) at birth is classified as having a low birthweight. Babies can be small because they have been born too soon and have not had enough time to grow and develop – they are called 'premature' or 'pre-term' babies and account for most of the work of intensive care units. Babies can also be small because although they have been born at the right time they have not been getting enough nourishment to grow properly inside the uterus. In a sense they have been starved before birth, and these babies are called 'small-for-dates' or 'light-for-dates'. Some babies can be both premature and small-for-dates. Doctors can tell by examining the baby, testing his reflexes and measuring his head, body and limbs carefully, whether he has been growing at the expected rate and how mature he is. Premature babies have different problems from small-for-dates babies and size is not always a guide to maturity. For example, the baby of a diabetic mother can be born prematurely but weigh as much as 4,000 grams (10 lbs) or more.

About 700,000 babies are born each year in Britain and of these about 40,000 will arrive prematurely. A baby is said to be premature if he is born before 37 weeks of gestation. In general, the earlier he is born, the more care he will need, although each baby's condition and maturity will be different. The reasons for his premature birth, if they are known, and the type of labour and delivery he has had will also make a difference. Because the lungs of premature babies have not yet matured, they often have trouble breathing (see page 188), and because they have scarcely any body fat they cannot keep themselves warm (see page 192). They may not have developed the reflexes to suck or swallow food, and the digestive system of very premature babies may still be too immature to work. They have reduced resistance to infection and become ill easily, and they can be prone to fits and sometimes to episodes of bleeding within the brain, though this may not be as alarming as it sounds (see page 195). Jaundice is a common problem for both small and premature babies as is calcium deficiency.

In most cases, small-for-dates babies have been deprived of nourishment only during the later weeks of pregnancy. This means their normally developed brains will give them a rather large head in relation to the rest of their body and can predispose them to becoming hypoglycaemic (low in blood sugar) rather easily. This is because the brain uses up a lot of the body's energy source, glucose, while the liver is too small to store much glucose. Serious problems in small-for-dates babies usually arise only if the babies have been deprived of nourishment from early pregnancy, while the brain and other organs are developing, but the use of ultrasound means that such babies may be detected during pregnancy, and continuing research is going on into ways of detecting very early in pregnancy babies who are likely to suffer in this way. Like premature babies, small babies also have difficulty keeping warm because they have so little body fat, but they are less likely to have breathing problems unless they are also premature. Although small, their lungs are mature enough to work efficiently.

WHY ARE BABIES BORN PREMATURELY OR SMALL-FOR-DATES?

'*My son was born eleven weeks early for no reason anyone could pin down. I felt I had been too casual about the pregnancy and looking after myself. Somehow if I had rested more or given up work and stayed at home it wouldn't have happened. It didn't help that my mother-in-law believed that as well.*'

It is usually the most terrible shock to parents when their baby is born prematurely – they feel very upset and anxious and often blame themselves. Although there are some known reasons for premature labour (see page 113) in nearly half the cases doctors will not be able to suggest or discover a reason. It is very unlikely indeed that a premature birth will have been caused by anything in the mother's lifestyle, whether it is carrying on working, pursuing an active life, having an alcoholic drink occasionally or enjoying sex. You have only to consider how many babies continue to term and are born healthy despite all sorts of adverse conditions.

The same feelings of guilt are also common in women whose babies are small-for-dates. Again, it is often very hard to pinpoint exactly why a baby fails to grow properly, although certain categories of women are more likely to have small babies (see page 113), even though the reasons may not be fully understood yet. Known reasons for prematurity and failure to grow often overlap so it is very common for a baby to be both premature and small-for-dates to some degree.

WILL MY BABY LIVE?

'We were told when my wife went into labour at twenty-seven weeks that our baby had only a forty per cent chance of survival and we prepared for the worst. But he did live and was taken straight into intensive care. On the third day we asked one of the doctors what the real problems would be – up until then we had hardly dared hope he would live. We were shocked and frightened when we heard of all the possible difficulties and formed an initial dislike for that doctor. But after a few days our opinions changed and in the end we were so glad we had been honestly informed. We now hold that doctor in the highest esteem.'

Each individual baby's progress and problems will be different, and the road to health will seem intolerably long and slow with each day bringing one step forward, only to be followed by two steps back. There are some general points which can be made, however. The first is that the majority of babies who go into a neonatal intensive care unit *do* go home. Most babies born at 32 weeks or later will live and grow normally. Only one in seven of babies born at 28 weeks (twelve weeks early) will not survive. Earlier than that the risks rise sharply, so that babies born more than fourteen weeks early may have a less than 50% chance of living, depending on their condition, weight and the reasons for their premature birth. In each case your paediatrician will tell you about your own baby's chance and answer your questions honestly.

Though this may seem harsh at the time, what often weighs most heavily with parents is not only the life or death of their baby but his chances of surviving normally without handicap. Of course, there are risks attached to the life-saving procedures that enable very small babies to survive, but although many more babies are now being saved, the level of handicap is the same as it was twenty years ago. It has stayed at a level of about one in ten, although this figure includes minor handicaps such as slight deafness, short-sightedness or squints, slightly slower development, clumsiness and shorter height, all of which still allow a normal expectation of life. Only about one in twenty of the very small babies is affected badly enough to need to go to a special school.

One of the problems of assessing how very small babies are progressing is that no one yet knows what is 'normal' behaviour for such premature infants, so there is nothing with which to compare their progress. In most cases, the only sure test that a baby has not been damaged is time. If, however, medical staff think there is a serious possibility a baby may have been damaged, they will discuss it in detail with the parents and decide with them whether to continue treatment.

In general, the first twenty-four hours of life are the most dangerous, and most deaths occur in the first ten days. Beyond that there is no definite point when parents can be told their baby is out of danger, though landmarks along the way bring that time closer. Being able to breathe unaided is obviously a crucial step – ventilator treatment can bring problems of its own, but 90% of babies on ventilators do make a full recovery. Usually parents are told to expect their baby to stay in hospital until the time he was due to be born, although he will not be receiving intensive care all this time, but will gradually be promoted through degrees of care until he is sleeping in an ordinary cot in a nursery, being looked after like any new baby. Don't be too disappointed if your baby appears to make slow progress — by being tube-fed instead of intravenously, or coming off a ventilator only to have to go back to needing this form of treatment again for a while. This often happens and doesn't mean he has become more ill, just that he is not quite ready for the next step yet.

WHAT DO PREMATURE BABIES LOOK LIKE?

'Like a newborn rabbit — I can say that now she is two, but at the time I felt guilty even thinking it. I just wanted to put her back inside me when I first saw how obviously unready she looked to be out in the world.'

Most premature babies do have a distinctly foetal look about them. If they are born before 26 weeks, their eyelids may still be sealed, though these will open naturally in time; their hands are almost translucent, and veins and arteries can be seen through the thin skin. The bones of a premature baby are still quite soft and the fontanelles (see page 140) are wider. Nurses change the position of babies regularly to stop pressure on one part of the body, and it is common to see that their heads have become flattened on the side they have been lying. Eyelashes and eyebrows may not be present, but will grow later. Normally ears lie close and flat to the baby's head, but the cartilage that forms the ear is still soft and can easily be pressed out of shape if the baby lies with them bent.

Premature babies have had no time to develop fat under the skin, which is why they have trouble keeping warm. It also makes their bodies look very bony and rather frog-like — pointed, bony bottoms without any buttocks to speak of, matchstick-thin arms and legs, a small chest and an abdomen which often looks proportionately too large are all normal for a premature baby. A very common posture is tummy downwards with arms and legs out to the side and the legs bent at the knees — adding to the frog image!

Premature babies may have scarcely visible nipples, though these will develop later, and in boys the testes have often not descended from the body into the scrotum. They usually move down as the baby matures. The genitals of premature baby girls can sometimes look odd because, although everything inside is perfectly formed, the outer lips around the vagina develop later in pregnancy and their absence makes the inner lips look bulging or even swollen. Don't worry, your baby's early birth will not stop the outer lips growing at the same time as they would have done inside the uterus.

Very premature babies will not have had time to develop lanugo, the downy hair which grows to protect their skin while they are in the amniotic fluid, but some later babies can still be covered with this, particularly on their backs and cheeks. It will be shed naturally as the baby develops.

Remember that your premature baby is not unformed, just immature. The baby is in fact perfectly formed by the end of twelve weeks from pregnancy and the rest of the time is spent maturing and growing. The job of special or intensive care is to give your baby the time he needs to complete the job of growing.

WEIGHT

Do not forget that normal term babies lose weight at first and take time to regain their birthweight. Exactly the same thing happens with small and premature babies, although you may be horrified to think they are going to get smaller still. Remember this is normal and not a sign of your baby's ill health.

Obviously your baby's weight is important information in assessing whether he is able to digest his food and is getting the right amount of fluid and nutrients. Babies are weighed regularly, but it is best to look at his overall weight gain for the week rather than become obsessed with each loss or gain: this is not as significant as the general pattern. The more premature the baby, the longer he will take to regain his birthweight. In the tiniest baby this can take up to a month.

BABIES IN SPECIAL CARE WHAT IT MEANS FOR THE FAMILY

You will have been shown your baby immediately after the birth, but may not have held him because there is a danger of premature and small babies getting cold easily and they may need help to breathe. As soon as possible after the birth you will be taken to see him in the special or intensive care unit. Try not to be overwhelmed if he looks very small or there seems to be a lot of equipment surrounding him. The nurses will be very pleased to explain everything. If your baby is very premature or ill, he may have to be transferred to a regional neonatal intensive care centre at a larger hospital. Care will be taken to keep the baby warm by wrapping him in gamgee and silver foil in a portable incubator and whenever possible you will be able to go with him. If there is no bed available for you to be transferred to or if you are too ill to be moved, the baby's father can travel with him in the ambulance and the staff will take some polaroid photos of your baby for you to keep.

Physical contact between you and your baby is a very important part of getting to know him and establishing a relationship. No baby is so ill you cannot put your hand inside the incubator and hold his hand. In most cases babies are well enough for parents to stroke and fondle them. At first you may be worried about disturbing the equipment, but nurses will show you what to do. The bright, noisy world inside an incubator could not be in greater contrast to the dark protected world inside your womb, and whatever human contact you can offer will help to reassure even the tiniest baby – just as skin contact, warmth and the movement of a mother's body is comforting for any newborn baby. Research is even being done about the benefits of holding a premature baby between a mother's breasts close to her body instead of keeping him in an incubator – an idea that comes from Bogota, Colombia – though there is a good deal of controversy about this idea. Positive physical benefits have been shown to be linked to close physical contact between parents and babies, so that gently stroking the baby in his incubator appears to help cut the number of apnoeic attacks (periods when the baby stops breathing) and even help weight gain. Premature babies can hear well and, like any new baby, will get to know the rhythm and tone of your voice, so it is important to talk to them as well. Very premature babies may still have their eyelids sealed, but once these have separated they can see quite well and, during alert periods, will be able to focus best on your face at a range of about eight to twelve inches.

Unfortunately, some of the procedures which save such babies cause temporary discomfort – for example having blood samples taken, mucus sucked from their lungs or tubes passed into their stomachs. Obviously staff will always be as gentle and careful as possible and keep interference to a minimum. Once in place the tubes and drips are not uncomfortable, but you should always tell a nurse if your baby has moved and you think he looks distressed or in discomfort, and she will help you to rearrange him in a better position.

Normally, premature babies can cry just as full-term babies can, although the cry will be feebler and not as prolonged because crying is exhausting and premature babies do not have so much strength. If your baby is on a ventilator, he will not be able to make any sound because the tube taking oxygen into his lungs passes between the vocal cords. Nurses will be watchful to notice if such a baby is in discomfort or distress and to find out what is the matter.

Premature babies usually sleep a great deal – between fifteen to twenty-two hours out of every twenty-four. Like normal newborns they drift easily between waking and sleep, and in their waking hours they vary from being drowsy to being very alert and aware. You can use these aware periods to talk to and especially to stroke your baby and later cuddle and hold him. You should talk normally during feeding just as you would to a full-term baby. You can encourage your baby to wake up when you are holding him by slightly loosening the wrappings and stroking his toes while you talk to him. Because their nervous systems are immature, the movements of premature babies will be rather jerky and uncontrolled, but this lessens as they develop. Small and ill babies are nursed without clothes on because it makes it much easier for nurses to spot any immediate changes in skin colour or condition and to treat them. As he gets stronger, your baby will be able to wear clothes, and you can put a bright soft toy or a picture or photo inside the incubator.

At first all the equipment will seem overwhelming, but never be afraid to ask questions of the nurses or doctors. Early mornings are busy times in the unit because doctors do a round of the babies to assess their condition, and there may be emergencies during the day when the staff have to see to one particular baby urgently, so pick a time when things are fairly calm if you want something explained. Don't forget the alarms often sound because a monitor that should be stuck to your baby's skin has fallen off — not because your baby's system is suddenly failing in some way.

Babies in special or intensive care often need a number of X-rays — to check their lungs, or to see that a feeding tube is properly in place. Understandably, parents may feel concerned about the number of times this happens, but it is always kept to the minimum and with modern techniques the risk to the baby is very small indeed.

BROTHERS AND SISTERS

Older children will have been expecting you to bring a new baby back with you that they would have been able to touch and hold. Instead, they may have had to cope with your unplanned and early departure to hospital, longer separation from you, and a new brother or sister who has had to stay in hospital. Units vary in their policy of children visiting, but if it is possible arrange for them to come and see the baby, even if they cannot touch or hold him. Generally, children are far less awed by the trappings of intensive care than parents, but take your cue from them and don't push them to do more than they want. It is as important for them to form a relationship with a new baby as it is for you — to do this they need to see, talk about, and if possible touch or hold the baby. They may like to bring the baby his toy to go in the incubator, and it is a good idea if the baby thoughtfully has a small present to give in return! Some children like the idea of putting a photo of themselves inside the incubator. Even if you are uncertain about your baby's chances of survival, it is probably better to bring your other children to see him. If he does not live, your grief will still be part of their lives and they will probably feel sad and upset too. Your sadness will have some meaning for them if they have seen the baby themselves and it will make any reference to the baby less confusing than if they have never seen him for themselves.

FATHERS

Individual reactions will obviously vary, but fathers who would have wanted to be fully involved with their baby's care in the event of a normal birth will be just as likely to feel the same if their baby needs special care. Sometimes one partner, either mother or father, tries to protect the other by shouldering most of the responsibility, but this is more likely to lead to stress and resentment later. Whenever possible, couples should see doctors together so that they can both ask questions, have a better firsthand understanding and share decisions.

Fathers need to be both supportive and sympathetic to the many difficult emotions their partners may feel – of course a premature or sick baby is a great shock to both parents, but it is still the woman's life which changes most. She has physically undergone the experience of birth and will usually be the one to stay and visit the baby most. Spending long periods in the timeless, isolated world of a hospital can increase her sense of unreality and loneliness, while going out to work or staying at home with other children can make it easier for fathers to keep a stronger grip on reality. If possible, it will help couples to take turns in staying at the unit so that they can understand more of what the other feels. This sharing of their baby's care will help couples to support each other when their baby comes home – a time to look forward to, but also one which can cause anxiety and some mixed emotions as well.

THE PROBLEMS OF BABIES IN SPECIAL CARE

FEEDING

Sucking reflexes do not usually develop until about 30 to 34 weeks, and the ability to co-ordinate sucking and swallowing perhaps a little later, though individual babies do vary. Babies born very early may not only be unable to suck and swallow but may have such an immature digestive system that they have difficulty in absorbing food through their stomachs. Fortunately, there is a variety of other ways in which they can be nourished until they are large enough to feed normally.

Intravenous feeding (also known as total parental nutrition, TPN) Babies who have prolonged breathing problems, who have had operations, or who are too ill or too immature to digest food through their stomachs can be nourished with a carefully balanced solution fed directly into their bloodstream through a tube inserted into a vein. If they are to be fed like this for only a short time, the solution will be given through a drip into one of the surface veins, sometimes in his scalp because his head moves round less than his limbs. To avoid damaging the tiny delicate veins, this kind of drip has to be resited every forty-eight hours. If a baby is to be fed intravenously for a longer period, the solution can be given into one of the larger veins by using 'a long line' – this means a long narrow tube which is introduced into a surface vein and then fed through one vein after another until it reaches a point in the chest where the veins are larger. The advantage is that more fluids of different types can be fed in without the worry of bursting tiny surface veins, and the long line can be left in place for some time and not resited frequently. Babies can be fed like this for several weeks if necessary, although there is a slightly increased risk of infection in using the technique – the doctor will need to dress in sterile operating gear when inserting the tube and afterwards take an X-ray to make sure it is properly in place.

Tube-feeding (also known as gavage feeding, naso-gastric feeding or polytube feeding) It is a simple and safe procedure to pass a tube down the baby's nose into his stomach and, if you wish, the nurses will be glad to show you what happens. When the tube is in position, the nurse will draw up some of the contents of the stomach to see if undigested milk is left from the last feed and to check the contents for acid – a sign the end of the tube is in fact in the stomach. At the first feed a baby will have only a tiny amount of acid present, but this will gradually increase. If a very premature baby is having breathing problems, putting food into the stomach may not be suitable because there is a risk of vomiting: instead food can bypass the stomach and be fed by a tube (called a 'naso-jejunal tube') directly into the duodenum or jejunum parts of the intestine beyond the stomach – a naso-gastric tube will also be inserted alongside through the same nostril so the stomach can be kept empty.

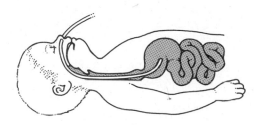

Combined tube and breast or bottle-feeding As the baby begins to suck and swallow, he can start to take feeds from breast or bottle. Because sucking is tiring work, he will start by just taking the first part of the feed like this and the rest by tube. Then he may progress to being fed alternate tube and sucking feeds. Before a baby is able to take any kind of milk, he can be fed a dextrose solution of colourless sugar and water given by drip as an interim measure to stop him becoming dehydrated and to give him some energy. Babies who have to be fed intravenously for a longer period need a more complete solution which will give them all the fluid, nutrients and vitamins they need. Once a baby is able to tolerate some milk, breast milk is the most easily digested and gives a premature baby what no formula milk can offer – added protection from infection by passing on antibodies from the mother. Extra vitamins and trace elements are needed by premature babies and it has been shown that the milk from mothers of premature babies is different from the milk of mothers of full-term babies and appears to have more trace elements and also a higher protein content. Naturally all the other advantages of breast milk over formula milk which apply to full-term babies apply just as much to premature babies. This will help you to understand why staff in special and intensive care units always encourage mothers of such babies to express breast milk to feed to their babies, even by a tube, until they are strong enough to suck at the breast themselves.

Breastfeeding a baby in special care Mothers often need a good deal of support, encouragement and help to breastfeed a baby who is premature or ill and in special care for a considerable amount of time, especially if this is their first baby. Even though breast milk is the best food for a baby, there will also be quite a number of mothers who cannot breastfeed because they are taking drugs to control illness, because they do not want to breastfeed for a variety of reasons, or who find it too difficult or stressful. They should not in any way feel guilty about this. A number of babies can still be fed expressed breast milk (EBM) from the reserves of the intensive or special care milk bank – this is milk collected from breastfeeding mothers in the area which is pasteurised before being given to the babies. There are also formula foods especially designed for low birthweight babies which are high in protein and energy and have extra minerals and trace elements. There are also special solutions which are high in calories to help small babies gain weight without having to try to take in enormous quantities of food. If your baby has some supplements of these foods in addition to your own breast milk, don't feel it is a waste of time expressing milk – the number of nutritional supplements needed will drop until he is having only your milk. Providing this milk is one of the most practical ways you can help your baby to health.

Unless there are definite medical reasons why you cannot breastfeed, or you know definitely you do not want to try, it is best to take each day as it comes and don't feel you have to commit yourself to a firm decision. You will be keeping all your options open and doing both yourself and your baby positive good if you begin by expressing milk. Even the small amounts of colostrum you can produce before the milk comes in are very precious: they have unique nutrients and antibodies which are the best help for your baby. If he had been born at the normal time, you would have been able to put him to the breast at birth and he would have been able to take a little colostrum, but if he is too premature to be given this straight away, it can be frozen and fed by tube as soon as he is strong enough.

Expressing milk is the only way to build up a good supply of milk so that you can feed your baby when he is strong enough to suck at the breast. In the meantime, the milk you express will be fed to him by tube or, if he is still being fed intravenously, frozen until he is ready. Little and often stimulates the body to start producing milk which usually comes in about the third day. Supply and demand is the rule which governs the amount of milk you produce. The principle works in exactly the same way when you are expressing milk – both to build up a supply and to feed him until he can be breastfed. Milk can be expressed by hand, using a hand suction pump, or by using an electric breast pump. Expressing enough milk regularly to be able to feed him later means using an electric pump. Your hospital will have their own electric breast pump and the midwife will show you how to use it – start as soon as you can after the birth. However, if for various reasons you do not start expressing milk until several days or even a couple of weeks later, you will still be able to stimulate your breasts into producing milk – it will just take a little longer.

At first you may not be able to produce anything but a drop or two of colostrum, but follow the little and often principle and use the pump for just a minute each side every two hours at the lowest suction over the next few days and your body will react just as if you were able to put your baby to suck. Around the third day the milk will come in and you can build up a good supply by continuing to follow the same routine – five minutes each side, six to eight times a day, is much more effective than ten minutes each side, four times a day. Few hospitals have pumps to lend mothers to take home, but they will put you in touch with a breastfeeding counsellor from the National Childbirth Trust (NCT) who can hire you a pump and also provide valuable advice and support about breastfeeding. Often the counsellor will also be able to put you in touch with other families who have premature babies and experience of special care units.

Once home it is much harder to keep up the little and often routine, but remember how precious your milk is to your baby. Babies vary as to when they begin to develop a sucking reflex but usually it is around 30 to 34 weeks. There is no reason why you should not hold your baby to the breast, even before this time, as long as he can be picked up and cuddled. Let him nuzzle at the nipple and be relaxed, and regard this as a pleasant opportunity for you both to enjoy some skin-to-skin contact which will help to comfort your baby and stimulate your milk supply. You can express a little milk and put a drop on his tongue and he may take the nipple into his mouth and lick or nuzzle.

Don't be upset or disappointed if at first when he begins to take a feed your baby is very sleepy and only sucks very weakly or won't suck at all: many full-term babies also take time to get established. It is important that he is hungry and has not just been given a feed by tube and is reasonably awake. The nurse will show you how to fix him properly on to the nipple so he is pressing on the area surrounding the nipple, the areola.

Feeding a baby, whether by breast or bottle, is a very emotional business and it is perfectly natural for you to want to be the one who gives your baby his first bottle if you are not breastfeeding. An experienced nurse will help you, but again don't be worried or upset if the baby takes a few sessions to get used to the idea of feeding from a bottle.

BREATHING

A baby who has difficulty breathing by himself is said to be suffering from respiratory distress syndrome (RDS) – sometimes called 'hyaline membrane disease'. This is very common in babies born before 32 weeks and it is estimated that 35 to 50% of babies born between 27 and 31 weeks will suffer some degree of RDS.

From about 22 weeks of pregnancy a fatty substance called 'surfactant' begins to be produced which coats the baby's lungs. It is this substance which enables the baby's lungs to expand easily, stretch and be flexible when he starts to breathe. Surfactant lowers the surface tension in the air sacs so that the same pressure blows them all to the right size, whether the sacs in the lungs are large or small. Because the air pressure is the same throughout the lungs, when the baby breathes out all the air sacs stay partially inflated to the same degree as well. When the lungs are not well supplied with surfactant to make them stretchy and flexible, a great deal more pressure is needed to blow up the large air sacs and in the process the smaller ones can get over-stretched. Because the pressure throughout the lungs is not equal, at the end of a breath these small air sacs can collapse in on themselves completely so that their sides touch together like cling-film.

The level of surfactant in an unborn baby's lungs can be measured approximately by testing the amniotic fluid, sometimes using amniocentesis, and if premature labour is likely or the birth has to be induced because of the condition of mother or baby, a 24- or 48-hour course of steroids may be given to the mother. It is thought that these steroids stimulate the unborn baby's lungs to produce certain enzymes which are needed to make surfactant. In addition, it would appear that certain mechanisms may also be triggered to have the same effect when a baby is likely to be born prematurely, perhaps because the placenta is ceasing to work properly. Certainly length of gestation alone is no absolute guide to a premature baby's ability to breathe.

Forms of breathing difficulties If a baby is immature or has already been deprived of oxygen he may have difficulty in breathing at birth. Pethidine given late in labour can also make babies sleepy and less able to breathe in some cases.

Wet lung (transient tachypnoea) is a term used when a baby still has some fluid in his lungs which is making breathing more difficult. The condition may also be due to a mild deficiency of surfactant, but usually disappears within twenty-four hours of birth. In the meantime the baby may need a little extra oxygen.

Hyaline membrane disease occurs when a baby is born without enough surfactant lining the lungs. It often appears in the first few hours after birth. The baby may make grunting noises in an effort to stop the air sacs collapsing as he breathes, and his chest becomes deeply sucked in at the beginning of each breath.

Apnoea simply means not breathing. It is very common for premature babies to have apnoeic attacks. Sometimes, because the nervous system is still immature, the right messages do not always get through and they simply forget to breathe. Usually, gently shaking or touching the skin is enough to start them breathing again, but if there is a more serious attack the baby needs to be given extra oxygen, usually through a face mask. Repeated or serious apnoeic attacks need further investigation because they can be a sign of fits, infection, metabolic imbalance or other problems.

How babies are helped to breathe The air we breathe contains 21% oxygen, and babies who are having trouble in breathing will not have to work so hard if they breathe air which contains an extra amount of oxygen. The easiest way to give this to babies is to pipe it directly into their incubators or into a plastic head box or plastic hood over their head. Babies who have moderately severe RDS can often be helped with a different method, called 'continuous positive airway pressure' (CPAP), when continuous air pressure is supplied to keep the air sacs expanded so that the baby can breathe more easily. This is done either by pumping air through a face mask or, more commonly, a small tube is inserted directly into the windpipe through the mouth or nose.

When neither of the two previous methods are enough, a baby can actually have his breathing done for him by a machine called a 'ventilator'. Ventilators vary, but they usually look like a box which stands on top or to the side of the incubator with a soft tube which goes into the baby's mouth or nose and between his vocal cords, so that the end rests just below the top of the windpipe into the lungs. It is usually secured in place with sticky tape or a bonnet around the baby's face and head. A mixture of air and oxygen is delivered in and out of the baby's lungs under carefully controlled pressures, just as in a normal breathing pattern, and it will be moistened as it passes into the lungs. With mechanical ventilation some sticky secretions begin to collect in the lungs, so the nurses will frequently take the baby off the ventilator briefly and pass another fine tube into his lungs to suck out these secretions. While he is off the ventilator, they can give him oxygen using a face mask attached to a hand pump. At the same time, the baby may be given physiotherapy to help clear any mucus from the lungs – this involves massaging the chest, often with an electric toothbrush with the end wrapped in cotton wool, and changing the baby's position. Signs that a baby may be ready to come off a ventilator are that he needs less oxgyen and begins to make efforts to breathe unaided.

While it is very important that a baby has enough oxygen, it is also vital that he does not have too much. Measuring the levels of oxygen and carbon dioxide in the baby's blood ensures this does not happen. A device called a 'transcutaneous oxygen electrode' can give an estimate of oxygen levels in the baby's blood by measuring the oxygen as it passes through the skin. This is achieved with a heated electrode which looks like a button and is stuck on to the baby's skin. It has to be moved regularly to stop the baby's fragile skin getting overheated. Other devices called 'oximeters' can be attached to a hand or foot to measure the percentage of blood fully loaded with oxygen; these do not have to be heated. Alternatively, an oxygen-sensitive electrode can be implanted into the tip of a very thin plastic tube, which, inserted into the baby's umbilical artery, gives a continuous readout on a display panel. The more traditional method is to take regular blood samples via a catheter into an umbilical or other artery and analyse them. Measuring oxygen levels very carefully has overcome what used to be one of the biggest risks – that of giving too much oxygen and damaging a baby's eyes.

As well as the lowest possible levels of oxygen, care will be taken that the minimum amount of pressure is used when giving CPAP or using a ventilator. Even so, because premature babies have such tiny fragile lungs,

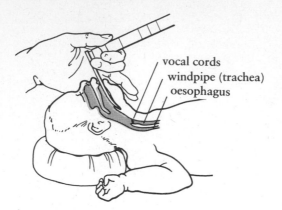

vocal cords
windpipe (trachea)
oesophagus

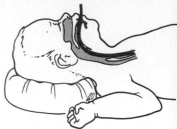

oropharyngeal intubation tube

Position of laryngoscope in preparation for inserting the breathing tube

Extra oxygen supplied through a pipe inserted directly into the windpipe through the mouth — naso-tracheal intubation tube in position

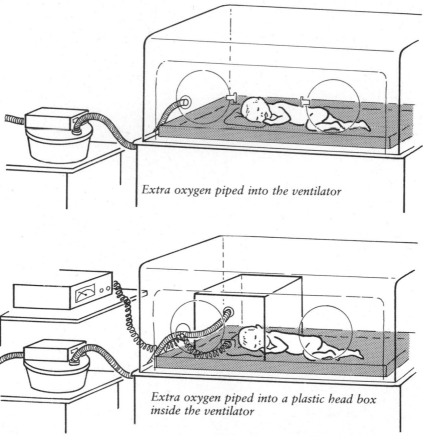

Extra oxygen piped into the ventilator

Extra oxygen piped into a plastic head box inside the ventilator

Methods of helping babies to breathe

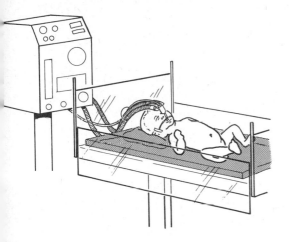

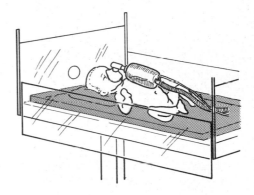

Extra oxygen supplied directly into the windpipe

Extra oxygen piped through a face mask

it is not uncommon for babies having this treatment to get a very small tear in one of their lungs. This is called a 'pneumothorax' and can happen anyway when a normal baby is making strenuous efforts to breathe. A small hole may mend by itself, but a large hole needs treatment (see page 140).

Sometimes babies needing to be ventilated or given oxygen therapy for a long time can become oxygen dependent and will not breathe unaided. It is thought that the pressure rather than oxygen levels over a long time may damage areas of tissue in their lungs – the medical name is broncho-pulmonary dysplasia (BPD). Such babies may need extra oxygen over months or very occasionally even for one or two years as the tissue recovers and they can gradually be weaned off to breathe unaided for longer and longer periods. It is also not uncommon to find that babies who have not been affected in this way but who have been ventilated for shorter periods and were very premature may be more prone to coughs, colds and chest infections for the first year or two.

TEMPERATURE – KEEPING SMALL BABIES WARM

Small babies cannot keep themselves warm because they have very little fat and a large surface area for heat to be lost from in relation to their body weight. One of the principal jobs of an incubator is to provide a constant temperature: it has carefully regulated heaters and fans to keep the air temperature inside at the right level. Very ill babies can be nursed in open incubators under a large radiant heater. Such incubators are also called 'infant care centres'. A plastic tunnel with one end closed, called a 'heat shield', can be put over the baby inside the incubator to keep heat from being lost. Sheets of bubble-plastic or a semi-circular plastic shield are also

191

good insulating materials and can be placed over the baby to help to keep him warm.

It may seem odd to parents with all this talk about heat loss that these very small babies are usually nursed without clothes but, as we mentioned, it enables nurses to notice easily any change in the baby's colour or breathing. Besides, if a baby's temperature does begin to fall, clothing will only keep the cold in – to get warm again the baby needs to be in direct contact with warm air. Inside the incubator the baby may lie on a sheepskin or a soft sheet to help to maintain warmth. Sometimes small babies may wear a bonnet or some kind of skullcap padded with gamgee wool, because a great deal of heat can be lost through the scalp which has a relatively large surface area. Once the baby is better able to maintain his own body temperature, he can be promoted from an incubator to a cot in a heated room. At this point he will be fully clothed with vest, stretch-suit and usually a cardigan and bonnet or cap as well.

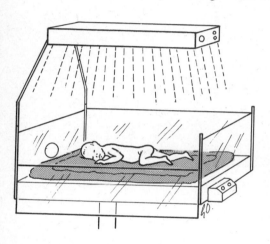

Radiant warmer

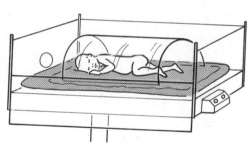

Heat shield

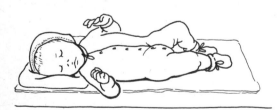

Clothed

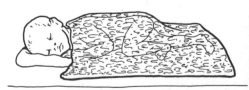

Thermal blanket

Methods of keeping premature babies warm

INFECTION

Premature babies have not had enough time in the uterus to acquire antibodies from the mother which will protect them against infection. This makes them especially susceptible, and all special and intensive care units take the greatest care to prevent infections and a possible spread to other babies. Precautions will certainly include careful washing of hands by all staff and visitors to the unit, and no one with any kind of illness such as a cold should visit. Some units also require visitors to wear gowns and possibly even masks, and restrict visiting to parents and siblings.

Signs that a baby has an infection may be obvious (for example, an inflamed eye) or vague (such as poor weight gain or lethargy). Infections can often make a baby suddenly and seriously ill, resulting in a 'collapse', and he may need intensive nursing care immediately. To avoid this happening whenever possible, a baby will always be started on a course of antibiotics if an infection is suspected. Samples of blood, urine, surface skin swabs and any discharge will be sent to the lab for analysis and their report will come back in two to three days – this is called an 'infection screen'. If an infection is confirmed, antibiotics will continue, but if not and the baby is better, they will be stopped. If it is not obvious where the source of infection lies, a number of other tests and samples will be taken. Taking a sample of spinal fluid to test for an infection of the central nervous system, such as meningitis, is called a 'lumbar puncture'. It will be done carefully by an experienced doctor under sterile conditions and he will use a fine needle to draw off some of the fluid surrounding the spinal column. An infection of the blood is known as septicaemia, one in the lungs is pneumonia, and in the eyes it is conjunctivitis. Most babies who have infections at this early stage respond well to antibiotic treatment and recover completely.

BLOOD AND HEART PROBLEMS

Bradycardia This is a slowing down of the heart rate, and usually the baby recovers if he is gently stimulated by rubbing his skin in the same way that an apnoeic attack is treated.

Anaemia Full-term babies lay down stores of iron which will last them for four to six months. Breast milk contains very little iron, but mixed feeding is usually started at around three to four months and provides extra iron. Premature babies have not always had the chance to acquire sufficient stores of iron, and because of this can more easily become anaemic. Fortunately this can be helped by giving extra iron and folic acid. Often such babies are also given top-ups of fresh donor blood. Blood banks now screen blood for AIDS.

Jaundice It is estimated that about 60% of full-term babies will become at least mildly jaundiced, and the problem is even commoner amongst premature and small babies. It is not dangerous as long as it is controlled, and can be treated either by phototherapy or exchange transfusion (see page 147).

Patent ductus arteriosus (PDA) Because he is not breathing air into his lungs and the blood does not need to pass through them to collect oxygen, an unborn baby's circulation is different from that after birth. With the first breath at birth, the circulation pattern changes and a large artery (the ductus), which has enabled most of the blood to circulate without passing through the lungs, closes. However, it is quite common in premature babies for the ductus to fail to close properly so that it is open or 'patent'. The doctor may tell you your baby has a heart murmur, meaning he can hear an unusual flow of blood when listening with a stethoscope. Usually the ductus closes of its own accord without treatment; if not, drugs may be prescribed to help it close and sometimes surgery is required.

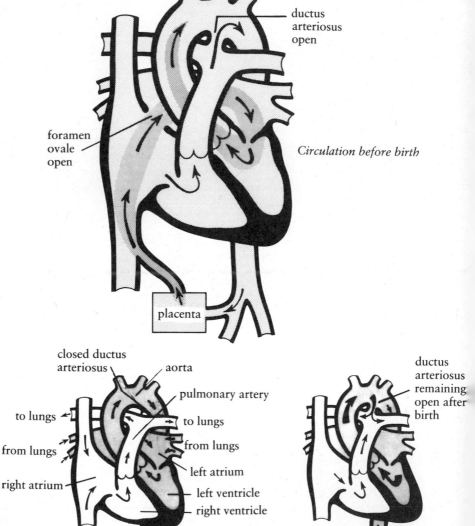

ductus arteriosus open

foramen ovale open

Circulation before birth

placenta

closed ductus arteriosus

aorta

pulmonary artery

to lungs

to lungs

from lungs

from lungs

right atrium

left atrium

left ventricle

right ventricle

ductus arteriosus remaining open after birth

Normal heart

Patent ductus arteriosus

THE PREMATURE BABY'S BRAIN

All parents of sick and premature babies worry about the risk of their child's brain being damaged. The brain tissue is made up of two halves or hemispheres in the middle of which are ventricles which are normally filled with a clear watery fluid (cerebro-spinal fluid or CSF). Because a premature baby's brain is soft and the tissues fragile, it is easy for blood vessels lining the base of the ventricles to burst, and a small amount of blood to leak into the ventricles (an intra-ventricular haemorrhage or IVH). Very often the amount is small and the tissues heal naturally, but occasionally it can be more serious and carry a risk of damage. In each case your paediatrician will always discuss your baby's condition and what it means for his development.

Many units use ultrasound scans routinely to check the baby's brain is growing at the right rate, and to see if there is any excess fluid in the cavities or signs of bleeding. Sometimes a special type of X-ray called a CAT scan (computerised axial tomography) can be used instead.

Fits are quite common in newborn babies, even if they are full-term, and can be due to biochemical imbalances such as hypoglycaemia (low blood sugar) or hypocalcaemia (calcium deficiency) as well as more serious reasons such as infection. Although fits alarm and upset parents, it is important to remember they do happen often with ill or premature babies and in many cases do not mean permanent damage. Your paediatrician will examine your baby carefully and carry out tests to try to find a cause.

TWINS – AND MORE

Twins are a common sight in special care units because the size the uterus has to stretch to in order to accommodate two babies makes premature birth or low birthweight more likely. As a rule, the greater the number of babies, the more premature the birth is likely to be, so triplets and the far rarer cases of quadruplets or quintuplets are certain to need some degree of special care. The same rule applies to the size of the babies. Twins tend to be smaller than single babies after about 32 weeks, and triplets after 28 weeks. One twin or triplet may be smaller and weaker, and the difference can sometimes be so great that one baby may need intensive care while the other scarcely needs extra attention at all. Usually the difference in size evens out, though very small-for-dates babies can remain smaller into adult life. If possible, units will keep both twins in until they can go home together, but if one baby has to stay for a long time this may not always be feasible.

All the difficulties already described apply in the same way if the babies are small or premature, but an additional problem is that blood can sometimes have crossed the placenta to pass between twins or triplets so that one may be anaemic (too few red blood cells) and very pale, while the other is polycythaemic (too many red blood cells) and a dark red colour. Fortunately this is treatable and your paediatrician will explain how if this has happened to your babies.

THE FUTURE FOR SPECIAL CARE BABIES

DEVELOPMENT

Your baby's age will always be taken from the day he was born, but his development for the first year or two will usually match more closely the dates he should have been born. It is important to bear this in mind when it comes to the milestones of development – sitting, crawling, walking and talking. Parents of premature babies often fear their child may have been damaged, despite reassurances from doctors, and they can feel particularly anxious when their child fails to do things at the 'right' age. If they make allowances for the baby's prematurity they will find their child is developing quite normally. The differences between the baby's true developmental and calendar (chronological) age will be most marked in the first two or three years but obviously all children are different. When it comes to starting school, your child will usually begin around his fifth birthday and by this time most premature babies are right in line with their peers developmentally.

The hospital will continue to ask you to come back for further checks for some time. There is nothing sinister about this. Some premature babies can suffer a degree of short-sightedness or a squint, slight clumsiness, smaller stature, slight deafness and slower development. These are in the minority, and such handicaps will not impair the child's quality of life. But some handicaps, like sight, need treatment to remedy the problem, and hospital specialists who know what to look for are best placed to do this. In addition, your baby will have the normal developmental and health checks at the local clinic. Always mention your child's start in life to the doctor or health visitor making the assessment.

IMMUNISATION

Premature babies should be fully immunised in the usual way starting at three months after the birth, whatever their gestation. Almost all can be immunised against whooping cough except for those who have had fits. As there are now major epidemics of whooping cough at regular intervals, this protection should be given whenever possible. If you have any doubts about this discuss it with your doctor.

A baby who has been in special care may be slightly more likely to develop infections than a healthy, full-term baby and so it is wise to keep him away from anyone with an obvious infection. It is important, though, that your other children play with and get to know their new baby brother or sister and they should be encouraged to hold him as much as possible.

PARENTS' REACTIONS TO PREMATURE BIRTH

Giving birth weeks or months before you expected to, producing a baby who may weigh only a quarter of what he should and who needs all the paraphernalia of highly technical medical care to survive is the most colossal shock. Every parent's story will be different, but it may help to recognise how common some reactions are. Often there is an overwhelming sense of loss – perhaps because they feel one of the most important events in their lives, and something which they have planned and looked forward to has 'gone wrong'. Parents may also feel a sense of loss because the baby looks so very different from the one they imagined. The disappointment continues with the realisation of what lies ahead. Instead of the triumphant return home with their baby, mothers very often have to leave hospital alone. This increases their isolation because their life as parents with a baby only seems to exist within the hospital. Neighbours and friends cannot share the experience or see them in their new role. Anger is another common reaction – with the baby, with themselves or with the hospital. Again, there is the sense of being cheated out of their expectations.

Leaving the baby in hospital when you go home is one of the hardest times – anger may turn to depression and a sense of unreality. Try to regard this time as an opportunity to rest and get yourself fit so that you will be better able to look after your baby when he does come home. Women often feel it is their fault their baby was born too early or too small. They may feel they have disappointed their partners, parents or put an extra burden on their other children by having a baby who needs so much more of their time and attention and takes them away from home for so long. This guilt can surface strongly at later times in their baby's life if he encounters setbacks, even though these are probably quite unrelated to his start in life.

Putting these feelings into words does help, as well as talking to unit staff and other parents. In all cases it is very important for couples to talk to each other about how they feel. Parents may also worry very much that their child will survive but be seriously mentally or physically handicapped. They feel frightened to say that in that case they would rather he or she did not survive, for fear of sounding callous and selfish. Parents need to be allowed to talk about these worries and be helped to understand exactly what it would mean if it seems likely that their child will have some disability. Where there is a possibility of serious handicap doctors will counsel parents as honestly as they can. Medical staff will not take part in euthanasia, but it is important that they know parents' feelings when making decisions about treatment of very sick babies. Always discuss such anxieties with your consultant or senior registrar. When mothers cannot touch and hold their baby freely they often feel jealous to see nurses so apparently in control. Moreover, parents can get on better with some members of the unit staff than with others. It helps to remember that caring for such tiny babies with the intensive care they need is highly pressurised work. Having parents so close to the staff, questioning every move, increases the tension. Trust is needed on both sides, and this is best arrived at by talking.

It might seem that the time when your baby finally does come home should be one of the happiest, after all the strain of seeing him ill and in hospital. Yet, surprisingly, mothers can frequently find this a very difficult period. They may feel low, depressed, weepy, lethargic and have difficulty picking up the threads of life again. Generally, the drama and the crisis of the birth, followed by weeks of uncertainty, have kept them going. Back home there is a chance for all the feelings they have kept at bay to flood in on them. Partners and other relatives can sometimes find this hard to understand and their impatience and even lack of understanding can make things worse. It may help to know that this is in fact a very common reaction. Don't forget that mothers of first babies often find it hard to adjust to life with a child anyway. Take things slowly and don't expect to slot immediately into a different way of life without any hitches.

Understandably, parents who have seen their babies needing expert care to survive will feel even more uncertain of their abilities to look after their baby at home than the parents of normal babies, but remember that all new parents feel nervous and uncertain in the early days. Many hospitals try to arrange for parents to come in and stay a night or two with the baby in the room with them before they go home. If possible, arrange for your partner to take time off so that you can both share your baby's first days at home.

When you leave hospital you may be given medicines and some vitamins in the form of drops of syrup. Premature babies are sometimes prescribed iron as well if they are anaemic. Although each bottle will be carefully labelled, it is a good idea to write out exactly what he is having on a separate piece of paper so that you can let other doctors (GP or clinic) know if necessary. The hospital will tell you how to give them, but it helps to make a chart of exactly what has to be given and when and tick off each dose through the day. Giving tiny babies a number of exact doses by spoon can be surprisingly hard, but you can get a plastic medicine measure from chemists and hospital pharmacies.

When you first come home you may find your baby needs feeding every three hours or so because he cannot take as much milk at each feed as larger babies can. Usually, he will also need night feeds for some weeks after coming home. Soon he will be able to take larger feeds and need to be fed less often. He will be ready to begin solids about four months from the date when he was due to be born. Some babies are ready for mixed feeding much earlier than others, and you will soon realise when he is not satisfied with milk alone. Your health visitor will advise at this time.

BABIES WHO MAY NOT LIVE

Parents can often be frightened to allow themselves to love their premature or sick baby because they are afraid he will not live. By withdrawing from him in anticipation of the death, they feel they will lessen the pain of losing him when it actually happens. Sometimes they have an almost superstitious feeling that if they invest their love in him it will be tempting fate. For these reasons they may be reluctant to see, to touch or allow themselves to feel close to their baby. Women may also feel very ambivalent about deciding to express milk — dreading to build up a supply of milk which will be such a real reminder of their loss if the baby does not live.

Experience has shown that holding back from loving a baby does not help to make his death any easier to accept. It used to be thought that playing down the loss of a baby could help to minimise the distress of parents, but we now know that doing this can deny parents the road to recovery — the opportunity to grieve. The process of mourning and grieving the loss of a child or someone close to us is very necessary, as anyone who has already experienced the death of a loved friend or relation will know. It is easier for parents to grieve for a baby they have known and loved, however short his life, than for a baby they never knew or tried to deny. There can be consolation in knowing you are giving your baby everything, and that he died surrounded by love. Suppressing that love can often lead to guilt later. Inevitably, some babies whose chance of life seemed very slim do in fact survive. If the parents have already withdrawn in anticipation of the baby's death, this can make it hard for them to reverse those feelings and to form a loving relationship with their child later.

Despite enormous increases in our knowledge and skill, some babies are still destined to live for only a short period of time. Some are born simply too soon to allow them to survive outside their mother. Occasionally a baby may be born prematurely because his body or brain has not developed normally and, as a result, he may be unable to live the usual length of time. In a few cases babies born after a very difficult pregnancy, labour, or delivery have suffered so much that they are not able to survive. Sometimes a baby is born with damage to his brain or body, and the severity of this is not immediately obvious. In all these cases, the baby may remain alive only with the aid of machines. When it becomes clear to everyone — the parents, doctors and nurses — that he will not survive without their aid, you may all agree that the help of the machines may be withdrawn. Often, for the first time in his short life, the baby can then be held and cared for by those who love him, without all the tubes and drips and monitors. Some parents may like to have a photograph taken of their baby at this point.

The death of a baby has a profound effect on all of those who cared for him. This is a time when parents need help from many different people — from each other, their family and friends, hospital staff, religious leaders and sometimes from others who have suffered similarly. Each one of us reacts differently, and some people find that they behave completely unlike their normal selves. It takes a long time to recover, you will never forget your baby, and no matter how many other children you may have afterwards, this baby will always be entitled to a very special place in your heart.

The funeral arrangements have to be made. Often there is a special member of the hospital staff who tells parents where to register the baby's death and how to obtain the services of an undertaker. If the baby's body is to be cremated, this can also be arranged. Help can also be given with any other problems and queries. The family doctor will be informed of the baby's death and parents are often helped by discussing it with him as well as with hospital doctors who were more intimately involved with his care. In many hospitals it is usual to ask if the baby's body may be examined after death in order to determine the exact cause of death and to help other babies with similar problems. At Great Ormond Street parents are asked to come back some weeks later when all the results of the examination are available and we explain why we believe their baby died. At this time parents often ask many questions because they have had some time to think about what has happened, and we try to answer them as fully and as accurately as we can.

The loss of a child, no matter how premature or small, is such a major event that in years to come you must expect to feel the pain more acutely on anniversary dates or around the same time of year. It is important to realise that this is not abnormal, but part of the very human process of mourning.

COT DEATH (SUDDEN INFANT DEATH SYNDROME)

This is the term given to the sudden and unexpected death of a baby which is not linked to any clear-cut cause, such as premature birth. Babies involved are almost always aged between one month and a year, with the highest incidence between four and six months. In the UK it is the commonest cause of death during the period, claiming two to three lives amongst every thousand babies.

Most typically the baby is found dead at home either first thing in the morning or after a period, often very brief, of being left alone in its cot or pram. 'Near miss' cot deaths where someone notices a baby has stopped breathing and resuscitates it by picking it up or shaking it also happen. In such instances parents should take the baby to an accident and emergency unit immediately.

Doctors do not understand why babies die like this, but it is thought that the baby stops breathing as a result of a wide range of different infective, circulatory, biochemical and immunological abnormalities. In about a third of cases there is a story of mild respiratory symptoms – runny nose or slight cough perhaps – in the previous two to three days.

Most recent research shows that babies should be put to sleep on their backs or side, not on their tummies. Smoking during pregnancy and after increases the risk of cot death. It is best if no one smokes in the house and you should try not to take your baby into smokey places. Babies should not be allowed to get too hot or too cold. Indoors, babies do not need more clothes than their parents, although they do need protection from draughts and need more clothes than adults outdoors. An ideal room temperature for a baby is 18°C (65°F). If your baby is unwell he may need less clothes (see page 542) and if he is sleeping a lot it is a good idea to wake him regularly for a drink and to check how he is. If you are worried contact your doctor – see page 517.

The shock to parents whose baby dies suddenly and inexplicably is obviously profound. They should be given the opportunity to see and hold their baby after death has been confirmed and they will need support to deal with the necessary official enquiries and funeral arrangements. Afterwards unequivocal strong support from their GP and health visitor is very important, as is a full explanation of the condition and some idea of possible causes. If a paediatrician has been involved in the care of the baby, it may be helpful to talk to him. Parents at first experience disbelief followed by deep grief – see page 199 for more discussion on the process of mourning. Some feel guilt that they were not present when their baby died, as though their absence was some kind of neglect. Many feel angry and this can be directed at each other, at professionals who had previously seen the child or even other children they may have. Friends and relatives need to allow the parents to talk and in some cases parents may need further counselling or psychiatric help.

All parents fear a cot death, and parents who have already lost a child in this way will be acutely anxious. There has been considerable debate about the value of home apnoea monitors (see page 285) which are special mattresses linked to an alarm which sounds if the baby stops breathing. The Foundation for the Study of Infant Deaths has an excellent supply of information leaflets (see address section, pages 673–6).

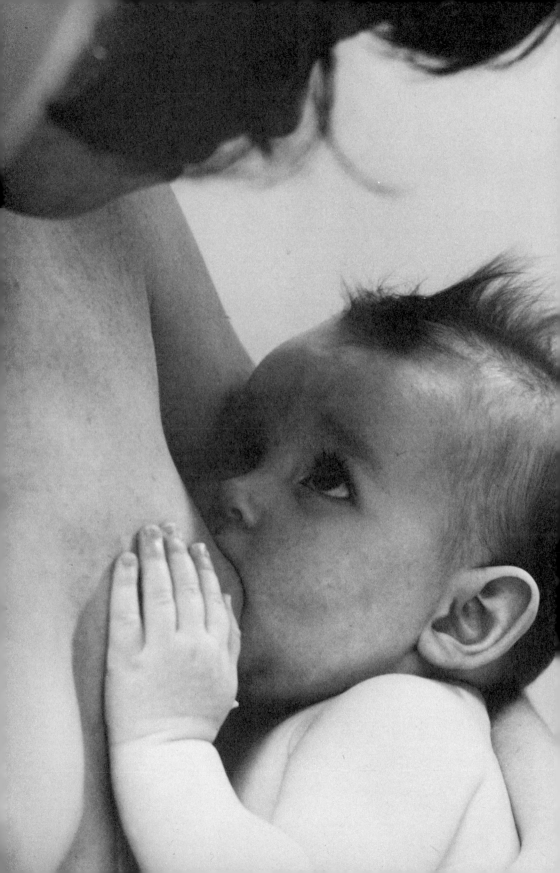

Chapter 6

FEEDING YOUR BABY

The big decision – breast or bottle?
Home truths about breast and bottle-feeding
Women who are not able to breastfeed
Women who do not want to breastfeed   Breasts and breastfeeding
Expressing and storing milk   Going back to work
Breastfeeding problems for mothers   Giving up breastfeeding
Breastfeeding problems for babies   Bottles and bottle-feeding
Vitamin supplements   Feeding second and subsequent babies
Problems with early feeding   Weaning   Eating out
Food intolerance

Many emotions are bound up in the whole business of preparing and giving food. Eating is not simply about taking enough fuel on board. In the beginning sucking milk is a source of great pleasure for a new baby, and feeding the baby is also a source of much satisfaction and enjoyment for a mother. Later, taking trouble to give a child or an adult what we think is something nice to eat is a way of showing love and affection – even if it is only a sandwich with a favourite filling. The flip side of the coin is that getting that food rejected – whatever the age of your baby or child – can feel like a very personal kick in the teeth for the giver. It is not surprising that most new parents have the occasional worry about the way their baby or child is feeding, nor is it surprising that later in life mealtimes are so often the setting for family battles!

The best advice for a new mother is to relax and enjoy feeding your baby in the way that gives you both the greatest pleasure – and later, as he grows into a toddler with the whole wide world to explore, don't take offence when the food you offer fails to hold the same fascination for him. By now both of you will have discovered a whole host of other ways of showing and sharing your love together.

THE BIG DECISION – BREAST OR BOTTLE?

At some stage early in your pregnancy you will be asked how you plan to feed your baby. The best food for babies to start life with is breast milk. It is

203

perfectly designed to meet their every need, has unique properties which can never be copied in formula feeds, and the act of breastfeeding itself helps form a close, emotional bond between baby and mother. But, having said that, very few women approach the subject with an open mind and objectively weigh up the pros and cons of breast versus bottle-feeding before making a decision. Our ideas on the subject have actually begun to take shape much earlier in life, and by the time we get to be mothers ourselves our attitudes can be deep-rooted. How you and your brothers and sisters were fed, what your partner thinks about breastfeeding, how your friends feed their babies, and how you feel about your body are factors which are far more likely to draw you towards either breast or bottle-feeding than the basic facts.

When it comes to weighing up the nutritional and emotional advantages of breast or bottle-feeding, breastfeeding is preferable. It is right, therefore, to state the case for breastfeeding and to encourage it, except in those few circumstances when it is not medically indicated. However, in the end, mothers must choose what is right for *them*. A woman who dislikes the idea of breastfeeding but is persuaded into it against her real feelings, or forces herself out of a sense of guilt, will not in fact necessarily be doing the best thing for her baby. Most important of all is that you should feel relaxed and able to enjoy your new baby in a way which suits you best. As long as you take care that feeding is always a time for quiet closeness and for comfort between you both, you will be doing the best whether you are breast or bottle-feeding.

THE DIFFERENCES BETWEEN BREAST MILK AND COW'S MILK

Breast milk contains:

Water in just the right amount to satisfy your baby's thirst so breastfed babies do not need extra drinks.

Protein for body building, again in just the right amount and in a form most readily absorbed. Colostrum and early milk have higher levels of protein and so does the milk of mothers of premature babies (see page 186). The protein is quickly digested and is vital for a baby's growth.

Fat for energy and growth. Breast milk contains more fat than cow's milk, yet it is more easily and completely absorbed by babies. This is one of many reasons why breastfed babies have different stools from bottle-fed babies (loose, without smell and yellow or mustard colour): they are not excreting any wasted fats. There is a higher concentration of essential fatty acids in breast milk and it has been suggested that the unsaturated fats may be important for the growth of the baby's brain and nervous system.

Carbohydrate in the form of lactose or milk sugar is an extremely important source of energy. Breast milk naturally contains more than cow's milk.

Vitamins and minerals are essential in the right amounts for your baby's health and development. As long as you eat an adequate diet that includes sufficient calories, water and some fresh fruit and vegetables, your milk will contain all your baby's vitamin and mineral requirements.

Protection from infection is contained in antibodies and iron-binding protein which make the baby's intestine far less vulnerable to bacteria and also give protection against a number of serious illnesses. Gastro-enteritis is unusual in breastfed babies.

Cow's milk contains:

Everything for a healthy calf, but it has to be changed in several ways before it can safely be given to babies under six months old. The same applies to goat's milk and sheep's milk which are even less suitable for babies.

Water content in formula feeds cannot change to suit the baby in the way breast milk can, so bottle-fed babies need extra drinks of boiled water, either from a bottle or a sterilised spoon.

Protein levels in cow's milk are three times higher than in breast milk, are of a different type and are less digestible. Giving this 'foreign' protein to some babies may cause allergic reactions (see page 253). The protein is diluted to a safe level in formula feeds, but this lowers the calorie content of the feed. Lactose must be added to give extra calories.

Fat in cow's milk is far less easily absorbed and again of a different type.

Carbohydrate has to be added to cow's milk in the form of lactose (milk sugar) to make up the same energy value as breast milk. So although natural cow's milk has less lactose, formula feeds end up containing the same amount as breast milk.

Vitamins and minerals are present in cow's milk, but not in the right amount for a baby. There are three or four times as much sodium (salt), potassium, calcium and chloride in cow's milk as in breast milk and six times as much phosphorus – another reason for having to dilute it before it can be used for babies. The iron and zinc in cow's milk is less well absorbed. Some vitamins in cow's milk are destroyed by processing and have to be added again artificially.

Protection from infection in the form of antibodies is not present and cannot be added artificially.

THE ADVANTAGES OF BREASTFEEDING

Breast milk is the perfect food for a baby with just the right amount of fat, protein, carbohydrate, vitamin and minerals ready-made, served at just the right temperature and in an ideal container! The composition of milk changes as the baby feeds in a way bottle-feeds never can: milk at the beginning of a feed, the foremilk, has fewer calories and satisfies thirst; the second part is the hindmilk which is released with the let-down reflex. It is richer in calories and satisfies his hunger. It is thought that this change may be important in producing a sense of fullness and controlling appetite. Milk also changes as the baby grows – colostrum and early milk have more protein and the milk of mothers of premature babies is also known to be different (see page 185).

Protection from infection is provided by antibodies and iron-binding protein which lines the baby's gut.

Protection from allergy Families with a history of asthma, eczema, rhinitis and so on are especially advised to breastfeed as a baby's immature immune system can react to the strong foreign protein in cow's milk by producing allergic symptoms.

Less likelihood of obesity because breastfed babies are able to follow the demands of their appetite more easily.

Easier digestion Breast milk is tailor-made for the newborn baby's still immature system. Some breastfed babies have a dirty nappy after every feed, but it is also common for a totally breastfed baby to have a bowel movement only once every five or even up to ten days because there is so little waste to excrete.

Much greater convenience There are no worries about infection, or keeping or carrying milk when travelling, including trips abroad. Night feeds are easier because it just means taking the baby into bed, and not having to get up to warm bottles. Breast milk is instantly supplied, and there are no tense waits for milk to warm while the baby screams. It leaves a free hand to cuddle or help another child or even pick up the phone. The convenience of breastfeeding increases the longer you carry on – the most difficult time is during the early weeks, but soon giving a feed just means sitting down for ten to twenty minutes, and there is no work at the end of the day with bottles to sterilise and make up.

An instant pacifier which can be a boon at awkward moments to calm a young baby who is frightened or upset.

Helps you return to shape because hormones stimulated in breastfeeding also help contract the uterus to its pre-pregnancy size and end post-natal discharge more quickly. Full or frequent breastfeeding usually delays the return of periods, a plus if you suffer from pre-menstrual tension or heavy or painful periods. Weight loss in response to feeding varies – some women lose weight more easily because of feeding, while others do not lose it until they finish. Nevertheless, stores of fat are laid down in pregnancy for the body to use when making milk and these can sometimes be harder to shift if you do not breastfeed, especially round the thighs. However, you should not try to slim while breastfeeding.

Money saving Even though feeding mothers need to eat more, about 500 extra calories a day, the cost of extra food is still less than that of formula food for the baby, bottles, teats and all the sterilising gear.

Emotional benefits for mother and baby Although this is listed last, it is not because it is the least important factor, but because it deserves more detailed consideration. As we have already mentioned, newborn babies need physical love and affection to thrive just as much as clean nappies and warm cots. Being held, cuddled, enjoying the sensation of skin contact and the feel of the human body comforts and reassures babies so they begin to relax, to uncurl and to respond to that love. Breastfeeding a baby is the closest physical bond between a mother and her child and combines all the sensations that give babies pleasure. Taking in food is one, but just as important is sucking – a source of great satisfaction and enjoyment to a baby.

Breastfed babies tend to be able to suck for longer and to control how long they continue, and sucking at a warm, responsive nipple is more rewarding than a rubber teat. Combining feeding, sucking, skin contact and being held and cuddled all adds up to bliss in baby terms!

All the time during a feed there is continual interaction between mother and baby – 'emotional feedback' is usually how it is described. The way the baby sucks, moves his hands, arms, body and the expression on his face tell the mother what he is feeling and needing and she responds. Most women who breastfeed for some time rate this harmony and closeness with their baby as what they enjoyed most. There can also be a physical pleasure for women in breastfeeding but that is highly individual and varies between just a physical satisfaction at being able to provide milk for the baby and the close contact, through all sorts of reactions to the women who find breastfeeding sexually exciting. Certainly the sexual attitudes of both men and women influence how they regard breastfeeding – some think it is beautiful, some disgusting, and some just a natural bodily function designed for feeding babies. You don't have to be someone who enjoys having their breasts stimulated in love-making to be able to enjoy breastfeeding, and it is quite possible for women who don't like having their nipples caressed at all to be able to enjoy breastfeeding and do it very successfully.

HOME TRUTHS ABOUT BREAST AND BOTTLE-FEEDING

* The most difficult part of breastfeeding is usually the beginning. After that it gets easier and easier.

* It may take two weeks to establish breastfeeding and another four weeks for the baby and the supplier to settle into a pattern – the feeding habits of bottle-fed babies will be just as erratic at first.

* Beginning to sleep through the night depends on the baby, not on whether he is breast or bottle-fed.

* Mothers who want to breastfeed but run into difficulties should get help

from a breastfeeding counsellor or community or hospital midwife who favours breastfeeding and is experienced. Most problems can be overcome or avoided.

* Mothers who switch from breast to bottle because they want to should not have to pretend it was because of problems, but rather congratulate themselves on breastfeeding at the beginning, even if it was only for a few days.

* Caring, sensitive mothers who have to or who want to bottle-feed will make sure they have just as close and loving a relationship with their baby.

* Similarly, women who have serious problems in becoming a mother and how they feel about their baby will rarely make things right just by forcing themselves to breastfeed.

WOMEN WHO ARE NOT ABLE TO BREASTFEED

There will be some women who cannot breastfeed, either because they are seriously ill, or have to take certain drugs or have a mentally or physically handicapped baby where breastfeeding is either impossible or very difficult without enormous dedication and support.

There will also be a larger group of women who begin breastfeeding and sadly give up because they run into problems, although many of these problems can be avoided or solved with the right advice and help. Recurrent bouts of infective mastitis or breast abscesses, or babies who, despite all your attempts to build up a supply of milk, fail to gain weight, or even lose weight, may in the end lead to partial or wholly bottle-feeding.

Finally, there will be women who feel very strongly that they do not want to try breastfeeding.

Women in all these categories should not feel they are giving their baby second best by bottle-feeding. Instead they can be confident in the knowledge that today there are good alternatives to breast milk which are used to feed babies safely and successfully. In addition, while it is felt that an emotional closeness happens automatically with breastfeeding, it takes only a little thought to foster a rapport between you and your baby during bottle-feeding. Many mothers will do this quite instinctively anyway.

ILLNESS

Serious illness in a mother may make breastfeeding impossible or undesirable. If you are ill and cannot feed, but want to try once you have recovered, you will still be able to produce milk, despite the delay, by putting the baby to the breast as frequently as possible. In general, the longer the interval after the birth, the longer it can take to build up a supply of milk, and if it is several weeks you may never have enough to breastfeed fully. Nevertheless, your baby can still benefit from your milk and you can enjoy the closeness of breastfeeding. If he won't suck at the breast because he has got used to a bottle, use a device called the Lact-Aid: this is a bag containing formula feed which hangs round your neck with a tube from the bag lying alongside your nipple, so the baby stimulates the breast, gets used to sucking at the nipple and still takes his feed at the same time. As your milk comes in, you can gradually reduce the amount of formula. Alternatively, you can use a breast pump to express your milk and stimulate your milk supply after the feeds. Use the expressed milk for your baby at another feeding time – it can be kept in the fridge for twenty-four hours or frozen.

DRUGS

Drugs which a mother takes are probably always excreted to some extent in breast milk, although in many cases the amounts are so minute they have no effect. As a general rule, breastfeeding mothers should try to avoid taking any drugs at all, but if they are needed, always discuss with the doctor prescribing whether they are suitable.

PREMATURE OR SICK BABIES

These babies may not be able to suck, but you can express milk to be frozen or fed to them through a tube until they are strong enough to feed (see chapter 5).

HANDICAPPED BABIES

These babies present two kinds of problem as regards breastfeeding. The first is the tremendous shock parents feel on giving birth to such a baby and the complicated emotions they may experience. Breastfeeding represents a long-term commitment which initially they may feel unable to cope with. The second set of problems are of a practical nature. Mentally handicapped babies have poor sucking reflexes and may be drowsy, and it needs dedication from the mother and good support and advice to breastfeed. Physically handicapped babies who are not brain damaged can normally suck well enough to breastfeed, but treatment which may entail operations and possibly splints, plaster or traction will mean breaks in breastfeeding when you have to express milk and then feed the baby who may not be able to be picked up or handled. Mothers have and do manage to breastfeed babies in such circumstances, and it is obviously a source of great comfort to a baby who is having to undergo treatment. The paediatrician should outline exactly what the treatment entails to help mothers make a decision, and good support, advice and encouragement is needed.

Abnormalities of the mouth will sometimes make feeding difficult, although a straightforward cleft lip should not produce any problems and mothers can usually feed babies with cleft palate too, provided again they get the necessary help (see page 627). It is only when a large area of the roof of the mouth is unformed that the baby has difficulty sucking and may need to be fed expressed breast milk or formula from a spoon. But even though cleft lips and palates can be most successfully repaired, the trauma of giving birth to a child with this problem can be quite as great for parents as in cases of more severe handicap, and the decision to breastfeed may often depend on the handling and counselling given at the time of the birth as much as on the degree of handicap.

FAILURE TO THRIVE

There will be some babies who do not gain weight, or even begin to lose weight despite all efforts, including extra breastfeeds and checking on techniques to increase the supply of breast milk. For more on changing from breast to bottle-feeding see page 227.

CONTINUAL PROBLEMS

If a woman has continual problems with breastfeeding in the way of abscesses, repeated cracked nipples, or mastitis, these may be related to the breastfeeding technique, so advice from an experienced midwife or breast-feeding counsellor is advisable in the first instance. Occasionally it may be necessary or preferable to switch to bottles.

WOMEN WHO DO NOT WANT TO BREASTFEED

'I dutifully breastfed my son for six months and even collected the drips from the non-feeding side to donate to the hospital milk bank. I hated every minute. I only did it because all my friends did and I was terrified of being branded a bad mother. In fact I did have real problems about becoming a mother and couldn't cuddle or show affection to my son at all. Thankfully, with professional help, that is now solved, but I was desperately embarrassed about feeding and no one except my parents or my husband ever saw me do it. I couldn't even feed my baby at a mothers' tea afternoon when everyone else was feeding their babies.'

Women who do not want to breastfeed will make this decision for a variety of reasons. What their partners, friends and families think about breast-feeding is certainly going to influence their decision. They may plan to return to work soon after the birth of the baby and leave him to be cared for by a child minder, mother's help or nanny, or in a day nursery. They may wish to share the feeding of the baby with their partner. Some women do not like the idea of being tied so closely to their baby, even in the early weeks. Women who have had successive pregnancies very close together can sometimes feel weary after a period of nothing but pregnancy and breastfeeding and be anxious for their bodies to get back to normal and belong to themselves exclusively again. Women with uncertain or unhappy partnerships can feel apprehensive at being tied and more vulnerable. Some women will feel repelled by the idea of breastfeeding, while others are open-minded about the physical act but very worried about the potential embarrassment of having to feed a baby in public. In fact this is, in practice, much less of a problem than many women imagine. Shops, restaurants and other public places can nearly always offer a room to use, and dressing in loose separates with a waistcoat, jacket or cardigan around your shoulders means you can feed a baby in a quiet corner without anyone noticing.

Women who feel positively repelled by the idea of breastfeeding may often find it helpful to talk over these feelings during pregnancy with their partner, a sympathetic breastfeeding counsellor or doctor they can trust who can help them understand why they feel so strongly while at the same time supporting them if their decision is to bottle-feed.

BREASTS AND BREASTFEEDING

THE BREAST

The breast is made up of fifteen to twenty segments – imagine an orange cut in half. The cells which make the milk, alveoli, lie at the back of the segments and have ducts leading down to the nipple. Just before the ducts open on to the nipple they enlarge slightly to form a reservoir. These reservoirs are at the point where the normal skin of the breast darkens into the pigmented ring around the nipple, the areola. Small glands in the areola called 'Montgomery's tubercles' produce a fluid that keeps the skin of the nipples and the areola soft and supple. The nipple has not just one opening, but several, which vary in number according to the number of segments and ducts of the breast. The size of breast does

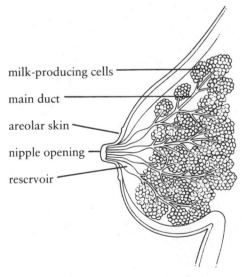

milk-producing cells

main duct

areolar skin

nipple opening

reservoir

not dictate its ability to produce milk – small ones can be just as efficient as large ones.

During pregnancy breasts become much larger as they prepare to make milk because of an increase in the milk-producing cells and ducts and a greater blood supply, but they do not actually begin to make milk until stimulated by a complex hormone reaction after birth.

Colostrum is the creamy, yellowish substance that is made before the breasts begin to manufacture mature milk. Unlike milk, this is made during pregnancy, and from about the fifth month and towards the end of pregnancy may leak from the nipple a little – it is not significant whether this does or does not happen. Giving your baby colostrum at the start of his life is important. Even if you do nothing more than breastfeed for those first two or three days you will still have given him something valuable that cannot be artificially reproduced. Colostrum is uniquely designed for the transition your baby makes from placental feeding, when the nourishment he needs is carried in the blood supply through the umbilical cord, to digesting food himself. Colostrum is low in sugar and fat, so it is easier for a baby's immature digestive system to cope with as it gently begins working. It also contains more protein than mature milk and has higher levels of antibodies. These protect the baby from bacterial infection, and this is perhaps the most valuable role of colostrum. It will also give protection from illnesses the mother has had or been immunised against. Colostrum goes on being produced for about ten days after the birth, but after about three days it begins to be mixed with mature milk which makes the milk seem creamier. Once the colostrum stops, breast milk on its own seems thinner and watery but do not think your own milk has become 'poorer' because this is its natural consistency.

Mature milk is usually present in the breast around the third day after the birth. Although the breasts have been ready to make milk since about the middle of pregnancy, it is actually the birth itself which acts as the trigger to milk production and this happens whether you plan to breast-feed or not. A drop in the hormones progesterone and oestrogen take the brake off, as it were, and cause more of the main hormone controlling milk supply to be produced – this is called prolactin. It is this hormone which starts the milk-producing cells working, although it takes a couple of days for the first milk to appear. This mechanism also operates in the case of miscarriage or stillbirth, because your body has no way of knowing there is no baby to feed, and can be very distressing, especially if a woman is not warned in advance. In the case of a live birth, it is the baby sucking at the breast which stimulates more prolactin and so 'orders up' more milk for the next feed.

Breast milk changes during a feed, from day to day and as the baby grows (see page 205). Your health, what you eat and drink, and even your feelings can also change the composition and quantity of milk. As mentioned, early colostrum and milk is higher in protein and antibodies than mature milk, but we still do not know all the ingredients of breast milk nor exactly how the composition changes as the baby grows.

Suckling after delivery has been shown to be a key factor in successful breastfeeding. Women who are able to put their baby to the breast within twelve hours of the birth and, even better, within four hours or as close to delivery as possible, are more likely to be able to breastfeed successfully and to continue longer. But if, for some reason, you cannot do this, it does not mean you won't be able to feed (see page 225 on Caesarean mothers and chapter 5 on babies in special care). The emotional and physical aspects of suckling after the birth are closely interwoven since milk production and the release of the milk are governed by hormones which are, in turn, affected by our emotions. The baby's suckling stimulates the nerve endings in the nipple. This sends messages to the brain to produce the hormones oxytocin and prolactin. These hormones make the uterus contract back to its normal size and get the milk-making cells in the breast working.

Supply and demand is the basic principle of successful breastfeeding. The more the baby sucks at the breast, the more milk the breast makes. In the beginning there may be too much milk and the baby's pattern of feeding will be erratic, but after two or three weeks this will settle down and as the baby grows your body will be able to match his needs by making just the right amount of milk, provided you let him feed whenever he is hungry.

PUTTING THE BABY TO THE BREAST

'I think men might imagine it's a natural instinct and you know exactly what to do. In fact I felt rather self-conscious and hadn't a clue how to get the baby fixed on. I was deeply grateful for a very helpful midwife who sat down and showed me exactly how. I was absolutely thrilled when my baby actually latched on and sucked. At first I still couldn't believe I was a mother and now here was this enormous, perfect baby, doing just what babies are supposed to do!'

If you can sit up, make yourself comfortable with pillows and hold the baby so his head is level with your breast; you can put pillows under him as well to support his weight. If you can't sit up you can still feed lying down and slightly turned to the side with the baby on the bed beside you (see advice for Caesarean mothers page 225). To help the baby suck properly without making you sore, put the whole nipple and part of the areola into his mouth with his tongue underneath so that the pressure of his jaws as he sucks is on the areola, not the nipple itself. The baby's father or a midwife can support the baby's head close to your breast and gently guide him into the right position. Touch your nipple or stroke your finger against the baby's cheek, and he will turn his head towards the breast – this is called 'rooting' – and open his mouth to take the nipple. If he does not open his mouth, touch your nipple against his bottom lip and then top lip – at this point you will need your helper to guide his head so that he takes the nipple fully deep into his mouth. If he is fixed on properly, the tops of his ears will

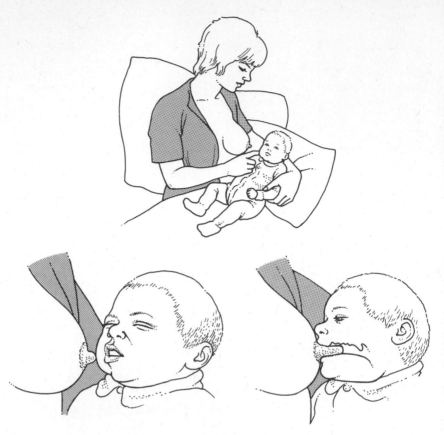

Putting the baby to the breast

wiggle slightly as he sucks. If this does not happen, and you can see his cheeks going in and out as he sucks, or it hurts, put the tip of your little finger gently into the corner of his mouth to break the suction and try again. Make sure when you are feeding your baby that he is able to breathe clearly through his nose. If you support your breast from underneath with the flat of your free hand against your ribs, this will direct your nipple and breast upwards into an easy feeding position for him.

A few hospitals may still recommend starting with two minutes each side and building up, but breastfeeding specialists now think this is not long enough to stimulate the let-down reflex. Instead they suggest following your and your baby's preference from the start. A rough guide is that a feed takes about twenty minutes, approximately ten minutes each side, although as a baby gets older and sucks more efficiently, he will take less time. You can tell when your baby begins to suck less vigorously and lose interest that it is time to swap him to the other breast. Babies are individuals and feed at different rates and your body responds differently too, but if each feed is taking much longer it is pretty certain that your baby is just enjoying comfort sucking, rather than feeding.

TAKING THE BABY OFF THE BREAST

Doing this the right way is just as important as fixing him on properly. Always break the suction first before withdrawing the nipple by sliding a finger-tip into the corner of his mouth – do not drag the nipple from his mouth while he is still sucking as this can cause soreness.

BABIES WHO WILL NOT SUCK

A baby who will not suck may simply need a little time and patience to get the idea. Loosen any wrappings while still keeping him warm and enjoy stroking his limbs, talking to him and generally discovering the delights of your new baby. Usually babies have a very alert, aware period immediately after the birth and they have a lot of new sensations to take in. Try him at the breast again when you feel like it and be relaxed about the whole business. If you have been expressing colostrum you can try putting a drop on his lips. If he seems very sleepy, let him sleep and try him again when he next wakes. If you had pethidine close to the time of delivery it can make your baby drowsy too and you may have to wait for the effects to wear off. Babies who are jaundiced are also sometimes slow to suck and fall asleep during feeds. Premature babies may not have had time to develop the sucking reflex of babies born at full term. Babies who have swallowed a lot of mucus during the birth may also be reluctant to feed. They may be sick, which will make them feel better: sometimes feeding water on a spoon or with a bottle can help them to bring up the mucus.

The paediatrician who gives your baby a full examination, usually the day after the birth, will ask about feeding so seek advice about any problems.

AFTER PAINS

These are caused by the womb contracting back to its pre-pregnancy size; they often happen during breastfeeding because this stimulates the hormone oxytocin which in turn causes the contractions. If they are very severe in the first days, take a painkiller half an hour before feeding.

WHICH SIDE FIRST?

Start on the breast you finished with at the last feed so that each side gets equal stimulation from your baby's stronger sucking at the beginning of a feed. When you change breasts sit your baby upright, supporting him with a hand behind his neck and thumb under his chin, and gently rub his back with your free hand to encourage him to bring up any wind. A muslin nappy is a good precaution as babies often bring up a little milk when they burp because the muscle that closes off the stomach is not yet very strong. If your baby does not bring up any wind, do not spend ages thumping him on the back, but carry on feeding.

FEED YOUR BABY WHENEVER HE SEEMS INTERESTED

If he wants to suck, you can be sure you are doing the right thing. He may wake and cry or just start to root around or make sucking movements with his mouth — you will quickly recognise the signs. At times this may be only half an hour after you last fed him, while at other times he may sleep deeply for much longer. Most babies gradually settle to a recognisable routine, and forcing a routine on them will only mean several hours with a miserable, crying baby.

WHEN THE MILK COMES IN

This is often the most difficult time because it usually causes some degree of engorgement and may coincide with a particularly emotional, weepy feeling around the third day. Signs are hard, swollen, hot breasts, with taut shiny skin and even some feverishness. 'I woke up with two rock-hard, aching boulders where my breasts should be — no one told me it would be like this,' is how one mother described it.

Don't panic if you do get very engorged because it really is a passing phase which never lasts more than twenty-four to forty-eight hours. The rest of breastfeeding is not at all like this. Engorgement at this stage is caused by a greatly increased supply of blood to the breast and it is thought that frequent suckling from birth can help to minimise this. The remedy is to feed the baby little and often to empty the breasts, and apply cold compresses or ice packs or spray the breasts with cold water to make the blood vessels contract and reduce swelling. Alternatively, try sitting in a warm bath and expressing the milk by hand.

Remember this does not last long and after this it all gets better! At some point, usually after about six weeks, your breasts will become smaller and softer — this is not a sign that you have no milk, rather that milk production has now settled down and is being made by the milk-producing cells but not filling the breasts until the baby starts to feed and stimulates the let-down reflex.

THE LET-DOWN REFLEX

This is stimulated by the hormone oxytocin and causes muscles to contract, squeezing milk out of the milk-producing cells into the ducts leading to the nipple. In fact the process will have been working before the milk came in, but is rarely felt. Once the milk comes in it is very important because although the baby can get what is called 'foremilk', which is present in the ducts of the breast, by sucking, two-thirds of the feed is contained in what is called 'hindmilk', which is only released by the let-down. The hindmilk has more fat in it and is therefore much richer in calories which your baby needs for growing.

The sensation of the let-down reflex varies, but is usually described as a tingling or slight ache and is always accompanied by a rush of milk. Usually milk begins to leak out of the non-feeding breast and you can see the rhythm of the baby's jaw action change as he begins to take deep swallows and does not have to suck so hard.

Problems with the let-down reflex are a common cause of babies not gaining weight and mothers of premature babies with a poor suck may be especially prone to difficulties. Anxiety, tension and stress can all inhibit the reflex so the circle gets worse. Try to relax and don't limit the baby's time at the breast, but continue to feed frequently. Bathing with hot water and expressing milk by hand can sometimes stimulate the let-down. You can also ask your GP or the hospital for a nasal spray of oxytocin which can be used effectively to prompt let-down – once the reflex has been experienced a few times the let-down will become easier.

COMPLEMENTARY BOTTLES

Complementary bottles can spell the beginning of the end of breastfeeding if you start giving them instead of letting the baby suck at the breast, or are too prompt to offer one as a 'top-up' without giving the baby enough time at the breast, because your supply will then decrease further. On the other hand, if the baby is driving you mad and won't settle and you feel completely shattered at the end of a day of apparently non-stop breastfeeding, then handing him over to your partner for the occasional bottle while you take time off to rest and relax can be a real life-saver. It is also useful to have a baby who will take a bottle if necessary to enable you to leave him sometimes. If you do not want to risk formula feed because of the possibility of allergy, you can express and freeze your own milk for bottle-feeds (see pages 219–22). Some babies accept breast or bottle equally well, others will take only the breast, or get used to bottle-feeding in hospital and will not switch easily to breastfeeding. 'Natural' nipple-shaped teats are available and have been suggested as more suitable for breastfed babies when they have the occasional bottle.

Cutting out complementary bottles can be done, but you need to be determined and prepared to accept a more unsettled feeding pattern for a few days. Aim to build up your milk supply as described on page 213 by putting the baby to the breast often and letting him suck as long as he wants. At the same time, try to get extra rest, take in plenty of fluids and eat well. Give the bottle after breastfeeds. Decrease the bottle-feed by half an ounce per feed per day until you have dropped all the complementary feeds. Alternatively, leave out the bottle at the feed when you have most milk, usually first thing in the morning. Continue to feed often during the rest of the day, but two days later drop the next bottle. Allow a week to make the change-over if you have been giving a top-up bottle at every feed. Alternatively, if you have been giving only one or two extra bottle-feeds you can try setting two days aside for nothing but feeding whenever your baby seems hungry and abandon bottles straight away – your milk supply will quickly catch up with your baby's demands in about forty-eight hours.

FOOD REQUIREMENTS OF BREASTFEEDING MOTHERS

Breastfeeding mothers need extra food and should eat regularly, with nutritious snacks between meals. During pregnancy stores of fat are especially laid down to be used to produce milk and in the early weeks you also need about 500 extra calories a day to offset the 600 or 800 calories a day your baby may be taking. Your appetite will usually be the best guide because breastfeeding invariably makes you hungry as well as thirsty — it is advisable to have a glass of water or fruit juice on hand while breastfeeding as some women get an overwhelming thirst then.

Examples of 500 calories are: a meal of meat, potatoes and vegetables; scrambled egg on two slices of toast with butter or margarine plus a rasher of bacon; one round of ham, or peanut butter or cheese sandwiches plus a yoghurt; a large slice of cake with a glass of milk. Breastfeeding is often a time when you can get away with the occasional indulgence in the cream cake or chocolate line, but do not rely too heavily on sugary and fatty foods to provide the extra calories as they have little nutritional value. As feeding is established, your body uses up fewer extra calories so you can gradually go back to normal eating, but still beware of going for long periods without food: this will affect your milk supply. What you should aim for is small amounts of nourishing food at regular intervals.

NOT HAVING ENOUGH MILK

This is a common worry among breastfeeding mothers. There are three rules to follow to build up your supply: feed your baby more frequently and let him suck as long as he wants; make sure you are eating and drinking enough through the day; take things easy so that the extra calories can be used for making milk. Usually forty-eight hours on this regime will summon up the necessary extra milk. You could try giving a weekend or some other couple of days over completely to trying to boost your milk supply.

Babies often go through a growth spurt at around six weeks and will need more milk. If your baby is suddenly hungry a couple of hours after a feed increase your milk supply in the same way.

TAKE ADVICE

Talk to your GP or health visitor about feeding if the following signs occur in your baby:

* Dry nappies at one or two feeds in twenty-four hours.

* Dark green stools, often passed frequently but only a small amount.

* Long periods of sleeping.

* No weight gain over two weeks, although if this is not coupled with other signs it may not be significant. However, it should be investigated.

EXPRESSING AND STORING MILK

You may want to express milk to relieve and soften engorged breasts, to provide your baby with a feed in your absence or because some problem prevents breastfeeding. If cracked or sore nipples or some other problem is making feeding temporarily impossible, a pump is not the answer and gently expressing by hand is best.

EXPRESSING BY HAND

Choose a time when you feel relaxed and unhurried, wash your hands and use a previously sterilised bottle or jar with a non-metal lid to collect the milk. After a bath is sometimes a good occasion for a first try, or you can help the let-down reflex by putting hot compresses on the breast before expressing. Start by stroking the breast with a light finger-tip touch from chest wall towards the nipple, moving all around the breast. Thinking about the baby and relaxing helps the milk to be released. The point at which you want to apply pressure is where the milk ducts open out into a wider reservoir which is usually where the dark skin of the areola merges into ordinary skin. Hold the breast between finger and thumb at this point using left hand to right breast and vice versa. Squeeze rhythmically inwards without letting your finger slide on the skin and without touching the nipple. Move around the breast to empty each of the reservoirs in turn and then swap to the opposite breast to give time for more milk to drain down.

You can also collect a certain amount of milk simply by holding a container to catch the drips which in the early days may leak from the breast the baby is not feeding from. Some people produce quite a lot when the let-down releases the main bulk of the milk. Usually this leaking tails off as feeding is established. But remember that drip milk is foremilk and therefore low in fat and calories. It is less satisfying when fed alone to your baby, and it is important to remember this if the baby is left for a baby-sitter to feed in your absence.

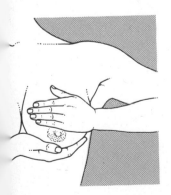 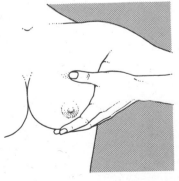 

Expressing milk to relieve engorged breasts needs to be done very gently to avoid bruising skin which is already stretched and tender. If you have problems ask a midwife, breastfeeding counsellor or another breastfeeding mother to show you how to express milk. Some people get very adept and use this technique even when having to express full feeds for the baby if they have gone back to work because it saves taking a pump around with them.

BREAST PUMPS

'I didn't like using the pump but it was the only way I could express enough for my baby who was eight weeks premature. I just used to switch off and imagine it was the baby sucking at the breast. I didn't like it in the beginning, but once I got used to it I could read a magazine and forget what was happening.'

Hand pumps These can be useful if you regularly express milk for someone else to give your baby. There are very many different designs on the market. One mother's ideal pump is another one's agony, so look around and take advice from other mothers and breastfeeding counsellors. Most pumps tend to be one cylinder inside another with a funnel shape at the top to fit over the nipple. Drawing out the inner cylinder creates a vacuum which puts pressure on the areola in the way the baby's sucking would. The exact shape and angle of the funnels, the ease with which they are operated and their ability to come to pieces to be sterilised vary quite a bit.

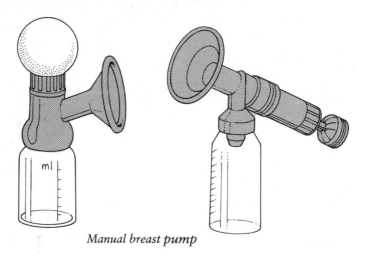

Manual breast pump

Breast relievers These are not the same as pumps. They consist of a glass funnel shape and a bulb and are not advised for expressing feeds. They are intended for expressing only a little milk to relieve pressure and are extremely difficult to clean and use.

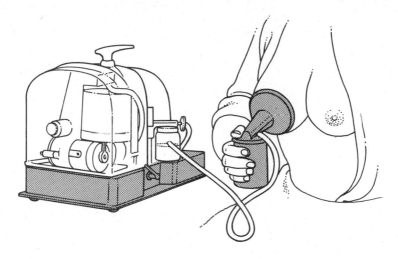

Electric pumps Such pumps are expensive but can be hired from breast-feeding counsellors and are usually the only effective way of building up and maintaining a supply of milk if your baby is ill or premature and needs to be given expressed milk regularly by tube (see page 186). In the beginning midwives will show you how to use one at the maternity hospital. As with all expressing it is important to relax. Hot compresses and stroking the breast in the same way as for hand expressing before you start can help the let-down reflex. Like the hand pumps, electric pumps have a funnel or cup which fits over the nipple and areola only; the rhythmic suction is provided by the machine. Milk collects in a sterilised bottle.

Containers and all detachable parts of pumps need to be cleaned and sterilised.

STORING EXPRESSED BREAST MILK

Milk can be kept for:

* Up to 24 hours in the refrigerator.

* Up to 2 weeks in the freezer compartment of an ordinary fridge.

* Up to 6 months in a deep freeze.

Always date milk if you plan to freeze it, and put it in a sterile container every time. Do not thaw frozen milk over direct heat on the stove because it will curdle and be unusable. You can stand the bottle in a jug of warm but not boiling water; or hold the bottle under the tap starting with cold, changing to tepid and then hand-hot water only as it begins to thaw. Do not allow it to thaw over a longer period at room temperature or leave it standing in the room once it has thawed.

Once thawed, breast milk should be used as soon as possible. Do not keep it for longer than four hours in a fridge before using it.

Never re-freeze milk that has been thawed.

Transporting expressed breast milk is best done in a freezer bag and this applies whether you are expressing milk at work to bring home to the baby or taking a bottle of expressed breast milk to give to a baby while you are out. Keep it as cold as possible by using more than one freezer pack and observe the storage times as if it were in the fridge.

GOING BACK TO WORK

Continuing to breastfeed fully or partially once you have gone back to work is perfectly possible if you have the motivation, although it is obviously easier to breastfeed in some jobs than others. Babies who settle quickly into a feeding pattern can make life easier, but a great deal depends simply on how much you want to do it. Determined mothers will usually plan carefully and make it work for them. Before you go back to work full-time you need to have established a supply of milk, and this can take about six weeks. Begin expressing milk and freezing it before you go back, both to build up a store so that you do not begin on day one without any back up, and also to learn the best method of expressing. If you get on well with expressing by hand, this has the advantage of doing away with the need to carry, set up and sterilise a pump. Otherwise find the best hand- or battery-operated pump to suit you.

It is usually easiest to express at the time when you would normally be feeding the baby. Finding the right place with privacy and enough comfort to express depends on your office – the health centre or medical room is often a good solution in a big organisation, otherwise find a free room. Usually the lavatory is not a good place though it may sometimes be the only answer.

A certain amount depends on having a boss who does not make you feel bad about disappearing for twenty to thirty minutes occasionally. Take ready-sterilised screw-top bottles to work and if possible store them in a fridge afterwards. If not, then use a freezer bag. If you work near home it may be possible to nip home at lunchtime or have the baby brought in for one feed. Make sure you wear breast pads or easy-access clothes that are loose and dark or patterned so they will not show if you do leak.

To keep up a supply you need to express as often as you would be giving a full feed – usually twice during the working day. Let your baby suck as long as he wants at other times – most babies do tend to take longer over the feeds you give to make up sucking time they may have missed. This will also keep up your milk supply.

Some babies may try to reverse day and night, to sleep longer in the day and demand feeds at night when they can be breast not bottle-fed. This is not to be encouraged as it is exhausting for a working mother. It is hard to control the waking and sleeping patterns of very young babies, but as they get older the person looking after your baby can try to keep him awake and amused during the day, and a nipple-shaped comforter can help a baby who seems to miss sucking at the breast. After a weekend you may find you have more milk because you have been feeding the baby yourself and by Friday your milk supply may be down again.

Don't worry too much about trying to accustom your baby to taking a bottle before you go back to work because breastfed babies often refuse a bottle from their own mothers but will accept one when they are hungry from someone else. A naturally-shaped teat with quite a small hole so they still have to suck hard will stop them preferring bottles to breast if you have to go back to work when they are very young. However, it is a good idea to start offering a bottle containing expressed milk or water occasionally right from the start so that the baby can learn both bottle and breastfeeding techniques.

PARTIAL BREASTFEEDING

'I did find that being able to come home and breastfeed my baby was tremendously comforting. It seemed an instant way of re-establishing the closeness and I think it helped me not to feel guilty or jealous about leaving her.'

A mixture of breast and bottle-feeding can be a pleasant way to continue enjoying closeness with your baby after you have gone back to work. Dropping one feed needs to be done gradually and you need to continue to allow the baby to suck for longer at other times, for example, at the morning and evening feeds, to maintain a sufficient supply. You will probably not be able to maintain part-time feeding for very long, unless your baby has had time to establish a pattern of full-time feeding, usually for at least the first ten to twelve weeks.

BREASTFEEDING PROBLEMS FOR MOTHERS

SORE NIPPLES

These can be caused by the baby sucking on the nipple instead of the surrounding areola, or being dragged off the breast without the suction being broken first. Other causes may be wet nipples from soggy breast pads; the baby sucking too long after the breast is emptied; use of too much soap which dries the skin; sensitivity to creams or sprays; or the baby feeding at an awkward angle.

The way to avoid these problems is to keep nipples dry and exposed to air as much as possible and to make sure the baby is fixed on and taken off the breast properly. Start each feed with the breast you finished with last time, so that alternate breasts are offered at the beginning of a feed when his suck is strongest. If you don't mind laughing at yourself a bit, a hair drier is a good way to dry nipples, and you can use the small nylon tea-strainers with the handles cut off inside your bra to allow air to circulate and prevent rubbing. Continue feeding, but cut comfort sucking until soreness has eased, and use a nipple shield if it helps. This is a sterilised rubber cap held over the nipple with a hole to allow milk through.

CRACKED NIPPLES

These can follow from untreated sore nipples or appear without warning. The nipple bleeds through a small crack or split in the skin. If it is not too bad it will not do any harm to carry on breastfeeding. You could use a nipple shield but, if it hurts, don't grit your teeth and carry on in agony – better rest for a day and allow it to heal and give bottles in the meantime. Express milk by hand to prevent engorgement and paint the nipple with Friar's Balsam mixed with lanolin or gentian violet.

Reintroduce the baby to the breast cautiously for a couple of minutes of feed at first and use a nipple shield until the skin has healed.

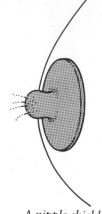

A nipple shield

BLOCKED DUCTS

Blocked ducts cause a tender lump and can make you feel feverish. This can follow engorgement or pressure on the ducts, perhaps from a tight or ill-fitting bra or even an awkward feeding position. Do not stop feeding because this will make it much worse – instead try to clear the blockage by massaging the lump gently in the direction of the nipple, applying hot and cold compresses and offer that breast first at frequent feeds so that the baby's strongest sucking at the beginning of a feed will help to get the milk moving through the ducts again.

MASTITIS

Mastitis can cause similar symptoms and may be non-infective, caused by milk leaking from the blocked duct and surrounding tissue. Feverishness alone is not a sign that the mastitis is infective, even though you may have a temperature. Infective mastitis also has the same symptoms, although you may feel iller, and it is often caused by a germ in the baby's nose which is trasmitted to the mother's breast and which may have been picked up in hospital. In both cases all the treatment described for engorgement and blocked ducts can help and the doctor will prescribe antibiotics. Remember to mention to him, even though it sounds obvious, that he needs to select an antibiotic suitable for a breastfeeding mother. If tests show the milk is infected you will have to stop feeding temporarily from the affected breast, and perhaps supplement with bottles, until the supply in the healthy breast is sufficient.

BREAST ABSCESSES

These are rare and sometimes confused with blocked ducts, but they can be nasty. Treatment is with antibiotics, and possibly surgical drainage if this is not enough alone. You will have to stop feeding from the affected breast in the same way as with infective mastitis.

BREASTFEEDING AFTER A CAESAREAN

This is easiest following an epidural because you will be fully conscious and alert and able to put the baby to the breast after delivery. Usually a cushion or two under the baby can prevent any pressure on your stitches, but don't be afraid to ask for help to get into a comfortable position and be handed the baby. Mothers who cannot sit in a propped-up position, either because it is too painful because of the restrictions of drainage tubes or drips, or because they feel ill from the effects of a general anaesthetic, can feed lying to one side with the baby's feet towards their head. Either offer the other side by leaning over the baby more, or get help to move the baby to the other side and shift position. Take special care when feeding in a less than ideal position that the baby gets properly latched on to the breast. Try to vary the angle at which he sucks so that the pressure is not always on the same spot. In this way you will decrease the risk of getting sore.

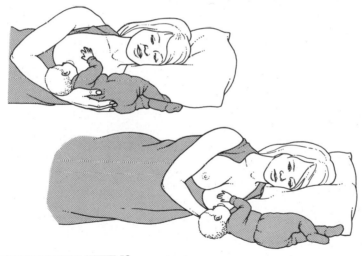

BREASTFEEDING TWINS

This is perfectly possible. During pregnancy, get in touch with the Twins Club in your area who can give advice and extra literature. Feeding both together saves a great deal of time and avoids the problem of one baby howling while the other is feeding, but in the early days you may want to feed each separately, both to give you experience of breastfeeding, if these are your first babies, and also to get to know each one individually. Put the baby that wakes first to the breast and wake the other to follow with a feed

so their hungry times stand more chance of coinciding. Totally demand feeding both babies will leave little time for anything else, so you will have to impose some kind of routine on them from the beginning – aim for feeds about every three hours.

Once you begin to give all or some feeds together, experiment with a helper to find the position that suits you and the babies best. Resting them on pillows on either side so their bodies are cradled under each arm and the head supported on more pillows on your lap is one way, or while they are small you can adapt the conventional nursing position with both babies lying in the same direction. If one baby has a much stronger suck, always alternate breasts so that each breast receives the same amount of stimulation and then produces the same amount of milk.

If one baby is very much smaller and cannot go so long between feeds, you may have trouble synchronising feeding times. Begin by feeding both separately and move on to joint feeding times. If the smaller baby wakes less than two and a half hours later, feed him again, but also wake him for a joint feed when the bigger baby wakes. If the smaller baby sleeps two and a half hours or longer, then try to spin a little extra time out by giving him a small drink and a nappy change and then wake the bigger baby for a joint feed. It will save more time to feed both babies every three hours than one baby at three hours and another at four. Gradually the smaller baby should catch up. The rule of supply and demand will ensure that as long as you let both babies suck as much as they want, your body will produce enough milk for both.

BREASTFEEDING TRIPLETS

It is possible to breastfeed three babies, but obviously it needs a lot of dedication and a great deal of extra help and support – as indeed does almost every aspect of caring for three new babies at once. One practical routine is to breastfeed with the third baby having a bottle on a rota system so that all the babies have some breast milk.

Whatever problems you may have with breastfeeding, try to take a positive attitude. Even if you manage to feed for only a very short time you will still have given your baby a valuable start which he would not otherwise have had, both from the anti-infective properties of colostrum and from the physical closeness. If you have to give up because, despite all your efforts, you cannot build up a supply of milk, or your baby does not gain weight or starts to lose weight, remember you can still combine breast and bottle-feeding and do not have to give up completely. If you do have to switch completely to bottles because of repeated serious problems or illnesses, do not regard bottle-feeding as second best, but concentrate instead on making feeding times a time of enjoyment for both of you.

GIVING UP BREASTFEEDING

CHANGING FROM BREAST TO BOTTLE

This should be done gradually. Start by dropping the breastfeed when you have least milk, usually the evening, and substitute a bottle. You may need to experiment to find the best teat and hole size to suit your baby. If he is very resistant to the bottle, you could try a natural-shaped teat, or better still get your partner or another person to feed the bottle for the first few times. If you are making the switch because your baby is failing to gain weight or you are returning to work, remember it is perfectly possible to continue with breastfeeding in the morning, during the night and evening or whichever suits you, in addition to bottles, so that you and your baby can still enjoy the closeness and comfort of breastfeeding (see page 207).

Extra drinks are not necessary for totally breastfed babies, but once you start giving bottles or solid food, your baby may get thirsty, so start offering plain boiled water in a bottle, cup or spoon. Don't fuss if he refuses, unless it is very hot weather, he has a temperature or is unwell. Babies from around three months can have diluted natural fruit juices and baby concentrated drinks – these must be diluted as recommended. Manufactured squash, fruit drinks and syrups which have a lot of sugar are unsuitable. Do not use dinky feeders filled with sweet drinks or dummies dunked in anything sugary as this will cause the teeth to rot.

Giving up breastfeeding because of problems may provoke mixed feelings – perhaps of failure if you very much wanted to breastfeed, or guilt if you are relieved to abandon the whole business.

BREASTFEEDING PROBLEMS FOR BABIES

Babies all feed differently, and their personality, temperament and maturity will affect the way they take to breastfeeding. Once you begin to understand and accept your own baby's foibles, the difficulties seem to diminish. Here are some of the more obvious types:

THE CLOCKWATCHER

This baby has a Quartz mechanism and wakes every three to four hours for a feed, sleeps regularly and for longer periods at night and is generally totally predictable. He also tends to be someone else's baby!

THE DREAMER

This baby likes to sleep and forgets to wake for meals. As long as he has at least six wet nappies a day, don't worry, but dry nappies between feeds may mean he is not getting enough fluids – seek advice and check he is gaining weight by getting him weighed weekly. Some babies will suck in their sleep, but if not loosen his clothes, bathe his face and talk and play with him to wake him up. If he falls asleep after one breast, change his nappy and try again. If he still sleeps, don't worry and offer the other breast next feed.

THE 'I WANT IT NOW' BABY

Such a baby comes to the breast in a panic; roots frantically for the nipple; sucks vigorously and then chokes and splutters when the milk lets down. He screams with frustration and gets more upset the more you try to feed him. Recognise this baby? The answer may be feeding in a quiet place – he is not the sort to latch on happily when you are chatting to friends around the kitchen table. A little water before the feed may stem his immediate thirst and help him to start feeding more calmly. If he still panics let him suck your finger until he establishes a rhythm; then slip the nipple in his mouth. He often appreciates rocking or movement while feeding, so try a rocking chair or walking around. Best feeding times are when he is half asleep at night in the dark or riding in the back of a car.

THE ANARCHIST

This baby wakes less than an hour after his last feed and seems ravenous, at other times hours pass and he is still uninterested. No two sleeps, feeds or days are alike and he is innocently driving you to distraction with his unpredictability. Demand feed at first, but gradually impose some sort of routine by feeding him when you are ready and distracting him with small drinks, pram rides, spells in a bouncing chair, baths and lengthy nappy changes with lots of exercise and chat when you are not ready. Keeping a diary helps because you can lose track of just when he was last fed – persevere and gradually a pattern will emerge.

THE PIRANHA

Some babies bite frequently, clamping down on the nipple with their gums towards the end of a feed. Take it as a sign he has had enough because he cannot bite and suck at the same time, so sucking can no longer be very important. Older babies may try it experimentally when teething – withdraw the nipple and say 'No' firmly each time. He will sense your disapproval. Between feeds provide teething toys, and if he is old enough a rusk or a crust of bread to satisfy the chewing urge.

THE CHOOSY FEEDER

This baby will take only from one breast and leave you lop-sided. Offer the less favoured breast when he is most hungry at the beginning of each feed so that his sucking will stimulate the milk supply. Try a different feeding position, more upright or lying down. Some babies can be fooled if they are fed tucked under the arm with head towards the front: the change of angle seems to help.

BOTTLES AND BOTTLE-FEEDING

Cow's milk, which is designed for calves rather than babies, is quite different from breast milk, and has to be altered before it can be used as food for babies. In fact, as has already been described, the composition of breast milk changes during a feed, as the baby grows, and from feed to feed in the same woman, so defining what an 'average' sample of breast milk contains is difficult. It is not possible to make up an artificial feed which is exactly like breast milk since we do not know all the properties of breast milk yet, the content varies and the immunising and anti-infective qualities cannot be reproduced artificially. But cow's milk can be modified to make a very safe food that your baby can thrive on, though it is necessary to get all the ingredients in the right proportions.

As we have already seen, although the calorie content of cow's milk and breast milk is the same, cow's milk has two to three times as much protein as breast milk, and this protein is of a different composition. Cow's milk contains less lactose (milk sugar), the fat is less easily absorbed, and the minerals are very much higher: sodium, potassium, calcium and chloride are three to four times higher. To make a baby's milk formula the levels of protein and these minerals are reduced by diluting the cow's milk. This will also reduce the calorie and vitamin content to levels much lower than in breast milk. To remedy this, extra lactose and other essential nutrients are added to make it suitable for your baby.

Commercially modified baby milks must be used for bottle-feeding. Your hospital or community midwife will advise you which brands to choose from and, having made your choice, stick to the same formula. Modified whey-based milks have been the most extensively modified to mimic the content of breast milk as far as possible. You must dilute the powdered varieties correctly by mixing the right quantity of cool, boiled water.

In the days before commercially modified milks were available, mothers simply diluted doorstep milk and added sugar but, while this will do in an emergency, formula feed is much better tailored to a new baby's digestion and should always be used when breast milk is not available. If you do get caught out and need to make up an emergency bottle from doorstep milk, it should be boiled first and then diluted with half as much boiled water (i.e. about 125 ml. milk to 75 ml. water). Sugar is added in a ratio of 15 g or 1 level tablespoon to every 200 ml. of diluted milk.

Bottle-fed babies have only a slightly higher risk of becoming fat than breastfed babies. It is important to offer properly diluted feeds, as well as extra water when your baby is thirsty. Make up more than the recommended amount for his weight. At some feeds he will take more, at others less, but do not try to force him to finish a bottle once his hunger is satisfied.

ESTABLISHING BOTTLE-FEEDING

'I loved taking a warm, fresh bottle of milk and seeing it disappear bit by bit as my baby fed.'

After delivery do not let the fact that you plan to bottle-feed deprive you and your baby of the pleasure of physical closeness and contact. Even if you do not want to put your baby to the breast there is no reason why you should not enjoy skin-to-skin contact in the same way. Loosen his wrappings while still keeping him warm and lay him on your tummy or between your breasts, gently stroke and caress him to help him uncurl and relax. See page 152 for more discussion of handling the newborn.

On day one it is sufficient to give a bottle-fed baby a glucose and water solution. There is no artificial replacement for colostrum, and at this stage he mostly needs fluid rather than food.

There is great pleasure in feeding a bottle to a hungry baby but you need to make an extra effort to see that feeding time stays a time for special enjoyment and closeness, not just another chore to be done by anyone. Always hold your baby very close – at night-time especially it is easy to cradle him against your skin – and support him in a fairly upright position.

Feed your baby whenever he seems interested in just the same way as if he were breastfed. Trying to force him into a routine of four-hourly feeds before he is mature enough will only lead to several hours with a crying, upset baby and misery for both of you. Remember that in the womb his body has been nourished continually and at first his pattern of feeding, just like a baby that is being breastfed, needs to be little and often. Offer him a bottle whenever he wakes and roots for food or cries. If he takes only a few sucks and goes back to sleep or loses interest, nothing is lost and you have given him the comfort of sucking. Do not think that offering him food whenever he wants will encourage him to go on asking for it at irregular intervals. The fact is that his digestive system is still immature and needs time to adjust – he is not able to cope with any other way of feeding. Usually, by about two weeks, some sort of pattern is beginning to emerge. He may sleep for three to four hours, perhaps in the morning, and have another time, possibly early evening, when he needs small feeds more often. Do not be tempted to add cereal to a feed in the belief that it will help

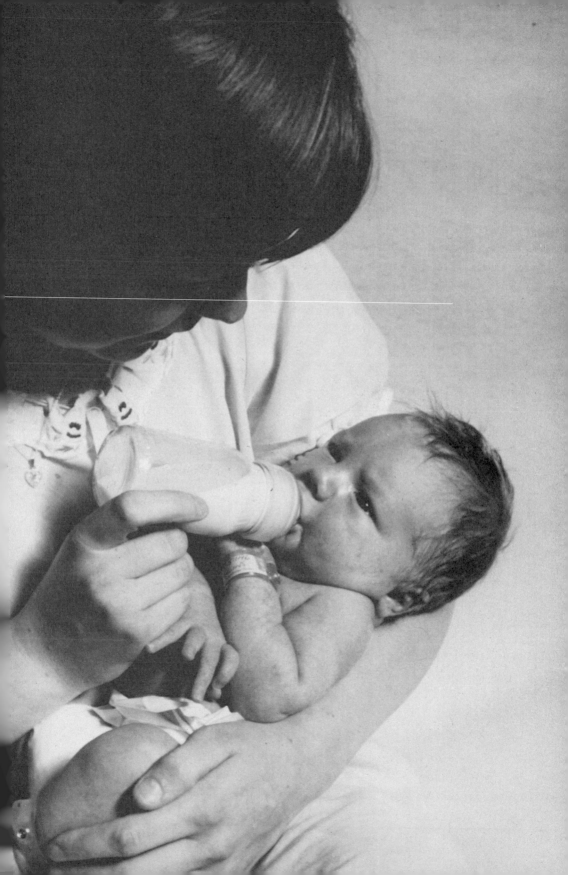

him to sleep through. Staying asleep for longer periods has to do with the maturity of your baby's brain as well as his digestion, and added cereal will just make him fat.

Extra fluid may be necessary for bottle-fed babies in hot weather. If in doubt offer boiled water or, after six to eight weeks, well-diluted unsweetened fruit juice on a teaspoon or in a bottle. If he does not want it you can conclude he does not need it. Avoid sugary drinks, which will rot emerging teeth.

EQUIPMENT

* Purpose-bought or improvised container for sterilising bottles, but it must be big enough to submerge everything completely. Steam sterilising units are available though more expensive.

* Eight wide-necked baby feeding bottles and teats designed for newborns.

* Large plastic or Pyrex measuring jug and plastic stirrer for mixing feeds, or you can measure the water into the baby bottles and add the correct number of scoops of powder directly.

* Sterilising tablets or liquid – check the instructions on how to make up the solution and how long it takes to sterilise bottles.

* Plastic knife.

MAKING UP FEEDS

Everything you use for making up bottles must be sterilised, including the jug and stirrer if used, so always start by washing your hands and freshly filling and boiling a kettle of water.

It is easiest to make up a day's supply of bottles in one go and store them in the fridge for up to twenty-four hours. Make up a little more formula than you think you need – a very rough guide is that babies need about 150 ml. of milk for every kilogram ($2\frac{1}{2}$ fluid oz. for every pound) of body weight per day, so a 4 kg. (10 lb.) baby will need approximately 600 ml. (25 oz.) milk in twenty-four hours. However, the real measure is your baby's appetite, and at some feeds he will take more than at others.

As long as you offer him milk whenever you think he might be hungry and do not try to force it on him when he does not want it, you will be giving him what he needs. Discard the rest of the feed and never save bottles to be reheated because warm milk is an ideal breeding ground for bacteria. It is now possible to buy ready-mixed cartons of formula, which, though expensive, can be useful for outings.

JUG METHOD

* Wash your hands.

* Take the measuring jug and stirrer from the steriliser. Do not rinse them

Jug method

under the tap because you will de-sterilise them again. Shake them to remove drops of sterilising solution.

* Pour the right amount of boiled water into the jug, make sure it is standing on a flat surface and check the quantity at eye level rather than from above.

* As hot water destroys vitamins, most formulas require the water only to be warm to mix easily, so cover the jug with its own lid or a plastic or glass saucer, which also needs to be sterilised, while the water cools.

* When the water is the right temperature, add the correct number of scoops – make sure there are no distractions because it is easy to lose count.

* Use the scoop provided and do not fill it by dragging it up the side of the box or otherwise compressing the powder – these are the commonest causes of over-concentrated feeding.

* The milk powder should lie loosely in the scoop; use the flat edge of a sterilised clean plastic knife (not metal) to level it off each time. Never heat powder. The common brands of baby milk are diluted with one scoop of powder added to 30 ml. (1 oz.) water. Do not be tempted either to increase or decrease the number of scoops recommended.

* Stir the milk until all lumps have dissolved: they could clog the teats.

* Take bottles from the steriliser. Again, shake to remove drops of sterilising solution and do not rinse. Fill to the right level – put slightly more in each bottle than you think your baby will need.

* Take teats from the steriliser, being careful to handle each teat by the edge and not the part you put into the baby's mouth, and fit them into the bottles upside down. Put the caps, rings and tops in place. Do not take out all these bits and pieces at the same time and lay them on the work surface because you will de-sterilise them, but take each item individually from the steriliser and put it directly on to the bottle.

* Put all the bottles in the fridge and leave them untouched until needed.

BOTTLE METHOD

* Wash your hands.

* Take the bottles from the steriliser. Again, shake but do not rinse them because you will de-sterilise them.

* Pour the right amount of boiled water into each bottle; make sure it is standing on a flat surface and check the quantity at eye level rather than from above.

* As with the jug method, make sure the water is the right temperature, warm but not hot.

Bottle method

* Use the scoop provided and add the right number of scoops of powder to each bottle — make sure there are no distractions so that you can count properly.

* Again, be careful not to fill the scoop by dragging it up the side of the box or otherwise compressing the powder. Level off the scoop with the plastic knife.

* Take the teats from the steriliser, being careful to handle by the edge and fit into the bottles upside down. Put the caps, rings and tops in place. Again, take out each item separately and put directly on to the bottle.

* Shake each bottle vigorously to make sure all the formula has dissolved and there are no lumps.

* Put bottles in the fridge and leave them untouched until needed.

GIVING A BOTTLE

* Take the bottle from the fridge and warm it by standing it in a jug of hot water.

* Check temperature and flow by testing it on the back of your hand or inside a wrist — it should feel warm, not hot or cold, and flow in rapid drips, not in a continuous stream or too slowly. Small holes can be enlarged with a red-hot needle but if the hole is too large you need another teat.

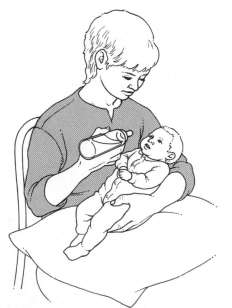

* Always get yourself comfortable, which means having your back and cradling arm supported — if you are getting uncomfortable you will get tense and be tempted to hurry the feed.

* Touch your finger against your baby's cheek nearest to you and, as he turns his head towards you, 'rooting' for food, touch the teat against his lips. Always introduce the teat fully into his mouth so that the action of his jaws as he sucks is against the lower half. Tilt the bottle so that the opening of the teat is always covered with milk and to ensure that the baby is not sucking in too much air.

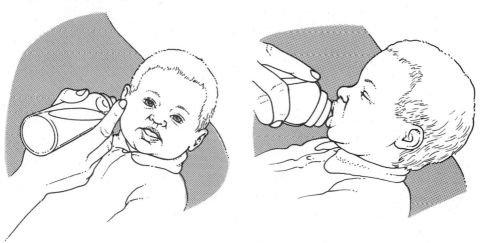

* You will need to stop feeding at least once to sit your baby up, allowing him to burp up any wind (see page 242).

* Do not try to force your baby to take more than he wants – his appetite is always your best guide.

* Never be tempted to keep the remains of a bottle. There is a high risk of germs contaminating warm milk that is left standing around. Throw away unused feeds.

* Never leave a young baby with a bottle propped for him to feed from because there is a real danger that he could choke. You are also denying him the closeness babies enjoy during a feed, which is also the time when they begin to learn the skills of communicating and taking turns that develop when an adult and a baby enjoy a shared task.

237

STERILISING BOTTLES AND EQUIPMENT

* As your baby finishes a bottle, rinse it out with cold water to remove any milk left inside and leave it ready for the evening washing-up session.

* At the end of the day thoroughly scrub all the bottles, caps, covers and rinse with hot soapy water – a bottle brush is essential, but remember to keep this clean too and leave it to dry afterwards.

* Rinse everything well.

* To clean the teats tip a little household salt on to the teat and rub it between your fingers; fatty milk deposits can cling to the rubber, making it feel slimy, and soapy water alone is not enough to shift them. Turn the teat inside out, thoroughly rinse off salt and any slime under running water. This also helps to reduce the risk of your baby getting thrush. Dummies should be cleaned in a similar way.

* Make up a fresh sterilising solution following the instructions on the packet or bottle and submerge everything needed for bottle-feeding including jugs, spoons and plastic knife or stirrer. Make sure there are no air bubbles trapped inside anything, or that the teats are not simply floating on top which will prevent them from being completely sterilised.

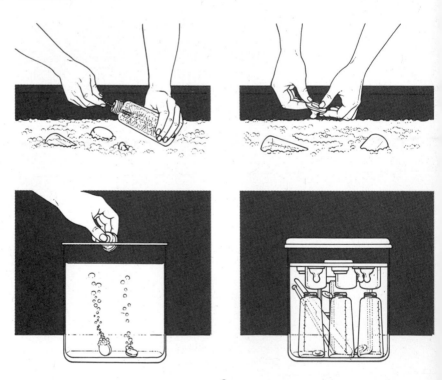

OTHER PEOPLE FEEDING YOUR BABY

'My mother was always saying, "Let me feed him so you can get on with things." In fact feeding my baby was the pleasure and "things" were just chores, but it was very hard to say that I wanted to feed him myself.'

Because there is a great deal of satisfaction to be gained from feeding a baby, you will not be short of willing helpers offering to do this particular job – from well-meaning grannies to friends and school-aged children. Indeed one of the reasons you may have chosen bottle-feeding was so that you could more easily leave him with other people at times, but remember that feeding time is not just an occasion when a baby receives the right amount of calories and protein. It is also an occasion of great pleasure to him and consequently to the person feeding him. It is a very important part of forming a relationship, of getting to know your baby as you and he respond to each other's touch, movement and facial expression. This is the main reason why breastfeeding has so many advocates – not only does it provide the best nutrition, but it provides a regular, continuing form of communication between a mother and her baby.

Naturally, you will be pleased that the baby's father can share in this experience and if it is to be he rather than you who is to stay at home and look after the baby then it is right for him gradually to take over most of the feeds. But early on guard feeding times for yourself. Do not be afraid to say that you want to feed your baby yourself because it is a time when you both get to know each other and feel very close. If any relatives threaten to get offended you could point out that it is a question that would not even arise if you were breastfeeding. Encourage them to help you with other chores, for example bathtime, washing, shopping and so on.

VITAMIN SUPPLEMENTS

BEFORE WEANING

If you eat a balanced diet and are healthy, breast milk will give your baby all the vitamins needed, but if you feel you have not, for whatever reason, been eating well, or have been ill, your health clinic can give you the right vitamin supplements in the form of drops for your baby. If you are bottle-feeding then the milks recommended by the hospital or community midwife do contain vitamins, but in addition most professionals advise the use of the children's vitamin A, D and C drops from six months old onwards. These, used in conjunction with modified milk or breastfeeds, provide a safe dose of vitamins, but never give two different vitamin preparations at any stage as this could be harmful.

AFTER WEANING

Once you change from formula or breast milk to cow's milk and mixed feeding it is recommended that you give vitamin A, D and C drops up to the

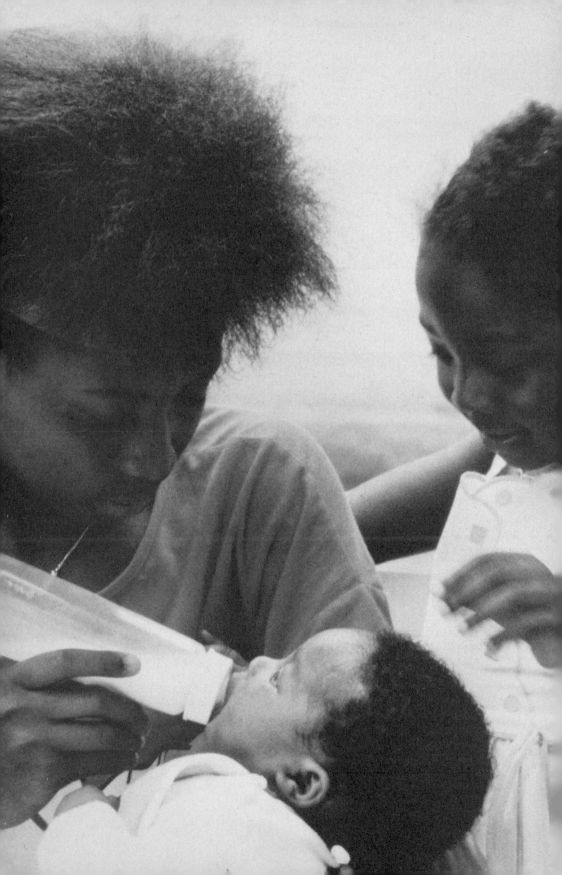

age of five. Again use drops that are supplied by the health clinic rather than over-the-counter brands.

Sunlight on the skin provides vitamin D, so in good weather give your child lots of opportunity to play outside, taking care to protect a baby's sensitive skin with a sunscreen and hat in summer.

After you begin mixed feeding make sure sometimes to include iron-containing foods such as kidney, liver, red meats, pulses and iron-fortified cereals.

Fluoride tablets or drops help to protect teeth if you live in an area where fluoride is not already added to your water. See page 536 for more on tooth care.

FEEDING SECOND AND SUBSEQUENT BABIES

You have the benefit of experience, know what to expect and have gained confidence from bringing up one child whether on breast or bottle-feeding. The differences with the second lie in the reaction of your first child to the new baby, your own desire to do the best by both children and the fact that feeding now has to be fitted into a much more complicated routine. You cannot always feed your baby at the time you expect him to be hungry because you want to see to another child's needs. The best policy is to feed him early, rather than hope he will last and then have to cope with a screaming baby in the background.

When you talk to your older child about the arrival of a new baby, talk also about how he will be fed. If you plan to breastfeed, photographs of you breastfeeding your first child can be a great help. He is quite likely to want to have an experimental suck himself at some stage and try feeding a teddy or dolly from his own nipples. The brother or sister of a bottle-fed baby is likely to want their own bottle and to try feeding toys. Both reactions are quite normal. One mother described how 'My daughter was always shoving her doll up her jumper in the greengrocer's or post office and latching it on to her tummy button saying she was giving it some milk.'

There is no evidence that breastfeeding provokes more jealousy in an older child than bottle-feeding, but because it is such an intimate act, mothers are often anxious and feel almost a sense of betrayal to the older child. The answer lies in giving the older child a period of exclusive attention ahead, although not immediately prior, to a feed, and being prepared with distractions while feeding. But it is a fact that however much you involve the first child in the care of the baby he is unlikely to be captivated by feeding sessions six times a day, and if a child shows signs of jealousy he can pick feeding times to be particularly disruptive.

Make sure you always have a potty, drink and small snack readily to hand and keep a treasure chest of interesting knick-knacks to be brought out at feeding times only. Boxes of old buttons or jewellery, different books from the library or special crayons are useful. Try swapping toys with friends and change the 'treasure' regularly – be innovative, they do not have to be new and expensive, just different. Empty margarine tubs can be stacked, or cut out to make a large hole to thread string through, or left with the lid on but with holes big enough to post conkers, stones or shells through. Breastfeeding mums have the advantage of a free hand to cuddle, draw pictures or turn pages. Older children may like cassettes or records, or you can time feeds to coincide with favourite television programmes, but avoid sending them off into a room on their own or they may feel excluded. Often just making them cosy beside you with a favourite blanket or teddy and talking, singing or telling them a story about when they were a baby can make feeding times less likely to be an occasion for trouble.

PROBLEMS WITH EARLY FEEDING

WIND

Some babies, whether breast or bottle-fed, take in more wind than others when feeding – you will soon get to know whether your baby needs a chance to burp midway through a bottle or when changing breasts. Hold him in an upright position against your body, or over your shoulder, and gently rub his back. Take avoiding action to prevent the odd mouthful of milk that is often regurgitated at the same time from ruining your clothes – babies have a wonderful way of depositing a trail of milk down the back of any smart blouse or dress! Alternative winding positions are lying face down across your knees, or sitting up with your hand behind his neck and thumb under his chin. If he is perfectly happy and does not pass any wind, carry on feeding. Beware of breaking feeds unnecessarily to wind your baby so that he starts crying and becomes upset and frustrated – it will be the crying rather than the feeding which makes him take in extra wind. If your baby seems unduly troubled by wind, try feeding him in an upright position; check that the hole in the teat allows milk to drip through rapidly and that the bottle is tilted enough for the milk to cover the entrance to the teat completely. If every feeding time or specific feeds are followed by lots of howling, your baby may have colic (see page 243).

SICKY BABIES

These are babies who regularly return part of their feed every time but generally are thriving and perfectly healthy. If you have any reason to suspect that the sickness may be a sign of illness or your baby is not gaining weight regularly consult your doctor. Otherwise you just have to be careful to cover clothes, carpets and furniture, and grit your teeth about the washing; he will grow out of it as his body matures and the muscle which closes the opening to the stomach becomes stronger.

PYLORIC STENOSIS

This is a condition where the muscle surrounding the channel at the end of the stomach (called the pylorus) thickens, narrowing the outlet. Five times as many boys suffer from it as girls and symptoms usually appear about two to three weeks after the birth when the baby starts vomiting, becomes constipated and stops gaining weight. The vomiting is often projectile – that means it shoots out and can land feet away. Although the baby does not gain weight, he usually remains bright and parents may initially think the sickness is due to unsuitable feeding. Such sickness can lead to dehydration so parents of babies under three months should seek advice rapidly if this type of vomiting occurs. Diagnosis can be made by feeling a lump in the abdomen over the pylorus which hardens and softens when feeding. Treatment is usually a simple operation. The baby can be fed only hours afterwards and makes a rapid recovery.

COLIC

> *'My baby never fed without at least an hour of screaming afterwards, then he would fall asleep exhausted. The evenings were the worst – he cried on and off from about four every afternoon until midnight. I had a toddler of twenty-two months and a husband who was rarely home in the evenings. On days when I had no plans to see anyone else I used to feel completely panicked by how I would get through the day.'*

All babies cry for a variety of reasons (see chapter 8), but babies with colic cry more – one study diagnosed colic if a baby cried for more than three hours a day and on more than three days a week. Usually such babies act as though they have stomach ache, drawing their knees up over their stomach during screaming fits and often punching their fists.

Normally our intestines contract in smooth, rhythmical undulations to move food along the digestive tract, but in some babies this gentle movement is replaced by spasms, causing the pain and distress termed colic. It rarely begins before about two weeks or after two months, and in the majority of cases stops at around three months, and in all but a very few babies at four months: this is why it is often called 'three-month colic'. Attacks can last anything from a quarter of an hour to several hours. There may be non-stop screaming, or bouts of screaming in between which the baby seems miserable or may briefly sleep. Some babies suffer only during the evening and the usual pattern is that as they get older and begin to grow out of it they begin to settle slightly earlier each night.

Research has shown that colicky babies are invariably healthy and thriving and basically no different from other babies except that they suffer from colic. The only slight factors to emerge are that weaning too early – before three months – makes colic more probable and that professional couples are more likely to have a colicky baby, though this probably just reflects the fact that such couples are more inclined to seek and get a correct diagnosis. No differences have been picked up between colic sufferers and others in terms of sex, birthweight, birth order, weight gain, feeding method or the amount of sickness, diarrhoea or constipation they may suffer. Wind used to be blamed as the main problem, but tests indicate that colicky babies have no more wind in their intestines than others, although what there is probably does contribute to pain by getting trapped in loops of intestine during spasms.

Why do some babies suffer from such jittery, jumpy intestines? A favourite theory is that it is simply caused by an immature nervous system which is not yet able to control the intestines properly; this would explain why the problem disappears as the baby grows and matures. Other suggestions include the possibility that it might be related to prostaglandin metabolism and intestinal hormones or to an allergic reaction, most commonly to cow's milk. Certainly amongst the colic sufferers there will be some babies whose distress is due either to a temporary or long-term intolerance of either cow's milk or other food. In babies whose problems do not disappear by five months food intolerance should be considered seriously. You will need to discuss this possibility with your health visitor or family doctor.

An inconsolably screaming baby places an enormous strain on parents: indeed such babies are more likely to be battered than calmer ones. Even though health professionals cannot usually do anything practical to help, just talking about the problem and letting them know the kind of strain you are under can be a relief and enable them to be more supportive. There are a number of things that may help to calm your baby:

Drugs for colic are now limited to gripe water or dimethicone – a mild antacid contained in Dentinox Colic Drops or Infant Asilone. Usually the psychological aid of actually having something to give the baby is more help than any pharmacological effect. Anti-spasmodic drugs containing dyclomine (Merbentyl) are no longer recommended for babies under six months because although they were used for over thirty years, in recent years there have been a number of reports of adverse side effects, mostly breathing difficulties.

Fennel is a herb said to have a relaxing, calming effect and it is contained in some drinks for young babies or can be taken as fennel tea. Some parents believe it helps, but there is no good evidence that this is so. Baby teas are not recommended.

Anti-wind teats and bottles are a waste of money because there is no evidence that taking in extra wind causes colic.

Sucking is often a tremendous relief for colicky babies, providing comfort and a distraction from pain. Sometimes these babies root as though for food, only to cry again when they begin feeding. As long as you are sure it is the comfort sucking provides, rather than food your baby wants, try offering him your little finger or a sterilised dummy to suck. He may suck furiously, begin to drift into sleep and then wake with a cry after a short while, wanting to suck again, so that you have to offer the finger or dummy once more. Natural-shaped dummies are available for breastfed babies, who are used to sucking with a slightly different technique to bottle-fed babies, but usually a baby who needs the comfort of sucking will not be fussy. See page 304 for more on dummies.

Traditional comforts like carrying the baby around, rocking, cradling, stroking and pacing will all be tried by harassed parents – rhythmic and constant stimuli distract from pain in the same way you use breathing exercises in labour. Swaddling (see page 303) can sometimes help, so can a continuous buzz of noise like the tumble-drier or television; a dark, quiet room is also worth trying. Long evenings with a colicky baby can be made easier with a rocking chair so that you can sit and rock the baby on your shoulder or knee to the accompaniment of a good television programme.

Keeping a diary over seven days in which you record the number of hours your baby cried, plus a systematic approach using one possible remedy each time can help you pinpoint which is most likely to be effective and when you most need to draft in extra help. Just writing down what happens can also help to make sense of what may seem one long nightmare and be therapeutic in itself. Resist throwing every possible remedy at your baby in one evening because you will not know which works (if any) and will have nothing left in reserve to try. Also, too much different attention can add to his distress.

Extra support is invaluable and so is support between couples. It is not unknown for men to stay out later or work longer hours just to escape from a screaming baby. You need to face the problem together, and this means talking and planning how best to cope. Ask a reliable friend or relative if they will come and stay with your howler just for an hour one evening a week so that you can get right out of the house together and go to the pub or just for a walk. Take turns with late-evening and night waking as far as possible so that you both get some decent stretches of unbroken sleep, even if it means sometimes turning in at nine o'clock. Make sure that each day you have one other person visiting or you are going out to see someone yourself. Talk to other mothers about your problem and let the health visitor know so that she can be as supportive as possible. If you reach crisis point and feel you could harm your child, put him in his cot or pram, leave the room and ring a friend, relative or health visitor. So common is the problem, an organisation, Cry-sis, has been formed to help parents to cope (see address section, pages 673–6).

WEANING

Weaning is the process of teaching a baby to take foods other than milk from a spoon or cup rather than just sucking at the breast or teat. At the same time the amount of milk being given gradually decreases.

WHEN TO START

Between three and six months is usually the right time. Feeding solids before three months is unnecessary because all your baby's needs can be met from milk and, if necessary, extra drinks of boiled water. Giving solids too early may make your baby fat which, in turn, may lead to other health problems. It also places a strain on the baby's still immature digestive system, and increases the likelihood of allergy (see page 252). Some mothers are very tempted to give solids earlier because they think it will make their baby sleep through the night – a thought often encouraged by well-meaning grannies. Although babies do wake from hunger, the length of time they sleep is also largely governed by the maturity of their brain (see chapter 8) and stuffing them with food only makes them fat and sometimes more fretful if they are already prone to colic. Cereal or any solid food should never be added to bottle-feeds.

However, just as there are good reasons for not starting too early, so there are also reasons for not leaving weaning too late. New babies carry a store of iron in their livers laid down during the last months of pregnancy (premature babies are different, see page 193) which can meet their need for the first four to six months of life. As this runs down they need other sources, and milk alone is not enough. There is also a belief amongst some paediatricians that babies have 'sensitive periods' when they are ready to move on to or learn a new activity – in this case chewing solid food – and that if they do not have the opportunity or are prevented at this time it is very hard to get them to do it later.

WHAT TO FEED

At first foods need to be very smooth indeed, strained or puréed. Egg, wheat and unmodified cow's milk may be causes of allergy (see page 253), and some doctors recommend that you do not give these until six months and not until a year if there is a history of allergy in the family. If you use a baby cereal to start with, choose one based on rice or other grain such as oats, rather than wheat, and mix it with boiled water, formula milk or breast milk. Alternative starters are puréed vegetables or fruit, but if you use vegetables from the family meal take them out of the cooking water before adding salt – extra salt is unnecessary for babies and it increases the risk of dehydration. Similarly, never add extra sugar to cereals because this may condition his taste towards sweet things. Use a non-brittle, smooth plastic spoon and sterilise both spoon and bowl before using. Offer just one teaspoon of the chosen food either before or half-way through the lunchtime feed and finish off with milk from breast or bottle.

FIRST TASTES – WHAT TO EXPECT

'I felt it marked a milestone the day I gave her a first teaspoon of solid food. I really enjoyed mixing up a tiny quantity of baby food and putting a bib on her – it seemed to be so much what I imagined having a baby was all about. I suppose it is pretty well what little girls do when they are

playing dollies! But actually feeding the stuff to her was like trying to put a teaspoon of water into the mouth of a hot water bottle that was already overflowing – it all just kept coming out again.'

Don't expect your baby to open his mouth and know what to do at first. Taking something from a spoon instead of sucking, having to move the food to the back of his mouth with his tongue, and the taste and the texture of the food itself, all adds up to a bewildering number of new sensations and at first most of the food does tend to get pushed out again. Let him get used to the whole experience gradually with just a teaspoonful once a day for a week – a bib is a good idea even though you are only giving a tiny amount to begin with. Be patient and relaxed. Some babies take very quickly to solids, others are not interested for some time, but if you persevere in offering a taste once a day, he will eventually get the idea and you can gradually increase the amount to match his appetite. Just as with breast and bottle-feeding in the early days, his demands are a good guide. Once he is taking some food at one mealtime you can begin to offer something at a second time in the day.

CUTTING DOWN ON MILK

His needs should still be met mainly by milk, and you need to make the change from principally milk to principally solids very gradually – too much solid food too quickly can also make him dehydrated. The first feed to be dropped will usually be the one following the solids – most babies can learn to drink from a cup or feeder cup from about five to eight months. Once a baby starts to have solids remember he will usually need extra fluids. Offer diluted fruit juice (not squash) or cool boiled water after the food and in between mealtimes if you think he may be thirsty. But remember that sucking is still an important source of pleasure and comfort to babies and make the change-over very gradually – it usually takes two to three months. Many babies continue with a last 'comfort' breast or bottle-feed for much longer.

COW'S MILK

Paediatricians now advise continuing breastfeeding or the use of a modified infant formula feed until a year old or at least until the baby is taking drinks from a cup or teacher beaker. But ordinary, whole-fat pasteurised cow's milk, provided it is fresh and has been kept in the fridge, could be given occasionally after six months, or if you want to be extra safe you can boil it and let it cool. However, cow's milk may be a cause of allergy and if you, your partner or a brother or sister has a history of this (eczema, asthma, hay fever, etc.) the modified milks are less sensitising. So delay introducing fresh cow's milk or take expert advice from a doctor or dietitian specialising in this field about an alternative – some babies can also be sensitive to soya and/or goat's milk. Specially manufactured follow-up milks can be used as an alternative to infant milk after six months provided a variety of weaning solids are included in the diet. Skimmed milks are not suitable for children below the age of about five years, and semi-skimmed below the age of two years.

CUTTING BREASTFEEDS

As your baby sucks less at the breast, so less milk is made. When you first miss a feed you may find your breasts begin to fill with milk as the let-down reflex works before the next feed time, but your baby will usually be happy to have the meal that follows early. Alternatively offer the breast after the baby has had his solids. After a day or two your supply will have adjusted. It is quite possible, and often convenient and a source of pleasure, to carry on with just a morning and evening feed for some time. This may even be advantageous to babies in continuing to provide protection from infection and allergy.

Some babies just finish breastfeeding of their own accord and seem to lose interest naturally – others would carry on, it seems, for ever, and it is you who want to call a halt. There is no 'right' time to end breastfeeding, and some mothers choose to carry on past the first year of life. There is often a tinge of sadness about the last breastfeed, but you can continue to enjoy holding him close and cuddling him just as often. La Leche League, the Association of Breastfeeding Mothers and the Breastfeeding Promotion Group of the National Childbirth Trust can give more information (see address section, pages 673–6).

LEARNING ABOUT LUMPS

From about three to six months your baby has been adjusting to taking some of his food puréed or strained instead of simply having milk. From about six to nine months he is in the next phase which enables him to make another series of changes so that by about nine months he manages to chew soft, mashed and minced foods and finger food. By a year old he can eat more or less what the rest of the family have with the addition of extra milk drinks and of course vitamin drops.

Begin to feed him meals with more solid lumps of food – at first you can make food sloppier and easier for him by mixing grated cheese, fish and minced or finely-chopped meat with well-cooked cereal or potato. Soon family meals need be only lightly mashed, although meat often continues to be hard for babies to chew. You have to mince it or cut it very small, and then mix it with gravy so it is not too dry.

If you are feeding mainly ready-prepared baby foods, begin using the junior or stage two varieties instead of the strained ones and start some home-cooked foods as well. Unless you have a special reason to worry about allergy, milk and milk products such as yoghurt and cheese and also egg should be introduced as an important part of his diet. Around a pint of cow's milk (whole pasteurised) a day is a rough guide to what he needs, and may be given as custard, yoghurt or in milk puddings, such as semolina, rice pudding, junket or blancmange. Three or four well-cooked

eggs per week should be included as egg dishes. By this stage at least one or two drinks should be given in a cup or feeder cup, and bottles should be discontinued by about ten to twelve months.

FINGER FOODS

'Once my children got on to the stage of being able to chew and eat lumps, I used to feed them almost everything by just putting pieces in front of them and letting them pick them up with their fingers – toast, fruit, bits of sausage and fish fingers, and I have to admit my daughter even used to eat spaghetti hoops like that! It made them slower to learn to use spoons, but it did save an awful lot of hassle.'

Once he can pick up and hold pieces of food in his hand you can offer your baby finger foods, which give practice in chewing as well as enjoyment – but stay on hand and watch in case he begins to choke on lumps bitten off. Obvious examples of suitable foods are rusks, toast fingers, pieces of peeled fruit and sticks of cheese, but a hungry child will eat almost anything with his fingers if you can stand the mess!

LEARNING TO FEED HIMSELF

Children learn by imitating and a baby who sits with the family at mealtimes or eats with older children will soon want to have a go at feeding himself with a spoon. Some mothers hate the mess this experimental stage involves so much they will not let their child try. But stopping children who are ready to learn a new skill may mean it will be more difficult to teach them later. It can also be frustrating for the child who may get cross and try to grab the spoon.

The best idea is to stand the highchair on a square of plastic or newspaper, cover your child with a plastic bib with sleeves, make sure he is hungry and let him get on with it while you eat your own meal. A small spoon with a deep bowl is easier for scooping things up than a flat, shallow bowl. His natural desire to copy you and any other members of the family, plus hunger, will ensure he gets some food in. Children who are allowed to try to feed themselves like this when they want to will soon learn to eat with a minimum of mess and save you hours of spoon feeding. Alternatively, you can give the baby a spoon and let him feed himself while you continue to pop in the occasional spoonful yourself.

Once playing completely takes over from eating, that is when he begins throwing the food on the floor or playing mud-pies with it, you know he has had enough and you can offer him some suitable pudding, some fruit, a milk drink or let him go and play. Do not try to get a young baby to stay in his chair as long as everyone else stays put round the table, unless he is happy.

EATING OUT

While babies and small children are unfailingly welcome in eating places abroad, we British are far less tolerant. Small babies in carry-cots do not usually present too many problems, although if you are nervous you can check with the restaurant in advance. Dressing with a little thought usually makes discreet breastfeeding possible – the table itself provides a screen – or ask beforehand if they have a room you can use.

Most restaurants which specifically welcome children provide high-chairs, otherwise ask if you can bring a portable one which fastens to the table or a chair. Taking suitable toys, diversions, drinks in appropriate containers and making sure your child is hungry, so that he spends at least part of the time eating, all helps. Timing of sleep to coincide with the meal and either rocking him off beforehand in a pram or reclining pushchair often works well, or one of you can nip out for a few turns round the block to lull him off between courses. Park the chair or pram inside and within sight or sound.

The most difficult age to eat out with children is between the onset of walking to around three years, although it depends slightly on your child's temperament. All the previous tips still apply, and in addition you can give him lots of exercise beforehand and keep his interest by telling him a bit about what is happening around him. Waiting for food is a sophisticated challenge for toddlers, so bring a private supply of mini-sandwiches or bits of fruit to ward off screams of anguish when the next table gets served first! Generally, though, if the meal out is meant to be something of a treat for you, arranging to leave a toddler with someone else for an hour or two may spare you both unnecessary trauma.

FOOD INTOLERANCE

Children may develop physical symptoms and (although this is more controversial) behaviour problems because of food they have eaten. The foods that cause the trouble may be natural, like wheat, eggs, milk or chocolate, or they may be artificial substances added to food for colouring or as preservatives.

The child's reaction may be caused in a number of different ways. The food may be infected or contain chemicals that are poisonous (toxic) to the child: bacteria and viruses may cause food poisoning in this way, but some foods may be chemically toxic to sensitive children, even though they are not infected. The child may be lacking in an enzyme to deal with the food in question, so that toxic substances build up and harm him, or he may have an allergy.

Normally, the immune system of the body reacts to substances or organisms it thinks are attacking it, such as bacteria, by developing antibodies. The antibodies are formed the first time the substance attacks the body, and the person is then sensitised. When the substance attacks the body again, the antibodies are released again. Usually the result of the antibody release is a healthy one, mobilising the body's defences effectively against attack. However, in predisposed children, the immune system of the body may also react by producing allergic symptoms such as asthma, eczema, hay fever, and, possibly, behaviour problems, like hyperactivity.

Doctors use the term 'allergy' in an exact sense to describe the body's responses when the immune system is involved, but many people use the term much more loosely: for example, they may say, 'I think I am allergic to my boss.' It is important to remember that allergy is only one of the ways in which the body can react unhealthily to substances in the environment.

Food intolerance can run in families, so if your husband or you or a close relative suffers from eczema, asthma, rhinitis (runny nose and eyes) or other symptoms of sensitivity there is a greater chance that your child may also suffer.

Some preventive action is possible in the case of food allergy or sensitivity. To show symptoms a baby must first have been exposed to the foreign protein antigen causing the problem – once he has encountered the antigen and begins to react he is said to be 'sensitised'. Some specialists suspect this can happen before birth if an allergic mother-to-be eats something which causes her to react. Her raised antibody level enters the baby's circulation and the baby could theoretically be born with a ready-made sensitivity to that food. Although there is no hard factual evidence to support this, there is some anecdotal evidence, and it is worth while for women with allergies to have their problem identified and controlled as effectively as possible before and during pregnancy and then follow a safe diet in pregnancy to avoid an allergic attack. Naturally this applies only to food allergy and not to inhaled substances such as pollen.

Cow's milk is one cause of food allergy. The importance of this lies in the nutritional role of milk in the diet, especially of young children. The immature immune system of new babies is particularly sensitive and may react to the foreign protein in cow's milk. If there is a family history of allergy, mothers are particularly advised to breastfeed, not to take in too much milk or milk products themselves, and if possible make sure their baby does not have any formula feeds at all – one bottle is quite enough to sensitise a baby. When breastfeeding is not possible a soya or modern modified (heat treated) formula feed may be advised, but soya can also affect some children, as can goat's milk which is not suitable for babies in any case. Your doctor or paediatrician should advise. It may be that you should not give any fresh cow's milk or milk products such as cheese and yoghurt or egg until your child is a year old but continue the formula feed.

Introduce a small quantity of these foods (a teaspoon or two) for the first day or two. Stop if there is any reaction. Symptoms vary but common signs are skin rashes, miserable behaviour, failure to thrive or gain weight and occasionally colic. Remember, however, that babies can get these symptoms from a number of other causes, and if symptoms have started suddenly after months of successful feeding with foods based on cow's milk, then it is unlikely that cow's milk protein intolerance is the cause. Remember too that if you reduce your baby's milk intake, the nutrients in milk like calcium, vitamins, protein and calories must be replaced in the diet to avoid affecting growth.

HOW CAN YOU TELL IF FOOD INTOLERANCE IS YOUR CHILD'S PROBLEM?

'My daughter was fine while breastfed but when I started solids she began getting a rash around her mouth and horrible nappies. I had a friend with a child that was milk allergic and wondered if this could be the same problem with the milk content in the solids causing a reaction. Sure enough, after three milk-free days the rash and the diarrhoea disappeared. I tested by giving her a small amount of cheese mixed with potato and by the end of the meal her skin began to look red around the mouth and within an hour the rash was quite noticeable.'

The only sure test of any food intolerance is elimination and challenge. This means eliminating, or cutting out, the suspect food from the diet and then, once symptoms have disappeared, challenging by reintroducing a small amount again with the symptoms reappearing. If symptoms do not disappear or reduce significantly within three to five days of completely cutting out the food, you can conclude this is unlikely to be the problem. If they do disappear and return with reintroduction of the food it seems likely that this is the cause. When this is done under the supervision of a specialist, it will be strictly controlled to make sure the suspect food really is being eliminated and not taken in other forms, and that the child's diet remains nutritionally balanced. However, more than one food may be the cause, and sorting this out is definitely a job for an expert.

Parents often try eliminating foods from their child's diet without any medical supervision in the hope that it may help a physical or behavioural problem. There are potential hazards with do-it-yourself testing and children should not be put on elimination diets without expert supervision. There are possible dangers in reintroducing foods to a child who is highly allergic, and it is also sometimes a difficult task to pinpoint exactly what is causing a reaction because it is often a combination of quite unrelated foods. Parents should seek medical advice and the correct diagnosis of symptoms. If they are to test their child safely for food intolerance, they must be careful to bear in mind the points made below:

* Symptoms must not be treatable by other means, e.g. 75% of children with eczema need ointment and emulsifiers and only if these fail should a diet even be considered.

* Be objective and do not convince yourself in advance that food intolerance is your child's problem.

* Cutting out cow's milk to test for a reaction by omitting milk temporarily will not do any harm in the short term: five days should be

enough to see if this is the problem. Some babies, however, react to goat's milk and soya-based formula given instead of cow's milk and others react more severely when milk is reintroduced as a test dose or by accident after it has been omitted from the diet for a period of time. So ask your GP, health visitor, hospital paediatrician or dietitian for advice. In the long term you need advice from one of these professionals if your child is to follow a safe milk-free diet to be sure he is still getting the nutrients he needs. They can also advise on the need for supplementary vitamins or minerals and brands of foods which are free from milk.

* If symptoms appear only after weaning keep a diary of what your child eats and the occurrence of signs such as rashes, diarrhoea, etc., but beware because not all of these are due to allergy. Get the co-operation of your partner or a friend to help you to be objective about the severity of symptoms. Study the diary to try to pinpoint troublesome foods. Wheat and egg are two very common antigens after cow's milk and occur in many foods, but if they are excluded nutritional replacements are necessary to ensure your child gets enough to eat and will grow.

* Cut out only one food at a time otherwise you will not know what an improvement was due to. Be careful to cut out all products with that item in. This may mean a lot of label reading. During the time this item is cut out, replace it with something from the same food group so that your child still has a balanced diet (see page 258), for example, if you omit wheat, replace it with rice or rice flour or rice cereals.

* Food addiction is often an aspect of food intolerance – we crave the things which make us ill. If your child regularly likes and eats a lot of a certain food, say oranges or milk for instance, try cutting out that item first.

* Be very cautious about reintroducing a supposed problem food. Two reactions are possible after a problem food has been eliminated for a period: either the child may lose what tolerance he had for the food so that even a very tiny amount can make him very ill and in extreme cases he may go into what is called 'anaphylactic shock' and collapse. For this reason you must test with only a very tiny amount of the suspect food for one to two days in case your child reacts severely, and then increase to a full serving daily for a week. Give the test dose with two adults present and watch your child for the first twenty minutes in case a severe reaction occurs. Alternatively they may be able to tolerate small amounts of the food again.

* Your child may grow out of food intolerance so do not keep the fixed idea that he can never eat a certain item again. Occasionally test him with a very small amount and if it seems safe gradually reintroduce it.

Chapter 7

FEEDING THE UNDER-FIVES

What is a balanced diet?   Good eating habits – lessons for life
Tips for feeding a young family
Good meals don't have to be a chore   Drinks   Sweets
Family eating habits   Eating problems   Fat children
Behaviour problems and food intolerance

A calorie (also called a joule) is a unit of energy. We all need energy and children need a great deal because they are not only naturally very active, but they are also growing. While a woman of average build, working at home looking after children and running the house, would burn up about 2,000 calories a day, her two-year-old son would need about 1,300 calories. When you consider that he probably weighs only two stone, perhaps a quarter or less of her weight, you can see just how many calories he uses up in the vital business of making extra tissue grow. Children, then, need a great many calories, but energy alone is not enough for the body to stay healthy and grow. We also need protein, vitamins and minerals. Some foods, like sweets, contain lots of calories but nothing else. Others, like meat, fish, cheese and cereals, provide energy along with protein and other nutrients. Bread, cereals (particularly the wholemeal varieties), fruit and vegetables, should make up the major part of the diet. Feeding the right mixture is called a 'balanced diet'.

WHAT IS A BALANCED DIET?

A little of everything, but everything in moderation, is probably the best way to describe a balanced diet. Imagine the body as a very complicated machine – different types of foods provide different kinds of nutrients which the body is able to absorb in just the right amount to provide the perfect fuel. Missing out on one type of food over a long period means that the body has to try to run on an incomplete or poor quality fuel. Just like any machine, that will inevitably mean a strain on the different parts which can finally show in malfunction or breakdown – in other words, poor health or illness.

The bodies of children need the best quality fuel even more than adults because as well as working in a very complicated way their body machines are also growing and expanding. A poor diet through childhood can mean a child's body never grows properly or has a number of built-in weaknesses. Children who regularly eat nothing but cakes, biscuits and sweets will be short of protein, vitamins and minerals. At the other end of the spectrum, a child who eats nothing but fruit and vegetables may take in large quantities of vitamins and minerals but miss out on protein and enough calories.

In recent years we have become far more conscious of the way in which our diet affects our health and of diet-related illnesses. The fact that we Westerners eat far too much sugar and too little fibre, or roughage, and starch in the form of wholegrain foods, fruit and vegetables has been said by some experts to be one of the main causes of illnesses like heart disease, diabetes and even some forms of cancer.

The government has recommended that the population as a whole cuts the amount of fat and sugar it eats and replaces the calorie deficit with wholegrain cereals, fruit and vegetables. But what some parents have overlooked is that *it has been specifically stated that these rules should not apply to the under-fives*. The reason is that their metabolism, the rate at which they burn up calories, is quite different from that of adults. It makes sense to keep down sweet consumption and the amount of very sugary drinks and foods your child eats because these are empty calories – they provide energy but little else. Too many will only give your child the habit of sugar eating which may make him fat, rot his teeth and deprive him of other nutrients. However, parents who mistakenly apply adult eating rules too zealously to their young children could unwittingly end up depriving them of the large number of calories they need to grow. If growth is affected during this toddler stage, it can have long-term effects on development. This is not a reason, however, to become over-anxious about hunger-striking toddlers who go through phases of refusing many foods they previously enjoyed.

Types of foods can be divided into five different groups (see below) for the nutrients they provide. Include some from each group each day to ensure that you are eating a balanced diet. Don't worry if children seem to go from hamburger and chips to sandwiches and cake on a day out – just make sure you cut down on fatty and sugary foods the next day and feed them more in the fruit and vegetable line.

FOOD GROUPS

Milk and milk products Milk, yoghurt, cheese and cottage cheese provide protein for body building and repair, calcium for teeth and bones and vitamin A and some B vitamins for good health.

Meat, fish, eggs and pulses Beef, pork, lamb, liver, kidney, chicken, herring, mackerel, white fish, sardines, tuna, shellfish, eggs, peas, beans, lentils, seeds and nuts all provide protein for body building and repair

— especially muscle and tissue. Liver, kidney and egg yolk are especially rich in iron for normal blood. Fatty fish (herring, mackerel and sardines) are especially rich in vitamin D for strong bones. Vegetarians can use pulses (peas, beans, lentils, nuts, etc.) to provide protein, iron and vitamins, but do not give whole nuts to any child under four years because there is a real danger of choking — peanut butter or ground nuts in cutlets are fine, though.

Bread and cereals Wholegrain bread, cereals, rice and pasta are better than whitegrain products which have been stripped of some of their nutritional content and also fibre. These are high-energy foods and contain some vitamins and minerals too. Fibre makes the bowel work properly and prevents constipation, and eating more fibre in the form of wholegrains, fruit and vegetables may be important in preventing certain types of bowel diseases. Most young children happily accept wholemeal bread, pasta and brown rice if everyone else eats them, but if your child will eat only white bread this is still a good basic food and he should certainly carry on eating this rather than go without bread at all. Bran is not necessary and should not be fed to young children, except that found naturally in wholegrain bread and cereals, as it can interfere with the absorption of important minerals like calcium and zinc. It may also give a child stomach cramps.

Children who do not eat sugar have healthier teeth without fillings. Liking and craving sugar is a habit which can be hard to break — you will be doing your child a big favour by not adding sugar to drinks and foods and by teaching him to enjoy dried or fresh fruit as treats, rather than eating too many sweets. Many sugar foods are high in calories but low in other nutrients, which increases the risk of getting fat without providing any of the fuel the body needs to function.

Fruit and vegetables All fruits and vegetables contain vitamins which are very important for our health and growth. Vitamin A, for example, is important for our eyesight and also for the health of our skin, hair and nails — like many vitamins it can also increase our resistance to infection. Carotene is a substance which is converted to vitamin A in the body and is supplied by carrots, tomatoes and all green and some yellow vegetables, for example swede or pumpkin. It is also found in dried apricots and prunes. Vitamin C increases our resistance to infection and is important for tissue repair and normal growth. It is found in citrus fruits like lemons and oranges, in berries, and also in green leafy vegetables. Unfortunately, the vitamin content of vegetables is easily destroyed by cooking or processing, so whenever possible let your child eat them raw and do not store fresh vegetables for a long time before using them. Remember that frozen vegetables are often as good as fresh ones and they do not lose their vitamins during the freezing process. Tinned vegetables will have lost far more of their vitamin content and may also contain chemical additives. While many children go through a phase of refusing cooked vegetables, they will often eat raw vegetables, such as sticks of carrot or celery, and also fresh fruit.

Fats and oils Our bodies need some source of fat to protect and insulate vital organs. Some fats also contain fat-soluble vitamins A, D, E and K. Fats can be either saturated, mono-unsaturated or polyunsaturated and recent research suggests that eating too much of the saturated type of fats, which come mainly from animal sources, can be bad for us and in the long term may be linked with heart disease. Red meat, meat fats and dairy products are high in saturated fats, so replace some of these foods with poultry, rabbit, oily fish such as mackerel and herring, and use cooking oils from plant sources such as safflower, sunflower, soya and corn oils rather than lard. These foods are all higher in polyunsaturated fats. Red meat is a good source of iron and zinc and should not be cut out completely though.

For the under-fives try to avoid feeding too much fried food, but there is no need to ban them from eating butter. Simply use fat for cooking sparingly, and replace some of the foods high in saturated fats with those rich in polyunsaturated fats. It could be positively harmful to give them skimmed milk rather than whole milk because the fat-soluble vitamins contained in milk are found mainly in the cream. Taking away most of the fat from milk not only lowers its calorie count but reduces the amount of essential fatty acids and vitamins it has to offer.

GOOD EATING HABITS – LESSONS FOR LIFE

Good eating habits are not to do with how you hold a knife and fork but about the kind of food you eat, your attitudes to food and the part it plays in your life. Our ideas start being shaped in the early years by what our parents teach us — both in the example they set and the food they offer. This early influence can be far-reaching and carries through into school years and possibly into adult life. Good eating habits lessen the risk of a weight problem and increase the likelihood of good health, so you will be doing your child a big favour if you look objectively at your own eating habits and try not to pass on the bad ones.

DO teach him to eat principally at mealtimes. It does not matter that the actual times may be a bit erratic or the meals informal — you are teaching that eating happens at specific times and that life is not a non-stop nibble. However, most young children need three small meals and three snacks a day.

DO NOT feed him endless high-calorie snacks between meals. He will not be hungry for the more nutritious food offered at the meal and is more likely to go short of the essential nutrients. To begin with, babies and toddlers need five to six meals and snacks a day, but that is different from untouched meals and endless rusks, crisps, biscuits and sugary drinks in between.

DO teach him to enjoy a wide variety of different foods. You need to persist when offering new foods to toddlers and babies and continue to give small amounts of new items until they get used to the taste.

DO NOT be defeated into giving only two or three particular foods in the early days to a fussy toddler because that is all he seems to want – keep trying different ideas in between the favourites and do not fuss when he refuses.

DO set the example you want him to copy with your own eating habits. Children are highly imitative and that applies to *what* you eat, not just *how* you eat. Share mealtimes and eat the same dishes once they are old enough for ordinary family food. If mum and dad do not have vegetables nor will their children!

DO NOT teach him to crave sugar. If you never add it to drinks and foods or give him foods with a great deal of sugar he will never miss it. Mothers often find it hard to feed their children drinks or foods they would not like, but if you already have the sugar habit resist the temptation to pass it on – too much sugar only rots teeth. Try to cut it out yourself.

DO teach him to enjoy fresh fruit and vegetables by giving him different varieties from an early age and by eating them yourself.

DO NOT condition him into eating extra salt by sprinkling it over food at the table – it is quite unnecessary. All convenience foods contain a lot of added salt, and not just the savoury items, so we are already taking in quite enough without adding extra. There is a suggestion that eating too much salt over a lifetime may predispose certain people to high blood pressure. Giving salt to babies, even in home-made foods, is not advised as it increases the risk of them becoming dehydrated.

DO let him follow his natural appetite in deciding how much to eat. If you do not let him fill up on continuous snacks between meals, his hunger is the best measure of how much he needs at any meal.

DO NOT insist that he always clear his plate or try to cajole him into eating more than he wants.

TIPS FOR FEEDING A YOUNG FAMILY

Do not be put off and think that feeding your child good food has to mean making everything yourself, expensive trips to the health food shop or spinach four times a week.

FRUIT AND VEGETABLES

Most children like some kind of fruit. Seedless grapes, bananas, melons, satsumas, apples and pears can all be cut into pieces as soon as they are old enough for finger foods. Once they get to the stage of noticing what they eat many children go off vegetables. Do not force them to try to eat vegetables because you will be enforcing the idea that they are unpleasant. Instead, make sure they have some fruit and fruit juice each day for vitamin

C and go on enjoying and experimenting with vegetables yourself. Children are tremendous imitators and at some stage their curiosity will make them want to try what is on your plate. In between you can occasionally try them with raw pieces of vegetables to eat with their fingers while waiting for the meal to be ready – carrot, celery sticks, chunks of cabbage or cauliflower, uncooked peas and beans in their pod, cucumber and tomatoes are all likely favourites.

CONVENIENCE FOODS

Manufacturers process foods in many ways to allow them to be kept for extended periods. In general, the more processing a food undergoes, the more additives it will contain. There may be chemical colourings, flavourings or preservatives. Thus frozen fish is a useful and nutritious buy, but by the time it has been turned into a ready-made frozen fish and potato pie it will probably need to contain a preservative to keep it fresh. It will also be more expensive. A rough guide is to go for convenience foods which still resemble their original state – that is, you can recognise them when they come out of a packet or tin! Frozen vegetables can be as good as fresh shop-bought ones because they retain their vitamin and fibre value, but tinned vegetables have had to undergo more processing and will usually have had salt added.

WEIGHT WATCHING

Only a small number of young children are overweight, but the tendency increases by the time they reach their teenage years. Children who are allowed to follow their appetite and are not encouraged or expected to eat more than they want and who keep active will rarely get fat, but it makes sense not to feed too much sugar or too much fried fatty food. Grilled and baked foods are preferable to frying – for example fish fingers, hamburgers and bacon, which are just as easily grilled. Natually this makes even more sense with a child who has a tendency to put on weight, but if you have a serious problem you may need expert advice to help him to slim down (see page 272).

GOOD MEALS DON'T HAVE TO BE A CHORE

Good food does not have to keep you tied to the kitchen and, if your child is going through a fussy or hunger-striking phase, you will save yourself much anguish by keeping meals very simple and spending the time sharing other activities with your child – like looking at a book, playing a game or going out. Sandwiches made with wholemeal bread and filled with peanut butter, yeast extract, cheese, tuna fish, meat paste, pâté, ham, bacon, tomato or whatever your child likes in the savoury, not the sugary, line, together with some pieces of fruit and a drink of milk or some yoghurt

Bread and butter with ham or cheese

Baked beans on toast

Bacon and egg on toast

Soup and wholemeal bread

Raw vegetables

Sandwiches, fresh fruit and yoghurt

Some easy and well-balanced meals

make a well-balanced meal. If he will not eat sandwiches, just cut up pieces of bread and butter and something like cheese or ham for him to eat with his fingers, or try egg or baked beans on toast with fruit to follow. In winter you can toast sandwiches and offer a cup of soup and wholemeal toasted fingers to dip in it if he is able to manage.

If you cook only in the evening, you can freeze a portion for him to have at a later date, but be sure to defrost quickly by standing the container in cold water, and then heat thoroughly to boiling point before allowing it to cool enough for him to eat. If you save a portion for the next day, cool it quickly and keep it covered in the fridge, again reheating to boiling point. Do not save cooked food longer than twenty-four hours in a fridge or reheat more than once for a young child – if he does not want it, throw it away and do not be tempted to heat it up again for tea.

Most young children have a particular time in the day when they are hungry and eat well – do not necessarily expect him to want a full-sized meal every time, but capitalise on his favourite eating session, whether it is breakfast, lunch or tea, and feed a variety of types of food. For example, if he always eats a large breakfast you can give protein in the form of egg, bacon, baked beans on toast or anything else he likes rather than just let him fill up on two bowls of cereal. If he does not eat much fresh fruit then offer this at his hungriest time too. If you suspect he eats well at a certain meal because he is especially fond of what is offered, such as cereal, do not cut this out completely, but feed slightly less, and include other foods or fruit that he may be less likely to take on other occasions.

Avoid very spicy food like fried onions or chilli powder for babies under a year, and do not feed whole nuts to children under four because of the danger of choking.

DRINKS

Children are usually more thirsty than adults because their bodies do not adjust well to a sudden loss of fluid, such as occurs for example in an attack of sickness and diarrhoea or during hot weather. A two-year-old needs at least half a litre of fluid a day and a three-year-old at least three-quarters of a litre with more in hot weather. The amount and concentration of urine gives a guide to the adequacy of the fluid intake.

Fruit squashes contain very little fruit and a great deal of sugar and additives, so get your child into the habit of drinking milk, fruit juice and water instead. The label 'natural unsweetened fruit juice' on a drink means it must contain 100% fruit and no added sugar or preservatives. Concentrated fruit juice is also pure fruit, but needs diluting because it has been thickened and reduced in quantity. Fruit nectar contains 25 to 50% fruit, up to 20% sugar and large amounts of water, plus possibly preservatives, but exact quantities must be given on the packet. Fruit drinks have even less fruit and more sugar and water. Fizzy drinks like Cola and lemonade are fine for treats, but are not good thirst quenchers because they are so sweet: this tends to make children even thirstier, is bad for their teeth and takes their appetite away for more important foods. The amount of sugar in Cola is about 8%, in Lucozade 15 to 17%. You need not be anxious about the caffeine content of Cola – the cup of coffee you drink has three or four times as much, and the amount of caffeine in Cola will not affect your child. Since most older children do learn to love fizzy drinks, you could let them mix fizzy mineral water with fruit juice to make their own concoctions – cheaper, healthier and more thirst-quenching – or make your own Soda Stream drinks with fruit juices.

SWEETS

'My mother-in-law loves giving the children sweets, but she won't consult me first, and doesn't stick at small items but hands over whole bags of chewy sweets and big packets of lollies. I have tried saying tactfully that it is too much, and after she is gone I secretly take half away, but I don't want to offend her by being blunter.'

If you do not give your child a lot of sweets or chocolate he will not expect them. Certainly sweets and chocolate for babies should be avoided. Once they know what sweets are, you will have to cope with their demands, even at the checkout point in the supermarket. The first time you pick up a packet of sweets while waiting in the queue at the cash desk and hand it to your child, you are showing him that he can sometimes have the sweets he sees – and 'sometimes' is a very hard idea for a young child to accept. When he sees them and remembers next time, he is more likely to make a fuss if you do not buy any. It is much better to save sweets for special occasions, rather than buy them or hand them out routinely so that they become an expected part of some regular activity.

In terms of tooth care, a binge of sweet eating is better than eating them over a longer period – always brush their teeth well immediately after a sweet feast. Chocolate is also bad for teeth, but unlike other forms of sweet does offer some nutritional value in the form of protein and iron; check the label to make sure it is real chocolate and not just chocolate flavour or a small amount of chocolate around a sugary sweet or toffee.

Spoiling grandchildren is one of the joys of being a grandparent, but spoiling their teeth, making them less likely to eat anything nutritious at mealtimes and teaching them to expect sweets is not doing them any favours. Exactly what you say to doting relatives who turn up looking as if they have just raided a sweet factory depends on your relationship with them, but you are more likely to get their co-operation if you phrase it as pleasantly as you know how and give them specific guidelines. This may mean saying that only one lolly or small chocolate bar (preferably give the actual brand name because their idea of 'small' may not be yours) can be handed over, but if they really want to give more they can be saved for a party, special occasion or to share with friends, though you had better check with the friends' mothers first! Steer relatives in the direction of treats from the greengrocer's instead, like a bag of satsumas or grapes, a coconut, strawberries, or a bag of dried fruit or monkey nuts if your child is four or over. Small packets of dried fruit like raisins or sultanas are an alternative, or a carton of good quality ice cream made from milk.

FAMILY EATING HABITS

Table manners differ in every home – example is by far the best way to get your child to behave as you want because he will inevitably copy your pattern of family eating. Children who are brought up from an early age to sit round a table with other members of the family will soon pick up on adult cues, learn not to interfere with other people's food, to ask if they want more and to handle cutlery as you do. If meals are sociable, chatty occasions, they will also eventually learn something about taking turns to talk, although this is quite a sophisticated task. Try not to make your baby or young child the focus of too much attention at family gatherings because he can become self-conscious or start to show off.

Remember that if eating off your lap in front of the television or snatching a snack on the move is more your family's style, you cannot expect a young child to know how to behave at the occasional, more formal meal, when visiting relatives, friends or at Christmas time, so make allowances for him.

Usually, we tend to follow similar patterns of both what and how we eat to those of our parents, but eating rituals vary with different cultures. Children of other nationalities may be brought up with the food and customs of their parents' country and only later learn about the different,

Westernised, habits they may see in the homes of friends or when they are out.

EATING PROBLEMS

'I made her a bowl of rice pudding and she looked at it, and then at me, and then quite deliberately picked it up and emptied it on to the floor. I really shouted at her and then felt quite tearful.'

Most parents have passing worries at some stage about how much their child eats, what he eats, or how he eats it. This is quite understandable, especially in first children when parents do not have any experience of childish idiosyncrasies. Sometimes it is also hard to make the transition from dealing with an utterly dependent baby who has to be fed little, often and just the right foods to dealing with a young child whose needs are suddenly different and who can let you know when he is and is not hungry and what he wants to eat.

Many emotions are bound up in the whole business of preparing and giving food. Getting food rejected can feel like a very personal kick in the teeth for the chef, and children quickly find out how much you care, even though they may not understand exactly why.

Toddlers can do all sorts of horrific things with food, some of them innocent, and some, as they get more knowing, rather more experimentally testing. Obviously, you have to let them know what is and is not acceptable, but beware of making too much of what would otherwise simply be a passing phase in how much or what they eat because that is often how something trivial can develop into a real problem.

CHILDREN WHO WON'T EAT

'My son stopped eating anything much at fourteen months – looking back I realise now it was because the weather was hot and he'd just learnt to walk. Eating was boring and he wasn't hungry, but at the time I couldn't see it so clearly and wasted hours following him around with teaspoons of food trying to get him to eat. It all became an enormous game. If only I could have ignored it all the whole thing would never have become such a problem. As it was he didn't eat normally until he was three and a half and going to nursery school.'

All children go through phases of not eating, eating very little, or eating only a few foods – commonly labelled 'hunger strikes'. They usually begin in the second or third year and reach a peak around four years, disappearing with the start of school. If you largely ignore the problem and do nothing but offer meals without making a fuss or letting your child continually nibble in between, his hunger will ensure he takes what he needs. The more you try to encourage or force him to eat, the more he will discover how important this is to you, and what power he has to command your attention.

No healthy child will allow himself to starve, so if you have any other reasons, apart from his lack of appetite, to worry about his health, see your GP. Probably the best test to find out whether he is eating enough is to see if he is growing properly. Your health visitor will be pleased to check his height and weight against his expected growth which can be plotted on a chart. If this is all right, as it will be for most children, then exercise supreme indifference to plates of untouched food, but do not allow him to fill up on extra snacks of any kind in between meals or offer puddings instead. Sometimes, parents who complain that their child does not eat do not look realistically at what is eaten between mealtimes in the form of sweets, biscuits, crisps and other snacks.

Do not forget that drinks are food, too, and often young children who seem to eat nothing are still drinking a great deal of milk. Liquids are also filling, so drinks of any kind before meals will take away his appetite. If this is the case, cut the amount of milk he drinks to one pint of whole milk per day and do not give sweetened drinks at all, only water. Remember that although after the age of six months milk alone is not enough to meet all his requirements, such as iron, milk is nevertheless an important source of calcium and other nutrients and that a pint a day should be given.

Often parents worry that even though their child seems healthy now, eating very little will lower his resistance to illness and infection – he will get 'low' and not have the right reserves of vitamins and minerals. Provided your child is healthy, this is not true. You should of course continue to supplement his diet with children's vitamin drops from your local health clinic. Very delicate mechanisms operate to ensure we absorb just the right amounts of vitamins and minerals, and eating a lot or taking massive extra supplements does not mean the body is able to store more; indeed an excess of some vitamins, such as vitamin D, is toxic.

EATING AND ILLNESS

Going off food is often the first sign of illness which is usually followed by other symptoms such as a temperature, tiredness, wretched or miserable behaviour, sickness, diarrhoea, complaints about pain or a rash (see page 517 for guidelines on when to call the doctor). As in health, the best guide as to what your child needs will probably be his appetite, but remember he will need extra drinks. If he does not want anything at all, just concentrate, especially in the case of sickness and diarrhoea, on giving him plenty of fluid to stop him becoming dehydrated. Packets of special salts and sugar are available from your GP or over the counter from the chemist to make up into a drink to rehydrate him. If his lips and mouth appear dry and/or he hasn't passed urine for a number of hours (the number depends on the age of the child, but as a guide 4 to 6 hours for a baby under one year and 8 to 10 for a child from 1 to 5 years) go to see or ring your GP for advice.

Generally, though, as appetite returns, illness is a time to relax some

aspects of eating rules, so try to tempt him with milky drinks or sweetened drinks and interesting but nourishing snacks. Eating problems can often follow an illness when fads have been indulged, and you need to assess carefully when to go back to the 'rules' by gradually re-introducing normal eating. This may mean weaning a child who has gone back to having mainly breast or bottle-feeds on to solids all over again, or re-establishing a pattern of regular mealtimes for a child who has been having odd snacks as and when he wants.

Frequently children are temporarily ravenous after a bout of illness and eat anything and everything. However, although they will need extra drinks and snacks, they sometimes cling to eating habits they were allowed when ill. Parents who have been worried about their child and nursed him through an illness are naturally more anxious and do not want to upset him. However, the same rules apply as at other times – keep him busy and distracted between meals so that he forgets about asking for in-between treats: offer such treats at mealtimes sometimes if you think he will like them, as well as two or three extra drinks or snacks for a week or two. Do not make too much fuss or comment if he does not seem hungry.

CHILDREN WHO WANT FOOD ALL THE TIME

Fridge raiders are not as common as hunger-strikers, but this can be a passing phase which develops into a habit because it gets so much reaction from you. Taking food without asking, especially in other people's houses, usually acts as a sure way of getting your attention. It can be a sign of jealousy, for example, about a new baby. Make sure you give your child plenty of attention at other times and keep him busy and occupied in order to take his mind off food. Offer foods and drinks he likes at meal or snack times, but explain that extras are not permitted, except water. Play down your reactions to his eating habits generally – often children who seem obsessed with food can also be very fussy and refuse food at mealtimes. This may be another way of gaining your attention or the result of nibbling in between meals. If you think the problem has become serious or your child is getting fat, discuss the problem at your health clinic (see also page 272).

IS FOOD TOO IMPORTANT?

'My mother never cuddled or played with us but spent all her time in the kitchen preparing meals. She would take it as the most personal affront if you weren't hungry or didn't like something she served, and to this day I still can't leave anything on my plate and both I and my brothers have weight problems. She also had a very martyred attitude to it all – serving up wonderful children's teas at parties but with a stony face that defied us not to enjoy every mouthful after we had caused her so much work.'

When long-term battles about food become established, it can often be that the whole relationship between parent and child has come to rest on food and eating alone. If you seem to be at this stage, think about how much of your attention your child gets in other areas of his life. Do you play games or join in activities with him? Do you read stories to him, go for walks together or just sit him on your knee and talk about what he is watching on television? It may be that food is very important to you in some way, or that you find it hard to show affection to your children in other ways and feeding them becomes either the only way to show affection or a substitute for love. Children may make more and more out of what they will and will not eat if it is the only way they can get your individual attention and a genuine response – the fact that you get cross and angry does not make any difference.

Try to take the emphasis off food and concentrate on sharing other aspects of your child's life. If you find this difficult, then talking to your partner, a good friend or a professional you trust, such as health visitor or GP, may be helpful.

USING FOOD AS PUNISHMENT OR REWARD

Once children are old enough to understand, it is reasonable to say 'no pudding' until they have eaten some of the first course – though there is no need to insist on a clean plate. This is a straightforward reward system and probably what you have been practising when they were younger. It is also reasonable to deprive a child of an edible treat if it is set in context – for example, if they behave badly in a shop or supermarket and you are buying them a lolly or crisps then forgoing the expected treat is an obvious punishment. However, banning sweets or puddings for bad behaviour in a situation that has nothing to do with the food in question, or handing out sweets and other treats for good behaviour, just puts too much emphasis on food and eating all the time. For more on encouraging good behaviour see page 457.

FAT CHILDREN

Exactly what being overweight is is difficult to measure and even harder to define. Causes may be many and specialists all have different ideas and approaches to the subject. However, there are some general points which can be made to help parents who think their child may be becoming fat, or is fat already, or who have a weight problem themselves and are anxious that their child may follow suit.

The first is that prevention is better than cure and it is probably easier to help a tubby child slim down in the pre-school years when parents still have greater control over what is eaten, eating habits are not as fixed and the child is distracted from food with less difficulty. Later, when a pattern of eating too much and being fat is established, it can be very hard to change.

So at what point should you begin to watch your child's weight? Start by seeing that your baby does not get too fat because this will make him more prone to respiratory illnesses and he may be slower to do things like turning over, sitting up, crawling and walking just because too many rolls of flesh make it more difficult. Most fat babies grow into normal-weight children and it is only a small proportion of them, about one in ten, who are still fat when they start school. Include a good range of fruit and vegetables, cereals and small servings of high-protein foods. Distract the older baby with finger foods and smaller quantities of spoon foods at meal and snack times. Usually rolls of fat start to disappear during the second year when the child learns to walk, becomes more active and able to do more, and is usually less interested in food. For these reasons parents should always let a child's appetite dictate how much he eats and not try to force or coerce him into eating more.

Probably the best way to prevent a child becoming fat is to teach good eating habits in the early pre-school years. This means eating a wide range of different foods and not just a very few favourite items — many fat children are also extremely fussy about what they eat, sticking to just a narrow range of foods, and have a tendency to dislike fruit and vegetables. Offer pieces of fresh fruit or raw vegetables instead of crisps, cakes or sweets as edible treats or mid-morning or supper snacks.

It is very important for you to teach your child that eating is something that happens at specific mealtimes and to give only a drink in between meals to the child who is overweight. Continual nibbling will also make children likely to refuse the more nutritious food you offer at mealtimes. Teach your child to drink water right from the start and keep very sugary drinks like Cola, lemonade or sweetened squashes for special occasions. If a child stays fat after the first year of life, or after being normal suddenly becomes fat and gets into the habit of eating sugary, high-fat, high-calorie snacks and drinks, his risk of growing into an overweight teenager and adult is greater. If a child is fat at seven he has an almost 50% chance of continuing to be fat into adult life.

Why do some children become or stay fat? We do know what makes them fat – taking in more energy from food than is needed so that extra energy is stored as body fat. But even at that point the matter becomes complicated because all children sometimes eat more than they need – so why do some stay slim and others become fat? Obesity runs in families, so a child with two fat parents has a much higher chance of becoming fat himself. Whether this is because of some inherited tendency to obesity or because families share similar eating habits and attitudes to physical activity is uncertain: probably both factors are involved.

A pattern of eating more than is needed may begin for various reasons – perhaps the child is very difficult and the parent finds giving food is one of the only ways of comforting or appeasing him. This may be true at night as well as during the day, so that a baby or child with sleep problems gets offered far more night feeds or drinks. A parent who cannot show affection except by handing it out on the end of a spoon may put great emphasis on feeding, and in turn a child may try to please a parent by eating everything offered. Parents can also overfeed to compensate for guilt because they feel inadequate about some other aspects of their relationship with the child.

HOW TO TELL IF YOUR CHILD IS FAT

Look at your child when he is next running around naked or with a swimming costume on with other children of the same age – at bathtime, on the beach, at the swimming pool or simply in the back garden. If he looks very fat, especially round the thighs and abdomen, in comparison with other children, then almost certainly he is overweight. Think about the clothes you buy for him – do they always have to be two or three age sizes bigger because the waist will never do up or the sleeves are always too tight? The waist in particular is a good guide because tall but slim children may need bigger age sizes because of their height, but in their case the waist invariably needs taking in to fit properly.

Parents with weight problems themselves can often have trouble recognising or acknowledging a child's problem – if you are not sure, ask a couple of trusted friends for their opinion, but phrase the question so that it allows them to answer honestly. 'You don't think John is any more than big for his age?' may get a different response from, 'I am not sure if I should be concerned about John's weight – tell me truthfully what you think?'

Weight adjusted to height charts are a good guide, though children who consistently take in more calories than they need tend to be taller than average as well. However, a GP may simply be able to decide whether your child is too fat by looking at him.

HELPING CHILDREN TO LOSE WEIGHT

Many parents do recognise, at various stages, that their child is getting a bit tubby and solve the problem without professional help by just cutting down on high-calorie foods and drinks like biscuits, cakes, puddings and sweets, keeping their child busy to take his mind off food and encouraging more exercise. For parents who recognise that their child is continually and persistently gaining more weight than other children of his age, the pre-school years are still a time when they can more easily adjust their child's eating habits before he becomes seriously overweight. These are some simple rules to follow:

* Teach your child to eat only at mealtimes — a young child may need four small meals rather than three, but make them recognisable and definable occasions.

* Sit down and eat the same food as your child — use your example and that of other members of the family or visiting children to try to encourage him to eat a wide variety of foods.

* Between mealtimes give only fresh fruit or fresh vegetables as snacks.

* Provide plenty of opportunities for activity — walking, running and playing with other children are the most easily arranged. Trips to playgrounds and swimming pools can be managed sometimes.

* Both parents must co-operate to ensure success, and it is also important to have the co-operation of relatives and grandparents as well.

If your child is already into the habit of nibbling at whatever he wants between meals, then putting these five rules into practice will demand energy and determination. Children who are accustomed to having whatever they want to eat at almost any time will need to be encouraged in the mealtime habit — for example, by making sure they are hungry and by providing appealing but nutritious food. They also need to be distracted from their usual continual nibbling by being kept busy and occupied. This may be particularly hard for parents who are not, for whatever reason, in the habit of spending much time supervising their child's day.

Tubby two-year-olds will probably slim down naturally as long as you do not try to encourage or force them to eat more than they want — if you have a demanding new baby, resist the temptation to palm off the older child with food for the sake of a bit of peace. Instead, plan a few distractions in advance which do not involve eating. By three years, children enjoy having friends round and visiting other homes, though you usually have to go too. Playing with other children is both distraction and exercise and, if the other child has good eating habits and is a normal weight, then sharing mealtimes can set a useful example. Enlist the help of sympathetic friends or relatives to keep your child busy — if you have a weight problem yourself it may be very hard to ask for help initially, but good friends with the same age children can be very supportive.

Professional help may sometimes be hard to come by — if your child is fat do not be tempted to ignore the problem because your doctor takes the view that it is 'puppy fat' which will disappear of its own accord. If your GP is unsympathetic try asking for a referral to see a hospital-based or community dietitian or see your health visitor at the clinic. Special clinics do exist in some large hospitals but are not widespread for children – if your GP is unable to tell you of the nearest one you can ring the dietitian at your district hospital or the regional health authority.

BEHAVIOUR PROBLEMS AND FOOD INTOLERANCE

Many young children show patterns of behaviour that parents find hard to accept. Among these, disobedience, feeding and sleeping problems, temper tantrums, restlessness and difficulties in concentrating are among the most common. It is often suggested that food intolerance or allergy may be a cause of these difficulties and there is some evidence that, in a small number of children, this is indeed the case. All the same, before jumping to the conclusion that your child is difficult because of something in his diet, it is sensible to be cautious.

First, what is problem behaviour? One person's uncontrollable home-wrecker can be another's adorable, lively toddler. Children do vary quite a bit in their personalities, and inevitably some are more active, restless and wilful than others. Second, our circumstances affect the way we view children's behaviour – single parents with many problems, little support and bad housing will naturally find the normal phases children go through more of a strain. Your child's behaviour certainly is a problem if you find your life is being spoiled by it, but the problem may be more in your child's behaviour or more in the way you see it. If the problem goes on for some time, and other people, such as neighbours or a playgroup leader, comment on it, then probably the problem is more in the child than in you. Even if this is the case, the way you are bringing up your child may be important, as well as his personality.

HYPERACTIVITY

'My son never settled to long sleeps and cried a lot as a baby, but as a toddler he became impossible. He was always restless and miserable and never settled to anything. He was continually destructive but didn't even seem to get pleasure from that, and the number of accidents he had would fill a book. At playgroup he was aggressive and would never sit down with other children for more than a few minutes at storytime. He just whined or wandered around, darting between activities. Then I read about how additives can make children ill. I changed his diet and within a week he began to sleep longer stretches at night, stopped wetting the bed and sat on my knee and let me read a book to him for the first time.'

One type of behaviour problem is 'hyperactivity'. Doctors and psychologists use this term to describe children who are quite excessively active, have very poor concentration, and are reckless and impulsive wherever they may be – at home, with friends or in a playgroup. It is often suggested that children with this particular type of problem are especially likely to be reacting to something in their diets, and occasionally this may be the case. There are some convincing stories which have been widely publicised, and information about additive-free diets is given below. Before applying a diet, however, do remember these points:

* Your child may not be unusual in his behaviour at all. The problem may be in the way you are seeing him. Check out with friends and neighbours.

* There are many causes, other than diet, for children's behaviour problems. Try to work out what situation seems to bring out the difficult behaviour and do something about that first. Are you being firm and consistent enough when he wants something he cannot have? Do you have enough time to give him the affection he needs? Does the problem occur only when his young baby sister is on the scene?

* Are there any positive signs his behaviour is likely to be caused by allergy? Does he, or anyone in your immediate family, suffer from other allergic problems, such as eczema? Is his difficult behaviour accompanied by physical changes, such as his face becoming flushed or pale? Have you already noticed his behaviour is worse after certain foods?

ADDITIVE-FREE DIETS

Additives are chemicals added to packaged food to make it keep safely, last longer, or taste and look as a manufacturer thinks people find most appealing. Preservatives in the form of benzoic acid and the yellow colouring tartrazine are said to be the commonest culprits as far as allergies are concerned. There is no harm, however, in trying your child with a diet which omits the common additives listed below for a period to see if physical or behavioural problems improve. In some children simply cutting anything with artificial yellow colouring such as orange squash, lollies, cakes, sweets and anything coated in bright golden breadcrumbs makes a difference.

A number of manufacturers and supermarkets are now producing additive-free foods: the presence of additives is shown in foods on the content label of the tin or packet by what is called an E number – this is a code number recognised within the Common Market. Not all E numbers are harmful chemicals, some are vitamins or preservatives, but the following do cause reactions in some people:

E102 (tartrazine)	E210–E219 (benzoic acid and
E110 (sunset yellow)	its salts)
E124 (ponceau 4R)	E320 and E321 (antioxidants
E127 (erythrosine)	BHA and BHT)

If your child's behaviour remains a problem after you have tried an additive-free diet, you should consult your doctor or health visitor. It is quite likely that factors other than diet may be producing the problem. Alternatively, if no other factors do seem likely and there are positive signs that diet may be the answer, then it is just possible that your child is reacting badly to naturally occurring foods such as milk, eggs, wheat, chocolate or some fruits. To take this further you must consult a doctor and a dietitian who will be able to advise you how to cut out certain foods or even, if the problem is a severe one, how to put your child on a diet limited to just a very few foods to see if this makes a difference.

It is potentially dangerous to put your child on a diet cutting out these foods unless alternative sources of calcium and so on are given, so this diet must be supervised by a dietitian.

Chapter 8

SLEEP, WAKEFULNESS AND CRYING

'Is he a good baby?' What is sleep and why do we need it?
A bed for a baby A book at bedtime Sleep problems
Crying in young babies Babies who won't stop crying
Nearing the end of your tether

'IS HE A GOOD BABY?'

There can scarcely be a parent who has not been asked this question about a new baby. What the questioner often means is: 'Does he sleep for long periods and does he cry a lot?' It is one of the biggest shocks of becoming a parent to discover that the right you took for granted to sleep when and as you wanted has been taken away, apparently for ever. No wonder that in any gathering of parents with young children there is so much comparing of notes about how much their child sleeps at night. Hearing that someone else's baby settles for the night at 7.00 pm and sleeps without interruption until 6.30 am the following morning is certain to bring gloom, total amazement and a sense of inadequacy to the many parents whose children seem to spring to life as dusk falls. If the child in question also cries a great deal and is very hard to console, the stress for the parents is intense. But be comforted. Before reading any further, parents of wakeful or crying children should take some reassurance from these simple truths:

* This is probably the most stressful and difficult time you will have to cope with. Things can only get better.

* You are not alone with your problem – most people with children have had terrible nights and miserable days at some stage as well.

* There are things you can do to solve some of the problems – in other cases time alone will bring a solution.

279

WHAT IS SLEEP AND WHY DO WE NEED IT?

Sleep is different from unconsciousness. When we are unconscious our brains hardly respond to any outside stimulation such as light, temperature or noise, but during sleep our brains are still active, aware of the passage of time, and respond to bodily states such as hunger or anxiety as well as to certain sounds. Exactly why we need sleep is not yet fully understood, but one possibility is that it allows chemicals used by the brain to build up again ready for the next day. Researchers have divided sleep into four stages – stage 1 being the lightest and stage 4 the deepest. During the night we go through several cycles of sleep, moving backwards and forwards from light to deep sleep. When in stages 3 and 4, the deepest sleep, we are much harder to wake, but when in the lightest stage of sleep we are more likely to wake and in fact most people, both adults and children, do wake during the night but slip back again into sleep without remembering this brief period of wakefulness. It is often the children who do not slip back again into sleep unless they receive some kind of attention who give their parents sleepless nights.

An additional division in types of sleep is between 'rapid eye movement' (REM) sleep and 'quiet' (non-REM) sleep. REM sleep happens in the lighter stages and is when dreams and nightmares are most likely. People who are deprived of sleep fall more quickly into the deeper stages of sleep and also spend more time in REM sleep as though they need to catch up on dreaming time.

That children suffer less from loss of sleep than adults is one of the unfair facts of life parents soon notice. This is because they can cat-nap at odd intervals during the day – most parents know how impossible it is to keep a drowsy toddler awake in a pushchair or car seat. For the adult it is hard to snatch a few minutes' sleep for themselves in a day filled with the demands of small children. Lack of sleep can make adults irritable and depressed, impair their judgement and slow their reactions. Naturally this makes them less able to see the problem of their child's wakefulness or crying in any kind of perspective or to act rationally. This is especially true of all of us when we are woken at night, because immediately on waking the mind is less alert – something most people realise only too well! This is also true for your child – the result can be two people who find it difficult to behave very rationally towards each other.

SLEEP PATTERNS IN THE NEWBORN BABY

'I expected my baby to sleep most of the time and only wake for feeds. It was a terrible shock when all she did was doze for an hour or two at a time.'

It is a common mistake to think that new babies are either asleep or feeding. In fact a newborn baby spends six to eight hours out of every twenty-four awake, often for an hour or so at a time, and some are more

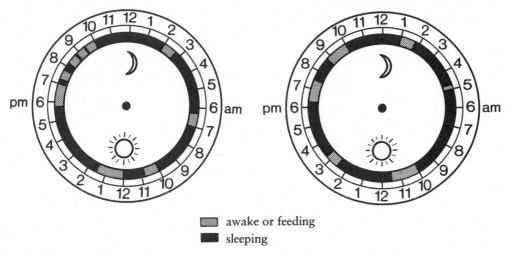

awake or feeding
sleeping

The twenty-four-hour clocks of two babies' sleep patterns can vary considerably

wakeful than others. The length of time they spend asleep depends on the maturity of the brain as much as their need for food. In the beginning, babies rarely sleep for longer than three to five hours, but by four months most can manage six to ten hours at a stretch and can also stay awake for several hours.

ENCOURAGING A DIFFERENT PATTERN BETWEEN DAY AND NIGHT

Manipulating the waking and sleeping hours of a young baby is not easy, but there are some things you can do to encourage longer stretches of sleep at night:

* Give your baby plenty of stimulation and attention by talking and playing with him when he is awake in the day.

* In contrast, make the night feeds as unstimulating as possible – do not encourage your baby to stay awake and play after a feed.

* Provided they do not have nappy rash, using double nappies, or liners in disposables, makes night-time nappy changes unnecessary and this reduces the chances of waking up your baby.

* From around ten to twelve weeks begin to develop a definite bedtime routine which he will get to know and recognise (see page 282). If your baby is very colicky this may not be possible until later (see page 243).

* Allow him time to settle on his own so that he begins to develop his own ways of going to sleep.

DEVELOPING A BEDTIME ROUTINE

'I used to spend hours trying to get my four-month-old son to go to bed in the evening when in fact he was having these great long sleeps late in the afternoon which set him up until ten o'clock at night. At the time I just couldn't see it because I was on holiday with friends with an identically aged baby who also had long afternoon naps and then went to bed each night at half past seven.'

Sometime between three and five months, depending on the baby, it will help good settling and sleeping habits if you establish a definite routine that leads to bedtime. The aims are to encourage the child to be in a calm, relaxed state which is likely to make it easier for him to go to sleep, to establish a sequence of events which the child recognises as signals that indicate bedtime, and lastly to enable the child to learn to make the transition from waking to sleeping. You will work out the exact nature of your own child's bedtime routine, but some points should always apply. First, the child should be in a clean nappy and not hungry or thirsty. Second, he should be ready for sleep. This may sound obvious but it is an essential aspect of establishing a successful bedtime routine.

Remember, no two babies are alike. The fact is some need a lot of sleep while others seem to manage on very little. But patterns can change, and the baby who never sleeps can grow into a toddler who needs two naps a day, while the baby who sleeps through the night from early on can become a wakeful child. In the beginning we all settle babies in the way they respond to best – rocking, stroking, patting, and so on. Various ways of soothing 'hard-to-comfort' babies are described on page 244. Something of this will carry on into the bedtime routine, but remember that you are instilling habits which will continue through into childhood. For this reason, it is much better to devise a routine that allows your baby to fall asleep without anyone else being involved. Hence cot-rocking, hair-twiddling, patting and stroking, which all entail you staying until he falls asleep, are not a good idea. Many babies fall asleep during a breast or bottle-feed, but again this is not a habit to encourage as a baby gets older. You will want to wean them at some point, and if they have only ever fallen asleep while feeding they will probably be harder to settle without the breast or bottle. For this reason it is much better to finish the last feed while your baby is still awake and then put him into the cot. He needs to be aware of this transition into sleep to be able to accept it without a breast or a bottle to suck. By all means sing your baby a lullaby, pat or stroke his back to help him relax, but leave the room and let him actually fall asleep by himself.

Here are some suggestions for a young baby's bedtime routine:

* Bath or wash, clean nappy and nightclothes.

* Take him to say goodnight to other members of the household.

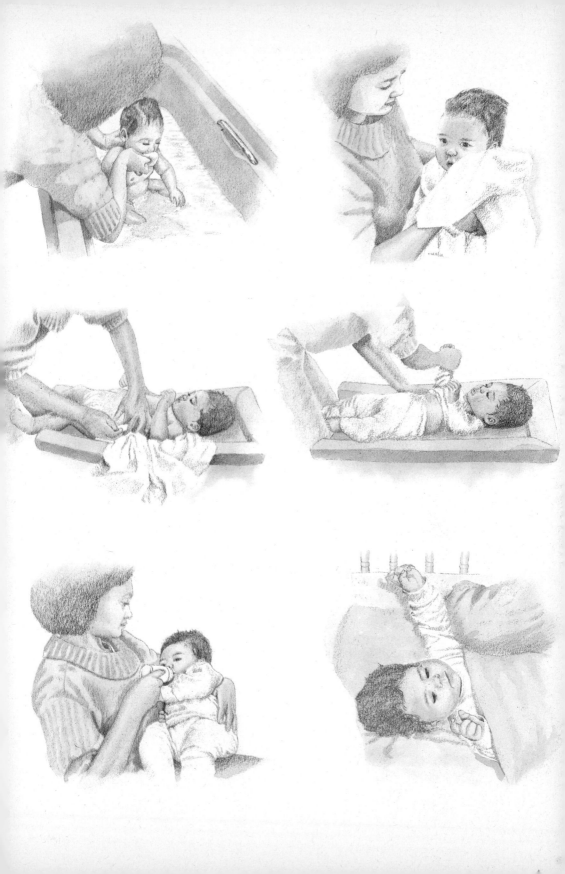

* Carry him upstairs or into his room telling him it is time for bed in a soothing voice.

* Last breast or bottle-feed in the room where he sleeps, but do not let him fall asleep during the feed.

* Song or lullaby while rocking him on your shoulder, but again not to the point of sleep.

* Settle him in the cot saying goodnight.

* Leave the room without waiting to see if he settles or using singing, rocking or patting to send him to sleep.

As your child grows, the bedtime routine needs to change to take account of age. From about twelve months, looking at a book may be incorporated into the routine (see page 289).

A BED FOR A BABY

It seems that small babies do tend to settle better in a fairly snug sleeping place. You can buy or borrow a crib or equally well use a carry-cot on or off its wheels. At a pinch a cardboard box will do as well, provided it has a mattress. A cot bumper is not recommended for babies under a year. Some parents like to take their baby into bed with them which is safe, provided neither parent is taking sleeping tablets or has been drinking.

New babies can lift and turn their heads to a certain extent, but they should never be put to sleep on anything soft, squashy or quilted, however comfortable you think it seems, because of the risk of suffocation if they cannot lift their heads clear of the material. For this reason do not use a pillow or duvet for a baby under one year old, and do not use a quilted baby nest for anything other than carrying or holding your baby. A fairly firm mattress covered with one or two layers of flannel, cotton or stretched towelling pulled taut is fine. Do not use nylon sheets because they do not allow air through and are likely to make your baby sweaty and possibly cause mild skin irritation. If your baby is the sicky type, then putting an extra layer of a muslin nappy or folded sheet across the head end saves changing the whole bed every time he burps up a little milk.

By about three or four months most babies begin to look rather cramped in a crib, unless they were very small to start with, and need moving to a cot. Using the same type of blankets and sheets and transferring familiar toys helps them to settle, and you can get them used to it by putting them in the cot for a few times during the day first. Most babies make the switch without any problems. When to move them into a proper bed depends on the child, space available and parental preference, but it is usually sometime between twenty and thirty months. For more discussion on moving children from cot to bed see page 288.

It is important that small babies do not get too hot or too cold. Premature babies are particularly bad at keeping themselves warm (see page 191). Several layers of light clothes are best. A vest, a stretch suit and shawl or cardigan is usually right indoors during the day. At night dispense with the cardigan or shawl provided you use about three or four blankets, keeping the room at a steady 18°C (65°F), see page 164. During the day, as long as the temperature is high enough to be comfortable for an adult wearing indoor clothes, that is fine, and a baby of over a month old need only wear the same amount of clothes as an adult. Choose a warm room for bathing young babies though. If your baby wears a vest, this will save undressing him completely when changing sleep-suits or nightdresses and help to keep him warmer. Unless your baby has nappy rash, is dirty or has wet nightclothes there is no need to change him during night feeds. Instead use a double nappy or disposable plus liner, plastic pants or ties, with a liberal coating of some kind of protective cream.

As they get older, babies can move out of all-in-one stretch-suits and into any kind of pyjamas, sleep-suits or nightdresses you fancy. Remember always to buy those that are flame-proof. Remember also that babies under two are especially likely to kick off bedclothes and something to keep their feet warm is a good idea in winter. Some people still think it is necessary to put mittens on babies to stop them scratching their faces. It is in fact much better just to clip their nails short. If you feel nervous about doing this, then baby nail-clippers may be easier to handle than scissors. Putting their hands and fingers to their mouths to suck is an important source of comfort and enjoyment for small babies and they should not be prevented from discovering their hands.

POSITION

Very recent research now suggests that there may well be a slightly increased risk of cot death if babies are allowed to sleep on their fronts. Instead it is now thought better to lay the baby on his back. If you put him on his side, make sure the underneath arm is in front of the body to stop him rolling on to his tummy. Babies develop their own preferences quite quickly though, and once your baby is able to turn over, he will naturally adopt the position he finds most comfortable. It is also important your baby does not get too hot while sleeping, so avoid duvets until he is at least one year old. Also make sure that the bedding does not cover the baby's head.

BABY ALARM SYSTEMS AND MATTRESSES

There is a lot of anxiety about cot death (see page 200) – quite understandably. However, some parents are so anxious that they buy expensive mattresses which are especially designed to give an alarm sound if the baby stops breathing – called 'apnoea mattresses'. If your baby really is at risk for some particular reason, then the hospital paediatrician will advise you if a mattress or alarm system is necessary, otherwise following the guidelines we have outlined is quite sufficient.

Baby alarm systems are designed to allow parents to hear if their baby is crying rather than a warning system to detect apnoea attacks. They can be bought from most baby specialists and department stores, and can be useful if you have a house where sound does not carry easily.

WHICH ROOM?

While babies are waking quite often and at unpredictable intervals for feeds, most people prefer to have them sleeping in the same room, preferably within arm's reach of the bed. If you find it easier still to have your baby sleeping in bed with you then go ahead. As long as neither you nor your partner are the worse for drink or drugs, you will still respond to your baby's movements while asleep and there is no danger he will get squashed. If you are breastfeeding, then having the baby in bed can be a way to snatch extra sleep while giving the breast.

There is no danger that taking a small baby under four months into bed with you will spoil him or get him into the habit of always sleeping with you. Most children go through a phase of wanting to sleep in their parents' bed, whether they were allowed in as a small baby or not. However, parents who do not want their babies in bed with them should not feel guilty or think they are being less loving; we all vary in the amount and type of physical contact we want with our children and it is simply a matter of choice for the individual.

Some parents worry that if their baby is not in the same room they will not hear him crying in the night. Provided sound normally carries between your room and where the baby is sleeping, that is highly unlikely because we all filter sounds in our sleep and parents usually respond very quickly to their baby's cry. In fact the opposite is sometimes true, and parents are too sensitive to their baby's night-time noises so that they wake with every rustle, snuffle and whimper, without giving the baby a chance to settle again. In the early weeks, when the new baby is not disturbed by light and noise but needs several night feeds, keeping him in your room is usually easier. Once he gets to the stage when you have to avoid making a noise or putting on the light for fear of disturbing him – which hopefully may coincide with longer stretches of sleep – it may help to have him in another room if possible. In many families that means moving them in with another child. If the child has to go on sharing the parents' room, it can sometimes be harder to be firm about sleeping problems which arise, but all the advice about trying to encourage good sleeping habits applies in the same way.

COMFORTERS AND COMFORT HABITS

'As a small baby my son got into the habit of rubbing a cotton cellular blanket against his face and sucking his thumb to go to sleep. When he

was two we went on holiday to Spain and left it behind on the aeroplane. It was total murder coping without it – every time he got sleepy he put his thumb in his mouth, reached for the blanket and then howled and howled when it wasn't there. I tried every kind of substitute but none would do. Fortunately we had a spare at home and the minute we got through the front door that was the first thing he went to find.'

Around six months of age babies often develop or can be encouraged to develop settling habits of their own. Perhaps the commonest is sucking – either at a thumb, a dummy or parent's finger. Thumb sucking in fact often develops much earlier and is the best of the three because the child can find his own thumb in the night without disturbing anyone else. A dummy can often be useful to soothe a colicky baby in the first four months, but it is better to transfer children to sucking their own thumbs after that. At what stage should you begin to discourage thumb sucking? The longer it persists, the harder it can be to stop, so by the age of three or four it is a good idea to discourage daytime thumb sucking. Continuous thumb sucking after the age when the second teeth begin to appear, usually around six to seven years old, may eventually push the top teeth forward, which may entail corrective dentistry later. There is no evidence that children who thumbsuck are emotionally deprived. Most children suck their thumbs only when they are tired, and the attitudes of other children generally encourage even the most addictive thumb sucker to give up, at least in public, by the time he gets to eight or nine.

Other comfort habits may be stroking something soft – such as silky material – rocking or twiddling someone's hair. Children can form an attachment to a special blanket or other piece of material or a particular toy. Some children naturally form their own comfort habits or latch on to a comforter, others can be encouraged to if you think it will help, and other children again are not at all interested. Two points are useful to remember – the comfort habits should not involve anyone else, and the comfort object should have a back-up spare or be easily replaced. As time goes on and the object gets battered and tattered, then it is unlikely an identical new one will be accepted – you might consider rotating identical blankets or whatever in the early days, so that if one gets lost or destroyed it is not such a disaster.

Comfort habits and comforters usually continue for many years, but eventually children do learn to settle without them. In the early years they can be a great help to soothe and comfort in times of stress and separation as well as when a child is tired.

MOVING FROM COT TO BED

Some children make it quite obvious when they are ready to move – they begin climbing out of their cot, refusing to go in it or simply starting to want to put themselves to bed in a brother or sister's bed. There is no right or wrong time to make the move in terms of age, although avoid moving them out of a cot just to make way for a new baby. It is more tactful to leave a gap of a few months and present the move to a bed as an achievement so they do not feel they have been pushed out of their cot by the baby.

Many children do not realise at first that they can actually get out of a bed, especially if they never learnt to climb out of a cot. Once they do realise, they will inevitably put this newfound freedom to use and keep hopping out every five minutes. The answer is to keep the bedtime routine the same and make sure they are ready for sleep. If they get up, keep calmly but firmly putting them back to bed – do not suddenly weaken and let them stay up or take them into your bed, because you are teaching them that if they try hard enough they can have their own way. It may mean hard work and broken nights again for a short time, but if you persevere for a couple of evenings or nights it will pay off in the long term.

You can put large cushions or chairs alongside the bed to stop your child falling out in the beginning. Check the room again for safety once the child can get up without you knowing in the morning. There should be no unprotected windows left open, for example.

A BOOK AT BEDTIME

As your child grows, looking at books together or telling or reading a story is part of a useful bedtime routine because it provides:

* A time of quiet closeness for parents and children together.

* Something enjoyable for the child to look forward to in the bedtime routine.

* An opportunity to learn to enjoy books and stories.

By the time they reach their first birthday, many babies enjoy books, although their attention span is short and they often get as much fun from turning the pages as looking at the pictures.

Small children naturally enjoy turning the pages of a cardboard book and often begin to look at the pictures by themselves. Very realistic pictures of things they recognise – like dogs, shoes or a cot – tend to mean more than stylised or cartoon drawings at this stage. Naming the objects and talking about them helps language to develop. Children like looking at the same book again and again, and a particular picture often holds a special fascination. At what stage you introduce simple stories depends on you and your child. Most children appreciate something more than just naming the pictures at some stage between one and a half and two years. Listening to a story and following a sequence of pictures is very much a habit, one which will hopefully give your child a good start in enjoying books.

When it comes to a bedtime story or book, take the child into a quiet

room so that you are not competing with the television, other children's activities or adult conversation for their attention. Make the child comfortable on your knee or snuggle him up beside you so that a cuddle becomes part of looking at books together. The child may enjoy choosing his own books for this session. You do not have to spend a fortune to get nice books for your child. Your local library or toy library will have a children's section with picture books suitable for babies and upwards, and jumble sales are also ideal places to pick up other people's outgrown books for just a few pence. If you enjoy making things you can even make an exciting book for your baby by cutting pictures out of catalogues and sticking them on to card for him.

SLEEP PROBLEMS

The commonest sleep problems are to do with settling at night or about waking and not going back to sleep in the night. It is very easy for a sleep problem to creep up on parents without them being able to see what is happening. Once the habit is established, they find it very hard to know how to change it. However, research has shown that by changing the way they respond to their child's behaviour many parents can succeed in changing the way their children settle and sleep.

Many children stay up very late, sleep in their parents' bed or will settle only if someone stays with them. If you do not mind, then it is not a problem, however unorthodox it might seem to another family. It is only when your child's sleeping habits are restricting your life in a way you do not want or creating stress and tension for you that it becomes a problem.

It is often difficult to see exactly what is happening when you get bogged down in what seems to be a never-ending battle over sleep. Your own tiredness often prevents you from seeing things rationally or having the strength to try changing the pattern. Start by keeping a diary of what happens at night, what your responses are and what the child does. Do this for at least a week or two before deciding on your strategy.

Some fathers are happy to share caring for a sleepless child at night, others expect to leave it to their partners. Sometimes it helps to break a pattern if the father, rather than the mother, goes to a child as part of the agreed plan. This may be especially so if the mother cannot bear to see her child crying without picking him up. The important thing is that both parents agree on the plan to be tried, carry it through consistently, and back up each other. One parent must not suddenly switch tack and begin to criticise and undermine the parent who is going in to see to the child.

Bringing up children alone is very hard work – both emotionally and physically. Single parents may often let children stay up late or sleep in their beds for company. But they also often need the freedom to go out in the evening to enjoy other adult company and leaving a child who is not used to a bedtime routine with a sitter can be harder. The methods described here work as well for one parent as for two and single parents should follow the same rules as couples in being consistent and determined to succeed.

ARE YOU ENCOURAGING YOUR CHILD'S BAD SLEEPING HABITS?

'My son was still waking twice or even three times a night for a breastfeed at eleven months. I was so desperate to go to sleep I used to take him into bed and fall asleep with him latched on rather than stand around for hours trying to get him back to sleep.'

In this case the eleven-month-old boy was being rewarded for waking in the night by being given a cuddle, a comforting suck of milk and being able to spend the rest of the night snuggled up to his mother. She was no longer breastfeeding in the day, and once she decided to stop the night feeds it was agreed that the baby's father should go to him and offer a drink of water from a feeder cup instead. Babies do not need night feeds after about five months of age. This is a fact that many parents do not realise and it is easy for the habit to continue. The first night the baby was upset and cried, the father had to go back to him eight times before he would settle on the first occasion, and seven times on the second. The couple admitted they thought it was not going to work and the mother was very upset to hear the baby crying, even though her partner went back to him at five-minute intervals. However, the second night the baby woke only once and after a short bout of crying, during which the father went in three times, he fell asleep until morning. The third night the couple had their first unbroken night for nearly a year.

It really does pay, once you have kept a diary for a week or two, to look at what you are doing in response to your child waking or not settling. Without realising it, parents are often rewarding, and thus encouraging, the very behaviour they want to discourage.

DECIDING HOW TO CHANGE YOUR RESPONSE

Each set of parents must work out the approach they think will work and with which they will feel happy for their own child. They must agree between themselves exactly what is to happen – if one parent is not to be involved he or she must not criticise the other. Parents exhausted by endless broken nights are often too shattered to try a new approach. Initially it is true that trying to change your child's behaviour could make for more difficult nights – but only for a very short period. If there is no improvement within five to six days, then the plan is not working and you must try something different. Pick a weekend or holiday time to try changing your approach, so that there is more opportunity to make up for missed sleep in the daytime. The aim of the plan must be to stop rewarding undesirable behaviour and to try to get the child to behave in the desired way by being consistent, calm and firm. In fact, once having made up their minds to try to change their child's behaviour, many parents have been surprised by how quickly the child has responded. The key is in their own determination. Being unsure, hesitant or inconsistent will only show the child he has to try even harder to get his own way. With older children of three, four or five, it is also possible to reinforce desirable behaviour with reward schemes (see page 294).

Often changing the child's sleeping habits will need to be done in stages. For example, the child who will not settle without a parent lying down beside him may need to be 'weaned' off this gradually so that the parent sits on the bed, then beside the bed, then at some distance from the bed and finally in the next room.

WAYS OF SETTLING CHILDREN AT NIGHT

Checking This is a system devised to replace taking the child into your bed, endless rocking, patting or other night-time routines and rituals. When the child cries, one parent goes — it sometimes helps if it is not the parent who normally goes to the child — but does not pick up the child. The parent keeps all interaction to a minimum and does not start chatting or playing with the child, but instead reassures him, and tucks him up firmly and deliberately. The parent then leaves the room, even if he goes on crying. The procedure is repeated every five minutes. The first night this may be very many times, but as soon as the child realises he is not going to be taken out of his cot he will almost certainly settle down.

Night drinks Breastfeeds, bottles or feeder cups are often given to settle babies who wake in the night. It is a custom which develops out of night feeds in the early months to become a habit. If your child is still having a breast- or bottle-feed after about six months, it is more of a comfort habit than a real need. After this age children are not hungry at night and rarely thirsty. There is no such thing as night starvation.

If the child is having drinks or juice from a bottle or cup, try gradually weakening the strength night by night until it is plain water, and also reduce the quantity. If a bottle is used and the child still wakes, try getting him used to a feeder cup in the day and offering that at night. When offering drinks in the night, always keep all interactions to a minimum and if possible avoid taking the baby or child out of the cot or bed.

Once they are about twenty months old you can tell them to take their own bottle or feeder cup. Tuck them up firmly, telling them to go to sleep, and leave the room, even if they cry, using the checking procedure until they settle.

Breastfeeding a baby or toddler at night poses a different set of questions. Is your child breastfed only at night or during the day as well? Do you want to wean him off breastfeeds totally or just to cut down the number of feeds? Obviously this does not apply to babies under six months who may still need a feed in the night.

If your child is not weaned at all then begin by weaning him in the day. Many children get into the habit of falling asleep while sucking at the nipple, so the breast becomes a comforter, like a dummy, which they need as part of their going-to-sleep routine. You first need to teach the child to settle to sleep without sucking at the breast. Begin by using daytime naps to do this and progress to settling at night. Once your child learns to fall asleep without the comfort of a nipple in his mouth, there is more chance of him going back to sleep by himself if he wakes in the night and of you settling him without a breastfeed if you do have to go to him. When trying to wean at night it helps if the father, rather than the mother, is the one to go to the child.

If you want to cut the number of night-time feeds, then agree how many feeds your child is still to have. At other times the father can go to reassure and tuck him in, using the checking procedure if the child goes on crying.

OLDER CHILDREN

'*My three-year-old son was coming into our bed every single night just after we had fallen asleep and then kicking and wriggling all night, making it impossible for us to sleep. I tried bringing a camp-bed into our room for him so he could be with us but not in our bed, and very often one of us ended up sleeping in that while he was in the bed with the other parent.*'

Older children can be given rewards in the form of star charts made out with days of the week when they are allowed to put a star or sticker up for every night of desired behaviour – for example, staying in their own bed. Five nights of stars can equal a small treat such as a special friend round to play, an outing to some favourite playground or duckpond or a small toy. Make sure the goal is within their reach so that they experience the reward of the star – if you set an impossible target and they never achieve the goal, they will soon be put off. Be firm about not giving stars for undesirable behaviour, but do not tell them off or make too much of it. Give them lots of praise and encouragement when they do succeed. Never take away or threaten to take away a star or reward won for good sleeping habits.

If you think it would be impossible for him to stay in his own bed straight off for a whole night, start by giving him a star if he stays in his bed once he has been taken back there during the night. At first you may need to take him back several times – the checking procedure of tucking him up firmly and leaving him even if he makes a fuss is the same as for a baby in a cot. If he finally settles and stays in his bed until the morning, that could be considered a success and he wins a star. The second night you will probably have to take him back several times again – always be firm and calm, keep interaction to a minimum and do not give him cuddles and hugs which will encourage him to keep coming back to you.

For a child who repeatedly comes into your bed, check that it is not because he gets cold at night, for example due to his cover slipping off.

CHILDREN WHO WON'T GO TO BED

Babies and children who have got into a bedtime habit which involves someone else – for example, being fed, rocked, someone lying down beside them – can refuse to settle with another person and take up hours of that person's time. Children who have never had a bedtime routine, but have been allowed to stay up until they fall asleep from exhaustion, often stay up until 10 pm or later with the result that their parents have no time to themselves.

For a child who has never known a bedtime routine, begin by introducing a set pattern of events leading to bedtime. Set a time that you think is reasonable – obviously you cannot go back from 10.30 pm to 8.00 pm in one swoop, but gradually move the time backwards. As long as you are determined, calm and firm that this is bedtime, your child will accept this, although for the first two or three nights you may have to take him back to bed many times.

Babies and children who are in the habit of settling only while sucking at the nipple, having someone lying down or any other procedure that demands the presence of a parent, need to learn to fall asleep by themselves. Begin with a daytime nap when you are likely to have more energy. Settle them in their cot or bed, stroking and speaking reassuringly and then leave the room. You may have to go back many times using the checking procedure to begin with, but persevere. You may have to make graded moves so that they are gradually 'weaned' off a routine they have been used to. For example, instead of rocking them quite to sleep rock the pram or cradle for a short time only so that they are still awake and make the transition to sleep without rocking.

No two parents or set of circumstances are the same and you must devise the plan you feel most able to carry out and one which will best suit your child, but the ground rules still apply – be consistent, be firm and calm, and change your approach in gradual steps.

TWINS

It is hard to devise a bedtime routine and to settle two children at once, especially if only one parent has to do this. Twins are also more likely to have had a difficult birth or to have been premature. But it has been found possible to use these methods successfully with twins as long as parents are both consistent and determined.

DRUGS

Doctors often prescribe drugs for children who will not sleep, or parents buy them for themselves. Those most often used are antihistamines, Phenergan and Vallergan. Different children react to them in different ways – some may be knocked out and also sleepy the next day, while with others they have no effect. It is common for children to acquire a tolerance so that the drug loses its effect, although if they have a period without it, the tolerance usually disappears. Sometimes drugs can make a child more hyped up and irritable rather than sending him to sleep. No one knows how much parents' belief in the power of a sleeping drug affects the way they handle the child – for example parents who think their child will sleep because he has had medicine may put him to bed more confidently, which in turn may encourage him to settle.

In general, sleeping problems are much better solved by management, and drugs, if they work at all, usually give only short-term relief without tackling the basic difficulty. Nevertheless, drugs can be used, together with management, in very difficult cases or with handicapped children to establish a new pattern, and they may be of help for short periods to give parents a break. Children with eczema or other irritating or uncomfortable conditions may sometimes be helped by drugs, but using a different approach to waking or settling will often enable the doses to be cut or reserved only for times when the eczema is especially itchy.

EARLY RISERS

'My eighteen-month-old always wakes at six in the morning and begins to scream if I don't get him up. By eight-thirty I feel as though I have already been up for half the day.'

It has been found that there are ways for parents to encourage their children to wake later or amuse themselves in their cots for longer once they do wake. For example:

Later bedtimes Most children manage to adjust to the hour's difference when clocks are switched from winter to summertime, although it takes a few days. Edging bedtime back ten minutes a day over a week can produce later waking, but is more likely to succeed with good sleepers – it rarely helps with poor sleepers.

Going to your child before he gets upset If you go to your child and get him up before he begins to cry, you will give him confidence to go on playing by himself for longer. If you do not go until he gets really upset, you are teaching him that he needs to cry before you will come to him.

Drinks and toys For children over about a year, a small amount of drink can be left in a trainer cup or bottle at the end of the cot – do not leave them more than they will drink because it will probably be tipped into the cot. Books and toys can be left for a baby of any age – for many parents the first sign that their child is awake is hearing a mobile being jangled or musical toys starting up.

Older children Once children can climb out of cots or are in a bed, it is best to set up some interesting toys in your bedroom the night before, plus a drink and a biscuit. You can then bring them into your room to play, which should mean another half an hour or so snatched in bed.

Cues Older children often respond well to being given an alarm clock – they can come into your room once the alarm goes off. Do not set it at an impossibly late time, but aim for perhaps the fifteen minutes they are likely to wait to begin with. You can gradually make the time later and later. Rewards in the form of a sticker or star chart help to enforce the idea. If you can arrange for a light-switch to go on at the desired waking time, this enforces the pattern and may be better than an alarm clock because the child is not woken by it.

THINGS THAT GO BUMP . . .

Nightmares Nightmares happen to most children at some time – most commonly around the ages of three to four. They can be sparked off by a television programme or story and are not themselves a sign of some emotional disturbance. If your child cries out during or after a bad dream, all you need to do is cuddle and comfort him and settle him back to sleep.

Night terrors This is the term given to episodes which happen in the deep stages of sleep. They are different from nightmares which happen in the light stages and often wake up the child. In a night terror the child usually screams out and often looks terrified and sweats but is in fact fast asleep so does not respond to anything you say. Although it may worry you to see your child like this, he will almost certainly remember nothing the next morning. Wait until it passes and settle him down again – don't try to wake him up. Night terrors are very rarely a sign of emotional disturbance – they happen more often with boys and can occur at any time from the age of three to four upwards.

Sleepwalking and sleeptalking These can also be very worrying for parents, but again they are rarely a sign of emotional disturbance. If your child sleepwalks often, the main concern must be safety, so make sure windows and doors out of the house are locked. Like night terrors they happen during deep sleep – the explanation seems to be that one part of the brain is active while the rest is asleep.

Fear of the dark There are many children who do not like sleeping in the dark – most commonly from around three years old upwards. A nightlight, landing light or ordinary bedside light with a low wattage bulb can be left on all night. Do not try to force them to sleep without a light because you will make any anxiety they would have grown out of naturally much stronger.

Headbanging Headbanging or rocking the cot violently can become bedtime settling habits for some children. In a few it may be a sign of anxiety, but if this is the case there will probably be other behavioural problems or indications of tension during the day – ask your GP or health visitor if you are worried. Such habits more often develop very early on and because they might persist and babies can hurt themselves when headbanging it is better to try to discourage the habit. Try introducing an alternative settling routine, or putting them in a bed which is not so inclined to rock.

WHEN TO SEEK HELP

Persistent nightmares, night terrors, sleepwalking and sleeptalking, headbanging or cot-rocking can be a sign of disturbance. For this reason it is a

good idea to seek the advice of your GP or other professional such as a health visitor or child guidance clinic, or ask your GP for a referral to the Department of Child and Family Psychiatry at your nearest hospital.

CRYING IN YOUNG BABIES

In the first few months, finding out why your baby is crying is largely a matter of elimination. These are some of the things which might make a baby cry:

Hunger Unless you have just fed your baby, this must be a first possibility. In the very early weeks breast as well as bottle-fed babies should be offered food on demand.

Colic If your baby cries after being fed or has long crying sessions each evening, he may be suffering from colic (see page 243).

Needs changing Some babies are more bothered than others by a wet or dirty nappy. Try changing them anyway if they will not settle. Nappy rash causing soreness is especially likely to upset some babies. Always change a dirty nappy to avoid this, whether your baby is one who minds or not.

Too hot or too cold Small babies are not very good at maintaining an even temperature. A baby who is too hot will look red in the face, feel very warm and may be sweating around the nape of the neck. A baby who is too cold will also be fretful – he may be pale and his hands and feet feel cold. To lower the temperature, loosen wrappings and take off a layer of coverings, but keep a check the baby does not cool down too much. To warm up a baby take him into a warmer room and hold him next to your body with a warm blanket around him. A warm feed can also help.

Uncomfortable position Until they can turn themselves over and become more mobile, babies have to rely on you to change their position. Most babies quickly show preferences for sleeping on their fronts or sides. A baby who has been in an unusual position in the womb will especially dislike being rearranged into the opposite direction in the early days.

Feelings Even day-old babies do not spend all their time asleep or feeding. They can spend up to one or two hours awake and can become bored, actually craving human company or something to look at – a human face ranks highest. A young baby may also feel anxious, frightened, or insecure.

Need for bodily contact All babies find the sensation of being held reassuring, and a baby who will not settle in his cot will often doze off contentedly in his parent's arms or while being carried in a sling. How much contact you give has to be balanced against the demands of other children, your lifestyle, your partner and your own needs for time to yourself.

Over-tired or over-stimulated Small babies can equally refuse to settle if they get over-stimulated and irritable. They have a limited attention span. If your baby has been awake for quite a while, is not hungry or uncomfortable, but cries and will not settle, this is a possibility. Take him somewhere quiet and not too bright and help him to slow down gradually with gentle rocking or other rhythmic stimulation like patting or singing.

Pain or illness Always consider the possibility of pain from some passing internal discomfort or illness in a young baby who will not stop crying. Other signs may be loss of appetite, slight feverishness, sickness or diarrhoea – for more on when to see a doctor see page 517. A cold which makes your baby bunged up and unable to breathe well through his nose can make him extra fretful (see page 550). Children with irritating conditions such as eczema will be extra miserable and hard to settle (see page 595).

Allergy When they have gone through everything else, many parents wonder if their child's crying could be due to allergy, initially to cow's milk. In a few babies this may be the case. If crying begins only with the introduction to solids, look for other signs, such as rashes, swelling or diarrhoea. Diagnosing food intolerance is a skilled and difficult task. Some children grow out of their initial allergic reactions. If you have reason to think allergy may be a problem, see page 252 for more discussion and ask your GP's advice.

BABIES WHO WON'T STOP CRYING

'Every day and most of the night seemed to be spent feeding, changing and pacing the floor with a screaming baby. In fact looking back I realise she did actually sleep for one good stretch most mornings, but I was so shattered from the night I hardly noticed that. Everything just got on top of me.'

Some babies do cry a great deal more than others and can be very hard to comfort. It is also true that some parents are much better equipped than others to cope with a crying baby. Your own circumstances will make a lot of difference to the way you see your child's behaviour and how you cope with it. A woman who has already had one or two babies, who has a supportive partner who is often on hand to help, plenty of friends with children and perhaps even relatives nearby to enlist as extra helpers is not too badly set up to cope with a rather difficult baby. On the other hand, a first-time mother whose partner is often away or not very supportive, who has no friends nearby because she has just left work and no relatives on hand is more likely to get upset by her baby's crying.

Events can spiral so that tiredness, a sense of inadequacy, tension between partners, loneliness and depression make the parents more and more unable to cope with crying. A loss of perspective can mean parents just focus on the one problem: 'My baby won't stop crying.' In fact other problems, such as loneliness or inexperience, may be separate issues running alongside and could be more easily solved, in turn making parents better equipped to cope with a crying baby.

HOW TO UNLOCK THE SPIRAL

* Recognise the problem. You are under great stress, you do need and deserve help.

* Don't feel inadequate or guilty. Your baby is not crying because you are a hopeless parent or because he hates you. Very many other parents are having exactly the same problem at this minute.

* Talk to your partner. Be honest about what you feel and work out how you can each help each other at this time. Single parents should talk to friends or relatives they trust and ask for help.

* Remember it will not last for ever. Perhaps the most important point is regaining a perspective. Babies do grow out of inconsolable crying – most by six months and many before that time.

* Involve other people. Tell your health visitor, community midwife or GP you are having a very difficult time. Do not expect them to offer a miracle solution, but recognise that talking about the problem and ways of tackling it will help.

* Get out of the house and talk to other parents. If you know no one or very few people, ask your health visitor to tell you about pram clubs. Ring the organiser in advance and tell her you do not know other parents. The National Childbirth Trust has post-natal support and holds get-togethers open to anyone (see address section, pages 673–6).

* Plan a way to get more sleep. Both of you waking all the time or leaving it all to one partner is not a good idea. Devise shifts or alternate nights. It may mean getting four hours between 8.00 pm and midnight sometimes. Single parents should ask another parent, friend or relative to give them a break in the day – remember most people are flattered to be needed.

* Accept that you have a temporary problem. Stop expecting your baby to sleep three hours between feeds. Stop expecting to get longer stretches of sleep. Behave and plan as though under siege and you may begin to be suddenly surprised by the odd lull.

* Be systematic in trying different approaches to solve the problem. Recording what you do each day helps. If nothing else, it will help to pass the time while your baby grows out of crying so much.

WAYS OF TRYING TO SETTLE BABIES WHO WON'T STOP CRYING

Assuming you have already checked whether your baby is hungry, wet, the wrong temperature, in an uncomfortable position or just wanting to be held and amused and he is still howling, what next? Well, there can never be a sure way of settling any baby and a method which works well on one occasion may go down like a lead balloon next time. But just having something to try does help morale, and while you are trying it he may get tired enough to drop off anyway.

If you have a young baby who cries a lot it is better to try going through possible ways of calming him fairly systematically. If you bombard him with everything you can think of in one evening, you are more likely to make him even more upset, and if he does finally fall asleep you will not know which particular trick was most successful. If crying is a regular feature, say in the evening, then keep a diary over a week. Write down when the crying begins, times of feeds, and record what method was tried to soothe him and with what success. At the end of the week you should be able to see which method or combination of methods is most likely to work – and at least he is one week further on to growing out of the problem.

Rhythmic movement Parents automatically rock their babies and have done from time immemorial. It can be done in a pram or cradle or by holding them. A successful position is often the 'parrot' stance (baby on shoulder) but type and speed of rocking is important – vertical rocking has been shown to be more effective and it should be as fast as possible. This means holding the baby upright and jiggling him up and down swiftly, either on your shoulder clasped facing towards you, or with his back against you looking outwards. Slings which hold the baby upright and facing you can be useful, but generally if babies do not get used to them while they are small, say under two months, they are less likely to accept them later. Some parents find rocking-chairs help for long, noisy evenings when their legs fail.

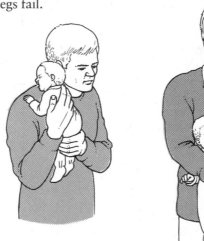

Patting or stroking Light, rhythmic pats or long sweeping, stroking movements can sometimes distract a mildly fretful baby enough to drift into the much-hoped-for sleep. You need to have calmed him down enough to lay him in his cot or pram without full-scale howling.

Sound Constant, moderate noise has been shown to calm babies under four months – in general the younger the baby the more effective it is likely to be. Despite lots of records and tapes of womb music (rhythmic heart-beats and pulsing sounds the baby was used to before birth), there is no evidence that this is especially soothing. Any constant background noise will do as well – the tumble drier, Hoover, television. However, there is no harm in investing in one of the tapes or records if you wish, or you can try your baby with a loudly ticking clock. Soothing music or your own crooning/singing is something parents often try as well – babies do not know if you sing out of tune! Nevertheless, research indicates that noise alone is not as effective as when tried together with one or a number of other methods of settling (see page 306).

Swaddling

'Both my mother and the fairly elderly health visitor suggested wrapping my baby up very tight in shawls to help her settle. I thought it seemed an awful idea and very old-fashioned.'

Some people may find the idea of swaddling unacceptable, but the fact remains that it does work as a way of calming and helping babies to slip into sleep. Not only has it been tried and tested over centuries, but modern research has also established that new babies often respond well to swaddling. The aim is to give the baby comfort and security by holding his limbs firmly without binding. The rationale behind this is that it resembles the restriction of life in the womb and stops the baby being upset and disturbed by the freedom of his own involuntary limb movements. The exception may be babies who have been in an unusual position in the womb and those who have congenital hip dislocation. Traditionally strips of material were used, but these days a large, stretchy shawl, a cellular blanket, or, in hot weather, a large piece of gauze will probably do the job just as well. If possible, begin swaddling when the baby is in an awake but calm state – if this is not possible, handle as calmly and deftly as you can, talking soothingly. It has sometimes been found that the distraction of handling involved in swaddling calms them anyway.

In cold weather, warm the material by ironing it or putting it on the radiator first. Lie the baby on his back on the material. Take a top corner and fold it downwards and across. Wrap the rest of the material firmly round the baby's body. Secure it by either lying the baby on one side on the loose end or use two safety-pins. Aim to secure the limbs, but leave hands and lower arms free so that he can suck his hand, fingers and thumb. Always keep a careful check on the temperature of a swaddled baby and remove layers and loosen wrapping if he starts to look red and hot.

In cold weather a vest, stretch-suit or nightdress and swaddling material plus one or two light blankets tucked firmly over the cocooned baby

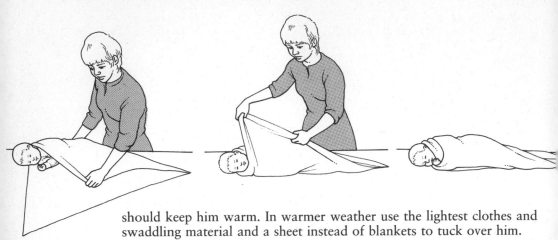

should keep him warm. In warmer weather use the lightest clothes and swaddling material and a sheet instead of blankets to tuck over him.

Sucking

'The only way of calming my month-old baby in the evening was letting him suck at my finger — feeding just made him worse. In the end I bought a dummy but I did hate seeing him sucking at it and only used it at home. I taught my two-year-old it was called a "sucky-thing" so he wouldn't talk about the baby's dummy when we were out.'

Sucking is a source of comfort and satisfaction to young babies as well as a way of getting food. Many babies fall asleep at the end of or during feeds and can be calmed if they are upset by being offered the breast or bottle to suck, even though they may not actually be hungry. Some babies need to suck more than others, and colicky babies in particular can often find comfort in sucking and cannot be consoled in any other way. It is possible to get specially shaped dummies for breastfed babies — the National Childbirth Trust can usually put you in touch with a supplier he makes any demand at all will deprive him of the attention he needs. However, there is nothing wrong in using a dummy for young babies who find comfort in sucking and cannot be consoled in any other way. It is possible to get specially shaped dummies for breastfed babies — the National Childbirth Trust can usually put you in touch with a supplier (see address section, pages 673–6). Treat the dummy as you would treat the teat of a bottle and keep it in sterilising solution in between use. Be consistent — if you let your baby suck at a dummy at home, take it with you when you go out. Always be sure it is not food, comfort or attention your baby wants before offering him the dummy.

If you dislike the idea of a dummy but your baby seems to take comfort in sucking, you can lend him your little finger instead. The disadvantage is that you have to stay anchored. Most babies can be taught to suck their thumbs by about four months and if they are the 'sucky' kind will often do so by themselves. Once your baby has found his thumb you can stop using the dummy and at this young age it will not have become a fixed habit. If you let your baby go on using a dummy for much longer it can be harder to break him of the habit and he may not find his thumb an acceptable substitute. The disadvantage of a dummy over a thumb is that it requires someone else to find it again when needed which applies especially at night. The disadvantage of thumb sucking over dummies is that sometimes the habit carries on into school age, although dentists now say that thumb sucking has to be carried on into adolescence and be almost a full-time habit to push front teeth outwards.

Leaving your baby to cry It is worth remembering that there is a danger of giving a small baby too much stimulation. Sometimes this makes the child very fretful and unable to settle and fall asleep. The baby's crying continues — the parent continues to try to soothe him in every possible way and the circle gets worse. It is worth putting your baby in his cot, tucking him in firmly and leaving him to cry for five to ten minutes to see if he begins to settle.

Driving

'I tried absolutely everything I could think of and finally in desperation I put her in the carry-cot in the back of the car and drove round the roads for an hour and a half.'

Many parents take to the roads in desperation in the small hours with wakeful or screaming babies. It is probably the combination of the drone of the car plus the movement which sends them off. It is a very bad idea to get an older baby or a child into the habit of being driven round at night in order to settle them, and much better to try settling them at home in the ways we have suggested. However, as a desperate last resort, it may be worth remembering. If possible, try not to drive alone with a screaming baby. This is very stressful and inclined to make you want to race over amber lights rather than stop! Always make sure the baby is secured in a carry-cot or baby seat and the carry-cot and seat is in turn secured in the car.

Herbs Fennel is said to have a calming effect, though there is no firm evidence of this: fennel drinks for babies can be bought from most chemists.

Massage Not a new idea, but one currently being rediscovered. Various articles and books have been written on the subject. Essentially the idea is that a relaxed baby will not cry and also that massage is enjoyable for both parent and baby. In fact many parents massage their children without thinking about it — stroking their temples, hair or nape of neck, squeezing and stroking hands and stroking their whole body to help them to relax. Massage, it is said, is best begun with the baby in an awake but calm state. If your baby rarely combines these two states, and is usually crying or asleep, you will have to pick your moment carefully — perhaps after a bath.

The room needs to be warm enough for the baby to be undressed without getting cold. Warm some baby oil on your hands to help them to slide on sensitive skin. Begin by lightly stroking hands, fingers, feet and toes. Go on to stroke the whole length of the limbs, making your touch a little firmer. Movements can be a mixture of stroking in circular or straight patterns and gentle kneading. Talk soothingly and reassuringly to the baby all the time. He can be lying on something soft in front of you, or cradled in your lap. If he is still enjoying it, move on to the body and reserve the head and neck, which is more sensitive, until last. Stroking the nape of his neck with straight fingers, brushing his temples with the back of your hand or kneading his earlobes gently between finger and thumb can all be relaxing and you can do this at any time, without having to undress your baby completely. If, when you begin, or during massage, your baby starts crying, pick him up and comfort him as you would normally, and try again at a later opportunity. Keep each session short to start with and finish before either of you loses interest.

Whether you and your baby come to enjoy regular massage sessions depends entirely on your individual temperaments and personalities. If, after a few tries, you have to conclude that although you may think it a good idea, your baby does not, then don't feel rejected or upset. Nothing has been lost by trying and if you are keen on the idea you can give it another go in a couple of months when he is more mature and settled.

Combining techniques For generations mothers have instinctively rocked, fed, sung to and patted their babies to get them to sleep. Now instinct has the backing of modern research which shows that babies are indeed more likely to be soothed by stimulation to several senses. It is important to remember this and also that too much stimulation can sometimes make a baby fretful. If you have tried every technique singly and waited to see if your baby is likely to settle if left to cry for a short period, it might be worth going on to work your way through a combination of two techniques at a time. Use the same approach for a whole evening or day and write down what happens, especially the time of crying and when it stops. This will enable you to work out the most successful formula. But do not leap to the conclusion that it will necessarily mean rocking, sucking, noise and swaddling all at once. Remember also that what works on one occasion may lose its charm another time and you will have to try a different approach.

NEARING THE END OF YOUR TETHER

Quite a lot of parents get so desperate through lack of sleep, personal problems and a continually crying baby, that they feel they just cannot carry on any longer or fear that they may actually hurt their baby. If you get to this point or have done something to your child – thrown him into the cot or on to the bed, shaken him or hit him – you need help. In an emergency these are some immediate measures you can take to stop you hurting your baby:

* Put the baby in his cot. However furiously he is crying he is unlikely to come to harm. Then telephone a friend or relative. Tell them just how bad you are feeling at the time – unless you ask for help, no one will know of your need.

* If you have no phone, wrap up the baby and go next door to a neighbour or nearby friend.

* If you have no one to call on, put the baby into a pushchair and take him out and walk around the streets. Just being out of the house and walking around usually has a calming effect.

* If you are able to, do something which changes the mood of the moment. Running a warm bath and getting in it together with your baby can be very soothing and often distracts the baby enough to make him stop crying. Alternatively, making you both something nice to eat and sitting down and watching television with a toddler or older child can be calming.

* If you are on your own or a single parent, ask a friend or relative if you can come to stay the night with your baby.

* Once the immediate crisis is past, sit down with a friend or your partner and try to work out what brought you to this state. Remember that tiredness and loneliness can make any problems seem worse.

What steps can you take, with the help of others, to make things easier? Talking to your GP or health visitor can be very helpful – such people are very well aware of the stresses that a crying baby can put on parents. Simply talking things over and knowing other people are aware of your problem and care how you feel can be a real help. There are also a number of self-help groups which try to put mothers in touch with each other – for example Cry-sis, or the National Childbirth Trust Post-Natal Support System, or simply the person who runs your local mother and toddler club. If you feel you desperately need a break from your child, ask your health visitor or social worker if it might be possible to organise more practical help – for example a place at a nursery or a child minder for a short period each day or week to give you some time to yourself. Don't be frightened to ask for professional help from doctors, health visitors or social workers – they are not going to brand you bad parents because you are finding the going tough.

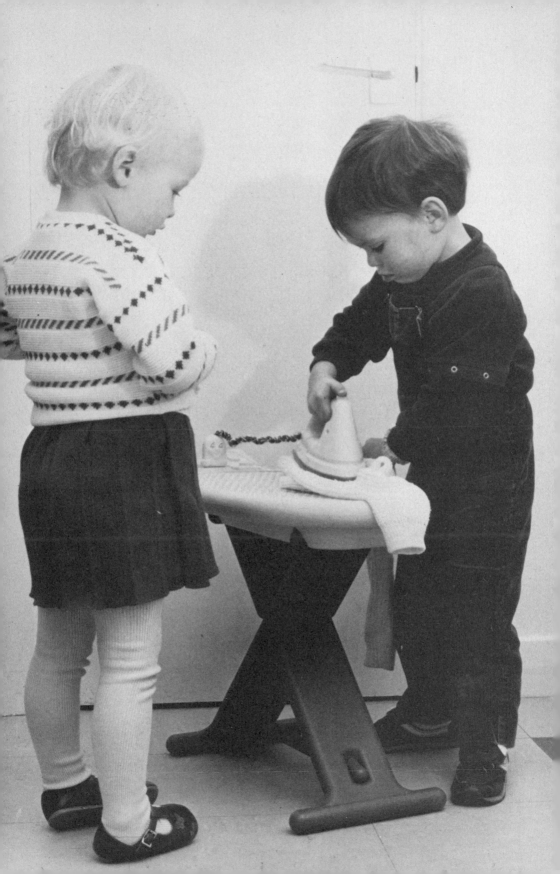

Chapter 9

GROWING AND MOVING

How your baby grows   Measuring growth
Growth in the toddler and pre-school child   Feeding and growth
Movement   How your child learns to move   Boys and girls

Most of us remember being visited by distant relatives when we were children and having to endure all those exclamations about 'Haven't they all grown!' One of the most obvious things about children is that they do grow, and at the most tremendous rate – in height, in weight and in different proportions. For instance, your newborn baby's head accounts for a third of his whole body weight, but of course the head of an adult is proportionately much smaller than this compared to the rest of his body.

All parents are concerned about their child's growth because it is an important sign of health and progress. However, other signs are just as important, such as intellectual development (see page 355), behaviour and general health. If you have a very large child you may worry that he is overweight for his age. Of course obesity, or excess fat, can be a health problem (see page 272), but if your child is simply big then this need not affect his health and progress. In general, exceptional smallness, particularly at birth, is more likely to be a cause for concern. However, even if your child looks very small and frail, if he has plenty of energy and can do the things that other children his age are able to, he is probably very well.

HOW YOUR BABY GROWS

The way we grow is governed by our inbuilt genetic and hormonal programming and also by environmental factors – events that happen to us. These outside influences, such as nutrition, love and education, interact with and affect our genetic programme, and the effects of these can never be completely separated. For example, a child who does not get enough to eat will not grow and develop normally no matter how genetically large he is programmed to be. And, not surprisingly, a child who is consistently deprived of love can also fail to grow. Lack of growth can be a symptom of illness, but, given a reasonably healthy, safe, loving home background, the process of human growth and development will unfold of its own accord.

HOW YOUR BABY GROWS IN THE WOMB

When your baby is first conceived he results from the fusion of two gametes (the sperm from the male and the female ovum). Everything the child needs to develop is contained in the genes that each parent has contributed. The chemical substances that contain genes are called 'chromosomes'. The 23 chromosomes in each gamete (or 46 chromosomes in the resulting cell) contain directions for the development of all the bones, organs, nerves, muscles and other tissues and for the physical and some intellectual characteristics that will make your child who he is.

Your baby will spend about 40 weeks growing in the womb (for more about this see chapter 2), but anything from 37 to 42 weeks is quite normal. Your baby's growth there will be measured in a number of ways – by your own weight gain, by the increasing height of your uterus, and by ultrasound scans. If your baby does not seem to be growing well, special measures can be taken to help to promote his growth, or, if the pregnancy is nearing its end, he may grow better outside the womb and the birth can be induced early.

Your baby grows very fast in the womb – reaching a peak rate of growth at around 20 weeks. At this stage he is growing at a rate of 10 cm. (4 in.) a month, but after birth the rate of his growth is only 20 cm. (8 in.) a year, and this steadily decreases. Obviously your baby could not continue growing at this fast rate or he would become a giant! As well as growing in length and weight he is also developing the various limbs and organs. It is during this very early stage that your baby is most at risk from external damage. There is more about this in chapter 1 on preconceptual care on pages 2–10, but basically you have to be very careful not to take any unprescribed medicines or be exposed to X-rays, and always tell your doctor you are pregnant if he is prescribing for you.

Babies of mothers who smoke are, on average, smaller than babies of mothers who do not. Being small-for-dates can be dangerous for the baby (see page 177). In addition, heavy drinking in pregnancy can cause damage and some doctors suggest that to be on the safe side pregnant women should drink no alcohol at all. It is important for women to eat a sensible, balanced diet during pregnancy, but in general babies take what available nutrition there is even if the mother is under-nourished – it is the mother who can end up being depleted and unwell. There is no evidence that morning sickness, however severe, will affect your baby's well-being.

FITTING INTO THE WOMB

One of the most remarkable ways in which nature ensures that your baby will have a safe delivery is that the growth of a baby adjusts itself according to how much or how little room there is in the mother's womb during the last weeks of pregnancy. The size a person will grow to is ultimately determined by the genetic characteristics he inherits from both his parents

— each contribute half of the genetic material. So if you are a small mother with a large husband, the baby, who has an equal contribution from both of you, might be too big to be delivered safely through your small pelvis and birth canal. Fortunately, during pregnancy the father's contribution is 'suppressed' and the baby grows just enough to fit comfortably into his mother's shape. After the birth, however, the baby will grow more rapidly to accommodate the father's 'largeness' genes and by the time he is two years old will represent this equal contribution more exactly.

In the same way, a larger woman with a generous-sized pelvis will give birth to a larger than average baby even if her husband is small. However, the baby will grow more slowly during his first two years until, again, his parents' contribution is equally represented. His ultimate size will probably be somewhere between the two parents. Growth after birth also depends on external factors, in particular nutrition. Even if both of you are large but your baby is undernourished (perhaps because of illness) he will not grow to his full genetic capability. Other environmental factors can also affect physical growth, as explained on page 309.

BIRTHWEIGHT

While he was in the womb it was difficult to assess exactly how your baby was growing. After the birth it is very important that he should be checked expertly as the starting point for the monitoring of his development, and also to see whether there are any immediate problems which need extra medical or nursing help. That is why some time will be spent in the delivery room weighing, measuring and checking your baby. One of the most important indicators of your baby's well-being is his weight. Most healthy full-term babies weigh between 2.7 kg. (5 lb. 13 oz.) and 4.3 kg. (9 lb. 6 oz.) if they are boys, and between 2.6 kg. (5 lb. 10 oz.) and 4.1 kg. (9 lb.) if they are girls. There will always be some healthy babies who come on either side of this range, but this is taken by doctors as a general guideline to what is considered normal birthweight. If your baby is one of the few individual exceptions outside this range he will be given special checks just in case there might be anything that needs extra care.

When your baby is born and you hear the doctor or midwife saying that he should be checked for smallness or largeness for dates, remember they are checking not diagnosing. These checks are important and in many cases all is well. Furthermore, if anything is potentially wrong it can usually be put right.

PRE-TERM BABIES

A baby born before 37 weeks of pregnancy is known as pre-term and he may need special nursing care because his life-support systems may not be working properly — his lungs, digestive system and nervous system may not be able to cope on their own. Such a baby will usually be below 2.7 kg. (5 lb. 13 oz.) but this in itself is not automatically a cause for concern. So long as he is the correct weight for his pregnancy (gestational) age, doctors will not be primarily concerned about his size. They will be more concerned about his immature bodily functions and check to see if he needs help with breathing, digestion, temperature control and so on.

SMALL-FOR-DATES BABIES

A small-for-dates baby is one who weighs less than he should do for his pregnancy age. Sometimes failure to grow properly in the womb can be picked up during pregnancy and the birth may have to be induced so that the baby can be fed and nurtured better outside the womb. Sometimes the placenta tends to wear out and stops working efficiently before the baby has completed his growth in the womb. A small-for-dates baby is not just small, he is undergrown, and this is why women should take seriously warnings about the dangers of smoking, which causes the risk of producing light babies. There is nothing wrong with being small if that is the way you are intended to be, but it is dangerous to be smaller and less well developed than you should be (see also page 178).

LARGE-FOR-DATES BABIES

Babies over the 4.3 kg. (9 lb. 6 oz.) normal limit should be checked in case their mothers have had undiagnosed diabetes during pregnancy (see page 62). Many very large babies are not large because of diabetes in the mother, they are simply genetically large, perhaps because their mothers are large in build. These babies will not have any problems and, contrary to what many people believe, they will not be unusually difficult to breastfeed. The only other possible danger with a large baby is that he can be difficult to deliver; if pre-natal tests show the baby is very large and the mother is rather small-boned by comparison, the birth may be induced a week or two early or a Caesarean delivery performed. However, it is quite difficult to make such a judgement antenatally and many doctors are happy to let large, fast-growing babies be delivered normally in their own time. It is quite possible for large babies to be safely delivered without even an episiotomy being needed.

MEASURING GROWTH

The commonest method of measuring a baby's growth is by weighing him. Later, when he can stand, his height will be measured too but by that stage (around 13 to 18 months) he will not be weighed and checked as regularly as he was in the first few months of life. In these first few months weighing can loom very large in the concern of parents, and health professionals too, because it is the simplest indicator of growth and whether your baby is getting enough to eat. This is particularly true of breastfed babies. A better indicator of healthy growth than weight is measurement of length. With babies this has to be done while the baby is lying down and can be quite difficult to do because babies cannot be

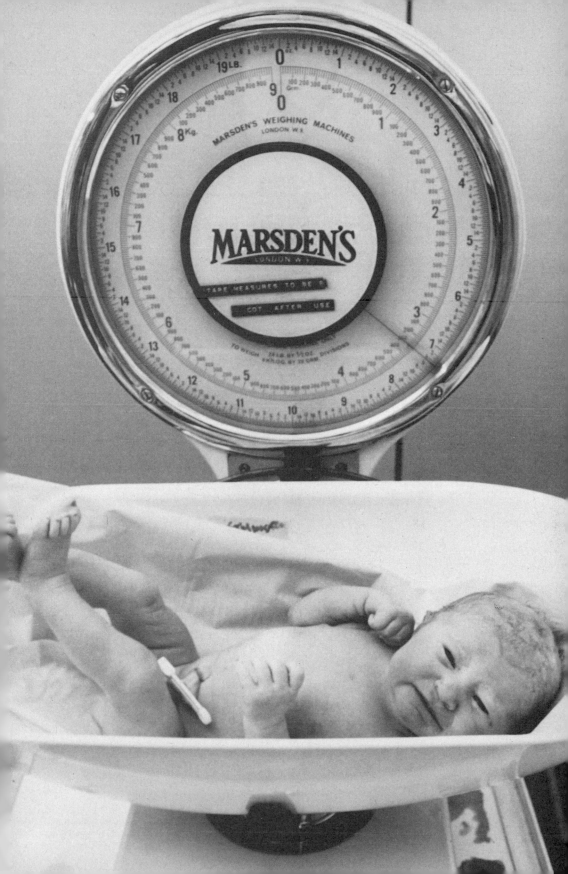

straightened out very easily! You can ask your health visitor or doctor to measure your baby's length for you or you can try it yourself with someone to help you when the baby is wakeful and relaxed. Length is a better indicator of whether a baby's frame is growing properly than his weight because weight can sometimes mean fat, and it is possible for a baby to be fat and still not growing properly in other respects. In general, though, you will find that regular weighing along with signs of well-being in your baby such as firm skin, alert behaviour and eagerness to feed, give you an indication he is growing.

HOW YOUR DOCTOR MEASURES YOUR BABY'S GROWTH

When you take your baby to the clinic to be weighed and checked you may hear your health visitor or doctor talk about centiles. They will note your baby's weight (and perhaps length) and check it against what is called a 'centile growth curve' which is based on the average of large numbers of babies. This gives an indication how your particular baby ought to be growing. A child on the 3rd centile means that if 100 children of the same age are measured, then 97 will be larger and 3 will be smaller. Being below the 3rd centile (or conversely above the 97th) is not necessarily abnormal provided the rate of growth is normal, i.e. the child follows along its own particular centile course. These centile measures are used to pick out the few babies (about 3% at each end of the size range) who might need special attention. Many of the children in the big category and the small category will turn out to be normal.

Your baby, when he is weighed and measured, will be placed on one of these centile curves according to how big he is. If, for example, two babies are both perfectly normal – that is, within the middle 80% of all babies – but of different sizes, they will be on different growth curves. The main thing about the bigger baby A is that he should grow along the curve appropriate for him, and the same thing applies to the smaller baby B. If baby A's weight and growth curve started to drop down towards baby B's and stayed there, it would be cause for concern that he was not getting enough to eat. Similarly, if baby B's weight gain suddenly shot up on to the level of baby A's and stayed there, whilst his height remained on its original growth curve, there might be concern that he was getting too much to eat. These curves can be used to measure how well your child is growing through his childhood and will continue to be used to check for the small minority at each end of the size range who may need special dietary help – either more to eat and better care, or less to eat because they are gaining too much weight.

INDIVIDUAL VARIATIONS IN GROWTH

It is important for you not to spend too much time worrying about and checking your baby's weight and size. Relaxed, happy parents help children to grow best! In the first few months of your baby's life fluctuation in growth rates may be quite marked – some weeks he will gain about 225 grams (8 oz.), other weeks less or perhaps none at all. This is particularly true of breastfed babies who control their own intake of milk in all kinds of subtle ways. The weekly weight gains of normal babies during their first three months are steadily upward but they are not always smooth. Other things may cause a fluctuation in weight gain – for example, your baby may have a cold one week and not be feeling well, or he may suddenly have a growth spurt, demand feeding every two to three hours and put on an impressive amount of weight in a short time.

You will soon develop the practised eye of an experienced father or mother, and you will know from the way he continually grows out of his clothes, from the changes in his face and body, from his skin tone, his eyes and his behaviour, that he is growing as he should be. There will be no need for constant references to scales and tape measure, although it can be fun, once your child can stand and understand, to measure him against the door from time to time, or against a special wall chart. These are often given away free in magazines, and more elaborate versions are sold in baby-care shops.

GROWTH IN THE TODDLER AND PRE-SCHOOL CHILD

Your child's growth is actually slowing down in its rate all through the years of toddlerhood and childhood. The amount of weight and height gained by your child gets progressively less over the years until adolescence – although of course overall he is still getting bigger all the time. During young childhood, other interesting changes, some noticeable and some less so, will also be taking place. The most obvious will be the changes in proportion. The head looks smaller in relation to the rest of the body; the arms and legs, fingers and toes grow longer; the limbs straighten out; the fat baby tummy becomes flatter; the face acquires its own unique characteristics and loses its baby chubbiness. Less visible changes occur in your child's bones, muscles, brain and nervous system.

BONES

The number of bones are still not complete when your baby is born: a one-year-old has only three bones in each wrist and hand; an adult has twenty-eight. The bones steadily become harder through childhood: the bones of the hand, wrist and head harden quite easily, but the long bones of the arms and legs do not become completely hard until the late teens. It is because his bones and ligaments around the joints are so soft that your baby can curl himself up into positions that would be quite impossible for an adult. In addition, the tone of the muscles is poor, which is the reason he is 'floppy' to start with and cannot hold his body straight until the end of the first year, or support himself on his legs without help until roughly half-way through his second year – although, as with everything about children's development, there are large individual variations. Some babies can sit up well at six months, others not until nine or ten months. Some walk before they are a year old while others do not walk until eighteen months.

The head bones in a young baby are special. He is born with several head bones joined together with soft cartilage or openings called 'fontanelles' which enable the head to be 'moulded' to fit into the birth canal during birth. These soft spots will gradually disappear during the first two years as the bones knit together until your toddler, like you, has confluent bone covering the brain.

As well as increasing and hardening, the bones grow in length, although different parts of the body grow at different rates. It is bone growth which contributes most to your child's ultimate height. These rates will vary from individual to individual. Contrary to what you might have heard, it is not possible to predict accurately what a child's adult height is going to be from his height at two years old. He may be three feet tall at two, but the old rule of thumb that this is half his adult height will not apply if he is an individual, for example, with medium-sized parents. In this case, he is unlikely to grow to six feet and, of course, it is extremely unlikely that a little girl will grow to this height. Boys and girls differ by 12.5 cm. ($5\frac{1}{2}$ in.) in average height at the end of adolescence, but when they are toddlers there is hardly any difference at all.

MUSCLES AND NERVES

Unlike the bones, your baby is born with all the muscles he is going to need, though they will develop in length and thickness as he grows. During childhood there is no difference between the muscles of boys and girls, but in adolescence and adulthood boys will normally develop more muscle than girls. It has been estimated that about 40% of the final body mass of a man is muscle, while it is only 24% in a female. Muscles are responsible for the strength and flexibility of the different parts of the body. This can be increased by exercise, and of course your little girl should be given as many opportunities to exercise and strengthen her muscles as your son (see also page 329).

The brain and nervous system of your baby have a lot of rapid growing to do after birth. Some part of the brain – the parts that control attention, absorbing new experience and the basic baby activities of sleeping, waking, feeding and getting rid of waste through bowel and bladder – are already working well. However, the parts of the brain that control more complex activities – controlled movement, thinking, language, under-standing – go on developing after birth and are nearly, but not altogether, complete by the time he is two. If you think how competent a two-year-old child is compared to a newborn baby, you can see for yourself how many changes have had to take place in his brain and nervous system in order for him to do the running, holding, planning, talking, demanding and control-ling that he can do now.

The brain controls the activities of the body through the nervous system. At first it cannot do this very well because the nerves, particularly those at the extremities of your baby's body, take some time after birth to become fully equipped to carry the brain's messages. Nerves have to be covered with a special sheath called 'myelin' in order to communicate effectively with the body parts that they control. The process of myelinisation in the nervous system outside the brain takes up to two years to complete and is not complete in the brain itself until the end of adolescence. Once the nerves are sheathed in myelin they can help your baby to control his movements much more effectively. You will notice that this process does not happen all at once – the baby gains control of his head first, then his limbs and trunk, and finally he gains the very fine control of fingers and limbs which enable him to do delicate and complicated tasks such as building with small bricks or holding a pencil and writing. As his nervous system matures he will also learn to gain control over bowel and bladder movements. There is more about this in chapter 13 on toilet training, but the important point to remember is that your baby cannot control his behaviour as you might like him to until his nervous system has gained the necessary maturity. This takes time.

FEEDING AND GROWTH

Feeding is such a vital aspect of looking after children and one which causes so much concern for parents that we have already given it two whole chapters to itself. Growth and food are fundamentally linked together. All the complex genetic, hormonal, physical and behavioural developments we have described cannot take place if your baby is not properly nourished. Nourishment is most important during the vulnerable last months in the womb and the first months after birth. If a baby is not fed at all he will die. If he is not fed properly he will not grow or develop properly. This is obviously a big responsibility for parents and it is why mothers worry so much about breast or bottle-feeding and if their children will not eat greens or drink milk. You will have read and heard a lot of different advice about eating enough vitamins, getting enough roughage, not eating sweet, sugary foods, being wary of foods that cause allergies or behaviour problems. It can all be very bewildering and make you understandably anxious. In fact the main point about giving your baby nourishment so that he grows properly is actually very simple – he should be given *enough* to eat. What is enough for him may not be enough for your friend's child, and what is enough for him when he is eighteen months old may not be enough for him when he is three years old, although at this stage he may actually want less to eat because children develop likes, dislikes, increases and decreases in appetite just as adults do.

Remember that growing takes a lot of energy, far more than adults use, and, of course, your child will be using energy for all his activities as well. Energy uses up calories which is why it is important that your child's diet contains enough calories. Different foods are required for different aspects of growth and health. The importance of protein, carbohydrate, vitamins, minerals and fibre are all explained in chapters 6 and 7. In general, if your child has plenty of energy for his usual activities, if his bowel motions and urine are normal, if he looks well, with clear skin, bright eyes and shiny hair, and if he very broadly follows his own centile curves, then no matter how little you fear he is eating, you can be sure that he is growing and developing normally. Similarly, even if your child eats like a horse and has a passion for what you consider to be unsuitable foods, so long as his growth curves do not rise above what they should be (which may indicate that he is too fat), and so long as his behaviour and looks are normal then you shouldn't worry either. More problems are caused by battles and rigid rules about food than are ever caused by food itself. Food provides your child with the energy to grow and to function. It is not a religion or a test of your love.

MOVEMENT

It is hard to look ahead from those moments when you hold a new baby in your arms and realise that within a matter of months this stage will be long gone, and before two years are up your child will have developed into a lively little toddler. Watching the way their baby is increasingly able to move different parts of his body and to control his movements is a subject of great fascination for all parents. This development depends on the physical growth of bones, muscles, brain and nerves. The first eighteen months of a child's life are often described as 'the sensori-motor period' of development. This means he is developing and learning about the world around him mainly through body movements and through senses. He cannot use language or abstract thought yet. Like most descriptions of childhood that divide progress into stages, this is a rather over-simplified view. Young babies *can* solve problems and work things out for themselves, as you will notice if you leave toys just out of their reach or do something they do not want you to do. Working out that because you have left the room he will not get his tea just yet and then yelling in protest actually involves quite a complicated thought process for your nine-month-old. And of course the reverse is true as well — movement does not stop being an important way of learning or an aid to learning after the age of eighteen months. Sport, dance, design, even writing or typing all require body movements that 'embody' intelligent processes. Being immobile can handicap mental as well as physical progress, and physical exercise benefits all our functions — not just our movement.

HOW YOUR CHILD LEARNS TO MOVE

Watching as your baby is first able to lift his head, then to roll over, to sit by himself, to crawl or to pull himself up and finally to walk is obviously exciting and rewarding for all parents. There are enormous variations in the way different children develop controlled, confident movement, but in general these developments follow predictable patterns. The medical term for the development of movement is 'motor development' and it takes place from the head downwards and from the central part of the body outwards. At birth your baby already has good control of eye movements and the movements that control sucking and feeding. He will first begin to gain control of head movements and, working downwards, he will stand on his feet and walk on them last of all. It means that he will first gain control of his trunk, then of his arms and legs, and finally of his feet, thumbs and fingers.

There are two other points to bear in mind about your baby's development of movement. First, it is not possible to speed it up. Babies who are given freedom of movement and encouragement to stand and walk do not walk any earlier than babies who are more restricted, though they do of course have a more interesting time! However, babies who are severely restricted, for example, children brought up in bad institutions where they are never taken from their cots or stimulated in any way, can be delayed in their development, and they may suffer muscle wastage too. Second, early crawling, standing and walking are not linked to intellectual development. Just because your child walks early does not mean he is more advanced than other children of his age. Nor does it mean that he is necessarily going to be unusually athletic or energetic later in life. However, it does mean, again, that he has a more interesting time. Once a baby is mobile he can explore and discover things for himself. He does not have to wait for them to be brought to him. And once he can walk he has the priceless advantage of having hands free which means he can move and hold things and arrange things with his hands all at the same time.

Of course, a baby who is on the move early is more work for you. Toddlers can play havoc with your household at any age, but a baby under a year old who is walking about cannot be told what to do, and can be a real handful. There is advice on arranging your home to make it safe and stimulating for a toddler in chapter 12. Nevertheless, the first steps at whatever age are an exciting moment – physical independence has arrived.

Some of the main stages of the development of movements are shown in the chart on pages 320–6. Your baby might not go through some of them: some babies never crawl, they just get straight up and walk; some babies shuffle on their bottoms instead of crawling; some support themselves on their feet on your lap at two or three months, others just flop down and wait until seven or eight months; some are eager reachers and graspers, while others have to be encouraged to hold things and look at them. Bear in mind with this chart that babies are very individual in the way they progress, and the range of what is normal is very wide. This is just a guide.

HOW YOUR CHILD LEARNS TO MOVE

AGE	LARGE-SCALE MOVEMENTS	DELICATE MOVEMENTS
Newborn	Unless picked up he can only lie prone, with limbs curled up and his cheek on one side. His head is floppy. He makes reflex movements such as 'walking' and 'grasping', but these are not controlled. He will begin to develop synchrony with your movements – setting up feeding rhythms and responding to your touch and handling.	He can turn his head to sound and light, control eye movements and blink. He can suck and time his own feeds. Although his movements are not well controlled, you will be fascinated by the delicate folding and unfolding of fingers and little movements and breathings while he sleeps. Already different babies have different body language.
Around 1 month	He still cannot support his body, but is beginning to hold up and control his head. He can turn it at will. He will press down with his feet on a surface or your lap. He waves his arms and legs rather jerkily, but already you will see that he does this at certain times – he may enjoy kicking in the bath, for instance.	He will turn towards sounds and your face out of interest. He can follow a moving object with his eyes and head. His facial expression will begin to show interest and excitement. First smiles come at around six weeks and sometimes sooner. He will open his hand to grasp your finger.

AGE	LARGE-SCALE MOVEMENTS	DELICATE MOVEMENTS
Around 3 months	He moves his arms and legs more gracefully now – his movements may be more purposeful, for instance, the beginnings of reaching. He holds his head up and his back straight if you sit him up. If you lie him down flat on his stomach he can raise his head and chest and support himself on his arms. He may roll over, so watch him carefully if he is on a raised surface.	He is doing a lot more watching and noticing with his head and eyes; he will study his hands, perhaps clasping them together. He may get hold of his feet, too. He will begin to enjoy play objects – things he can hold on to for a while, such as rattles and things he can bash and kick. His movements will express his feelings – he may start kicking, arm-waving and waving his head vigorously as he approaches the breast or bottle, for instance. If he is a thumb or finger sucker he will have become one by now.

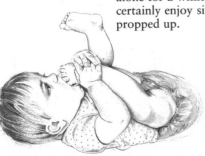

AGE	LARGE-SCALE MOVEMENTS	DELICATE MOVEMENTS
Around 6 months	He now has much more control of the upper part of his body. He can lift his head and shoulders when lying on his back, can roll over, will raise his arms to be picked up, can bounce with his feet on your lap, and he may even be sitting alone for a while. He will certainly enjoy sitting propped up.	He reaches out with his hands to grasp things and holds them confidently. He can pass them from hand to hand. He may deliberately drop them for you to pick up! He watches and monitors everything that is going on. His mouth is an important testing ground now – everything will go into it, including his precious thumb if he is a thumb sucker. Sucking his thumb will indicate whether he is tired or thoughtful. He may deliberately bang and rattle things to make a noise. He can hold and suck a spoon, rusks and large pieces of food.

AGE	LARGE-SCALE MOVEMENTS	DELICATE MOVEMENTS
Around 9 months	He is almost certainly on the move by now – either wriggling along on his stomach, or crawling or even walking. He will try to pull himself up to a standing position and may take a few steps with support. He can sit up on his own and lean forward to pick things up. He may be a 'bottom-shuffler', in which case he may not crawl, but go on shuffling until he can walk.	He can grasp things well and is beginning to use his finger and thumb to pick things up and to pull them towards him. He can poke with one finger and may be pointing a lot as a way of drawing attention to things, or asking for something. He will take things when offered, but may not be able to give them back. When he drops things he will follow them with his eyes and try to get them back. He manages spoons and finger foods quite well, although with some mess (which he will probably enjoy!) He can play games which involve body movements such as hand clapping, imitating your actions and peekaboo.

Around 1 year	He can sit well, pull himself up and sit from lying down, walk round the furniture, walk holding your hand or by himself, and can stand alone now. If allowed to, he may crawl upstairs or on and off low items of furniture, so check your house for safety well before this stage is reached. However, he may have difficulty getting down and will still need careful watching. He may bounce rhythmically in time to music.	He can use forefinger and thumb more delicately to pick up tiny objects, and he will still put them in his mouth, so make sure everything is safe. He can pick up, hold, drop and throw toys with both hands and may have a preference for one hand now. He will be playing more, putting small toys into bigger toys and picking them out again. He will show he knows the uses of things by drinking from toy cups, combing with combs, and so on. He will be able to obey your instructions to do things.

322

AGE	LARGE-SCALE MOVEMENTS	DELICATE MOVEMENTS
Around 15 months	He will probably be walking now – staggering might be a more appropriate description. He is likely to fall over and sit down suddenly a lot, but will show amazing persistence in getting up and carrying on. He can probably manage stairs and steps but will need a lot of supervision. This is a peak age for accidents.	Both hands are much more efficient at picking things up and manipulating them. He can probably build with a few bricks and arrange toys on the floor. He may show interest in drawing or painting, holding pencils, crayons or brushes in his fist. He is less likely to put things in his mouth now, unless of course it is his spoon, which he should be managing quite well by now.

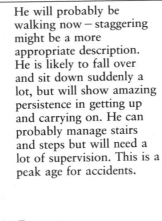

Around 18 months	Much more confident now, walking with arms swinging, able to stop, start, sit down, stand up, kneel, squat, climb and carry things around with him.	He will be doing many things with his hands, including some skilled tasks, perhaps with some help, such as threading large beads, building, attempts at drawing, helping you, using toy tools such as hammers and pegs.

AGE	LARGE-SCALE MOVEMENTS	DELICATE MOVEMENTS
Around 2 years	He can run, walk with confidence, pull wheeled toys around and safely negotiate obstacles around the house. He can probably walk up and down stairs properly, can push himself along on a pedal trike and can throw, aim a kick if not actually manage it, but will not be able to catch yet.	Hopefully, increasing skills in language and thinking mean he has many more opportunities to exercise physical abilities too; he can look at a book, turning the pages over properly; can arrange things neatly; perform useful tasks such as wrapping and unwrapping parcels; can, perhaps, use scissors, and will be increasingly skilful with hand and eye tasks such as jigsaws, painting, threading and construction-toy play. Of course, a lot of practice helps and so to some extent his skills depend on having opportunities and playthings to practise on. He will probably have some control over bowel and bladder, maybe even complete control, but it will still be variable at times.

Around 3 years	He is quite an athlete now, can jump from a low step, climb on climbing frames, walk backwards and sideways, stand on one foot, stand and walk on tiptoe, throw, kick and maybe even pedal his trike. He can carry and manoeuvre large objects and toys such as prams or trains.	He will be doing all the things he did as a two-year-old, but better. He may hold a pen or pencil properly now, and draw or paint simple shapes; he will probably be able to model shapes with plasticine or dough. He can eat with a fork and spoon and make a reasonable attempt at washing and drying himself and also at dressing and undressing, but with some things he will still need help. He may be dry at night.

AGE	LARGE-SCALE MOVEMENTS	DELICATE MOVEMENTS
Around 4 years 	He will now be walking, running and climbing confidently. He can manage stairs and obstacles, and find his way round with ease. He can hop, bend, clamber and swing on climbing frames and is getting better at throwing and catching – he may even be able to use a bat.	He will have a good control of fingers and thumbs now – holding pens and pencils properly, able to draw and build from memory and to copy other people's drawings and buildings quite efficiently. He should be doing many things to look after himself now: taking himself to the toilet, washing and drying himself, dressing and undressing (still with some help), helping you and doing all the things for his own toys.
Around 5 years 	By now, you may well have a gymnast on your hands – although children do vary a lot in their physical agility and confidence. A confident child will be climbing, balancing, attempting handstands, somersaulting, hanging upside down from the bars of the climbing frame and probably causing you some considerable nervous strain! Less confident children will still have good control of their limbs, begin to be able to skip, hop, bend, grasp things strongly, throw, kick and dance or show an awareness of rhythm when moving to music. Physical differences between children will become more apparent, particularly with the more organised activities of school. Some children are never going to be	As well as doing all the things mentioned above but better, the five-year-old may well be writing, drawing and painting with confidence and skill. He will be quite good at copying and colouring. He may be able to sew by now – perhaps even to knit or crochet given help. He can manage tools, hammering nails, using screws and nuts, screwdrivers and spanners – again with your help. He can manage gardening and cooking implements too. All these skills depend on you giving him opportunities to try his hand and being very patient with him as he learns. However, it is worth spending time teaching your child skills – it will provide a bond between you. as well as increasing ability and confidence. He will

AGE	LARGE-SCALE MOVEMENTS	DELICATE MOVEMENTS
	very good at games, or graceful dancers; some may be clumsy or slow or need extra help and patience. Nevertheless, all healthy five-year-olds have, in their bodies, a very efficient instrument for movement, making, controlling and mastering the environment that you provide for them.	also enjoy constructive, creative play with other children – planning large-scale models, digging and tunnelling in soil or sand, modelling and painting on a large scale. All these activities will increase and blossom at school, but you can still continue to foster them at home.

HOW YOU CAN HELP YOUR CHILD

The way your baby gradually gains control over his body – his motor development – proceeds fairly automatically, and there is not much you can do to speed it up or hinder it. However, you can do a great deal to encourage and help your child to develop the skills involved in learning different aspects of controlled movement. The most obvious example is giving him plenty of opportunity to practise and exercise each new aspect of movement as he becomes capable of it – for example, providing times for kicking and wriggling on the floor without being hindered by nappy or clothes; scope to look around, reach and grasp; freedom and safety to roll, crawl, walk round the furniture, and eventually walk alone; many safe, interesting objects and playthings to exercise hand and eye skills. He will need liberty to explore the world he is discovering, which may mean mud and puddles in the garden or park or the ever-fascinating contents of your cupboards.

Later, as he becomes more controlled, deliberate and purposeful in his activities, he will want more organised play and events in his life. Having an active child around the house makes a huge impact on your life and it can be quite a strain to give your child opportunities for free movement and at the same time keep your own life and home in a condition that is comfortable for you. For more on this see chapter 12.

You may want your child to learn a sport or have dancing lessons. Swimming is an excellent sport and you can begin to help your baby to be confident in the water as soon as you start to give him his first baths. Once he has had his first triple vaccination (see page 529) you can take him to the local swimming pool – ask at your local baths for details of parent-and-baby swimming sessions. Many sports and leisure centres have special facilities for under-fives – for instance baby bounce sessions with trampolines, floor cushions and climbing bars.

If you enjoy it, it is never too soon to introduce your three- to five-year-old to the delights and disciplines of more organised group games such as simple versions of football, cricket, rounders, races and obstacle courses.

By the time he is five years old your child should have a good grasp of rules, though he will probably still sulk when he is out.

If you are not a sporty type, then walking, climbing and making trips to the swing park together are just as good exercise if you do them regularly.

If your child is agile or graceful or simply very keen, he or she may enjoy dancing or gymnastics. There are many dancing schools in most neighbourhoods and you can get information about them from the library or local education authority. Local sports centres will have information about gymnastics and other sporting facilities for under-fives. However, if your child is not keen do not try to force it. Sport, dance and other organised activities at this age are only for fun. Too intensive coaching could spoil enjoyment and may even do damage to developing muscles and limbs. Again, the value of many sporting activities is that you can do them together as a family. Playing games together, so long as you all enjoy it, is a good way of uniting family members and giving younger members who may have surplus energy a way to let off steam.

BOYS AND GIRLS

In the first five years there are virtually no differences in physique and growth rates between boys and girls. They have the same endowment of bones, muscles and nerves and on average they are almost the same in height and weight, although, as with everything else, we all know of individual exceptions to this. Yet on some measures of physical skills there do seem to be differences between the sexes. On short runs, girls are faster than boys at the age of five years. Boys are better at throwing and catching and seem to have more strength; girls are better at jobs that involve judgement and precision such as playing hopscotch. In every playgroup you visit you will see groups of boys doing heavily physical things such as running about, rough and tumble, playing with cars, trains or large-scale layouts; and you will see groups of girls arranging the Wendy corner, reading books, doing jigsaws and helping the teacher.

The question of sex differences is a very controversial one and every family has to decide for themselves how they want to bring up their children. Just because research might show that girls are more likely to become scientists if they are given more opportunity for play with numbers or building toys is no reason for you to deprive your little daughter of a much loved doll or deny her the opportunity of helping you in the kitchen. It depends on whether she actually wants to be a scientist – and even scientists need to learn to cook and look after babies. Similarly, just because research suggests boys can throw and catch balls better than girls is no reason for you to exclude your daughter from games of cricket or rounders. Physically, she is just as well equipped as your son, provided she is given plenty of practice, and could be as useful as a bowler or batter. The reverse is also true: if your son is very keen to become a ballet dancer don't

hit the idea on the head because you think it is not the sort of thing a boy should be interested in.

The question of sex differences has been raised in this particular chapter because the very different ways in which we treat boys and girls are most marked in the amount of physical freedom or restriction we give them. Running, climbing, fighting, riding bikes and playing ball games are all tolerated or encouraged in boys, but may not be in the families of some girls. Similarly, quiet, orderly, table-top activities which involve co-operation with an adult are often felt to be more acceptable for girls. There are no physical reasons why this should be so – although you should remember that your child will have considerable pressure from his or her friends to behave in the same way as they do.

However, it is important for you to give both your boys and your girls opportunities to do whatever physical activities they are capable of. If you do not encourage your son to talk to adults, take care of other children, help you to cook the lunch and learn the basics of cookery, he will miss out on important chances to learn skills he will need later in life. If your daughter never gets the chance to climb trees, or if you never buy her a bike, she will not get the chance to become physically daring and adventurous.

One of the most valuable reasons for becoming physically skilled is the confidence it can give a child. If he feels comfortable in his body, if he feels he can make it do what he wants it to, then he can be helped to be a more confident person. Both boys and girls need to be brought up to accept and be proud of their bodies. There is no genetic or physical reason why little girls should be encouraged to be timid and shy, modest and passive, quiet and still; and there is no genetic or physical reason why little boys should be the opposite. You need to give them the opportunities to do all the activities they might be capable of. It is then up to them to take what opportunities they want to develop into the person they are going to be.

Chapter 10

THE SENSES

Your baby's eyesight   Hearing   Touch   Taste and smell

From the day your baby is born he begins to look around him for information about the world. He explores through his other senses too: he is soothed
by touch; he enjoys the taste of milk, but might make a face at something salty; he listens and turns towards sounds; he soon recognises your smell.

YOUR BABY'S EYESIGHT

Vision is the richest of all the senses for helping your baby to understand
the world. The development of other skills, using his hands, moving
around in a controlled way, understanding speech and learning to relate to
people all depend very much on what your baby can see.

The eyes provide a direct pathway to the brain for information about the
world. They are the first outpost of the brain to develop in a tiny inch-long
embryo. The eyes of a newborn baby receive lights rays from objects in the
surroundings and build them into an image which is transmitted along the
optic nerve to the brain. The brain 'sees' the image, but although your very
young baby can see what you see – for example, a rattle – he does not yet
know what this is. The message his eyes have received has passed to the
brain, but it is not until he has more experience of the world that his brain
will recognise the image as a rattle. The newborn baby can see, and it takes
only a few months for him to recognise, to choose and to focus on details of
all the many objects he sees. This process is known as perception and it
begins to develop from the moment of birth.

SIGHT AT BIRTH

It is one of the most common misconceptions that a new baby cannot see.
He naturally sees best near to because he cannot yet adjust the focus of his
eyes for different distances. For example, he sees his mother's face most
clearly when she is nursing him in her arms. This first eye-to-eye contact is
one of the most important ways in which a relationship is built up between
the baby and the person looking after him.

New babies react to very bright light by closing their eyes and turning
towards other more diffuse sources of light. During the first weeks a baby
begins to learn to use his eyes to follow moving objects, for example, a
dangling mobile. He quickly develops preferences: human faces are more

331

interesting to him than mere abstract shapes. Babies like to be held where they can see faces, and especially your face, clearly.

You may notice your new baby seems to be squinting – that is, one eye looks in a slightly different direction from the other. This may just be due to an early weakness of the eye muscles and correct itself, but it is sensible to ask your doctor about it straight away.

By around four months some important developments become notice-able. Your baby's sight and his ability to perceive and recognise different objects have been improving all the time. By now his eyes and the visual part of his brain have developed enough to see clearly and three-dimen-sionally. He can focus on near or distant objects and recognise them, and his interest and ability to see detail far away will continue to improve for some months. While he is immobile, learning will benefit if objects such as toys, spoons and human faces are brought nearer and people carry him around to broaden his horizon.

However, one important change happens at around four months which begins to give your baby more control over what happens to him and shows an important link between seeing/perceiving and other skills. At this age your baby has realised that what he can see is a tangible object he can reach out for, touch and grasp. At first he will notice his hands waving in front of his eyes and gradually he will deliberately bring them up to where he can see them and will start to play with them. Or he may catch sight of his foot without realising it belongs to him. If you hold a toy or a spoon or his bottle close to him, he will begin to reach out and try to get hold of it. At first he is not very good at this. His aim is not always accurate and he will not always be able to grasp the object because he has not yet got sufficient control of his fingers, but it is an important step because it shows the baby is making the link between himself and the outside world. He recognises there is an outside world and that the things he sees are not just pictures in his head. When he reaches out to touch and grasp he is saying to himself, 'That's for me. The world is my oyster and I am going to explore it.'

Make sure your young baby has plenty of safe things to look at and which are within his reach from a few weeks old. A cradle gym suspended over his cot or pram is great fun: you can make your own and change the objects on it from time to time if you wish. Babies like variety, so give him a mixture of textures – soft and furry, wood, plastic and rubber. Include a few things that make a noise so that he can make things happen. All these experiences will increase his sense of control over the world around him and make him eager to explore more. They will also help to keep him happy and amused. Make sure you carry him around too, so that he sometimes sees the world from an upright position. Some babies enjoy being carried in a sling, and most mothers get very good at doing a great many tasks with one hand!

RECOGNISING AND REMEMBERING

When a baby realises that things and other people have a separate existence from himself, he then has to learn that they go on having a

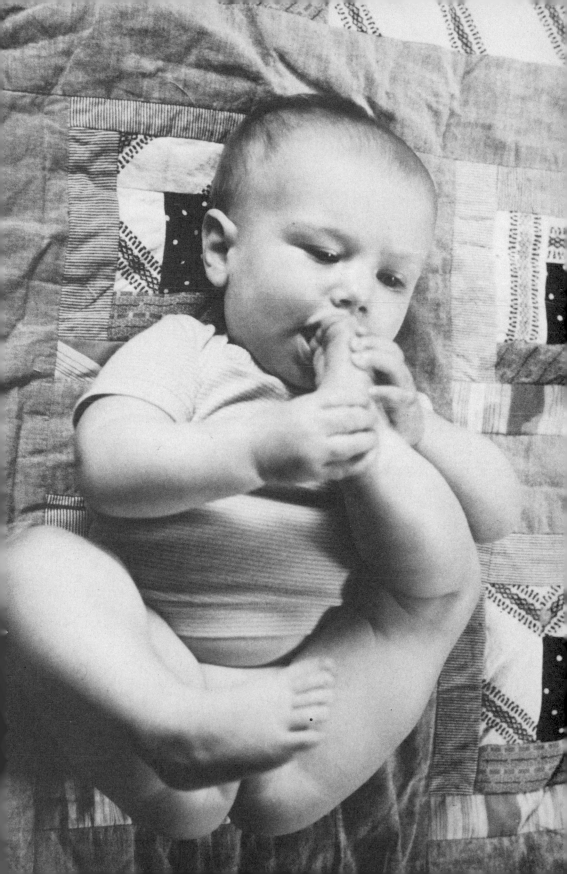

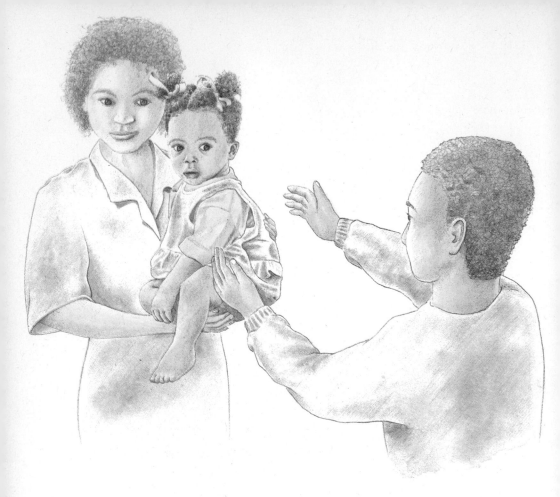

Your baby may become wary of strange faces

separate existence, even when he cannot see them. You will probably notice that when your young baby of four or five months drops a rattle, or when a person disappears from view, he seems to forget about their existence. At some time between six and nine months you will notice that the baby's memory for objects has improved. When he drops his rattle, he will look over the side of the pram to see where it has gone. If you hide a toy under a blanket he will pull the blanket away — and probably urge you to go on playing this game until you are exhausted! At this age peekaboo games in which you hide your face and then show it again are great fun for a baby who has just made the important discovery that people and things are still there — even when they cannot be seen.

From six months onwards babies are full of curiosity for the things they can see around them. They love to look at things and reach for them and, if they get hold of them, usually put them in their mouths. The link between sight and touch becomes closer and closer at this time. The baby's ability to grasp objects improves, although he will not be able to pick up very tiny things until he can co-ordinate his forefinger and thumb, which happens at around nine months. He likes new things and by about a year will point and babble when something catches his attention.

He is sensitive to faces and their expressions too. Watch when other adults hold your baby – they usually go to an enormous amount of trouble to get a response from him, by smiling, nodding, wrinkling their foreheads and talking. Watch how the baby follows, imitates the expressions and responds. You do this too, although you are probably not aware of it at the time. From a very early age babies become unhappy and distressed at a sad or angry looking face and respond happily to smiles and animated faces.

At about nine months, although it may be earlier or later, babies will stop responding happily to all friendly faces and may begin to show wariness of strangers' faces, no matter how friendly they appear. Although this may be inconvenient for you, it does show that your baby has made another important discovery – that the world can be a dangerous place and that caution and suspicion are sometimes needed when he is faced with new experience.

NAMING AND PLAYING

As your baby begins to notice and be interested in different objects around him, you will automatically begin to name them for him. Mothers do this even for newborn babies: they will say, 'Here's Daddy', or 'Look at that

lovely car', even though they know the baby cannot possibly understand. However, when your baby begins to point and reach and grasp and show likes and dislikes then you can start using his visual behaviour to build up his understanding and awareness of language.

Mothers have many ways of doing this: you may just point and say the single word very clearly, 'spoon', or 'teddy' or 'biscuit'; or you may give the baby a running commentary on what he is doing, 'Oh dear, you've dropped your spoon. Let's pick it up and try again'; or you may encourage his ability to learn that out-of-sight objects are still there by saying, 'Where's the spoon? Is it on the floor?' and looking down yourself and picking it up with a triumphant cry, 'Here's the spoon.' Never feel that this kind of behaviour is silly or that talking to a baby who cannot yet talk back is pointless. It is not. It is the most valuable learning experience you can give him – and mothers are very, very good at it. There is more about language in chapter 11.

Babies begin to understand the names of things quite a long time before they can say them. If you say, 'Where's the cat?' your year-old baby may look around and point or babble if the cat is there. Giving your baby plenty of experience of the 'Where's the . . .' and 'What's that?' variety, encourages him to learn and build up his store of words and names. Many babies between six months and a year begin to enjoy looking at pictures too. Simple board picture books can encourage his recognition of objects and their names. Generally young babies like pictures which are very realistic rather than those which are done in a stylised or cartoon design. Good sources for these kind of pictures are catalogues and magazines and babies enjoy turning (and tearing) the pages as well. Pictures help him to learn that objects not only exist outside him, they can also be represented. A picture may look very like the real thing, but it is not the real thing, it is just a representation of it.

Television pictures are too complicated for a young baby to understand – he cannot reach out to grasp and handle the objects represented there as he can with real things and, unlike a book, the image changes very quickly. Although older babies may like to look at television for short periods, they will learn very little from it at this stage, so do not leave your baby in front of the set for long periods.

ON THE MOVE

Once your baby begins to crawl and then walk, he no longer relies on you to show him things or bring them to him. He can decide for himself what he wants to look at and then go and take a closer look, and if possible get hold of it. It is just before this stage that you need to take a look at your house in terms of safety (see also chapter 15). Babies will obviously be attracted to things at their own eye level, so you will have to move all dangerous and fragile things steadily upwards from the floor as your baby gets older.

The information he receives through his eyes is the foundation for all sorts of other learning, and the means of learning at this stage is play (see chapter 12). From twelve months onwards, and certainly once he can walk and has his hands free, the co-ordination between your baby's eyes and hands become more and more skilled. He will play with things in a more purposeful way, pick up tiny objects and examine them, try to put one object on top of or inside another. He will throw, push and pull; he will turn things into tools – for instance, he will use a piece of string to pull a toy car towards him. He will observe and imitate. If you give him the chance, the young toddler will also show interest in holding a pencil or crayon and scribbling on paper. He will be able to use a paintbrush, but expect him to enjoy simply making a mess with the paint rather than actually painting! He can now recognise familiar things and people at a distance of twenty feet or so. The world of the toddler is full of colours, shapes and sights to be explored and learned about.

VISUAL IMPAIRMENT

Very few babies are born completely blind or with severe visual problems. The majority of those who are often have other handicaps as well, because something that interferes with or damages the formation of the eyes or optic nerve may affect other parts of the baby's or embryo's nervous system, for example German measles (*rubella*) in pregnancy or breathing problems at birth. In some cases severe eye problems can be inherited.

It is very important that such problems are identified and treated early because, as we described above, so much of the baby's early development is linked to his ability to see and perceive. Some visual handicaps are detected immediately after birth, particularly if doctors have been alerted by problems occurring around the time of delivery, by the mother's illness in pregnancy or by a family eye problem. Sometimes the baby's visual behaviour is the only clue. If your baby's eyes roll a lot, if he is startled when he is touched or hears a voice because he has no visual clue that someone was approaching, if he does not meet your eyes or begin to respond to your smiles and movements, then it could possibly be that he cannot see properly. These signs will become more and more noticeable during the first three or four weeks. If you are worried by your baby's lack of visual response, then do not hesitate to seek medical advice immediately.

•

Curable conditions Some eye problems can be cured and it is important that they are because after about eighteen months the brain's ability to learn to interpret messages from the eyes decreases sharply. The first six months of life are the most important time in this learning process.

Some conditions like cataracts and squints are treatable. *Cataracts* affect the lens of the eye and prevent the light rays falling on the retina. They can now be operated on successfully in very tiny babies: the baby is given a contact lens to help him focus. A *squint* means the eyes do not look in the same direction and therefore cannot operate together. With normal binocular (two-eyed) vision, the two independent images received by each eye are fused by the brain into one. The child with a squint cannot do this and therefore relies on the information coming through only one of his eyes and does not use the other one. Eventually the sight in the unused or 'lazy' eye, as it is sometimes called, becomes very poor because the brain does not register the information coming from it. Squints can be treated by putting a pad over the good eye thereby encouraging the active use of the lazy one; by glasses; by an operation; or by a combination of these. If you think your baby squints, ask your doctor to advise whether you should take him to see an ophthalmologist for full diagnosis and treatment.

EYE TESTS

Most babies and young children in developed countries are routinely tested for sight from six months onwards. First tests are designed to find out whether your child has a squint or a minor visual defect such as *short-sightedness* (myopia). In myopia the eyeballs are longer than normal and the image is blurred because it falls in front of the eye's retina instead of on it; the child cannot see things that are far away from him, but can focus on things that are near. *Long-sightedness* (hypermetropia) creates the opposite problem: the image falls behind the retina. Severe long-sightedness causes great strain because the eyes have to work to focus on images, even when they are across the room. Normally we only need to make our eyes work to focus on near objects. Both conditions can be corrected by wearing glasses. Another problem is *astigmatism* in which the light rays entering the eye are bent because of an irregularity in the eyeball creating a distorted image. This too can be dealt with by glasses. Glasses early on can also prevent the development of squint and lazy eye, as well as helping your child to see clearly.

If any of your family have needed glasses in childhood, or if your baby or young child has not been routinely tested and you suspect there is something wrong with his sight, make sure you ask for a test. The sooner treatment is begun the better. For more on eye problems see chapters 17 and 19.

GLASSES FOR CHILDREN

Parents, especially if they themselves have never worn glasses, may feel a pang of protective anxiety if their young child needs glasses. The common worry is that their child may feel self-conscious or that other children may comment adversely. In fact these protective anxieties are nearly always entirely adult based and usually a remnant from our own childhood memories of unattractive flesh-coloured frames for children. It is very important that parents, and any grannies or other older relatives, keep any such feelings very strictly to themselves, as children, and especially pre-school children, will usually accept wearing glasses quite happily provided they are introduced to them in a positive fashion. There is now a wide range of bright, attractive frames for children. Find an optician, rather than simply a glasses shop, who stocks a good selection. Those with bendy wire sides which curl behind the ears are usually best for under fives as they stay put during handstands, head rolls, and so on. An alternative is a style with sprung sides for a firm grip. Let your child feel he has chosen the style of frame, though obviously a little tactful manipulation may be needed to see that his choice comes within your budget. Make sure they are fitted correctly so that they are comfortable, with no red pressure points when they are taken off.

At first glasses will feel a little strange to the child, so it helps to plan some busy days with plenty of activities to help him to forget he is wearing them. Try not to let him get into the habit of taking them off during the day because he will be likely to forget to put them on again and there is a higher chance of them getting broken or lost. The mother of a three-year-old who wears glasses because long-sightedness made him squint recalled:

'At first I did feel a bit choked about him wearing glasses even though it's a tiny thing compared with real disabilities. It was seeing him crying because he had fallen over, and trying to rub away the tears but finding the glasses got in the way that slightly got to me. But now they are so much part of his personality, to the extent that the other day he came and said, "Mum, I can't find my glasses anywhere," and he was actually wearing them. He's not at all the sort of child I used to think of as "speccy" from my childhood days either – he's very sporty, chunkily built and really popular with other kids.'

The eyes are the most sensitive information receivers in the whole body and are able to deal with literally millions of bits of information every time they look at something. Most of this information is screened out and discarded because it is not needed. The process of becoming ever more selective and discriminating in the perception of all the many objects and people in the world around him is a vital part of your child's intellectual and social development. It is also a source of wonder and delight. Some of the happiest shared experiences between a baby and adult begin with the word, 'Look'.

HEARING

Although sight is the most important co-ordinating sense, hearing is a most valuable sense for human beings because it is through hearing that we learn language and are able to communicate with each other. A child or person who cannot hear is cut off from other people and this will affect his ability to make relationships, as well as the way he learns, unless prompt help is offered and maintained.

The ears work by collecting sounds from the environment and channelling them down into the inner ear via the eardrum. The sounds make the eardrum vibrate, and these vibrations are converted by the organs of the inner ear into electrical impulses which are then passed along the auditory nerve to the brain. The brain converts these impulses into meaningful information just as it does with the light waves coming through the eyes. We take the skills of the brain so much for granted we do not always appreciate what an impressive performance it is to turn sound vibrations into the lines of a poem, or rays of light into patterns, shapes and designs, but this is what your baby's brain is equipped to do. And as with vision, his brain will set to work on the task of learning to interpret sounds right from birth.

YOUR NEWBORN BABY

Once the newborn baby's ears are drained of fluid which is left over from his life in the womb, his hearing is acute and it will get even better as he grows older. If he hears a sudden noise he will startle. He may also move his head in response to noise, but he cannot yet tell exactly where a sound is coming from and look towards it. He learns to do this more accurately at around five or six months. New babies soon learn to recognise their own mother's or special caretaker's voice. If your baby is crying and hears you speak to him, he may stop and listen. A strange voice will not be so reassuring. Babies are also sensitive to the sound of other babies. If your baby is in a ward or a nursery with other mothers and babies and one baby starts crying, it is not long before your baby and all the others begin as well.

Many sounds seem to have a special quality for soothing babies – especially rhythmic sounds. Lullabies are an age-old way of sending a baby to sleep and so is rhythmic rocking. We do not quite know why this should be, but since the ear controls the sense of balance as well as hearing there is an obvious connection between rhythmic movement and rhythmic sound. You will probably notice you quite automatically sway backwards and forwards when holding your baby, you will pat his bottom rhythmically, and you will say simple phrases over and over: 'There, there. What's the matter?' and so on.

By about seven months your baby will be well able to recognise and discriminate between different sounds: for instance, the sound of a spoon in a dish will mean food to him; the door opening will mean someone is coming; he can tell angry from cheerful voices, will be most upset if you speak crossly and will perk up if you speak brightly. So although he cannot understand words or sentences or speak them yet, he is well on the way to linking meaning with sound – an important part of learning to talk.

SOUND PLAY

Being able to hear is vital in order to learn to talk, but we do not express ourselves only through speech. Language can also be expressed in signs and gestures (as used by deaf people) and of course through print and the written word. There is more about language and its development in chapter 11.

During his first year your baby will learn to distinguish words from other sounds he hears and to associate them with meaningful things, but he will also enjoy being talked to. As you talk to your two- or three-month-old, you will notice he responds by waving his arms and kicking his legs and smiling and gurgling. Babies enjoy being sung to as well, no matter how unmusical you think your voice is, so do sing and hum to your baby, and let him hear other music too.

However, babies can be upset by too much noise. Sudden loud sounds can startle them and make them cry. They may get very upset by the vacuum cleaner or the washing machine. We all have a mechanism known as habituation which enables us to screen out unnecessary sounds once we have heard them a few times: although the noise may be continuing we simply do not hear it. Babies learn to do this in the first few days of their lives, but new sounds may still have to be introduced gently.

Babies and young children in today's cities live in a very noisy environment, with cars roaring past and perhaps the radio or television as continual background noise. You do not want your child to screen out all sounds, so once he is old enough it is sometimes good to be quiet and encourage him to listen for particular noises: leaves rustling; a dog barking; a train passing; a car in the distance getting nearer. Talk about the noises as you hear them and tell him what they mean. As he gets older you can use his hearing skills to introduce important ideas such as loud/soft or high/low. There are plenty of ways of introducing sound play around the home – although most adults find it hard to habituate to sounds such as saucepans being banged! Five minutes will probably be as much as you can stand.

Most toys are designed to encourage hand–eye activities, but remember babies play and learn through their ears too. Once your child is talking, sound remains crucial. This is especially true for blind or partially sighted children who have to learn everything through hearing, touch, smell and taste.

HEARING TESTS

New babies do not have many ways of letting us know whether or not they can hear. If you have any hearing problems in your family, however, or if you had German measles or any other illness during early pregnancy, you should tell the hospital paediatrician or your own doctor.

Your newborn baby may be tested using an 'acoustic cradle' to see if his hearing is working. Different hospitals vary in their policy, but this is especially likely if there is anything in his medical history which might cause impaired hearing. During the test the baby wears a special belt and lies in the acoustic cradle, which looks like an ordinary cradle, so that any changes in his breathing in response to a variety of sounds can be detected and recorded. A newer test for hearing called the 'cochlea echo' is also becoming more common. The cochlea is the snail-shaped organ in the middle ear which is full of fluid, sound receptors and membranes and is able to covert the vibrations of the eardrum into nervous impulses which send messages to the brain. In this test a probe bounces sound into the ear and a fraction of a second later is able to pick up an echo bouncing back from the cochlea. If there is no echo, this may indicate that the complicated hearing mechanism is not working properly.

Different health authorities operate slightly different community health screening programmes, but most see babies at six weeks and then again between about eight to nine months. At the first check, which may be done by your GP or at a health centre, hearing can only be tested in a fairly elementary way to see if the baby responds to a loud level of sound. At eight to nine months the hearing test usually consists of sounding a high frequency rattle and whispering low frequency words to see if the baby makes a turning response. A baby with a history indicating a greater chance of hearing impairment would be observed more carefully.

The test at eight to nine months involves you sitting with your baby on your lap while the health visitor or her assistant makes test sounds behind him, to his right and then to his left. If the baby turns towards the sound, it is assumed his hearing is all right. If he does not turn, then it does not necessarily mean he is deaf – he may have caught sight of something more fascinating across the room. Bear in mind also that hearing can be temporarily affected by colds and illness. If he does not respond to this first test, you will be asked to bring him back again.

If you are sure that he responds to sounds, for instance, you know that you have only to tiptoe across his bedroom floor for him to leap up in his cot, then tell the health visitor. A parent's own reports on the child are usually taken very seriously, because as one paediatrician with years of experience of testing has put it, 'The mother is usually right.' Of course, if you are worried about your child's hearing, perhaps because he does not respond to the soothing noises and sounds in the way described above, if he startles when he sees you as if he has had no warning from footsteps or the door opening, and if he is not woken by sounds, then be persistent in getting his hearing properly checked. Your worries will usually have some foundation as you know your child best and you will be well aware if he does not seem to be developing in the same way as other babies you know.

Your child will also usually be tested as part of a community screening programme at the local health centre or GP's surgery before he goes to school, when more sophisticated electrical equipment will be used to measure how well he hears high and low tones. The age when this is done varies according to regional health authority policy, but most see children between three and four. Some children have 'high tone deafness' and cannot hear consonants properly; the speech they hear will seem blurred

343

and will affect their own speech. If your child does seem to have difficulty hearing some sounds (although not so much as to make him partly deaf), or if he is prone to ear infections and colds which also affect his hearing, ask for the test and tell his playgroup leaders and teachers so that they sit him near the front of the group and make allowances for it. If he says 'What?' all the time or ignores half of what you say, he may not be being difficult. Never rule out the possibility that he cannot hear properly and make sure he is tested by an audiologist – a specialist whose job it is to check hearing.

THE CHILD WITH REDUCED HEARING

Some children are deaf from birth through an inherited disorder of the auditory nerve or through damage during pregnancy, for example, from *rubella*, or from a shortage of oxygen at birth. Other children may become deaf later, perhaps because of a severe illness, such as meningitis, or from other childhood diseases such as mumps. Many children suffer some temporary deafness during their childhood from middle ear infection (*otitis media*) or by a build-up of wax in the ear, but do not use ear bud cleaners, as they stimulate wax production. If in doubt ask your doctor to check hearing – occasionally the ear may be blocked by something your child has inserted, such as a glass bead.

As mentioned on page 342, above, good hearing is very important for the proper development of speech. It follows that poor hearing may affect social relationships, so always be aware of the possibility of hearing loss if your child suffers from any of the illnesses mentioned above or from subsequent coughs and colds. Also consider it if his behaviour seems absent-minded or indifferent, or if his speech is slow to develop. Few children have total hearing loss, and what hearing they have can be the basis for very specialised speech and language training. Once hearing loss, whether partial or severe, is diagnosed, it is important for this treatment to begin straight away.

HEARING AIDS

As with glasses, parents usually find the idea of a hearing aid for their child much harder to accept than he does. It is important to keep such feelings from the child and to take a positive and optimistic view of the hearing aid as a real benefit. All hearing aids work on the same principle: they are amplifiers which make the sounds around louder. In this amplification there is a risk of distortion, but the quality of aids is improving all the time.

Small hearing aids worn behind the ear consist of an individually made ear mould in the ear which connects to a small box containing amplifier and micro battery. Under long hair it is invisible. However, some audiologists still favour body hearing aids, which have batteries in a box worn at waist level to power the amplifier in the ear, as they feel they are more robust. Whether a child has a hearing aid for each ear or only one depends on their particular circumstances, but it is more common to give babies and young children bilateral (two) aids. Young babies easily accept a hearing aid, but more tact and encouragement is required between the ages of eighteen months and three years when many children can be unco-operative about almost anything, ranging from putting on their coat to taking it off again!

OVERCOMING DEAFNESS

Parents of children who cannot hear properly have to work much harder to stimulate them, drawing their attention to objects and events and associating them with language. You cannot just throw casual remarks over your shoulder — you have to look at the child and speak very carefully so that he can learn to read your lips.

Together with advice from audiologists, ENT specialists and specialist teachers of hearing impaired children, early language training at home is vital with regular help from the teacher. We all use language in our thought processes and it is important that hearing impaired children are able to develop an inner language to use in this way. Specialists feel that both lip reading and sign language should be used to communicate with a child. There is some evidence that babies of deaf parents who learn sign language early on do better at reading and writing later than do deaf children who can only lip read by the time they learn to read. Young children have a greater facility than adults for learning language — children of bilingual parents are able to absorb both languages easily, while an adult finds tackling a foreign language for the first time far more difficult. In this way the mastering of what is two languages — sign language and lip reading — may be easier than an adult imagines for a young child.

Depending on where you live and the degree of handicap, a child with hearing impairment may attend a special school for the deaf to which transport is provided. Alternatively, he may go to a special unit for hearing impaired children attached to the local primary school. This allows him to live in a hearing community and helps hearing children to be aware of the problems of the deaf. Some partially hearing children go to ordinary infant schools, but they need a great deal of specialist teacher help if they are not to miss out. For more on hearing problems see chapters 17 and 19.

TOUCH

We learn through our eyes and ears, but we feel through our skin. We will learn through feeling too, and this is particularly true of young babies whose vision and hearing are still limited, and even more for blind children. However, much less attention seems to be paid to the sense of touch than other senses.

The skin gives us a great deal of information about what is going on around us — whether our environment is hot or cold, wet or dry. A most important function of the skin is to control temperature. In warm conditions the blood vessels expand, bringing blood to the surface of the body and cooling it. We also excrete sweat though the skin and as the sweat evaporates our bodies are kept cool. In cold weather the blood vessels contract to conserve the body's heat. New babies cannot control their temperature through their skin as effectively as older babies, children and adults. That is why it is important to keep them in a constant warm temperature, as well as keeping them warmly wrapped up when the weather is cool. There is more about keeping your baby in the right temperature on page 164.

Our skin also tells us, through its sensitive nerve endings, whether the sensations we are receiving are painful or pleasurable: a caress is pleasant, a blow is not; warmth is pleasant, sunburn is not. Pain is an important signal of danger to the brain. When we get a sudden blow, cut or other painful contact we instinctively recoil. Pain also indicates illness and damage, and crying can be a sign that your baby is suffering. Always check for uncomfortable bumps in the cot, a sore bottom or a tightly constricting garment if your baby is miserable.

Babies and young children have more sensitive skins than adults. What seems pleasantly warm bathwater to you may feel scaldingly hot to a baby. What seems a pleasantly cool breeze to you may be really chilly to a baby. A firm grasp of a toddler's hand may actually hurt him quite a lot and you cannot really blame him for protesting. A good general rule to remember is that babies and young children often feel things more intensely than adults. Although they are resilient and well equipped for survival, they can easily be hurt so they need to be treated gently and sensitively.

As well as responding to the environment around you, the skin is affected by the emotional state inside the person. Blushing and sweating when you are embarrassed, excited or afraid are obvious examples. Some children with skin diseases such as eczema, psoriasis and acne can be made worse by emotional stress, and emotional upset may even be the trigger to an attack. When you are happy your skin looks glowing and healthy; when you are miserable it can look sallow and lifeless. The colour, condition, feel and state of the skin are important signs as to whether or not a person is well. If your baby's skin changes very markedly and suddenly in any way — whether it is a change of colour or temperature, or if there is a rash — take him to the doctor, especially if there are other symptoms such as fever or loss of appetite.

THE IMPORTANCE OF CONTACT

As soon as a baby is born one of the first things a mother does, provided she is well herself and has access to her baby, is to reach out and touch him. Research has shown that many mothers have a systematic way of doing this — starting with finger-tip touching of hands and feet, and then going on to stroke the baby all over with the palms of their hands. Of course whether you do this depends on whether you have the baby near you and whether he is naked or wrapped up. Nowadays many doctors and mid-wives deliver the baby straight on to the mother's stomach so that they are lying skin to skin straight away.

Some research has suggested that such skin-to-skin contact repeated regularly in the first days after birth may improve the mother's relationship with her baby later on. No one would suggest that if you do not have skin-to-skin cuddles with your newborn, you will not have a good relationship with him later, but the importance of touch to babies and their parents is beginning to be emphasised more and more. It is certainly true that many mothers, given the choice, love to hold and stroke their babies, to press their cheek against their baby's cheek, to smell and even to lick their babies – after all humans are animals too. They want to be as close as they possibly can to their baby's body.

Young babies are also soothed by touch. They like to be held firmly or wrapped up securely. When they are miserable, being carried around in a sling in close contact with their mother's or father's body can sometimes cheer them up and send them off to sleep. Gently stroking their stomach, limbs or temples can often calm them and, as with other rhythmic behaviour like rocking and singing, can get them off to sleep. This need for comfort through cuddling and touching does not stop with babyhood. A sympathetic touch – just a grasp of the arm or a stroke of the head – can make adults as well as children feel happier and more confident.

Because children frequently have to be carried and have things done for them they automatically come in for a lot of touching, but special forms of touching such as cuddles, a kiss or throwing up in the air, are ideal forms of reward for children, much better than sweets. When your child is being peaceful or co-operative, remember to pat him on the head or give him a hug. If he is having a tantrum, however, cuddles may infuriate him even more: it may be better to stay with him until he has calmed down, and then to touch him gently, perhaps just by holding his hand.

INDIVIDUAL DIFFERENCES

Many experienced mothers or nurses will tell you that some babies are more cuddly than others. Some babies curl cosily into your body while others go stiff and rigid, take their feeds in a businesslike ten minutes and want to get off your lap. Some adults are like this too – including mothers. It seems to be a matter of personality and it is no good quoting research at a baby who does not like people grabbing him all the time! If you have a non-cuddly baby or child, or if you are a non-toucher yourself, don't waste precious energy feeling guilty about it. It should become clear to you from other sections of this book that babies and parents learn and receive mutual pleasure from all the senses in hundreds of different ways. If your baby does not like being on your lap, he may love sitting opposite you in a babychair while you talk to him. If you do not feel you can manage full-scale skin-to-skin contact at regular intervals, or if you do not want to

carry your baby around in a sling all the time, don't worry. Perhaps the father can do the carrying instead of you, or there might be a grandmother or friend around who does like cuddling and carrying. You can give your baby what you feel you want to give him – it might be conversation or games or outings. However, touching and carrying and cuddling are absolutely unavoidable with human babies for many months and even years. If you feel you are not getting any pleasure out of these things and that you see your baby as a burden, do talk to somebody about it. Your doctor may be able to help you or you can contact one of the organisations listed in the address section, pages 673–6.

Touch can also be especially important to newborn babies in incubators. There is more about how parents can meet their babies' and their own needs for contact in these circumstances in chapter 5.

One of the most important sensory experiences for a baby is through his tongue and mouth. Sucking is not only necessary to obtain milk, it is also a source of comfort and satisfaction for a baby (see page 207). Once a baby can begin to hold things in his hands, he automatically puts almost everything to his mouth for further exploration. By about nine months a baby may still put things in his mouth, but he will show that he is also able to appreciate the sensation of different textures which he can touch with his hands – stroking a pet, putting his fingers in his food, playing with sand or water. As he grows you can help to develop his understanding of different materials in his environment, both natural and manmade, through everyday experience and play.

If your baby develops an attachment to a toy, blanket or other object as a 'comfort' object you will see clearly how his sense of touch is being exercised. Not only will he clutch the comforter to him or enjoy stroking it, he will often pull it across his face or hold it against a cheek. Later, if he inadvertently comes across the same texture in a fabric when he is tired – a similar silky or soft piece of material for example – he may immediately clutch it in the same way and show other going-to-sleep habits such as thumb sucking. Your baby naturally explores and tests out the textures of rattles and other toys and as his awareness grows will increasingly enjoy playing with the water in his bath. Look for textures and sensations to introduce in play – being aware that young babies automatically put most things in their mouths – so your child experiences hard followed by soft, rough/smooth, angular objects like bricks and round ones like balls. When you are out in the garden or park let them touch the roughness of tree bark, scrumple green leaves and crunch crackly autumn ones. You sometimes see parents getting angry with small children for grubbing around in the earth getting dirty, but while it is understandable that parents don't want children covered in mud or worse after every outing it is also part of a child's natural curiosity continually to explore and discover.

TASTE AND SMELL

Much less attention has been given to the senses of taste and smell by experts in child development than to the other senses. We do not therefore know so much about them, but this does not mean they are not important. Just consider:

* The word 'taste' also means a person's own particular preference for things.

* Parents can have battles with their children for years over particular foods because the children do not like the taste or the smell.

* A bad smell is one of the most revolting experiences people can have – literally making them sick.

* Pleasant smells have a powerful effect in attracting people to each other.

New babies can tell the difference between drinks of different degrees of sweetness – they suck most eagerly at the sweetest drink. But since sugar is harmful for children's teeth, an apparently inborn taste for sweetness does not mean a child should be fed on sweet things. Breast milk is sweet and babies obviously like it, but the sugar (lactose) in it is not harmful to teeth. Babies do not like and spit out sharp or acid tastes.

When you begin introducing solids to your baby, you should aim for a variety of tastes in what you give him so that he gets a balanced diet and learns to develop his own tastes. There is more about starting to feed your baby solids and about the problems of food battles and food faddiness in chapters 6 and 7.

There is evidence that new babies can tell their own mother's smell from that of other mothers. A paediatrician who studied them noted that they turned their heads much more often to a breast pad used by their own mothers than to pads worn by other women. A new baby with limited vision, hearing and understanding of the world may rely on smell as a source of information about where he is and who he is with and also as a source of comfort. A baby may refuse to feed because his mother smells different, perhaps because she is using scented soap. Mothers sometimes comment enthusiastically on the special smell that their own babies have. Parents can tolerate the smell of their own baby's nappies, but find it very difficult to change another baby. It does seem, therefore, as if we use smell as part of the process that helps to attach parents and babies to each other.

The human baby has a potentially wonderful mind – able to use language, to invent, to create, to make jokes, to solve problems – but, especially in the early years, the mind is nourished through the body. What your child sees, hears, touches, tastes and smells are the raw materials of his intelligence and his personality. Young children try to experience things through all these senses at once. They will see something, reach for it, rattle it and talk to it, and then they will put it in their mouths. Their huge appetite for experience can sometimes be inconvenient but it is most essential and it can help you too to see and experience the world again as if for the first time.

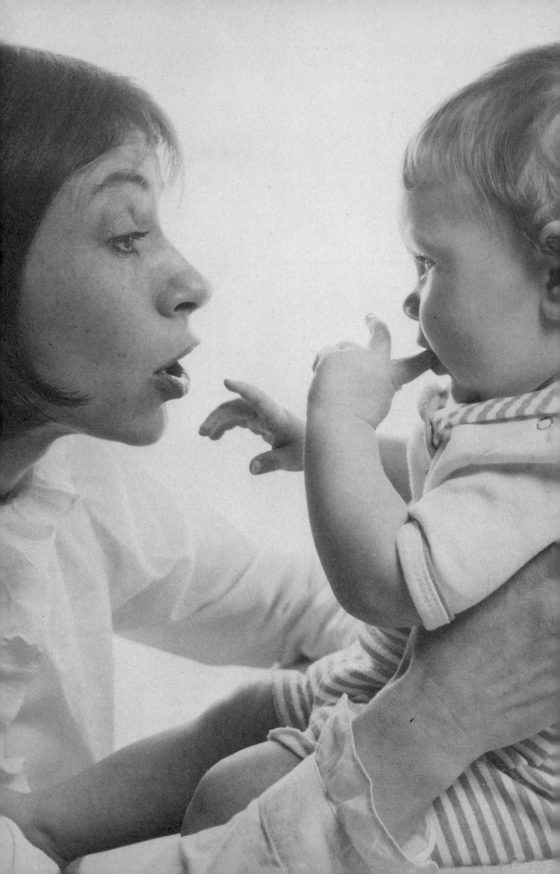

Chapter 11

LANGUAGE

What is language?   How language develops   Stages of development
First communications   First words   Talking with your child
Stories, books and television   Reading and writing
Early language problems

If someone asked you what you thought was the most impressive human achievement in using the English language, you might answer that it was Shakespeare's plays, Dickens's novels or the *Oxford English Dictionary*. However, the scope of achievement, even in these great works, is not as great as the difference between a newborn human baby whose main form of expressing himself is to cry and the speech of that same baby three years later.

A new baby cannot understand what you are saying and cannot talk back to you. A three-year-old can say, 'Daddy says I can have some sweets tomorrow.' In this simple sentence a three-year-old is showing he can report another person's speech, anticipate the future, use a complex combination of verbs ('can have'), hold a conversation, and in this case even use language not quite truthfully as a form of persuasion ('Daddy says'). If you disagree with him he will probably go on to conduct a sustained argument with you!

Children seem to pick up language so quickly and it is so basic to our everyday lives that it is easy to take it for granted and to overlook what a vital and complex skill it is. However, there are good reasons for recognising how important it is to your children and to you. In the first place it gives contact and closeness between you: it is through talking and listening that you get to know each other and eventually to share each other's experience. In the second place it is an important vehicle for learning. For instance, language is the tool which enables a child to tell Mummy what happened at Granny's while she was out. Later on language will be used in abstract arguments ('Supposing that . . . ?') and also to solve logical problems. Still later your child will learn the more formal skills of reading and writing as well as talking and listening. Language, or verbal ability, is one important factor in success at school, although it is not the only one.

The roots of your child's verbal ability lie in the early years between birth and four years old. By the end of this period most normal children have mastered the basic rules of their own language and are able to produce original, creative sentences in any number of combinations. And they do it without any systematic training on your part, though this does not mean you have no part to play.

WHAT IS LANGUAGE?

Language is a system of symbols – they can be sounds as in speech or they can be marks on paper – but language is more than a long list of signs which mean something, that would just be a dictionary. Language is also a system of rules used to create new meanings. Through language we can not only produce sentences that are completely original and that nobody has ever heard before, but we can also understand statements we have never heard before, as we do every time somebody talks to us.

So when a baby learns language he is not only learning lists of words – mummy, daddy, cat, and so on – he is also learning to use the rules that help him to combine words into completely new and often very delightful statements such as, 'Look, I didded it myself.' As the word 'didded' shows, the way he uses the rules may not be the way grown-ups use them but it is sensible as far as he is concerned.

Human babies and young children seem to have a natural ability to learn and use language creatively, but of course your child's enjoyment and mastery of language also depends a lot on you and the other people around him continuing to talk and listen to him.

HOW LANGUAGE DEVELOPS

All babies and small children learn first to understand and then to use language in a fairly standard developmental sequence, but there are big individual variations in when these developments happen. One child may say his first word (as distinct from babbling 'mummum – daddad' sounds) at 9 months, for instance, he may say, 'bye' and wave, so you know that he realises the sound 'bye' is associated with somebody leaving. Another child will not be able to do this until 15 or 16 months. Yet another might not bother with many single words like 'bye' or 'gone' or 'teddy', he will keep fairly quiet, understanding what you say to him, then suddenly start producing short sentences at 20 months. Some children may be very slow at understanding and producing language, which could be a sign of problems as discussed below. However, by the time they are four or five years old, most children are using language almost as adults use it, although with smaller vocabularies.

The main stages of development are summarised in the following chart. These are a rough guide as to what you might expect, but the ages are obviously approximate. Do not be surprised if your baby does something much earlier than the chart shows, although if he is very much later – by several months, say – in reaching these stages, you should discuss this with your health visitor or doctor. There is more about language delay on page 374.

STAGES OF DEVELOPMENT

BABY'S AGE	BABY'S UNDER-STANDING	BABY'S MEANS OF EXPRESSION	YOUR RESPONSE
0 – 1 month	Responds to sounds, especially familiar voices; goes quiet when picked up. Establishes feeding rhythms and patterns.	Crying, grunting, sighing, blowing bubbles. Feeding rhythms develop as 'cues' for you to respond to, for example, breaking off to gaze at you when he is less hungry.	Picking him up, talking to him face to face. Responding to his 'cues' while feeding by talking, smiling or staying silent.
1 – 4 months	First smile, in response to approaches and talking from you – usually around five to six weeks. Recognition of you and familiar faces and objects (e.g. bottle). Anticipation of being picked up – excited arm-waving and kicking.	Non-crying noises such as cooing and gurgling, also first laugh. Cries become more expressive – of hunger, tiredness, impatience, etc.	Learning to distinguish his cries and to respond to them differently. Still talking sensibly to him, you may imitate his sounds which may encourage him to make them again. You will probably tickle and tease him to produce smiles and laughter.
4 – 6 months	Recognises and responds to familiar sounds, voices and objects. Reacts to tones of voice – is upset by anger, cheered by brightness and jollity.	Babble begins – 'ga' and 'goo' sounds joined together. Makes noises to show his feelings of pleasure or distress.	You will continue talking to him, but particularly in response to his own noises. He will be having more varied experiences – with solid food, learning to hold toys, etc. – which gives you more to talk about.
6 – 9 months	Understanding signs – e.g. bib means food. Also understanding 'up' or 'down' or 'Daddy's coming'.	Makes appropriate gestures, such as raising his arms to be picked up. Continues	You are getting a lot more pleasure out of him now, and you will tailor your speech much more to his under-

BABY'S AGE	BABY'S UNDER-STANDING	BABY'S MEANS OF EXPRESSION	YOUR RESPONSE
	Responds to his own name and other familiar names.	babbling – tries out a few single syllables, can imitate, clap and play peekaboo.	standing, using clear single words to help him learn. More games, less face-to-face chat as he may be mobile. You will talk to him as he does other things.
9 – 12 months	Understands games like dropping and picking up a toy. Understands 'Give me' and 'No'. Follows instructions like 'Kiss teddy'. Enjoys songs, action rhymes. Understands own daily routine.	May produce first words – probably 'dada' or 'mama' or 'bye'. Much expressive babbling as well. Plays with toys and objects and shows he knows what they are for.	Your own speech will be much more designed to respond to his, for example, naming things repeatedly, giving him instructions, asking him questions, checking his knowledge – 'Let's get dressed', etc. Other people, like friends and grannies, will be talking to him and getting a response.
12 – 15 months	Follows simple commands. Can point to pictures of things he knows, knows parts of body, listens carefully to you and others. Laughs at humorous events, e.g. funny faces, falling, etc.	May say 2 or 3 words, but still much speech-like chatter with no meaning. Shows he knows use of things by more complex play, expecially as he becomes mobile.	Still echoing his words, pointing out new ones, questions, commands and, as he becomes mobile, more 'no's' and 'don'ts'. In addition conversation increasingly based on real events as he becomes more active.
15 – 20 months	Recognising many objects and pictures of objects. Can make plans, anticipate future. Begins to understand 'in', 'on', 'me' and	Vocabulary goes up to 6 to 8 words, though some children may say more. Words will be familiar objects, such as 'ball',	A fascinating period for you as your child is now physically independent, very enquiring and beginning to respond much

BABY'S AGE	BABY'S UNDER-STANDING	BABY'S MEANS OF EXPRESSION	YOUR RESPONSE
	'her'. Understands things and events in his own daily life almost completely.	'cup', etc. Asks for things with question intonation, imitates you.	more verbally. Also a lot of work! Many more occasions for conversation through play, outings, shared activities.
20 – 24 months	Understands longer sentences, recognises objects and pictures in greater numbers. Can match familiar objects. Understands 'more', 'here', and 'now'. He will enjoy and follow very simple stories.	Vocabulary increasing from 30 to 60 or 70 words, some of them joined to make two-word sentences. Makes up own words, tries to tell you about things that have happened.	More for you to listen to. You may have to interpret much of what he says to others, particularly special words. You will not be doing all the initiating, he will be talking to you and telling you things.
24 – 30 months	More understanding of concepts – 'big', 'small', 'one', 'a lot'. Can pass on a message. Enjoys stories and will remember details. If asked can name pictures, match pictures, define where things are – 'in', 'under', 'over', etc. He will begin to understand cause and effect: 'If you bounce on the bed, you'll fall off.'	Vocabulary becomes impossible to keep track of – 200 to 400 words, many of them in short sentences and phrases. Uses verbs, plurals, possessives ('Mummy's', 'teddy's',) and question words such as 'where?', 'what?', etc.	You are much more equal in conversation now. He is no longer a language learner, he is a partner in conversation. You can begin to reason with him: you can say why and how things happen. Stories, games, television programmes, all mean more to him now: he will be able to follow a plot with your help.
30 – 40 months	Can describe pictured actions, understand size differences, remembers events and can tell you about them. Recognises and corrects	Can anticipate, tell you what he is going to do. Vocabulary 500 to 1,000 words. Many sentences are proper grammar, with a few childish	You will not be the principal person he talks to now. He can explain things to anyone, joining in with other children. He is a person you

BABY'S AGE	BABY'S UNDER-STANDING	BABY'S MEANS OF EXPRESSION	YOUR RESPONSE
	inaccuracies in stories or messages. Can put words into categories, e.g. 'A cat is an animal.'	errors. Remembers nursery rhymes, can play Let's Pretend games.	converse with. He may have a brother or sister too with whom he will be talking.

FIRST COMMUNICATIONS

If you were alert and well when you had your baby, one of the first things you probably did was to say hello to him. You might then have commented on his nose or his eyes, gently scolded him for being late or giving you a difficult time. Later, when you picked him up for a feed, you probably asked him if he was hungry, or if he was screaming you may have told him that he was impatient and he ought to calm down or neither of you would be able to manage. In short, you talked to your new baby as you would talk to another adult. You treated him as if he could understand, although you knew he could not.

When adults talk to new babies they use normal adult speech, but they tend to raise their voices and use rather sing-song rhythms. Later on, when your baby begins to understand what you say and starts producing his own words, you will not talk to him as you do to another adult. New babies respond to the sound of human voices and seem to prefer higher-pitched tones. They will respond to other sounds by blinking or turning their heads or starting, but human speech seems to have an especially soothing quality for them. One researcher who filmed babies while their mothers were talking to them, and then slowed down the film, found that the babies' arm and leg movements seemed to correspond with the rhythms of the mothers' speech. New babies cannot understand adult speech, but they certainly seem to respond to it, so talking to your baby as you do things for him is probably important. It is also important for you as a way of expressing your feelings, so don't feel inhibited in case other people think you are odd. Almost everybody talks intelligently to new babies, without even being aware of it. Just watch, next time you are at the clinic!

TAKING TURNS

Most people use language in the form of conversations with other people. We talk in order to tell people something we want them to know, and we listen so that they can tell us what they want us to know. We then answer back and develop the conversation, and people respond to what we have said. We need to know when it is our turn to speak in order to have an effective conversation, we have to wait until other people seem to have finished. We notice when they pause or accentuate their voice as if to ask a question, or raise their eyebrows as if to invite us to comment.

All these signals about whose turn it is to communicate begin to be learned when your baby is very young. They often happen at feeding time because you are close to your baby and noticing his behaviour very attentively to see if he is sucking properly, or taking enough from breast or bottle. While your baby is busy sucking, you may just watch him, but when he pauses for breath and comes off the nipple or bottle, you will take your turn to communicate. You may talk to him, smile and ask if he has had enough. He may then widen his eyes and gurgle and kick his legs and then, suddenly, he will dive back to the business of feeding and start sucking again.

These exchanges can happen at other times too, of course, and mothers cannot always gaze down at their babies when they are feeding, particularly if they have older children, or the baby has his eyes closed and is oblivious to the outside world. Nevertheless, feeding is a good time to develop communication skills with your baby because it is a shared activity which is important to you both, and it gives many opportunities for the baby to let you know how he is feeling and for you to respond.

This is why it is a good idea to feed the baby yourself for most of his feeds, even if you are bottle-feeding. It is never safe to prop up a bottle for a young baby and leave him on his own with it because he might choke, but, apart from this, propping him up with his bottle denies him the opportunity to learn the skills of communicating and taking turns that develop when adult and baby are close to each other and enjoying a shared task. These 'turn-taking' sessions are the beginning of conversation.

CRYING

In his first few weeks, your baby's main means of expressing himself is through crying. Of course if you are near to him you can pick up his signals and gestures, but babies also need a way of bringing people to them from a distance. Crying does this. Language does the same thing: words enable us to communicate with people in another room and even across time and space through the printed word or electronic message. It is much more convenient and efficient as a form of expression than physical gesture.

Most mothers learn to recognise their own baby's cry from that of other babies. They can also detect different kinds of cry – hunger, boredom, fear, habit. Some babies, for instance, seem to need a good yell just before they drop into a deep sleep. You will quickly learn from experience how to tell this kind of non-urgent cry from a cry of real hunger or distress. Crying is meant by nature to be disturbing – even adults who are not related to a baby find it difficult to ignore, and if you are his mother you will probably find it almost impossible. There is more about crying and comforting in chapter 8.

FIRST SOUNDS

By the time he is a few weeks old, your baby will be producing more pleasant sounds, usually in response to attention from you, but sometimes when he is just lying in his pram or cot, looking at objects in the room or at his own hands and feet. These first sounds will be little cooing noises and gurgles; many babies also seem to enjoy blowing loud raspberries. These are his first exercises in expressing himself vocally and of course they will bring a response from you, which will give you both more practice at conversational turn-taking. However, even if there is nobody around, the baby may enjoy making noises and listening to his own sounds.

Between three and six months these little sounds gradually become more like speech – they turn into babble. Your baby may say one sound over and over, 'bababababa' or 'gagagaga', as if fascinated by the noise. He will begin to raise and drop his voice as he makes these noises as if he were really talking. This babbling is not really like the adult speech he hears – even babies with severe hearing loss babble, although they do not develop the speech-like rhythms that hearing babies do. In the early babbling stages, babies produce sounds that do not belong to their native language: babies from all countries seem to make exactly the same kind of noises. It is only later on that they make English-sounding noises or French-sounding noises.

These babbling sounds can give you a lot of pleasure. The fact that the first noises are often 'mamama' or 'dadada' is also rewarding to parents. Although they are not true speech, you will be encouraged to look at your baby and talk delightedly to him when he makes them. Other people also talk back to babbling babies. These experiences enlarge the baby's social world and set the scene for the verbal communication which comes later.

Even after the first true words appear in your baby's chatter, he will still continue to play with noises that sound like speech but are not. A toddler of 14 or 15 months will wave his spoon and address the rest of the family from his highchair in a long stream of incomprehensible jargon, just as if he were making an after-dinner speech. The rising and falling of his voice will be just like yours, but no words are present. This is very amusing for everybody else, but it is also important for him to practise speech sounds and rhythms and of course to take his turn in holding the floor and joining in family conversation.

LISTENING AND UNDERSTANDING

A baby has to do a lot of listening and working out what goes with what before he can produce a word of his own. It has been estimated that he needs to have heard a word 500 or 600 times before he says it for the first time. This applies to the first early words he uses: later, when his grasp of the language is better, he will start soaking up new words at a greater rate, including words you would probably rather he did not say!

Before a baby starts talking you will notice he seems to understand many of the things you say. If you ask a 'where?' question, such as 'Where's Daddy?' or 'Where's the cat?' he will look round as if to search. He will understand phrases that are accompanied by gestures, such as you holding out your hand and saying, 'Give it to Mummy.' He will recognise his own name and the names of familiar people, he will respond to simple instructions such as 'Clap hands', and he will understand 'No' and 'Don't touch', although he will not always obey them.

When a baby is at this stage – from 7 or 8 months to the time when he is managing simple sentences – you will notice the way you talk to him also changes. You now use very simple language and repeat things over and over again. Obviously you do this unconsciously, without thinking about it. You will ask a lot of questions and speak very clearly, saying the names of things distinctly. All this, linked with the gestures you use, helps your baby to learn the names of things and associate words with meaningful actions.

Other processes help him do this too. As his brain and nervous system are physically developing, which enables him to behave in a more complicated way, he is also learning more and more about the outside world. He knows objects have a separate, permanent existence, he knows that they have uses. When your ten-month-old baby picks up a cup and offers it to his teddy to drink from, he is making a vital connection in learning that the cup has an identity, 'cup', and a purpose, 'drink'. The next step is to realise that the sound 'cup' means the object cup.

FIRST WORDS

Your baby's first real words are just as exciting as his first steps, but they may be harder to pick out from all the babble and chat that has gone beforehand. The first real word is a sound made by your baby that is only associated with one meaning – it may be one object, or a set of objects, but it always means the same thing. Sometimes 'mummum' or 'dadadad' is the first real word – that is, the baby uses it only when Mummy or Daddy is around. Often the first real word will be something quite different, and indeed it can be a word that the baby has made up himself. Thomas, aged one, coined the word 'menem' to mean food. It may have been made up from 'mmmm' or 'yum yum', but he used it to apply only to food, or to the dish or bowl in which food came, but not to the spoon or the drinks. It was therefore a true word, although not English! Most babies' first words refer to objects – 'cat', 'ball', 'dad', and so on, are favourites. Genevieve and Oscar, aged one, both hit on something different which for them meant 'dog' as a first word. For Genevieve all dogs were 'gogs' and for Oscar every dog was a 'woof woof'. Babies may also run two or three words together to make one word – for example, combining 'what', 'is' and 'that' to say, 'wassat?' Although Elinor had

no idea that this should be a phrase made up of these words, 'wassat' was simply a question sound. Another common combination first word is 'allgone' which is used simply to mean 'gone'.

The first word is a very exciting milestone – at last your patient conversations, your pointing things out, your peekaboo games, your explanations of what you were doing, have paid off. Your baby has answered back. New words will be added in the next three to four months – usually you will be able to keep a track of them, and many parents like to keep a record of the words their babies use. They will usually be words that mean something particular to that baby, so they will probably be to do with food, people, special toys, shoes, the car, or a pet. By the time he is 18 months your baby will know about fifty words and will have added some instructions, 'look', 'down', 'gimme', 'again', as well as some adjectives, 'big', 'pretty', 'naughty'. He will also have some useful words like 'what?' and 'where?' He will have some idea of himself – 'mine' – as distinct from another person – 'he' – although he will not say 'you' very much.

Don't worry if your baby has a smaller vocabulary than this, as long as he is understanding what you say and is able to grasp the meaning and the purpose of things; he is probably just taking his time about speaking up for himself. However, if he does not appear to understand and does not do what you tell him readily, you should ask your doctor to have a look at him and have his hearing checked.

If your baby's vocabulary is greater than this, and he is already using short sentences by 18 months, that is wonderful. You can communicate with each other much better and share games and stories that you could not share before, but don't assume your child is a genius and put pressure on him accordingly. Rapid language development is a good sign that you have a bright child, but it is not the only sign, and you will find that other, slower, children catch up a little later.

The great advantage of having an early talker is that it is so much easier to explain things to him, so you are less likely to have misunderstandings, and there are many ways of entertaining him once he has a good grasp of language. This can make for a smoother and pleasanter relationship.

FIRST SENTENCES

The very first sentence may be only one word, but it means more than one word. For instance, your fifteen-month-old may call out 'bicky'. Depending on the way he says it he may mean: 'I want a biscuit'; or, if he is leaning out of his highchair and staring sorrowfully at the floor it may mean, 'I've dropped my biscuit'; or, if he is looking at the television and suddenly notices a child eating, he may mean, 'Oh look, there's another biscuit, the sort of thing I eat.'

You will soon be able to interpret what he actually means and you may put it into words for him. For instance, if he has dropped his biscuit you say, 'Oh dear, you've dropped your biscuit. Mummy will get you another one.' Then, if he angrily throws the biscuit down again, you might say, 'Oh, so you don't want that biscuit, you want this biscuit,' and you will give him back the one he dropped. If you see the picture on television that he is talking about, you might say, 'Oh yes, clever boy. That's like the biscuit you had, isn't it?' During these chats, you are not only encouraging his efforts to tell you things by listening and interpreting carefully, you are also repeating back to him what he probably means in the correct speech and so giving him the chance to learn the right way of saying things, although it may be months, even a year or more, before he actually puts it as grammatically as you do.

If you are worried about your child not speaking when he should and you know his hearing and general development are all right, think about how you respond to your child's attempts to communicate. Sometimes when we are busy it is very easy to say, 'Wait', or 'Here you are', and not use the opportunity for conversation. Young children need adults to give them careful individual attention and listen and talk to them during the day for short periods so that they can learn language and communication skills. Remember too that they only like talking about what they know – conversations about biscuits, toys, buses, shoes and animals may not be riveting to you, but they are the best things for encouraging him to talk. He will not bother to talk about things he is not interested in or does not understand, so it is wise not to talk too much over his head. There is nothing wrong with baby talk if that is what he enjoys.

PUTTING WORDS TOGETHER

Putting two words together to make something closer to a real sentence is a very big step. It shows your child is beginning to grasp the rules. The first simple sentences will still be about familiar objects, for instance they might indicate belonging: 'Mummy shoe', meaning 'Mummy's shoe'. Then verbs will be added. These sentences show your child understands the importance of word order – a big step. For instance, 'go shops' means 'Let's go to the shops' or 'I am going to the shops.' On the other hand, 'shops gone' with the 'go' verb after the word 'shops' means that perhaps a picture of shops has disappeared, or the bus has gone past the shops. The child understands that the subject of the sentence (in the first case 'I', and in the second case 'shops') has to come before the verb. This is a big advance in understanding and you can help it through conversation and fantasy play, for instance, with dolls going to and from shops, or model shops being on and off the table. On many occasions we automatically do these sorts of things when we are playing with children.

USING THE RULES

Once your child starts using these first sentences sometime in his second year, you will find it very difficult to keep a record of the way his language develops. This is because his vocabulary increases in leaps and bounds and will number hundreds of words by the time he is three, but more than this his use of words will not be just statements you have to interpret. He will start using them grammatically. For example, he will learn to say 'going' instead of 'go shops'. He will learn that you have to put an 's' on the end of words to make them express more than one, which shows a development in his knowledge of mathematical concepts as well. He will learn that past tenses usually have 'ed' on the end – 'played', 'jumped', and so on – and, being logical, which young children are, he will put 'ed' on all kinds of other words as well. He will say, 'hitted', or 'goed' or even 'wented', indicating that he knows 'go' becomes 'went' when it is in the past, but he sees no reason why the rule should not apply here, so he puts 'ed' on the end for good measure.

If you try to correct your child's mistakes, you will probably find he is very resistant to doing it your way. 'Wented' fits with the way he sees the language in his particular state of development. He will gradually work out that 'went' is the right way to say it, and so long as you keep saying 'went' yourself he will finally get the message. Remember, these errors are not really errors, they are his way of teaching himself the rules and the exceptions to the rules. He will master most of the rules, including turning sentences round to make questions or negatives ('Are we going?', 'We are not going') by the time he is five or six. But you could help and encourage his early use of language in many ways – you do not have to leave it all to him.

TALKING WITH YOUR CHILD

The main point of being able to talk and listen is to enable the child to communicate with other people, and he will not want to communicate if it is not enjoyable and rewarding for him. The best way you can encourage language skills in your child is to give him plenty of opportunities to practise in ways that arise naturally out of the things you do together. There is no need to sit him down and say, 'Right, now we are going to have a conversation.' Conversation comes naturally out of mealtimes, playing with toys, going out, visiting friends or programmes on television.

Here are a few ways in which you can think about helping your child to learn to talk:

* Talk to him about what you are doing: 'I am going to put the kettle on now because I am thirsty and want a cup of tea.'

* Ask him to tell you what he is doing: 'Tell me about the house you've just built with your bricks.'

* Ask him what things are for, for example, hold up a fork and ask, 'What's this for?' A three- or four-year-old will be able to use the right

verb in his construction. 'It's for eating.' If you say, 'What do we do with this?' he will say, 'We eat with it.' There are several different ways of saying the same thing and he will enjoy experimenting with them.

Talk to your baby about what you are doing

* Help him to learn what 'in', 'on', 'under', 'over' mean. There are many games you can play with toys being put in various places.

* Help him to understand what the words 'up' and 'down' mean — on the swings, for instance.

* Help him to learn the words to use when he wants to compare things: 'Which is the biggest brick?' or 'Is that doll thinner than this doll?'

* Have fun helping him to understand and learn the word which means the opposite of something. For example: 'The water is too hot. I need to make it . . . ?'

All the time you are helping him to use language in a more sophisticated way and these are also aids which will encourage his intellectual development. For instance, knowing the meaning of 'big', 'bigger' and 'biggest' is going to be important when he starts learning maths at school. At the end of the day, make a point of talking about what happened during the day. Get him to remember what happened in the morning and then after lunch which will also help his understanding of time. Ask him what was the best thing that happened that day. What was the nastiest thing? Children need to be encouraged to put their feelings as well as their thoughts into words.

Don't feel rebuffed if he does not feel like talking, but be ready to listen when he does.

Give him opportunities to talk to other people besides his parents, especially other children. This will encourage him to tailor his speech to be appropriate to different kinds of people, an important social skill. He will need to learn that formal politeness is right with other grown-ups, but that he should scale down his conversation for a child who is younger than he is. Children can have a lot of fun playing language games with each other that they would not do with an adult. Listen to your three- or four-year-old playing a fantasy game with a friend, and notice how they imitate adults or use nonsense words or spontaneous little rhymes they have made up themselves. When a child is socially ready, then playing with other children is vital for teaching conversational skills such as taking turns in speaking, and asking and answering questions appropriately.

MORE THAN ONE CHILD

Conversation does not only go on between one adult and one child. In everyday life there are not that many occasions when there is only one adult and only one child. Most families have at least two children, and there are very many occasions, even in families where there is only one child, when both parents are present, friends or relatives or other children are visiting, or when the mother and child are talking to people like bus conductors and shop assistants. In other words, it is very common for a child to be in a situation where he either has to compete for the attention of his own special adult, or has to join in with the general conversation.

It is commonly recognised that firstborn children have a head start in many respects because they have your undivided attention for those early months or years, and various studies have shown that firstborn children tend to be more developmentally advanced in the early years. It is harder to find the same amount of time to talk with your younger or youngest children, especially on a one-to-one basis during the early pre-speech and first-word stages. To make sure younger children do have a fair chance of listening, understanding and replying to you, you have to teach your older children or child not to interrupt when you are talking to the little one. The older child must take his turn, not only as part of a two-person conversation, but as part of a three- or four-person conversation. This is quite a hard lesson to learn. Mealtimes are sometimes good occasions to help children to learn to talk like this if you are all sitting round a table, but make sure that the baby is not ignored, or that the older child does not keep chipping in when you ask the younger one something.

Simple games which involve taking turns, such as picture dominoes, or coloured dice games, or very simple card games like snap can sometimes help once the younger child is able to join in, which is usually from about two and a half or three onwards. Both parents and other adults such as grandparents can help to make sure that each child gets a chance to practise his conversation alone with an adult now and again.

In fact, in some circumstances, a sympathetic granny or the lady next door can actually encourage a child's speech skills far more than his mother can. After all, Mum already knows what he got for his birthday, but Granny has to ask, and the child can really enjoy the opportunity to tell her all about it. That is why it is important for you to give your child a chance to make friends with other adults as well. Apart from their social value for you, these friendships can help your child to practise his growing social and communication skills on a wider circle which will be a great help when he goes on to playgroup and to school.

STORIES, BOOKS AND TELEVISION

Stories, books and television programmes help the child to learn that information does not come only from his very direct experience – in other words, he not only learns from actually doing things himself but he will also learn about them from hearing them described in other people's words. In the case of television, he can also learn from watching other people experiencing something.

Babies can start looking at picture books as soon as they can sit up and enjoy spending time on somebody's lap, usually sometime towards the end of the first year. You do not need to invest in a lot of expensive books – big catalogues are very attractive to babies of this age. Recognising an object in a picture when you ask – 'Where's the cup?' 'Where's the cot?' – and pointing to it is a useful skill in learning language. Your baby is learning that some items like a cup or a cot can be shown in different ways – for real, in pictures and also in words. Babies love looking at things they recognise and this means that realistic pictures and familiar objects are more likely to catch their attention and give them enjoyment than stylised or cartoon drawings.

Telling and reading stories to your child is one of the most valuable ways of giving him attention and helping him to learn. Pick a time when he is likely to be interested in sitting down quietly with you   not a time when his favourite television programme is coming on, a friend is round to play, Granny is visiting, and so on. The time when a child is getting a bit tired, but does not actually want to go to sleep is an ideal moment for a story. It also gives you a very useful opportunity to sit down and enjoy a cuddle as well. Make sure other distractions are not competing for his attention – that means switching off the television or radio and letting older children know that you are not available for fifteen minutes or so. Sit your child on your lap or beside you with your arm round him.

All libraries have children's sections where there are a number of good simple stories you can borrow to read to toddlers. When you choose a book for your child, remember it will make more sense if it has something to do with his own experiences. In the very beginning, with a baby, pictures of familiar objects which you can both talk about are probably enough, but by about a year, a very simple story will be enjoyed. Choose one in which the storyline is straightforward – without any subplot – and about something he understands, for example, going to bed, meeting a cat, going in the car. Do not worry if you think your child cannot understand every one of the words that you are reading: that is how children pick up interesting new words, by hearing them read in a context which they understand. You can also make up simple little stories about things that you and your child did together and draw them with your child – he will not mind if you are not a skilled artist! Older children can really enjoy hearing about what they did and what they were like when they were a baby, which is especially true around the time when a new baby has arrived in the family. Looking at family photograph albums is also an all-time favourite with children, although in the beginning do not be surprised that your very young child does not recognise himself in pictures, but points to 'baby'. Do not think stories have to be new all the time because children love repetition of old favourites, and that is especially true of pre-school children. They will soon become familiar with a favourite story and will know immediately if you try to leave out anything or change one word. Nursery rhymes, simple poems, finger rhymes, see-saw games, all help your child's language development and of course can give you both great pleasure and amusement.

If you have a tape recorder there is a great variety of children's stories, nursery rhymes and songs on cassette which you can either buy or borrow from the library. Several pre-school children can enjoy listening to one of these together at a time when they are a bit tired but do not want to have a sleep. They are also a great way to keep children amused on long journeys if you have a small tape recorder with a head-set. Do not forget that it is quite possible to buy a blank tape and make up your own cassettes with favourite stories read to children, or something about the child himself or even a very simple I-Spy or quiz game, but do not let cassettes become a replacement for reading books with your children when they can look at the pictures and share the experience with you.

Television programmes are often very popular with young children but they give a rather different experience from books. The biggest difference from a learning point of view is that the child has to follow the programme at the pace dictated by the programme makers. If he misses something or does not understand something, he cannot stop the programme and ask about it, but he can do this when someone is reading to him or telling him a story. This is why it is a good idea to sit with your child sometimes when he is watching television so that you can talk to him about what he sees and hears. Television can give children many new topics to talk about and widen their knowledge of the world, but it needs to be backed up by you talking about it and by direct experiences of the child's own.

Can too much television or the wrong kind of television be harmful? The answer is almost certainly yes. Sitting a small child in front of a video tape of his favourite cartoon programmes for two or three hours on end is denying him valuable opportunity for learning by direct experience – that is, by playing, by exploring, by finding out about things for himself.

What about seeing violent or frightening scenes on television? There is no doubt that these can be disturbing and frightening for a young child. It takes a long time to understand the difference between fantasy and reality, and school-age children can still be very confused by realistic scenes staged in television fiction, despite all your reassurance that it is only pretend and actors. A simple example of this is of a two-year-old who saw the video of *Superman III* because it was a wet day and his older brothers and sisters were watching it. It had the most marked effect on his behaviour immediately – he went around making 'bam' and 'wham' noises and punching everyone who got in his way in a good imitation of Superman fighting the baddies. Amusing perhaps when he tried it with an adult, but not at all funny when he directed well aimed blows at a few of his mates at playschool the next day.

On an even more worrying level, it is true that a lot of very young children almost certainly see some of the worst horror movies in their own living rooms, and this applies especially to toddlers and young children who are hard to get to bed or who get into the habit of staying up very late in the evening. Parents may think, because very young children do not voice any questions or worries, and do not understand everything that is happening, that these images on television have no effect. Older children are all too easily disturbed and frightened by seeing such scenes and can become worried about the dark, begin to have nightmares, be worried about being left alone in a room or going upstairs to bed on their own. There is no reason to think the effect is any less on a younger child. At the very least, it must give them a curious view of the world to see their parents sitting and watching scenes of people being tortured, terrified or attacked on television. It encourages them to grow up with the view that such acts are acceptable and in this way they could be said to be becoming desensitised to violence.

Television is a very powerful influence and is an everyday part of our children's lives. We need to make sure it is used constructively and not harmfully:

DO NOT use videos or television for hours on end just to keep your pre-school children quiet.

DO make your children be selective about what they watch on television. A reasonable rule as they grow older may be that they can watch for a limited period of time, or two or three programmes a day, and that they have to choose these programmes at the beginning of the day. Obviously, when they are very young you can take a hand in the choosing of these.

DO NOT let children see horror movies or be playing in the same room when a horror movie is being shown on television.

DO make a point of knowing what they are watching on television. A very simple question to ask yourself, if it is a film or video, is 'Would I be allowed to take them to see this at the cinema?' The use of videos means that we as parents have to be our own censors now. Do we care less about what our children watch than the British Board of Film Censors? You never saw horror movies on television as a child — is it really fair to subject your child to them?

DO be positive about the good side of television. There is a lot to enjoy on television and videos — you just need to make sure you are selective.

DO NOT be pressurised by the views of other parents. Make your own decisions in agreement with your partner.

DO remember that other rules may apply in different households that your child may stay in or visit, including those of relatives. It is worth finding out, tactfully, whether television is used as continual background or if they are likely to be having X-rated videos on at a time when your child will be around, or perhaps just reminding them, in the case of relatives, that you would rather your child did not watch anything you consider to be unsuitable.

READING AND WRITING

Talking and listening to your child are two of the best ways you can prepare him for school and formal education, and they cost nothing at all. A child who has had plenty of experience of conversation, stories, language games and play generally is much better equipped to start learning reading and writing when he goes to school than the child who has not been talked with very much and does not know that experiences, knowledge, events and feelings can all be expressed in words. If your child talks well and can mix with other children easily and readily and also relate to adults, that is the best way to prepare for a good start at school.

Some children are keen to start reading and writing before they go to school, although most do not begin to get the idea until they are five or six. These children will start asking what the words on the side of the breakfast cereal packet are, or perhaps when they spot an advertisement in the street, they will say: 'Look, Kellogg's.' Many four-year-olds can recognise letters of the alphabet and numbers if they are given the chance. Children with older brothers and sisters are more inclined to do this than the firstborn child because they like to copy and will want their own books, pens, pencils, rulers and rubbers so that they can be just like the others. Some infant teachers do not like the idea of parents teaching pre-school children to read, because they say it may result in confusion when the child starts school. However, if a child is recognising letters and words and asking what they are, then it is impossible to stop him reading. Learning to read is a bit like learning to ride a bike or drive a car — once it is learnt you cannot unlearn it. You can test this yourself by looking at the advertisements on a bus or a train next time you travel and not reading the words. Try to see them as a collection of shapes with no meaning. You will find it impossible.

If your child is showing an interest in making sense of letters and words,

encourage it by using books, reading stories, letting him see the text, showing him when it is time to turn over the page, pointing out letters or words he might know. A common mistake that parents make is to teach children capital letters and to teach them the names of the letters in the way that they may have been taught – for example, a, b, c, etc. Instead, talk about the *sounds* of the letters, for example, the sound 'b' as it is at the beginning of the word 'book', and the sound 'a' as it is at the beginning of the word 'apple'. If he begins to want to know how to write something – his own names for example – teach him to form all the letters the right way and to use capital letters where it is appropriate – at the beginning of his name, for example. If children get into the habit of writing and making the shapes of the letters the wrong way then it is very difficult to break this habit later. If in doubt about the correct way to form a letter ask his nursery or playgroup leader. There are many good books available which show the correct letter formation.

Do not buy a school reading scheme and work through it with him if he really wants to learn to read because this can result in confusion when he starts school if the teacher's methods are different from yours, and also boredom if he has seen the books already. Instead, you can make your own books with him about things that have happened to him using very simple words, or pick picture books with a clear simple text.

Like learning to crawl, to walk and to talk, parents can find great excitement on the day their child learns to read, but remember, reading is not just an end in itself. The point of it is to convey information and also to entertain. If your child learns to read but does not enjoy reading books, then he is not going to gain very much. On the other hand, if your child sees books as a source of shared pleasure, excitement and a way of finding out about things, he will not need to be forced to learn to read, he will want to. If your child does not seem to be learning to read very easily when he starts school, don't put pressure on him because, like all the other stages, it is a developmental skill and when a child is ready he will often do it very quickly. However, if he does not seem to be making any start at all by the end of his sixth year, then discuss it with his teacher and ask about ways in which he can be helped.

Most children want to start drawing, which at first they see as being just the same as writing. You will probably find that your two-year-old can hold a pencil properly and, once he can do this, he should be given plenty of opportunities to practise. You can encourage him to copy simple shapes such as circles and squares and to try drawing a circle with eyes, nose, mouth, and so on, in the centre. Working with a pencil is more useful for learning to write later on than working with a paintbrush, although this can be very helpful in developing artistic skills.

Writing involves having very good control over body movements to work the muscles of the hand and the fingers in the correct way. Other skills, like understanding language, are also involved. Writing is therefore usually more difficult to learn than reading. Just as your child understood a great deal of what you could say to him before he could reply clearly, so he may be able to read several things before he can write clearly.

EARLY LANGUAGE PROBLEMS

HEARING LOSS AND LANGUAGE

Hearing is essential in learning to understand and use language and there is more about helping children with hearing loss in chapters 10, 17 and 19. If your baby does not seem to respond to sounds or is slow to talk and understand language, then his hearing will be carefully checked (see page 342). Hearing loss may not be present at birth, but may develop later on, perhaps because of ear infections. So if your child's language progress seems to be at a standstill, he should have a hearing test. If he does start to speak, but his speech has certain uncommon abnormalities (not the normal lisping that many young children have, but one in which some consonants are missed out), then he may have partial hearing loss. If other people find it very difficult to understand your two- or three-year-old, it is worth getting his hearing checked.

SLOWNESS TO UNDERSTAND OR SPEAK LANGUAGE

If your child is not making vowel sounds such as 'oo', or 'ah', etc. by five months, babbling by eleven months and using three or four words apart from 'Dada' and 'Mama' by two years, there is cause for concern, and you should talk to your health visitor or doctor. Indeed, even if your child is more advanced than this, but you are worried about his hearing or language development, it is worth mentioning it at a clinic visit.

Slowness in language may be occurring because your child is slow in all aspects of development. You can check whether this is the case by noting his progress in movement and co-ordination against the chart on pages 320–6. General slowness may be due to some form of brain damage that may have been discovered already, so that you know your child is handicapped. Alternatively, slowness of language may be the first sign that is noted before it is realised that a child is generally backward. Handicapped babies and children need special help to encourage language skills as much as possible, and you should receive help and advice from a speech therapist (see page 647).

Some children are not generally slow but have a particular problem with language – they have a 'specific language delay'. If the child is just a little behind, one can expect him to catch up, but if his language is only at a level one would expect from a child about two-thirds his age, then you will need to discuss the problem with your health visitor or doctor and advice from a speech and language therapist may be needed. Programmes of therapy and intensive training have helped many handicapped children to become more fluent in language than people at first thought possible.

Some children who are especially slow in language also have unusual difficulties in making relationships. They may show little or no interest in other people, turn their eyes away when people look at them, and pull away when cuddled. Such children are autistic or may be generally backward with autistic features (see page 649). You will need to discuss this with your doctor, who is likely to refer you to a psychiatrist or psychologist. Again, advice from a speech therapist will also be needed.

PROBLEMS WITH ARTICULATION

Children may be able to understand well and use sentences but not be able to speak clearly. This may be because they have difficulty saying the various speech sounds or in working out the rules for the speech sounds.

There may be a physical problem or difficulty in co-ordinating the movements of lips and tongue which may affect how a child produces a sound. For instance, children with cleft palate may need therapy to help them pronounce certain sounds. Children with cerebral palsy may also need this type of help: they are able to understand and express themselves but the physical control of jaw, lip and tongue movements is hard for them.

In a similar way to learning the rules of language children also have to learn the differences between sounds and how to use them in words. For example, in English there is a difference in the way we use our vocal cords to form consonants such as p, t, k and the consonants such as b, d, g. There are rules governing the use of consonants in English which allow us to have three consonants at the beginning of a word, for example 'splash' and 'string', but we cannot have six consonants.

Some children have difficulty learning to recognise and use the different consonants and rules – their hearing may be normal but they find it hard to work out, for example, which sounds go at the end of a word. Because the pronunciation or articulation and the correct use of consonants are complex skills, it is to be expected that many children make mistakes when they are learning to talk. For instance, young children often muddle or miss out a consonant and say 'b' for 'f', 'fing' for 'thing' or 'poon' for 'spoon'. If you listen to other children talking, you will realise how common such mistakes are. Some children will mix up consonants and syllables so that 'cat' becomes 'tat' and 'animal' becomes 'aminal'. It is not usually helpful for a child to be made to say a word over and over again in order to change the way he says it: he views words as whole units and probably cannot recognise that there is a difference only in one consonant between the right way and the wrong way.

If your child continues to make many mistakes of this kind and is difficult to understand you should seek advice from a speech therapist who will be able to explain whether the mistakes are part of normal development or whether help is required.

PROBLEMS WITH VOICE AND FLUENCY

Some children may have voices that sound hoarse or rough, even though they do not have a sore throat or a cold. Others may sound as though they are 'talking down their nose'. It is important that you see your doctor about these problems: he may refer your child to an ear, nose and throat (ENT) specialist for an examination of the throat.

Many children between two and four years trip up over words or repeat the first syllable or consonant of a word before saying the rest of the sentence, for example 'b-b-b-book'. When you think about all the new developments that are happening to a child at that age, particularly in language skills, then it is not surprising that they make the odd mistake – as we all do. However, if the non-fluent speech lasts for more than six weeks or if it is distressing to you or your child, then again seek the advice of a speech and language therapist.

There are many reasons why a child can have a speech or language problem. It is important that he receives appropriate help from the specialists at the right time and that you receive advice about the nature of the problem. Your doctor or health visitor will refer you to a speech therapist, but most district therapy services also have an open referral system through which you can contact a therapist directly. The therapist will recommend various activities to help your child to overcome his problems and you will be expected to work on the therapy activities with him at home in order to get the maximum benefit and effect.

The ability to understand language and to talk seems to be one of the strongest and toughest forms of human behaviour – it is very hard to destroy it. Even children who have been badly neglected and isolated for years can learn to use and understand words once they have been rescued. From the first cry your baby is longing to understand and communicate, and the first time he turns his head towards your voice he is already expecting an answer. Although most of the skills of his own language will be learnt in the first few years, the pleasure of talking to other people will hopefully go on for the rest of his life.

Children with language problems developing their listening skills in a mainstream nursery

Chapter 12

PLAY AND EARLY EDUCATION

Different types of play
How parents can help children have richer play experiences
Play stages   Organising play   The importance of messy play
More than one child   Routine   Making friends
Play for sick children   Playgroups and nurseries   Schools

Play is a serious business. It is important in every single aspect of your child's development and education, and is the way he will acquire the skills and knowledge he needs to prepare him for adult life.

DIFFERENT TYPES OF PLAY

PHYSICAL, ENERGETIC PLAY

This helps a child to learn how to control his body and co-ordinate his actions, for example, in climbing up and down and around playground equipment, up trees and over rocks; throwing, catching and kicking balls; roly-polying down grassy slopes. Watch your child and you will discover many more of these types of activities.

EXPERIMENTAL PLAY

In one sense all play is an experiment for young children – they are testing their powers, finding out what can and cannot be done. But particular kinds of play can lead to more discoveries than other types, for example, putting objects into containers, stacking different sized and shaped objects and sorting shapes. By watching what they are doing and talking to them you can help children to find the right words to describe their discoveries.

CREATIVE PLAY

There is great joy and triumph to be had from making something all by yourself when you are very young. Household 'junk' such as empty

379

margarine tubs, the inside of toilet rolls and polystyrene food trays can be used for gluing and sticking. Under-fives will need help, but resist the temptation to take over – the end result is always a masterpiece, whatever it actually looks like.

FANTASY PLAY

Acting out with friends, or with toys, things that happen in their lives, helps children to make sense of the world around them. Children everywhere play at schools, shopping, mummies and daddies, hospitals, babies and making houses, and the subject matter of these games has not changed since parents themselves were young because this is the stuff of life. Fantasy and pretend games can also be flights of pure imagination – witches and wizards, flying fairies or underwater fish. Children also play imaginative and fantasy games in miniature – setting out farmyards, dolls' houses, Legolands, and so on.

MESSY PLAY

A session spent playing with playdough, sand, water, or some other substance can have a very soothing and calming effect on young children. It also helps them to explore the properties of many different materials and to discover, experiment with and sometimes create things. Having a second, younger child who wants to join in but who needs much more supervision can often make organising this more difficult. One solution is to try to pick a time when you can give your full attention to supervising and put a time limit on the whole affair so that you do not lose patience.

PLAYING WITH FRIENDS

This teaches children how to co-operate, to develop social skills and also to have a sense of fair play. They learn how to make friends again after a disagreement, to keep rules, and also to develop a sense of humour.

HOW PARENTS CAN HELP CHILDREN HAVE RICHER PLAY EXPERIENCES

Perhaps the simplest way to enrich children's play experience is by talking to them about their discoveries through play, and sometimes, though not always, to play with them. Playing with your child helps him to learn the skills he needs to play with other children and is an important part of learning about relationships. Games and playing are also an important part of the way in which children learn to talk and to understand what is being said to them. Early baby games, like peekaboo, round and round the garden, pat-a-cake and this little piggy, are all great fun for parents to play with their children and at the same time the child is learning about listening, anticipating and responding. There is more

about how children learn to understand and use language in chapter 11.

As all parents quickly learn, small children do not have to be encouraged to play. In fact, once they're on the move, you may feel you want to *discourage* them, since everything in the house is fair game as a plaything! However, long before they are big enough to decide for themselves what they want to play with, babies and small children are observing, listening and absorbing information about the world. The fuel for their behaviour is curiosity – they want to find out what is going on, and they will explore and discover in the best way that they are able at each stage of development. What a baby does with the objects he is interested in is often described as play, for example, when we see him holding a rattle and chewing on it we may say, 'He's playing with his rattle.' But the baby does not know he is playing. He is exploring naturally and instinctively. To him the rattle is not a toy because it is no different from the spoon or the bunch of keys. It is simply a hard thing which makes intriguing noises.

New parents soon discover that the most obvious effect a child has on their lives is the impact he makes on the home. Once their baby begins to move, rooms have to be arranged so that they are safe and interesting for a child to play in, whilst still being a comfortable place for the parents to work or live in. Arranging your home so that children can play safely but still leaving clean, comfortable spaces for adults is an important contribution you can make to your child's play.

From a safety point of view it is important that parents make changes to their home *before* children progress to the next stage of mobility. With a first child it is not always easy to anticipate what this may be, but chapter 15 on protecting your child gives some helpful suggestions. Being one step ahead of your baby's growing abilities means being careful about putting him down on sofas even *before* he has learnt to roll over, and not leaving him on the floor near potentially dangerous objects although he has not yet begun to make those first wriggling movements forward. Later it is important to keep chairs tucked underneath the table, anticipating the time when he will learn how to climb on to them and reach cupboards or work surfaces which were previously out of reach.

Obviously the way that children play and what they need changes considerably as they grow. The chart opposite gives some ideas of what your baby might require at different stages and some suggestions for playthings. It also lists some ways in which you might meet these needs. As you can see, giving children things to play with does not have to be expensive (and that is especially true at the baby stage), but it does take a certain amount of thought and planning.

PLAY STAGES

AGE	WHAT HE CAN DO	PLAYTHINGS	WHAT YOU CAN DO
0 – 3 months	Listen, observe, begin to recognise people, objects and places. Smile and coo.	Colourful, tinkling mobiles to look at and listen to; cradle gym in cot; pictures or postcards inside cot or pram to look at; music boxes, music from records or songs; mirrors.	Carry him around on your front or back. Talk, play and sing. Lie him where he can see things – trees, people, moving objects, other children. Give him changes of scene.
	Kick, wriggle, turn head, try to roll.	Warm rug to lie and kick on. Jingle toys that he can bat with hands and feet.	Give him exercise times – take clothes and nappy off after bath or when he seems restless and bored to allow him to kick and move more freely.
3 – 6 months onwards	Reach, begin to grasp, chew, put things in mouth, roll, squirm. Follow objects with eyes.	Rattles and smooth objects he can hold and gnaw on. Different textures – rubber, plastic spoons, wooden spoons; different cloths – like furry teddy bears, leather gloves, woolly blankets, cotton scarves. These must be safe for baby to be able to put in his mouth. Different shapes – balls, square board books, cubes, squashy toys that change shape.	Floor play. Sit him in a reclining chair with a tray with different objects on it. Vary toys – give different things at different times. Put things just out of reach so that he has to wriggle and reach for them. Look through your kitchen drawers for safe wooden and plastic utensils. Use crackly greaseproof paper – not plastic bags or wrapping.

AGE	WHAT HE CAN DO	PLAYTHINGS	WHAT YOU CAN DO
6 — 12 months onwards	Make sounds and communicate with others. Recognise people. Learn that things and people go and come back.	Other people, teddies, dolls, soft animals, etc. Simple games with others such as 'peekaboo'.	Talk and listen to him. Take him where he can see other people, e.g. shops, toddlers' club, friends' houses. Play games with him.
	Crawl or wriggle across floor. Pull himself up. Decide what he wants and go to get it.	Safe, stable furniture to hold on to. Warm rugs and carpets to move about on. Walker-trucks to push, baby-walker to move about in (under supervision).	Once a baby is on the move arrange all rooms he is likely to be in so that they are safe (see page 391). If you cannot supervise all the time, playpens may be necessary plus safety-gates on the stairs or in doorways.
	Reach, grasp, pick up small objects, pass them from hand to hand or to mouth. Give and take objects. Increasing hand control and co-ordination between eye and hand.	Things he can put other things into and take out of — stacking beakers, plastic cartons, boxes, saucepans with lids, bricks, cupboards and drawers with safe objects such as pans, plastic dishes and utensils in them.	Give him freedom to explore; increase your tolerance of the level of mess very considerably! Learn from his exploring behaviour what he's most interested in and talk about it — language is developing now.
	Understand the use of things.	Ball to roll, activity centres which require different actions — a ball and ring, a flap to lift. Simple books or pictures from catalogues of objects he will recognise.	Play giving and taking objects, showing him how to put things inside other things, stacking towers for him to knock down.

AGE	WHAT HE CAN DO	PLAYTHINGS	WHAT YOU CAN DO
12 – 24 months	Walking, climbing, greater control over all movements, including hands. Activities now purposeful; he wants to get somewhere when he moves and to do things with the objects he handles — not just explore them. Hold crayons and brushes.	Walker-trucks still, other push-along toys, wheeled trucks, trains, pull-along animals, low, stable furniture to climb on and off. Greater control means he can now enjoy some messy materials: sand; play pastry; water; earth in the garden; painting with large brushes, thickly mixed powder paint and old newspapers or rough paper. 'Painting' with plain water in the garden is a favourite. Big crayons and chalks for drawing. Simple puzzles; posting shape boxes. Balls to kick or throw.	Give him toys to encourage all these new abilities. Make sure gifts from others are suitable, safe and sturdy. Keep some back, let him get the most out of each new plaything. Arrange a corner of the kitchen or garden for messy play (see page 395). Put him in sensible clothes and invest in large plastic bibs and aprons.
		Pretend household objects such as tea-sets, model cars, lorries, trucks, also dolls and their equipment begin to be used in make-believe play. Picture books of familiar objects and those with a very simple story.	Buy him toys that encourage these skills — not just girls' or boys' toys. Join the local children's library for him.
	Language developing from single words to short, conversational sentences.	Other people, other children — for conversation, singing, finger-rhymes and simple stories.	Talk and listen to him; give opportunities to talk to others, e.g. keep him up later in the evenings to

AGE	WHAT HE CAN DO	PLAYTHINGS	WHAT YOU CAN DO
	Enjoyment of songs and rhymes and beginnings of fantasy play.	Toys which encourage fantasy such as models (e.g. Lego, Duplo), toy cars, houses, dolls, dressing-up things. Books to look at. Bricks and toy telephones.	talk to Daddy or both parents together. Join a toddler club or some group where you meet other parents and children. Read and sing to him, encourage others to do so too.
	Toddler tantrums and sudden changes of mood.	Comforters, toys he had as a baby. Unbreakable things. Musical toys — drums, shakers; banging toys — hammer toys.	Sympathy, firmness, a supply of novel playthings and safe objects as distractions.
24 – 36 months	Walk and climb confidently. Good control over hands. Can pay attention to activities that interest him for a long span now, but may still get bored and moody. Throw, kick a ball.	Toys to ride and climb on such as trikes, safe climbing towers and frames. He needs space to run in — a garden or trips to the park. Water, sand, dough, paint, will give more creative opportunities now. Also enjoyable are threading beads, building models with construction toys, simple jigsaws, wheelbarrow, books, glove puppets.	Give opportunities for more outdoor play and exercise. Second-hand trikes and large outdoor toys will do if you cannot afford new ones. Garden can now be adapted — a sandpit, safe climbing frame and/or swing, plus space to dig and make a mess. If you have no garden, try to take him out regularly. He will need his own space to play in the house or flat. You can start teaching him how to arrange toys and put them away.
	Beginning to learn colours, numbers (at least 'more' or	Use everyday life to talk about colours. 'Your red	Your conversations will be more natural

AGE	WHAT HE CAN DO	PLAYTHINGS	WHAT YOU CAN DO
	'less'). Language will be more conversational and adult. May be able to sing now. Recreate domestic situations, make-believe and role play.	socks today, not blue ones.' Count the stairs, the knives and forks as you use them. Simple musical instruments, records and songs. Story and picture books and children's television will give him new ideas and experiences. The garage and cars and other 'miniature worlds' will become deeply interesting.	now, but still be aware of ways in which he is learning. Be ready to answer many questions; listen and watch him when he is playing to help you to understand what he is trying to ask. Read to him and talk about what you see together on television. Let him play with other children whenever possible. Join in the make believe games with him.
3 – 4 years	He will have many skills, both physical and mental, which he will need in adult life, but they still need developing, refining and specialising. For example, he can perform delicate tasks with fingers, although he may still have trouble with hand—eye matching — he will not see why a jigsaw piece is the wrong way round. He can run, skip, balance, climb and may be able to hop.	He will enjoy some activities for real — swimming, and running, although walking long distances depends on the individual child — most three-year-olds still want to play. Talking, being read to, watching television, preferably with you as much as possible. Doing things for himself; having own clothes, hangers and storage spaces, own soap, towel, toothbrush in their own places. A peak age for dressing-up clothes which continues through to six or seven.	You are finally resigned that a large part of your house will be permanently occupied by toys and children's equipment, plus children themselves! Give your child a wide variety of playthings, not forgetting the cheap, reliable standbys of waste material, dough, water, sand, and safe household utensils.

387

AGE	WHAT HE CAN DO	PLAYTHINGS	WHAT YOU CAN DO
	Will talk more fluently, understand more than he can say, be sensitive to other people's feelings, able to show sympathy and helpfulness, as well as anger or hurt. A three-year-old still often indulges in parallel play – playing alongside rather than with other children – but he is beginning to be able to co-operate with other children in pairs or groups now.	Toys which need more skill such as basic Lego, more complicated picture-jigsaws, modelling games, memory games and board games which require turn-taking. Other children will be important partners, but in more sophisticated activities like board games he is best playing with you to begin with. Playing board games with another child and no adult supervision comes later. He will enjoy 'helping' to cook and using safe implements and tool sets. Doll and model play is very important – pretend houses will be made in all sorts of corners. A Wendy house is a good toy now.	He will enjoy going to places of interest, and animals become fascinating now. Make sure he has opportunity to be with and to play with other children, perhaps in a playgroup or nursery school. This is usually the stage when he can spend a regular part of some days of the week away from you in a supervised setting such as this. Normally around this age he begins to have friends back to tea and to go out to visit other people's homes – perhaps without you if he feels confident enough.
4 – 5 years	Now he will be able to co-operate far better with other children, either in pairs or in groups. He has a better understanding of games which have specific rules – at this age children understand well and love party	A lovely age for toys – he can manage a bigger range of board games, is safe with toys with smaller parts, and messy play becomes much less messy as he learns better control, so that organising painting, sand and	Children this age have the stamina and understanding to enjoy more sophisticated days out. Take advantage of the last year before school to visit places like museums in quiet term-time periods. Safety rules you

AGE	WHAT HE CAN DO	PLAYTHINGS	WHAT YOU CAN DO
	games like musical statues, dead lions, and hunt the thimble or other treasure. Drawings with properly held pencil will give clues about how he sees the world. Some children may begin to recognise written words by now, especially their own names, but just like all the other milestones of learning to crawl, walk and talk, so learning to recognise words and write them develops at very different ages with different children.	water and playdough activities at home is easier, although you still need to cover up and be prepared for some mess. 4 to 5-year-olds are also better able to manage some gluing and sticking on their own, although you need to be on hand – most children can manage to cut out with blunt-ended scissors around this age. Pedalling a first bike with stabilisers or a three-wheeled trike can usually be managed now. A good age to fix up rope-swings from garden trees or think about investing in some kind of outdoor climbing frame – an expensive buy but one which should last through to 9 or 10 years old and can be used by brothers and sisters as well.	have already instilled can now be passed on with some of the reasoning behind them. For example, talk about crossing the road, not swallowing dangerous substances like bleach, or running around with sharp pointed objects, although you still need to be vigilant in safety precautions. Now it can be an adventure to stay away from home for a night with a friend. Looking at wildlife around brings great pleasure – the birds in the garden, collecting tadpoles or following an ant trail. By now your child will be aware of the stage ahead, big school. Making sure he can manage to go to the toilet by himself, change for PE and recognise his name are essential skills to give him confidence.

ORGANISING PLAY

The way you organise your life and home when you have a young child makes a great deal of difference to their freedom and ability to play. The following points all have to be considered:

SAFETY

There is more detail about this in chapter 15 but remember the following points about play safety:

* Choose playthings and activities which are right for your child's age and stage of development – see the chart on pages 383–9. A general rule is that the smaller the child the larger the toy needs to be, apart from large exercise-type toys. When buying toys, look for British Standard No 5665. Check toys you buy or those given as presents for loose parts, sharp edges or pins, and loose fluff which could be swallowed or inhaled. Make sure all soft toys are washable. Never let children play with plastic bags; paper ones, especially greaseproof which does not dissolve, are fine, but you need to supervise any children under 18 months.

* Once your child starts to move around, make sure that all dangerous, small, breakable or poisonous things are kept well out of reach. Keep one step ahead of your child's increasing mobility and anticipate when he may begin to be able to pull himself up, climb on to chairs, and so on. Once a child can climb, dangerous things must be locked away. Small children do not know the difference between cleaning fluids and cosmetics which can be poisonous and bottles of drink, so keep all such items well out of reach – putting them under the sink or on the dressing table leaves them accessible to a young child. A secure fireguard around any fire, including gas or electricity, is a must, and so is a safety gate on the stairs until you are sure he can manage them. Block off low electric points so that he cannot put his fingers or other objects into them – use dummy plugs. If you have another child or have to leave the younger one unsupervised – for example, if the telephone rings or if your cooking area is too small for you to work safely with him under your feet – you may find a playpen (BS4863) useful. Children usually accept being in a playpen more readily if they have got used to it from early days.

FREEDOM

Babies, toddlers and small children all need increasing amounts of freedom to move around and explore for themselves. This is why making your home safe is so important. If you are constantly saying 'Don't touch' or 'Keep out' to your child, you are not only making harder work for yourself, but you are inhibiting his natural curiosity about the world, which enables him to learn about it and test it. Every small child needs the freedom to:

391

* Move, and that means space, both indoors and out, where he can kick, crawl, roll, toddle, climb, bounce and run. If you live in a flat without a garden, then daily outings to a park or other open area are especially important.

* Explore, and that means having things he can open, empty, dig into, spread around, tear up, pile up, spill, drop, pick up and, hopefully, put away.

* Learn from his own mistakes how to do things instead of having others always do them for him. He also needs to be free from too much interference, criticism and control so that he can learn the limits of his own attention and concentration and be given plenty of time to get on with what he is doing without interruption. He needs to be praised for his own efforts. Later he also needs a different kind of space for displaying his artwork. You need not ruin newly decorated walls with Sellotape — the front of the fridge is just as good for sticking up toddlers' pictures.

ORDER

Anyone familiar with lively toddlers will know that the list of freedoms above would sound like a recipe for chaos if it were not for the reverse side of the coin of freedom, which is control. A child cannot really be free if he cannot learn how to make order in his life, how to find things that are lost, how to arrange things so that they do not get broken, how to correct mistakes, how to ask for an adult's help, how to win adult approval by co-operating with his parents' requirements, how to make and keep friends because he knows when to compromise and sympathise with other people's needs.

Important points to remember about order are:

* Storage. You will soon discover as the collection of toys grows that being able to find things and put them away easily is crucial both for you and your child. It teaches your child a great deal, like knowing that each set of objects, whether it is crayons, bricks, toy cars, sticky shapes or building blocks, has its own place, and this helps him to learn that things belong in groups. He can also learn that small things can fit together into bigger things, for example, crayons, felt-tips, drawing books all go on the shelf for writing and drawing materials; cars go in the white box, lorries go in the blue box, and both boxes are stored on top of the model garage — these are all transport toys.

* Help your child not only to be tidy and to find things easily, but also to learn about sets and groups, by giving each set of toys its own storage container. You do not need to spend a lot of money: plastic ice-cream boxes or cardboard shoe boxes are excellent. Make a picture label to stick on the outside, and a printed label with its name which will help him in pre-reading skills. Just cut the pictures off the container the toys came in for the labels. Your child will enjoy looking for the right labels with you. Obviously there is no need to be too rigid about this and get cross if he puts the crayons in the car box. So long as everything gets put away in a place where it can be found again at some stage, this is the main thing – for your peace of mind at least!

* Small containers are better for general tidiness than putting all the toys in one big box, basket or drawer. To find anything, your child has to tip the whole lot out on the floor every time. It also becomes impossible to keep small pieces of toys or games assembled together in their right group. It is preferable to make only some toys available at any one time, and to keep others put away so that you can rotate them every now and again. Bringing out a toy he has not seen for four or five weeks is as good as giving him a new present and can be especially useful when either you or he are not feeling well, it's the third rainy day in succession, or there is just some special occasion.

THE IMPORTANCE OF MESSY PLAY

Playing with sand, earth, water, dough and clay, paint and glue is both relaxing and soothing for children. Messy play, as it is generally known, does not actually have to make a tremendous mess and is a very acceptable outlet for a child's feelings of frustration and anger. It also gives children a marvellous chance to experiment, by pouring, sifting, measuring, moulding, moistening, hardening, colouring, sticking and unsticking. Working with these sorts of materials, as opposed to structured and specific toys and playthings, a child is able to impose his own ideas, which is not only satisfying and rewarding, but also stimulates imagination. For parents the plus side is that these activities cost virtually nothing and mean with a little planning that children can be happily occupied for hours. Messy play brings so much pleasure and contentment that you will find some kind of session of this activity built into your child's day will have a beneficial effect on his temperament and make him calmer and much easier to cope with.

If you have a garden and the weather is fine these activities can take place outdoors where there is more space and you do not have to worry so much about protecting furniture or floors and about clearing up afterwards. However, it is also possible to give children a chance for messy play indoors, however small your house or flat, if you plan in advance. Decide

where in the house it matters least if water, paint, glue or playdough gets dropped on the floor. The bathroom and the kitchen are naturals because they usually have lino or tiles which can be easily cleaned. Always cover up your children's clothes so that you do not have to keep nagging them about not getting dirty — cutting the sleeves off an old T-shirt of yours and tying a belt around the middle makes an effective overall which can be put over whatever they happen to be wearing. Give them a reasonable area to work in and cover it all with old newspaper, or better still invest in a couple of pieces of plastic cloth which can be bought by the yard to cover floor or table. You need to stay on hand to help and supervise under-fives with messy play, although the older they get the more they can do unaided, and their actions also become far more controlled, thus minimising accidental mess.

Simple ideas for messy play include:

OUTDOORS

* A sandpit — make one yourself with an old box sunk into the ground or buy one from a shop, but make sure it has a lid to stop neighbourhood cats using it as their lavatory at night. Silver sand from garden centres or DIY shops is best — do not use builder's sand which is yellow and stains clothes and skin. Adding water to the sand adds a whole new dimension to the game and provides children with magical experiences as they watch the sand change and the water soak away. Remember though that small children do not know when to say 'when', so you need to supervise to make sure the whole sandpit does not get flooded. You can make cardboard combs to use for patterns in dry or wet sand and almost any plastic household containers and implements, including teaspoons and plastic knives, will add to the fun. Turning an old cardboard box on its side beside the sandpit and telling them it is their 'cooker' into which they can put all their sand-pies and cakes will increase their pleasure.

* Water is marvellous entertainment for all ages, but you must always stay on hand to supervise. Never leave a young child alone in a paddling pool, even for a minute to go and answer the telephone. Once he can sit up, a small baby will enjoy sitting in a couple of inches of water, perhaps in a washing-up bowl, or you can invest in a paddling pool. Again, plastic household containers and implements, including bottles and jugs for pouring, are all good playthings. Make holes in the sides of margarine tubs or plastic containers so that the water pours out of the sides in little jets. Washing dolly or teddy's clothes or bathing dolly with real soap or a drop of shampoo is another favourite game.

* Painting for young children is something they will not usually spend as long doing as they will playing with sand, water, or modelling materials, but there is tremendous excitement and value to be had from

it. The simplest way is to invest in a few paint pots with lids and holes for brushes so that they cannot be tipped over and spilt, or make your own out of old washing-up liquid bottles. To do this pull the cap off the top of the bottle and cut through the empty container about three inches from the top. Turn it upside down inside the bottom part of the bottle, having put the paint inside, and insert the brush through the hole. Overalls are essential and even in the garden you may want to cover the ground with old newspaper. Don't think your child has to paint a specific picture. Young children have tremendous fun from painting cardboard boxes or other junk material. You can cut a door and windows in the box. Don't invest in an expensive upright easel to pin their paper on because in fact painting on an upright surface is quite difficult. Laying the paper flat on the ground is probably easiest to begin with.

Another easy outdoor colouring activity is chalking – little ones do need you to supervise, but if you can give them a little square of backyard or paving stone to chalk on, the result will be washed away later by the rain. You do need to explain carefully that this is the only area they can chalk in, though, because it is confusing for a child to be told he can chalk in one place, and then find you are very cross when he does the same thing indoors on the kitchen floor. Keep chalks, paints and crayons safely put away to avoid mistakes.

INDOORS

* Home-made playdough is softer for little fingers and much cheaper than harder shop-bought modelling clays. The recipe is two cups of flour to one cup of salt plus two cups of water, two heaped teaspoonfuls of cream of tartar and two dessertspoonfuls of vegetable oil. Mix all this together in a saucepan until it is smooth – mixing and stirring it is all part of the fun for small children. Colour it any shade you wish with food colourings, and then cook slowly over a low heat stirring all the time until it binds together and forms a soft dough. Store it in a plastic container with a lid or in a plastic bag to stop it from drying out in between play sessions. You could use a small rolling pin and shape cutters plus cut-up straws for 'candles' when making a birthday cake out of playdough, while a plastic container with a lid and a few holes in the top as a flour shaker, and some blunt plastic knives for cutting complete your playdough cooking set. Again, adding a cardboard box as a 'cooker' increases the fun. Playing with playdough is a very easy messy activity to set up which does not actually make much mess. Avoid the problem of children walking dropped bits of playdough over the rest of the house on the soles of their feet by sweeping all round the table before they get down at the end of the session.

* Washing-up. Cover them in something waterproof and fix up a secure chair for them to stand on at the sink. If you fill an old washing-up liquid container with water and tell them it's soap and give them a few plastic cups and saucers they may keep happy for hours. Alternatively, you can give them the sort of plastic utensils and playthings mentioned earlier as suitable for the paddling pool. You need to stay closely on hand when a young child is standing on a chair, but this sort of activity can easily combine with preparing vegetables for a meal and so on.

* Bathtime can happen at any time in a dull day and does not need to be at the end of it. Putting two young children in the bath together is a good way to let them enjoy water play even in the middle of winter. Of course you need to stay in the bathroom with them, but it can be an opportunity to have a cup of coffee or clean the rest of the bathroom. Do not use up all your hot water by making it as deep as you would for a bath, just a few inches and all the toys and plastic containers mentioned earlier will give them great fun.

* Gluing and sticking can happen outdoors or indoors, but is perhaps well thought of as a wintertime activity. Again, you do not need any equipment. Paste made from flour and water plus a couple of paste brushes and some household junk such as egg cartons, cereal packets, polystyrene meat trays and so on can all be glued together to make fantastic sculptures. Cover your child in an old overall of the kind already described and protect the table and floor with newspaper from the inevitable dropped globs of glue. Don't forget that scraps of material and wool as well as pasta, rice, and other dried foods are fun to glue as well. Mothers who enjoy handicrafts themselves can get quite carried away, but try to let the child do as much as possible himself, even though you can see easy ways to make it look better. Other parents may find the urge to meddle only too easy to resist, but children do need one or two ideas to get their imagination working. Could they make something that looks as though it might fly? Or, very simply, could they make something that was as tall as their teddy? Will something made of polystyrene float? And can it be made into an extra special boat? Older children love making very simple toys – for example binoculars by Sellotaping two cardboard tubes from the inside of toilet rolls together, or a telescope that folds up from several different sized tubes fitting inside each other, or taping together several tubes to make a great long run for marbles or little cars.

These are just some suggestions – you will probably have many more ideas of your own.

MORE THAN ONE CHILD

If you have more than one child, particularly when they are at different and equally demanding stages, you need special patience and ingenuity to provide regular opportunities for messy play. The oldest child may well be able to manage something without too much difficulty – for example a three- to four-year-old can enjoy painting, gluing and sticking and all sorts of activities without your continual supervision, but having a one-year-old butting in can mean disaster. Choose opportunities when the youngest is sleeping to do these activities alone with the eldest. This is true in other areas of play, not just with the messy materials. More than two children means giving quite a large amount of your home over to the children's needs, both in storage and space. Twins create their own special demands – you only need to multiply the problems of an energetic and exploring toddler by two to understand the impact they can have. When you have children at different stages, the older child's toys may be dangerous for the younger child because a crawler can easily put small bricks, marbles, or dolls' house equipment into his mouth, and the older child's toys can be spoiled or broken by a curious, energetic toddler. Such disasters are the basis for much squabbling between brothers and sisters. Until they learn to play together, it is better to keep their playthings on different levels, putting the older one's small models on a high table or on their own desk, and the younger one's things on the floor, if need be in a playpen.

When you have two or more children sharing the same play area there is all the more need to ration the toys. Just keep a few of the most popular and hardwearing unbreakable toys within reach and swap them round for different ones every so often. Toys which can be used by both or all of them, such as bricks, dolls, waste material and sturdy plastic models (with no removable small parts), also come into their own at this time. Later, when the younger one is more sensible, you can allow them much more choice in what they want to do.

Many toys come as presents from friends or relatives. In several cases these people may not have young children of their own and be out of touch with the sort of toys that are useful. It is well worth having a chat with them about the kind of toys which make the best presents, because fiddly, breakable, losable toys and games are simply not worth the money. Sometimes foreign imitations bought in street markets can actually be dangerous as they do not conform to the same British standards. Good hardwearing standbys such as bricks, push-along trucks and cars, construction toys, balls, dolls, jigsaws and masses of paper and writing materials, colours and painting equipment cannot fail. Good, well-written picture books are always welcome too.

ROUTINE

A little thought at the beginning of the day as to how you will structure and pace the day with different events can make it pleasanter and easier for both of you. If you start by looking at what you have to do and then looking at what it would benefit your child to do, you may be able to arrive at something which suits both of you. For example, your child needs to get out of the house and have some fresh air and if possible some exercise – can a trip to the post office or shops be combined with a visit to the park or the ducks? It is also important that at some point in the day you give your child a certain amount of your undivided attention. If you keep fobbing him off with only minimum attention or 'Wait a minute' for too long, he can easily become whining and seem extra demanding. After having you to himself for a while, a child is usually happier to play on his own for some time following this. Your own mood, your child's mood and the weather will all be factors which help you to decide how to plan the day. Don't, for example, start on something which is likely to tax your patience on a day when you are particularly low and feeling unable to cope. On other occasions you might feel you want to spend a lot of time with your child and take short cuts with the housework and cooking. A day might begin, for example, by your child 'helping' you to wash up the breakfast things with his own bowl of water and plastic cups. He will continue to be absorbed with this while you go on to prepare some food for the evening meal. After this period of messy play he may be ready to sit down and do some drawing or colouring with you beside him – a chance for you to enjoy a morning cup of coffee, provided you keep it well out of his reach. Having had your undivided attention he may be content to play with his toys while you are nearby getting on with other chores. On some days your child may be content to play in a very absorbed way without much intervention from you; on other days he may want to be with you all the time. The secret to getting anything done is to involve him – so, for example, can he 'help' you to make the lunch? The afternoon might be a time for a nap, plus an outing to a friend's, to a toddlers' club or just for a walk to the park or shops or to visit the library.

Evening can be a time for songs, stories, play in the bath and whatever bedtime rituals your child finds comforting. This may be the time when either both of you, or one of you, comes home from work so perhaps the person who has been out at work might like to take over. If you both work, it is worth keeping a child up sometimes in the evening so that you can have some play time with him. Get whoever looks after him in the day to let him have a nap if you are worried about him being too tired. Children learn and develop so much through play that you will miss out on a vital and enjoyable part of his growing up if you do not have regular times when you play with him.

Then of course there are times when routine and order need to be forgotten and you can enjoy something spontaneously. If the sun is suddenly shining, give your child a nice surprise (small children like surprises just as much as you do) and take him out to the nearest open space, or just for a bus ride. If the weather is awful and you are both fed up, forget what you were planning to do and curl up with a book together, or make some biscuits, or a camp where he can dress up and pretend to be characters in a story. Of course, some of these activities are better for an older child if they have another child to share them with sometimes. One of the best things you can do to encourage your child's play is to find playmates.

MAKING FRIENDS

Babies begin to have social interaction with their parents right from the word go — but most of us think of a social life as something rather different. In fact your baby's first contact with other babies and young children is likely to be through your own need to meet friends with babies of a similar age. Many long-term friendships between women stem from first meetings in antenatal classes or in hospital. Some hospitals now run post-natal classes when you can go back afterwards with your baby, or you may meet another mother living near you during one of your visits to the local clinic. Most towns have pram clubs in church halls and com-munity centres — if you are new to an area the best way to find out is to stop a mother with a pram and ask. You will probably make one or two close friends with whom you will spend a lot of time and whose children you consider to be your own baby's 'best friends', yet even at eighteen months your baby may play alongside another but is unlikely to interact a great deal — he still turns to his mother for real enjoyment. At two he will acknowledge the existence of a friend, but often most of the 'playing' takes the form of disputes over who owns which toy. However, by the age of two and three-quarters to three years many children begin to enjoy the prospect of other children and are often happy to join in playing with them. He still needs you on hand to help to organise these early social interactions, and you can gently show young children how to take turns, or how to enjoy simple activities together. There is more about this in chapter 14 on relationships.

PLAY FOR SICK CHILDREN

When your child is ill, he probably will not want to play or do any of the usual things at all, but needs to be close to you and perhaps able to watch his brothers and sisters playing. As he gets better his interest and need for play will return. Because his concentration is less active, he will probably want to play with easy toys and activities that give quiet satisfaction and are not too tiring. These may include toys he grew out of several months ago such as simple jigsaws, colouring books or the shape posting box,

instead of the more complicated building toys he has been used to recently. He may also want more babyish stories too. Don't be surprised if your child goes back to wanting a bottle, or a special comforter. You need to be tolerant of this behaviour because it is just his way of coping with the fears, weakness and strangeness of feeling ill.

If your child cannot move around, perhaps because he is in traction or plaster, you will need to choose play activities which he can do easily despite his limitations. Sticking activities, colouring or drawing, jigsaws, modelling material such as dough can all be used on a tray. Model figures, cars, trains, bricks and dolls can create a miniature fantasy world for a child who cannot move around. He will also appreciate different things to look at and listen to – stories, records, cassettes, a television set, a computer, even hand-held electronic games – all in moderation. You can also play guessing games such as I-Spy and memory games with him.

Sick children need to be kept as mentally and physically active as possible. If they are not, they can lose a lot of ground and their development may be slowed down if they are sick for a long time. Illness will always slow down your child to some extent, but his recovery will be quicker if you do all you can to make the best of the skills and abilities that he can use. Play is important to help your child recover the use of injured limbs or a body that's been kept still in bed for a long while. Exercise on climbing frames, bouncing on trampolines, running, jumping, balancing and learning to hold and handle small objects in his fingers are all more important than usual for your child's well-being when he has recovered from an illness.

PLAY IN HOSPITAL

Babies and small children can find hospitals strange and bewildering. Familiar play activities and toys reduce the strangeness and make it seem a more homely place. The opportunity to play in hospital will enable normal development to continue and the enjoyment it brings will help them to cope better with illness and being away from home.

Hospitals understand the importance of play and provide playrooms and play equipment on the wards and in the out-patient areas. Many hospitals employ trained play specialists to organise the play. The play specialists will find the activities your child enjoys and will show you where the toys are stored so that you can play with him too. He may want to do some hospital play with dolls or teddies, and it is important that he has an opportunity to do this as it will help him to become familiar with the strange equipment and to understand his own treatment.

Special toys can help to keep the link with home. Your child should always be allowed to keep his own teddy, comforter or other familiar thing with him. Ideally, one of his parents should be with him too, but if you cannot be there all the time, familiar toy-friends from home can help to remind him of you. There is more about children in hospital in chapter 20.

PLAYGROUPS AND NURSERIES

When your child is about three, he may be ready to start at a playgroup or nursery school, where he will get different, more organised play experiences from the ones he has had at home. A few children in the United Kingdom are in group care from babyhood – they are the very few children for whom state day nursery places are available, and those cared for in private crèches or nurseries. But most children in this country spend their first three years being looked after by their mother, or by a child-minder or nanny, in a home setting. The move to being part of a group can be quite a big one, but it has advantages.

At a playgroup or nursery school your child will have a much wider variety of play equipment than you can give him at home. He will get the chance to use big adventure toys, such as climbing frames, that you might not be able to provide. He will also have the fun of playing with others on this equipment, learning to take turns, pretending to be on a spaceship, in a hospital, school or whatever anybody feels like doing. As well as having the companionship of other children his own age and learning to play with them, he will have the chance to make relationships with other adults and to learn that other people, as well as his parents, can be trusted and liked. It is also an enormous adventure because for most young children it is the first time they leave their parents to go and do something on their own with other adults who are not relatives or very close friends. If your child settles happily at a playgroup or nursery he will gain valuable experiences of happy separations, learning to do without you and knowing that you can go and come back reliably. Having your child in a playgroup or nursery increases his independence and confidence and also has advantages for you because it gives you some time to yourself. It may also involve you in activities with other parents and children which are rewarding.

THE OPTIONS OPEN TO YOU

State nursery schools These are run by the local education authority and have fully trained staff. Attendance is voluntary from the age of three onwards. There are no fees and nursery schools, or nursery classes which may be attached to the local infants' school, enable children to move on easily to full-time education when the time comes. Most nursery schools offer the kind of learning through play that a playgroup does, the main difference being that the nursery schools are staffed by teachers and nursery nurses and are less likely to need, or perhaps want, parental involvement, although a good nursery school should be just as welcoming to you as a good playgroup. Some have parent-helper rotas and you can offer to help on outings or at fêtes. Generally, nursery schools are of a high standard and if a place is available for your child it is well worth considering. However, the number of nursery school places is limited, so this option may not be open to you. Nursery education provision varies greatly from one local authority to another and in some areas places are only offered to children from families with special circumstances.

Private nursery schools Such schools are run for profit and fees are generally quite high. They are not state controlled, do not necessarily have trained staff, and a full range of facilities cannot be guaranteed, so it is up to you to satisfy yourself that one is suitable. Some private nursery schools are certainly excellent. They have small numbers, several helpers and manage to fulfil some of the goals of companionship between children and creative development. Some are more formal and put great emphasis on teaching the three Rs at an early age. The idea of giving your child an edge over his peers may be appealing, but a head start in reading and writing does not mean your child will stay ahead through his school life. Most children learn to read and write quickly and readily in primary school and have the experience of a number of years of enjoyable and imaginative play beforehand. Many private nursery schools are attached to prep schools and if the assumption is that your child will continue his education there you need to look at both carefully.

Playgroups Most playgroups in this country belong to the Preschool Playgroups Association (PPA, see address section, pages 673–6) whose motto is 'Playing is learning for living'. Mother and toddler clubs and nursery schools are also able to join the PPA. Playgroups emphasise the value of free, creative play in a framework of planned sessions of different kinds of play: constructive; imaginative; organised (e.g. song and story sessions); active; outdoor, and so on. Playgroups are run by groups of parents and usually involve mothers and, if they have time, fathers in the running of the group on a rota basis. The PPA runs training courses for helpers and supervisors, sets down guidelines and provides newsletters and advice to helpers. Most of the pre-school group provision in the United Kingdom is provided by playgroups. You usually have to pay for your child to attend and the playgroup may operate every morning, or mornings and afternoons, or only a few mornings a week. Local social services departments may pay for your child to go in cases of particular need. If you want your child to go to a playgroup but cannot afford it, do ask the organiser, your health visitor or social worker, if you have one, about special places.

CHOOSING A PLAYGROUP

You can find out about local playgroups by asking your health visitor, social services department, reference library, the PPA or just by asking other mothers. It is worth taking time over choosing a playgroup or nursery school, but if you have a choice in your area it might be sensible to put your child's name on several waiting lists while you make up your mind because the best ones are often oversubscribed. As well as asking other mothers about the playgroups you are most interested in, make sure you go along and spend a morning at each group, together with your child – this is quite an enjoyable thing to do with your two-year-old anyway. Points to consider are:

* You are made welcome and introduced to the helpers and other mothers. If the supervisor does not like the idea of you staying to watch, be suspicious. By talking to the staff you can quickly find out their views on discipline, anxious children and free play and ascertain whether they match with yours. Even if you feel they are staging something special for your benefit, their general attitude to the children usually shines through.

* Your child is also made welcome, perhaps introduced to other children, but no attempt is made to force him to join in or do anything until he is ready.

* Look at the space the children have to play in. Church halls can be bleak, but interesting activities and a happy atmosphere can transform them. Does the place seem crowded? Numbers are governed by insurance and also local authority regulations, but some playgroups and schools let their numbers creep up. Somewhere for outdoor play on fine days makes a tremendous difference.

* Look at the toys, equipment and play materials on offer. Do you get the impression that the same old jigsaws are put out in the same area every single day? Are a number of activities like painting, sand, water play, playdough and dressing up on offer all the time? You may have to drop in one or two times to find out if they bother to vary the week's activities, and introduce woodwork or cooking or a special handicraft. Do the children look excited and seem interested in what is there? Look for a Wendy house or corner; dressing-up clothes which are imaginative and in good repair; plenty of construction toys and puzzles; large layout-type toys, such as railways and big building blocks; toys which encourage fantasy play such as models, dolls, vehicles, road layouts, toy villages, etc. Look also for large equipment such as climbing frames, slides, play-tunnels; for books and a quiet corner where children can go and look at books; for ideas such as theme tables which involve the children bringing their own contributions – such as a nature table, or a colour table.

* There should be a good ratio of adults to children (one to eight is a minimum, but in a playgroup which encourages parents' involvement, it may be one adult to five children or less). Are the adults listening and talking to the children? How do they deal with squabbles and destructive or disruptive behaviour? Do they seem to be calmly in control? Do they seem to be affectionate with the children? Do they make a point of helping the shy, lonely or aggressive child to join in more constructively? Do they spend most of the time with the children rather than gossiping to each other? Do they welcome and involve rota parents rather than leave them to find their own way about? If they do most of these things

most of the time (nobody is perfect!), then this is a good playgroup. The atmosphere at the group should be busy and buzzing, but you should not feel the place is out of control. Hordes of children on bikes and cars zooming up and down the middle of the room is a hallmark of a few less supervised playgroups.

* Are boys and girls treated without discrimination? Do boys get encouraged to do the quiet, creative activities that promote language skills and prepare for schoolwork as much as the girls? Or are they allowed to run about in gangs and spend a lot of time with sit-on toys and cars without much adult attention? Similarly, are girls encouraged to join in with the physical play and large-toy activities? Do boys and girls play together? Both boys and girls need physical, energetic play, construction play and quiet, creative periods with adult attention. If both sexes are getting these things, you are in a good playgroup. If they are not, and you are concerned for your daughter or son, have a word with the playgroup leader. Often, busy teachers and supervisors are not really aware of what is going on and, if you say, 'I'd like my son to have the chance to paint, thread beads and dress up, as well as run about,' the playgroup leader may suddenly realise that she has not done these things yet, and will arrange for them to happen.

* Singing sessions and storytime can tell you a great deal about the playgroup. Singing sessions should always be varied and fun with lots of action rhymes and percussion and be obviously enjoyed by the children. If you get the impression that this is a session that most children would like to miss out, then something is not going well. Storytime should also be something children look forward to. The story should be chosen so that it holds the children's attention, and be well read so that it keeps their interest quite naturally without continual interruption from helpers telling the children to pay attention or sit up. Unfortunately, a few playgroups use storytime as a way to keep everyone still while the helpers tidy up or take it in turns to shepherd the children in and out to go to the toilet and wash their hands.

If the playgroup seems happy and potentially welcoming to your child, but there are a few things that do not measure up to what you would like, why not approach the playgroup leader and offer to help? The great strength of playgroups is that they can use the ideas and skills of parents, so you may be in a position to change things.

PREPARING YOUR CHILD TO START PLAYGROUP

Before your child starts playgroup, it helps to read him some books about it and perhaps to have a pretend playgroup at home with a drink and a biscuit mid-morning. Providing him with a friend to start with or making friends with a child who is already at the playgroup can often make life easier. On his first day you may perhaps feel a little apprehensive, or even sad when you are confronted with this first step to independence, but don't let him know this is how you feel. It may be better for a child to start going two mornings a week rather than one at first, to avoid such a long time elapsing between visits that he may become anxious all over again every time he goes. Some children sail into this experience without a backward glance, but often your child will want you to stay for the first few times. A playgroup which does not welcome parents to stay as long as they like is one to be suspicious of.

Any value of playgroup is wiped out by leaving a screaming, terrified child, or an unwilling one. If this problem arises, talk about it with the playgroup leader because there are many ways around it. It is true that some children will always cry when their mothers leave and calm down instantly the moment they have gone – it is as if the moment of parting is too much for them to bear. If you suspect your child is one of these, leave him with a trusted playgroup assistant who can distract him the moment you have gone. However, you know your child best, so do not be overpowered by a supervisor or nursery school teacher who has seen it all and insists you are making it worse by lingering around. A star chart can often work wonders for a child who finds it hard to say goodbye, but basically enjoys the playgroup once you have left. Make a simple poster and stick a gold star on every time he manages to be brave and not to cry when you leave, and give him a little reward at the end of the week. Be sure to be back in good time to meet children in the early days – being late can cause great anxiety, and try to collect him yourself until he is well settled. Remember playgroup and nursery school are not compulsory, and if you have real problems settling your child it may be a good idea to leave it for a month or two, and then try again.

Once your child starts at nursery school or playgroup he will probably come home very tired and may go back to having an afternoon sleep, particularly if he is going every day. Much as you want to know what he has been doing, don't badger him with questions. Sometimes there has been so much going on he will be too confused to reply, and as likely as not he will remember the best bits later in the day and tell you of his own accord.

If he goes off playgroup and suddenly refuses to go, check first that nothing has upset him – perhaps a fight with another child or a telling off from one of the helpers. If you have not been helping at the playgroup at all, ask if you can come in occasionally, it will cheer him up enormously. Alternatively, give him something interesting from the garden or park for him to take in and show, or suggest he has a friend back to lunch after the morning session. If he is getting near school age he may just be feeling bored and a bit too big for the playgroup, particularly if some of his friends have already started school. Many playgroups and nursery schools have rising fives groups once or twice a week to cater for this age group and give them an idea of what big school will be like.

Don't linger too long over your goodbyes

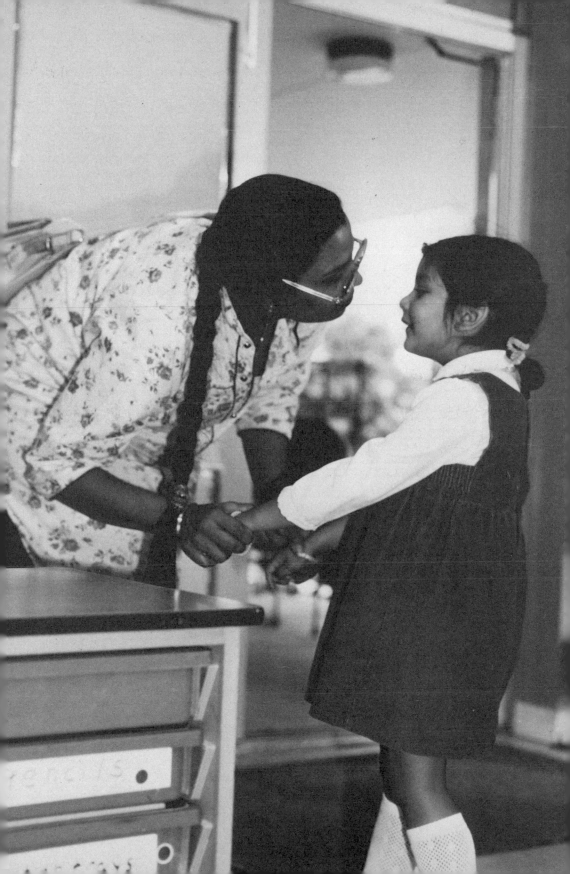

SCHOOLS

CHOOSING A SCHOOL

Not many parents are far-sighted enough to think, in the first year of their baby's life, about the school which he will eventually go to. But each state primary school has its own catchment area, so that where you live dictates which school will offer a place to your child. It is possible for you to ask the local education authority if you want your child to go to a school outside your catchment area. Each authority has its own rules, but in general you will only be offered a place at such a school if there is room.

If you wish to send your child to a school outside your own catchment area, you can make your request in writing to the local education authority, but you are not assured of a place unless there is one free after all the children within the other catchment area have been accommodated. Remember too that numbers fluctuate and policies change and there is no guarantee that a brother or sister may be able to follow on at the same school if you are still outside the catchment area. It is also a great advantage as children grow and become more independent to live in an area where all their friends are close at hand.

Under the 1988 Education Act schools can 'opt out' of the control of the local authority and instead administer their own affairs and answer directly to the Department of Education. Such schools are not allowed to change their status and basis for admission for five years, so a comprehensive cannot suddenly become a grammar school with entry by exam overnight, but opting out may allow them more flexibility in taking children from outside their own immediate area – in this instance you should apply directly to the school to enquire what the position is.

In choosing a primary school, apply the same guidelines as you did for choosing a playgroup or nursery school. Go and have a look round the school, talk to the teachers and parents of children who go there. Is the headteacher available and pleased to talk to you and show you round? Is there a friendly, happy atmosphere in the school with plenty of lively art and project work on show? What are the sizes of the classes? Does the school have any particular strengths, such as music or drama? Are there out of school activities and clubs for junior children? What sort of grounds and sports facilities do the children have and what kind of sports can the juniors expect to take part in?

People obviously expect different things from a first school. One set of parents may disapprove of children roaming from one activity to another in an open-plan classroom, while another set of parents may applaud the relaxed attitude of the teacher. It is worth remembering as well that the views of parents who already have a child at the school vary enormously according to how well their child has fared there. Good and bad reputations linger long after the headteacher who has established them has left, and you may be told something totally contradictory about the same school by two different sets of parents. The attractiveness of the school building itself is less important than work seen around the classroom. The coats may not be hung in immaculate rows, but classes should be bustling and happy without seeming noisy and out of control. You will quickly form an impression of whether the school is welcoming, and be wary if it is not. The headteacher can give you a copy of the curriculum which will show if the general educational aims of the school match up with your own ideas. In general it is best to trust your instincts. If you like the headteacher and are pleased with what he or she tells you about the school, and this is backed up by the impression you form when you are given a tour, then that is probably a better guide than what other parents may tell you.

Private schools do not have catchment areas so children tend to live in more scattered localities – again, think carefully before committing yourself to a school which may mean years of difficult travelling and less likelihood of playmates living nearby. Entry to private primary school depends on putting your child's name on their list early enough – there is usually a non-refundable registration fee. These schools usually take children from four or sometimes even younger if they have a nursery class, and instances of parents putting a child down for a place even before birth are not unknown. In general, private primary schools tend to offer a more structured, formal style of education earlier, but talking to other parents and looking at where children go on to at secondary stage may help you to decide if the end result will be very different between state and private education in your particular area. If you do not have a fixed view on choosing a private versus a state education, make sure to visit as many of both kinds of schools and compare facilities and class sizes as well as the general attitude and feel of each school. Fees tend to be similar within an area – your bank or accountant can give advice on investment schemes to defray the cost over a period.

STARTING SCHOOL

Moving up to big school with a group of friends from a playgroup, or, even better, from a nursery school attached to a big school makes the changeover easy, but not all five-year-olds are so lucky. However, you can help by inviting a few likely friends round to tea in advance of the big day. The school secretary will be able to supply some names, or you may meet some mothers when your child is invited up to the school in the afternoon of a previous term for a visit. There are a number of good books about starting school which you can read with your child, and some playgroups and nurseries have a video which describes what happens at school. Talking about changing for gym, what happens at playtime and school dinner times all helps, as these are areas which are likely to cause most problems. Don't look for trouble, though, because some children will sail through everything without any worries, and don't bombard him with information at one sitting – it is best to answer questions as they arise or chat about subjects when it is appropriate. For example, when you go to buy his lunch box or are having lunch together at home, you can talk about what all the children will be doing at school.

Some schools start with mornings only or insist parents take their children home to lunch in the first week. If, however, all the other children stay to lunch, it is probably better if your child does as well because this is an important time when they can begin to make friends.

Even if your child has been settled happily at nursery school, he may still feel nervous when it comes to leaving you on the first day at big school. Don't be surprised or get cross if there are a few unexpected tears. The sheer numbers, noise and different smell of the classroom can seem foreign. Most good reception teachers are adept at dealing with upsets and, just like nursery school, you can always telephone the school secretary afterwards to make sure everything is all right.

MAKING A GOOD START

Make sure your child is well used to going to the lavatory without help, and is able to dress and undress himself for PE. It helps to have clothes that are easy to get in and out of: elasticated waist trousers and skirts instead of difficult buttons; pull-on T-shirts instead of buttoned shirts. Not many children can tie shoelaces at this stage, so velcro fastenings or buckles are helpful. If possible, forget the tie to start with – it just means more work for the reception class teacher! Make sure all clothes are clearly labelled and that a child can recognise his own name – whether it is on a piece of clothing or a picture. It does help if he can write it himself as well. If he is having school lunch, make sure he can manage cutlery, or if he is taking a packed lunch that he can open his own lunch box.

Children who have just started school often find playtime bewildering – at the nursery or playgroup there may have been plenty of sit-on toys to ride about with outside, but now they have to make their own games without the help of any other toys. Sensitive reception class teachers often take their class on a tour of the playground before the first breaktime, showing them all the little areas and making sure they know just where to come back to when the bell rings. Children quickly latch on to the reception teacher and what Miss says can become more important than anything coming from their parents. At playtime, however, children often have to get used to someone different taking over, while their own teacher takes a much-needed break, and this can be disconcerting.

Remember that at first the long day is usually quite exhausting and your child will probably be tired when he comes out. Try to restrain your curiosity to know every detail of his day, even though it is frustrating to be told that he 'can't remember' anything that happened. He will probably tell you a little more in his own time if you don't quiz him too hard and instead try to have an informal chat, perhaps at bathtime or after the story. Don't make the mistake of thinking he is not learning anything if he says that they did nothing but play all day – the reception class is all about learning through play and it does not mean he is not making progress with reading, writing and number work. Of course, it is quite right to be worried and ask to see the teacher if your child seems to have learnt very little even after several months have passed.

As classroom numbers grow, teachers usually welcome parent helpers, although this slightly depends on the policy of the school. Parents can give teachers time to give extra attention where it is needed and it is very pleasant for a mother or father who has time to be able to go in and help out sometimes because it gives them such a clear picture of what the child's life is like at school. In addition the Parent Teacher Association will always welcome enthusiastic newcomers who can help with fundraising.

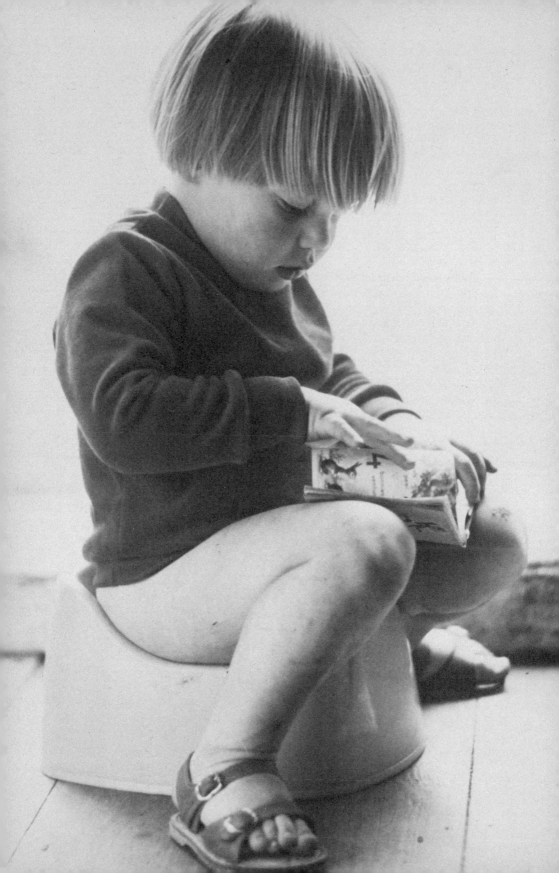

Chapter 13

TOILET TRAINING

Body waste
How do you know when your child is ready to start toilet training?
Early setbacks in toilet training   Potty or lavatory?
Common problems with toilet training   Illness and infection

Understandably, all parents look forward to the day when their child is toilet trained – partly because nobody enjoys dealing with dirty nappies, and partly because it really does seem to signal the end of babyhood. So the day when your child first steps out in a smart pair of pants or knickers (*and is still wearing the same pair at the end of the day!*) is just as big a milestone as when he learns to walk or to talk. Just like those other developmental milestones, there is a wide variation in the age range at which children achieve bowel and bladder control.

Mothers used to spend hours holding their tiny babies over potties. If the baby was regular in passing a bowel motion the mother hoped to strike lucky by providing the potty at the right time and saving a dirty nappy, though of course this did not mean that the child was able to control bladder and bowel movements. There are still some parents who want to start training their babies in the first year by trying to catch regular bowel motions, for example, by potting after meals. If a baby is regular, this may condition him to open his bowels when he sits on the potty, although he still does not have conscious control. The danger of this approach is that when he does learn to understand and control what is happening, in his second and third year, he may decide not to co-operate and you have to start training him all over again. Nowadays, with disposable nappies designed for toddlers making life much easier, most parents prefer to wait until their children show some signs of becoming ready to use the pot or lavatory. But before we embark on the whole subject of how your child learns control, it is useful to know a few of the basic biological facts.

BODY WASTE

The food that healthy people eat is automatically processed by their digestive system. We eat fats, sugars, proteins, carbohydrates, vitamins, minerals, and we drink liquids. These are distributed through the blood-stream to fuel growth and to give us energy to function. But there is some waste matter that the body does not need and this has to be passed out at regular intervals. Liquid waste, urine, is produced by the kidneys and stored in the bladder until a feeling of fullness signals a need to pass urine. It is then passed out through the urinary tract. Solid food is passed from the stomach through the small and the large intestines which are responsible for extracting what the body needs and which then push out the waste through the rectum and its external opening called the anus. Normal people vary in the number of times they need to pass this waste — most urinate several times a day and have a bowel motion from once or twice a day up to every few days. Obviously these functions vary according to what and how much you eat and drink. This may vary depending on the weather (when it is hot you may drink more and excrete more fluid, or if you do not drink, you will sweat more and pass less urine), or on your state of mind (when you are nervous your digestive system becomes more active), or of course when you are ill.

Newborn babies produce and pass this waste automatically and indeed have started doing so in the womb. Although they often seem to know what they are doing — they usually go very quiet or red in the face when passing a motion — they actually have no conscious control over the process. Conscious control means being able to recognise the signs of wanting to empty bowels or bladder, and then waiting until you are in the right place to do so — lavatory or potty — which only comes with age and maturity. It happens because both the parts of the brain and the nervous system supplying the bowel and bladder become more mature. The rate at which this happens is under control of the genes, so it is not surprising that delay in gaining bladder control tends to run in families. Most children are able to achieve this conscious control at some time between eighteen months and three years with a few exceptions either side. Bed wetting at night goes on longer in most children, although a few whose bladders can hold urine for long periods are dry earlier. Wetting at night isn't abnormal in children under five years, although if a child has been dry and then starts wetting again you need to check there is nothing wrong physically or emotionally.

HOW DO YOU KNOW WHEN YOUR CHILD IS READY TO START TOILET TRAINING?

Sometime during his second year your child may give you some clues that he is ready to start learning how to use the potty:

* He may show that he is aware when he passes urine or a bowel motion. For example, he will tell you when he has done something or he will stop what he is doing and look uncomfortable.

* There may be longer intervals between wet nappies so that when you go to change him the nappy is either completely dry or suddenly absolutely soaked through. You may notice he starts being regular with bowel motions, for example, always after breakfast, when he wasn't before.

* He shows an increased interest in passing urine or a motion, for example, looking at it and talking about it.

* He may want to copy other children or parents and may play with the potty, if you keep one around, or play at sitting his toys on the potty or lavatory.

If he does not show any of these signs by the time he is about 20 to 22 months, you can start introducing the idea of the pot yourself. There are all sorts of stylish potties available now, often designed as cars, turtles, and so on, and one with a lid is very handy for travelling. Show him the potty and explain what it is for. It is sometimes a good idea to buy a pair of smart grown-up pants at the same time, for the idea that he is moving on from the baby stage can be especially attractive if your child has older brothers or sisters. However, it is probably a bad idea to start potty training a child just at the time when you are expecting the birth of a new baby, or immediately after the birth, because this is a time when he may want to be babied himself as a reaction. Remember that it is also quite common for toddlers who have been dry for some time to start wetting or soiling again when a new baby arrives. If this does happen, don't get cross and angry, but be patient and prepared for accidents with several spare pants or knickers, or, if necessary, put the child back into nappies for a while. The phase will usually pass if you make sure you give the older child plenty of love and attention at other times. Alternatively, some children become very independent soon after the birth of a baby and start managing to use the potty or go to the toilet by themselves. It is not a good idea to start potty training a toddler around the time when there may be other pressures – for example, if you are moving house, or if either you or he is likely to have to go into hospital shortly, or if you are planning a holiday somewhere where accidents would be a particular problem, like going to stay in the newly carpeted home of friends or relatives!

Probably the best incentive for a toddler to start using the potty or toilet is to see other children slightly older than himself using it. If he has no older brothers or sisters, or you do not know older children who can be invited round and encouraged to demonstrate, then it helps to get some books which show pictures of children using a potty. Let your child sit on the pot with his nappy or pants on – many toddlers feel very insecure about sitting down on what appears to be a seat with a hole in it without nappy or pants, so do not force him. If he wants to play at sitting teddy or dollies on it, that is fine as well. When you think he understands what the potty is for, you can start sitting him on it at regular intervals – shortly after meals is a good time. At first you will probably only catch a 'wee' or a 'poo', or whatever his name is for it, by accident. This is a big milestone, and when it happens you should take the opportunity to praise him, and tell him how clever and grown up he is, and generally make a big fuss of him. It is much easier to potty train a child in fine summer weather because you can let him run around outside with no nappy or pants on and the potty ready to hand. In winter you will have to accept that some accidents are absolutely inevitable, and try the same technique in rooms where you do not value the floor covering too much! It helps if you can have more than one pot around so that there is one in every room where he is likely to need it — perhaps you can borrow one or two from friends. Some people like to give a child a positive reward when he actually manages to produce something in the potty — such as crisps, a piece of apple, or a chocolate button. Usually your praise and a big hug are a child's greatest reward — plus the pride in becoming grown-up — and he does not need any more than this. If he does

not do anything, or does it in his pants soon after he gets off the potty, do not blame, scold or get angry, which will give him the idea that potty training is a big issue and a possible battleground. Instead, just say, 'Never mind, better luck next time', and keep persevering with good humour and plenty of encouragement. Once you have started pot training, as long as you are sure that your child has shown signs of readiness, it is best to keep going and remain consistent despite accidents and setbacks. The very first time you leave the house with your child in a pair of pants or knickers it can feel rather like a trapeze act without a safety net, but be brave — trainer pants with plastic coverings can serve to stem the flood and it helps to have regular potty stops on every outing. Nevertheless, taking several sets of pants, trousers and socks with you is pretty essential in the early stages. Naturally, as soon as he begins to get the hang of using the potty, dressing him in dungarees, trousers with a tight fastening or any other complicated clothes, is out — what you need are fairly baggy tracksuit trousers or dresses which are easy to manage without help. Children of this age do want to learn and to co-operate with parents, despite bouts of awkwardness, so capitalise on this and keep going.

EARLY SETBACKS IN TOILET TRAINING

If the process is very slow or does not happen at all, then ask yourself if perhaps your child is not yet ready — check again that there have been signs of readiness (see page 416). If your child seems to have pain passing urine, if his urine dribbles away rather than passing in a proper stream, or if there is blood in the urine, this may be a sign of an infection (see page 424) or other problem, so you must certainly consult your doctor. Usually children gain control of bowel motions first and take a bit longer to make it to the potty or lavatory every time they want to pass urine. However, some children become dry first and are more reluctant to 'let go' of their bowel motion — they may prefer the safer feeling of performing in their night nappies.

When children begin toilet training and are really ready and able to co-operate, the whole process can be very quick — only a few days for some children. This is much more satisfactory from the parents' point of view than starting much earlier, but taking months or years over the whole process with a great many accidents on the way. Becoming dry at night takes longer, but most children are able to achieve this before they are five and, at most, before they leave the infants' school. About one in ten children are not dry, even by this time, so if your child is one of these, remember there are many others like him. This problem tends to run in families, and is commoner in boys than in girls. It occasionally occurs because the child is upset and cannot get into a routine, or alternatively because the child is generally slow to learn and is showing this in other ways besides being slow to obtain bladder control. Round about the age of five years, or on school entry, it is a good idea to ask for advice from your doctor to see if the process can be speeded up. He may wish to rule out an infection by testing the urine, and will also want to know whether the child is wetting because he is upset — perhaps because there is too much pressure on him to be dry, or for some other reason.

Probably, trying to remain relaxed about the problem and just being confident that eventually, if you don't get too anxious about it, the child will become dry, is the best treatment. However, there is no harm in cutting out a drink before the child goes to sleep, or, for a few days or weeks, waking up the child before you go to sleep yourself and getting him to pass urine. It is important to try not to be angry in the morning after a wet night if you possibly can, as bed wetting really is not the child's fault. Of course it is even more important to show pleasure if the child does have a dry night.

POTTY OR LAVATORY?

Most people find it easier to start their child on a potty as it is more comfortable and feels safer. The lavatory can feel rather insecure and

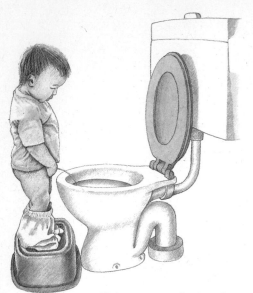

alarming to a small child, and he may be worried by the flushing noise. He can also be encouraged to use a pot himself: as already mentioned, it is a good idea to have more than one around the house. When he becomes confident and reliable he can be introduced to the lavatory, either sitting on a special child seat or, in the case of boys, standing on a step. Boys can be encouraged to urinate in the potty standing up from the start, but don't worry if he'd rather sit down. If father or an older brother will do a bit of demonstrating he will soon get the idea of standing up to do a wee! Remember that all children are different – while some toddlers accept the whole idea very readily and are quickly dry with scarcely an accident, for others it takes a lot longer.

Using strange lavatories can sometimes be a problem, so if your child is worried about passing urine at playgroup or nursery school, explain or write to the teachers so that they can help to reassure him.

COMMON PROBLEMS WITH TOILET TRAINING

CONSTIPATION

Constipation is actually a common problem in young children but it is not always recognised. Constipation means an abnormal amount of waste matter has built up in the lower bowel which then becomes so hard and uncomfortable the child is afraid or unable to pass it. Once a child has had pain or difficulty passing a bowel motion, he is more likely to hang on to subsequent bowel motions and this vicious circle makes constipation yet more likely.

What causes constipation in the first place? It can be a poor diet with too many bland, sweet and fatty foods and not enough roughage. It can also occur after an illness; it may follow a bout of diarrhoea in which the child has been deliberately holding on to the motions. Sometimes a hard motion can cause a crack in the anus – if you see little specks of blood in the stool it may come from such a crack. The pain of this can make the child want to hang on to his bowel motions.

Constipation can also result from over-enthusiastic toilet training by parents. If you put too much pressure on a child to perform in the potty, he can deliberately choose not to do so to thwart you when he is angry.

Inconsistent toilet training, when it is not clear to the child what he is expected to do, can have the same result. Sometimes a child just isn't ready and you need to let up in your demands a little and not worry about accidents.

Mild or occasional constipation can be put right by stepping up the amount of roughage in the diet and giving more fluids, particularly drinks like prune juice. Some doctors may prescribe laxatives; others may not be happy about giving them regularly as the bowel needs to be encouraged to make its own muscular efforts to expel waste, and laxatives can make the passage of the waste too easy. If your child is prone to occasional bouts of constipation, make sure his regular diet has a lot of wholegrain bread, cereals, fresh fruit and vegetables in it. You should also encourage him to go to the lavatory regularly. Be careful not to be too insistent about this, though, as it can increase his anxiety. Reward him when he does go. With a child who is having problems, an external reward is sometimes necessary. A child old enough to understand such a system can have a chart with stars for success on it. Children who are too small to understand a chart can just be given praise or a little treat every time they sit on the lavatory or pot and try to pass a motion, until the habit is established.

Untreated constipation can go on for weeks and become a serious physical and emotional problem. When this happens the child becomes completely incapable of opening his bowels because the muscles have become overstretched and will not work to push out waste. The sensation of wanting to pass a motion may be lost as a result. Liquid waste matter may dribble out from around the hard mass in his system; this may look like diarrhoea but is in fact due to constipation. It is very distressing for the child because he cannot help it, and yet may be scolded by parents and teased by other children. If your child is soiling his pants in this way, think back to what his bowel habits have been in the past. Busy parents may not notice a child has not passed a motion for a while.

When constipation gets to this chronic stage medical treatment is needed. Laxatives may work or the child may need admission to hospital so that the waste can be removed manually or with an enema. Ideally the child should be kept in hospital — along with a parent — so that he can be retrained in healthier bowel habits. Fortunately, the stretched muscles do recover their elasticity and can be retrained to work normally.

BOWEL MOTIONS – IN THE WRONG PLACE

Sometimes children who have no physical problems with their bowel motions deliberately pass them in their pants or on the floor, although they are quite capable of getting to the potty or lavatory. This condition (the medical name is encopresis) happens in children who are old enough to be toilet trained and know the difference between the right and wrong place to go.

It does *not* apply to young toddlers in their early stages of toilet training — who often go and hide behind the sofa or at the end of the

garden when they are passing a bowel motion. Do not get angry when this happens because what the young toddler needs is understanding, sympathy and patience from you. Some children feel very vulnerable when sitting on the potty to pass a bowel motion and ensuring that they have secure privacy is often a great help. You could put the potty behind the sofa or let the child sit on it alone in the bathroom – making sure of course that he cannot lock himself in! Soiling is a very common problem in young children and there is nothing shameful about it – so don't make the child feel ashamed as this will make the problem worse.

In an older child, passing a bowel motion deliberately in the wrong place is sometimes a sign that the child is disturbed or unhappy about something, or he may be wanting to get his own back on you if you have been scolding or punishing him. Alternatively, he may simply be teasing you to see if you rise to the bait. Annoying and worrying though this may be, it is important *not* to rise, but to stay as cool and unconcerned as possible, pointing out that the floor is not the right place to put bowel motions and encouraging and rewarding him when he does go in the right place.

If your child starts doing this regularly – having been toilet trained previously – think whether anything could have upset him recently. A big change in his life such as the arrival of a new baby, separation from one of his parents, a spell in hospital or other upset can produce this reaction. If you cannot work it out or you feel you cannot cope with this behaviour, do seek help from your health visitor or doctor – referral to a child guidance clinic or psychiatric department may be necessary on rare occasions.

TODDLER DIARRHOEA

Some one- to four-year-olds, particularly boys, can have bouts of very loose stools for a few days. The loose stools may contain bits of undigested food. The condition passes, stools are normal for a while, and then there is another bout of looseness. It is probably caused by the intestinal muscles being over-active, perhaps because the nerves which supply them are not working properly, and the food gets hurried through without being fully absorbed. The condition is not dangerous, though it sometimes occurs when the child is under stress. It passes with age, so if your doctor can find no other symptom of illness don't worry about it. Just be sure to remind the child to go to the lavatory regularly so that he does not have an accident. If he does have an accident, be reassuring and sympathetic because it can be very upsetting for him – particularly if it happens somewhere like playgroup.

ACCIDENTAL WETTING

When a child has been dry for a while and starts wetting again, this is usually because the habit of being dry has not been very well established in the first place, and something has happened to upset the child's routine. He may have had flu or one of the infectious illnesses of childhood, such as chicken-pox. Alternatively, some upsetting event – a period in hospital, a parent being away from home, or the birth of a younger brother or sister – may have occurred. Occasionally a recurrence of wetting may be due to an infection – this is a possibility if the child has pain passing urine, if the urine is cloudy, smelly, has blood in it, is passed more frequently, or if your child dribbles urine after passing it in a proper stream. If you notice any of these symptoms, you should consult your doctor. Accidental wetting after a period of dryness can be annoying both to you and the child, but it will usually stop after a few days or weeks. Just use the techniques you worked out to help the child become dry in the first place. If it persists beyond a few weeks, but the child has been dry previously, you should talk to your health visitor or doctor.

ILLNESS AND INFECTION

GASTRIC INFECTIONS

As most parents quickly learn, stomach bugs are common – few children reach school age without having had at least one bout of sickness and/or diarrhoea. The cause is either a virus or bacteria in the intestine, and mild cases usually cure themselves. Children do not usually want to eat when they have a tummy bug, but they should be given plenty of fluids as the biggest danger of gastric infection is dehydration – the smaller the child, the greater the risk.

Mothers of breastfed babies sometimes worry that their babies have diarrhoea because the normal stool is so liquid, can be very frequent, and often seems to come out in a great explosion! But as long as the motion is the usual yellow colour and there are no other signs of illness, there is no need to worry. A continuing change in the colour and the consistency of the bowel motion could be a sign of illness and should always be checked with your doctor.

Once children are old enough to be having solid food, there is usually no doubt about when they have diarrhoea. The first signs of a gastric infection are vomiting or stomach pains and/or diarrhoea – loose, watery stools that will look and smell differently from normal stools.

A child who is being sick and has diarrhoea can easily lose too much fluid and become dehydrated. These are the warning signs:

* No urine is passed.

* The eyes become sunken.

* Skin loses its elasticity.

* The child becomes floppy.

* Rapid breathing with a dry tongue.

* Rapid pulse rate.

* In a young baby the fontanelle or 'soft spot' on his head will be sunken.

Because dehydration can develop so rapidly, a child with these signs will almost certainly need to be taken to hospital. There they will be able to replace the fluids, sometimes through giving drinks, but in some cases a drip may have to be inserted into a vein.

Breastfeeding helps to protect babies against gastric illness and if your breastfed baby does catch such an infection breast milk will help his recovery. (For advice on treatment see page 582).

However, a regular routine of washing hands after handling nappies or going to the toilet, and before handling any food docs help to prevent the likelihood of such infection and stop it from spreading. As children grow, it is useful to get them into the handwashing habit as well.

URINARY INFECTIONS

One cause of wetting, particularly in girls, is an infection in the urinary tract or bladder. If your daughter starts wetting her pants when she has been dry, check with your doctor for the presence of an infection. A sample of the urine will need to be tested. Other signs of such infection are smelly urine, complaints of pain when passing urine, dribbling urine rather than passing it in a stream, and general symptoms of ill health, such as loss of appetite and vomiting. Abdominal pain and vomiting may also be caused by an infection in the urine. If you have any reason to suspect that your child is particularly prone to urinary infections, you should see your GP who may refer your child to hospital for a special X-ray. Continual bouts of infection can be a sign of an underlying abnormality such as vesico-ureteric reflux. This means that some urine is not passed out of the body but goes back from the bladder into the kidneys. If this is not diagnosed and treated it can cause damage to the kidneys. Fortunately, once it is detected this condition can be treated with antibiotics or by surgery. Your child will be taught how to empty the bladder completely and to drink plenty of fluids.

You can help your child to avoid the chance of infection by encouraging her to pass urine regularly and to make sure the bladder is really empty. Try not to let your child get constipated since this may interfere with bladder emptying and can increase the chance of bladder infection. Nylon underwear is best avoided, as it may cause soreness and predispose to infection. Let your child have plenty to drink.

SERIOUS KIDNEY DISEASE

The kidneys are vital in getting rid of waste from the body, so if they stop working or are seriously damaged a person cannot survive. Nowadays many people with kidneys that do not work can be helped by transplants or by having regular dialysis – a machine artificially does the work of the kidneys in cleaning the bloodstream.

Signs of kidney disease include slow growth or failure to grow well, being very thirsty (especially at night), and passing much more or much less urine than normal. Blood in the urine, frothy urine or swelling of the child's eyelids and feet (due to a build-up of fluid in the body) are all signs that the kidneys may not be working properly. Such symptoms need careful specialist investigation and hospital treatment. In fact, complete kidney failure is very rare and most of these illnesses can be medically treated.

CONGENITAL DISORDERS

The earlier in life that symptoms of gastric or urinary illness show themselves, the more likely it is that there may be some underlying disorder that the baby has been born with.

The first bowel motion normally passed by a new baby is called 'meconium' and looks black and sticky. After a day or so the baby's bowel motions change to the normal colour and texture according to how he is being fed. Breastfed babies have soft, sometimes almost liquid stools which are bright mustard-yellow. They can be very frequent – every nappy change – or, particularly as the baby gets older, only every few days. In a breastfed baby this does not mean constipation. The bottle-fed baby's bowel motions are paler, firmer and smell slightly unpleasant. A bottle-fed baby may become constipated, or the stools may become harder, and the baby shows signs of straining and discomfort. In this case, check that you are making up the feed absolutely correctly and try to give the baby more water or fruit juice in between feeds.

If the new baby's bowel motions do not show normal patterns, this could be a sign that something is wrong with the bowels or digestive system. A baby who does not pass meconium in the first twenty-four hours may have a condition that prevents his bowel muscles working properly which needs putting right with an operation. Some babies are born with blockages in their intestines, and these too can be operated on. Some babies have the opposite problem and have a condition which gives them continual diarrhoea. Because they are losing too much fluid and too many essential chemicals from their bodies, they need to have these substances replaced by a drip into their veins as well as normal feeding. However, once they are past the first few vulnerable weeks these babies can grow up normally and live with their condition, provided they are careful to drink enough and follow the instructions of the doctor and dietitian about diet.

Babies can be born with urinary problems too. Boys in particular can sometimes have an extra valve in their urethra (the tube leading from the bladder to the opening at the tip of the penis) which prevents them from passing urine properly. If urine in the newborn baby boy only dribbles out instead of shooting out in a stream, it may be a sign of this condition, which can be corrected with an operation. Babies can sometimes get urinary infections which show themselves through strong-smelling urine, apparent discomfort when wetting, and other signs of illness such as vomiting and being generally off their feeds. Continual infections could mean that there is an underlying abnormality which causes some urine to go back from the bladder into the kidneys instead of being passed out of the body – this is called vesico-ureteric reflux (see page 425). It is important that this is diagnosed and treated as early as possible. Urinary infections are much more common in girls, so if you are at all worried about your daughter or if she seems ill for no other apparent reason, it is important to have her checked for underlying problems.

The most common of the serious inherited illnesses (that is a disease which is passed on through the genes) is one that also affects the digestive system: cystic fibrosis. This affects the pancreas and prevents the body from absorbing fat. It also affects the lungs by making the mucus which is normally present in them very thick and difficult to cough up. Fibrocystic babies are very sweaty, have large amounts of salt in their sweat and have very offensive-smelling bowel motions. The disease can be controlled in childhood by special diets, physiotherapy and courses of antibiotics. For more on cystic fibrosis see page 619.

Chapter 14

RELATIONSHIPS

Your baby   How your baby learns   You and your baby
Separation   Leaving your baby   Your baby and other people
Social problems   Aggression   Sharing
Good behaviour   Fears
Going back to work – who minds the baby?
Communicating with children – marriage difficulties, separation and
divorce, death, illness and handicap, religion, sex

'When I have my baby I shall feed her whenever she cries. You have to organise your life round the baby, don't you? You have to meet their needs.'

'I am very worried about spoiling the baby. I don't want to give in to every demand. That would be bad for him, wouldn't it? I want to still be able to carry on with my life and the baby will have to learn to fit in.'

These are two mothers-to-be talking in an antenatal class before the birth of their first babies. Both are already thinking ahead to how their babies are going to become part of their lives and using words like 'organise' and 'fit in'. They already see their babies as people who have needs, who can be upset, who can be spoilt. All expectant parents have these sorts of ideas about their babies, while parents who have already had children may base their expectations on the children or the child they already have. In fact the baby always seems to turn out at least a little different from the one that was imagined, and parents also often behave in ways they would not have predicted for themselves. How will you adjust to each other?

YOUR BABY

A baby arrives in this world with certain features that parents often interpret at once as a personality. He may be a large baby who sucks strongly and yells loudly for feeds. 'He's quite a pig,' you'll say affectionately. 'He doesn't like to be kept waiting, he's got a will of his own.' Another baby may be very calm and placid, with slow movements and a deliberate way of doing things. You will adjust your own movements to his, speaking slowly and softly. 'He's so calm,' you'll say. 'He's as good as gold.'

You can probably think for yourself of hundreds of other examples of the ways in which parents attribute personality characteristics to babies. If

429

you do not yet have a baby, you will probably think these people are quite mad – all new babies seem to look the same. But they are not, they do have their own ways of looking and behaving and these influence in turn how people around them treat them. Thus your baby will contribute just as much to his own upbringing as you do.

As well as the way your baby behaves and reacts, physical factors make a difference – the sex and size of the baby, for example. A tiny, weak baby will arouse more protective feelings than a big healthy one and will also need much more physical attention. The position in the family can make a difference to the sort of person he is going to become, and so can the fact that he has an older brother rather than an older sister, or vice versa. Many factors contribute to mould and form a baby's personality and the way he relates to other people. But just as there are various recognisable stages in his physical development so there are certain stages of becoming sociable that all babies go through, although at different rates and with their own individual ways of doing things.

The table shows your baby's social development in the first five years:

HOW YOUR BABY LEARNS

BABY'S AGE	WHAT HE CAN DO	WHAT YOU DO
Birth to 4 weeks onwards	Hear and respond to voices, turn towards them. Show signs of recognising you. Respond to touching and being picked up. Move in rhythm with you and your voice. Cry.	Respond to crying, pick him up, talk and sing, exchange long looks with him, feed, clean, clothe and become confident in handling him.
4 – 6 weeks onwards	First smile – a genuine, pleasurable reaction to your face or voice.	Talk and smile back to him, which encourages more smiling.
6 – 12 weeks onwards	The first laughs. Noises and gurgles other than crying. Beginning to enjoy play, e.g. in the bath; activities such as splashing, tickling and hearing songs.	Respond in the same way. Talk back to the baby as if his noises meant something. Give opportunities for play – splashing him, rocking and so on.
	Can grasp something put in his hand; turn his head to interesting noises and objects, but not yet with accurate focus.	Give him things of different textures to hold, different shapes, colours, noises to look at and listen to.
	Can wait for feeds. Is awake for longer without crying.	Life becomes more predictable, and you may feel more relaxed.

BABY'S AGE	WHAT HE CAN DO	WHAT YOU DO
4 – 6 months onwards	He can use his eyes and control movements to reach for things and focus attention. He will be showing pleasure in you with special smiles, reaching out to you.	You may be pointing things out, watching to see when he learns to follow where you are pointing – a big step. You will learn to recognise more the type of baby you have – if he likes company try to provide it, if he is wary do not force him to go to other people.
	Solids introduced – this means he can join in mealtimes, a real social occasion.	Other people can now feed your baby if he has been breastfed. Take care not to start fighting over food. Early solids often introduced, but not vital nutritionally yet.
6 – 9 months onwards	Begins to show wariness of strangers. On the move – perhaps crawling; probably rolling towards things and people. Enjoys games like peekaboo, which shows he realises people are still there even when out of sight. Laughs in response to play. Will give you things as well as take them. May become more clingy, protesting when you leave the room.	You have to be much more vigilant and make the home safe. More playthings needed and more mess will be made. More impact on your life now. You can make up games to play which will test skills such as crawling after an out-of-reach ball. You may have to take a clingy child everywhere with you at this stage and your life may seem very baby-dominated.
9 – 12 months onwards	Babbling begins to turn to word-like sounds such as 'mama' or 'baba'. Understanding of what you say: 'Where's Daddy?' will make him look round. Will imitate your actions, become more adventurous and need more supervision.	Respond to early word sounds and encourage by repeating and saying the things that have caught your baby's attention. You may find you have to start checking him, and the word 'no' will enter both your vocabularies – yours first and then his!

431

BABY'S AGE	WHAT HE CAN DO	WHAT YOU DO
12 – 18 months onwards	First words will come soon. He can feed himself if allowed to, holding his own cup and spoon. Will probably be weaned from breast and perhaps bottle. He will understand much of what you say and may do things for you, for example, he will 'go and get the cup' for you. Can wave bye-bye and perhaps hug and kiss you.	When language comes you will begin to hold conversations. Your baby will also delight other people at this stage as they can enjoy talking to him and getting answers. Weaning may have made you sad, but independence gives new pleasures. He can also amuse himself more and do more things for himself so you feel freer.
18 – 24 months onwards	Tantrums and refusals may start now. He develops a will of his own. May be destructive or aggressive but there are compensations. Chat is developing fast and toilet training may begin.	A lot of patience needed now, and recognition that this is a phase that will pass. Other people can be a great help, so cultivate them. Positive achievements in language or first use of potty may emerge.
2 years onwards	Tantrums and arguments may continue, but he becomes more competent at everything now and you can distract him by giving him new things to play with. Talking is becoming more like yours, short sentences and connected conversations. He can answer questions and follow instructions and give his own. Fantasy play with dolls, models and household objects. He imitates you and helps with chores. Begins to understand others' point of view, e.g. in stories and through sympathy for other people. Can play with another child for short periods.	You will be helping him to do more in the way of taking care of himself by now as he will be able to feed himself, perhaps help to dress himself, amuse himself and make more of his own decisions. Try to find ways of sharing pleasant activities together – conversations, books, outings, visits to friends. Treat him as a person living in your house and not just a baby under your control. You will certainly need a break from him from time to time.

BABY'S AGE	WHAT HE CAN DO	WHAT YOU DO
3 years onwards	Still needs help with some things, but has at least the beginnings of the social skills that you have, for example, conversation, doing things with others, helping, hindering, deciding, and organising. May be able to be away from you at playgroup or nursery.	The range of toys, books and play activities you can give are as great now as they will ever be. He still enjoys baby toys, but also skilful ones and playing with other children. You may have another baby by now, but do not try to force independence too early.
4 – 5 years	He can probably be independent for a part of each day and will do most things for himself, although coat buttons and shoe fastenings still need help. He will be able to go to the toilet by himself, may be able to tidy his own things away, partly depending on your help and attitude in this respect. His language is almost as articulate as yours although the number of words he knows is still less. He will choose his own friends, maybe become more attached to another grown-up such as a teacher than he sometimes seems to you. In a safe setting he can even take simple responsibilities like running an errand – his memory and sense of responsibility will be good enough. He will be ready for school and the start of his own 'career'.	You will be handing him over to other people on a much more regular basis. Teachers and playgroup leaders are not substitutes for you; they are part of his life and they will be *his* grown-up friends, not yours. The same is true of friends he chooses at nursery school or school. He is much less work for you now and more of a companion, but he will still need babying sometimes, especially if he is ill or sad, and he may still have moods and tantrums.

Note: There are wide variations in the rates at which children achieve these abilities, but parents should be concerned and consult their health visitor or doctor if their children are definitely behindhand.

YOU AND YOUR BABY

ADJUSTING TO MOTHERHOOD

However much you have wanted one, there may be times after the birth when you feel completely overwhelmed by the responsibility of caring for a helpless little baby. However equal a mother's relationship with her partner, the change in her life is still greater because carrying the baby in pregnancy, giving birth and suckling at the breast *do* give you a special relationship with your baby when he is first born. Physically mother and baby are often very wrapped up in each other. Because mothers have undergone the most change, their difficulties in adjusting to having a baby may be greater. But don't be dismayed – there are qualities in both babies and mothers which help with this adjustment.

Anyone watching parents in different delivery rooms with their new-born babies would be struck by the similarity with which they often behave. They keep saying 'hello' to the baby and then go on to talk about the way he looks and whether he has got his father's nose or eyes. Straight away parents begin treating their baby as part of the family and as a person – although the baby cannot answer back yet. New babies can answer you in other ways, though. It is now recognised that parents need to spend time with their new babies, and that babies should not be taken away immediately and put in a nursery. When you are able to lie next to your new baby, to pick him up, to watch him and talk to him, you will soon notice that he responds to you in all sorts of special ways. He will gaze steadily into your eyes, react to the sound of your voice and stop crying when you pick him up. When you feed him you will gradually develop a pattern of feeding that allows you time to rest and talk. You will learn to know from the faces he pulls, or the way he draws up his legs, or the sound of his cry, whether he has got wind, or is about to start yelling, or is just about to drop off to sleep. Most mothers-to-be worry about whether they will know what to do with their babies: 'How will I know if he's hungry?' 'How will I know if he's just tired and about to drop off to sleep?' In fact most mothers do know and they learn surprisingly quickly how to read their own baby's signals and tune in to them. A new baby means lots more hard work, broken nights and a big change in lifestyle, but being sensitive to your baby's needs and meeting them half-way cuts the stress in this early period. There will be time enough later on for your baby to have to learn to wait and to fit in with others as inevitably he will.

A happy, mutual understanding between mothers and their babies often takes time to develop, though. Most healthy mothers and their babies have begun to be sensitive to each other and pick up each other's signals by the time they are discharged from maternity care. However, even when things have been going well there will always be times when the baby starts behaving differently – for instance, suddenly wanting to be fed every two hours again just when you thought you had got a bit more organised (see

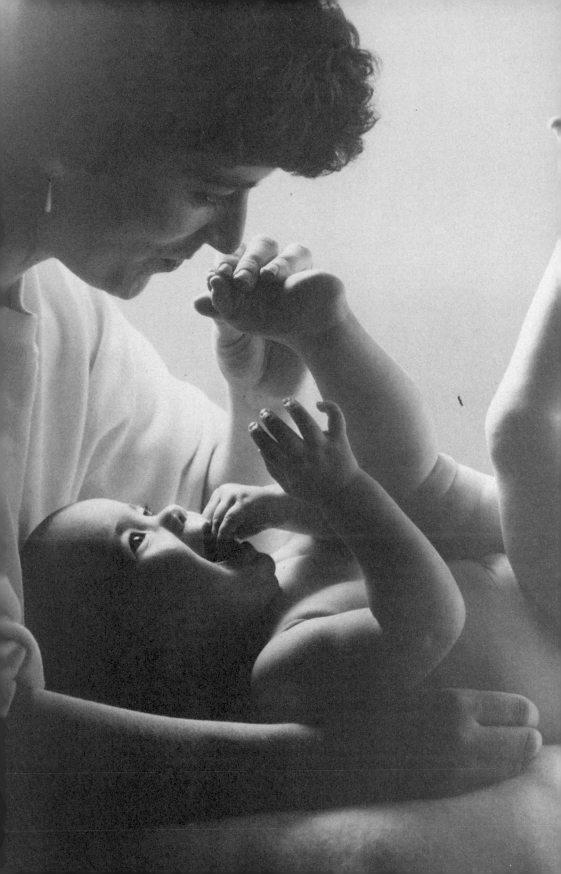

page 216). Further, there will be times when it is difficult to be responsive to your baby's signals – if you are tired, depressed, preoccupied, ill or have sore stitches just after the birth. Babies are very sensitive and quick to pick up what is happening around them and often become more demanding just at the time when you are least able to cope.

What do you do when the baby is screaming for no apparent reason and you are feeling low yourself? The first thing to remember is that you are *not* failing as a mother by asking other people to take over now and again. Even if you are breastfeeding, the baby's father, grandmother or a friend can bring the baby to you for a feed and then take him away afterwards to rock him, play with him or take him out for a walk. Don't fight shy of willing offers to help if you feel in need of a break just because you are worried someone else will take over your special role with your baby.

SEPARATION

Sometimes it is not possible for mother and baby to be together immediately after the birth. This may be because your baby has to go to special or intensive care (see chapter 5), and even if you are well enough to be able to go and visit the unit you may not be able to pick up your baby or cuddle him straight away because of life-support machinery and equipment. Obviously this will make it more difficult for you and your baby to get to know each other in the first hours or days, and when you do have him to yourself at last you may have to work hard to try to understand his signals and needs. He may be a difficult baby and need a lot of patience, but it is important to know that such difficulties are usually overcome and good relationships established.

There may be other separations in your child's life later – for example, you or he might have to go into hospital for a few days. You may have to go away for a short time, or he may be going to stay with relatives or friends. Perhaps you are going back to a part-time or full-time job soon after the birth. All mothers, whether they work or not, need to have some time away from their babies. It may be simply a shopping trip, a chance to read a book, or an opportunity to take an older child to the cinema or swimming pool.

A great deal has been written about 'bonding' – the way in which a close relationship between you and your baby is formed in the early days – but bonding is certainly not affected by successful separations from your child. What is a successful separation? It is one where both parties – child and parent – feel secure and are not upset. Obviously a great deal depends on the reason for the separation. A day spent with a grandmother the child knows well is quite different from a child suddenly being rushed into hospital with awful pain and being left among white-coated strangers. If separation is linked with pain, illness and fear then of course it will be distressing and upsetting to the child. This is why it is always a good idea to try to stay with your child in hospital as much as you can – for more on this see chapter 20. Nevertheless, giving your child secure, happy experiences of being away from you, such as regular outings with grandparents or occasional afternoons with a friend, is important for both of you and will stand you in good stead as preparation if you should be unlucky enough to have to be separated in the event of an emergency.

How can you tell if arrangements for leaving your child are successful? After all, a baby cannot tell you what happens when you are not there. In deciding this your instinct and common sense should go hand in hand. Is the person with whom you have left your baby someone you trust, who understands how to look after him and is physically able to do so? Did they pay attention and ask questions when you were telling them about your baby's routine? Be slightly wary of the person who brushes aside details of your baby's likes and dislikes with a cheery, 'Don't worry. We'll be fine.' Are you happy that your baby will be safe where you have left him? First-time mothers who are not used to the curious and boisterous ways of toddlers can be horrified at the thought of an eighteen-month-old let loose anywhere near their tiny newborn baby, and the friend who takes the trouble to reassure you that she *will* make sure her own children do not take liberties with your baby is a good friend.

Do not forget that grandmothers and friends with older children may not have homes that are geared to crawling babies or lively toddlers, so do not be afraid to remind them tactfully about the dangers of trailing kettle leads, low level glass and china ornaments and electrical sockets, and bring your own stair-gate for them to use. Again, it is reassuring if they have already thought of all these things in advance. Some people may be fine for looking after your child for an hour or two while you go shopping but not suitable to leave him with all day. For example, another mother who already has a baby herself as well as a toddler just simply will not have the time and energy for another baby on a regular basis, however willing she may be. Grandparents who may have adored sitting cooing and chatting to a new baby may find a lively toddler just too taxing, but may not want to admit it.

There is more about leaving your baby with someone else while you go back to work on page 462, but in general any separation from your baby will be much more successful if the person who looks after him is loving and familiar and makes sure that your child has a good time with them. It is also potentially damaging if a child is switched from one person to another and never has the chance to build up a permanent long-term relationship with any one person. This may happen not only with children in institutional or foster care but also in a family situation. In some disturbed or disorganised families a child can be handed from one person to another and never really gets the chance to attach himself to anyone in particular.

LEAVING YOUR BABY

Sometimes a mother can feel very unsure about leaving her baby, even when she wants time to herself and knows that the person she is leaving him with is trustworthy and loving. Anxieties about leaving your baby may hark back to your own, unhappy separations in childhood. These feelings may also be caused by guilt instilled by other members of the family or friends – perhaps your mother-in-law thinks you should not have a part-time job, or a close friend has told you she does not think the crèche at your local keep-fit class is a very good place to leave a small baby. First-time mothers who do not have a wealth of experience to fall back on can be easily unsettled by casual remarks!

Whatever the reason, it helps to remember that babies are like blotting paper, tremendously good at soaking up your feelings. Hovering around anxiously, making too much of saying goodbye and generally behaving in an over-anxious, out-of-character way when you leave will immediately give your child all the clues he needs to become clinging and anxious in return. A mother confident of leaving her baby is more likely to have a baby confident of leaving her.

Allow yourself time to separate, so that you do not just dump your baby and rush off, but make sure, when you first begin to separate, that he is properly settled and that the person looking after him has everything needed and knows what stage the baby has got to in his day with sleeps, feeds, etc. Always make a point of actually saying goodbye and telling your baby where you are going and that you will be back soon. This may seem silly with a very tiny baby who will not understand your words, but children very quickly do get to understand your feelings, both from the tone of your voice and your actions as well as your actual words. Do not linger too long over saying goodbye – a quick cuddle, a kiss and 'Bye-bye, Mummy's going out now but she will be back soon' is fine. Do not try to force children into waving bye-bye or make the whole ritual unnecessarily drawn out and long as this is much more likely to prompt tears.

When your child enters the phase when he is more sensitive about your absences and may become clingy and cry when you leave, usually between six and eighteen months, do not be tempted to slink out secretly without saying goodbye because you are afraid of a scene. Again, your anxiety fuels his. Sensitive caretakers will have a distraction ready on hand such as a game, a drink or something really fascinating and new to look at such as their cat or a pretty flower in the garden. If saying goodbye does get hard, then talk about the routine with the person who is going to look after your child and suggest ways that the child can be cheered up and distracted once you have gone. If you just suddenly vanish without telling your child you are going, you will make him much more anxious. Children will also be fearful and less trusting in other situations, for example, when you are visiting friends or going to the toddler club, because they think that you may suddenly vanish again. They may also spend a great deal of their time while you are away looking for you in the house.

It can be just as upsetting if there are tears again when you return. This does not mean your child has had a bad time. You can tell this yourself when you come upon a peaceful, happy scene, with your child

439

sitting in his pram or being amused on the floor, but then suddenly he looks up to see you and his face crumples into tears. Try not to allow reunions to become too emotional – snatching up a baby, hugging and kissing him and clinging to him is going to make your child think his experience was much worse than it really was. By all means pick him up and cuddle him, but then make a point of letting him get on with some activity while you chat to the person who has been looking after him. This changeover time where the child has both of you sitting there is quite important as it takes the emphasis off the fact that you go and come when the other person is present and makes for a more normal, everyday atmosphere for the child. You will also want to know how your child has been behaving and how he and the caretaker have got on together in your absence. A good caretaker will tell you exactly what has been happening and how long your child was distressed after you left and not try to pretend that everything has been straightforward when this has not been the case.

Always give the person who has been looking after your baby a good idea how long you will be away and come back at the time you said. Leave a phone number whenever possible or the phone number of a relative, your partner, or someone else to be contacted in an emergency if you are leaving for more than a couple of hours. Make sure there is a good supply of bottles, and in the case of breastfed babies express the milk and leave it in a bottle, or leave a bottle of fruit juice or some food if the baby is more than about four months old.

YOUR BABY AND OTHER PEOPLE

The intense feelings a mother has for the little creature to whom she has given birth can be overwhelming. This is just as true (sometimes even more so) for mothers who give up their babies to be brought up by adoptive parents as for mothers who have difficulties with their babies, who may sometimes even hate and abuse them. A baby arouses *very* strong emotions in his mother, but other people besides his natural mother can become very attached to him too. Adoptive parents are an obvious example, and other people in the family and amongst your circle of friends and acquaintances will form relationships with him as well. From the baby's point of view, the person he feels closest to is the person who cares for him, talks to him, loves him and remains constant through his life. This person may not be his natural mother. Although babies and children can have happy relationships with several other people it does seem to be important for their well-being and security as they grow up that they have at least one constant, loving person in their lives who does not go away or abandon them. This 'mothering' relationship is a foundation for good relationships with other people. In practice it is usually provided by the child's own mother, but we turn now to some of the other people in the life of a small child.

FATHERS

Most fathers are present at the birth of their babies nowadays – a survey in 1986 showed that over 90% of births in the UK had fathers present. Even as recently as ten years ago this figure would never have been reached, but it is now accepted by professionals that *both* parents may want to be involved in the birth of their baby and the preparation for it. Fathers are invited to antenatal classes; they may shop for baby clothes, read baby books and feel more free to talk amongst themselves about the pros and cons of natural childbirth or epidural anaesthetic.

If you are a father reading this, how important do you think you are to the well-being of your child? And what can you do in practical terms to bring him up? There is plenty of evidence to suggest that children from homes where there is no father can be at a disadvantage, although for single mothers reading this it should be remembered that these disadvantages are not only due to the absence of the father. Families with only one parent often face financial difficulties: financial security coming from at least one wage-earner, and a mother who feels supported, both financially and emotionally, is obviously going to be better for the children.

A father also provides a masculine example for his children – a man for his son to model himself on and for his daughter to begin to learn about the opposite sex. At certain times most children prefer the company of their fathers to that of their mothers. As a child gets older, he may be the person who is sought out to dry tears or 'mend' the cut knee. This may be especially true when a second baby comes along and fathers can do a great deal to help an older child come to terms with not being the baby of the family any more, especially if he has built up a good relationship beforehand. Mothers cannot do everything and be everywhere, particularly when there is more than one child in the family. Children suffer if their mothers are depressed, overworked or feel isolated, so this is another important reason for fathers to share child care from the beginning.

There is evidence that children do better at school when their fathers take a close interest in what they do, and this is especially true of boys. However, fathers cannot expect to become involved in their children's lives suddenly when they start school or when they become teenagers if they have not been involved in the early years. Fathers do need to start getting to know their children and to read their signals right from birth, just as mothers do. Of course, this is all to the child's advantage, but it can also be to yours. There are many rewards for the father who looks after his baby and small child. Those first beaming smiles, first brief sentence – 'Daddy kiss' – the triumph as your toddler struggles to his feet and stands on them for a few seconds are just as exciting for fathers as they are for mothers. It may be harder for men to express these feelings, but far more men now talk amongst themselves about how their baby is gaining weight or cutting first teeth.

Feeling left out Because they are often the main wage-earners, fathers can sometimes feel left out after the birth of a baby, both in their relationship with their partners and in their relationship with their children. Mother and baby may seem locked into a perfect mutual understanding and the father does not quite know where he is supposed to fit in. One important issue which highlights this is breastfeeding. When a mother breastfeeds her baby she is actually physically joined to the baby in the most intimate way. If her partner feels strongly about this it may have something to do with the way he regards her sexually, perhaps feeling possessive about her body or breasts. But many men do not feel excluded in quite such a personal or physical sense, just a little superfluous to the whole exercise.

However, although feeding is a very important part of caring for a baby in the early stages, there are many other things fathers can do for their babies. It is also worth remembering that many mothers lack confidence when they are breastfeeding their first (and sometimes later) babies and need the father's support and encouragement.

Sharing the workload Because babies increase the workload of the household all round, fathers will be needed to do their share of other chores. This is even more necessary if the mother works or when a second or subsequent baby arrives. This should not be a matter of father 'helping', but of sharing the workload fairly. If practical arrangements have to be made for substitute child care, assistance in the house or babysitting, it will be a contribution if the father takes some responsibility for these too. Below is a list of some of the regular things (as distinct from occasional things such as decorating) that fathers need to think about when having a baby, a young child or more than one child. Look through it with your partner and see how many each of you does or shares responsibility for.

Mark each box with your initials and at the end tot up to see how many jobs are shared or fall to one person and if so to whom.

If one of you is doing nearly everything on this list, perhaps you should

CARE OF HOME		CARE OF BABY		FINANCIAL AND PRACTICAL RESPON-SIBILITIES	
Shopping	☐	Feeding	☐	Wage earning	☐
Preparing food	☐	Changing	☐	Paying household bills	☐
Cooking	☐	Bathing	☐	Paying other bills	☐
Washing up	☐	Dressing	☐	Arranging babysitters	☐
Cleaning kitchen floor	☐	Taking to clinic	☐	Babysitting yourself	☐
Hoovering	☐	Taking to doctor	☐	Inviting friends' children to play	☐
Dusting	☐	Making up bottles (if applicable)	☐	Cooking tea for friends' children and own	☐
Putting rubbish out	☐	Putting to bed	☐	Other family responsibilities (e.g. elderly relatives)	☐
Laundry	☐	Playing with	☐		
Ironing	☐	CARE OF OLDER CHILDREN		Choosing childminder/ childcare arrangement	☐
Sorting children's clothes	☐	Taking to/collecting from playgroup/ nursery school	☐		
		Reading stories	☐		
		Listening to children read	☐	Paying childminder	☐

443

CARE OF HOME	CARE OF BABY	FINANCIAL AND PRACTICAL RESPON-SIBILITIES	
	Attending playgroup /school special events ☐	Liaising with household help/ paying household help	☐
	Choosing playgroup/ school ☐	Cleaning the car	☐
	Talking to playgroup/ school teacher ☐	Cleaning the inside of the car	☐
	Putting to bed ☐	Taxing/insuring car	☐

both ask why. Of course it may be that you have consciously decided to do things this way, perhaps because one of you works shifts or does very heavy work or because the mother is not going out to work. Nevertheless, from a child's point of view you both need to be seen as people who care for him and take responsibility for him if your relationship is to be close and trusting. You will also need to be seen by him as generally agreeing with each other or at least sorting out any disagreements you may have in a friendly way, and this means discussion and co-operation. It may mean too that extra commitments at work or in your sporting or social life will have to be dropped for a while. This is a difficult decision, particularly regarding work if one or both of you are ambitious. With some couples, the wife exchanges some of the chances of fulfilling her work ambitions for the rewards of a close relationship with her children. Couples will work out solutions like this in their own way, but there are advantages in talking about the problem, preferably before you have children and as they grow up.

If fathers are to share the work and the rewards of parenting on an equal basis, they need a partner who is prepared to relinquish some of the special mothering responsibility – and this can be harder than some women realise or are prepared to admit. There are some men who deliberately make such a performance out of doing any job involving the baby that in the end their partner stops asking them, but there are also women who complain that their partner has not done something right, meaning they have not done it *their* way. Women who feel they are married to someone who never helps out with the children at all may want to ask themselves if they are really able to let go of that special mothering responsibility and accept their partner's different way of doing things with the children. There are undoubtedly some women who need to remember that in order for their partner to take on more responsibility for their children's upbringing they in turn have to learn to give up some of that responsibility.

Some decisions need to be reached by mutual agreement, as it would be totally confusing for a child if both parents had completely different ideas about what sort of behaviour was acceptable. But women who expect their partner to stick rigidly to their patterns in all the more mundane aspects of child care — for example, how children are fed, what they are dressed in, or even how they are bathed — are setting their partner up for constant criticism and taking away some of the rewards involved in child care. On the other hand, fathers who rarely look after their children should not adapt the routine simply to suit themselves. For instance, a father who usually goes out to work but is looking after the children for one Saturday may feel perfectly happy about feeding them on crisps and a sandwich, and letting them watch television most of the day because he wants to get on with something himself. He knows perfectly well that the rest of the time his children are being fed balanced, nourishing meals and encouraged in stimulating, interesting play so that one day of a different regime will not harm them. Similarly, it does not matter to him if a father allows a baby an unaccustomed sleep in the afternoon, perhaps because he knows his mate will be home in the evening to help out with a lively toddler who is not going to go to bed much before midnight! If the same father had to look after his children for most of the week he would probably behave quite differently.

BROTHERS AND SISTERS

For many mothers expecting a second baby the effect on their first and older child is their biggest worry. However much they want another baby many women can actually feel a little bit sad at the prospect of losing that special one-to-one relationship they had with their first child. 'I feel I'm almost betraying her by having a second one,' said one mother, and this feeling is quite common. Parents worry that the older child will be jealous of the baby and about how they are going to manage the work of two children while still giving enough individual time to each. With so much attention given to the problem of jealousy and rivalry it is sometimes forgotten that children can have a relationship between themselves which really may not have much to do with the adults at all.

The extra work that second-time mothers fear can be much more of a reality than the jealousy problem. Second-time mothers may get little sleep, have far more work and much less time to spend with the new baby than they had with their first, but although most of their concern may be for the older child often it is actually the second one who misses out on their attention — he may be left to cry longer for a feed, or be parked in a babychair while his mother does a double load of ironing instead of being played with quite so much.

In this situation major compensations are the extra opportunities and interests the children provide for each other and here much depends on the age gap. Even quite young toddlers can be protective and helpful towards a new baby. As the baby grows up and begins to move around and be capable of doing things, many activities can be shared together. The baby also has the distraction of a bright, noisy toddler bouncing around.

One very valuable aspect of being a brother or a sister is mutual teaching and learning. The older child shows the younger one how to do something and in the process learns himself – he has to put into words exactly how you make a tower by putting one brick on top of another, he has to break down a process into its different parts in order to show this poor incompetent baby how it is done. He learns to understand the point of view of someone who is less able than himself, for he can see that baby sister or brother is not as advanced as he is and he has to work out how to explain things simply in terms the baby can understand. Of course some of this teaching/learning process may go on in directions you will not find very helpful – like the time the toddler shows the baby exactly how to haul everything out of the cupboard for the umpteenth time! – but in general it is a valuable process that is often overlooked by parents.

You may worry that with more than one child you are not doing as much with either of them as you did when you had just one baby. Relaxed sessions when you could let the baby kick without his nappy or lie down beside him on the floor chatting, the hours of letting him sit on your lap while you talked to friends, or looked at stories with him, or simply the amount of time you carried him about and talked to him – all these may seem things of the past. The loss of this one-to-one closeness can be quite sad for both you and your first child. Be prepared for tears and tantrums sometimes (and some strong emotions on your part as well), but make sure that you talk to your child about what is happening and about what you feel, and listen to what he has to say to you. Remember, small children understand far more than they can put into words.

You may be tempted, in your efforts not to upset your older child, to make out that tasks and chores involving the baby are nothing more than a bore – 'Oh that baby's crying *again*,' or 'Silly baby needs his nappy changing, what a nuisance.' The thinking behind this approach is quite understandable, but it can lead to the older child thinking that the baby himself is nothing more than a nuisance and a bore, and will not help the two children to form a relationship. Research findings suggest that a better relationship develops between older and second children when the mother talks to the first child about the needs of the baby and about the baby as an individual. She should also seek the older child's opinion about what is happening and what she should do, inviting him to think about and to share the experience of looking after the baby: 'She's crying now, what do you think she wants? What can we do?' The older child may think the baby wants a toy, or a feed, or rocking in the pram – try out his ideas with him so that he can, with you, find out which idea works. Help him to understand what the baby thinks and sees of him – 'She's looking towards you because she's heard your voice,' or 'She likes looking at you jumping around because you've got that nice, bright jersey on,' or 'She doesn't know my name or your name yet, but she is going to get to know her name the more often we talk to her and say it.' Talking about what the baby sees, understands, feels and begins to learn about the world around her and especially about her very important older brother or sister all seems to help the older child in understanding and being interested in his younger sibling. This is the start to a good relationship between the two. Of course, talking like this about the baby and inviting the older one to share the decisions and help is not always appropriate and sensitive mothers pick the right time. If your toddler is tired, engrossed in play, in a hurry to go out somewhere, or has a friend visiting, he is unlikely to be interested.

Once you have more than one child, sharing bathtimes, mealtimes, outings, sessions at the dentist, all become a way of life, and of course it is sensible to share as much as possible so that you are not having to do everything twice over. But sharing can be fun for children too — even a very new baby can enjoy splashing in a bath with an older sister or brother. However, do not think that private times between you and your older one or you and your younger child are impossible or a thing of the past. It is very important to create opportunities when each child has some time alone with you. The founder of the Methodist movement John Wesley's mother had seventeen children and one of her principles was to give five minutes each day to each child individually! With fewer than seventeen children you could probably spare more than five minutes — perhaps ten or fifteen, or even the occasional hour. For instance, you might go on a special outing with the older child while grandmother looks after the younger one. As the younger one grows up he too needs times alone with you. This may happen naturally when the older one goes to playgroup or out to visit a friend. Of course, the children will often be happy playing together, making secret and appalling chaos and having their own private world which their parents do not know about, and this does give you a break. All the same, it is worth trying to give each one a special time — it may be a television programme watched with you, a story or two at bedtime, a private conversation in the bedroom away from everybody else.

Dividing up the work of looking after children often means that fathers take the older child off and leave the mother to look after the baby. Why not make conscious efforts to do it the other way around sometimes? This means that fathers will be able to spend time getting to know their new baby by changing his nappy, dressing him and so on while the mother cares for the older child. Giving older children individual attention even for a short time will make them feel less need to demand attention in ways that are irritating and upsetting such as tantrums, whining or being aggressive towards the younger child.

GRANDPARENTS

'A few days after I came out of hospital with my first baby, I was really down and miserable, and when my mum came to see me, she could see I wasn't right. She took him off me for an hour or two a day, and in a few weeks I was fine again. Now she is really fond of my two-year-old and it's lovely to watch them together. I don't know what I would have done without her.'

'My mother-in-law had never breastfed any of her children and although she said it was a good idea I don't think she did really. It was her

447

first grandchild and she was desperate to take him off to show all her friends and even talked about him coming to stay with her when he was only a few weeks old. She didn't really like the fact that he was still tied to me because of feeding times and used to talk to him, saying things to him that she really meant to say to me, like "When you have finished with all those feeds you are going to come and stay with me, aren't you?" I don't think she was aware of what she was doing consciously, though.'

Grandparents are often very important people in children's lives. The part his grandparents play in your child's life depends on how near they live, on the type of people they are, how physically able they are, as well as on the sort of relationship you have enjoyed with your parents or your parents-in-law before the first baby arrived on the scene. If that relationship was already a bit fraught and had tension in it beforehand, then there may be clashes between you and them as they take on the grandparent role. But whatever your own personal feelings, try to stand back a little and let them develop a separate relationship with your child because there are big rewards to be had on both sides.

How soon, how often and in exactly what way you want your older relatives to be involved with their grandchild is highly individual. Some mothers welcome their own mother or mother-in-law moving in straight away on the return from hospital and helping to hold the fort. Others very much want to keep their relatives at bay until they themselves have found their feet and have become confident in their new role as a mother. It is very common in the early days for new parents to feel just a bit tense if a slightly domineering grandmother gives too much forceful advice or wants to start taking over responsibilities.

Some issues, like potty-training, table manners, the giving of presents and discipline generally are especially likely to be sensitive and provoke strong feelings between grandparents and parents. But on the plus side grandparents can often be the most tremendous source of support and comfort. If they live nearby they may be able to give you a break from babycare, babysit in the evenings, and help out in all sorts of practical ways. Be careful not to abuse their goodwill and start 'dumping' your children on their doorstep more often than you think they want. Part of the joy of being a grandparent is being able to indulge your grandchildren and then to hand them back to their parents after a relatively short time! If grandparents are forced into taking on a more regular childminding or substitute parent role that special relationship may change and can even become soured. If your own relationship with your parents-in-law or parents works well, then none of these problems are likely to arise, but if the going does get difficult at any stage it is worth remembering just how much your own children will get out of what their grandparents can give.

It is especially worth maintaining contact with grandparents if you and your partner separate or divorce, for it is in these sad circumstances that grandparents most often fear losing touch with grandchildren. And it can be an additional loss to children who no longer live with both parents if they also lose regular contact with grandparents and other relatives who love and care about them. Obviously, in order to maintain that contact it is important that grandparents show tact and sensitivity by not taking sides, criticising or putting undue pressure on couples to get back together again.

On a purely practical note, do not forget, when you are visiting older relatives or leaving them in charge of young children, that however many children of their own they may have had they might have forgotten about some of the safety aspects of child care. So do not be afraid to point out, gently and tactfully of course, about the need, for example, to keep stair-gates in place, and to cook with saucepan handles turned in towards the centre, not jutting out where they can be pulled down by a toddler.

FRIENDS

Other parents with children of a similar age can be a great support. Lifelong friendships often spring out of meetings at antenatal clinics, hospitals or the health centre, and your child's first encounters with other babies or toddlers will probably come about as a result of your need to see your friends. Even babies can enjoy themselves by gurgling at each other, touching each other and imitating each other's sounds and movements. As your child gets older you may also take him out to more organised play activities such as toddler clubs and then playgroups or nursery schools. At first he will want to play with others only within sight and even touch of you, and you will need to be there to sort out squabbles over toys and prevent accidents, but there will come a time when your child definitely does not need you – for some of the time anyway. He prefers going off with his friends to play shops, make camps, or play schools. He may have a special friend to whom he will become very attached. Even in very young children such special friendships can be longlasting. If the friend moves away your child may remember him or her for years to come.

Same-age friendships are very valuable, and not only for your child's emotional and social well-being – children also learn from them. In order to get through to each other children have to learn to tailor their conversation and reactions to the other one. Listen, for example, to a three- or four-year-old talking to a friend and note how the subject matter is sustained, then changed and how friends react emotionally to each other. For example, here is a four-year-old sympathetically listening to her slightly older friend David telling her about his first day at school:

KATY: *'What did you do at school?'*

DAVID: *'We played a game called Superfriends. It was Paul Bryant's game. There were twelve boys and twelve girls. The boys chased the girls.'*

KATY: *'Did you chase the girls?'*

DAVID: *'No, I didn't want to play.'*

KATY: *'What did you do?'*

DAVID: *'I played with a girl and we hid in a corner of the playground. The teacher looked out of the window and told Paul off. He had to go inside.'*

KATY: *'What did you have for dinner?'*

DAVID: *'We had peas and carrots and potatoes and meat. What did you have?'*

KATY: *'I had fish fingers and baked beans.'*

It is unlikely that David would have given his mother so many of the details about the game or expressed his anxiety about Paul – another older friend of both children – getting into trouble. Moreover, few adults would have had the tact to ask for the supremely important details about school dinners at just this point in the conversation.

How do you help your children to learn the skills of making friends? In the beginning you need to be on hand when they have another child of the same age round visiting with their mother. It is very difficult for them to start learning about taking turns with toys and sharing at this stage. A mixture of gently telling your child to give things to the other child or saying, 'Now it's Mary's turn,' together with distraction if there is going to be a dispute over a toy, is the sort of guidance in their play that will set toddlers on the right lines for later on. Distracting a toddler by presenting a different toy is much better than head-on screaming scenes, with both children yelling and tugging at the same toy. At the toddler stage, children tend to play alongside each other rather than together, but you can help them by showing them little simple games they can play with you – like building a tower of bricks and then both of them knocking it down, or getting a big cardboard box that they can both fit inside and pretending it is a car or a boat, or even just pulling it along to give them a ride. Showing them together how to play traditional games like peekaboo or 'Round and round the garden like a teddy bear' can be useful. If you do something simple like this with one child, the other child will probably stop and watch and then may want to come and have a go or join in himself. The first child will then stop and watch the other one. They are learning that the same things make other people laugh, as well as observing and noticing what other people do. As they grow older they will begin to do some of these things together without your help.

Do not expect just to put two children of any age in each other's company and see them immediately hit it off and start playing together. Left alone, two very young children are more likely to end up having a clash over the same toy. Your help with introductions and easing them into a game together is nearly always necessary. Encourage your child to show the newcomer where the toys are kept for a start, then get something out and help your child to demonstrate how it works so that the visiting child can have a go. Talk to them about what the other child wants to do – 'Have you got one of these at home?' or 'Do you know how this works?' – and then you can invite your child to show them or to help them, a role which he will probably enjoy. Once your child can see that the visiting child is friendly and is not going to take all his things away, he may relax and begin to learn that there can be a great deal of fun in showing off his own things to a newcomer, rather than just grabbing them back all the time and saying 'No, mine!'

Young children also need to be shown how to share very simple games. If it is summer, for example, you can put them in the garden with a small bowl of water and demonstrate how they can get plastic tumblers and pour the water in and out of different containers. If children never experience any of these very simple skills in turn-taking, enjoying activities together and showing other children how to use toys or playthings, then their behaviour may appear very antisocial when they are first put amongst a group of same-aged children, at a toddler club for instance. Children quickly learn to watch each other to see what sort of reaction they are

Children have to learn to take turns

likely to get. If one child immediately grabs a toy in a possessive way or takes it away from another one, the same kind of reaction will be sparked off in the other child and before you know it there is a full-scale row going on.

What do you do if your socially skilled toddler, who is normally very friendly and sharing, finds himself on the receiving end of grabbing, snatching or aggressive behaviour? Most mothers feel terribly upset when this happens – there is more about it in the section on aggression later in this chapter – but in general it is best to explain to your child that this little boy or girl does not yet know about sharing or is not yet used to playing with a lot of other children and does not understand about taking turns. If you find it easy to encourage children into sharing kinds of play then perhaps you could stay on hand and help this other child learn the ropes a little.

When children are worried or in trouble, having another child they can talk to freely is a very important safety valve, which is especially true if the trouble is with the adults in their lives. When his parents are cross with him, or when they are cross with each other, your child needs a friend he can turn to. This process can begin to work at a very young age if your child has the chance to meet other children regularly. Brothers and sisters can also be confidants for each other, although they are sometimes the source of trouble! Other grown-ups, such as the lady next door or the teenager who comes to babysit, can be friends as well.

SOCIAL PROBLEMS

DIFFICULTIES IN MAKING FRIENDS

Some children find it difficult to make friends. They cling to their parents when they are at a party or at a friend's house. They sit by themselves in a corner at the toddler club or playgroup and seem to prefer solitary activities such as reading or playing with Lego to joining in make-believe games with the crowd.

Others have problems for quite different reasons. They seem to have no idea at all about taking turns. They barge to the head of the queue for the slide, snatch the Superman outfit from the child whose turn it was to wear it, and push over anyone who gets in their way. If another child protests, he is hit. Aggressive children like this can be just as lonely and friendless as the shy ones.

Children need to learn the *skills* of making friends and these do not come automatically. They need to learn to ask the right questions at the right moment, as Katy did of David in the passage quoted above. They need to show tact and sympathy. They also need to be trusting and confiding, to show liking for the other child, as David did for Katy. If your child has difficulty getting on with other children it may be he just does not know how. You can help by giving him opportunities to talk about what he has been doing, asking him the right tactful questions, and telling him what you have been doing.

Sometimes a younger child in the family is always getting shouted down by the older one, or has everything done for him by an overbusy mother, and he never gets the chance to take the initiative himself. It can be helpful to invite other children of the same age home to play, but avoid pushing them into each other's arms. The ideal companion is a more confident, generous child like Katy or David who will be sympathetic to the shy child and will set an example of friendliness, or a younger child to whom the shy child will appear grown up and important. Children who have difficulties making friends for whatever reason are usually better with just one friend around than when they are one of a crowd of other children.

You might also ask yourself about your own social life. Do you have a circle of other mothers that you see? Do you have people coming to visit your house bringing their children along so that your child has the chance to meet new people on his own home territory? Sometimes, if a mother is shy and finds it difficult to make friends herself, her child may have fewer chances to learn all the social skills of friendship just because he meets fewer people. The time when you have young children is often a key one for making friends yourself and even if you are not naturally very chatty or sociable, you can often enjoy an untaxing hour or so in the company of other women with whom you may not have anything basically in common except the children. Try finding out about a pram club or mother and toddler club in your area. Ring the supervisor and tell her you do not know very many people, or anyone at all in the neighbourhood. If it is a friendly, well-run group, she is sure to invite you to come along and make a point of looking out for you on your first visit so that she can introduce you to one or two other mothers. This may be easier than simply turning up and hoping that someone will talk to you, for even in the friendliest such group newcomers can sometimes be overlooked at the first visit just because it is such a busy, slightly chaotic place!

AGGRESSION

Aggression shows itself in various ways and at different stages. Children who have learnt to walk are often tempted to give a younger, tottering toddler a little experimental shove. They can then be quite amazed by the amount of attention this attracts when the toddler falls flat and starts yelling, bringing both mothers running up making an equal amount of noise. If your child does this, say 'no' very firmly but without shouting, and then immediately take him away into another room on your own and tell him again quietly but firmly that he must not do this. Aggressive action from you will not help, so stay calm and resist any temptation to punish a child for such behaviour by being aggressive in turn and hitting or shaking him.

Hitting is easily imitated and children learn hitting from each other as well as from adults. Be prepared, for example, for your child to become more aggressive if he sees this demonstrated by older children once he starts playgroup. In a well-run group this will not go unchecked by play leaders, but in calm moments it helps to tell your child why this kind of behaviour is not allowed and give him some guidelines for coping with problems which lead to hitting.

However, if your child is the subject of aggression from another child or children, you may find yourself in something of a quandary. We generally teach children not to hit back, on the principle that two wrongs don't make a right, but you do not want to find your toddler unable to cope in a boisterous group and becoming a target for attack. The social rules of the group that you belong to must inevitably be your guideline and if you do not like the rules in action – for example, toddlers left to sort out their own quarrels with little adult intervention – then it is worth investigating alternative playgroups or pram clubs where adults are quicker to step in to help toddlers resolve quarrels without fighting.

Biting As an aggressive act, biting is not any different from hitting or pushing, but it deserves separate attention because parents are often more shocked if their child starts biting or is on the receiving end of such action. Some parents believe that biting the child back to show them how much it hurts is the best way to stop such behaviour, but it is better to try a form of management which enables your child to learn some sympathy and understanding for other people's feelings which they can apply on a larger scale. Such management consists of responding to your child when he is hurt in a way which gets this message across. Simple actions like a cuddle to help the injured person to recover and kissing the bad place better is something you can both do for each other. Toddlers are capable of understanding quite a lot about how another person is feeling, and saying 'Sorry' and 'I didn't mean to hurt you' is part of social learning at this age. Again, your example and the example set by other members of the family is the starting point.

Some children start biting in response to another child biting them, some begin through play which gets out of hand (pretending to be biting monsters, for example) and many more give experimental bites, perhaps to a parent, initially without aggressive intent. Give them a clear indication of your feelings if they indulge in such 'trial' biting by saying 'no' firmly and removing them a slight distance from you.

In general, the same reaction to biting as to hitting or pushing will work as long as it is applied consistently. Tell the child firmly but without shouting that biting is not allowed because it hurts other people and immediately remove him to a place on his own – the other end of the hall or another room. Allow him back when he seems to have calmed down, usually after about five minutes, or earlier if he seems frightened.

If biting seriously develops out of an excited game, then calm things down and show the children how to play the game without actually biting, again making it clear that real biting is not allowed. If they cannot play the game without things getting out of hand, switch their attention to another activity instead. If your child starts to bite after being bitten by another child, you will need the co-operation of the other parent or playleader – it is possible for epidemics of biting to spread through playgroups and then the play leader needs to manage events carefully to stop the habit.

AGGRESSION BETWEEN BROTHERS AND SISTERS

Seeing your own children being unkind or aggressive to each other can be the most hurtful experience and one which many parents say is guaranteed to make them feel angry. Invariably parents get most upset when they see an older child being aggressive to a younger one. Jealousy and rivalry are triggers and it is important for you to be seen to be fair and not to demand all the time that an older child gives in or allow the younger one to get away with provocative behaviour. Codes of behaviour between brothers and sisters are set very early on and sharing objects, activities and also time and attention is the basis of family co-operation. If, for example, one parent is bound up with supplying the needs of a new baby and has no time for the other parent or other members of the family, they are likely to feel neglected and resentful.

SHARING

The demands of a baby and then a young child are self-centred, and learning to understand that other people have needs and that not all possessions belong to him is a long process of social learning which begins towards the end of a baby's first year and is especially important in the second and third years. As with all behaviour, example is the first lesson: share the biscuit on your plate with your baby; talk about 'Mummy's shoe' which psychologists maintain is a less aggressive phrase than saying 'That's mine'. Remember that a one-year-old thinks everything belongs to him, and 'me' and 'mine' are often among the first words. First children may have a less well developed sense of possession as they are often given quite a lot by their parents and other relatives and, since adults tend to use avoidance tactics, may take possession for granted. This phase passes quite quickly, however, as they begin to have more contact with other children who want their toys. Sometimes parents can get too involved in disputes about sharing, especially between brothers and sisters, and where possible it is best to let the children sort out sharing disputes unless you see one child consistently coming off worse. Older children should not always be made to give way to younger children, and it is reasonable that possessions belonging to older children, which may be broken or which are unsuitable for the younger one, be kept out of the way. It may help younger children accept this if they in turn have some prized possessions which are special to them and not freely available in the collection of household toys.

Practical solutions to sharing problems

* If you are not sure who had the toy or item first and neither are willing to give it up, take it away from both and distract them with another activity.

* If one child has grabbed a toy from another, take it back and give it to the child who had it first for a short time before letting the other have a go. Waiting and asking should be seen to be rewarded.

* If the owner of the toy simply cannot be persuaded to give it up, the other child should be distracted with a similar or more interesting toy.

* If the toy in question is of special emotional value to the other child – for example, a cuddly toy they take to bed, or something always brought to nursery school – the other child should still give it up and the special significance be explained. It is very important to lavish praise on the child when he gives it up, making sure you offer an enticing alternative game or toy as a distraction.

GOOD BEHAVIOUR

HANDLING YOUNG CHILDREN

The problem of trying to get your child to co-operate and to behave in the way you require on certain occasions usually only arises when he has learnt to walk and is fully mobile. Once this happens, so many more activities are within his range that you begin to need him to take more notice of what you say for his own safety as well as the necessity of getting certain things accomplished. This does not mean you need to watch him any less carefully: for example, you need to be able to tell him not to climb up on the table and have him accept that this is not allowed, even though you should still take safety precautions like keeping all the chairs pushed in and checking what he is doing very frequently. Other issues, like accepting he cannot have sweets or crisps every time you go into a shop, co-operating with putting outdoor clothes on or waiting until you have finished laying the table or helping another child before getting him a drink, are all just as important to a good relationship between you and your young child.

How should children be handled so that they are likely to do what they are told? First-time parents learn by trial and error and few of us escape those embarrassing public scenes when a child stages a major tantrum because he wants to be allowed to push the pushchair when you are in a hurry or does not want to hold your hand when it would be unsafe for you to let go. However, there are some general principles which are the basis of all child management, whatever the situation:

* Your love and the expression of your love in the form of cuddles and praise is more important in helping your child to be 'good' than threats or punishments. Always make a point of expressing your pleasure and telling your child he is good when he stops touching things when you ask or climbs into his car seat obediently. We all have a natural inclination to notice the times children do not do as required and tell them off far more often than we notice good behaviour and give praise.

* Cut back on the number of demands you make. Children become less receptive to a continual stream of 'Don't do that' and 'Stop touching those', and if you look carefully at the commands which really matter you will find they are relatively few. Try to use other means of encouraging your child to behave in the way you want in trivial matters, for example by playing or distraction, and reserve commands for those instances when it is important your child takes notice.

* Carry through what you say. This means when you tell him to stop doing something you must be prepared actually to go and intervene if necessary and brave the ensuing screams. If you say 'no' to something and then give in after the child makes a fuss you are teaching that 'no' means 'All right, carry on' as long as he makes enough protest.

* Be consistent. Firmly stopping a child doing something one day then allowing it the next is thoroughly confusing. Talk to your partner about what is and what is not allowed – if parents cannot agree then a child can easily play one off against the other.

* Remember that it is possible to be firm and loving. Saying 'no' to something does not have to be done in a cross or unkind way and can be followed by affection when your child complies.

* Playfulness and humour are important weapons in managing the behaviour of young children. Most children have a strong sense of play and can be joked out of behaviour you do not like – going on telling them to be as difficult as long as they want, for example. Humour also

helps them learn to make the best of things and not to get upset about trivial matters.

DISCIPLINE

There can be few parents who have never hit their child, some in the belief that smacking or slapping is the best way to correct behaviour, but most in moments of exasperation which they usually regret the next minute.

In all dealings with our children we are trying to teach them principles and behaviour which will enable them to make judgements and to decide for themselves on socially and morally acceptable forms of behaviour, whether in the matter of relationships or practicalities. Hitting children teaches them only that you are angry with them at that moment, and it may encourage them to hit other children and possibly to indulge in the behaviour you have disapproved of the minute your back is turned. If your child is generally fairly well behaved then he would respond to another form of discipline, and if he is usually naughty then smacking him probably has no effect. It certainly does not help children to develop any form of social understanding and code of conduct. Further, since children are strong imitators, it does not mirror any behaviour which we find acceptable in other relationships. We do not approve of children hitting each other or adults settling matters by violence.

If you do lose control and slap your child, it is best to tell him afterwards that you are sorry and that it was wrong, explaining at the same time why he drove you so mad. Remember that all children go through difficult phases and all parents suffer times of stress and lack of confidence. Talking to other parents of similar-age children is a great help because so very many problems are extremely common and hearing how other people cope can help.

The importance of your praise and approval has been stressed, but do not underestimate the impact of your disapproval and withdrawal of affection. This does not mean you should 'cold shoulder' your child for a long period or make disturbing threats that you will cease to love him, but saying firmly, 'I don't like you doing that because it's making a big mess,' or whatever the reason is, and stopping him does have an effect with a young child. In general, deferring punishments, such as not allowing something he enjoys, is not very effective with two- or three-year-olds, who live very much in the present and will have forgotten the incident an hour or two later. Even with older children, if you are withdrawing a privilege or treat, it is better to pick something due to happen in the next hour or so and not at the end of the day or even the next day. It is reasonable to withdraw edible treats if the bad behaviour occurs in relation to the treat – for example, if a child stages a scene in a shop, not to give him crisps or whatever item has been promised. It is better, however, not to use food too much in punishment (e.g. no pudding) or reward (e.g. extra sweeties) as it lays too great an emphasis on the enjoyment and the importance of eating which in a few children can make problem eating phases extend into something more permanent (see page 271).

Probably the most effective and immediate punishment for young children is that described in the section on aggression, simply to isolate them for a few minutes from the scene of the crime. Physically distancing a young child from yourself, by putting him out of the room you are in, should only be done for a few minutes as such separations quickly register your disapproval, and keeping him apart from you for longer than a few minutes can be very frightening for a young child. Afterwards, try to change the mood with a distracting activity and help him to calm down. Do not expect him to be mature enough to be able to say sorry – this will only prolong the scene without any benefit to either you or the child. Later, when he is calm, you can say why you put him outside the door and tell him it does not mean you don't love him, only that what he was doing was wrong. Obviously, different situations call for different tactics – distancing yourself from the child who is refusing to let you put a coat on him is unlikely to work because you have to return to the same battleground. Making a game out of it is much more likely to be successful.

Humour is a very powerful weapon in managing young children, who have a strong sense of fun and playfulness, but summoning up the ability to be humorous is not always possible. Parents have to be endlessly resourceful and able to use a wide variety of skills to manage their young children and it is not surprising that it is when we are under pressure or feeling tired that we find children most difficult to handle. Although already mentioned, it is worth stressing again how important it is to praise and show your affection and pleasure when your child does comply with your wishes or is helpful. This gives much greater emphasis to the times when you show displeasure, while an undiluted stream of negative commands and criticism makes children switch off.

LEARNING TO WAIT

One of the things which is particularly exhausting when caring for small children is the non-stop stream of demands for assistance and attention. The process of growing up is largely one of children learning to develop some awareness of other people's needs and feelings and to control their own demands and behaviour accordingly. Helping your child to learn to wait means picking the right occasion – when a toy is trapped and he cannot free it is not a good moment because your child's frustration will make him oblivious to anything else. Other requests, to come and see something, to help with a jigsaw, to give him a biscuit, may not be so pressing. Try not to say 'Just a minute' all the time because this does not have any meaning in terms of time for your child. Instead be specific – say 'When I've finished laying the table/writing this card/hanging out the washing, I'll do that for you,' so that the child can see for himself when you will be ready. Do not ask him to wait for everything or make the waiting time too long, and remember to praise him when he does wait.

Young children tend to amuse themselves best if you put a little thought into the planning of their day so that activities and pace are varied and periods when you give them little attention are interspersed by times when you give them some of your undivided interest — for more on this see chapter 12.

FEARS

Fears of the dark, of insects, dogs, thunder, water and the noise of the vacuum cleaner or even washing machine are very common in toddlers and can often lead to what parents see as difficult behaviour. It is true that sometimes children can pick up a parent's fears, and many adults quite rightly struggle to control their natural reactions to spiders or going to the dentist in an effort to show calm unconcern to their child. Most such fears need only reassurance and calmness and will fade or pass. It is only when the fear is so strong that it seriously disturbs your child's normal behaviour that it is termed a phobia — for example, a child who becomes hysterical at any prospect of getting in the bath or other water. These are some guidelines for helping children overcome fears or phobias:

* Take your child's fears seriously and do not laugh, disregard or tease him about them. Your sympathy is important.

* Do not force contact with the feared object, but rather try gentle tactics, allowing the child to have some control over his approach so that he can retreat or draw closer as he feels able.

* If your child's fear is so intense that even a gradual approach sparks panic, avoid the object of anxiety and only try to approach it again when he is happy and relaxed. Stop before he becomes anxious again.

FEAR OF THE DARK

This is more common in school-age than in pre-school children and can be sparked off by a story in a book or by television, by a change from summertime to wintertime or by some other event. Pointing out that your child can still call for you in the dark, talking to him about where everything is in the room while his eyes become accustomed and making the room less dark with a night light or landing light left on can all help. As with all other fears, never force a child to confront the fear by leaving him in the dark. For more on sleep problems see chapter 8.

FEAR OF DOCTORS AND DENTISTS

Familiarity with the doctor or dentist's surgery on occasions when treatment is not required is the best preparation for small children, so when possible take them with you on your own check-up visits. If some treatment is required, a little explanation in advance is helpful for older pre-school children, and there are a number of well-illustrated books you can read together. If your doctor or dentist has children or grandchildren of his own, mentioning this and talking about them in a family context is sometimes reassuring for three-and four-year-olds. For more on children in hospital see chapter 20.

GOING BACK TO WORK – WHO MINDS THE BABY?

When mothers want to return to work, it is sometimes possible for fathers to take over, especially if the mother only wants to work part-time. But this is not always the case, and other plans have to be made. The effect on their child's relationships with them, and with other people, will be one of the main factors which influence what parents do in these circumstances.

Making arrangements so that someone else can look after your baby and enable you to return to full- or part-time work is a highly personal business and one about which you will probably have some strong, instinctive feelings. There are many questions to consider in trying to choose the best arrangement:

* Are you still breastfeeding and do you plan to continue? It is perfectly possible to return to work and continue to breastfeed – for more suggestions, see page 222. Even if you are not breastfeeding, the age of your baby is a key factor in deciding who it is best to leave him with.

* How long will you be away, including travelling time, and how often? There is obviously an enormous difference in the kind of arrangements you need to make for a part-time job as opposed to a full-time job with long hours spent travelling to and from your place of employment.

* What choices do you have? They will not be the same for everyone – for example, is there a relative or a friend who can help? Is there a crèche or nursery at or near the place where you work? Does your local authority run its own nurseries whose hours fit those of your job? How much money will you be able to afford to pay someone to look after your child?

Obviously it is better if any arrangement you make can adapt and grow with your child so that he does not have to cope with too many changes, but that is not always possible. It may help to consider the different needs that arise at different stages.

In the first year of life a baby needs to relate to one person and for that person to get to know him and his wants. This does not mean that it always has to be a one-to-one relationship exclusively, but if your child is to be cared for in a nursery, then look for one which enables the same person to look after the same babies, and has time to give your baby enough individual attention. A constantly changing flow of different people looking after a great many babies so that there is not time for them to get to know each one individually is not a good arrangement.

Obviously you will want the person who looks after your baby to know all about the requirements of babies, to have some experience of them, and also to be keen to know about your particular baby and his or her needs and wants. This can be very labour intensive — as you know yourself! — so make sure the person you choose has enough time to spare. For example, a child minder who already has two other small babies to care for is unlikely to be able to spend much time talking to and playing with each one on their own. Find someone who can provide the kind of day that you would like your baby to enjoy, which may mean some time spent in the open air, some time being played and chatted with and an environment as loving and stimulating as the one you would provide yourself.

How can you be sure what will happen when you are not there to see what goes on? There is more public scrutiny and accountability in a nursery, but a child minder who takes three children from different parents and where the parents arrive and leave at different hours will have a busy and open house that should give some reassurance.

If you can afford it, employing an individual to come to your own home may be the best arrangement. If this is what you plan, it is sensible to start the new arrangement at least two weeks in advance of when you plan to return to work, so that the two of you can exist alongside each other and get to know and establish a trust before you go back. It also helps to introduce the person you employ to as many of your friends as you can, as well as places to take the baby out to such as pram clubs.

In the second year of life, continuity and closeness of attention are still very important, but other factors now come into consideration. This is the year that your child takes off from baby to toddler — he will begin to run around, to explore, to get into everything. A baby needs a lot of nurturing, but with a toddler continual but less intensive attention and a different kind of caretaking come into operation. Is the person who is going to look after your child fit and active, and alert to danger without being repressive? The care of a doting grandparent may have been ideal in the first year of life, but they can find that a lively toddler is just too much to cope with for a full day. Obviously their love and attention is still invaluable, but could the day be rearranged so that part of it is spent with somebody else? Most toddlers enjoy the bustle, excitement and lively atmosphere that surrounds other children, although they play alongside rather than with each other at this stage. It is also important for their own social development that they begin to mix with and see other children. Could a friend or one of the grandparents take your child out to a toddler club for an afternoon? A crèche or nursery which you may have dismissed as being unsuitable to care for a baby may now be worth investigating for an older child.

Playgroups, nursery schools, crèches and full-time nurseries differ in the ratio of caretakers and the type of care that is offered for the children. It is usually thought that a child needs to be about three years old to go to a playgroup or nursery school without you or another adult closely supervising his activities. Once a child reaches this stage, your care arrangements may need to be reviewed again. Could the child minder take your child to the nursery or playgroup of your choice? And while it means that your child is amused and looked after for the mornings, there are still the rest of the day and holidays to consider. By now, however, your child will really love having other children around. A rather solitary arrangement where he or she is cared for at home by one person who comes to the house is only satisfactory if that person can invite the child's friends round and provide the sort of social life that you would offer if you were at home. Sometimes working parents may find it easier to juggle hours with a young baby or toddler, so that they can keep him up late in the evening and spend time with him, but once a child begins to go to playgroup, nursery or school regularly each day, he obviously needs to have a more stable routine and go to bed at a reasonable hour. As the child's week begins to become more structured, so weekends, other times off and holidays begin to be more important as opportunities to spend time as a family.

The most economic and the commonest form of childcare for working mothers in this country is a childminder. These are people, usually mothers themselves, who look after other people's children in their own homes. They have to be registered with their local authority. Common sense plus the recommendation of other parents are the best guide in choosing a minder and you can ask minders for the names of people such as other parents, their GP or health visitor who can give a character reference. Children in the minder's care will follow her routine, going shopping with her and meeting older children from school so you need to feel happy with the daily life your child would lead.

Nannies, mother's helps and au pairs are all options for working mothers, depending on their circumstances and how much they can afford to pay. Trained nannies have the Nursery Nurse Examination Board certificate (NNEB), which can be obtained by doing a two-year course at one of the private top three nanny-training establishments (Norland Nursery Training College Ltd, Princess Christian College and Chiltern Nursery Training College), or a college of further education. Although the qualification is the same there are some variations in the course, for example, some colleges and all the private training schools send girls for an attachment to a local maternity unit while others do not. Girls straight from college have the advantage of not being set in their ways, so mothers can train them in their particular style, but often they will have much less idea of what a muddle and how unlike theory family life proves to be. They

The home of a good child minder can provide the company of other children and plenty of stimulation

also cost less than a girl who has experience plus training. Nannies who have only experience but no training can be just as good or sometimes better. A nanny only deals with extra jobs relating to the children, such as cooking for them and doing their laundry, but any extra helping has to be negotiated at interview stage. A live-out nanny will ask a higher salary than one who lives in and has her keep included.

Reputable nanny agencies charge quite high fees but in return should vet girls thoroughly. However, because supplying child care has become a booming industry, some agencies simply act as an introductory agency, passing on numbers of clients and girls without any checking. Alternative ways of finding a nanny are to advertise in the columns of the *Lady* magazine, in your local paper or to contact the tutor in charge of the NNEB course at a local college around April or May.

Always ask for character as well as work references, if relevant, and follow them up. Decide in advance exactly what time you want your nanny to start and finish work, and exactly what jobs you want her to do; also whether she has to take her holidays at the same time as you and what your policy is to be on sick pay, should you be unlucky enough to hire a nanny who then breaks her leg on a ski-ing trip. In the end, though, parents should trust their own gut feelings about who the right person is for the job. Find out what the going rate of pay is in your area, then calculate what she will get in her hand and what you will have to pay in tax and insurance on top and work out what extra perks the job offers – for example, a car, occasional flexible hours, a specially nice room if she is living in or perhaps holidays away with you sometimes.

Less expensive than a nanny is a mother's help. These are girls who have no training in child care but will also do some housework. Provided you find a girl who is intelligent and reliable and is using this as a way into nannying, rather than someone who is not so bright and has fallen into such work because she cannot think of anything else to do, this can be a good solution. The sources for finding mothers' helps are the same as for nannies and, again, parents should decide exactly what they require before interviewing.

Au pairs are cheaper still but not suitable for parents who are working full time and need someone to take sole charge of a baby all day. Usually families take them on through an agency on the basis of a letter, references and a telephone call, so it is very hit and miss what kind of girl you get and how much experience she has had with young children in the way of baby-sitting. Au pairs can, however, be a good solution for parents with older children who are at junior school, or to help out by baby-sitting to bridge the odd hour for parents who are trying to overlap their working arrangements with evening jobs and just need a little extra help. Many au pair employers make the mistake of expecting the girls to do too much and are then disappointed. Au pairs are supposed to do five hours a day of light housework and some baby-sitting with at least one day free, but preferably two. If you imagine a niece coming to stay to help out and fill in time between school and college and treat them accordingly

you have a better chance of making the relationship work.

Whenever employing somebody to look after your child, whether in your home, in their home or in a group such as a crèche or nursery, ask for references or ask if you can talk to at least two previous employers or clients. Make sure at least one of these is recent (within the last 12 to 18 months), and always follow up all references. Anyone who has left a lot of child care jobs suddenly and without apparent reason, or who cannot give you the name of at least two employers who have found them satisfactory in a similar job will not give you the kind of confidence you need. In the case of newly registered child minders or newly trained nannies, ask for character references as well as contacting the place of training.

It is important from the start to be very specific about the kind of care you would like for your child – this may be more difficult to talk about with relatives who are giving their services free than with people who are being paid. It helps to write down a plan of the kind of day you would like your child to spend, which should include not only details of feeds, sleeps, and so on, but also the kind of fun and playtimes you would ideally expect him to be able to enjoy. Good communication is the key to a successful relationship between you and your child's caretaker. You need to be honest, detailed and accurate from the outset in explaining and writing down just what you expect from that person.

Continuity of care is important, but if you are worried about some aspect of your child's care it is better to trust your instincts. If the problem cannot be resolved by talking to your child's caretaker you may have to make changes. Inevitably the burden of having to choose a caretaker and form a relationship generally falls primarily to the mother, but it is much better if the job can be shared between both parents because they can then discuss any worries between the two of them rather than let any problems become one person's sole responsibility.

SINGLE PARENTHOOD

Financial restrictions limit the choices of child care arrangements as full-time nannies require that the employer has a high earning capacity – less likely with one rather than two wage-earners in the family.

The facilities on offer in a particular area or by an employer will be especially important to single parents and it is well worth investigating the possibility of moving areas or changing jobs in order to take advantage of good quality, economic child care. This may take the form of council-operated day nurseries or later nursery classes attached to primary schools, or to workplace crèches, flexible hours or allowances paid towards the cost of child care by an employer. Single parents who work part-time may be able to consider teaming up with another parent to operate a swap system, but otherwise the most available low-cost child-minding arrangement is to leave the child with a registered child minder. For more on choosing a minder see page 465.

In practical terms, single parents can try to lessen their workload and the strain of bringing up children alone by building up as effective a support system as possible. It will be beneficial for your child if he can continue to know and have a relationship with the parent he does not live with, but other relatives and friends who want to take an interest in him or help you can make a great difference to a single parent's quality of life. It is very common for single working parents to feel that finding a baby sitter and arranging to go out is just too much trouble. This simply increases their isolation, however. It is important to have some kind of adult social life and ultimately to make an effort to organise a balance in your life.

All parents, whether single or in a permanent relationship, find the friendship of other parents with similar age children, with whom they can share and compare experiences and perhaps offer practical help by looking after each other's children, a valuable source of support. Hospital ante- and post-natal classes, National Childbirth Trust tea afternoons, pram clubs and clinics are common spawning grounds for such friendships. In addition local branches of organisations such as Gingerbread and the National Council for One Parent Families are worth exploring.

COMMUNICATING WITH CHILDREN

'When my mother, who lived nearby and was very close to us all, died, my three-year-old son asked if he could go and see her and when I tried to explain that her death meant he wouldn't ever see her again, she was gone, he asked if he could have her car when he was older. I found it very upsetting.'

'I never married the father of my two-year-old daughter and we separated when she was six months old, but he has tried to get custody and comes to see her once a fortnight. On most of these occasions he and I end up rowing in front of her. She sometimes says things like "Daddy bad," but I worry that what happens may affect her in the long term.'

All parents find some subjects much harder to talk about with their children than others, although exactly what they are will vary from household to household. Common topics which cause us to stumble are death, religion, divorce and separation, and sex.

We know that the understanding of children under five is more advanced than their language development and this is especially so with very young children of two or three whose ability to put into words questions and worries may be limited, but whose awareness and anxiety about events they cannot fully understand is nevertheless real. The result is that quite often when parents come up against a subject which is difficult or painful for them to talk about and which may make them feel guilty or anxious, they either avoid young children's questions or fob them off with something which has a weak link with the truth. Studies of children whose parents separated when they were under ten, for example, show that in a great number of cases the children were never offered any explanation at all. Often the parent remaining with the children felt that what had happened was obvious and no words were needed, but the children's version of events showed that this was far from being the case. Obviously, exactly what parents choose to say to their children on difficult subjects will always depend on individual circumstances, but there are some broad guidelines which hold true in most instances:

Children can understand more than parents realise This means not only are they likely to be aware of changes in their lives or pick up information from television, overheard conversations and things they see, but that they can understand simple explanations better than we often realise.

Children will ask questions or give cues to discussion but are very sensitive to parents' reactions If everything about an adult's manner and behaviour tells a child this is a 'no go' area of conversation, if parents ignore first questions or get angry if the subject arises, a child will quickly pick up on this and generally avoid the topic.

A child's interest in a subject is generally entirely self-centred The under-five's view of the world is self-centred and learning to take account of other people and think about how they feel is a slow learning process. This means adults do not need to burden a child with long, involved explanations relating to their own feelings. Rather, a child usually wants his questions answered directly and related always to how something will affect him. This child's-eye view can often lead to him asking questions or making statements which may upset parents – for example, 'Can I have Granny's car?' on learning of her death, or 'Will my Daddy still come to see me on my birthday?' Don't think it is just your child being selfish or unfeeling, all young children share this view.

Explanations need to be kept simple Do not think that because a child's understanding is in advance of his language he will want to know all the complexities and adult issues involved. Taking a deep breath and launching into a carefully thought out and planned explanation of something you dreaded tackling, only to find your child has lost interest after half a sentence and gone off to play is a common parental experience. Keep it simple and answer the question he has asked.

Information needs updating Parents often breathe a sigh of relief once they have tackled a difficult subject, feeling that now their child has been told there is no need to go over it again. The fact is, though, that children forget, sometimes events change, and, as their understanding develops, they need more sophisticated and fuller explanations. Telling a three-year-old everything about how babies are made and are born does not mean you will not have to cover the same ground in different terms for your child as his understanding develops through childhood and adolescence.

MARRIAGE DIFFICULTIES

There may be times when you and your partner are not getting on well. This may mean you are often quarrelling and arguing, or alternatively not speaking much to each other and angry or tense silences ensue. These emotional difficulties will affect the way you are able to look after your children. If you yourself are unhappy and under pressure, it is much harder to cope with the demands of young children and to be the same source of stability in their lives. There are, however, various ways in which you can reduce the effect that your relationship traumas will have on them and minimise the chance of long-term emotional damage.

* Do not run down the other parent when you talk to the children, or indeed to friends in their presence. However you may feel personally, it is important for children to be able to appreciate the good sides of their father or mother and presenting the other person as an unmitigated villain will be confusing and in the long term potentially damaging for children.

* Do not threaten to leave home – this is very frightening indeed to children and undermines the very core of their security.

* If events have actually arrived at a point where you are going to leave, then it is vital that you talk to them, prepare them as far as possible and reassure them that you will still love them and be their father or mother. Give them details about who is going to look after them and when and where you are going to see them.

* Try to carry on talking to your partner about the welfare, care and future of your children.

SEPARATION AND DIVORCE

It is often hard to put aside your own feelings about your ex-partner and events, but whatever has happened a child still needs to go on loving and being loved by both parents. If something has happened which shows that the other person is not able to fulfil that parental role then you will have to try to explain this in simple terms. Expect your child to be sad and to grieve this loss, even when he has been abused in some way. Make it very plain that events are not the result of the child's action – a young child sees everything in terms of himself and thinks it is his fault if Daddy or Mummy goes away – perhaps it has happened because he was naughty. At the same time emphasise your love and reassure him that he will not lose you. If you feel bitter towards your partner, it can be hard to find that your child still loves and wants that other person, but do not feel angry that your love alone does not seem to be enough – your child's reaction is a plea for more reassurance.

In the long term it is better for a child if he can maintain a relationship with both parents. It is one of the hard facts of life that long after love has changed to loathing or indifference you both still have to go on being parents and the

471

more you are able to communicate, to set aside differences and make arrangements based on your child's needs, the better it will be for him.

It is at times like these that other relatives and friends can be very helpful, so make use of them if you can. Grandparents, aunts and uncles, as well as close friends can all give your child extra love and security and can often talk more dispassionately than you can about events. Their detachment may enable a child to ask questions he senses are taboo with you.

If your young child does not ask you direct questions, don't assume he has not noticed anything. Trying to make sense of events and feelings through play is common. Uncertainty may show in changed behaviour, for example, wanting a bottle when he has left that stage behind, wetting the bed at night, disturbed sleeping or simply difficult behaviour. It is also common to find that children in this situation often start to be more clingy and do not want to let the remaining parent out of their sight, whereas before they were happy to go to playgroup or play in the garden on their own. Patience plus reassurance that you will return to collect them or, in the case of playing in the garden or another room, that you are not going to leave suddenly, is necessary. There is a fine line to be drawn, however, because parents can often assume that every little problem with their child is due to their own marital difficulties and end up doubling their guilt load. Remember, children do go through difficult stages anyway, irrespective of family life.

DEATH, ILLNESS AND HANDICAP

Young children can seem very insensitive when talking about death, especially the death of a loved grandparent. They often ask very practical questions like 'Where is Grandpa?' and 'Can I see him?' after hearing of his death because their concept of people is rooted in the physical reality of the body. The idea of a personality and a spiritual presence which can cease to exist is beyond their grasp. Talking about the way in which plants or flowers grow and die, or the way animals die, can help them to understand. Although the finality of death is beyond their understanding so that they do not show the grief which an adult feels, young children may still miss and feel the loss of a loved friend or relative who dies. They may ask about the person some time after his death, even though you thought they understood that they would not see him again. Be prepared to be patient and explain simply – exactly what you say will be tempered by your own religious or other beliefs. If the child enjoyed happy times with the person who has died, recall those occasions.

When someone within your child's life is ill you need to explain the facts simply to him so that he understands the changes in that person's behaviour towards him. The way in which you answer your child's questions about people he may encounter personally or see in the street who have some noticeable disability or handicap is also important in influencing long-term attitudes. If he embarrasses you by pointing and asking loudly in front of the person concerned, give a simple explanation – for example, that person is in a wheelchair because his legs do not work well enough to walk. Later you can tell him that not everyone is as lucky as he is to have a perfect body and mind which work so well. Go on to explain that people whose bodies do not work as well as his may look or behave differently, but they probably get tired of children asking what is wrong so it is better to ask later instead of in front of them. Young children are simply curious – prejudices such as fear or pity will be picked up from the way you and other people respond to that curiosity.

RELIGION

How you answer questions about God as well as about death will naturally depend on your own religious beliefs. If you are ambivalent, expect children to be influenced by the much more definite views which may be presented at playgroup or nursery with the telling of the traditional story of the birth of Christ and the enactment of the Nativity. It is probably best to be honest about your own feelings while giving them an idea of the prevalent religious beliefs they will encounter.

SEX

With widespread public advertising about the threat of AIDS, more young children may ask specific questions – 'What is a condom?' is just as likely from a four-year-old as 'Where do babies come from?' The arrival of a second or third baby in the family or the birth of a friend's baby may prompt questions. There are many good books if you need help in explaining how babies begin and grow in the womb but remember children will forget and need a fuller explanation as they grow older.

Young children are very interested in babies – though it is important to teach them to touch and hold them (under supervision) with care and gentleness and not allow them to view a baby as a dolly to be played with. Strangely, though, young children are often quite unperceptive about the changing shape of their mother or a friend during pregnancy. Most parents find the growth of the unborn baby inside the womb quite easy to explain to young children, using one of the many picture books which are aimed at under-fives. It is often less easy to answer questions about exactly where and how the baby gets out and just how 'Daddy's seed' got into the womb in the first place. Even if you find it easy to furnish toddlers with facts including the correct anatomical terminology, instilling a sense of discretion as to the time and place for discussion can still prove difficult. One mother, in the seventh month of pregnancy, remembers her four-year-old daughter's clear and merciless questioning in the queue at the green-grocer's: 'When exactly did Daddy give you his seed?' In fact young children accept factual information about intercourse and birth without any of the embarrassment of much older children. Again, be led by your child's questioning and do not burden him with more information than he wants. Inevitably parents will use the language and the words they feel comfortable with and will also follow their instincts about how and what they tell their children.

473

Quite separate from the question of how a baby is made, is the question of warning children about sexual abuse. From a very early age – certainly by about two – children have a good understanding of what their 'private parts' are. Parents will choose the language and words they are comfortable with, but the simplest message to give pre-school children is: 'Your body is special and it is your own – if anyone touches you in a way you don't like, tell them not to, and tell me as well.' Growing public awareness that child sexual abuse appears to be relatively widespread and the resulting media attention have left many parents both fearful for their child's safety and uncertain about what is normal sexual development in a child. A degree of healthy suspicion and awareness on the part of parents is no bad thing, and certainly paedophiles do seek out positions of authority and trust which will put them in close contact with children. But at the other end of the spectrum a few parents may begin to feel anxious about enjoying what is simply a child's natural sensuality. This may take the form of hugging, caressing and stroking, all of which are perfectly normal. There is nothing wrong in finding pleasure in the sensation of a baby's soft cheek against your own face, in stroking their limbs or admiring the perfection of diminutive bodies. What is not normal is to find the natural sensuality of children sexually exciting.

What should parents do if their child says something which may indicate he has been a victim of sexual abuse? The most important thing is not to panic and over-react: the moment a parent goes over the top the chance of ever discovering what happened recedes. Parents should take what their children say seriously, but they should also remember that while children do not make up stories they do say funny things which, on investigation, turn out not to mean what they may think. For example, a three-year-old who said, 'I don't like snakes because they go up your bottom,' revealed, after a bit more chat, that this was based on a story from an older child about how a snake could live in the lavatory. Parents must also be careful, in their desire to coax a child into telling the truth, not to prompt them with leading questions or to put words into the child's mouth. This will obviously not happen if the parents let the child tell them what happened in his own time and in his own words, but it is all too easy for an anxious parent with a not very forthcoming child to ask questions of the 'Did he put his willy up your bottom?' type. There is good evidence that young children are likely to say 'yes' to this sort of question, and then the question may be repeated by the child as a statement and become part of 'the history' of what happened – irrespective of the facts. Cultivating a natural patience when talking with young children and allowing them to volunteer information at their own pace and in their own words is a valuable skill for any parent to learn and a general principle to be remembered whether talking about what they did at playgroup or potential sexual abuse. A child under five is, however, unlikely to be able to make up a sequence of events, including a person and a place.

Physical signs of sexual abuse may be a sore bottom, vaginal discharge in girls, or disturbed behaviour such as wetting or soiling in a child who has been potty trained for a long while, a disturbed sleep pattern, refusal to eat, anxiety, clinginess, or awareness of sexual acts in speech or behaviour.

Sexual abuse may have occurred inside or outside the home. The latter is easier to deal with, because the child is still able to continue to trust those people he loves and still has their support. Abuse inside the home by a member of the family entails an abuse of power and of trust. Insensitive investigation can be traumatic for children and it has come to be recognised that steps taken to ascertain the truth and then to protect the child from further abuse can in themselves cause so much distress to the child as to constitute secondary abuse. In deciding to take action, parents must make their own decisions and these must be based on the future welfare of their own and other children. Can their child be protected from further abuse? If no action is taken will other children be safe?

Sexual play and exploration involving looking and touching without the use of force with children of the same age is a normal part of growing up; sexual abuse is not. Sometimes sexual play can get out of hand, and, for example, a brother can seriously abuse a younger sister. Parents should find out what has actually happened by talking to their children separately. If parents are worried about this or any other sort of sexual abuse, but have difficulty talking to their children, or if they are convinced that there has been a case of serious sexual abuse, they should contact a social worker, or talk to their GP, who will put them in touch with a social worker.

Research has shown that the attitude of the mother is relevant to the long-term effects of both the abuse and the investigation, and that children fare best when the mother is very supportive but stays calm. To do this she may need a good deal of support herself, particularly if such an incident revives memories of sexual abuse she may have suffered as a child. Research shows that parents who were sexually abused in childhood are more likely to talk to their own children about sex in general, probably because they are specially aware of the need to educate and protect early.

Children are naturally very curious about bodies — talking about what they can and cannot do in the way of developing skills, about what different parts of the body are called and how they work, and about how a child's body differs from an adult's helps to foster a sense of pride and confidence in their own bodies that will lead towards having a good self-image. This curiosity can also be encouraged naturally to help them to learn the basic skills of looking after themselves — brushing teeth and hair, washing, going to the toilet, choosing the right kind of clothes according to the weather and season and eating healthy food. You can explain that smoking and eating things which may be harmful — toxic substances which occur naturally like berries and leaves, for example, as well as household poisons — can damage a healthy body.

Chapter 15

PROTECTING YOUR CHILD

Safety
Parents' check-list – how to protect your child from accidents
Emergency first aid   Hygiene

SAFETY

'My eighteen-month-old climbed up on to a stool to try and reach something on a work surface and knocked a cup of boiling hot coffee all over her chest and tummy. She had never got up on to a stool before and I didn't even know she could manage it so I thought the coffee was perfectly safe.'

'We were at a family wedding when my three-year-old began to choke on some peanuts she had helped herself to. Fortunately there was a nurse among the guests and she told us to go straight to hospital. In the end she had inhaled a peanut right into her lung and had to have an operation to get it out before it splintered and did serious damage. I had no idea peanuts could be so dangerous.'

'I left the front door pushed to but not properly shut while I was taking rubbish sacks out for the dustman. I was only out the back for a second when I came through and found the front door wide open and my two-year-old had gone right out into the street and was standing on the pavement. I managed to get to him before he stepped off, but I was trembling for ages. We live on a busy road, but I had no idea he could pull the door open because even when the catch isn't on it's quite stiff.'

Very many accidents which happen to children could be prevented. With the under-fives the problem is that dangers and risks change daily as the child grows and becomes more mobile and able. It is harder for first time parents to anticipate and look ahead to spot potential dangers when they have no experience of the way children develop. Generally parents tend to react to the threat of danger, rather than anticipate it. Once their child has

477

managed to climb over the stair-gate and fallen down the stairs, or moved enough to roll off the table, they know those things are dangerous and will not rely on the stair-gate or leave their baby on the table again. What we all need to do is to protect our children by being one step ahead and spotting the dangers before an accident happens. Your health visitor will be pleased to give any advice and help you to plan safety measures in your home when she visits. When you have a small baby in a cot it might seem a long way off before you need to think of stair-gates, the dangers of electric plugs, trailing kettle leads and all the other hazards that might harm a crawling or walking baby. But in fact it is not – very many babies are mobile by seven to eight months and can pull themselves to their feet with whatever comes to hand before they are one year old. Further, once you have a baby, you are more likely to be visited by people with slightly older children as well. It will be better to child-proof your home from the start. Accidents are the single most common cause of death in children aged one to fourteen.

WHAT ARE THE MOST COMMON ACCIDENTS?

Road accidents where the child is a pedestrian are the most common cause of accidental death in children under five. Fires rank second, with most deaths being due to breathing in smoke and toxic fumes in house fires. Nearly three-quarters of all burn accidents (as distinct from deaths from fires) happen to children under five with the most at risk age being one- to two-year-olds. Suffocation and choking is the third commonest cause of accidental death in pre-school children – babies are most at risk, but older children can be as well when left playing alone. Nearly half the children who drown each year are under five years old and with these very young children the accident is likely to happen in a garden pond or swimming pool. Deaths from traffic accidents while they are passengers in a car, rather than pedestrians, happen slightly less among very young children, probably because parents are becoming more conscious about safety straps for babies and toddlers, but are the fifth commonest cause of accidental death. Children from one to four years are most at risk from deaths from falls, as they begin to crawl, climb and want to explore and adventure more. Less common causes of accidental deaths are electrocution, scalds, and poisoning.

PROTECT by taking safety measures around the home and when out. Always be one step ahead of your child's ability and anticipate what he will soon be able to do.

TEACH about avoiding dangers by what you tell him and by the example you set.

BUYING GOODS

The British Standards Institution is an independent national organisation that publishes technical documents – British Standards. Its aim is to make sure that what you buy does its job and with products for children it is important they are both safe and, in the case of equipment, work properly.

What to look for A British Standards (BS) number on a product means the manufacturer is claiming that his product meets the requirement of that standard, but it does not mean that the British Standards Institution has approved the product. If you have any problems with something carrying a BS number, you can ask your trading standards office, consumer advice centre, or trade association which can be found in your local phone book.

Household electrical equipment which meets standards of the British Electrotechnical Approvals Board (BEAB) also carries its own mark of safety. The Institution tests samples of electrical appliances on behalf of the BEAB. If you have a complaint you can go to the BEAB (see address section, pages 673–6).

The British Standards Institution (see address section, pages 673–6) will be pleased to advise on which products carry safety or kite marks and on standard numbers.

The kite mark This mark means that the British Standards Institution has checked the manufacturer's claim that the product meets the specific standards. If you have a complaint about a product carrying the kite mark, the Institute will investigate.

The safety mark The safety mark indicates that a product has been checked to see that it meets the British Standards specification for safety only. Again, if you have a complaint, the Institute will investigate.

The lion mark This is the symbol of the British Toy and Hobby Manufacturers Association and is widely applied to toys. Beware of toys bought off market stalls or cheap foreign imports which may be copies of well-known toys without the same safety standards.

During the 1990s a European safety standard mark is to be introduced, but importers as well as manufacturers of foreign goods have an obligation to ensure their product meets the necessary safety standards. When buying second-hand or foreign goods if in doubt about the safety mark to look for consult your local trading standards officer who can be contacted through the local authority listed in the phone book.

PARENTS' CHECKLIST – HOW TO PROTECT YOUR CHILD FROM ACCIDENTS

CHOKING AND SUFFOCATION

Babies are most at risk, but older children can be at risk when playing on their own.

DO NOT use a pillow for babies under a year old or leave them alone in quilted material because they are not able to lift their heads. Use a firm mattress which meets British Standard No. 1877. It is very important to check that the mattress does not leave dangerous gaps between the edge of the mattress and the sides or ends of the cot. Baby nests must meet British Standard No. 6595 and have a flat head area, which allows unobstructed breathing and avoids any risk of suffocation, has no handles, ties, cords or elastic, and carries a label warning against the use of soap-based washing powder which might clog fibres and stop air passing through the fabric. They are suitable for carrying but not for leaving a sleeping baby unattended. For children over a year old, pillows should meet British Standard No. 1877 (the same as the mattresses) and should be porous and allow air to pass through freely whatever position the baby is in.

DO NOT ever leave a baby alone with a propped-up bottle because he can easily choke on it.

DO make sure babies cannot get anything pulled tight around their necks – always pin a dummy or teething biscuit on a short ribbon, not a long one. Watch for open-weave cardigans and jackets, especially with ribbons or threads around the neck which can catch on a hook or knob and pull tight. Open-weave or lacy shawls, blankets or clothes can also allow fingers to be caught and trapped – babies have actually lost fingers which were trapped and cut off like this. Beware of potentially lethal tie-strings on anoraks for older children.

DO check that there are no hanging cords, for example from a window, which can catch around a child's neck and strangle him if he falls – again such tragedies have happened. Make sure no cords or threads are within reach of the cot and keep string and rope away from children. Teach toddlers never to put things around each other's necks in play and make sure older children grow up with this message.

DO keep all plastic bags away from babies and children and teach children never to put such bags on their heads. If they do they can suffocate. Very flimsy plastic, for example on dry cleaning, often attracts babies and toddlers because of the rustly sound and could obstruct breathing if held over their faces – keep it well away.

DO NOT let your baby or young child get hold of tiny items like coins, small marbles, Lego, hearing-aid batteries, dried peas or chickpeas and buttons, because once he can pick up things it is an automatic reflex to put them into his mouth and he can easily choke on them.

DO check that all toys you give to babies and young children are safe with no loose parts which can come away or sharp points which may be dangerous.

DO NOT leave babies alone with finger foods such as carrots, cheese, and so on, because lumps can break off and cause choking. Always be on hand when your child is eating. Make older children sit down to eat, do not let them run around when there is more chance of choking. Always chop up babies' food to a size small enough to swallow.

DO NOT give large, hard sweets to babies or young children and always supervise eating and drinking.

DO NOT give peanuts to children under four years because they can easily choke on them or inhale them into their lungs, often without anyone realising at the time. A child who has inhaled a peanut or other object will usually begin to wheeze or cough after a time. Take him to your doctor immediately, or to the nearest accident or emergency unit if you know he has inhaled something. Peanuts can splinter and cause infection and the risk of local lung damage rises the longer the nut stays in place. In cases where the peanut is left longer than seven days, over half the children suffer some such damage. Be especially careful on occasions like weddings or parties or when visiting other homes that your young child does not eat peanuts.

SCALDS AND BURNS

As children learn to crawl, climb and walk, the risk of burns or scalds increases – be one step ahead of your child's curiosity and make safety measures a habit from birth.

Hot drinks and hot water can scald badly enough to scar permanently and children have died from severe scalds. Never take a hot drink with a child on your lap and do not pass hot drinks over the heads of children. Keep all hot drinks in drinking containers or teapots away from the edge of tables where they can be reached. Do not use tablecloths which young children can pull down on top of themselves.

Kettles should always be well out of reach with a short flex which is not hanging down – curly flexes which curl up on themselves are now available. Remember steam can be dangerous and scald badly so do not leave a kettle simmering unattended.

Cookers can be made safe with a guard round the edge. Make it a habit always to turn pan handles inwards and use the rings at the back if you are cooking with only one or two pans. If possible, keep a young child in a playpen or chair while working.

Do not take things off the cooker, for example to strain vegetables, with a child under your feet. Never leave a child alone in the kitchen with the cooker on. Turn things off and take the child with you to answer the phone or the door. Teach him not to touch the oven door or try to open it.

Do not let your child get into the habit of climbing on chairs to reach cupboards or anything else near the cooker.

Irons are a common cause of burns. Use a coiled or sprung flex, do not iron where children are likely to run through, and always unplug and put the iron away completely out of reach to cool down. Do not leave an iron unattended with a child around – remember an unplugged iron which is still hot can burn badly. Young children are highly imitative and love to copy things they have seen grown-ups do. A toy iron and their own ironing board is fine, but hammer home the message that they should never, never try to iron with your iron.

Baths should always be tested before putting a child in – children have died in baths of very hot water. Always put cold water in first and then add the hot. A plastic strip thermometer is now available to stick to the inside of the bath to indicate the temperature. Do not leave a baby or toddler alone in a bath, even for a minute when answering the phone or door. Instead wrap him in a towel and take him out with you.

Do not set the thermostat so high that water is very hot when it comes out of the taps because it can burn older children when they go to wash.

Matches and lighters must be kept well out of reach. Do not let children play with matches – again they will try to imitate you and strike them. Do not indulge in any 'blowing out' games with matches or lighters.

Fires must always be protected with a fixed fire guard which has safety hooks to secure it to the floor or wall, fine mesh to stop children putting hands through and a fixed covering over the top. Government regulations state that such guards must be fitted to electric, gas or paraffin heaters.

Do not use gas or paraffin heaters in children's bedrooms, use only a BEAB approved electric or gas convector heater with a safety guard. Be careful when visiting friends' or relatives' houses where fires may not be guarded. Start using fire guards (British Standard No. 6539) before your baby crawls – later may be too late.

Petrol or paraffin must be kept away from children and not stored in large amounts.

Nightclothes and dressing gowns must be flame resistant. The UK law requires all nightdresses to be made from material which does not flare up or burn easily and new regulations have come into force which also cover dressing gowns. Pyjamas and night-shirts are not covered by these regulations. Flimsy cotton is the most dangerous material. Check that you buy nightwear for your child covered by the British Standard No. 3121.

Fireworks are more likely to be a problem with daredevil school-aged children, but younger children need careful supervision on firework night. Follow the firework instructions and keep children a safe distance away with another adult. Do not try to stage a backgarden firework display if you are the only adult at home and you have young children – join forces with a neighbour or another family instead.

Do not let children walk around holding sparklers – children have burnt their faces by falling or by another child putting the sparkler in their face by accident. Be careful they do not touch the end when it has just gone out but is still hot.

Preventing fires

* Use a thermostatically controlled deep fat fryer.

* Keep a fire blanket in the kitchen.

* If a small fire breaks out smother it with a blanket or rug.

* Do not leaving burning cigarettes in ashtrays.

* Never smoke in bed.

* Do not leave paraffin heaters in draughts or where they may get knocked over.

* Check you have no highly inflammable furniture – Part I of British Standard No. 5852 studies the effect on upholstered furniture of a smouldering cigarette and a flame equivalent to a match – red triangular labels displayed on the furniture warn of failures and green rectangular ones show the match test has been passed.

* Install automatic smoke detectors – alarms which go off in reaction to smoke.

* Check plugs are wired correctly and sockets are not overloaded. Consider installing a circuit breaker which makes it impossible to electrocute yourself.

TRAFFIC ACCIDENTS

Pedestrians Outside the home traffic is the single greatest danger to your child's life. Children under five years old need continual close supervision and it is worth remembering, as your child grows, that children are not totally reliable in traffic as pedestrians until they are about twelve years old. Judging the speed and distance of traffic from several directions and reacting quickly is a very complex business.

A great many children are killed each year just a few hundred yards from their own homes – remember accidents do not only happen on busy roads. Be just as careful on quieter roads.

Hold your child's hand or use reins if he is out of a pram or pushchair near a road. Make sure you always cross roads in a safe place and do not let your child go half-way across and then run over by himself. Example is an important way of teaching road safety.

Talk about traffic and the dangers when you are out with your child. Children of three years and over can join a 'Tufty' club run by the Royal Society for the Prevention of Accidents – the road safety officer at your local authority can give details.

Teach your child the Green Cross Code and follow it yourself. Safe places to cross are subways, foot bridges, zebra or pelican crossings, traffic lights or with the aid of a lollipop man or lady, traffic warden or the police. Failing this, choose a place where you can be clearly seen both ways.

Playing out in the streets is not safe for any child under five, even if there are older children there as well. The Royal Society for the Prevention of Accidents recommends that children under eight are not safe on their own. You cannot rely on young children, however sensible they may seem, to follow instructions or understand dangers.

When your child is old enough to ride a trike or bike on the pavement with you beside him, teach him to be careful of other people walking on the pavement. Do not let him ride across the road – always make him get off and either carry the trike over yourself, holding the child with your free

hand, or get him to wheel it across beside you at a safe crossing point. Children should be encouraged to wear cycle helmets from an early age.

Roads in the country without pavements can present a special hazard. Keep children between you and the side of the road and walk so that you face oncoming traffic. At dusk or after dark make sure you can be seen clearly by wearing light clothes and a reflective arm band, coat or disc.

Children as passengers in cars We all dread the possibility of a serious car crash, but you can give your children a much better chance of surviving or escaping an accident without serious injury if you ensure they are safely secured every single time they travel in the car.

Babies If a baby cannot sit up yet and weighs less than 10 kg the best system for transporting him in your car is in a rearward facing restraint. This is a relatively new design and is essentially a portable chair which cradles the baby in a reclining nest. The chair fits in the front passenger seat using adult safety straps and the back of the baby's head is towards the dashboard. In the event of a crash the restraint tilts towards the back of the passenger seat and the baby, harnessed in the restraint, is protected in the space in between. The standard is BS AU202 and specifies that the restraint can be used in conjunction with an approved adult seatbelt in the front or rear seat of a car. The restraints can also be used as baby seats in and around the house or when visiting friends, which is useful. Many hospitals and a variety of other bodies have combined to provide loan schemes so that rearward-facing restraints can be hired as some babies quickly grow out of them – this means that parents can be sure their child is safely secured in the car for their very first journey home from hospital. An older system for transporting babies is a carry-cot, secured in the back seat with carry-cot restraints made to British Standard No. AU186a. In this case the baby's head should face away from the door: use either a harness or carry-cot cover to secure the baby in the cot – it is no good fixing the cot securely if the baby can be thrown out in the event of an accident. The restraint straps need to be fitted into the car.

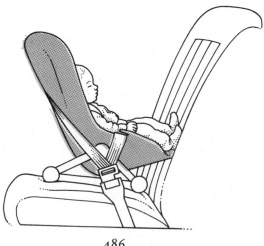

Toddlers and young children Once your baby can sit up on his own then you can move on to a child safety seat. The seat should be made to British Standard No.3254 or EEC regulation 44 and usually suits children up to about four years old or those weighing between 9 kg. and 18 kg. (24 and 48 lbs). Make sure the seat you buy carries the BSI kite mark. Straps securing the seat to the car are usually bolted on to the car structure and need to be fitted by a garage. Make sure you insist on your child going in his seat every trip, no matter how short the journey. Many toddlers go through a stage of making a fuss, but if everyone else in the car wears seat straps they are more likely to want to copy.

Do not be tempted to let him travel unstrapped 'just for once' because it will be much harder to get him into the seat next time and could be the one occasion when straps might save his life.

Older children Once your child weighs more than about 18 kg. or is four years old or over and is too large for a child safety seat, you can progress to a child harness made to British Standard No. 3254 or EEC regulation 44 or a special adult belt adjustable for children. All types of restraint should have a quick release button. A special booster cushion (British Standard No. AU185) can make them high enough to see out of the window, but do not use just ordinary cushions which will not have the same safety effect at all.

It is a popular myth that there is a law giving a specific age at which children can legally travel in the front of cars. The guidelines are simply that children under fourteen should use safety restraints appropriate to their size. Children are not safe in adult seat straps until they are big enough for the chest strap to fit properly across their chest and prevent them from slipping out of it. Nor should the strap be able to slide up so that it passes across their neck.

Travelling in other people's cars This often poses a problem. When possible, children under fourteen should travel in the back using seat straps, but, if the child is large enough travelling with a seat strap in the front is better than sitting unstrapped in the back if there are no rear seat straps. A BSI approved booster cushion can make adult seat straps, preferably in the back, but otherwise in the front, fit better. As a last resort, if there is no other means of securing a young child, he should be held by an adult in the back. Always use child safety locks on the back doors if your car is fitted with them. These enable the door to be opened only from the outside.

NEVER hold a baby in your arms in the front seat or put a seat belt round yourself and a baby or child in your arms.

DO NOT let a child stand on the back seat or lean out of the window when driving along.

DROWNING

A baby or toddler can drown in a very shallow amount of water, far less than you normally put in the bath, so do not let a young child play with water on his own and never leave a baby or toddler alone in the bath, even for a second. If the doorbell or phone goes or another child needs attention, lift out the baby first. If you have a garden make sure you check it for safety. Ponds need to be fenced, covered with wire mesh or filled in. Other water containers can also be a danger to the very young, so clear away or fence off water tanks, butts, or ditches which fill with water after rain.

Whether children are paddling in a pool or playing at the seaside, at the swimming pool or beside a river, stay nearby and watch them closely. Insist that they wear arm bands all the time, but remember that these are not life-saving buoyancy aids and children should be supervised even if they are wearing them.

Teach children to swim as soon as possible and make sure they learn about water safety, but when your child has learnt to swim do not assume that he is drown-proof. Being confident about water does not mean he is necessarily safe.

Do not try to take two very young children swimming when both need close supervision – wait until another adult can join you.

Teaching your baby to swim Most babies love water. All that splashing and bobbing about is exciting stuff when you are not yet fully mobile on dry land. It is not surprising that swimming is just about the most popular out-of-home activity for small babies and toddlers

Feeling confident and enjoying water can begin with bathtime sessions at home. Encourage your baby to enjoy water by making him feel safe, holding him securely, and be sure the water is the right temperature for his age (see page 482). There is a question mark over the practice of completely submerging babies under a year old in water as has been taught in Russia and America because there is a suggestion that it may be possible for a young baby to swallow too much water and suffer a type of brain damage, although no cases have been recorded in this country. This does not mean you should worry about your baby getting the odd faceful or mouthful of water, but the benefit of deliberately submerging young babies seems dubious. Instead, get your baby used to the feel of water on his face and encourage breathing control by gently sprinkling some water over his face in the bath and later in the pool. Even the temperature of a small 'trainer' pool will be too cold for a very new baby, but once he is about three months old he will be able to enjoy short dips in trainer pools which are generally warmer than the large main swimming pool. Pick a time when he is well, wide awake and not hungry. Your baby's swimming gear should be towelling pants or a little costume. If he wears plastic pants or nappies he will sink. Pick a swimming pool which has a separate shallow pool for beginners and ask another adult to come with you on your first time swim. Your helper can hold your baby while you climb in and out of the pool, but if you have no one to help, then lie your baby on a towel at the pool's edge and keep one hand on him while you manoeuvre yourself in. Then lift him in too, once you are standing safely.

If you are taking an older baby or toddler swimming who can sit up by himself, make sure he will sit still on the edge while you get in: older toddlers can be taught to use the ladder steps while you stand below them. When your baby is small you can lie him on his back in the water with one hand under his head and the other under his bottom. When he feels secure take your hand away from his bottom and his own buoyancy should allow him to float. Another good position is to put your baby's head on your shoulder while you hold him under his arms, encouraging him to kick in the water. As your baby gets older, he will want to go on his front. Crouch down for eye contact and hold him under his armpits, bringing your wrists together under his chin thus supporting his head. Then move him around so that he can get used to the feel of moving through water. To encourage him to move his arms, support him sideways on, holding him under the armpits, and float a brightly-coloured toy or ball in front of him to entice him to stretch out for it. Even young babies will stretch out as long as they feel safe. Encourage him to blow bubbles in the bath and swimming pool which will get him used to breathing out in water. Your baby can 'go solo' right from the start on the water surface with a simple push and glide between two adults. However, neither of you should let go at first. As he grows bigger and stronger your baby will start to make leg and arm movements – his first try at swimming properly. Use inflatable arm bands and as your child gets bigger and more confident you can gradually decrease the amount of air in the arm bands. But whether swimming with your child in a pool, at the sea or in a lake, always stay close and keep a careful eye. Ask at your local swimming pool or write to the Amateur Swimming Association (see address section, pages 673–6) for the address of your nearest mother and baby swimming class or for swimming classes for older children on their own.

CUTS AND OTHER ACCIDENTS THROUGH PLAY

Glass around your home is one of the biggest safety hazards to a young child. It may be in a front or back door, and is in most patio and french doors. Every year about 7,000 children end up in hospital because they have been cut by glass, often very badly. Toddlers can easily totter and go through a glass door and older children can crash into a sheet of glass in a door when they get excited and run around. All this may seem a long way in the future when you have a small, helpless, newborn baby who cannot even turn over for himself, but as we said at the beginning – anticipation is the key to preventing accidents.

Check your house and either replace glass indoors with wooden panels or with special safety glass. While ordinary glass easily breaks into lethal jagged pieces and splinters, safety glass does not. There are two types – laminated glass is two sheets of ordinary glass stuck to a layer of plastic in between. Although laminated glass rarely breaks, if it does the pieces stay in place. The second type of safety glass is made by a special process of heating and cooling which makes it less likely to break – it is called 'toughened' or 'tempered' glass and must be ordered to size. If it does break it will shatter into small cuboid pieces which are relatively harmless. As well as panels of glass in doors or glass doors look at low level windows, especially interior ones, and glass panels or doors in showers or bathrooms. Glass which is frosted or patterned is unlikely to be safety glass.

Measures can be taken to make glass safer by fixing a plastic film over panels in doors or other areas. Mark dangerous glass with coloured strips to make children notice it is there or board up the area. Do not let toddlers or young children walk around with a glass or anything made of glass in their hands as they could easily fall.

Keep all knives, scissors, tools and other dangerous objects out of the way of babies and young children. As they get older teach them to use dangerous tools safely and only with you on hand. Remember again that children are highly imitative and keep scissors and razors in the bathroom well out of reach.

Teach children:

* Always to carry scissors, screwdrivers, sharp pencils or anything else pointing downwards, and to walk, never run with them.

* Never to run with a pencil or lollipop stick in their mouth.

* Never to touch electric sockets or plugs. Socket covers are a cheap and useful way of securing floor-level points.

* Not to slam doors or play with doors. Fingers easily get pinched in hinges as well as by the door itself. A device which can be fitted at the top of the door can prevent doors from slamming – ask at your local hardware shop.

TOYS AND PLAYGROUNDS

Toys should not have sharp edges or points which can cut. Be particularly careful to inspect foreign toys closely and make sure there are no heads which can come off leaving lethal spikes, glass eyes that can be pulled off, or other dangerous aspects. Be especially careful and watchful when young children have access to toys meant for older ones. Check toys for British Standard Nos 5665 and 3443 – all toys sold in the UK must comply with government safety regulations which refer to these British Standard numbers.

Playgrounds In general these have become safer and better designed places but there are still many around with old style equipment where much closer supervision of young children is needed. Never let a pre-school child go to a playground without an adult.

These are some points to watch for when assessing the safety of a playground:

Swings These should be made of rubber or plastic, not metal or wood. Ideally they should be on the edge of the playground enclosed by a safety barrier. Always teach your child never to step into the path of a swing where they can be easily hit on the head.

Slides These should be built into the side of a slope so that children cannot fall off the top. If you have to use a playground with a traditional slide, climb up behind very young children and seat them safely on the slide.

Swinging and rocking equipment Apparatus such as see-saws or rocking horses should have a limited amount of movement. In many playgrounds heavy swinging equipment like the witches' hats or boats still exist. Any swinging equipment should have a handle which a child can grip.

The ground This should have an impact absorbent surface in the immediate area of the equipment: many newer playgrounds are being designed with surfaces such as sand, peat, gravel or grass interspersed with impact absorbent material. Beware of playgrounds which still have concrete or asphalt.

If your playground has equipment in a dangerous state or of a dangerous design report it to the local council.

ELECTRIC SHOCKS

Simply fixing socket covers or putting dummy plugs in all your sockets could save your child's life. As he grows older teach him never to touch plugs or sockets or to poke anything into the sockets. Make sure the plugs in your house are correctly wired and safe. Be especially vigilant when visiting other people's houses which are not geared to young children which may especially apply around Christmas time when Christmas tree lights could be within easy grasp of a toddler. When buying Christmas tree lights look for the British Standard No. 4647.

POISONING

The under-fives are most likely to swallow poisonous things they find around the house and every year thousands of small children end up in hospital. Some even die as a result. The peak age for accidents with poisons is one to three years old – just the stage when children are highly mobile and inquisitive but have absolutely no idea that taking medicines is any more dangerous than the sweets they resemble or that a bottle of bleach is anything more than a drink.

Keep all medicines in a cupboard that locks, and keep it locked. Try not to take medicines, pills or potions in front of small children – they will be intrigued and want to copy.

Ask the chemist to put medicines in childproof containers and make sure that you shut them properly. British Standard Nos for packaging are BS 6652 and BS 5321.

Be careful with tablets when your child goes to stay in other people's houses, particularly those of elderly people, and when people come to stay with you. Old people may be especially likely to take some form of medicine and may be used to leaving it about.

All dangerous household chemicals should be kept out of reach of a young child, in a locked cupboard if possible. Never transfer dangerous products into other containers, for example weed killer into a lemonade bottle.

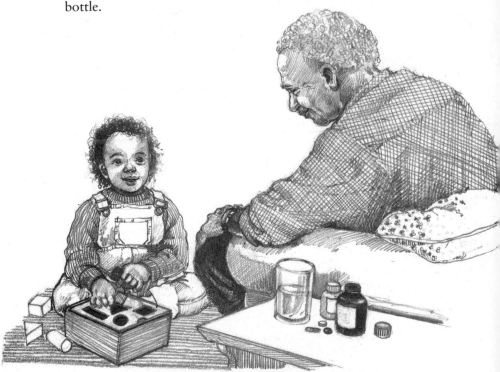

Check whether your child could reach any of these items in your house or garden:

Battery acid	Lavatory cleaner	Slug pellets
Bleach	Methylated spirits	Turps
Caustic soda	Paint stripper	Weed killer
Disinfectant	Paraffin	White spirit
Insecticides	Rat poison	

Teach your child never to put any berries, fungi or plants in his mouth because some of these are very dangerous.

FALLS

All children fall, but there are things you can do to try to make sure they do not fall too far or too hard. Babies most often fall because they roll off table tops or other raised areas, so never leave them alone on a table, work surface, bed or sofa, even if they have not learnt to roll over. The time you turn your back to go to answer the phone may be the first time your child learns to roll over. Nor should you leave them in bouncing chairs on a high surface because they can easily bounce off. Be careful about leaving them, even in fixed baby chairs, if there is another young child who may try to climb up beside them and accidentally pull the child over. Do not leave your child in a baby-walker near steps or stairs.

When your child begins to crawl you need to guard stairs and doors out of the house that might be left open with a safety-gate; British Standard 4125 is the number to look for. A playpen (British Standard No. 4863) can be useful to put them in when you need to leave a door open for a short period, for example, while taking rubbish in and out, or when you want to answer the phone or see to another child. Check that there is no room to crawl under the banisters at the top of the stairs and board up horizontal banisters to prevent climbing.

As your child becomes more mobile check there are no standard lamps or wobbly free-standing cupboards he can pull down on top of himself. Keep chairs pushed into the table or well away so that he cannot climb up. Falls from windows, balconies or roofs are likely to be much more serious, so check that windows are fitted with safety catches to ensure they cannot open wide enough to allow a child to climb through or fall out. Dangerous windows should be fitted with vertical bars: horizontal ones encourage climbing.

Use a harness when you put your child in a highchair, pushchair, pram or other seat – British Standard 6684 is the number to look for on safety harnesses. For more on buying baby equipment see page 74. Remember to anticipate your child's growing ability to climb and move. Things which could once be easily put out of reach on a table or low shelf may suddenly come within reach when he learns to climb. The stair-gate which kept him safe may suddenly become an obstacle to try to climb over, especially if he has seen older children do this. Once your child starts to crawl teach him to come down stairs backwards on all fours.

Beware of dangers such as balconies, stairs and windows when visiting other houses, or in holiday homes which may not be geared to a young child.

EMERGENCY FIRST AID

However carefully you watch your child, accidents still happen. Number one rule is – don't panic. A calm manner may help to comfort the child as well as helping to save his life.

It is often very hard for parents to decide how serious or urgent an injury is. In general, you should go to the nearest hospital with an accident or emergency department.

CHOKING

* Do not waste time trying to get hold of the object the child is choking on unless it is very easy to reach – it will usually be too far back and too slippery and you risk pushing it further down the throat.

496

* Hold a toddler or baby upside-down by the legs and slap him smartly between the shoulder blades with the heel of your hand. If the object he is choking on does not fall out, do it again. A child who is too big to be held upside-down should be laid face downwards across your knees.

* If you try this several times without success, as a last resort you can give the baby's tummy a short, sharp squeeze which should push the object out of the baby's windpipe. If all else fails, take the child immediately to medical assistance – to a GP or hospital if possible, getting someone to phone in advance.

SUFFOCATION

* Immediately take away whatever was covering the child's face, causing the suffocation, and if the child has stopped breathing give mouth to mouth resuscitation (see below).

ARTIFICIAL RESPIRATION

Mouth to mouth resuscitation can save lives in any emergency where breathing has stopped such as electric shock, drowning or smothering. Do not attempt this if the child is still breathing, however faintly, but where breathing has ceased every second counts. Send any bystander for help, but if alone begin immediately without wasting time searching for a pulse or calling for help:

* Turn the child on his back, remove obvious debris from the mouth, and with one hand under his chin and the other on the crown of the head pull the chin forward, arching the neck and tilting the head far back. This stops the tongue blocking the windpipe.

* Open your mouth fully and seal it over the child's mouth, pinching the nostrils closed. You may be able to cover both nostrils and mouth with your mouth if the child is tiny.

* Breathe out gently, looking sideways to see if the chest rises. If the chest does not expand or the abdomen rises, arch the child's neck more, tilting the head further back to open the windpipe.

* Between each breath remove your mouth, breathing normally, and watch the chest fall. Give the first six breaths quickly, then continue every three seconds (six for an adult).

* Do not stop until the child breathes. Many have revived after more than an hour of artificial respiration. If he begins to breathe, put him in the recovery position (see page 500), keeping him warm and quickly phone or call for help. If this is not possible manoeuvre the child between breaths towards a phone or window to call for help but don't stop giving artificial respiration.

SCALDS AND BURNS

* Immediately carry the child to the nearest cold water tap and run plenty of cold water over the scald or burn – it is very important to do this for at least ten minutes to reduce the heat in the skin.

* Only remove clothes that are not stuck to the skin, as will be the case with a scald. Do not try to remove any cloth which is stuck to the skin if the child has actually been burnt.

* Because burnt or scalded skin can swell up take off anything tight like a belt or jewellery.

* Cover the burn or scald with clean cloth which is not fluffy, such as a freshly laundered cotton pillow case or linen tea towel. This helps to protect the damaged area and cuts down the risk of infection.

* Call an ambulance or take the child to hospital yourself. You should take children to hospital for anything other than a very small scald or burn.

* Do not put any fatty substance, such as butter, oil or ointment on a scald or burn because it only has to be cleaned off before the area can be treated. The most important step is to reduce the heat in the skin which you will have done with the cold water.

* Never prick any blisters because this will let germs in.

FALLS AND KNOCKS

* The key things to check are whether your child is conscious, whether he is breathing, and whether there is any bleeding.

* If the child has stopped breathing give mouth to mouth resuscitation immediately (see page 497).

* If the child is breathing but is unconscious or very drowsy it can be dangerous for him to go on lying on his back because the tongue or any vomit may block the throat and stop breathing. For this reason it is important to place him in what is called the recovery position (see page 500).

* If your child is conscious but you think he may have broken a bone or have some kind of internal injury don't move him unless you absolutely have to – for more on broken bones see page 500.

* If you don't know what is wrong or you think the child may be seriously injured, always call an ambulance.

BLEEDING

* Small cuts or grazes simply need to be cleaned carefully with water and cotton wool and you can use a mild antiseptic cream as well. In cases of

severe bleeding the aim is to staunch the flow of blood as quickly as possible. Do this by pressing firmly on the wound with a pad of clean cloth. In an emergency, when a cloth is not available, use your fingers. It may take ten minutes or more to stop the bleeding, but keep pressing until this happens. In the case of a large wound, try to press the edges of the wound in towards each other.

* Provided you do not think your child has broken any bones, lay him down and raise the injured limb on a cushion or anything to hand: this will help to stop the bleeding.

* Do not use a tourniquet or tie anything so tightly that it stops the circulation.

* Toddlers and older children may be especially frightened by the sight of blood, so remember to stay very calm yourself. Cover the wound with a clean dressing.

* After you have done all these things call an ambulance or take the child to hospital yourself.

* Even if the cut or wound is not sufficiently serious to seek medical advice you need to ask your own doctor about a tetanus injection if the accident happened outside or the wound is dirty. Phone your surgery for advice once the child has been made comfortable.

POISONING

* It is sometimes difficult to know for sure whether a child has swallowed pills or medicine. In the case of pills, check on the floor to see if any have rolled away. If you still think something has been swallowed do not waste time but take your child to your own doctor or the hospital – whichever is the quickest. If possible take with you a sample of whatever has been swallowed and its container.

* Do not give your child salt and water to drink to make him sick because salt in large amounts can be dangerous.

CHEMICALS

* If your child has drunk any household or garden chemicals such as turps, petrol, paraffin, acid, or any kind of caustic then the first step is to give him a glass of milk to drink – if there is no milk give water instead – this dilutes the poison.

* Immediately take the child to hospital, again, if possible take a sample of whatever you think has been swallowed and the container with you.

DROWNING

* If the child has stopped breathing give mouth to mouth resuscitation immediately (see page 497).

* If possible send someone for medical help.

* Keep going with the mouth to mouth resuscitation for a long time – breathing can start again more than an hour after it has stopped.

* If the child is still breathing but is unconscious, then place him in the recovery position (see below).

The recovery position

ELECTROCUTION

If your child receives an electric shock in the home:

* Use a dry non-conducting item such as a wooden chair or broom to remove the child from the source of the electricity. Send for an ambulance.

* Do not try to remove the child from a source of high voltage electricity because you risk being electrocuted yourself.

* If the child has stopped breathing give mouth to mouth resuscitation (see page 497) and place a clean dressing or handkerchief over any visible burns.

BROKEN BONES

* It is hard for parents to tell the difference between a fracture and a bad sprain because both will cause swelling and be very painful. The general rule is not to move the child unless you have to; this is particularly important when you think there may be a risk the child has injured the spine or neck.

* If the child *has* to be moved, be as gentle as possible to avoid causing further damage. An injured arm can be supported in a sling and an injured leg can be supported with padding in between the legs and then tied gently but firmly to the good leg.

* Whenever possible try to get medical help before moving a child with a broken bone.

* Do not give a child anything to drink or eat after an accident if you think they may need to have a general anaesthetic later on.

HEAD INJURIES

* It is better to play safe if you think there is a risk that your child may have injured his head. Again, it is very hard for a parent to make a diagnosis because a child's skull can be fractured without suffering a head wound and a serious head wound does not necessarily mean the child has fractured his skull. Signs to watch for are drowsiness, vomiting or pale or bloodstained fluid from nose or ears following a blow to the head. If your child hits his head and loses consciousness, even for a short time, it is best to take him to the accident and emergency unit at your nearest hospital.

FOREIGN BODIES

* Babies and young children have been known to swallow all kinds of foreign bodies such as buttons, small pieces of Lego, tiny batteries, coins, and so on. Fortunately, most of these pass through the bowel and come out the other end without causing any damage and within a day or two. The risk to the child is when the object gets stuck in the gullet (oesophagus). The child will begin to choke and gag and tissues around the object can swell up making it hard for him to breathe. Stay calm; immediately hold him upside down or lay him across your knee so his upper body is hanging down and slap his upper back to dislodge the object. If your child has swallowed a mercury battery this needs urgent medical assessment.

* Rarely children can inhale an object which can go right down into the lungs themselves or get stuck high up in the larynx. This can happen with peanuts, which is why it is unsafe to give peanuts to any child under four years old. Signs may be that the child begins to cough repeatedly. You need to get your child immediately to an accident and emergency unit at a hospital. If necessary the child will be given a general anaesthetic so doctors can pass a special tube down the airways and look directly into the lungs.

* Young children often stick beads and similar items into their ears and up their noses. If you can see the object sticking out of the ear then remove it gently, but do not dig around if it is deep inside the ear because you can risk damaging your child's eardrum. The same applies to objects wedged up the nose. A continuing discharge or bleeding from one nostril can often be a sign that a foreign body has been lodged up the nose.

* Discharge from the vagina may also be a sign that the child has pushed something inside. Again take your child to the doctor who will be able to remove the foreign body.

SPLINTERS

* Use tweezers to remove wood splinters or thorns sticking out of the skin.

For a splinter that is lying visibly under the skin use a needle sterilised in a flame and then cooled to squeeze it out.

* Glass or metal splinters are much more serious and you should take your child to the doctor.

EYES

* Injuries to eyes can be especially frightening and again you need to stay as calm as possible.

* If your child gets a chemical in the eye then use cold water to rinse out the eye as quickly as possible – do this by leaning a child back against your arm, holding a towel under his chin and literally pouring water on to the eye. Then cover the eye with a clean linen cloth and get him as quickly as possible to the accident and emergency unit of your local hospital.

* Foreign bodies in the eye can be flushed out in the same way. If you cannot remove the item take your child to the local hospital or, if it is small and the child is not distressed, to your GP. If your child has a serious accident damaging the eye, hold a clean cloth to the eye and call an ambulance.

SHOCK

* A child can become shocked following any severe accident or injury. The signs are that he may be pale and feel unwell. His skin may be colder than normal and clammy to the touch.

* Make the child lie down and if he has lost a lot of blood keep the head down and raise the legs. This makes more blood and therefore more oxygen go to the head. However, do not do this if you think there is a risk of head injury or a broken leg.

* Loosen tight clothing and jewellery and keep the child covered up and warm with a coat or blanket, but not too hot.

SPRAINS

* It is often difficult for a parent to tell a sprain from a fracture and if in real doubt you should seek medical advice. General rules for sprains are to remove tight clothing or jewellery from the area, which will swell up, and to treat the swelling and pain with ice packs or cold water.

* Bandage firmly but not too tightly.

BITES AND STINGS

* Grasp a bee sting low down near the skin with fingers or tweezers and pull it out. Use a cold dressing or some calamine lotion. Wasps do not leave a barb in the skin but you can treat the sting with lemon juice,

vinegar or one of the anaesthetic sprays which are available from chemists' shops.

* Try not to make a big fuss about insect stings and bites because they are not usually serious and will make your child extra frightened of every insect in the future.

* Very rarely a child can have an allergic reaction (anaphylactic shock) to a bite or a sting. Signs are sickness, difficulty in breathing, swelling of the face, runny eyes and sneezing. In severe cases the child may actually lose consciousness. Get medical help as soon as possible and in the case of an unconscious child place him in the recovery position (see page 500). Serious risk arises if the tissues in the airways begin to swell up making breathing difficult.

* If your child is bitten by an animal or another child and the skin is punctured, seek medical advice because there is a risk of infection from teeth.

* Snake bites – we have only one poisonous snake in this country (the adder) and although bites from it are painful they rarely cause death. Adders can be easily recognised because they are grey, yellowish or reddish brown, and about 30 in. long with a broad head. The distinctive sign is the black zig-zag marking on its back. If your child is unlucky enough to be bitten by a snake, keep the part that was bitten still and below the heart if at all possible: this should help to stop the poison spreading. Either get him to a hospital as soon as possible or send for medical help.

CONVULSIONS

* The most common type of convulsion is caused by high temperature and happens most often between six months and three years – for more on this see page 545. If high temperature is the cause of the convulsion, it is important to cool down the child by tepid sponging as described on page

503

543. If your child has a convulsion, your only concern is to prevent him from injuring himself – not by holding him still which is impossible, but by making sure there are no dangerous objects around and that he is not going to fall on to anything that could hurt him. Do not try to put anything between his teeth which could cause him to break his teeth.

* When the jerking has stopped, lay the child on his tummy with his head to one side in the recovery position (see page 500). Seek medical advice.

HYGIENE

While he grows and matures in the womb, the unborn baby is protected from outside infection by the sterile amniotic fluid in which he swims. This fluid is contained within a membrane or sac known as the amniotic sac.

However, once the baby leaves the sterile and watery world of the womb and is born he quickly becomes host to millions of invisible, teeming micro-organisms – or germs. This happens in the cleanest of hospitals or homes. Fortunately, most of these germs which cover not only our skin, but also the lining of noses and throats, respiratory tracts and intestine are quite harmless. In a few cases, some of them are actually helpful, for example, certain bacteria present in digestive juices help in the processing of food. But of course there are also germs which cause disease – in understanding why, and how it is best to protect babies and children from germs which can cause infection and disease, it helps to know a little both about germs and about the body's way of protecting itself.

GERM KNOW-HOW

Germs come in three basic types:

Bacteria These are very tiny, single-celled organisms and although some can actually be useful and essential as described above, there are very many more which can cause an enormous range of illnesses. Fortunately, our bodies can cope very well with the vast majority of bacteria which are around – skin and the mucous membrane lining prevent most bacteria from invading. In addition, natural antiseptics are contained in body fluids such as saliva, breast milk and tears. Inside the body the bacteria or the poisons that they produce can be conquered by antibodies – these are produced by our immune system (see page 505). If the body's own natural defences fail to cope and illness or disease results, then antibiotics can be used – certain types of bacteria are more easily defeated by certain types of antibiotic. However, in just a few cases using antibiotics too frequently has resulted in a strain of bacteria becoming resistant (see page 525).

Viruses These infective agents are very much tinier than bacteria. They work by getting inside the cells of the body and altering the way the cell functions. Our bodies can produce antibodies to defeat them and both this and immunisation helps our resistance to viruses. They cannot in general be treated by antibiotics.

Fungi Certain types of fungi occasionally cause infection, the commonest of which is thrush, caused by the fungus *Candida albicans*. However, fungus infections are usually easily treated, though not with antibiotics.

It also helps to know that it takes more than the mere presence of germs to cause illness. If a doctor takes a swab from your child's throat, he is likely to be able to grow all kinds of germs which are capable of causing a variety of illnesses from pneumonia to sore throats. Yet your child stays healthy. This is both because changes need to occur in germs to make them more likely to cause infection, which is called 'virulence', and also because the body has a natural defence mechanism which keeps germs under con- trol – our immune system. At birth a newborn baby's immune system is still very immature and it takes several months before it begins to work reasonably effectively, and even longer before it works as well as that of an older child or adult. Fortunately, new babies are not born completely unprotected. During the last three months in the womb, antibodies from the mother cross the placenta and enter the baby's bloodstream so that the baby is born with a ready-made set of antibodies to protect him against certain infections which the mother has already suffered. This is called 'passive immunity'. In addition, colostrum and breast milk are very rich in both antibodies and anti-infective agents which lessen the likelihood of gastro-enteritis and other infectious illnesses. This passive immunity does not last for ever but, as it fades, so the baby's own immune system begins to work more efficiently and is able to produce its own antibodies. Further protection can be given with a vaccination programme which gives your baby a lifelong immunity from certain diseases (see page 526).

YOUR NEW BABY – HYGIENE IN THE FIRST SIX MONTHS

New parents usually feel rather anxious but also quite confused about what sort of safety measures they should take to protect their new baby in terms of cleanliness and hygiene. In fact the basic rules are very simple:

* Wash your hands before handling a baby under three months old and ask other people who look after your baby to do the same. This very simple measure really does help to stop the spread of germs. It is especially important to wash your hands after changing a baby's nappy, wiping another child's bottom or going to the lavatory yourself because the bowel/hand/mouth is one of the commonest ways that germs are spread, usually causing diarrhoea and sickness. It is also essential to wash your hands before making up bottles or preparing any food.

* Do not let people who have colds or other illnesses breathe all over, cuddle or kiss your new baby and tactfully discourage visiting toddlers

and older children from doing the same. However, your baby is at far less risk from germs that are within the family, so there is no need to be quite so restrictive with older brothers and sisters who have a runny nose.

* It will reduce the chance of infection if in the first three months you try, tactfully, to cut down on the number of people who handle your baby. Obviously, this does not bar all the family who want to have a look at the new arrival, but it is probably better not to have him passed around at large gatherings, such as someone else's christening or the local toddler club.

* Breastfeeding is generally much safer than bottle-feeding. However, if you are unable to breastfeed, be meticulous about sterilising bottles and making up feeds (see pages 232–6, 238). Milk is an ideal breeding ground for bacteria which is why you have to be especially careful. Bacteria grow most quickly when in warm milk – boiling kills bacteria and storing at fridge temperature slows down the rate at which bacteria can multiply. This is why you should always cool milk quickly and not leave warm bottles of milk standing around or reheat or warm up a bottle which has already been used. For the first five months, dummies also need to be sterilised, but when mixed feeding is introduced at about four months, plates and implements just need to be washed well in hot water in the usual way.

* Toys and other playthings are not usually the carriers of germs because germs which cause illness do not live in the dust found on a kitchen floor, but are more likely to thrive in cooked food or milk. There is no need to sterilise playthings – once your baby begins to hold and grasp things and put them in his mouth (usually around four to five months) just keeping them socially clean is enough. However, try not to let playthings which have been sucked or played with by babies or toddlers who have illnesses be passed on to your baby without thoroughly washing them first.

* Do make sure your baby is given the vaccinations to protect him against potentially harmful illnesses, unless there is a medical reason to the contrary. Your GP, health visitor, or the local health centre will advise you about this.

How long to go on sterilising bottles By about five months your baby has become a human vacuum cleaner, taking hold of almost anything that comes within reach and putting it automatically into his mouth. Fortunately, by this time the immune system is better developed and beginning to work more efficiently. By five months most babies can begin to take drinks from a feeder cup and bottles can gradually begin to be phased out. There is no need to carry on sterilising bottles after six months as long as they are kept scrupulously clean; and unless there is a history of allergy babies can take cow's milk from this age. However, you still need to be just as careful about cooling milk quickly and storing it in the fridge, and not leaving warm bottles of milk standing around or reheating a bottle that has already been warmed up.

KEEPING YOUR BABY CLEAN

If you carry out the suggested procedures on page 160 for topping and tailing your baby every day, and change his nappy regularly so that the skin does not get sore, then a bath once or twice a week is fine, but most babies quickly begin to enjoy bathtime and then it is up to you whether you bath him every day or every other day. However, once babies begin to move around or to sit on the floor and be able to reach for toys and to eat solid food they very quickly become far more dirty and most mothers find that a bath at the end of the day is a good prelude to the bedtime routine.

OLDER CHILDREN

After about the age of five months there is no need to go on trying to keep your child away from colds and coughs, although serious illnesses are different. If you keep your child wrapped in cotton wool for too long, he will only go down with a worse bout once he comes into contact with his first infectious bug as he has had no chance to build up any immunity.

Safety, rather than hygiene, dictates that you gradually begin to teach a toddler not to put absolutely everything into his mouth. Tiny pieces of Lego, the cat's food or something unmentionable he found in the garden are obvious examples. However, one habit is important to instil in him for life – to wash his hands before handling food, before having a meal, and after going to the lavatory to pass a bowel motion. The same applies to other adult members of your household who have not already picked up this habit!

PETS

Children can pick up worms from dogs and cats – these are roundworms (toxocara). The eggs are transferred when a child puts his hands in his mouth and they then hatch out into larvae in the child's intestines. This is why it is important to worm your dog or cat regularly. The rear end of pets is potentially more harmful than the front end, and children are more likely to become infected after touching an animal's excrement and then putting their hands to their mouth than by having a dog or cat lick their face. However, it is better to discourage animals from getting near babies' faces and to tell children not to let animals lick their faces for safety reasons. Toxoplasmosis is an infection which can be spread by cats and is also in uncooked or not properly cooked meat. It can cause serious damage to an unborn baby in the first three months of pregnancy. Fleas can also be passed on to children from animals so make sure your pet is kept free from fleas and when buying a pet of any kind have it checked over first by a vet.

YOUR HOME – HOW CLEAN IS CLEAN ENOUGH?

Most people have vague worries from time to time about whether their home is kept clean enough and this is especially likely when a new baby comes along. It is also an anxiety well recognised by the makers of cleaning agents for use in the bathroom, kitchen and toilets, whose advertisements go a long way to suggest that without their product your home will be a hot-bed of highly infective germs. In fact, as with most aspects of hygiene, common sense is your best guide. If the lavatory looks dirty, then it probably does contain more germs, but keeping the toilet bowl looking clean and the toilet flushed is all you need to worry about. In fact water in toilets – provided the toilet is kept flushed – has been found to contain surprisingly few germs. Do not waste time worrying about 'invisible' germs and remember that germs do not live in household dust, but rather in food and drink. Keep your home socially clean to your own standards, but don't go into overdrive when a new baby arrives.

PREPARING FOOD

Scrupulously clean and careful preparation of food is the best way to avoid stomach upsets. Food prepared in this way that is put in the fridge straight away can simply be warmed up when it is needed. Food less carefully cooked and then reheated is likely to carry germs which can cause stomach upsets, so always reheat such food very thoroughly to as high a temperature as possible rather than just warming it up. Then allow it to cool so that your child or the rest of the family can eat it. Always wash your hands before preparing food, and never prepare food if you have a septic finger or some kind of infection on your hands as this is a very likely way of passing on germs. Even touching your nose when you have a cold and then going on to prepare food is a way of giving your germs to the rest of the family. If you are storing the leftovers of any cooked food, always cover it and keep it in the fridge. Alternatively, food which has been cooked can be frozen and then thawed and reheated thoroughly, but do not freeze food a second time.

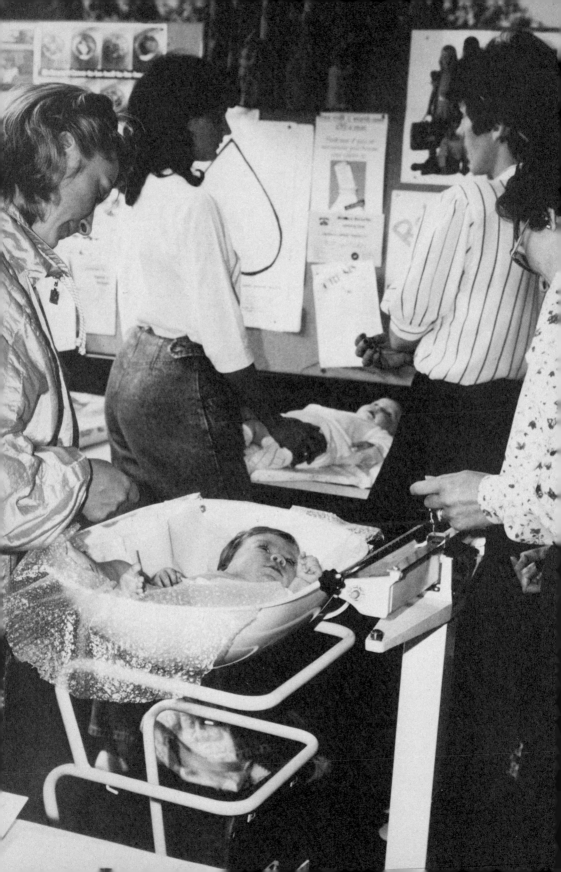

Chapter 16

DOCTORS AND MEDICINES

Doctors – choosing a GP, changing GPs,
how to get the best from your GP, referrals, when to call the doctor
Medicines – your attitude to drugs, giving medicines,
taking the medicine, antibiotics, allergic reactions,
the pharmacist, over-the-counter medicines, immunisation
Health visitors and health clinics – developmental check-ups
Your child's teeth – teething, looking after teeth,
food for healthy teeth, going to the dentist

DOCTORS

CHOOSING A GP

'I was expecting my third baby and saw my GP for most of my antenatal care. My morale sank below zero the day he prodded my tummy and said: "Hm, of course your stomach muscles are shot to pieces – that's why you're so big." '

We all remember the bad moments from medical encounters for many more years than the good ones and it is specially important that your general practitioner is someone you like and trust. Women having babies and then caring for small children are among the most frequent visitors to GPs' surgeries and their family doctor can be a valuable source of support during these high pressure years.

How do you make the right choice of doctor? The success of the relationship will depend on what you expect from a GP, whether that matches up with what that particular GP aims to provide, and on how you both get on together as personalities. The Post Office can give you a list of doctors in the area and you can see from that whether they all work together in a large health centre, in a small partnership of two or three, or by themselves; big, though, as far as a practice is concerned, is not necessarily beautiful. There is also a *Local Directory of Doctors*, which is available from Family Practitioner Committees or Local Health Boards. It contains not only a list of the doctors in the area but details of the service provided and the number of employees in the practice. You may already

511

have some feelings about whether you would like a man or a woman doctor, someone recently qualified or more experienced. You can find out when they qualified, and whether they have any specialist qualifications by going to the library and looking them up in the *Medical Register*. If you have not yet completed your family you will probably want your GP to be able to provide antenatal care – this means he or she must be registered on the obstetric list of the Family Practitioner Committee of your Regional Health Authority. GPs who work with a health visitor and organise their own baby clinic are more likely to be specially interested in the needs of young children.

Call in at the practice and ask the receptionist or practice manager about the services offered – just looking around the waiting room and picking up the general atmosphere will help you to decide. Is the receptionist easily available across a counter or locked away behind a glass partition or closed door with a 'Please Knock and Wait' sign? Are there toys for waiting children and interesting and useful notices and information around the walls? Many GPs put up photos of themselves in the waiting room with their names so patients will know who they are, and practices are now required to produce their own information leaflet explaining how to make an appointment, how to contact a doctor out of surgery hours and special services available. But the real low-down on what a doctor is like inevitably comes via the local grapevine – in other words by asking parents of young children whose attitudes and judgement are in sympathy with yours. Your local pharmacist, health visitor and possibly community midwife may all be useful sources of information too.

While you may hope to pick the ideal doctor, he is not obliged to accept you, however perfect a patient you think you might prove. It is quite common for a GP to ask to see you before taking you on his list. As well as giving you a chance to see if you like his approach, the doctor will also want to know about special conditions which need long-term care – for example, epilepsy, heart condition or diabetes – so mention anything of this nature when you make a first enquiry with the receptionist. An average GP's list consists of about 1,700 patients and if he already has what he considers to be enough in terms of work load then you may be told new patients are not being accepted.

Temporary patients can sign on for care for up to three months if they are staying in the area, but if you do visit a GP in these circumstances remember it is not the best way to judge his approach. He will only be aiming to tide you over, and few doctors in these circumstances want to meddle with treatment already prescribed by another doctor.

CHANGING GPS

If you fall out with your GP, find he no longer provides the kind of service you need or just lose confidence in his ability for one reason or another you can ask to register with another doctor in the area instead. But you should be aware that unless you are actually moving to a new district your application may be greeted with a certain amount of suspicion. It may be you have a perfectly legitimate reason for wishing to change – perhaps you grew up in the area and the GP your parents were registered with does not provide any family planning service. Perhaps you would prefer to have a woman doctor. But the thought may also wander across your prospective doctor's mind that perhaps you are an unreasonably demanding or difficult patient who has simply exhausted the patience of your previous GP. Naturally there are always several sides to such cases and the new GP will usually take you on and see how the relationship works out, although he will probably want to see you first and ask why you want to change. But if problems arise and dissatisfaction becomes rife on both sides then a GP can tell an individual or a family he will no longer take them as patients. In such cases the Family Practitioner Committee has a duty to find them another doctor. Unfair as it may seem, a GP does not have to give a reason for refusing to take a patient or for asking them to be taken off the list.

HOW TO GET THE BEST FROM YOUR GP

* Find out how the practice operates by asking a receptionist who can tell you about the appointment system, contacting doctors out of surgery hours, and special services such as baby clinics or family planning services. Making friends with the receptionist can be the key to getting on with the doctor – she can often give useful advice when you are unsure about bringing a child to the surgery.

* Keep appointments and be on time. Always phone if you are likely to be delayed or no longer need the appointment.

* Take your child to the surgery whenever possible, rather than calling out the doctor. Babies and small children are highly portable and provided you can wrap them up warmly in a pram or put them in a car they will come to no harm even if it is raining or snowing. If you do not have a car, see if a friend can help with a lift – community care schemes can often lay on transport. Remember that if your child was very ill and had to be taken to hospital he would still have to go outside and be moved in a draughty, bumpy ambulance. If your child is so ill that physically moving him is difficult, ring the surgery and explain – no doctor minds being called to see a really sick child. In this category are children with severe vomiting or diarrhoea, or bigger children who are delirious with fever. However, apart from such cases, a doctor can usually do far more for your child at the surgery where there are more facilities and equipment than at home, and a doctor can see many more people at the surgery in the time that one home visit would take.

* Warn the receptionist if you make an appointment to bring in a child with a rash or a suspected infectious fever such as measles. She may arrange for you to wait in a separate room or come at the beginning of the surgery to avoid passing it on to other people.

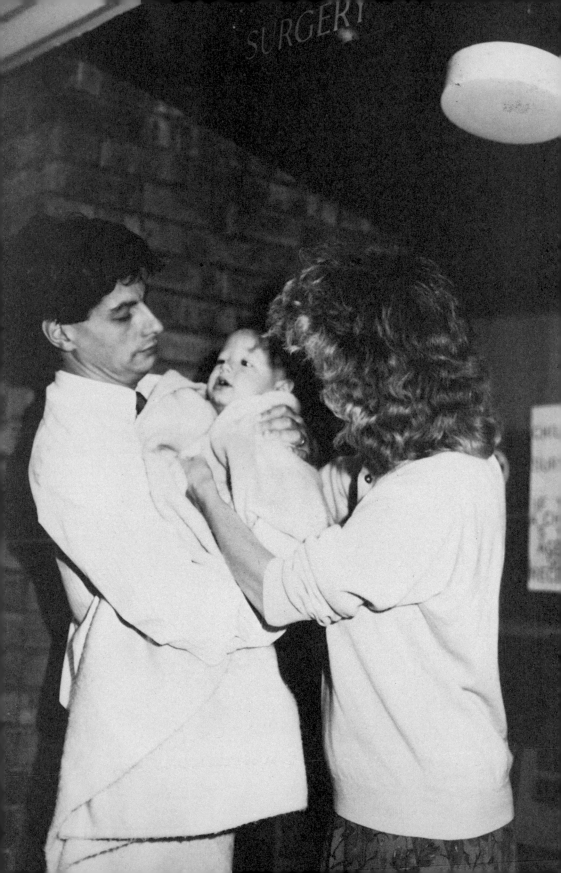

* Calling the doctor at night is something people usually feel worried about. Although most GPs can come up with stories about the odd call for something totally unnecessary – cutting an old lady's toe-nails at midnight was an example that stuck in one doctor's mind – in general parents know when their child is ill and needs attention. Obviously parents tend to learn with experience, and first time parents are likely to be more anxious and make more calls than seasoned veterans of childish illnesses, but it is best to trust your instinct. If you feel seriously worried about your child's condition, then ring for advice.

The majority of calls tend to be made between the time of the surgery closing and about 11 pm and far fewer are actually made in the small hours. People also call more often when GPs use a deputising service to cover at night – obviously they do not feel so bad about calling out a locum who is getting paid specifically to cover at night and who they are unlikely to meet again.

It is worth remembering that a child's temperature usually rises in the evening, and coughs are likely to get worse when the child lies down. Parents who have dithered all day about whether to take a child to the doctor see the symptoms getting worse and panic about getting through the night. Tell the doctor on the phone what it is you are most worried about and answer questions as accurately as possible. Do not necessarily expect him to run straight round – this may be a case for telephone counselling. For example, the doctor might tell you how to try and lower your child's temperature, but he will always ask you to ring again if the suggested treatment does not work or you are still anxious.

What should you do if you are very seriously worried and the doctor you have rung, either your own or a locum, refuses to come and see your child? Well, it may be that they are justified and your fears are needless.

However, young babies in particular can deteriorate very rapidly. If you can drive a car and the doctor lives locally then offer to bring the child round to him. If that is not possible, ask a friend to take you to the nearest hospital accident and emergency department. If your trip turns out to have been unnecessary then be prepared to learn from experience and listen to advice, but do not feel ashamed or guilty. If, on the other hand, it transpires that your child does need treatment then be relieved that you had the courage to trust your instinct and that your child has been helped.

* Do not expect your GP always to have an answer, because for many problems there is no one single answer but a variety of possible solutions or causes which you need to discuss together, or even no obvious answer. A relationship between a GP and patients or parents today is a two-way business, not simply a matter of pronouncement and a few pearls of wisdom plus a prescription. A doctor has expert knowledge about how bodies in general work and about some aspects of how people behave – you have expert knowledge about your own or your

child's body and behaviour. Pooling the two can arrive at some possible answers. If you always expect a definite solution you put pressure on a doctor to come up with one, instead of being able to say he is not sure or does not know, which can lead to a more honest attempt at finding one.

* Do not expect a prescription every time you see a doctor because it will not always be necessary. Explanation, advice and/or reassurance can be far more valuable in many instances than drugs. Do not feel your visit was unnecessary or unsuccessful because you leave without a prescription – the doctor will certainly not have felt that. Sometimes a patient's expectation and unjustified faith in medicines can put pressure on a GP to hand out a prescription he knows is medically useless simply to reassure a parent or patient. Remember that there is not a drug for every problem and teach your child the same outlook.

* Always ask if you do not understand anything. Parents are less inclined now to talk about the 'red pills' or the 'yellow medicine' – they are better informed and they generally welcome a doctor who takes time and trouble to explain something about their child's condition and treatment. Doctors in turn now view a large part of their work as education, and the old-style GP who feels threatened or affronted by parents or patients who ask informed questions is becoming rarer. Remember, though, that while a doctor will be happy to discuss a problem, he will have good reason for advocating a particular course of action, even though you might feel that you disagree with his advice.

* The real reason for your visit may not actually be your child's cough/cold/behaviour but some vaguer or less tangible emotional problem that is much harder to ask for help with. Some GPs would not think to look for extra work by delving for difficult problems, and at other extremes there are a few doctors who seem to suspect that deep-seated sexual dissatisfaction must lurk behind every presenting sniff and twinge! In general, though, a good GP will try to exercise a sixth sense to pick up less obvious anxieties, but if you do have some insight into the real reason for your visit, try to help short-cut the detective work and say what it is.

* Make separate appointments for each person needing treatment. Do not turn up to an appointment booked for only one child, then suddenly say, 'While I'm here . . .' and launch into details about your own or other children's ailments. If you need attention as well as your child, or have other children requiring attention, tell the receptionist when booking – she will not only allow the proper time, but make sure all the relevant notes are in front of your doctor. It may be helpful to jog your memory by writing down in advance particularly important questions that you want answered, but this is more likely to apply when seeing a hospital consultant.

* Listen to advice and carry it out. Doctors are trained to listen to what

patients say – we need to take in what is said in return. This is not always as easy as it sounds when at least half your attention is on your child, and often we only pick up part of a sentence or latch on to a few words without taking in the rest. Taking advice is also a relatively new skill patients have had to cultivate in place of simply picking up a prescription. Before you go back with a problem which has not been resolved think whether you have actually tried what was suggested.

REFERRALS

If your child needs specialist help, for example for a squint or a hearing problem, or your GP is not sure what is causing the trouble, he can refer you to a hospital specialist. However, many conditions which used to be reasons for referral are now dealt with by GPs themselves as they can arrange most tests and these days have many more facilities and resources at the surgery. Your doctor will usually ask if you have any special preference for a hospital, but if he is strongly against sending you to a particular consultant or hospital then be guided by his advice because almost certainly he has a good reason. GPs get to know a great deal about specialists in the hospitals by feedback from patients, by the kinds of letters consultants send and by the general treatment and management patients receive.

Occasionally you may be reluctant to ask your GP for a referral, for example, if you feel he may disapprove of your wish to see someone practising alternative medicine – a homoeopathic doctor or someone specialising in allergy. If you really feel your doctor is totally opposed to such ideas and would oppose your interest, then that may be a reason to consider seeing another doctor in the practice or even to change doctors. But give your own GP the benefit of the doubt first and go and explain why you are worried and what you hope for. His referral is very important because he is your protection against medically unqualified or un-scrupulous practitioners who may take your money and do nothing or else do positive harm. He is also your protection against going to perfectly good specialists, who may not be suitable for you for various reasons. In general, any consultant who will take you on without a GP's referral letter is suspect.

WHEN TO CALL THE DOCTOR

In general parents should trust their instincts – no one else knows their child as well as they do. If your child's condition is worrying you, then it is right to call a doctor.

Babies under six months   Because young babies cannot yet move around, talk or understand questions, spotting that they are ill and finding out what is wrong has to mean detective work and picking up clues. Most parents quickly notice changes in their baby's behaviour and condition. Because a young baby's condition can deteriorate very quickly in certain circumstances it is best to play safe and see a doctor if you are worried. The following symptoms are certainly reasons to seek advice:

'Not himself'

Not responding to you, not smiling or 'talking' as much as usual, not as interested in his surroundings, or sleeping more than usual.

Fever

This may be accompanied by other signs. Try reducing temperature in the ways described on page 543. If the baby cools down, is still feeding and not otherwise distressed just keep a watch. If he stays feverish or has other symptoms listed here, call the doctor.

Not taking his feeds

If he takes less than usual for several feeds or does not wake up for feeds at usual times.

Vomiting

If there is more than normal regurgitation on several occasions, particularly if it shoots out to a distance of 3 to 4 feet in babies less than 3 months old (called projectile vomiting), or is green (bile-stained vomiting), or contains blood.

Diarrhoea

If this is profuse and watery, with or without blood, on several occasions. If you are breastfeeding and you have taken any laxatives or eaten more fruit than usual, etc., this might cause temporary diarrhoea.

Dry nappies

If his nappies are much drier than usual because he has not passed urine, which may indicate that he is dehydrated – usually as a result of poor feeding, vomiting, diarrhoea, or a combination of all three.

Rapid or difficult breathing

His ribs may appear sucked in with each breath or he may make an unusual noise with his breathing. He may find it difficult to feed as well.

Persistent coughing

If he coughs in spasms lasting more than a few seconds. Long spasms often end with vomiting.

Blue coloration of lips and tongue

A lot of babies have blue hands and feet if they are cold. However, if the baby's lips and tongue look blue or mauve (compare with yours) after a bout of coughing, or with breathing difficulties or feeding, he needs to see the doctor urgently.

Fits (also called convulsions)

During a fit a baby either goes stiff or else rhythmically jerks his arms or legs for a period lasting up to several minutes. His eyes may roll up, he may dribble or go blue and he is unresponsive to you. All babies jerk their limbs once or twice, for instance if they are startled by a sudden movement or a loud noise, but this is quite normal. It is only if the jerking continues that you need to worry. After a fit the baby may be floppy and sleepy and needs to see the doctor urgently.

Screaming   If this is continuous and unusual, even after you have checked that he is not hungry or thirsty, wet or dirty, too hot or cold, etc. The doctor may not find anything wrong, but it is reasonable for the baby to be seen.

Accidents   Head injury. If your baby bumps his head and loses consciousness, no matter how briefly, or vomits or remains floppy and lethargic, take him to the doctor.

Burns   These happen particularly when the baby reaches out for the cup of tea you have just poured – so remember to keep it well out of the way. Remove clothes immediately because they retain the heat and make the burn worse, keep the affected part under the cold running tap for five minutes, dry very gently and cover with a clean, dry cloth. Then take to the doctor. Some people recommend rubbing the burn with butter, but this is not helpful.

Any other injuries should be seen by the doctor unless very minor. For more detail on accidents see page 496.

If your young baby is obviously ill and your doctor cannot come at once then play safe and take the child to the nearest hospital accident and emergency department – check by phone first that they are open.

Babies six months to a year   Much the same rules apply to this age group although changes in behaviour and clues as to the cause of an illness may be easier to pick up. As babies get bigger and stronger they are better able to withstand bouts of illness, but breathing difficulties and persistent coughing, vomiting and diarrhoea need to be treated seriously and acted on promptly. If your baby has vomiting and diarrhoea always take this seriously (see page 580) – stop feeding him solids and milk and just give him plenty of Dioralyte, a salt and glucose compound available from chemists, until the diarrhoea stops and his symptoms may well have settled. If they have, then give him feeds of half-strength milk (for instance 4 oz milk added to 4 oz water) for a further 24 hours and then gradually reintroduce his normal diet. He may lose weight very slightly but will rapidly regain it once he starts feeding normally again. If his symptoms do not settle after 24 hours or if he vomits everything, including water, he needs to see a doctor. In the case of slight fever in a baby who is still taking fluids and is otherwise alert, try giving paracetamol for babies (Calpol, for example) and sponging down with lukewarm water to reduce fever. Seek advice if the baby continues to refuse food and drinks, seems in pain or is reluctant to move an arm or leg, or is listless and unresponsive.

Children aged one to five   Loss of appetite is a good guide to how ill your child is – if he begins to eat something it is usually a sign he is getting better. Make sure always to give plenty of fluids – a child who is so ill he will not drink anything during a day needs to see a doctor. Fever which does not respond to paracetamol for babies, which is accompanied by other worrying signs of illness such as pain or crying, which is bad enough to make a child delirious or which continues for more than 24 hours needs treatment. There are, however, no hard and fast rules – again, trust your own judgement. Breathlessness due to croup or asthma can be serious and needs treatment.

Between the ages of one and five years children become increasingly able to tell you what is wrong – although not always accurately! They may describe pain felt anywhere as 'tummy-ache' and, conversely, a wide variety of illnesses – such as infections, pneumonia, urinary infections or gastro-enteritis may give them abdominal pain, so the site of the pain does not necessarily indicate the cause. Call a doctor in the following cases:

Severe or prolonged pain	Judging the seriousness of your child's pain is not always easy. However, if he complains of tummy-ache but continues to play football, there is unlikely to be anything seriously wrong, whereas if he just wants to be cuddled or lies on the settee all morning, he is unwell.
	Children's ability to tolerate pain varies quite a lot, just as in adults, and you will know best whether your child is the stoical sort who does not complain until the pain is very severe.
Diminished level of activity or generally 'not himself'	This is a good, though non-specific indication of illness.
Loss of appetite	Another non-specific indicator of illness. Conversely, once he starts to eat again, you know that he is feeling better. Parents sometimes worry that their child may lose weight and try to make him eat while he is ill. However, this is not necessary and he will not come to any harm provided he drinks plenty of fluids. Once he is better, he will rapidly regain any lost weight.

Fever	Particularly if he is generally unwell without anything obvious to account for it. Fever almost always causes loss of appetite. However, he may be developing one of the childhood illnesses such as measles, mumps or chicken-pox, so it is worth asking friends or the nursery if there are any cases about.
Not drinking, prolonged vomiting, or diarrhoea	Children may become dehydrated, although not as quickly as small babies. Indications include a dry tongue and passing very small amounts of concentrated (dark) urine.
Urinary symptoms	Pain passing urine; 'fishy' smelling urine; funny colour – pink or like Coca-Cola; not passing as much urine as usual while drinking normally.
Puffy eyes, face or ankles, particularly in the morning	This is usually associated with other urinary symptoms.
Severe earache	This may be due to ear infections, but can also be due to a sore throat or teething. Ear infections need treating with a full course of antibiotics because if left untreated there is a risk of some hearing loss. Not all children with ear infections suffer from earache – fever and vomiting can also be signs. Bright red ears may occur if your child is hot or has been crying or rushing about and do not indicate an ear infection.
Severe sore throat	This may make swallowing painful. Give fluids, ice-cream, yoghurt.
Dribbling	Particularly if your child has become very unwell, often with a fever, over a period of a few hours he needs to see a doctor quickly.
Difficulty in breathing	Or making extra noises when breathing in (stridor) or breathing out (wheezing). He will usually have a cough as well.
Fits	With or without a temperature.
Not walking, putting weight on one leg or using one arm	When previously normal and no obvious accident to account for it.
Bleeding or bruising	Again, if you are unable to account for it.

Accident   Unless it was very minor, your child should be seen by a doctor, particularly after a head injury, if he has been knocked out, or vomits, or if he has eaten or drunk any medicines or household items.

If your child has any of the symptoms described above, he ought to see a doctor within 24 hours. However, he may have other symptoms which worry you and need discussion with a doctor, though not so urgently. Some of these worries, for instance, about your child's hearing or vision, may be serious. Others, such as 'fussy' eating or constipation, may be less serious medically but still important to you, and it may be helpful to discuss them initially with your health visitor.

MEDICINES

YOUR ATTITUDE TO DRUGS

Drugs include not only aspirins or antibiotics, marijuana or heroin. We all use a variety of drugs in our everyday lives. Coffee, tea, fizzy drinks and chocolate all contain varying amounts of caffeine – a stimulant. Tobacco contains nicotine – a very powerfully addictive drug, as smokers who have tried to give up will know. Alcohol is a drug which for many of us is an instant aid to relaxation, enjoyment or getting through the tough times.

The problems of cigarette smoking, heavy drinking, glue sniffing or heroin addiction may seem a million miles away when you have tiny children, but one factor which may make children more likely to abuse drugs of any type when they are older is the example they are set in childhood. Obviously this is by no means the only factor, but because small children subconsciously absorb attitudes and ideas from the way the adults around them behave it is worth considering. There is a much greater likelihood of children smoking if both their parents smoke. The children of heavy drinkers are themselves more vulnerable to following suit.

It is no good saying 'Don't you ever do this' while lighting up a cigarette. Children quickly pick up hidden or double messages and are more likely to follow example than empty exhortation. So what does this mean in practice when it comes to the under-fives? Parents who are very dependent on some form of drugs, whether alcohol, tobacco, tranquillisers or one of the illegal varieties, need to think seriously about the effect this will have in the long term on their children's attitudes. Talk it over with your partner and, if possible, with a doctor you trust or one of the organisations aiming to help with advice, see address section, pages 673–6. But all of us can be more aware of the messages we are giving in word and deed by looking at this list of dos and don'ts.

DO NOT teach that for every problem there is a drug to cure or soothe.

For example, by coming back from a hard day at work and immediately reaching for a large drink or cigarette, saying, 'I needed that.' Instead, make an effort, and some considerable effort may be required, not to present a drug as the answer to stress or problems.

DO NOT give your child an infallible belief in the power of medicines. If you always expect a prescription every time you go to the doctor, you may give your child the same idea. Do not teach that medicine is the only answer, that it always works and nothing will get better in any other way.

DO be honest about your own use of drugs. If you smoke and cannot give it up, tell your child you wish you had never started because smoking can give you a bad cough and may make you ill. Most children are very anti-smoking and want their parents to stop. Even a young child can understand something about addiction. Once you start taking something your body gets used to it and you just cannot do without it, even though it is bad for you. It is better not to start. It may be much harder to be honest about dependence on alcohol. Try not to set the example that adults can never be happy or have fun without a glass in their hands.

DO NOT develop medicine rituals. Small children can think taking medicine is 'grown-up' and therefore attractive, so do not develop elaborate procedures around medicine taking or make too much fuss about it. Don't encourage children to believe a medicine always makes everything better so they ask for cough medicine, for example when they are just tired, or for vague 'off' days.

DO teach that the right amount of medicine can sometimes help – but twice as much is not twice as good. Young children can understand that a little may make them feel better, but too much can be bad for them. When they get older you can explain that drugs always have more than one action and should therefore be treated with caution.

DO make sure always that all medicines, especially brightly coloured pills which look like sweets, are kept safely out of reach.

GIVING MEDICINES

Here is a list of essential points when medicines are prescribed for your child.

* Store all medicines well out of reach of children and in child-proof containers.

* Store medicines at the right temperature – i.e. in the fridge or away from direct heat if that is the direction on the bottle. When the course is finished destroy any remaining or return to the chemist.

* Know what you are giving. If your GP forgets to explain what he has prescribed, do not be afraid to ask. The days of talking blindly about the 'red pills' and the 'yellow medicine' without having any idea what they

are supposed to do are over. If you leave the surgery without knowing whether it is antibiotic or decongestant you are spooning down, ask the pharmacist.

If your child is taking any medicines and you have to see another doctor, for instance a hospital consultant, make sure you know the name and the dose, or take the medicine with you.

* Make sure you understand the instructions for giving the medicine before leaving the chemist, how much, how often and when. Lots of people misunderstand instructions without realising. For example, four times a day does not mean four randomly spaced doses but one dose every six hours. Giving it wrongly can make medicine less effective. Check whether the medicine should be given before or after meals.

* Measure doses of medicine accurately, using a marked medicine spoon for liquid.

* Make sure the medicine is swallowed – sometimes easier said than done with babies or protesting toddlers. Vomiting or diarrhoea may mean medicine never has a chance to get into the system – if this is a continuing problem ask your doctor's advice.

TAKING THE MEDICINE ... WITHOUT TEARS

* Do not try to give medicine to a baby or child who is upset – calm him first if at all possible.

* Measure medicine into a spoon before picking up the child yourself, or getting someone else to hold him for you. You can balance it on a clean plate with something under the handle to level it up or use a test-tube-style medicine spoon which stands up by itself. Bottle-fed babies may take thin, though not syrupy, medicines from a feeder or small bottle.

* Do not give medicine to a child lying flat as he may choke, nor to one sitting bolt upright as he is more likely to dribble or spit it out. Lie him back slightly with your arm supporting his head, trapping his arms so he does not grab at the spoon. With a small baby put him in a baby-relax chair.

* Babies who have been weaned will usually open their mouths for a spoon – give the spoonful in one go so they do not taste and decide they do not want it, although most children's medicines are very sweet. Smaller babies will open their mouths if you touch the spoon against their top and then bottom lip.

* Once the medicine is in the mouth use your free hand to gently lift their chin upwards – this will keep their mouths closed, stop it coming out again and encourage them to swallow. Very lightly stroking a finger across the outside of a baby or small child's throat will usually produce a swallow.

* If the child begins to choke do not carry on trying to force him to

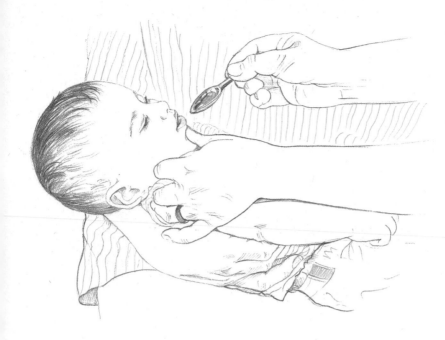

swallow and holding his mouth shut – let him sit up and gently stroke his back while he recovers and do not worry about the medicine. Try again when he has calmed down – giving it in two smaller doses may help, or pouring it into his mouth more slowly.

* If your child needs to take medicine contained in syrup regularly, remember to brush his teeth afterwards to prevent dental problems developing.

ANTIBIOTICS – WHY THEY ARE NOT ALWAYS THE ANSWER

Antibiotics have revolutionised medicine, but do not make the mistake of thinking they will cure anything and everything. Their use is in fact strictly limited – they work by killing off bacteria. So if it is bacteria which are causing an ear infection or sore throat antibiotics can be the answer. But if a virus is causing illness then antibiotics will not be any use. Viruses are smaller organisms than bacteria and, although research continues, so far there are few successful anti-virus drugs.

How does a doctor know whether illness is due to bacteria or a virus? Only by looking at the symptoms and using his medical knowledge. In general, pus indicates bacterial infection, but redness and soreness could be due to either. If an antibiotic is given by mouth in the form of medicine or pills this is said to be a 'systemic' form of treatment – that is, it treats the whole system. If an antibiotic in a cream or ointment is just applied directly to the skin then the treatment is said to be 'topical' – it does not affect the whole system but just one area.

Antibiotic medicine is always prescribed for a specific period of treatment – 5, 7, 10 or 14 days. Although symptoms may disappear very soon after taking antibiotics it is important always to complete the course. Otherwise not all the bacteria may have been killed off and the symptoms will start to return as soon as you stop the medicine.

Different antibiotics work better against different bacteria. Repeated use of the same antibiotic encourages bacteria to become resistant so they are not killed off. Bacteria that survive an only partially completed course of antibiotic may be specially likely to develop resistance. Giving medicine at irregular intervals instead of the prescribed interval also allows germs to fight back and multiply when the level of antibiotic in the system sinks and this can also lead to resistance.

ALLERGIC REACTIONS

If your child starts to show signs of allergy while taking medicine, stop giving it and ring the surgery for advice. Skin rashes and swelling are the commonest signs – rashes may be raised or consist of red blotches. Swelling may show as puffiness round the face or limbs. If possible take the child to the surgery so your doctor can see the reaction – it could be due to something else altogether. If it is thought to be an allergic reaction a note will be made on your child's medical notes because once a sensitivity develops, he will probably react to that drug again and could be more seriously ill next time. For this reason you should be sure you know what it is your child is thought to be allergic to so you can tell any other medical staff who may need to treat your child in the future.

THE PHARMACIST

The pharmacist at your local chemist can be a valuable help – he can advise about over-the-counter medicines and will always tell you if he thinks you should take your child to see a doctor. It is part of the pharmacist's job to make sure you understand how a prescription is to be used and he will tell you exactly what it is if you are unsure. Just ask the counter assistant at the chemist if you can speak to the pharmacist if you need this kind of advice.

OVER-THE-COUNTER MEDICINES

Do not give any medicines to a baby under six months old except on the advice of a doctor or health visitor.

IMMUNISATION

The body's immune system is its defence mechanism against potentially harmful bacteria and viruses. When the body is invaded by bacteria there may be a localised response in the form of inflammation and a general reaction including fever. There is also a specific immune response when the body recognises the bacteria as foreign and, along with other defensive measures, produces antibodies which combat the particular bacteria. Once antibodies to particular bacteria have been produced the body retains a 'memory' of the invading foreign cells so if the body encounters the same bacteria again the antibody system is immediately ready to combat the disease.

We do not have to wait for our children to catch potentially life-threatening diseases, though, to acquire an immunity. Instead we can protect them by having them vaccinated or immunised. There are two forms of immunisation – active and passive. Active immunisation means a weak form of the infection is deliberately given to a child which stimulates his body to produce antibodies so he will be able to resist future, more severe, infections. With passive immunisation the antibodies are produced by another person or animal and injected into the child to give temporary immunity. Some immunisations, like diphtheria, last a lifetime while some, like influenza, only last a short time. The programme of immunisation for pre-school children is designed to give them lifelong protection from nine diseases which are potentially life-threatening or can do permanent damage. Babies are born with some natural immunity because during pregnancy some of the mother's antibodies pass over into the baby's bloodstream, but the immunity usually lasts only for a few months. Breast milk also contains antibodies, so that babies who are breastfed are also more immune to infections than are the bottle-fed.

Very many parents today do not even know what diphtheria is because it has been so successfully combated by the use of vaccines (for a description of symptoms see page 605), but this may create a sense of false security which could make parents less conscientious about having their child immunised.

Before vaccines were available, many thousands of babies and young children became ill each year with serious infections such as polio, diphtheria, smallpox and whooping cough. Some of these affected children died and others were left permanently damaged. Since the introduction of vaccination, and improvements in hygiene and sanitation, these terrible illnesses have become rare in the UK and developed countries. Polio, diphtheria and tetanus still occur commonly in under-developed countries where vaccination is not widely available. As these diseases are now rare, it is easy to forget how devastating they were in earlier times. However, diphtheria, tetanus, whooping cough and polio *are* still present in the UK, and could again cause serious illness and death to many children if widespread vaccination did not occur. Even in recent years, there have been cases of polio in Europe and the United States in children who did not receive vaccination. Although there has been some publicity given to the side-effects of vaccination, the dangers of the diseases which are prevented by vaccination are many times greater than vaccination, which is now extremely safe.

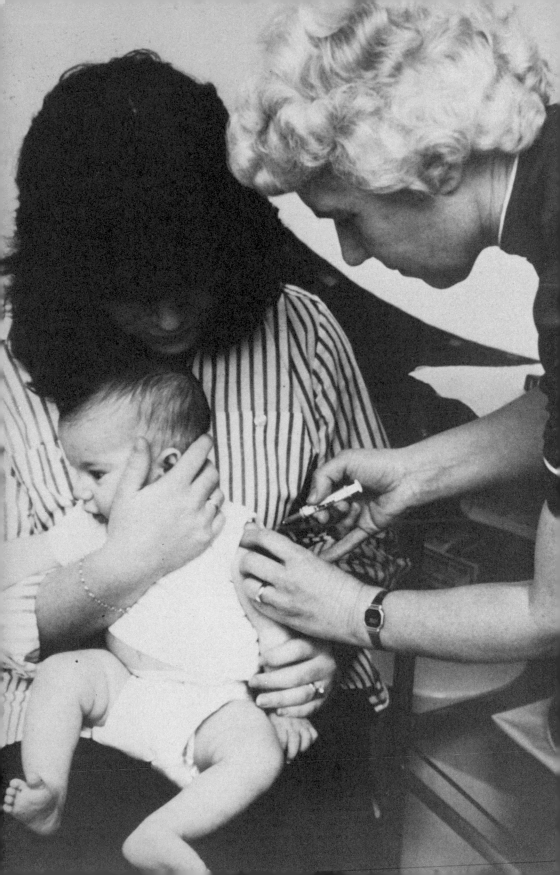

Why bother immunising against rare diseases? You may ask why you should have your baby immunised against a disease like diphtheria, which is very rare nowadays. The problem is that when a disease becomes rare, but is not completely wiped out, an unexpected outbreak could damage large numbers of babies if they are unprotected. Of course, when a disease has been completely wiped out worldwide, as has smallpox, then vaccination is no longer necessary.

How is it done? Most vaccinations are given by injection into the upper arm, buttock or leg. The exception is polio vaccine, which is given by mouth.

Most parents hate taking their children along for any procedure that may cause pain or discomfort. One mother said: 'I felt I was betraying my baby by taking her to the clinic for something that was going to hurt her. It seems awful to let someone stick a needle in them when they are so trusting and unsuspecting.'

If you yourself dread injections or the dentist, you may be especially reluctant. However, it is worth remembering that the vaccination is being given to prevent serious illnesses, and the small discomfort of the injection is very minor compared to the severity of illnesses like whooping cough or polio. Remember that some babies are scarcely upset at all, and most cry for less than a minute. They certainly will not be permanently upset by the experience or have painful memories, and it really is not worth putting your child at unnecessary risk to avoid minor discomfort. If one parent feels reluctant to take the baby, perhaps this is an occasion when the other can take over.

When is it done? Doctors sometimes differ slightly in the ages at which they recommend immunisation, but the following is the timetable recommended by the Department of Health in 1990.

Triple vaccine	1st dose	2 months	
(D/T/P) and	2nd dose	3 months	
polio	3rd dose	4 months	
Measles/mumps/ *rubella* (MMR)		12–18 months	Can be given at any age over 12 months
Booster D/T and polio		4–5 years	
Rubella		10–14 years	Girls only
BCG (tuberculin)		10–14 years or infancy	Interval of 3 weeks between BCG and *rubella*
Booster tetanus and polio		15–18 years	

Reactions

Triple vaccine A few hours after the injection there may be a small lump where the injection was given, and some reddening and tenderness around it. About half of all children vaccinated have a mild fever and many seem fretful. Very occasionally the fever may be quite marked and the child may seem quite unwell. Most of these symptoms subside within a few hours or settle after giving paracetamol for babies, but very occasionally (less than one in every 100,000 children vaccinated) more severe illness may occur with convulsions or even coma. If you are worried consult your doctor. If it is decided the baby has had a reaction to the whooping cough part of the vaccine, the baby can still have diphtheria, tetanus and polio vaccines, but should not have further whooping cough immunisation (see below).

MMR vaccine (Measles, Mumps, Rubella) Some babies may have a slight fever and a faint rash for a few days about a week to 10 days after the injection. A few get swollen faces, like mumps, about 3 weeks after. This will gradually go down. If your child is hot and grizzly during the first days after the injection, you can give a small teaspoon of baby paracetamol to lower the temperature. None of these reactions are infectious. If you are worried about a vaccine, consult your doctor.

A special word about whooping cough (pertussis) immunisation Whooping cough is a very unpleasant condition, but usually it does not leave any after effects in older children. However, in very young children the illness may be severe, with pneumonia, convulsions and sometimes brain damage. Each year, in the UK, children actually die from whooping cough. Unfortunately these are always children who were not immunised, and the number of deaths from whooping cough has increased recently as more children have not received the vaccine.

Children can be safely protected against whooping cough. Immunisation usually causes no reaction at all, though occasionally mild irritability may occur. Some doctors believe that, in a tiny number of babies, serious complications may follow immunisation. Luckily, it is nearly always possible to avoid giving immunisation to babies who are at risk of serious complications. Babies should not be immunised against whooping cough if:

* They have had a severe reaction to a previous whooping cough vaccination.

* They have an illness affecting the brain or suffer from epilepsy (fits).

It *may* be sensible for them not to be vaccinated against whooping cough if:

* A parent, or brother or sister of the child has had epilepsy.

* The baby has a neurological condition, such as cerebral palsy or *spina bifida.*

Although there are often concerns about whooping cough vaccination if a family member has epilepsy, or if the child has cerebral palsy or *spina bifida*, your doctor may still advise vaccination. Ask for your doctor's opinion on this matter. In some areas, there are special vaccination clinics to advise on children who present difficult immunisation problems.

In these cases your doctor may want to advise against whooping cough immunisation or ask for another opinion. If your baby has an acute illness with fever (not just a cold), your doctor may want to wait until the baby is better before immunisation is carried out. Babies can be safely immunised if they have an allergy or there is allergy in the family.

The important point to remember is that the chances of your baby being damaged by whooping cough caught naturally are many, many times greater than the chance of damage following immunisation.

HEALTH VISITORS AND HEALTH CLINICS

If you think your child is ill you will go to your GP, but there is also another level of health care designed to help parents and to monitor children's development. Community health care is the general term for this, although the way in which it works will vary slightly according to the practice of different Health Authorities and GPs. Essentially the aim of the service is to provide a surveillance system which can both offer support and advice to parents about their child's health and be watchful to pick up any developmental or health problems which may need further investigation or treatment. Much of the work of the community health service is aimed at preventing ill health — ensuring that all children are covered by a programme of immunisation to protect against certain dangerous diseases is a most important aspect. The member of your community health team you will have most contact with is your health visitor. Health visitors are State Registered Nurses who have taken an approved course in midwifery and a twelve-month course in health visiting and they have a statutory duty to visit every mother and child. You will probably have met your health visitor during pregnancy and she will visit you at home after the birth, usually on the eleventh day. This is the time when responsibility passes from the midwife, who has to visit mothers and babies from the time they leave hospital until the tenth day, to the health visitor, who is responsible up until the twenty-eighth day if necessary. An increasing number of GPs, especially those in group practices, now run their own child health clinics so your health visitor may work from a room at your GP's surgery or from a community health centre, or both.

Your health visitor can be a valuable source of support in the early days. As well as wanting to know if you and your baby are well and making good progress she will also have time to talk about the more intangible aspects of parenting. If you feel a bit low, disorientated or overwhelmed by the changes in your life, she can be a sympathetic and often constructive support. Unfortunately there are rarely any magic solutions to age-old problems of babies who cry a great deal and do not sleep, but it is

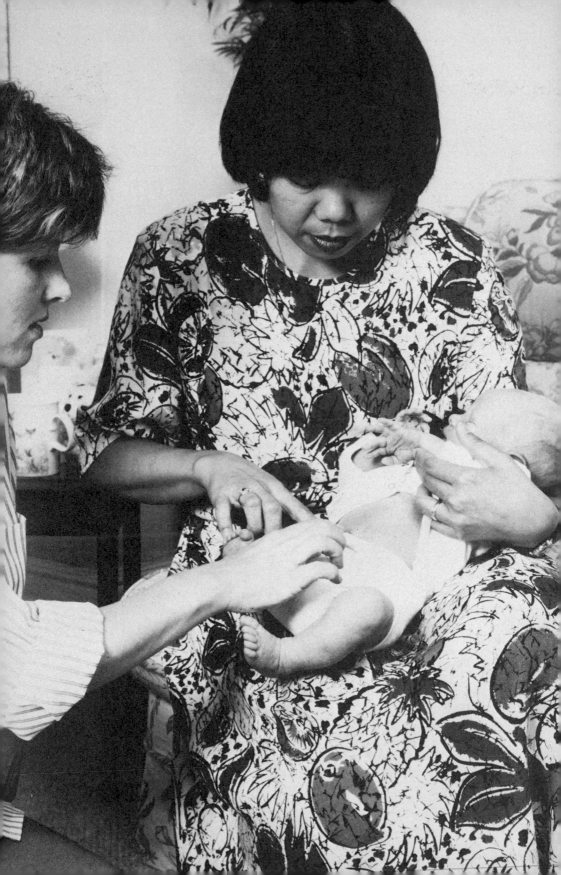

surprising how someone looking objectively at what is happening can often make helpful and positive suggestions. She will also be able to suggest ways in which you can meet other new parents, although very often such friendships spring from meetings at the health clinic where you will go to visit her once you get out and about. At her first home visit your health visitor will tell you all about the clinic and how often to bring your baby along. At these future visits, as well as discussing your baby's progress and any problems, the health visitor will weigh your baby and although weight gain will not be regular week by week, over a longer period it should show a steady increase which doctors can check against the expected pattern of growth for a baby of that age. Growth charts are explained in more detail on page 314 in chapter 9.

DEVELOPMENTAL CHECK-UPS

New babies should receive their first check-up within forty-eight hours of birth and this will either be done by a paediatrician in the hospital or by your GP in the case of a home delivery or early discharge – see page 140 for more detail. The next check is at six weeks, again either by a doctor at your surgery or at the local health centre and your health visitor will make the appointment for you.

On this occasion the doctor will ask about your baby's feeding and sleeping routine and will be looking to see how alert and responsive he is. He will see how well your baby is beginning to support his head, listen to his heart and check to make sure the hip joint fits properly into the socket (see page 144). The doctor will see if your baby follows objects with his eyes, look in his ears and ask if you think he reacts to noises, but screening for hearing defects is not usually done until the baby is about seven or eight months old unless there is cause for suspicion.

Exact timing of further developmental check-ups varies according to the practice of different Health Authorities, but in many areas the next check will be at about eight months and will be carried out by a health visitor. Again she will be looking to see how generally alert your baby is and ask about patterns of eating, sleeping and behaviour as well as about any illnesses your baby may have had. By eight months most babies can sit unaided, push themselves up on their forearms when lying on their tummies, and will reach out to grab an object such as a brick placed in front of them. She will test his hearing by making a series of sounds behind him and seeing if he turns his head in response. If the child fails to respond to the noises it is more commonly because he is tired, distracted by something else, not interested, not familiar with the test sounds or has wax blocking his ears than that his hearing is actually impaired, but the test will be repeated a few weeks later and if he fails to respond again he will be referred to an audiologist. All the same, if you are worried about your baby's hearing at any age, you should tell the doctor or health visitor so that, if necessary, checks can be carried out earlier.

Your health visitor can be a valuable source of support and advice

After this age Health Authorities vary considerably in their practice of developmental checks, some ask health visitors to see children at eighteen months and then at three and a half years, but all children should be seen by a doctor for a pre-school check-up before they are five. Depending on your child's age the doctor or health visitor will be looking to see if he has reached various developmental milestones and using a variety of tests to measure this, as well as making sure he is in good health and has no problems with hearing or sight. The age at which children learn to walk, talk, are potty trained and so on varies tremendously, but the chart in chapter 9 gives an idea of what to expect at various stages. Most doctors or health visitors will be happy to explain the point of various tests. If you have any specific worries about your child, always ask, and if you are not happy subsequently, always go to see your GP. Parents who still think there is some abnormality in their child's hearing, sight or development need to be reassured by a detailed assessment by the relevant specialist and very often their instinct about their child is right.

YOUR CHILD'S TEETH

Your baby's first set of teeth, or milk teeth, are forming in his gums before birth. Rarely, a baby is born with the first tooth and if this is wobbly it may have to be taken out. But, if it is firmly embedded, it may be left because removing it means the child may have a gap until his second teeth begin to come through. An early tooth may also interfere with breastfeeding. Usually babies cut their first tooth, which will be one of the middle upper or lower teeth (called a central incisor), at about six months. Do not worry, though, if your baby does not produce teeth until a little later – some babies are still giving toothless, gummy smiles at the end of their first year! Total absence of teeth is very rare.

TEETHING

Babies may become a little disturbed when teeth start to erupt. They like to bite on something hard, such as a teething ring. Rubbing the gums also gives relief. Do not give teething powders or junior aspirin but discuss any forms of medication for teething with your doctor or health visitor.

This is the order in which your baby's teeth will usually appear:

AGE	TEETH	POSITION
6 months	Incisors	2 central top and 2 central bottom teeth
8 months	2 more incisors	Top and bottom, making 4 top and 4 bottom front teeth in all
10–14 months	First molars	Double teeth for chewing
18 months	Canines	The eye teeth or 'fangs'
2–2½ years	Second molars	The second set of double teeth

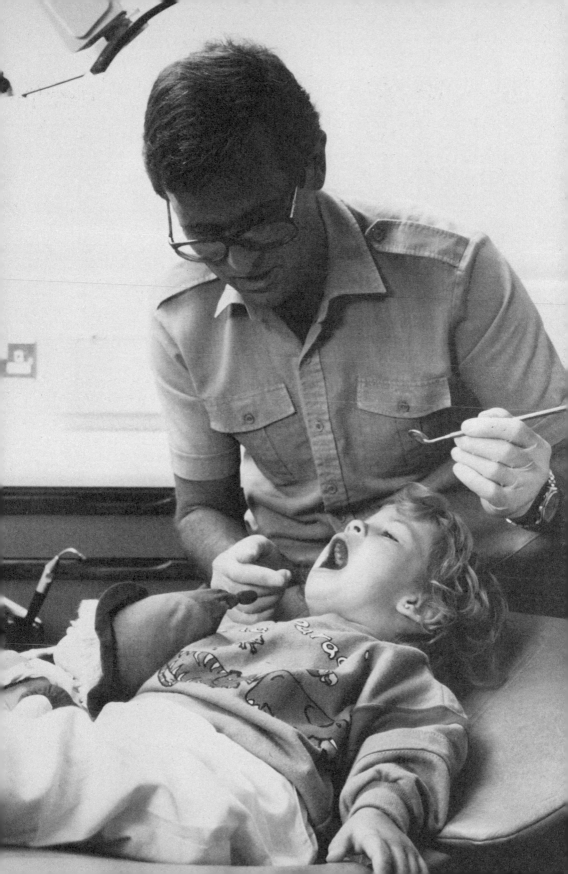

In total there are 20 milk teeth – 12 less than the full set of 32 permanent teeth we have as adults. Most children have a full set of milk teeth by the time they are about two and a half years old and these last until around the age of six, when the teeth which were the first to appear, the middle front or central incisors, become loose and fall out as the second teeth begin to push through the gums. These milk teeth continue to fall out until the age of about twelve.

LOOKING AFTER TEETH

Teeth are made up of a soft, sensitive centre called pulp which is well supplied with nerve endings and is protected by hard outer casings of dentine and then enamel. Dentine is less hard than enamel. Enamel does not have nerve endings and is therefore not sensitive. Teeth become decayed when acid eats through the protective coating of enamel and begins to attack the sensitive inside of the tooth – this causes toothache. So toothache is not the first warning of decay, but actually means the enamel has been eaten away at some point leaving the less hard dentine vulnerable to decay.

How does the acid which eats through the protective enamel coating come to be on our teeth? The answer lies in a substance called plaque, which cannot easily be seen by the naked eye, but which forms a sticky film covering the teeth. The attacking acids are produced when bacteria that are present in the plaque react with little bits of food leftovers. Cleaning plaque off the teeth, therefore, is the most important protective measure you can take to safeguard your child's teeth.

When to start cleaning teeth? Teeth need cleaning as soon as they appear, and that is true of milk teeth just as much as of second teeth. The idea that first teeth do not matter because they are going to fall out is wrong. First teeth need taking care of just as much as second teeth, first, to avoid pain and distress and unnecessary extractions; and second, if milk teeth are allowed to become rotten so that they have to be taken out long before the second teeth are ready to come through, this may lead to loss of space for the permanent successors, and thus to crowding.

If children have not been encouraged to take care of their teeth by cleaning them carefully and not having too many sweets and sweet drinks, they are unlikely to change their ways when they reach the age of six, and their second teeth start to come through. Sound teeth look good. Your child should have a nice smile, so why risk a mouth of discoloured stumps instead? Toothache is horrible and children do not have to suffer from it if their teeth are properly looked after.

Your baby's first teeth are best cleaned by wrapping a clean, non-fluffy piece of material like a flannel round your finger and simply rubbing the teeth and gums gently to wipe away the plaque.

In the second year, you can introduce a toothbrush – choose one with soft bristles and brush the teeth starting at the base of the tooth and moving away from the gum, i.e. upwards if you are brushing the lower jaw and downwards if you are brushing teeth in the top jaw. As your child grows, he will want to take over some of the brushing himself. Teach him to brush in the same way that you do and always insist that you have a turn at the end to make sure his teeth are properly clean.

When is your child old enough to brush his teeth completely by himself? It depends slightly on the individual child but usually not before five years old, although obviously he will have been taking over more and more of the brushing, with you supervising and having a turn at the end to reach those difficult back molars.

How often should you brush a child's teeth? The ideal would be every time he eats something, but obviously this is not practical. Compromise with a routine where you brush morning and evening and always make a point of brushing teeth after a sweet-eating session. You must make sure that the last tooth-brushing session at night is never followed by anything else to eat or drink which will leave a coating of plaque and bits of food in his mouth during the night. Be very firm about this from the start and it will become a routine with your child.

Toothpaste Toothpastes are mixtures that have a slightly abrasive action to aid cleaning. There is one active ingredient which is added to nearly all toothpaste nowadays, and that is fluoride. Fluoride is a mineral which occurs naturally in the water in some areas. It has been found that fluoride can cut down dental decay, although too much can cause teeth to become mottled – mottling varies from small white flecks to brown staining, and large amounts are needed to cause the latter. In this country, it is left to Health Authorities to decide whether to add fluoride to their water. You can find out by asking the local water board, the health visitor at the clinic, or by ringing your Health Authority, whether yours is an area in which the correct amount of fluoride is added to the water. If not, taking fluoride during pregnancy will not help make your unborn baby's teeth extra strong and you should give fluoride drops or tablets to your child from the age of six months until he is twelve years old, the period in which teeth are developing in the gums. The fluoride has been shown to strengthen the developing enamel against tooth decay. Where the water contains an adequate amount of fluoride or you are giving the child drops or tablets, restrict the amount of toothpaste you put on the toddler's toothbrush, as most of this is swallowed.

FOOD FOR HEALTHY TEETH

Sugar is a natural enemy of teeth and the biggest single cause of tooth decay. Children who do not eat sweets or drink sweet drinks do not get decayed teeth which need fillings as often as children who are continually bathing their teeth in syrupy solutions. But ruling sweets and sugary foods out of your child's life completely can be very hard. You will be doing well to protect your child's teeth if you follow the simple rules which are listed on page 538.

DO NOT make sweets a habit, save them for special occasions and treats.

DO encourage children to think of other foods as edible treats – for example, fruits, savouries or cheese.

DO NOT give children sweets to be eaten slowly over a long period – for example, a tube of toffees or a lolly to be sucked. It is far better to have a sweet-eating binge and then clean teeth thoroughly afterwards.

DO save sweet treats or sweet drinks for after meals when a tooth-brushing session can take care of all the plaque.

DO NOT give anything to eat or drink after teeth have been brushed last thing at night.

DO feed your child a healthy, balanced diet.

This last rule means plenty of the kind of food which needs chewing. Whole-grain foods such as wholemeal brown bread tend to need more chewing, as do uncooked vegetables such as carrots or celery and fresh fruit such as apples. These all exercise jaws and make for healthier teeth and gums.

Do not forget that fizzy drinks and most of the fruit drinks which have to be diluted with water contain a tremendous amount of sugar, which is just as damaging for your child's teeth as actually eating sweets. Even when the label says no added sweeteners, some drinks are naturally very high in their own sugar content – for example, blackcurrant juice, which is best rationed to drinking at mealtimes only and then made up in very weak solution. A steady supply of these very sweet drinks in between meals has the same effect as regularly giving your child sweets to eat. Because they are so high in sugar they are also very poor thirst quenchers.

Never ever dip a dummy in syrup or give your child a comforter which is made like a tiny bottle filled with sugar water, or some super-sweet fruit juice. This is the quickest way to rot teeth and your child will end up with a row of blackened stumps instead of pearly white, gleaming teeth.

GOING TO THE DENTIST

Try to pick a dentist whose manner is sympathetic and friendly towards children and who is prepared to take trouble with junior customers. The best way is to ask other parents about a dentist where children are made welcome. If you make an appointment as a family and take your baby with you, he will grow up being used to visiting the dentist and seeing his parents sitting in the dentist's chair. Try hard not to convey any apprehensive feelings or fears you may have yourself – parents can find themselves putting on their most convincing acting performance when they find themselves in the dentist's chair under their child's watchful gaze! In fact, it is important that you remember that modern dentistry has come a long way since you were a child. Your child does not have to end up with a mouth full of fillings, as you may have done, if adequate preventive methods have been taken. Modern treatment using local anaesthetic is rarely painful. If your child does need a filling in his first set of teeth, remember that milk teeth are far less sensitive than second teeth.

In the beginning, the dentist will just want to look at your child's teeth as he sits on your knee – as he gets older he will learn to open his mouth so the dentist can see better using a small dental mirror, and he can progress to actually sitting in the dentist's chair, but do not force this until he is ready. Some health centres have visiting dentists who are used to dealing with small children, and have more time to deal with a nervous one. Although milk teeth may show minor irregularities like crowding, there is very rarely an indication for treatment until the permanent teeth start to erupt.

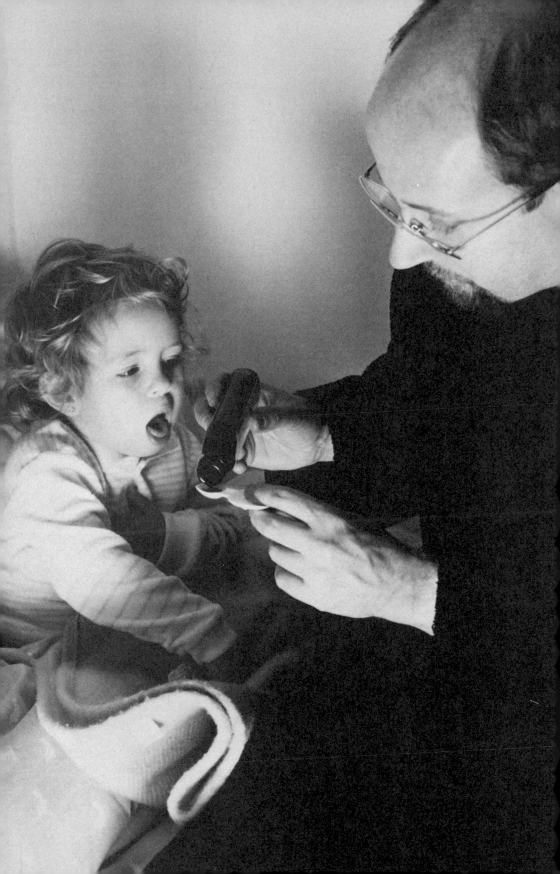

Chapter 17

COMMON
HEALTH
PROBLEMS

Raised temperature and fever   Infectious diseases causing fever –
chicken-pox, *rubella*, measles, mumps, scarlet fever, whooping cough
   Colds, coughs and sore throats   Tonsils, tonsillitis and adenoids
   Croup   Skin problems   Stings and bites   Parasites   Mouth
   problems   Ear problems   Eye problems   Urinary and kidney
      infections   The gut and its problems   Minor orthopaedic
               problems   The clumsy child

Reading descriptions of symptoms and wondering if they fit your child's
complaint – often in the small hours of the night – is an experience few
parents escape. Usually they will not find it difficult to decide whether to
ask for help from a doctor or health visitor, and there are some suggested
guidelines in chapter 16 about when to consult a doctor. In reading this
chapter and the next, however, it is important to remember that all
children are special individuals, which means the body of each one will
react slightly differently when there is something wrong. Your child may
be unwell yet have quite different symptoms or reactions from the ones
described. In general parents should trust their instincts and if they are in
doubt or really worried get professional help anyway. Doctors and health
visitors understand that children's ill health is a major source of anxiety to
a parent. If the problem turns out not to be serious or does not require
treatment they will still feel your visit is justified as they will have been able
to offer information and reassurance.
    When using these chapters to seek information about a complaint,
remember that the same condition can, in its mildest form, be a common
health problem, while in its more severe form it merits classification as a
serious illness – eczema and asthma are just two of the conditions which
fall into this category.
    If your child is unlucky enough to suffer from a long-term condition
with severe symptoms, the whole family will inevitably end up becoming
experts on the subject, but do not make the mistake, if your child does start

541

to show mild symptoms of being unwell, of leaping ahead and assuming a host of problems inevitably lie before you.

RAISED TEMPERATURE AND FEVER

A raised temperature and feverishness are symptoms of so many childhood illnesses that it seems helpful to set out the general principles for treating the problem, even though the cause will naturally vary.

Normally a temperature control mechanism in the brain keeps the body's temperature constant – this is the body's thermostat. When bacteria or viruses attack, the toxins they produce affect this thermostat and stop it working properly. The result is often shivering, shaking and feeling alternately hot and cold while the body temperature is actually raised: this is a fever.

A child's temperature can often rise without him being particularly unwell. Running around, getting upset and screaming, hot weather or being wrapped up too warmly may all make his temperature rise temporarily. It is very important to look at his overall condition, not just his temperature alone, to assess how unwell he is. Children can run quite high temperatures which would make an adult feel very ill and still have nothing very much wrong with them. Conversely, small babies may have only a slight temperature but still be quite seriously ill. Most parents can tell just by feeling how hot their child is and looking at his appearance and behaviour whether he has a temperature. Probably if you cannot be sure in this way, the temperature is either normal or only slightly raised.

If your child is under six months old fever alone is usually a good enough reason to see a doctor. However, as long as he is still feeding, has no other symptoms and is not distressed you can see if you can cool him down by loosening clothing and tepid sponging (see page 543). Do not think a baby or child with a temperature needs to be wrapped up warmly, whatever other people may say, because excessive covering with clothes and blankets will send the temperature even higher.

Babies and children over six months can be given paracetamol for babies in the dose recommended for their age. If the fever continues, and is accompanied by any other symptoms, you need to take a child to the doctor. How promptly you act depends on the child's age and the severity of symptoms, see page 517. Babies may safely be taken to the doctor's surgery.

Aspirin, in any form, should not now be used for any child under the age of twelve years without a prescription because it has been associated, although only in a few cases, with a very rare and serious condition – Reye's syndrome – which causes inflammation of the brain. Do not worry if your child has had aspirin in the past, there is no danger now.

TAKING YOUR CHILD'S TEMPERATURE

Modern thermometers measure temperature in Centigrade, older ones in Fahrenheit. Degrees of temperature are marked off along the thermometer, sometimes with an arrow or an N to mark the normal point. Normal body temperature is 37° Centigrade or 98.4° Fahrenheit.

Make sure the mercury column (the thin line) starts well below normal. To do this hold the top end of the thermometer and shake it with a wrist-snapping action, rather like cracking a whip. For children under three put the bulb end of the thermometer under their armpit and keep it there by holding their arm across their chest or tummy for one full minute before reading the temperature. Older children may be able to manage to keep it under their tongues — again, it needs a full minute — but if you have problems put it under the armpit. If you are telling a doctor the temperature mention if it is an armpit temperature because this is slightly lower than a mouth reading.

After using the thermometer shake it down again, wash it with cold water and store it well out of children's reach. It is important that the child understands he is not to bite the thermometer before you put it under the tongue.

Fahrenheit and Centigrade Comparison Chart

F	C	
95	35.0	
96	35.6	
97	36.1	
98	36.7	
98.4	37	Normal
99	37.2	
100	37.8	
101	38.3	
102	38.9	
103	39.4	
104	40	
105	40.6	
106	41.1	

TEPID SPONGING TO LOWER TEMPERATURE

* The air in the room should be comfortably warm — not hot or cold and draughty.

* Lay the child on a towel on your knee or the bed and gently remove his clothes, talking soothingly.

* Sponge his body, limbs and face with tepid water. As the water evaporates from the skin it absorbs heat from the blood and in so doing it cools the system.

* DO NOT be tempted to think that the colder the water the more effective the treatment. Cold water makes the blood vessels in the skin constrict, so less blood flows through and less heat can be lost. Consequently the temperature will stay high.

* As the child cools down, pat his skin dry with a towel and dress him only in a nappy. Cover him with a cotton sheet.

* Keep checking his condition to make sure he does not get too cold and shivery. If he does, give him more light clothes and wrappings.

* His temperature may begin to climb again. If he starts to get hot and distressed keep repeating spongings every ten minutes.

NURSING CHILDREN WITH FEVERS

Your best guide as to how to treat a child with a fever is the child's behaviour. As has been said, it is possible for a young child to have a raised temperature and not be particularly unwell, in which case there is no need to do more than keep a careful eye on him to make sure he does not suddenly deteriorate, and wrap him up warmly when going out in cold weather. He may be incubating an infectious illness so it makes sense to give places like the toddler club a miss until he is well and to warn other mothers whom you would normally see in case they have a special reason for avoiding infection.

Children who feel ill will naturally limit their own activities. Young children like to be near their parents, so make a bed up on a sofa downstairs if he wants to sleep so you can be on hand to keep a check on him and still get on with something. Try to get a child with a temperature to drink plenty of fluids but do not worry if they do not want to eat. If you have to take them out in cold weather, for example to the doctor's or because they have become unwell while you are away from home, they will come to no harm if you wrap them up warmly, but because they can quickly become cold and shivery it makes sense to limit other outdoor trips until they are feeling a bit better.

FEVERISH (FEBRILE) CONVULSIONS

'My eighteen-month-old daughter ran a high temperature very suddenly because of a sore throat. I was alone in the house, except for another toddler of two and a half, when she had a fit. I was completely panicked. She went stiff and rigid and began to turn blue in the face. I ran next door with her to the neighbours, who called the doctor and began giving her the kiss of life, though I don't know if that helped. After that I learnt a great deal about fits and two years later when my son began to make jerky movements while running a high temperature I recognised the signs. In this case he just went pale and limp, not stiff, and quickly came round.'

The words convulsion, fit and seizure mean the same thing. We all have electrical activity going on in our brains the whole time, but a fit happens when there is a sudden unusual release of electricity in the brain. Although it is very frightening for parents if their child has a fit, be reassured that they are rarely dangerous. About one in 30 to 40 children will have a fit as a result of running a high temperature – medically these fits are known as febrile (meaning feverish) convulsions. A young child's immature brain cannot cope with the sudden rise in temperature – it is the suddenness of a sharp rise in temperature which seems more likely to provoke a fit than the actual level the temperature reaches. Such fits are most common between the ages of 6 months and 3 years. About a third to a half of all children who have one feverish convulsion will have another and there is sometimes a family tendency to have such fits. These are not harmful in the long run.

What are the signs? While running a high temperature a child may begin to make jerky limb movements, seem distressed or frightened or cry out beforehand. In other cases there may be no such warning signs. The essential feature of a fit is that the child loses consciousness. Usually his body and limbs go rigid, and rolling eyes, clenched teeth, trembling or jerking limbs are all typical signs. During this phase his breathing may be interrupted and, more unusually in children, he may become incontinent. Some children may go rigid only briefly and then be limp and very pale. After regaining consciousness your child may seem confused but then go to sleep.

545

What to do if your child has a fit

* Stay calm.

* Turn his head gently to one side and put something soft underneath.

* Do not try to put anything into his mouth or to restrain his movements.

* Stay with him while the fit lasts.

* When he regains consciousness, reassure and comfort him.

* Take immediate steps to lower his temperature by taking his clothes off, giving paracetamol for babies and sponging him with tepid water (see page 543).

* When his temperature is lowered and he is comfortable, telephone the doctor although there is rarely any need for further treatment.

When emergency action is needed

* If a fit continues for more than 10 minutes or if the child has a second fit after the first you should immediately try to contact a doctor.

* If no doctor can visit then take the child straight to the nearest accident and emergency unit where, in the majority of cases, it will be possible to stop the fit within a few minutes by giving an injection of a drug.

Long-term treatment Nearly all feverish convulsions which are not associated with other problems are quite short and straightforward and will not harm the child or make any difference to his development. Even children who have several such fits will usually grow out of them without any problems, although if they are very frequent your doctor may discuss giving anti-convulsant medicine to prevent the attacks occurring until the tendency to have convulsions is outgrown.

A useful alternative to giving regular anti-convulsant medication to a child with a tendency to have febrile convulsions is to give diazepam (Valium) rectally (by the back passage). Until recently it was thought that diazepam had to be injected directly into the blood stream to stop convulsions. However, it is now known that it often works almost as quickly when given into the rectum. The best preparation is one which allows the liquid to be pushed in by squeezing a plastic container rather like a 'squeezy' bottle – your doctor will explain how to use it. Suppositories do not seem as effective since the outer coat has to be broken down before the drug can be absorbed. Many parents whose children suffer from convulsions now make use of this method in an emergency and it will usually control the fit and make admission to hospital unnecessary. In the case of children who give warning signs of a possible febrile convulsion, as some children do by seeming unwell, the same method will often prevent the fit from happening. However, this is not helpful in all cases, and you should discuss it with your doctor. In most children with febrile convulsions, the risk of later epilepsy (see page 600) is probably about one in a hundred.

INFECTIOUS DISEASES CAUSING FEVER

CHICKEN-POX

This illness is caused by a virus which has an incubation period of 12 to 17 days. First symptoms are a general feeling of being unwell, and possibly headache, slight fever and a blotchy rash which disappears when the typical chicken-pox spots appear. These look like little red pimples and the first ones may be mistaken for midge or flea bites, but they change into oval blisters filled with clear fluid which come to a head and then crust over. The spots usually take 3 to 4 days to appear fully and the child is infectious for 24 hours before the first spots and until all the spots are covered with scabs, which usually takes about 7 days.

Treatment is to make the child as comfortable as possible, choosing non-itchy clothes, give him plenty to drink and a light diet. It is better if he does not scratch, but do not get cross if he does because it is very itchy. Calamine lotion or Caladryl dabbed on the spots helps, plus a tepid bath with 2 cupfuls of sodium bicarbonate dissolved in it. Keep nails short and try to distract your child with not too taxing amusements.

Scratching can sometimes lead to the complication of infected spots which might leave small scars. More serious complications are rare, but occasionally chest infections can develop or, very rarely, inflammation of the brain or nervous system. If your child begins to have fits or is inexplicably drowsy and confused, contact your doctor at once. Adults can catch shingles from children with chicken-pox and vice versa.

RUBELLA (GERMAN MEASLES)

This is a very mild disease for children caused by a virus, but it is potentially very dangerous for the unborn child of a pregnant woman. The incubation period is 14 to 21 days and during this time the child may have mild catarrh and possibly tender, swollen glands behind the ears. The child may be a little off colour for a day before the slight pink rash begins behind the ears and on the forehead and then spreads to cover the whole body. The spots may join up so the skin looks flushed but in some children this is very faint or hardly perceptible. It is not itchy and no special treatment is needed for children with this mild disease beyond giving them plenty of fluids. The danger, however, is to pregnant women because if they catch *rubella* during the first 3 months of pregnancy it may seriously damage the unborn baby. Deafness, cataracts causing blindness, and malformations of the heart can result, while some women will miscarry. Unfortunately a child with *rubella* is infectious for 7 days before the rash appears, as well as when the rash is present and for up to a week afterwards. If you think your child may have been in contact with the disease or has it, warn friends and relatives and avoid contact with pregnant women as far as possible. Warn the surgery if you are taking your child for a diagnosis, and they will usually arrange an appointment at the end of surgery hours when the waiting room is empty.

Because *rubella* can be so dangerous to the unborn baby *all* girls should be vaccinated – having had or thinking you have had the disease is no guarantee of immunity because you can catch it again. Vaccination used to be routine for all girls between the ages of 10 and 14, but this is now being gradually replaced by the new MMR vaccine against measles, mumps and *rubella* which is given to all babies at about 15 months.

MEASLES

Also caused by a virus, this is a very infectious illness which is easily passed on by tiny droplets from the nose and throat which are inhaled from the air. The incubation period is 10 to 14 days and the rash often appears on the fourteenth day after exposure. Children are vaccinated against measles during their second year because this can be a nasty disease, and is very serious particularly in undernourished children in Third World countries. The first symptoms are fever, a cough, a running nose and red, sore eyes. There are often small white spots on the lining of the cheeks inside the mouth and they may also extend down the throat. The rash appears 3 to 4 days later as small red, flat spots which join up to form irregular patches. Usually the rash begins behind the ears and on the nape of the neck, spreading down to cover the whole body. As the rash erupts, a child's temperature usually rises sharply and he can be very ill. The rash itself is not itchy, but it is common for children to suffer tummy pain, diarrhoea and sickness, earache and swollen glands in the neck.

In an unvaccinated child seek your doctor's advice, keep his temperature down by giving paracetamol for babies and, if necessary, sponge with tepid water and give plenty to drink. Eyes may be sore and will be soothed by dimmer light, but no harm will result from bright lights.

Measles can cause eye, ear or chest infections which need treating with antibiotics, and more rarely complications of the brain and nervous system are possible, including convulsions. If your child seems unusually drowsy or confused or begins to have fits call the doctor at once. A much milder version of the illness is still possible in a child who has been vaccinated.

MUMPS

Mumps is not as infectious as measles but can be passed by droplet infection in the same way. The incubation period is 14 to 21 days and children are infectious immediately before the symptoms appear and for about 10 days after. Mumps is caused by a virus which attacks the parotid glands which produce saliva and are situated just below the ears. Usually the first sign is swelling and pain on both or one side of the face close to the angle of the jaw, as other associated glands can be affected. Sometimes the swelling may be prefaced by muscular pains (especially in the neck), fever and a headache. The glands do not work properly to make saliva so the mouth is dry and eating and drinking are painful – particularly first thing in the morning. Giving paracetamol for babies usually eases the pain, but hot compresses can also help if necessary. The exact location of the swelling may vary slightly depending on the glands involved and can affect both sides sequentially, only one side, or both sides simultaneously. The illness can be mild or can make a child very miserable for a day or two. Now a triple vaccine, MMR, against measles, mumps and *rubella* is given at about 15 months to prevent this illness.

The most common complication of mumps is mumps meningitis (1 in 400), with headache, stiff neck and sometimes sickness about 10 days after the onset of the original illness. There is no special treatment for this and fortunately most children recover well, but consult your doctor if you suspect your child has such symptoms. In adult men especially, the infection may spread to the testicles, which can be painful but is fortunately unusual and even if this happens it rarely affects both testicles to cause infertility. In women it may spread to the ovaries, but again this is rare. Sometimes the pancreatic gland in the abdomen can be affected in both adults and children, causing stomach ache. Mumps can occasionally also affect the hearing nerve, leading to deafness, usually only in one ear, but this is very rare.

SCARLET FEVER

This disease has an incubation period of between 2 and 4 days and is caused by bacteria called haemolytic streptococci. These bacteria can cause throat and ear infections without a rash or be carried without producing any symptoms at all. Scarlet fever itself is usually a fairly mild illness which is spread by droplet infection and results in a sudden fever, sore throat and loss of appetite. A day or two later a pin-point rash spreads over the face and body, except for the area round the mouth. The skin becomes quite dry and flaky.

If you suspect your child has scarlet fever, see your GP and he can take a throat swab and give a course of antibiotics. It is not nearly such a virulent disease as it used to be, although your GP will keep an eye on your child to make sure he makes a full recovery and does not suffer one of the rare complications. These include ear infections or, more unusually, a subsequent kidney inflammation. This is most likely about 3 weeks after the rash first shows – signs are vague and include general malaise, abdominal pain, passing red-brown urine and puffiness of the face and limbs. A very rare complication in the UK is rheumatic fever, which makes joints ache and causes general feelings of being unwell 2 to 3 weeks after the rash.

WHOOPING COUGH

Whooping cough has 3 distinct stages, beginning with a snuffly phase with a runny nose, slight cough and mild fever. After 7 to 14 days the child develops the characteristic whooping cough – this is a series of short coughs followed by a 'whoop' which is caused by the noise of air being breathed in through a partially restricted windpipe. The child suffers uncontrollable spasms of coughing and may go blue or grey during an attack because of lack of oxygen. The spasm is often followed by vomiting. This phase may last 2 weeks or more. The final phase is when the child ceases to be seriously ill but continues to cough and whoop more mildly – this can last for up to 3 months. In subsequent coughs the child may continue to whoop simply out of habit. Giving an antibiotic (erythromycin) in the snuffly phase may help to cut short the illness but there is no medicine which will cure the cough.

Small babies are most at risk of serious complications including developing a hernia, convulsions, pneumonia, brain damage, and even, in rare instances, death. Severe cases of whooping cough may have to be admitted to hospital for special nursing care. Patients may need to have their air passages sucked out and also be tube fed.

It is important that all children are protected against the disease with the triple vaccine first given at 2 months. By doing this the incidence of the disease will decline and tiny babies of less than 2 months will be at very little risk of contracting it. There are a very few specific reasons for not vaccinating, which are outlined on page 530.

COLDS, COUGHS AND SORE THROATS

COLDS

Most babies catch a cold some time in their first year – they are more likely to do this if they have older brothers or sisters at playgroup or school because there is more chance of a cold being brought home. It is reasonable to avoid known infection in the first 3 months as far as possible, but as long as your child is normally healthy it is not worth turning your life upside down to keep away from minor coughs and colds.

Why do we catch colds? Not from actually getting cold or not wrapping up warmly enough – although it is important to keep your child warm. Colds are infections of the nose and throat caused by cold viruses. Because there are so many different strains of these viruses and the immunity we develop against one strain only lasts a short time, it is not possible to protect by vaccination. Nor, as has been suggested, has any research shown that taking vitamin C makes us less likely to catch colds or to shake them off more quickly. Obviously a good diet and general good health make us better able to resist or to fight viruses of all kinds, including cold viruses, but sadly the cure for the common cold seems as far off as ever. If your child catches a cold all you can do is to relieve the symptoms and make him as comfortable as possible.

Babies under six months When a small baby catches a cold, the most serious problem is usually that the nose gets blocked up and the child cannot breathe through it – this in turn makes it very hard to suck at the

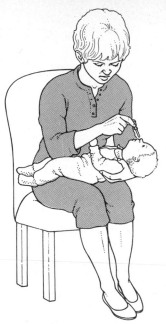

breast or bottle. Your baby may begin to feed and then break off, crying with frustration as he tries to breathe in through his nose and cannot. Take him to your doctor, who can prescribe decongestant nose drops. Given twenty to thirty minutes before a feed, these work by constricting the blood vessels inside the nostrils and drying up the cells producing the mucus. Your doctor can also tell you about giving some form of baby paracetamol if the cold is making your baby feverish – do not dose small babies yourself without advice. Be prepared for your baby to be more fretful and demanding and for feeding routines to go by the board.

He may have a sore throat as well, so offer frequent breast feeds or extra drinks of water if he is bottle-fed. Coughs that go with colds in small babies are usually a reflex action to clear mucus that trickles down the back of the throat – using nose drops to dry the mucus may make him cough less too.

Obviously babies cannot blow their noses, so keep gently clearing away mucus from around the nose with soft tissues. If he wakes clogged up with dried crusts of mucus after a sleep, wash them off using cotton wool and warm water. Smearing vaseline or white soft paraffin BP around the nostrils waterproofs the skin and helps to stop it getting sore. It looks a bit messy but gives the skin a chance to recover. Make sure it does not block the nose itself.

Some babies seem extra prone to nappy rash when they have a cold – be particularly careful to change nappies frequently and use protective cream if the skin starts to redden.

Babies over six months and older children   Decongestant nose drops can be useful for bigger babies too as they will probably still be taking some breast or bottle feeds. Sucking is also an important source of comfort, and some children are very reliant on thumbsucking as a bedtime habit. They can get very distressed by a blocked nose, so if the cold is making it difficult for them to breathe one dose of drops before bed may help them settle. The drops should only be used for a few days at a time.

A baby over 6 months old can be given paracetamol for babies in the correct dose for his age if he is feverish, but in many cases dressing him in loose, comfortable clothes which are not too hot and giving plenty of drinks will be sufficient. Fevered babies should not be wrapped up tightly or given extra covering. If you are at all worried by his condition or if the fever lasts more than a day it is best to ask your doctor's advice.

Over the age of a year paracetamol for babies is still probably the best way to relieve fever if the cold is bad. Not many children under three years old can blow their nose, so keep using soft tissues to catch the drips and use a cream locally (see page 551) if the nose starts to look sore.

Do not try to force your child to eat if he does not want to, but make sure he has plenty of drinks – if he will not drink either and seems unwell seek advice from your doctor for babies under a year. In older children seek advice if they are still not taking drinks and seem unwell the following day.

Be prepared to be patient when children are under the weather with colds. They may be more clingy and want to sit on your lap instead of going off to play by themselves. Your undivided attention and a bit of cosseting will be as useful as any medicine in making them feel better.

If a child has a cold or cough but does not seem unwell and is eating normally, there is no need to keep him indoors in cold weather provided he is dressed warmly. A child who is unwell or feverish will not want to play outside, but it will do him no harm to leave the house to go to the doctor's or on any other necessary trip – again, make sure he is well wrapped up against the cold and if possible take him in a car or arrange a lift. If possible avoid taking a child who feels ill on a bus or train as it involves so much more disruption, although babies and small children can be more easily wrapped up and taken in carry-cots or their parents' arms.

COUGHS

There are many different types of cough and various reasons for coughing. Many people believe that the answer to any cough is cough medicine, but this is not the case. No cough medicine can cure a cough, although some can suppress coughing. However, in many cases coughing is a reflex action to some form of irritation in the throat or lower air passages and often a way of clearing or coughing up mucus. This will help recovery, so suppressing a cough is not always useful.

While colds are infections of the nose and upper air passages, coughs may result from infections of the throat and lower air passages. These are the areas which may be affected.

There are various types and causes of coughing:

Coughs that happen with colds	These are usually a reaction to mucus trickling down into the throat and are a way of clearing it. They may be worse at night when the child lies down. Suppressing such a cough with cough medicine is not a good idea.
Coughs that follow colds	This usually means the virus causing the cold has moved down to infect lower air passages as well. If mucus has dried up but the cough is irritating and disturbs sleep at night, then a cough suppressant may help.

Throat infection	Colds often begin with a sore throat, but viruses or bacteria can also limit their attack to the throat alone. It is up to your GP to decide whether the infection is caused by bacteria, in which case it will respond to antibiotics, or to a virus, in which case antibiotics are no use. Sore throats in children are often due to mild tonsillitis, see page 554.
Short, hacking coughs	These can be the first sign of one of the infectious childhood fevers – such as measles or whooping cough, see pages 548, 549.
Chest infections	Chest infections can often follow colds or sore throats and mean that the bacteria have travelled downwards. The cough sounds 'chesty', the child may be short of breath and wheezy. It is up to your GP to decide, by listening to your child's breathing and looking at his condition, whether antibiotics will help.
Bronchitis and wheezing	Bronchitis is a specific form of chest infection meaning that the air tubes in the lungs (bronchial tubes) are inflamed and full of mucus. It can develop out of an infection higher up in the air passages, such as a cold. It begins with a dry, hacking cough which changes into a chesty, rustling one in one or two days and the child begins to cough up phlegm which is often swallowed. This, together with the coughing, can make the child sick.

A child with bronchitis may begin to wheeze – wheezy bronchitis is different from asthma. It is more common in children who are overweight but tends to be far less common after about the age of seven. Usually bronchitis is due to a virus and so will not respond to antibiotics. Coughing up the mucus to clear the tubes is important – in bad cases physiotherapy can be used to help.

For more on wheezing see asthma (page 589).

It is important to remember that persistent coughing can occur because a child has inhaled something into the lungs without the parent knowing – such as a peanut, bead or piece of a toy. This is potentially dangerous, so if you know or suspect this has happened take your child to the nearest accident and emergency department, where an X-ray can check if this is the case.

TONSILS, TONSILLITIS AND ADENOIDS

Tonsils and adenoids are made of special lymph tissue – an important part of our defence against diseases. It is their job to 'mop up' germs which threaten to enter the system by being breathed in through the throat or nose. Tonsils guard the throat entry to the body. Adenoids guard the nose route.

Taking tonsils out (tonsillectomy) used to be the commonest operation for children before the 1960s, so many parents today have had their tonsils taken out as children. Now we know that if a child's tonsils are enlarged it is usually just a sign that they are working well. Between the ages of about one and four years they are likely to be larger because they are specially active as the child begins to come into contact with more potentially harmful bacteria and viruses.

Sometimes, however, the tonsils are overcome by the germs and become infected. Tonsillitis can be very mild and simply part of a passing sore throat, but it can also be severe and make the child feel generally unwell. Children under the ages of five or six years hardly ever complain of a sore throat even when it is very inflamed. This may be because a bad throat does not hurt as much in young children, but probably also because small children cannot locate exactly where the pain is coming from. They may say they have tummy-ache instead, partly because they know where their tummy is, and partly because glands in the abdomen can be enlarged and tender as the system tries to fight off infection.

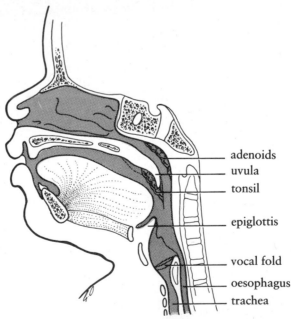

adenoids
uvula
tonsil

epiglottis

vocal fold
oesophagus
trachea

A young child's nose, mouth and throat in cross section

Treatment of tonsillitis is only effective if it is caused by bacteria. Antibiotics can then very quickly make the child feel better. If the tonsillitis is due to a virus, antibiotics will not work and a doctor can only treat the symptoms – paracetamol for babies lowers the fever, and iced drinks will ease soreness. Only a throat swab sent to a laboratory to analyse the germs can tell for sure if a sore throat and tonsillitis are due to bacteria or a virus infection, but if a child is very ill doctors will usually start treatment with antibiotics anyway while waiting for the result.

An operation to remove tonsils is rarely done now before the age of four years because tonsils are an important defence against germs. After that age an ear, nose and throat surgeon may suggest taking them out if they have become scarred and pitted and are no longer doing their job but instead seem to be the source of infection. Adenoids are usually removed at the same time. Tonsils and adenoids are sometimes removed because of very severe snoring and blocked breathing.

There may also be ear problems, and a specialist may suggest that adenoids are taken out at the same time as the middle ear is cleared of fluid and grommets are fitted (see page 572). This is because it is thought that without adenoids the eustachian tubes may drain better. If your child has a history of sore throats as well as ear infection, tonsillectomy will probably be suggested at the same time with the idea that the tonsils may not be working very well and may even have become a source of infection which is spreading to the middle ear.

Having both tonsils and adenoids taken out means children staying about 2 to 5 days in hospital, depending on the practice of the specialist. They may be nursed on a general children's ward or a children's ear, nose and throat ward. It is well worth asking if you can stay in with them, especially for the night before the operation and the night after when they may be feeling most apprehensive and then uncomfortable. Tonsillectomy makes a child feel miserable because obviously the throat is painful afterwards. But the quicker a child can begin to swallow food, the quicker it will heal. We now know that salty foods like crisps have far more healing power than the ice-cream and jelly that used to be fed to patients traditionally, although there is no harm in treating them to some of that as well.

CROUP

If your child begins to lose his voice and his breathing sounds hoarse or has a high-pitched croaky noise when he breathes in then an infection has affected his larynx. This can lead to attacks of croup – spasms of coughing which sound like crowing or sea lions barking, and difficulty in breathing in so that the child fights for breath. A croup cough can sound very similar to whooping cough – the main differences are that whooping cough has three distinct phases (see page 549) while the croup cough often starts soon after or at the same time as the child becomes unwell. An attack can be very alarming, but keep calm because if you make your child panic this will make things much worse.

If you imagine that a child's windpipe is only the width of a drinking straw, you can see how easily it can be narrowed further by swelling and inflammation. Panic makes this worse.

Attacks of croup happen most often at night. This is what to do:

* Pick the child up, speaking soothingly and reassuringly.

* Holding him upright, take the child into the bathroom and start to fill the bath or basin up with hot water.

* Keep the door shut and sit with the child, fanning steam towards his face, still talking soothingly.

* Usually, as soon as a little moisture in the form of steam is breathed in, the breathing will become easier.

* Continue to sit with the child in the steamy atmosphere for at least 10 minutes or so until his breathing is easy again, although it may still sound noisy.

* If you have no hot water on tap then boil a kettle (only put a little water in because you want steam quickly) and when it boils take the lid off and waft steam towards your child's face while holding him upright in your

other arm. Be very careful indeed not to get your child too close to the kettle because a direct cloud of steam can scald.

* After the immediate attack has been relieved, phone your doctor if you are still worried or if you think breathing is still very laboured.

* You need to keep a watch on your child's condition to take action if another attack threatens. If it is night time bring his cot into your room or take him into bed with you, making him more upright by raising a cot mattress or propping him up with pillows.

* Steam the room up by boiling a kettle before you settle down again. Alternatively, you may want to decamp to a smaller room — the smaller it is, the easier it is to fill with steam.

* Do not fall asleep and risk the kettle boiling dry.

* Keep a kettle full of water in the bedroom in case your child gets distressed again, but for a bad attack steaming the bathroom is usually quicker if you have hot water on tap.

Croup often follows on from a cold because the virus has spread downwards. Antibiotics are no use against viruses, although if the croup continues for several days, or the child has become suddenly very unwell or is under six months old, you should see your doctor, who can decide whether it may be due to bacteria and therefore treatable.

If the breathing is getting rapidly worse take the child to hospital for emergency treatment which involves either putting them in a steam tent or, in more serious cases, passing a small tube down the windpipe to give air or oxygen directly into the lungs.

Prevention is not always completely possible, but once you know your child is susceptible to croup there are certain measures you can take. Watch for signs that a cold has begun to move down to affect the larynx — loss of voice is the most obvious. Burning vaporising fluid in a specially designed vaporiser really helps — ask at any large chemist for a vaporiser and all the parts needed for it to work — candles, fluid, and a special stone which absorbs the fluid. Light the vaporiser half an hour before bedtime, making sure it is sited well out of reach of the child. If an attack seems likely, steam the bedroom using a kettle before his bedtime and again before you go to bed yourself. Keep central heating low and leave the window open a crack to make the air less dry — cover your child with extra blankets if it is a cold night.

SKIN PROBLEMS

The skin is a waterproof barrier which keeps germs out and body fluid in. It also assists with temperature control to help us cool down or warm up. The layer of fat just under the skin provides a fuel store for emergencies.

SKIN PROBLEMS IN THE NEWBORN AND THE YOUNG BABY

Newborns and young babies often have tiny yellowish-white spots on their faces, especially around the nose. These are quite normal, and are due to little glands. Nearly always the spots disappear in a few days, although the glands may become blocked and the spots larger ('milia'), in which case they last a little longer. There is no need to do anything about them.

Nearly half of all babies develop a blotchy red rash, sometimes with tiny white blisters as well, about one or two days after birth. It shows over the chest, back and face. It is called *erythema toxicum*, and goes away in a few days without treatment.

The skin problems of newborn babies are discussed in more detail in chapter 4.

Heat rash and sweat rash Young babies may also show a heat rash or sweat rash because their sweat glands are not yet properly formed and working. This red rash, in which there may be some raised bumps, is called milaria, and is more likely to appear in hot weather. It occurs especially in the groin and armpit. All you need to do is to keep the baby as cool as possible and the skin dry.

Nappy rash Almost all babies get some occasional bouts of redness and soreness in the area of their nappies. Treatment for skin which is irritated by being wet and in contact with urine and stools is to use disposable nappies and change them frequently. Whenever possible, allow your baby to go without a nappy to let the air get to his skin as much as possible, and use a zinc and castor oil cream at every nappy change. If the rash does not begin to clear in a week, it may have been complicated by a yeast infection – *candidiasis* or 'thrush'. This turns the skin a more fiery red colour with a scaly edge and does not respond to the usual treatments for nappy rash. Instead it needs cream prescribed by your doctor (usually Canesten or nystatin) and usually responds well to this.

Reactions to washing powders, especially the biological ones, can cause rashes, so if your child keeps getting sore and you are using terry nappies it is worth trying an enzyme-free powder.

SKIN PROBLEMS IN INFANTS AND OLDER CHILDREN

Dry skin If your child has dry skin this may become extra sensitive in the coldest part of the winter. Try using a water soluble cream (Unguentum Merck, aqueous cream or emulsifying ointment) instead of soap for washing; it will leave a protective, waterproof film. A thin smear of vaseline or zinc and castor oil cream will help to heal lips, cheeks or noses that have become sore. Avoid pure wool or nylon next to the skin if these irritate, and use cotton or cotton mixtures.

Eczema Doctors use the word eczema as a label for a group of skin problems, but there are actually different types of eczema with different causes. The common type dealt with here is called atopic eczema. About

one in eight of all children will show symptoms at some time and these can vary from transient dry patches to very severe symptoms which persist over years. For a full description of symptoms and treatments see page 595.

Itchy skin This is very common and there are a large number of different causes. Some of them are infections, usually produced by organisms such as bacteria and fungi, themselves invisible to the eye. Some are infections caused by worms or tiny insects – threadworm and scabies are examples. But there are also other skin conditions not caused by infections, of which eczema is the most common.

Impetigo This is a bacterial skin infection. It is itchy and very infectious and can easily spread through a playgroup, school or family. It begins with small blisters, and these turn into areas of pus covered with very thin skin. Raw, weeping patches then occur, and finally drying produces yellowish golden crusts. Healing usually starts from the centre and leaves temporary rings of red skin. Treatment with antibiotic cream or antibiotics by mouth will usually be necessary. Do not attempt to pick the crusts off or wipe them off. Be careful to wash hands very thoroughly after touching an infected area and keep the child's towels and flannels separate because impetigo spreads so easily. It is best to keep playgroup-age children at home and steer clear of other children until it is under control.

Molluscum contagiosum These are little whitish-yellow, pearl-like spots up to about half an inch across, but usually much smaller. They may occur singly or in clusters. They are caused by a virus. As they always go away within a few weeks or months, they do not need to be treated. If treatment is required, it involves freezing or the application of a drop of acid and both these procedures are uncomfortable. Even after treatment, it may come back and need treating again.

Moles These can be flat, raised, hairy or smooth. Moles present at birth should be seen by a doctor for checking. Moles appearing after birth in children are almost always harmless and should be ignored, unless someone in the family has had a malignant melanoma. In this case the opinion of a dermatologist should be sought.

Pimples and boils Redness, heat and pus-filled spots are signs of a skin infection. Sometimes infected spots occur when bacteria have been let into the skin after it has been broken by an injury, so keep cuts and grazes clean.

These infections do itch, but try not to let your child scratch because the infection will spread to other areas. Keeping pimples and boils covered with loose cotton clothes, so they can dry out, is better than putting plasters on. If the infection does not clear, visit your doctor, as an antibiotic cream or a course of antibiotics by mouth may be needed.

'Ringworm' This is not due to a worm at all, but a fungus, and in childhood it is often caught from an animal. It is most likely to affect the scalp, and little patches of hair may come out, leaving a sore patch. Your doctor will need to see it, and it can be successfully treated with medicine (griseofulvin) which your child may need to take for some weeks. Griseofulvin should be taken during the largest meal of the day.

Warts Warts are raised growths caused by a virus and are quite harmless. Children get them most between the ages of 6 and 12, although they can occur in younger children. Over half disappear by themselves within 2 years. If they do persist or grow very large they can be removed by your GP or local hospital outpatients' department, usually by freezing them. A verruca is a wart on the sole of the foot and may hurt because of pressure. They are readily picked up in swimming baths, but swimming pool attendants warn against wearing rubber protective socks because there is such a danger of slipping on wet tiled surfaces. Verrucas can be treated either by lotions or removed by freezing, but the treatment often fails, and unless a verruca is painful it is probably best left untreated, as it will eventually disappear naturally.

BIRTHMARKS

Babies may be born with a whole variety of marks on their skin, sometimes called *naevi*.

Skin Problems

Stork marks These are pink areas that may appear on the back of the neck, the upper eyelid, the forehead or knee. They are not caused by bruising from the bird that carried the child to the labour ward, but that is how they got their name! Those on the knee, eyelid and forehead go away after a few weeks, but those on the back of the neck are usually permanent.

Strawberry marks These are raised red patches with white marks that may occur anywhere on the body. They are usually not present at birth, but begin to appear in the first month or six weeks. They may become quite large but then usually just fade away completely over the first few years of life, first going white in the centre. See chapter 4 for more details. If bleeding occurs, it can be controlled by pressing a wad of tissues hard over the bleeding area for about ten minutes.

Port-wine stains These are present at birth, usually on the side of the face, and they are much less common. They tend to be permanent, and, especially if they are large, your child may need cosmetic surgery later in life.

SUNBURN AND HEATSTROKE

Babies and children can easily get sunburnt because their skin is more sensitive – fair or red-haired children are likely to be specially susceptible. Skin only begins to burn and redden *after* the damage is done, so do not wait for signs but take preventive action in advance.

DO NOT leave a baby in a pram or pushchair in direct sunlight.

DO introduce children to sunlight gradually at the start of the summer or on holiday.

DO NOT let them go out in the midday sun abroad or for more than an hour or so on the first day of a holiday.

DO protect them with light cotton clothes and hat in strong sun and use a good protective cream with a high sun protection factor at other times.

DO NOT ever leave a child in a closed car in warm weather – the temperature inside can rise very quickly and could be dangerous.

DO give children plenty to drink in hot weather.

If they do get sunburnt, use a cold wet flannel to reduce pain and moisturiser to relieve tenderness. Find a cool place out of the sun and keep sunburnt skin covered with clothes until it has recovered.

Heat rash can appear as a reaction to the sun or because a baby has been wrapped up too warmly and has become overheated. Cool down as for a fever by loosening clothes, fanning and tepid sponging (see page 543). Heat rash produces itching, so calamine lotion may help to ease this.

Don't leave your child in a closed car in warm weather

Heatstroke can be serious in babies and children. Children may not have sunburn but still be suffering from heatstroke. They look flushed and feel very hot. Their movements are often unco-ordinated and they may seem confused. In serious cases where nothing is done they may even become delirious and fall into a coma. Early stages of heatstroke can be treated by tepid sponging and fanning, but very rapid cooling can cause other problems so if your child has heatstroke seek medical advice rapidly.

STINGS AND BITES

STINGS

If your child is stung by something in the back garden stay calm and reassure him first – fright rather than pain is usually what will make him most upset. The only occasions when you need medical advice are if your child has been stung several times by bees or wasps, if he has been stung in the mouth or throat, or in the rare event of him being allergic to the sting. In a very few individuals this latter can cause sudden swelling of the lips, mouth and throat and needs emergency medical treatment, so if this should ever happen take him to the nearest accident and emergency unit.

Bee stings Bees leave their sting, complete with poison sac, in the skin. Pick it off carefully with tweezers aiming for the point nearest to the skin so you do not squeeze more poison into the puncture. Treat with cold water to take the poison out together with an anaesthetic spray such as Wasp-eze to ease the pain.

Wasp stings The barb is not left in the skin, so there is no need to do anything about it. Again, cold water and Wasp-cze spray are best for killing pain.

Jelly-fish These do sting but only a sting from a Portuguese man-of-war needs medical treatment. This species is easily recognised by the transparent bluish-white bladder that floats on top above the water level. Otherwise cold water and anaesthetic spray to take the pain away are the only treatment.

BITES

Mosquitoes Insects like mosquitoes that bite rather than sting are more interested in quietly feeding off the person they bite than hurting them. This means neither you nor the child may know when the biting is going on. The first sign may be a series of itchy bumps, or a rash. You can protect children with an insect repellent if you know there are likely to be mosquitoes around. Anaesthetic sprays (ask your pharmacist) are more effective than calamine for stopping the itching, but surgical spirit is an alternative.

Snakes The adder is the only poisonous snake in the UK and is easily recognised by zig-zag markings on its back. If your child is unlucky enough to be bitten by one give him the highest recommended dose of baby paracetamol and take him to the nearest doctor or hospital. Do not suck the poison out. See also page 503.

PARASITES

FLEAS

Flea bites can produce itchy red bumps on the skin, usually in clusters on the shoulders, arms, or the child's bottom. Nearly always the fleas have jumped on to the child from a cat or dog. The child may be the only person affected in the house, because though other people may be bitten, some children are hyper-sensitive and their skin reacts more to the bites.

If fleas are suspected, then regularly use a spray on your cat or dog or take it to the vet for checking. You may need to suggest this course of action delicately to neighbours, if you suspect their animal is involved! The child's skin is best left alone to get better by itself. Antihistamine medicine from the chemist may reduce the itching, but it may make your child a bit drowsy. If in doubt about the cause of the skin problem, take your child to the doctor.

HEAD LICE

> *'When my friend's child had head lice I was horrified. Then it turned out my daughter had them as well – we all began to feel itchy all over immediately.'*

Although parents are always horrified when they first encounter head lice in their children, it is in fact a very common complaint that usually shows up when a child complains of severe itching on his scalp.

Lice cannot jump or fly but move by climbing along the hairs. They can only spread from one head to another if the hairs are actually touching, so they are passed on when children put their heads together. Although they live on the hairs, they actually feed off blood by making pin-pricks in the scalp and sucking blood through the little hole. Soon after moving on to a head the louse, a six-legged insect the size of a match-head, lays eggs which are cemented to the hair with a special glue-like substance. The eggs are called nits and after the lice hatch they show up as white pin-head-sized specks. To check if your child has nits look behind the ears, on the nape of the neck and the crown for any dots stuck to hairs close to the scalp. Try to remove them by running finger and thumb up the hair – if they come off, this is probably dandruff and not nits.

Do not panic if you find them – treatment is easy and effective. Your local health clinic will supply you with free lotion or you can buy some from the chemist (gamma benzene hydrochloride). Do not use a shampoo, lotions will work best. Sit your child on a stool with a towel round his shoulders and, if possible, an old headband round his forehead to catch drips. If you do not have a headband another old towel will do. Soak the dry hair thoroughly with the lotion. It is very important to let the hair dry naturally, not blow it with a hair dryer, and although the smell may be off-putting you must leave it on for 12 hours afterwards. Do not go swimming or wash it until this period is up; then use an ordinary shampoo. It is important that all affected children and adults in the family are treated, or the problem will recur.

There is no need to go through the head with a nit comb – an unnecessary and unpleasant experience for the child. Health visitors or clinic nurses will always be happy to check for nits, but parents should also do this themselves as an ordinary part of child care.

THREADWORMS

'I first knew my daughter had worms when I went to empty her potty and saw these two tiny white threads waving at me. I felt revolted at first – that live "things" could be wriggling around inside her. Then I felt terribly guilty thinking that only a child who wasn't looked after properly could have worms.'

Most parents are horrified at the idea of worms – as with head lice they are socially taboo, linked in our minds with unhygienic homes. But, as with lice, this is misleading. Threadworms are so common that nearly half of all children under ten have them at some time and so do many adults, often without knowing at all.

To get worms a child has to swallow the microscopic eggs – these are usually picked up on hands or under fingernails and passed to the mouth on food or when the child sucks its thumb or puts a finger in its mouth. Once inside, the juices from the intestine stimulate the eggs to hatch and the tiny worms travel through the body feeding on the contents of the intestine. After mating occurs in the gut, the males disintegrate, having fulfilled their purpose in life, and the females then travel to the rectum. They emerge to lay their eggs on the skin of the perineum and around the anus – this is what causes the itching which is the main symptom of worms. The egg-laying usually happens at night when the child is still and warm. Girls are more likely than boys to get worms and they can also get into the vagina, causing even more itching. The cycle is continued when children with worms scratch their bottoms because of the itching – often without even waking up – and the eggs are caught under their fingernails again, ready to be transferred back into the mouth. There's a suggestion that threadworms can make people more vulnerable to appendicitis by burrowing into the mucous membrane and making infection more likely.

Treatment is simple and effective. A strawberry-coloured drug called piperazine, or an orange-coloured drug called mebendazole is taken, which paralyses the worms so they cannot lay eggs and are passed out of the system – the drugs may stain the stools red or orange. A second dose is taken two weeks later to catch any worms which may have hatched in the meantime. Because the eggs are so easily transmitted by hand the whole family should be treated at the same time. To make sure the cycle is broken, scrub carefully under the fingernails of the sufferers in the morning and put them to bed in cotton pants to prevent scratching in the night. All members of the family should be careful to wash their hands after going to the toilet and before meals, and anyone preparing food should wash their hands before starting.

ROUNDWORMS

These are much more unusual than threadworms. The only way you would know if a child has roundworms is to see one passed in a stool or vomited out – they are like earthworms but whitish. Although rare, they are not particularly harmful and can be easily treated with drugs. They are more common in hot, humid climates where there is poor hygiene. If someone who has roundworms handles food without carefully washing their hands, they may contaminate the food with the worms' eggs.

ROUNDWORMS FROM DOGS AND CATS (TOXOCARIASIS)

These are different from human roundworms.

Puppies which have not yet been wormed should not be allowed in too close contact with small children, nor taken out for walks in places where children play because their excreta contain large numbers of eggs from these worms. Infection can, occasionally, be serious, with a risk of it affecting the eyes or causing epilepsy.

SCABIES

This is caused by a tiny insect, an eight-legged mite which burrows into and under the skin. There may be just a few small itchy bumps, sometimes filled with pus, on the skin. This occurs particularly on the hands and feet of young babies, but often spreads over other parts of the body too. It may look like eczema (see page 595) and it may become infected. It is very infectious and other family members and friends often catch it.

Scabies needs treatment with a lotion, and you will need to see the doctor so that the rash can be diagnosed and you can get a prescription. Everyone in the family should be treated at the same time. The itching may continue for a week or so even after the rash has been successfully treated. In babies the treatment needs to be applied to the face and scalp as well as the rest of the body.

MOUTH PROBLEMS

THRUSH

This is common in babies under a year old and shows as white furry patches or spots on the tongue and inside the cheeks which cannot be wiped off. Babies with thrush often feed less well as food makes their mouths sore.

Thrush is caused by an organism called *candida albicans*, which is normally present in our bodies but which can sometimes get out of control to produce these symptoms. Babies most usually get it because many mothers have *candida albicans* in the vagina at the time of delivery, so that the baby's mouth becomes infected during birth. It can easily be cleared up with a variety of treatments. Most commonly prescribed are nystatin drops, but there are many alternatives.

MOUTH ULCERS AND COLD SORES

A virus called *herpes simplex* often causes an attack of mouth ulcers between the ages of one and five years. They show as little, flat, yellowish-white spots and can appear anywhere inside the mouth. They may make it so sore that the child will not eat and is reluctant even to drink. The attack can take up to two weeks to disappear completely. After that first attack the virus may persist in the skin around the mouth and may cause cold sores. These are not actually caused by the cold virus, but are likely to show when the child is a bit low or run down – often the case when they have a cold. Cold sores can also be triggered by cold wind or sunshine.

Severe attacks of mouth ulceration caused by *herpes simplex* can be treated by a drug called Acyclovir, and if your child has such an attack take him to the doctor as soon as possible. Local anaesthetic lozenges and sprays can help him drink and eat more comfortably. Try giving drinks through a straw and avoid fruit juices because the acidity will be painful. If a child is having trouble eating anything at all because of the pain, try junket, jelly, rice pudding and ice cubes to suck if the child is old enough.

Single mouth ulcers These are not usually due to the *herpes simplex* virus, but can also be painful and last a week to ten days. Their cause is not known, and treatment is rarely helpful. Try to give smooth foods which are not salty or acid and will not be so painful to eat. Ice cubes can help to deaden the pain in older children.

NAIL PROBLEMS

These are not common in the under-fives, but sometimes young children do get infections of the nails. There may be an acute, painful swelling, and this will probably need antibiotic medicine from your doctor. If your child sucks his thumb or bites his nails, there may be chronic infection with swelling and redness around the nail area.

EAR PROBLEMS

'My six-month-old baby became feverish and miserable and wouldn't feed. I thought she must have a sort of flu bug, but the doctor looked in her ears and said it was an ear infection.'

Ears come in three sections. The job of the outer ear – the part you can see – is mainly protective. It is separated from the middle ear by the ear drum. This is a sheet of membrane which vibrates in response to noises. The job of the middle ear is to amplify that noise vibration. It is filled with air and has three tiny bones stretching in a chain through from the ear drum to the inner ear. When the ear drum vibrates it sets off a reaction in these bones which transmits the noise vibration to the inner ear. This part of the ear is filled with fluid, and here the noise vibration finally stimulates a nerve so a message is sent to the brain. A tube called the eustachian tube leads from the air-filled middle ear to the top of the throat and allows the pressure in the middle ear to equalise. We are most aware of this happening when we go up in an aeroplane and our ears start to 'pop' as the pressure drops. The same thing happens in reverse when coming down and the pressure rises again. Because the eustachian tube opens into the throat, swallowing can help to counteract the changes in pressure which give that popping sensation.

MIDDLE EAR INFECTIONS

Earache is most usually caused by an infection (medical name *otitis media*) in the middle ear. Because it is so common in babies and young children a doctor will always look inside their ears with an instrument called an auroscope during an examination.

An ear infection causes pus to build up in the middle ear, putting pressure on the ear drum and causing the pain of earache. Looking inside the ear a doctor can see if the ear drum is inflamed and red or if it is bulging.

The reason young children so often get earache is because their eustachian tube is narrow and lies horizontally so it very easily becomes blocked, especially after a cold. The end of the tube also emerges into lymphoid tissue next to the adenoids so germs from sore throats can very easily travel up to the ear. Babies spend a lot of time lying down, which makes the problem of drainage worse. But even the most trouble-prone ear sufferers grow out of infections because, as children get bigger, the

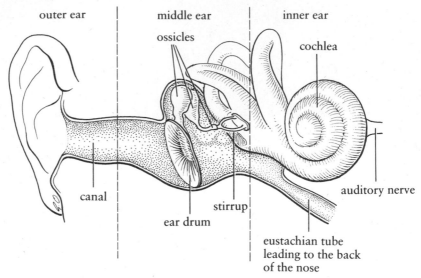

The ear in cross section

eustachian tubes become wider and move into a more sloping position, thus facilitating drainage during a cold.

Some children with ear infections may run a fever, be miserable, go off their food, be sick or have diarrhoea. Others may not seem particularly unwell but may still be found to have an ear infection. Even if they are old enough to talk children rarely say they have earache – although it can be very painful indeed. This is because they are not good at locating exactly where a pain is coming from, though sometimes they may put a hand to their ear. The only way to be sure if there is an infection is for a doctor to look inside, for a middle ear infection will not make the visible outer ear look any different.

A burst ear drum (perforation) may result if a child with a middle ear infection is not treated. After a period of acute pain, which may come on very quickly, the child may suddenly seem better but blood and mucus will start to pour from the affected ear. A burst ear drum is nature's way of relieving the pressure and hence the pain. However, perforation should be avoided if at all possible because each time it happens it leaves a small amount of scar tissue when the ear drum heals. Scar tissue is thicker than normal tissue and makes the ear drum slightly less flexible to noise vibration, and repeatedly burst ear drums can therefore make a child's hearing poorer.

If you cannot get treatment in time to prevent a burst ear drum, clean the discharge from the outer ear with cotton wool and cooled boiled water but do not poke around in the ear canal. Take the child to a doctor as soon as possible because antibiotics may still be needed to clear the infection. The ear drum usually grows back in about two weeks or less – your doctor will want to see him again to check that it has healed properly. In the meantime, do not let water get in the ear for this may stop the infection clearing – take care at bathtime and avoid swimming.

Treatment for middle ear infections is a course of antibiotics. If you suspect ear trouble take the child to a doctor without delay. Children over six months old can be given the maximum recommended dose of paracetamol for babies because the pain is severe. Do not cancel the doctor's appointment if the painkiller works and your child suddenly seems all right again – the ear infection is still there and he will get wretched again when the effect of the paracetamol wears off. Holding a warm, soft cloth next to the ear can be comforting – put it on a radiator or iron it to make it warm. Older children may use a hot water bottle wrapped in soft cloth. Even if the ear drum has not burst, avoid swimming and try not to get water in the ear during a bath as this may make the infection slower to clear.

Other causes of earache include infections of the outer ear canal, which will then look red and inflamed and be painful or itchy. There may be a discharge. Treatment is antibiotic drops or medicine.

FOREIGN BODY IN THE EAR

A bead or other tiny object in the ear is always a possibility with small children. This will cause infection and pain. They may even have poked something into the ear canal which has damaged the ear drum. One of the reasons parents should never poke around with cotton buds in their children's ears is that it encourages the child to do something similar – it is also unnecessary. If you know your child has put something in his ear take him to the local hospital accident and emergency department. In some cases a light general anaesthetic may be needed to get it out again.

GLUE EAR

This condition is being diagnosed in many more children today, partly because of better hearing tests and greater skill by doctors in detecting fluid in the middle ear.

In order to amplify noise properly, the middle ear should be filled with air. But very often the eustachian tubes get blocked and the ear fills up with fluid. Recurrent middle ear infection can contribute to this, and it is thought that in some children allergy may also be partly responsible. Unlike the pus caused by an infection, this fluid is sterile, although it can cause short periods of mild earache. But, because the bones and ear drum cannot vibrate so well, it can cause some hearing loss. It is reckoned that 17 out of 20 children will have had this condition at some point by the time they are 6 years old. Usually the fluid is thin and eventually drains naturally, but sometimes it becomes thick and glue-like – hence the condition is commonly known as 'glue-ear'. The danger is that poor hearing may affect a child's speech development and his ability to learn and to form relationships at a most crucial period. At school a child who cannot hear may well be branded slow or lazy unless the real problem is picked up. Getting through to a child who does not hear well can place a great strain on the whole family.

Doctors can tell if there is fluid in the middle ear by looking at the condition of the ear drum, testing the hearing and measuring the middle ear pressure with a machine called a tympanometer. The ear, nose and throat specialist will usually want to wait for several weeks to see if the fluid will drain by itself, and may sometimes prescribe a decongestant to be taken during this period.

If the fluid does not drain by itself, then the only way to remove it is by making a tiny opening in the ear drum (called a myringotomy) under an anaesthetic, and sucking it out. Specialists vary in their exact approach to the problem, but most suggest fitting grommets in the ear drum at the same time as the fluid is drained. These are tiny hollow tubes of plastic which are fitted into the ear drum allowing air to circulate freely in the middle ear and any further fluid to drain down the eustachian tubes. Some surgeons

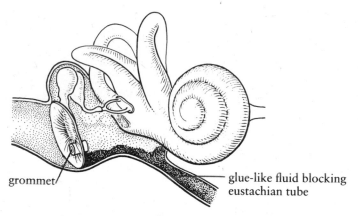

grommet

glue-like fluid blocking
eustachian tube

Grommet inserted into ear drum to allow air to circulate freely in the middle ear

recommend taking out adenoids at the same time to help drainage. Depending on the policy of the surgeon, having grommets put in usually requires a one-day stay in hospital, though it can be longer if the adenoids are to be taken out at the same time. Grommets normally stay in place for between six and eighteen months and are then rejected by the ear and fall out naturally. The hole in the ear drum heals up in about two weeks and, hopefully, the middle ear stays free of fluid. The child's hearing is restored to normal within about a week of the operation, but if he has been very deaf he may notice a difference immediately and think everything sounds very loud.

Sometimes the ear fills up with fluid again after the grommets come out and another set has to be put in. If this seems likely to keep happening or if the grommets fall out very quickly the surgeon may put 'long-stay grommets' in — these work the same way but have a different design, opening out into a wider shape behind the ear drum so they cannot fall out naturally, and will have to be taken out by another operation.

Most children grow out of the problem as the eustachian tube widens and becomes more upright, and glue ear is very unusual after about eight years old. For more serious ear problems see chapter 19.

EYE PROBLEMS

Always see a doctor if your child's eye seems infected, the cornea is hazy, vision is affected, or there is swelling and redness of the eyelids, especially if this spreads to the surrounding skin and he complains of sore eyes.

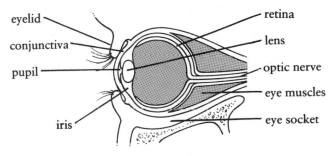

The eye in cross section

Sticky eye is very common in the first forty-eight hours after birth, see page 141.

CONTINUALLY WATERING EYE

If this occurs in the first four months of life it may be because of a blocked tear duct and the baby needs to be taken to the doctor to check on this. It usually clears itself over a period of time.

BLOODSHOT OR SORE EYES

These are sometimes due to a smoky atmosphere, which can make an eye bloodshot, or they may be caused by something irritating the conjunctiva, the moist lining over the eye. Such problems are more often uncomfortable than serious. The first step is to check if there is anything in the eye, such as a speck or an eyelash. Usually the eye waters so the tears wash it away or at least move it to the outside of the eye, where it can be picked off the lid with a clean tissue without touching the eye itself.

To look at your child's eyes wash your hands and gently pull the skin below the eye slightly downwards to reveal the inside of the lower lid. To look under the upper lid hold the eyelashes between finger and thumb and very gently pull the lid forwards and upwards. Ask older children to look up while you check the lower lid and down while you check the upper lid. Do not try to remove anything still in the middle of the eye but wait for it to move to the outer edge — blinking helps this but rubbing is likely to make it worse.

If you cannot see anything, the soreness and inflamed blood vessels which make an eye look red may be due to infection from bacteria or a virus. See your doctor, who will probably prescribe antibiotic drops or ointment.

To give eye drops, lie your child down, speaking soothingly, and try to put the drops into the inner corner of the eye so that blinking sweeps them across the eye. You can ask older children to tell you what colour the ceiling is or how many spiders they can see on the lampshade to get them to look up — asking them to blink ten times afterwards often distracts them and stops them getting upset.

To ease the discomfort for them, try pressing warm compresses or a clean cloth wrung out in warm water and wrapped round a spoon over the eye. Clean away discharge using cotton wool and cooled boiled water. Wipe away from the eye and use separate swabs for each eye to avoid continually reinfecting each side. Children with eye infections should not share flannels or towels, and try to stop them rubbing their eyes.

Sometimes conjunctivitis caused by a virus can spread through a group of children at nursery school or playgroup, and there is not much that can be done to prevent this. Viral conjunctivitis can be accompanied by fever, mild rash and sore throat and it often occurs with measles, see page 548.

CRUSTY EYELIDS

The eyelids may be sticky and irritated or have crusts of dried discharge, especially after sleep. This can be caused by specks of dandruff or a tendency towards eczema or allergy. If your child has dandruff, treat this with shampoo and cleanse the eyes in the way described above. If this does not seem to be the problem seek your doctor's advice — antibiotic cream may be needed for infection, or short-term use of steroid cream if the trouble seems to be eczema.

RED EYE

This is due to a burst blood vessel and looks far more alarming than it is — it shows as a bright red spot which then spreads out making half the eye look red. Red eye can happen as a result of pressure from fierce nose blowing or from a bad fit of coughing (especially in whooping cough) or violent vomiting. It can also happen for no apparent reason. It is not painful and there is no need to do anything — it will gradually fade.

STIES

Sties are the result of an infected eyelash hair follicle. They show as red swollen lumps on the upper or lower eyelid and can be painful. Warm compresses help discomfort, but if they are very sore see your doctor, who can give some antibiotic ointment.

ALLERGY

Allergy to some kind of pollen, fungus spores, mites in house dust or animal fur can show as watering, swollen, sore or itchy eyes. There may or may not be other symptoms. Allergy tends to run in families, so if close relatives have hay fever, asthma or eczema, your child is more likely to suffer. Allergic rhinitis is the medical term for inflammation of the nose due to allergy. You may find the complaint is seasonal, coming on when a particular pollen or fungus spore is in the air or it may occur only when the child is in contact with a particular animal.

There is no cure for allergy. Some children may grow out of it, though sometimes it returns in adult life. In bad cases antihistamines can be taken by mouth. Steroid drops or cream may also be used, but only for a very limited period under strict supervision. Sometimes the eyelids can become so puffy they start to droop, and a slight muscle weakness may make this more severe on one side. Your doctor may suggest you consult a specialist both to rule out other causes and discuss possible treatments.

SQUINT

A squint is present when the two eyes do not point in the same direction when the child is looking at something. It may occur for a variety of reasons – the child may be long-sighted (hypermetropic, see page 338), or there may be a defect in the eye itself or in the nerves supplying the muscles moving the eye. There is a hereditary factor and other members of the family may have been affected in a similar way.

Squints may be diagnosed at child health clinics when routine testing for them is carried out, but, much more commonly, parents are the first to notice them, and it is important to take a child for treatment as soon as you do. We need the use of two eyes (binocular vision) in order to see things properly in depth. If a child has a squint, only one eye is used. The 'lazy eye' gradually loses its function, and unless the squint is corrected, the child will have defective sight in that eye. Of course, it is also important to correct squints for cosmetic reasons.

If your child has a squint, he will probably be referred to an ophthalmo-logist, a specialist eye doctor. Treatment may involve cutting off the light to the good eye with special glasses or a patch, to ensure that the lazy eye has to work. Young children, and even some older ones, may find this difficult to tolerate, and it may instead be necessary to put drops in the good eye each day to paralyse it to produce the same result. Children may need glasses anyway to correct a refraction error if they are myopic (short-

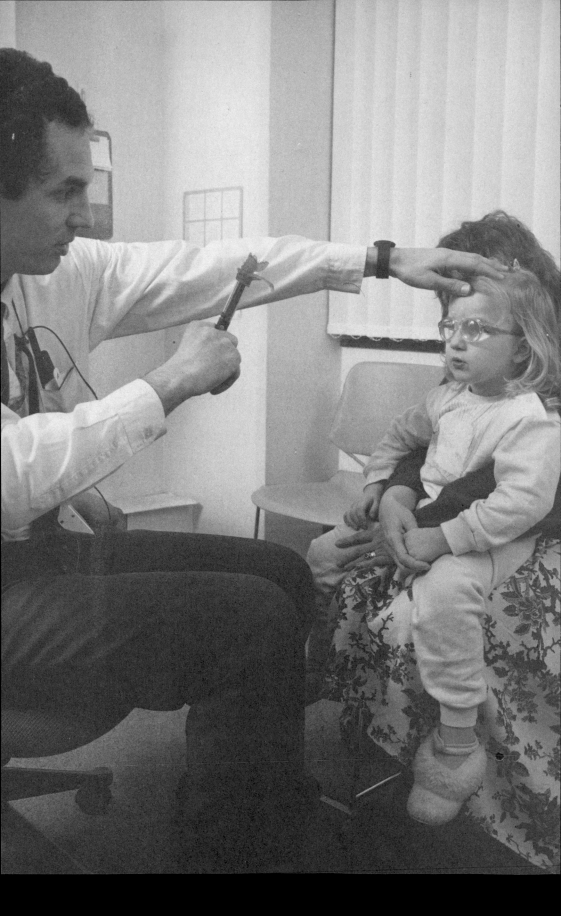

sighted), astigmatic or hypermetropic (long-sighted). Older children may benefit from exercises, and the advice of an orthoptist will be helpful here. Finally, it may be necessary for the child to have an operation to correct the squint. This will correct the appearance, and, if carried out early enough, may also help the lazy eye to work better. Admission to hospital for surgical treatment of a squint usually only lasts one or two days, but treatment by any other method for squint is really a childhood-long process.

LONG SIGHT – SHORT SIGHT

Children will not be able to see clearly unless the light coming into their eyes is focused exactly on the retina – the light-sensitive screen at the back of the eye from which messages are sent to the brain. The eyeball may be slightly the wrong shape, so the distance between the front of the eye and the back is too long or too short. If the eye is relatively short, the light coming into the eye will be focused behind the retina causing long sight (hypermetropia) or, if the eye is relatively long, the light is focused in front of the retina causing short sight (myopia). In either case the child is said to suffer from a refractive error.

A refractive error in one or both eyes is sometimes first detected because it leads to a squint. In other instances parents may notice the child cannot see clearly unless he puts objects close to his eyes. He may seem clumsy because he is not able to see things clearly. Alternatively, vision testing at the child health clinic at the eight-month or three-year screening examination may show that the child's sight is not as good as it should be.

If any of these problems arise, the child should have a proper eye test to check out how severe the refractive error is. For the young child this is done by retinoscopy – examining the eyes with a special light after paralysing drops have been put into them so that the pupil stays wide open and the eye cannot focus. Trial lenses are then held between the light and the front of the eyes until the error is corrected. Spectacles can be prescribed which will bring objects into focus when the child looks at them.

Small children vary quite a bit in how well they tolerate glasses, but most manage surprisingly well, particularly if their eyesight is greatly improved (see chapter 10 for more on introducing glasses to under-fives). Explaining to an older child why glasses are necessary, and giving praise when they are worn, is more effective than applying heavy pressure. It is important that young children who need glasses have their eyes checked every year, and occasionally more frequently, as the refractive error can change quite rapidly when they are growing fast, and new lenses may be required: older children usually need less frequent testing.

Children with squints are often long-sighted and, in this case, the glasses do not usually greatly improve the vision, but are used to control the squint. For more serious eye problems see chapter 19.

URINARY AND KIDNEY INFECTIONS

URINARY INFECTIONS

Girls get urinary infections far more often than boys because the tube leading from the bladder to the outside (the urethra) is much shorter and germs from outside do not have as far to travel as they do in boys. In girls the opening of this tube is very close to the back passage and it is therefore easy for germs from the bowel to get into the bladder. This is the reason why it is very important always to wipe a little girl's bottom from front to back and to teach her to do this too, so that germs are not wiped from the back passage forwards into the vagina and urethra, causing infection.

Symptoms of a urinary infection in children are not the same as in adults, and infection is much harder to diagnose. It is impossible to tell whether a baby in nappies is passing water more frequently or has pain when doing so, and the only signs of urine infection may be feverishness and vague ill health, or complaints suggesting a tummy upset such as vomiting or diarrhoea. If checking for other sources of infection such as ears or throat reveals nothing, then a urinary infection may be suspected. Occasionally the urine smells different, but this may be just because the child is drinking less and the urine is more concentrated and stronger. It sometimes also smells of ammonia which does not mean that it is infected.

Ideally a mid-stream sample of uncontaminated urine should be collected and sent off for analysis, and after this the child may be started on a course of antibiotics. In practice some GPs prescribe antibiotics without sending off a urine specimen first, since this can be awkward to collect properly until the child is old enough to use a pot or lavatory. Unfortunately, if the doctor does this no one knows whether there is a urine infection present or not, and if possible, a sample should be checked before treatment is started.

Urinary infections are easier to diagnose in children past the nappy stage who may complain of pain when passing water and may need to do so more frequently. The suspicion of a urinary infection always needs prompt treatment with antibiotics, but a urine specimen must be sent for analysis first, even though a laboratory may not confirm it for several days. If left untreated there is a danger of the infection spreading upwards to the kidneys with the risk of permanent damage.

Children who get urinary infections will need to have an ultrasound scan and X-rays to make sure that there is no blockage or delay in the passage of urine from kidneys to bladder or, in boys, no blockage in the urethra. Their kidneys will also need to be checked to make sure that they have not been damaged by the infection (see also kidney infections, page 579).

FORESKIN INFECTIONS

There is not thought to be any medical reason for circumcision at birth.

Before the age of about four years the foreskin is joined to the penis and trying to force it back can cause infection. Infection of the foreskin can occur in older boys after it has separated. There is then a risk that it can become 'fused' back on to the penis. Symptoms of infection are soreness, especially when passing urine, redness and a yellow discharge. The infection can be treated with antibiotic cream and if the foreskin has become fused it is worth trying to ease it gently back as far as it will go each night in the bath and then covering it with zinc and castor oil cream. It may take several months for it to separate again fully. If this does not work then a small operation is necessary to remove the foreskin.

Circumcised babies can get ulcers on the tip of the penis from contact with wet nappies. This can spread into the opening of the urethra and be very painful when passing urine. Treatment is to change nappies frequently – one-way liners in terry nappies or disposables help. Protect the tip of the penis with cream to allow it to heal.

VAGINAL DISCHARGE

If this comes with soreness, redness and itching it is usually due to thrush. Babies can get it if their mother has thrush at the time of the birth and the *candida* organism can spread from mouth to bowel, where it easily infects the vagina, especially in a baby in nappies. In older girls the *candida* organism can also be spread from bowel to vagina easily because the openings of the back passage and vagina are very close. Always teach little girls to wipe their bottoms from front to back after a bowel motion to avoid this. Treatment involves using one of a number of creams – usually Canesten – and is very effective.

Threadworms can also cause vaginal itching and soreness – see pages 565–6 for details of treatment.

Persistent vaginal discharge may be due to the child putting something like a bead or small piece of a toy inside her – she may have forgotten or be too shy or ashamed to let you know.

Some little girls may develop itching and discharge as a reaction to biological washing powders, so make sure all pants are well rinsed and use cotton in preference to synthetics. Bubble baths are also a frequent source of irritation.

KIDNEY INFECTIONS

The kidneys perform a number of vital functions: they excrete waste, which is passed out of the body as urine, but they keep some useful substances in the body which would otherwise be left in the urine; they produce a substance which stimulates bone marrow to make red blood cells; they maintain the body's balance between acidity and alkalinity, and also play a part in controlling blood pressure. So you can see that any infection which might damage the kidneys has to be taken seriously.

Kidney inflammation can follow throat, or more rarely, skin infections from bacteria. The inflammation is not caused by the bacteria themselves, but is a result of the body's reaction to fight the infection, so antibiotics are not usually necessary. Children with this problem pass small amounts of blood in the urine which make it look darker and brownish rather than red, and also have slight swelling of the face and hands and feet, and possibly fever, headache and a tender tummy. Treatment may just involve rest and observation, although if a child is very ill he might be taken into hospital for observation.

Inflammation of kidneys caused directly by infection is usually the result of infection moving up the urinary tract from the bladder. Much more rarely it can reach the kidneys via the bloodstream. Treatment in this case is antibiotics.

A common cause of repeated kidney infection is faulty valves in the tubes leading from kidneys to bladder so urine is allowed to flow back upwards, spreading any infection from bladder to kidneys. This can be detected by doing a special X-ray in which a radio-opaque dye is placed in the bladder through a fine hollow tube or catheter via the urethra, and X-ray pictures are taken while the dye is passed back out again. In older children it may be possible to give the dye by injection into a vein instead of needing to pass a catheter. Sometimes this problem is easily corrected by surgery, but since it has a tendency to resolve as the child gets older, treatment may be by giving an antibiotic regularly to stop the child getting infections until the problem has sorted itself out. For more on kidney disease see page 607.

THE GUT AND ITS PROBLEMS

The first bowel motion passed by a new baby is called meconium and looks black and sticky. After a day or so the baby's bowel motions change to the normal colour and texture according to how he is being fed. Breastfed babies have soft, sometimes almost liquid stools which are bright mustard-yellow. They can be very frequent – at every nappy change – or, as the baby gets older, occur only every few days. In a breastfed baby this does not mean constipation. The bottle-fed baby's bowel motions are firmer and smell slightly more and may be a variety of colours. A bottle-fed baby can become constipated, the stools may become harder and the baby shows signs of straining and discomfort. In this case check that you are making up the feed correctly and try to give the baby more water or fruit juice in between feeds.

If the new baby's bowel motions do not show these normal patterns this could be a sign that something is wrong with the bowels or digestive system. Some babies are born with blockages in their intestines or at the anus and a baby that doesn't pass meconium in the first twenty-four hours after birth may have a condition which needs putting right with an operation.

INFECTIONS IN THE GUT

As most parents quickly learn, stomach infections are common – few children reach school age without having at least one bout of sickness and/or diarrhoea. The cause is either a virus or bacteria in the intestine and mild cases usually cure themselves. Gastro-enteritis is just a word which means an infection of the bowel – the cause of most cases of tummy upset.

Dysentery is acute gastro-enteritis caused by a number of specific bacteria which invade the bowel wall. It is not as common as viral gastro-enteritis but is just as infectious and can spread through a playgroup or nursery quickly. If laboratory analysis confirms certain types of dysentery then treatment with antibiotics is occasionally suggested.

Germs are spread from the bowel of someone with the infection to someone else, usually via unwashed hands touching food. It is all too easy not to wash your hands very thoroughly after a bowel movement or after changing a dirty nappy. A contaminated hand may then touch an apple or another person's hand before that person puts their hand on food or in their mouth. There is no need to take undue precautions, but it does make sense to follow these simple preventive measures, especially when someone in the family already has a stomach upset.

Wash hands thoroughly

BEFORE   preparing food, making up babies' feeds, eating meals.

AFTER   a bowel movement (not so vital after passing water), changing a dirty nappy, wiping a child's bottom.

Germs causing diarrhoea and vomiting can also lurk in the nose and infected spots or cuts, so try to remember not to touch your nose or the source of infection while handling food.

The first signs of an infection are vomiting or stomach pains and/or diarrhoea – loose, watery stools that will look and smell different from normal ones. Mothers of breastfed babies sometimes worry that their babies have diarrhoea because the normal stool is so liquid, can be very frequent, and often seems to emerge with a great explosion; but, as long as the motion is the usual yellow colour and there are no other signs of illness, there is no need to worry. On the other hand, a continuing change in the colour and the consistency of the bowel motion could be a sign of illness and should always be checked with your doctor. Once children are old enough to be having solid food there is usually no doubt about when they have diarrhoea.

However, diarrhoea or vomiting or both can signal the beginning of an illness other than a stomach upset – for example, whooping cough, meningitis, a urinary or ear infection. If your child is drowsy and floppy, in pain or feverish as well as having diarrhoea and vomiting, see your doctor.

TREATMENT FOR BABIES

There is a serious risk a baby or small child with diarrhoea and/or vomiting can quickly lose too much fluid and become dangerously ill because of dehydration. The smaller the baby, the greater the risk, so very young babies who are seriously ill with diarrhoea and sickness may need nursing in hospital. How soon you consult your doctor depends on the age of the baby, whether they are taking any fluids at all, how severe their symptoms are and whether they have other sorts of symptom as well (see page 518). As a rough guide, do not let a baby under 4 months go longer than 12 hours if they are not taking in any fluids and have both diarrhoea and sickness. With an older baby you can afford to wait 24 hours to see if their condition improves with treatment. But if you feel very worried for whatever reason then ring your doctor for advice. Worrying signs are present if a baby stops passing urine, his eyes become sunken, his skin loses elasticity, or he becomes floppy and breathless. Babies with these signs will probably need to go into hospital.

The actual treatment of diarrhoea and vomiting is the same whatever the age. Stop all milk and solid forms of food for 24 hours and give fluid to prevent dehydration. For babies a number of carefully designed glucose and salt mixtures can be bought at the chemists in single dose sachets (e.g. Dioralyte or Rehidrat). These will prevent dehydration and are much safer than home-made mixtures, which should not be used. Frequent small sips rather than one large drink are best if you want to avoid further vomiting. You should aim to give at least as much as the total daily feeds, and sufficient to satisfy thirst. A very small number of babies may not like the salty taste, and the flavoured varieties that are available may also be rejected. If you have problems getting it down, try mixing the plain version with very small amounts of squash or fruit drink.

Once the diarrhoea and vomiting stop, milk and solids should be reintroduced – half strength for bottle-fed babies for the first 24 hours, then use normal strength. Breast-milk feeds can be continued while the baby has diarrhoea, but he should be offered extra water or glucose as well. Solids should be cautiously reintroduced as soon as milk feeds are tolerated and a normal diet introduced over 3 to 4 days. If diarrhoea and vomiting begin again go back to clear fluids for another 24 hours and see your doctor if the diarrhoea continues after this. Once better, your child may be extra hungry, so feed him as often as he wants to help recover the weight that has been lost.

HOSPITAL TREATMENT

Hospital treatment may be necessary for very small babies in cases where there is severe dehydration and where intensive nursing cannot be given at home. Fluid and basic nutritional requirements can be given directly into the blood stream using a drip.

OLDER CHILDREN

Treatment is the same – stop all food and milk drinks for 24 hours and give plain water, dilute fruit juice or fizzy drinks only. Frequent sips are best. Once the symptoms stop, gradually reintroduce food, beginning with something quite plain like a piece of toast or a dry biscuit. If diarrhoea or vomiting begins again go back to plain fluids only. See your doctor if the child does not respond after 48 hours of fluids only, or if you cannot get him to take any drinks. If there are other symptoms such as fever, drowsiness and lack of response to pain, see your doctor at once. Again, once recovered, the child may be extra hungry and will quickly regain weight if adequate food is given.

DRUGS

Most cases of diarrhoea and vomiting are due to viruses and so antibiotics are no use (see page 525). The commonest cause is the rotavirus which often causes respiratory illness (cold or cough) and ear infections as well as stomach upset. Laboratory analysis on samples (your doctor will tell you the best way to collect them) will show if a bacterium rather than a virus is the cause. For some bacterial infections your doctor may prescribe an antibiotic. Anti-diarrhoeal drugs such as kaolin, Lomotil or Imodium should not be used for acute diarrhoea in children.

NURSING CHILDREN WITH STOMACH UPSETS

'My two-year-old was seriously ill with diarrhoea and vomiting for a week and I had a four-month old baby as well. At the time I kept going because she needed me so much but as soon as she began to recover I felt totally collapsed. Being stuck in a house that smelt of disinfectant and sick for so long and doing nothing but soak and wash piles of horrible clothes and sheets got me down almost as much as the worry about her health.'

Nursing any sick child is a strain, but continually clearing up after children with bad stomach upsets can be specially demoralising. Even though you may not like leaving your child with someone else, try to get out of the house once a day because you will be more use to them if you stay reasonably sane. Ask a friend or relative to sit with them for just an hour in the day or wait until your partner is home in the evening.

MINOR ORTHOPAEDIC PROBLEMS

IN-TOEING

This means that one or both feet point inwards – hence the name in-toeing. It can affect just the foot, the foot and lower half of the leg, or the whole leg. In a new baby who is otherwise normal this can be due to an awkward position in the uterus during pregnancy. Naturally parents worry about any problem in their child which might affect development, and they may consult a doctor when the child begins to walk. In 90% of cases the foot will straighten out by itself by about three or four years old. In the few cases that do not right themselves treatment can still straighten the foot out and waiting will not have jeopardised this.

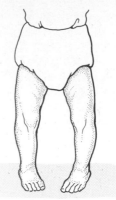

In-toeing

CLUB FOOT

As opposed to in-toeing where the foot is otherwise normal, club foot involves a structural abnormality in the bones of the foot so that it is twisted out of shape. The foot may be turned in so that the sole of the foot faces to one side and the child walks on the edge of the foot and heel instead of in the normal way. This is a congenital abnormality which requires early advice and treatment.

BOW LEGS

All babies' legs bend outwards at the knees to some degree and nearly all of them straighten up by the time they are five years old. It is only in cases which are so severe that they interfere with a child's walking that treatment may be needed. Rickets, caused by a deficiency of vitamin D, can very occasionally be the cause. There is no evidence that baby bouncers or early walking cause bow legs.

KNOCK KNEES

Three-quarters of all children between two and four and a half years have knock knees to some extent, but as long as it is not part of a more widespread problem there is no need to do anything. The majority of cases will correct themselves and the children will walk and develop quite normally. There is no evidence that special shoes, splints or exercise make any difference. If it is still a problem after the start of school your doctor will refer you to an orthopaedic surgeon, but even then treatment is unlikely to be considered before about ten or eleven years of age.

FLAT FEET

All children begin life with flat feet and only develop an arch when they are about two or three years old. Among the children whose feet continue to be flat, the majority are otherwise quite normal and will not have any special problems from being flat-footed.

However, a few children may have other symptoms such as pain, stiffness, floppiness or muscle spasm. In this case a flat foot can be due either to a bone irregularity or to an inflammation of the foot itself. It may also occur in conditions such as cerebral palsy or Down's syndrome.

LOOSE JOINTS

When someone can bend a joint in both directions – for example, bending fingers backwards as well as forwards – people often say they are 'double jointed'. In fact all it means is that the joint is very lax or loose so it can bend in both directions. This can often be no more than a familial characteristic causing no problems, but in a few cases widespread joint looseness can be part of a more general disorder.

THE CLUMSY CHILD

'Kevin was a worry. He had been a good baby and his talking had come on very early. But at four years old he seemed so backward in some ways. In particular he was always knocking things over, he was not able to manage a tricycle and showed no interest at all in playing with bricks or kicking a ball.'

No child is born perfectly co-ordinated, even one who grows up to be a champion ice skater will stumble over early steps. This leads some people to assert that all young clumsy children will 'grow out of it', a prediction that is true for most but by no means for all.

Clumsiness can be seen in large movements, like walking or throwing (gross motor skills), or finer skills, like using scissors or doing up buttons (fine motor). 'Motor' here means what makes movement. It is sometimes not realised that clumsiness involves more than just body movement: children also have to learn to judge their world visually. If they are trying to catch a ball they must first learn to watch it, anticipating its speed and direction. This kind of judgement is usually referred to as a perceptual skill and some authorities would rather talk about children with perceptual motor problems, arguing that the word 'clumsy' carries with it immediate ideas that the child is inferior. In everyday experience there is, indeed, a danger that clumsy children will be seen as generally backward and they may even come to think of themselves in this way.

Recognising clumsiness is not always easy, for the general pattern is that the affected children can move around well, but the quality of their movement is poor, rather like the child who can swim but has not progressed beyond the dog paddle. They seem to have great difficulty in organising and planning movements, so that, although they may know what they want to do, they are not able to organise their bodies to produce a smoothly planned set of movements.

Rhythm and force are two further difficulties: the accomplished child

The clumsy child can irritate other children

will learn to skip at an even pace, while the clumsy child will rush the rope round far too fast. Dealing with tasks in a sequence may be an obstacle as well, as anyone who has watched a child put on shoes before trousers will appreciate. Slowness is another characteristic and if they are hurried such children usually become flustered – they are no different from many adults in this – which leads them to greater problems.

Another distressing consequence is a lack of friends. Other children may be intolerant of the clumsy child constantly bumping into them; they will shun the butterfingers at games, and this can easily produce loneliness leading, possibly, to behaviour disturbance.

The causes of clumsiness are, as might be expected, several. It is always worth having a child's vision tested, but the central area of difficulty is more likely to be that the brain is not working as efficiently as it is in other children. It is important to note that it is *not* appropriate to refer to these children as brain damaged or spastic. Children with cerebral palsy are often clumsy, but not all clumsy children have cerebral palsy.

If parents have anxieties they should discuss these first with their health visitor or family doctor, who may feel that an opinion from an occupational therapist or physiotherapist would be helpful. When helping so-called 'clumsy' children it is useful to follow certain ground rules:

* Spend some time on what the children *can* do, to maintain their confidence.

* Keep practice to short periods, with tasks in short, manageable steps.

* Allow children to go at their own rate.

* Never ask them to do something that they clearly cannot. This sounds obvious but some adults think they can teach by humiliation. This is a mistaken approach.

Children with severe problems in this area are unlikely to become ballet dancers or carpenters. But if helped they can learn to reach acceptable levels of skill and if they escape the hurtful labels so often given much will have been achieved.

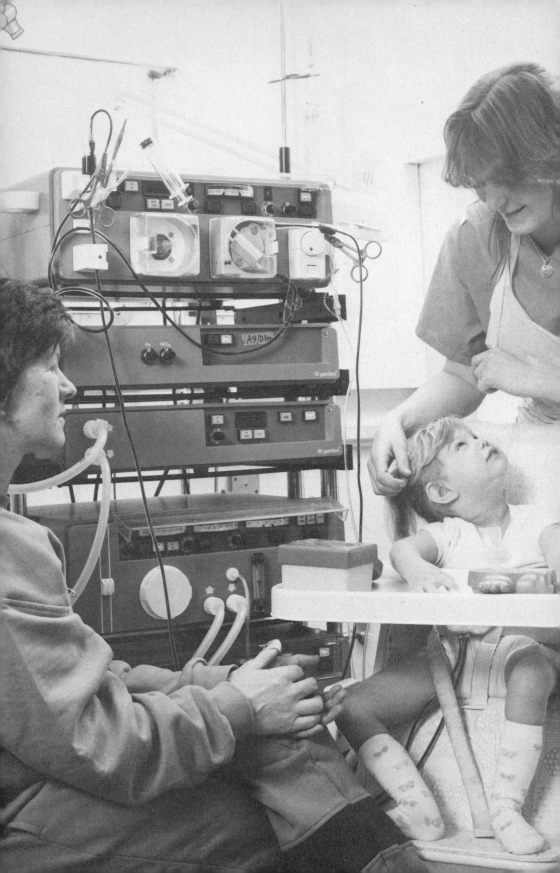

Chapter 18

SERIOUS ILLNESS AND TREATABLE CONGENITAL DEFECTS

Asthma   Eczema   Epilepsy   Serious infectious
illnesses – tetanus, poliomyelitis, diphtheria, meningitis and
encephalitis   Kidney (renal) problems   Jaundice   Haemophilia
Childhood cancer including leukaemia   Sickle cell disease
Thalassaemia   Short stature   Diabetes   Cystic fibrosis
Coeliac disease   Heart problems   AIDS   Cleft lip and palate
Genital problems

In this chapter we look at a variety of illnesses and conditions which are potentially more serious than those described in chapter 17, which dealt with common childhood illnesses. Some pose only short-term problems, others are more long term and some life-long, but none of them need necessarily impair the quality of life, and many can be treated successfully. We have also included some minor congenital defects which are easily treatable.

Obviously, in their most severe forms, each of these conditions poses far more difficulties than cases where children are only mildly affected, and each child must be assessed and catered for individually.

ASTHMA

'I had asthma badly as a child and still get occasional attacks. My son also gets it now. I think it's important to remember that generally an asthma attack doesn't feel nearly as bad for the sufferer as for the person watching.'

A child receiving dialysis treatment – see page 607

589

About one in ten children will have an asthma attack at some time. When this happens breathing becomes more difficult because the branching tubes (bronchi) leading from the windpipe through the lungs become narrower. It is hard to make enough air pass through these narrowed tubes and the effort of forcing air through causes the laboured breathing and wheezing sound of an asthma attack. It is easier to breathe in than to breathe out so some of the air gets trapped in the lungs and makes the chest expand more than normal.

No one knows the cause for sure, but it seems that the airways of asthmatic children are oversensitive or possibly hyper-reactive. They react to various triggers by producing excess phlegm and coughing and by narrowing through a muscle spasm in the airway walls. In more prolonged attacks, part of the narrowing or obstruction may be triggered by swelling of the walls of the tubes.

There are two types of asthma attack — one where the airways tense up and go into spasm and the other where the lining of the airways get swollen and sticky mucus plugs block the tubes. The second type is more difficult to treat and takes longer to clear.

CAUSES OF ASTHMA ATTACKS

Allergy
: Most children with asthma are allergic and, in most, allergies to pollen, house dust and furry animals may produce coughing and sneezing. Grass pollen, which is around from mid May to late June, is the worst offender among pollens. Cats are the commonest animal causes of allergy, but dogs, birds, horses, guinea pigs and hamsters can also cause reactions — sometimes horsehair alone in the form of upholstery padding can be enough. In dust it is the dust mites which cause the trouble — they are little creatures which live in bedding and furniture and feed off human or animal scales of skin which are shed. Food allergy may also act as a trigger for asthma.

Infection
: This can act as a trigger to asthmatic wheezing or a full attack. Respiratory infections, such as colds and coughs are particularly common triggers for asthma in the toddler age group and may cause prolonged flare ups lasting for several days.

Emotion
: Great excitement or upset can bring on an attack of wheezing in an asthmatic child, and general tension or anxiety often results in more frequent episodes of wheezing.

Smoke
: Smoke can trigger wheezing, so it is very important not to smoke if your child is asthmatic. Obviously smoking is a harmful habit for asthmatics of any age. Some industrial fumes, paint smells and perfumes can also be irritating.

Weather   Sudden changes in climate can provoke asthma. Sudden sharp cold or wind are particularly likely to irritate.

Exercise   Exercise, especially running around, can make asthmatic children start to wheeze, but is not a reason to avoid sports and games as the wheeze usually settles rapidly on resting. Treatment taken beforehand can enable asthmatics to take part in any sports.

Any of these factors can work together or singly to bring on asthmatic wheezing or an attack. Parents soon learn which conditions are likely to make their child specially susceptible and give preventive treatment (see below).

TREATMENT

Prevention Where possible avoid likely triggers to asthma – for instance, smoky atmospheres or specific animals that cause an allergic reaction.

Drugs

Bronchodilators are drugs which make the muscles around the airways relax and so widen or dilate the bronchi or airways, and the most common of these is salbutamol (Ventolin). It is up to you and your doctor to work out the most effective treatment for your child, for these drugs can be used in various forms including syrups, tablets, aerosol sprays, inhaled powders and mists. Theophyllines are also bronchodilators, but cannot be taken by inhalation.

Sometimes a bad wheezy attack fails to respond to bronchodilator treatment. This should be regarded as a warning sign that you should contact your doctor or local hospital.

Sodium cromoglycate (Intal) is a drug which can prevent asthma attacks by its action on the lining of the airways. It has to be taken regularly and is inhaled deeply into the lungs as a dry powder, spray or mist. A device called a spinhaler is used to deliver the powder and children can be taught how to use it from about three to five years old. Alternatively, before this, treatment can be given as a mist using a nebuliser. Older children can manage the spray.

Steroids are hormones that affect the body's reactions to infection. They can be very effective in the prevention of asthma, and are also useful in the treatment of acute attacks when bronchodilators are failing to work well. If taken by inhalation, the steroid is delivered directly to the lung, and only a small dose is required. Inhaled steroids may be used on a long-term basis to prevent asthma as an alternative to Intal. If steroids are given in the form of syrup, tablet or injection, a larger dose is required, and given in this way they need to be treated with caution. If taken regularly for a

long time they can affect a child's growth. There is no need to worry about this if your child needs just a short course of steroid treatment, but if he needs longer-term treatment, discuss all aspects with your doctor, who will keep a careful check and use the lowest possible level of these drugs.

Antibiotics do not make any difference to an asthma attack but may be prescribed if an infection due to bacteria has triggered the attack.

WHAT TO DO IF YOUR CHILD HAS AN ASTHMA ATTACK

At the first signs of an attack (laboured breathing and wheezing) sit him down, speaking calmly and reassuringly because if a child gets frightened or panics this can make matters worse. If he fails to settle, give him a dose of the bronchodilator prescribed. Stay with him and tell him to breathe deeply and regularly – it helps to sit young children on your knee and do the breathing alongside them.

If an asthma attack does not begin to respond to increased use of the bronchodilator always call your doctor at once. Parents with asthmatic children soon get to recognise when an attack is not responding to treatment.

Hospital treatment involves the use of oxygen and nebulised bronchodilators. Extra fluid may be needed, and is given, if necessary, in the form of a saline drip. Steroids can be given through a drip or by injection.

LIVING WITH ASTHMATIC CHILDREN

Provided you learn how to handle their condition properly, there is no need to mollycoddle asthmatic children or to stop them taking part in games or activities suitable for normal children. Together with your doctor work out the best way of preventing attacks and of treating them if they occur.

Preventive drugs such as Intal must be given regularly if they are to work – do not try to make your child manage without them in the belief that it will toughen him up. It will not – but it *will* make an asthma attack more likely.

Give preventive treatment with drugs such as salbutamol before events which may trigger wheezing – for example parties, games or sports.

Treat symptoms of wheezing calmly and in a matter of fact way and help your child to have a sensible attitude to his condition. Do not undermine his confidence by panicking and being obviously over anxious.

Learn as much as you can about asthma so you are best placed to help – the Asthma Society helps with very valuable information as well as contact with other parents (see address section, pages 673–6).

Children can learn to use a nebuliser by themselves

There is no need to prevent an asthmatic child from playing normally

WILL MY CHILD GROW OUT OF ASTHMA?

Only one in five asthmatic children will still have persistent symptoms in early adult life, but predicting in which children they will persist is difficult. Perhaps it is more important to remember that today's treatment of asthma is so effective that the great majority of asthma sufferers can lead just as full and active a life as anyone else.

These are a few indications about the likelihood of asthma continuing, but they are not hard and fast guidelines.

For growing out:

* When the main cause of wheezing is infection, resistance to the infection often develops around the ages of seven to eight.

* When the cause of asthma is allergy there is a good chance of growing out of it during the teen years.

594

* Breastfed children are more likely to be free of asthma in adult life than bottle-fed children.

Against growing out:

* If a child with other allergies, for example eczema or hay fever, develops wheezy attacks or a persistent cough in the first two years of life, then the chances of it disappearing are not quite so good.

* If the asthma is very severe, and the child often needs to go into hospital, or if a close relative or relatives have asthma, this seems to lessen the chances of it disappearing in early adult life.

ECZEMA

'My son was covered from the age of about eight weeks until approaching five with an agonisingly itchy red rash that was often raw and weeping. The irritation drove him so mad he used to tear at his skin even when it was raw and bleeding. He couldn't sleep at night and one of us had to stay with him every single night. It was terrible to see him suffering so much.'

The word eczema is a label doctors use for a group of skin problems. There are many different types of eczema that have different causes. The common type dealt with here is called atopic eczema – about one in eight of all children will get it at some time. Usually it covers only a small part of the body and only lasts a few months, but occasionally it is more severe, and it is the severe type that is mainly described here. See also page 558.

WHAT CAUSES ATOPIC ECZEMA?

No one knows for sure and there are many different schools of thought. But one explanation, which many leading skin specialists (dermatologists) subscribe to, is that the immune system of atopic people is oversensitive. Our immune system is our defence against disease, but if it is oversensitive reactions occur to normally harmless substances. These can be foods or airborne substances, like pollen, house dust, minute scales from animal hair, skin or feathers or fungus spores. For more on allergy, see page 252.

An atopic person is one whose body makes extra amounts of a certain type of antibody. The tendency to do this is inherited, and is passed on from parents to children in their genes. Some atopic people may be perfectly healthy all their lives and never know they are atopic. But it seems that making extra amounts of this antibody does make such people more likely to suffer from asthma, eczema and hayfever. Tests can be done to find out if someone is atopic and has extra amounts of the antibody. Even if they do, it is only a problem if the person suffers from one of the atopic diseases.

Eczema can affect children very badly over a long period, or it can be mild and disappear quite quickly. Usually the rash begins to appear on the cheeks at the age of about three to four months and can get raw and weeping. It may start to fade or appear later on other areas of the body. Typically it occurs in the creases at the elbows, wrists, buttocks, knees and ankles.

The hallmarks of an eczema rash are:

Itching	This is the worst aspect because it can be so upsetting for the child. It also makes him scratch, which itself can lead to more rawness, soreness and infection.
Redness	This is caused by extra blood flowing through the blood vessels in the skin in the affected area.
A bubbly, grainy appearance to the skin	These are tiny fluid-filled blisters just under the skin called 'vesicles'.
Weeping	This happens when the blisters burst, either by themselves or because of scratching, and the fluid oozes out on to the surface of the skin.
Crusts	These are scabs which form when the fluid dries.
Scaliness	Children with eczema often have a dry, scaly skin. This may be a result of the disease but may also be the natural skin type of that family which, in some people, can predispose them towards developing eczema.
Pigmentation	Pale patches of skin can appear because eczema can disturb the production of pigment which controls our skin colour. The effect does fade and disappear.
Lichenification	This means a leathery, thicker skin area in response to scratching. Again it does fade.

Other effects of eczema can be:

Infection	Skin which is broken and damaged is more likely to be infected by bacteria or yeasts. One very common type of bacterium (*staphylococcus aureus*) produces yellow crusts or pus-filled spots.
Thirst	If eczema is widespread, too much fluid can be lost through the skin.

Poor temperature control	Too much heat is lost through inflamed skin so the body tries to compensate by 'turning up the heating'. The result is the child can feel too cold and then when moving into a warmer atmosphere very quickly get too hot. Eczema also stops the sweat glands working properly and sweating is another way of losing heat when we get too hot.

TREATMENT

If a child's eczema is not so bad as to disrupt his own and his family's life it can probably be managed by avoiding likely sources of irritation and using bath preparations, moisturisers and suitable steroid creams (see below and pages 598–9). It is up to you and your GP to work out what suits your child best and to remember this may change. But in severe cases where the eczema is so bad as to interfere with the child's life and put a strain on the family, your GP may need to refer you to a specialist who can help.

In treating eczema there are various lines of approach:

Avoiding irritants Various things can irritate sensitive, eczema-prone skin and avoiding them can make a great difference.

Fibres	Use pure cotton or cotton mixtures instead of wool or synthetics.
Soap	Do not use any soap at all. Instead add bath oils to bath water and use emulsifying ointment or a

Moisturising or other creams may help to soothe your child's eczema

597

	water-dispersable cream instead of soap. Examples are aqueous cream, E45 cream or Unguentum Merck. In mild cases this will probably be enough by itself. Avoid enzyme detergents in washing clothes.
Chemicals	Some acid fruits and vegetables like tomatoes and citrus fruits and also very salty foods cause a reaction on hands and around the mouth; avoid all direct use of antiseptics and solvents.
Heat, sunlight and cold	Can irritate some children so protect from them or avoid them as far as possible if this is your child's problem.

Moisturise the skin Washing with water alone rapidly results in drying off, but adding oil to water (see soap, page 597) will moisturise dry, eczema-prone skin very effectively. Your doctor can tell you what is available and you may need to experiment to find the best product for your child.

'Weeping' eczema Once patches of eczema begin to weep, moisturisers may not be the answer. Instead the area may initially need drying up with diluted solutions of potassium permanganate either in a bath, bowl or applied with wet flannels 2 to 4 times a day for 15 to 20 minutes.

Treating infection As mentioned, eczematous skin is prone to infection. This can be treated by a course of antibiotics taken by mouth. Some doctors initially use antibiotic cream, but serious infections always need treating with an antibiotic internally. Some steroid creams also contain antibiotics, but because resistance can develop which makes the antibiotic useless it is best not to use them for more than four weeks at a time without a break or change to another antibiotic. Once infection has broken out antiseptic solutions may sometimes be added to the bath. Seek your doctor's advice about whether to use antiseptic to try to prevent infection in children who seem specially prone.

Steroids These hormones can be very useful for their power to 'damp down' the inflammation the body produces in an allergic reaction. Unfortunately they can also have other undesirable side effects if not used properly and so parents need to pay close attention to advice about using them. We now know that taking them internally (by mouth or injection) regularly for long periods can stop the body producing its own supplies of steroid hormones and can also slow down growth. However, steroids can be useful in controlling eczema and safe if they are used as creams or ointments directly on to the skin. It is important to use the minimum amount of the least potent preparations to keep the condition under reasonable control. They should not be put on like face cream but instead only the very thinnest smear which can hardly be seen should be applied to the rash. The best time to do this is after a bath containing some form of oil because the skin is better able to absorb it then. There are about sixty brand names of different steroid creams and ointments available on prescription and they come in different strengths. The mildest is hydrocortisone, which goes under various brand names, but in various strengths which are marked on the tube as a percentage beginning with $\frac{1}{2}$% and going up to $2\frac{1}{2}$%. 1% hydrocortisone is most suitable for long-term use for babies and for use on sensitive parts of the body such as the face. Eumovate, Haelan and Modrasone are slightly stronger, but suitable for longer-term use in older children, if the affected area is not large. Medium-strength preparations include Synalar 1 in 10 and 1 in 4 and Betnovate RD which can be used short term for sensitive areas (but not on the face). Strong steroids are Betnovate, Propaderm, Synalar and Metosyn and the most potent of all Dermovate. Most skin specialists now think these should not be used undiluted on children for more than a few days, and only very occasionally. Because they are easily absorbed some of the hormone from these creams and ointments will enter the bloodstream, so if very strong preparations are used over a large area the risks are the same as for steroids taken internally. Too much of a strong steroid can also thin and stretch the skin itself, which shows rather like stretch marks after pregnancy – skin creases and loss of elasticity. Thinning of the skin means blood vessels show through. This can show as a reddish complexion on the face. Ask your doctor if you think your child's skin shows signs of damage – going on to a non-steroid cream or a weaker steroid can often reverse damage if it is caught in time. But coming off a strong steroid suddenly can make the rash much worse, so weaker preparations need to be given over a week or two.

Other treatments Tar is soothing for inflamed skin and comes diluted as ointment or paste, sometimes mixed with steroids. Tar paste bandages can be very helpful.

Elimination diets are now very popular in treating eczema. Probably only a few children with eczema can be helped by special diets, but in these cases they may make a great deal of difference. Avoid artificial colourings and benzoate preservatives. For more complicated diets, especially those in which natural foods such as milk are eliminated, you should consult a doctor and dietitian.

Antihistamines do not conquer bad itching but may take the edge off it, and the drowsiness they cause can be useful at night to conquer sleeplessness caused by irritation. In some children they stop working after a while so it is best to reserve them for bad periods and have times in between without them. In a few children antihistamines do not work at all. They may even have the reverse effect and make a child overactive.

Bandages can be used to stop scratching at night and, in particular, tubular bandages made into cotton mittens can be very helpful. Children often begin scratching in their sleep and then wake because of extra irritation and soreness. Medicated bandages impregnated with paste can also be very soothing in specially troubled times.

HELPING YOUR CHILD COPE WITH ECZEMA

'One of the worst things about having a child with bad eczema is other people's reactions – they do stare and look repulsed and horrified. The older and more aware your child is, the more protective you feel.'

Once you have learnt about eczema, explain to relatives and friends what it is – people do still tend to think any kind of skin rash must be catching. As your child gets older there is a good chance he will grow out of it – if the eczema appears in the first year of life there is a 50% chance it will not be a problem by the age of five. Even if it continues into school age only one in twenty will still have trouble in adult life. In general, the later it first appears the greater chance there is that it will persist. But even children who first develop eczema at five years old have about a 50% chance of it clearing within the next five years. There are no hard and fast rules and each case is different.

Eczema only very rarely leaves physical scars – however long it continues. Parents can be vital in protecting their child from psychological scars. This involves allowing a child to lead a normal life, even if some activities do make the rash worse in the short term. Help your child forget his skin problems by keeping him busy and encouraging his interest in other people and activities. As he gets older explain, in simple terms, that the rash is caused by an allergy – he will certainly be asked by other children and possibly adults and needs to know how to answer. Do not be overprotective or hide your child away. Talking to other parents can be a great help and in particular the National Eczema Society offers great support and information (see address section, pages 673–6).

EPILEPSY

'We had so many muddled fears and anxieties about the epileptic fits our son had – we worried about brain damage, about him being less intelligent, about his future hopes. In fact there is no reason why someone with epilepsy should be less healthy or less intelligent than anyone else, but it took counselling to help us understand this and sort out our fears.'

There is a great deal of ignorance and misunderstanding about epilepsy and this in turn often leads to fear. In fact there are about 60,000 school-age children in the UK with epilepsy, and the vast majority go to ordinary schools. If there is no other associated condition, there is no reason why they should not be as intelligent and healthy and lead as full a life as anyone else. Epilepsy is not an illness in itself but a symptom of several different conditions with different causes, and in a great many cases the reason for its appearance is not known, even after intensive tests. So there is no such thing as an 'epileptic child', rather a 'child with epilepsy'.

Electrical activity takes place in everyone's brain, but an epileptic fit happens when there is a brief disruption of this normal activity and a sudden unusual release of energy – a sort of electrical storm which sends the system out of control for a few seconds or minutes. Anyone could have fits in theory, and those who do simply have a lowered resistance to certain stimuli, not all of which can be identified. Unlike feverish convulsions (see page 545) which may affect one in thirty to forty children at some time, an epileptic fit is not usually triggered by high temperature and typically occurs out of the blue, though sometimes emotional or physical stress, or infections, may provoke it. There are several different types of epilepsy, all of which can affect children, but the most common are *petit mal* (minor) and *grand mal* (major). These names are the French for 'little illness' and 'big illness', and are used because French doctors were prominent in writing about epilepsy years ago when the different types were being recognised and described. Many doctors today prefer a more modern, scientific classification, but these old names still have some value and seem to be familiar to many non-medical people.

In fact *petit mal* is rare – less than one in twenty children with epilepsy suffer from it.

Petit mal attacks involve a brief lapse of consciousness, so that the child may seem to be daydreaming or going blank for a few seconds, often with rapid blinking of his eyelids, but he does not usually fall down, and may even continue to perform simple actions such as walking, though he is not really aware of what he is doing.

Afterwards he will have no recollection of what happened, but may be aware that there has been a gap in his experience. Usually he can pick up the threads of his conversation or activities at once, but sometimes needs to be reminded. If the attacks are infrequent they are unimportant, but if they are frequent the child may be literally 'peppered with unconsciousness' and his school work may suffer as a result. Schoolteachers often suspect *petit mal* as the reason for a child doing less well than they think he should. Sometimes they are right in their suspicion – but not often! Much more often the child is just not paying attention because he is uninterested or anxious.

These attacks seldom occur under the age of three, and rarely persist beyond adolescence, so the outlook is usually very good. They also tend to respond rather well, even dramatically well, to appropriate medication.

Grand mal corresponds to the kind of fit which most people think of as epilepsy and it often generates fear because of ignorance. The child may have a warning of some kind; this may be a feeling in his tummy though often he cannot describe it. He then goes rigid and stiff, loses consciousness and may have trouble breathing. His limbs jerk convulsively and he may produce bubbles of saliva, with blood if he has bitten his cheeks or tongue, and may be incontinent. The movements gradually stop and the child may fall asleep for a few minutes or even longer before waking, often confused and irritable. There is no set pattern to how often fits happen and it varies with every individual. Some children have warning signs – an 'aura', which they learn to recognise before a fit, which older children may be able to describe. One mother said her three-year-old used to sense when an attack was about to happen and would lie curled on the floor in readiness.

WHAT TO DO DURING A FIT

* Loosen any tight clothing round the neck which might be dangerous and remove surrounding objects which might also endanger the child.

* Turn him on to one side.

* Stay with the child while the attack is taking place, but do not try to put anything in his mouth or restrain his limbs.

* After the fit, making sure the child is still on his side so he can breathe more easily, put him somewhere comfortable to rest or sleep until he wants to get up.

In the rare event of a fit lasting for more than five minutes or fits happening one after the other without the child regaining consciousness it is best to call a doctor, or an ambulance if your doctor is not available, although it is most unlikely that any harm will result.

TREATMENT

There is no cure for epilepsy in the sense that penicillin is a cure for tonsillitis or pneumonia, but treatment of the tendency to have fits with anti-convulsant drugs is often highly successful in preventing them from happening. It is a bit like giving a cough medicine to suppress a cough, rather than giving treatment to cure the cause of the cough – bronchitis, pneumonia, or whatever.

Many effective drugs are now available and the more modern ones have the advantage of being less likely to cause troublesome side effects than the older ones. The dose is always carefully calculated for each child, based on his weight, and the aim is to produce and maintain a level of the drug in the blood which is neither too low to be effective, nor so high that it produces drowsiness or other side effects. Obviously to be effective the drug must be taken regularly, and the child's co-operation is important. Sensible older children can often be entrusted with their own medication. The doses are usually taken two or three times a day (occasionally only once – at bedtime), and do not need to be given at precise intervals, though a routine is obviously desirable and more reliable. The drug should never be stopped suddenly as this can sometimes provoke more fits. If you are unhappy about the medicine, perhaps through fear of side effects, you should discuss it with your doctor. Sometimes a change to another drug proves very helpful.

Unfortunately it is not possible to predict just how long a child will need to continue on treatment. Each case is different. It is rather like asking, 'How long is a piece of string?' In some cases, and with certain types of epilepsy, the attacks come under control very quickly, whereas in others they respond less well. There is a tendency in children for spontaneous improvement with age, and many children grow out of their epilepsy. This has something to do with maturing of the nervous system. The fits can cease at any age. The popular idea that they stop at 7, 14 or 21 has no basis in fact; they could just as well stop at 6, 12 or 18! There are many children, but few adults, who have epilepsy, and somewhere along the line a lot of children have stopped having it — the same is true of two other 'paroxysmal' disorders, migraine and asthma.

LIFESTYLE FOR CHILDREN WITH EPILEPSY

Being over-protective so that the child is stopped from taking part in normal activities, or giving in to every whim for fear of causing upset, will do more damage in the long term than the epilepsy itself. Parents need an opportunity to discuss their worries and to find out about the condition — the British Epilepsy Association has an excellent counselling service (see address section, pages 673–6). In general children with epilepsy should be treated quite normally, although simple safety measures must become a way of life — do not, for example, leave the child alone for a long time or let him lock himself in the lavatory or bathroom. These precautions apply to all under-fives anyway, though obviously as the child gets older and more independent the questions get harder. But parents of ordinary children have to keep making decisions about what is and is not safe, based on their child's age and ability and the circumstances of the activity. Parents of children with epilepsy have to make the same decisions but also have to take into account the nature and frequency of fits.

Swimming and cycling may be specially difficult to decide about, and again the child's condition, age, ability, the level of supervision and place of the activity must be considered. One specialist with several decades of experience suggested children with frequent fits should only swim for brief periods in a pool with a competent assistant alongside them all the time. Children with occasional fits or with controlled epilepsy could swim for longer periods in a pool if an informed lifeguard or competent swimming companion is present. Such children should also not be encouraged to cycle on busy roads, though cycling in the back garden or, with young children, on the pavement, is safe enough. Children with frequent fits should not be allowed to climb trees or use climbing frames.

EDUCATION

As has been said, there is no reason why the vast majority of children with epilepsy should not go to an ordinary school. As long as your child has no associated problems which may need special attention go ahead and pick a playgroup or nursery school as you would with any child. Naturally you should tell the organiser of your child's condition.

Young children with frequent fits should only swim with a competent assistant alongside them

Some parents want to conceal the fact of the child's epilepsy from the teachers, and though understandable this is unfair both to teachers and child and is most unwise. If he then has a fit at school, the panic and alarm which will result will be far greater than if you had been frank.

It is important to make sure the teachers understand what to do in the event of a fit – obviously that also applies to other helpers who will be in charge at different times. Young children need careful supervision anyway when using paddling pools, climbing frames, swings and so on – as long as a helper is always on hand there is no reason why your child should be restricted. Usually your instinct will tell you if this is the kind of playgroup or nursery which will suit his needs. If he takes drugs which may make him drowsy, make sure the playgroup or nursery staff also know about this. When it comes to primary school activities much the same applies – as long as there is good supervision most activities are suitable though you may need to use your judgement about swimming. If you feel drowsiness due to drugs may cause a problem, talk to the teacher, though be aware that most children whether or not they are on anti-convulsant drugs can feel tired when faced with something they do not want to do!

THE FUTURE

Each case is so different that again there can be no certainties but many possibilities. Most people with epilepsy do marry and have children, do drive cars, do get insurance cover and mortgages and do take up the careers they hope for. The possibilities depend on the nature of the individual's condition as well as all the other factors which influence all of us, such as personality, temperament and talent.

SERIOUS INFECTIOUS ILLNESSES

TETANUS

Another name for this is lockjaw, so called because the bacteria cause the muscles of the jaws and neck to go into spasm. Fortunately immunisation has now made this disease very uncommon, but even so some people still get it each year in the UK and a few die. A common misconception is that tetanus can only be caused by a wound from something rusty. In fact bacteria grow in the soil so any cut can potentially allow the bacteria to enter. Symptoms can show any time between twelve days and six months after the infection, which makes diagnosis difficult. A sore throat and pain in the muscles of the jaw and neck are first signs. A child thought to be suffering from tetanus would immediately be admitted to hospital, but immunisation as part of the triple vaccine is routinely given to all babies to protect them. Three doses of the vaccine are given during the first year with a booster before starting school.

POLIOMYELITIS (POLIO)

Thanks to routine vaccination (see page 527) this potentially fatal or crippling disease is now very rare in the UK. It is caused by a virus which affects the brain and central nervous system, causing paralysis of the lower limbs but sometimes of the whole body so that breathing is affected and the child needs a respirator. The first symptoms, seven to ten days after infection, are mild fever with sore throat, headache and vomiting. Before a vaccine existed many children died of this horrible disease and others were left crippled because limbs that suffer paralysis often become deformed and wasted. Because immunisation has largely conquered polio it is easy to forget just how frightening the threat of it can be and consequently to become more casual about immunisation. Once children begin to be unprotected against polio it is possible that it might occur again because it is still common in other countries and could be re-introduced. The vaccine is given in the form of drops at the same time as the triple vaccine three times in the first year of life, with a booster before starting school.

DIPHTHERIA

There are many parents who have no idea what diphtheria is because, like polio, it has virtually disappeared from this country since routine immunisation was introduced. It is caused by bacteria which multiply in the throat, sometimes blocking the passage of air and forming a greyish membrane over the tonsils. Sometimes the nose is the main site, causing a bloodstained discharge. The bacteria produce a potentially lethal poison which affects the heart and nervous system and can cause heart failure or paralysis of the muscles used for breathing. The first symptom, two to seven days after infection, is usually a severe sore throat. Immunisation is provided by the triple vaccine, which includes diphtheria, and is given three times in the first year and once before starting school. Like polio and tetanus, it is essential that parents do not become complacent about immunisation just because the disease is now very rare.

MENINGITIS AND ENCEPHALITIS

'A child at my daughter's play group had meningitis and although he made a complete recovery I don't think there was a mother there who didn't begin to have passing worries if their child complained of a headache or a stiff neck. It may not be catching among children, but fear of meningitis is certainly infectious among parents.'

The meninges are the covering of the brain and spinal cord and in meningitis they become inflamed because of infection by bacteria or a virus. Bacterial meningitis can be treated with antibiotics, and if it is diagnosed and treated early the outlook is good, although there is a very low risk of brain damage, deafness and blindness. There is no special treatment for viral meningitis, which can follow virus infection occurring elsewhere in the body, such as mumps, but usually children make a complete recovery.

What are the symptoms? Unfortunately, in children under two years old and in babies in particular they can be very vague and so missed or mistaken. Poor feeding, drowsiness and vomiting and extreme irritability are general signs that may be due to meningitis, or other causes. A high pitched cry, convulsions and tension or bulging of the fontanelle (the soft spot on top of the head) are much more definite signs. The only sure way to diagnose meningitis is to test the fluid surrounding the spinal cord, and this is done with a lumbar puncture (see below). In older children more adult symptoms such as a headache or stiff neck may show, but do not leap to the conclusion your child has meningitis every time he complains of either of these, especially if he seems well in all other ways. Sudden mood changes and irritable or uncharacteristic behaviour coupled with vomiting and possibly fever, stiff neck and headache are reasons to call a doctor. Again, the only sure way to make the diagnosis of meningitis is to do a lumbar puncture and examine the fluid under a microscope.

Another condition needing a lumbar puncture to confirm its presence is encephalitis — inflammation of the brain, usually caused by a virus. This is a rare complication of infections such as measles, *rubella* (German measles), chicken-pox or whooping cough. Symptoms are rather similar to those of meningitis.

Lumbar Puncture The process is somewhat similar to having an epidural anaesthetic except that fluid is being drawn off instead of injected. The baby or child needs to lie curled on one side so that the knobbly ridges of the spinal vertebrae stick out. In young children these are not close together and there is plenty of fluid surrounding the spinal column so the procedure is not difficult. The doctors and nurses will dress in sterile gowns to avoid any risk of infection and the co-operative child needs only

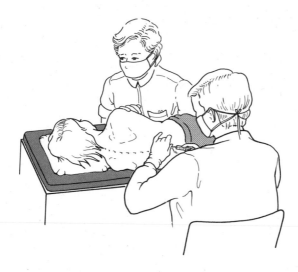

to be held gently so he does not move. Local anaesthetic will be used to deaden the area before a needle is inserted into the area surrounding the spinal column to draw off some of the fluid which surrounds the spinal cord. It does not hurt although it may feel strange – so reassuring and comforting the child to ensure he is not frightened by what is happening is important.

KIDNEY (RENAL) PROBLEMS

Apart from infections, most kidney disease in young children arises from conditions present at birth. These include malformation of one or both kidneys and obstruction or malformation of the urinary system. Blockages in the tube leading from the kidney to the bladder can often be successfully treated by surgery. Other conditions can be tackled by a combination of drugs and diet.

If one kidney fails to work, the other kidney, if normal, can take over its function very satisfactorily. However, if both kidneys fail, the child will either need dialysis or a new kidney, transplanted from a donor. Complete kidney failure is rare: it only occurs in one or two children in a million and often occurs after a prolonged period of decreasing function. Many kidney diseases can be completely cured by treatment, but a few are long term and chronic, and may require nursing and medical treatment throughout life.

Dialysis either involves passing fluid into and out of the abdomen by a special tube or passing the child's blood through a machine which carries out all the functions of a normal kidney. When the abdomen is used the process is called peritoneal dialysis. When blood is passed through a machine it is called haemodialysis. For haemodialysis needles need to be inserted into the child's arm, sometimes by means of a permanently fixed shunt, so that the blood can flow through the machine.

Both forms of dialysis can now be carried out in the home, but it is an exhausting process because it can take up many hours each week, and the ideal situation is renal transplant.

Long-term problems with the kidneys (chronic renal failure) do involve much stress, both for the child and the parents. The lighter burdens fall in those cases which can be treated without resort to prolonged dialysis. This means either, as mentioned on page 607, a successful transplant or, if the disease is not so severe, drugs or diet, alone or in combination. Stress for the child arises either from the direct effects of the disease or from its treatment. One effect of kidney disease is that the child tires easily and so cannot keep up, in games or work, with children of the same age. Growth can be stunted in some cases. Stress from treatment comes especially when dialysis is needed.

In the longer term children who have experienced kidney failure may be more prone to anxiety. It has been suggested that this may be because, at a time when they should be taking a pride in increasing control over their body, they find instead that it is not functioning to such an extent that they have to undergo dialysis of one form or another. Sympathy and support helps, but parents also experience considerable stress in view of the endless time-consuming nature of the treatment. If home dialysis is not possible, treatment in hospital can be extra stressful for the parents because of the burden of organising a programme to allow for the constant journeys to and fro. The British Kidney Patients' Association (see address section, pages 673–6) can provide much helpful information to parents of children with serious kidney disease.

JAUNDICE

The word jaundice describes the yellow skin that develops when a yellow pigment in the bile builds up in the blood. This happens when the liver, which produces bile, is not working properly. The pigment which gives bile its colour is dammed back and begins instead to turn the whites of the eyes yellowish and the skin a sun-tanned colour. Jaundice can be caused by a variety of factors and newborn and premature babies are especially prone (see page 146). But there is one type of jaundice, known correctly as infective hepatitis, which can be passed on in the form of a virus just like a cold or flu. There are various kinds of hepatitis virus. Most cases in Britain are due to A virus, although outside this country the B virus is also widespread and this is why vaccination to give temporary protection is advised before visiting certain parts of the world.

Symptoms of infective hepatitis are: loss of appetite, headache, sickness, abdominal pain due to an inflamed liver and sometimes fever. The yellowing of the skin does not usually begin for a week and once it does the child generally begins to feel a bit better. The urine becomes dark because it is also stained with bile, and bowel movements are pale because the bile is not finding its way into the intestines. Because it is caused by a virus there is no specific treatment, but viral hepatitis is a mild childhood infection and children usually recover well. Rest and a high protein diet are the treatment.

The virus is very infectious, so take care to wash hands after nappy changing or taking a child to the toilet in order to avoid catching hepatitis yourself.

HAEMOPHILIA

'At first we just thought Peter bruised very easily. I had one very unpleasant session with our health visitor when it was obvious she thought that all these bruises might be the result of us actually ill-treating him. I got very upset, but it was after that she suggested we should take him to the doctor. We were referred to the local hospital where there was a haemophilia centre, and where the diagnosis was finally made.'

Of course, nearly all bruising in children is caused by minor injuries, usually accidents, but occasionally inflicted by parents, so the health visitor's mistake was understandable. A very small number of children — about 8 in every 100,000 — do have an abnormality in the mechanism that causes blood to clot and the flow to be staunched when a blood vessel is damaged. By far the most common variety is haemophilia A. This is caused by the lack of one of the substances (Factor VIII) that is involved in clotting. In this and other related conditions, spontaneous bruising occurs in the absence of injury.

Children with haemophilia vary a good deal in how many times they bleed spontaneously — in some it occurs several times a week, and in others only two or three times a year. The bleeding often occurs into joints, which may become painful and stiff, and then red, swollen and tender. Bleeding episodes usually come out of the blue, but sometimes they seem to be brought on by a change in the weather or emotional stress, and there is sometimes an increase in the frequency of bleeding around adolescence.

Haemophilia is inherited as a sex-linked recessive condition. The defective gene is carried on one of the mother's two X chromosomes, and only boys are affected. If a couple have a boy with the condition, there is a 50% chance of any subsequent boys being affected. If a woman in this situation becomes pregnant and would prefer a termination if she is carrying an affected boy, it is now possible, in some specialist centres, to carry out a test round about the tenth week of pregnancy to check on the presence of the abnormality in the unborn baby.

Parents are understandably shocked when they first learn of haemophilia, especially if it has never been detected in the family before, and many women feel guilty because they have carried the defective gene but are healthy themselves. It is a very natural reaction to want to protect a child with this condition, but being over-protective, for example not letting children play with scissors, can lead to additional emotional and social problems. Parents with young children obviously have to be more watchful, and letting toddlers lead an ordinary life while trying to avoid knocks is very stressful. Extra back-up to help with housework is important because parents of haemophiliac children need to be more watchful. But there is no reason why children should not go to playgroup or nursery and the vast majority go to ordinary schools, which is the best course if possible.

Living close to a haemophilia centre helps, as does learning to give treatment at home, because after a while parents feel more confident and this in turn gives their child confidence. In the pre-school years parents can find it hard to leave their child with babysitters or relatives, but it is important that they continue to have a life together and sensible precautions like making sure the sitter is fully briefed are sufficient. Later in life the choice of job for a man with haemophilia may be limited if the haemophilia is severe, but most affected men find and keep satisfactory jobs.

TREATMENT

Although there is no cure for the condition, it is possible to stop the bleeding when it occurs, and indeed it is most important to do so — repeated bleeding into joints can result in crippling arthritis. So when an episode of bleeding occurs, children should receive an infusion of the missing clotting factor into their blood stream as soon as possible. Until recently this could only be carried out in a specialist centre, but, increasingly, home treatment is becoming possible. Tragically, a number of children with haemophilia who received such infusions were infected with the AIDS (Acquired Immune Deficiency Syndrome) HIV (Human Immunodeficiency Virus) because they were given contaminated blood products. Infusions are now carefully checked to ensure this will never happen again.

Children with problems in their blood clotting mechanism also need special care when they have dental treatment or more serious surgical operations for other reasons, so their families need to keep in touch with specialist centres. The Haemophilia Society can provide further information (see address section, pages 673–6).

CHILDHOOD CANCER INCLUDING LEUKAEMIA

Many adults do not realise that children can have cancer, and just hearing the word can be a great shock. It is still a life-threatening condition, but modern treatment means that the chances of cure, or at least of long-term remission of the illness, are very much more likely now than they were even ten years ago.

Normally the cells of the body increase in number to replace those that die off. In children more cells are produced as the body is growing, but the process of cell multiplication is very much under control. Cancer is a condition in which the cells in the body do not obey the rules; they multiply in an uncontrolled way, sometimes spreading to other parts of the body.

Although the causes of some cancers in adulthood are now known – the link between cigarette smoking and lung cancer, for example – the causes of nearly all cancers in children are still unknown. There is no evidence that anything children or parents themselves have done could be a cause.

In theory, the cells of any part of the body can get out of control and a cancer develop, but, in practice, in children there are only certain organs that are affected. Leukaemia, a cancer of the white blood cells, is the most common variety, but occasionally cancers of the brain, the eye, kidney, bones and connective tissue also occur.

The signs that a cancer is developing will obviously depend on where it is situated. Most children with leukaemia first show tiredness or a predisposition to infection because of anaemia – the blood is not able to carry enough energy-giving oxygen to the tissues. But, of course, leukaemia is a very rare cause of tiredness.

Pressure from swellings is usually the first sign of other sorts of cancer. One of the commonest forms of brain cancer affects the cerebellum, a part of the brain which is important in helping the child to keep a sense of balance. So cerebellar tumours often show themselves with the child starting to stagger rather than walk properly.

To make the diagnosis of a cancer, it is sometimes necessary to take a biopsy – to remove a tiny part of the body to examine it under the microscope. If leukaemia is suspected, a biopsy of the bone marrow, where blood is manufactured, is taken, usually from the hip.

The treatment varies, not only according to the type of illness, but also according to the age of the child. There are three main approaches which can be used:

Surgery to remove a malignant growth. This is not possible in leukaemia.

Chemotherapy (drugs) to shrink a growth or to control blood cells.

Radiotherapy to kill off 'blasts', that is the malignant cells in the blood.

The outlook for children varies according to the type of cancer and what stage it has reached. Some have over a 90% chance of cure – for others the prospects are much less good.

For most children the side effects of treatment are the worst part. They may lose their hair (something that does not upset young children very much at all, but which can be distressing for teenagers), and they may feel very ill as a result of the drugs rather than the illness. This can lead to them asking why they have to go to hospital since they go in feeling well and are then made, as they see it, worse.

The psychological care of children has to take into account the stress caused to the whole family. Uncertainty about the outcome is character-istic of many cases, if not all, and is one of the most powerful causes of distress. It is better if parents prepare children as much as possible for investigations and treatment.

Children are resilient and can cope, providing they trust those who are caring for them. Older children should be reassured that the doctors and nurses will be able to take away any pain or other sorts of distress-ing symptoms they may experience by giving medicines or injections. Brothers and sisters need support as well, and, if they are older than the affected child, may need to be given more detailed information so that they understand what is going on. The hospital doctors, nurses and social workers will be pleased to discuss how to talk to children about the illness – they have often had a good deal of experience of these situations.

Further information can be obtained from the Leukaemia Society (see address section, pages 673–6).

SICKLE CELL DISEASE

Sickle cell disease is a term covering a group of inherited blood disorders in which there is an abnormality of the red blood cells causing them to become rigid and sickle shaped, hence the name. Sickle cell anaemia (Hb SS) is usually the most severe and common form, but there are other types called for example, Hb SC disease and sickle beta-thalassaemia. Sickle cell disease mainly affects people of African and Caribbean origin (about one in 200) and is also found in people from the Mediterranean, Asia and the Middle East. Although there is no complete cure for sickle cell anaemia as yet, research has improved the treatment now available.

A child is born with sickle cell anaemia because he has inherited a gene from both parents, each of whom is a carrier with sickle cell traits. People who have sickle cell trait are not affected and have no symptoms them-selves. This is because people with sickle cell trait still have another identical back-up gene which is healthy to do the job (see pages 15–17 on dominant and recessive genes). But if both parents have sickle cell trait then there is a one in four chance that every child they have will be born with sickle cell anaemia. There is a one in two chance that each child will inherit sickle cell trait, that is be a carrier of the gene but not be affected themselves. If only one parent has sickle cell trait, each child has a fifty–fifty chance of inheriting either the trait or normal haemoglobin. If one parent has sickle cell anaemia and the other has sickle cell trait there is a fifty–fifty chance again that the child could be born with sickle cell anaemia or sickle cell trait. A special blood test can tell if a person has sickle cell trait and it is now possible to test the unborn child for sickle cell anaemia, although at present this is only being done at certain specialised centres.

SYMPTOMS

The rigid sickle-shaped blood cells cannot flow smoothly through small blood vessels. This can cause blockage of the blood supply with subsequent pain and, more rarely, damage to bones, muscles and lungs. A further problem is that these sickle-shaped blood cells do not live as long as the normal 120 days of healthy red blood cells and this causes chronic anaemia. The episodes of pain are known as crises and can be prompted by dehydration, strenuous exercise, infection, pregnancy and anaesthetics. Both the symptoms and their effects can vary greatly from one individual to another. Symptoms very rarely start until the child is more than six months old and may include painful swelling of hands and feet. As a child gets older, sickling, causing mild or more severe pain, may occur in any part of the body, with the joints, abdomen and chest being common sites. Anaemia is always present but can become dramatically worse, so a child may become jaundiced at times because of increased destruction of red blood cells. Young children with sickle cell anaemia are prone to bacterial infections and during adolescence other features may occur such as leg ulcers and delay in growth.

TREATMENT

Drinking extra fluid regularly helps to keep the blood flowing smoothly and taking folic acid tablets compensates for folate deficiency. Taking penicillin regularly protects against serious infections. Parents need to learn how to let their child lead as normal a life as possible while avoiding triggers which may cause sickling such as dehydration, sudden change in temperature, infection or strenuous exercise. They also need long-term support from skilled and sensitive professionals to help them cope with their own emotions and be as supportive as possible to their child. Genetic counselling can help them understand the long-term implications of the disease and equip them with information regarding future pregnancies. During a crisis, children need pain-killers to give pain relief and, depending on the severity of the attack, bed rest and possibly antibiotics and blood transfusion. With help and advice parents can learn how to recognise the early warning signs calling for urgent medical attention, such as raised temperature, pallor, lethargy and swelling of the abdomen, as well as how to manage mild symptoms at home. The most vulnerable period for those with sickle call disease is early childhood, but improved treatment means the prognosis is much better and most sufferers live into adulthood.

THALASSAEMIA

This is an inherited abnormality of the blood which is found amongst people from Mediterranean countries. As with sickle cell disease, people can carry the thalassaemia gene without being affected, but when two adult carriers of the gene have children there is a one in four chance with every pregnancy that their child could have thalassaemia. The blood of thalassaemia sufferers cannot produce haemoglobin efficiently, which makes them anaemic. They can also suffer skull deformities, fail to reach their full height, be of shorter than normal stature, and fail to enter puberty.

The symptoms, which usually show in the first six months of life, are anaemia and failure to thrive. As yet there is no complete cure, but with babies bone-marrow transplantation may be successful: this is a new field. The prognosis has improved with better treatment to combat symptoms so that many thalassaemia sufferers now live to adulthood. Treatment consists of blood transfusions, which children need to have every two to four weeks to prevent them developing anaemia. It is now often possible for this to be done as a day patient, cutting the number of hospital stays necessary. However, because these children's bodies cannot process iron efficiently, there is a build up of iron deposits in the tissues and a drug has to be injected to induce a process called chelation, the freeing of iron deposits. This substance has to be injected either into the vein or under the skin.

Obviously the treatment is not pleasant for children and they need a great deal of support and help from parents and other members of the family both to minimise the stress of medical procedures and to help them have as full and enjoyable a life as healthy children as possible. Parents and relatives in their turn will need counselling about the disease and opportunities to talk about their feelings. In common with most inherited diseases, parents may feel great guilt and parent support groups have proved of value. Fortunately genetic counselling, fetoscopy and amniocentesis to detect thalassaemia in the unborn child mean that the incidence of the disease is declining.

SHORT STATURE

Obviously children vary in height, and the great majority of small children are perfectly normal. Such children have a normal rate of growth. They usually have parents who are not very tall either, and have probably inherited a tendency to be small.

Some children however are very small, so that, for example, a five-year-old might only be the height of an average two-year-old. There are various reasons for this. The child may have a definite, inherited syndrome in which failure to grow is one feature: such children are often small at birth even if they are born at the expected time. Very occasionally, there is a lack of the growth hormone normally produced in a gland at the base of the brain (the pituitary gland), and necessary for ordinary growth to occur.

TREATMENT

Tests can be carried out to see if the child is suffering from growth hormone deficiency, and, if this is the case, the child can be given injections of artificial hormone to stimulate growth. Children brought up in socially stressed conditions also tend to be small, and, in circumstances of severe deprivation, the amount of growth hormone put out by the pituitary gland is sometimes reduced. This situation is reversible if the child is placed in a more suitable social environment.

Education   Unless failure to grow is part of an inherited syndrome which has other problems, small children are of normal intelligence and go to ordinary schools.

Lifestyle   Children who are tiny for their age have all sorts of problems to put up with – in particular, they are often taken to be much younger than they really are and talked down to. They may develop ways of coping with this that are not very helpful, such as acting much younger than their age. Parents will usually have no problem dealing with this themselves, but they need to be able to help others treat their children more appropriately if secondary difficulties are to be minimised.

Helpful information can be obtained from the Child Growth Foundation (see address section, pages 673–6).

DIABETES

'Our daughter became very listless and then sleepy. It was a terrible shock when she actually went into a coma. All sorts of awful worries went through my mind, so when they came and told us at the hospital that it seemed likely she had diabetes but would be all right our first reaction was tremendous relief. In fact neither of us knew anything at all about it, otherwise we would have recognised classic warning signs like thirst and going to the loo all the time, and we had a great deal to learn about how it was to affect her life.'

Every year more than 1,500 children in Britain develop *diabetes mellitus*, sometimes called sugar diabetes. There is no cure, but medical advances mean it is no longer the killer it once was and with good management a person with diabetes can lead a perfectly normal, full life. Most people know that diabetes is to do with sugar, but unless they have a relative or friend who is diabetic they are often understandably hazy about the exact nature of the problem.

First of all, diabetes is not caused by eating too much sugar, nor is one of the symptoms a liking for sweet things. The problem lies with a gland called the pancreas, which is positioned near the stomach. The hormone, one of the body's chemicals, which the pancreas should produce is called insulin. It is insulin which breaks down the body's fuel, glucose, and enables it to be used as energy, to repair the body tissues or to be stored in the liver. You may think that you do not actually eat much glucose in the form of sugar, but a great deal of ordinary food and especially carbohydrate is broken down into glucose by the digestive juices. In children with diabetes the pancreas fails to work properly and either produces very little insulin or none at all. Because no insulin is made to convert the glucose it stays in the bloodstream until it reaches the kidneys when it is passed out of the body in urine. Because glucose carries water with it, this means passing a great deal of urine and this in turn leads on to another symptom, excessive thirst. Finally, since the body is being deprived of the fuel it normally has in the form of glucose and begins to use up fat stores, it sends out signals for more food by making the sufferer extra hungry. So the symptoms of diabetes are: excessive thirst, passing urine very frequently, eating a lot but losing or failing to gain weight, and glucose in the urine.

Of course the last of these can only be detected if the urine is tested, but if your child has the other symptoms seek your doctor's advice. If diabetes is not diagnosed early on then children can become very drowsy and tired and go into a coma; in which case they need urgent hospital treatment.

TREATMENT

Because the body cannot manage to make its own insulin this has to be given by injection. Adult diabetics can sometimes manage with diet and tablets alone, but children always need insulin injections, usually twice a day.

Normally the balance between the amount of insulin produced and the amount of glucose to be converted is regulated by the checks and balances of the body's own systems. But when insulin has to be given artificially it is much harder to keep the balance right and that is where diet comes in. Diabetics must try to keep the levels of glucose in their body fairly constant, which means eating little and often. Three main meals with snacks in between so that there are five regularly spaced intakes of food are needed and a diabetic child must not be kept waiting for meals.

Because diabetics' bodies cope so poorly with glucose they must avoid loading the system with sudden surges of it – for this reason sweets and chocolate are out and the intake of carbohydrate food, such as potatoes and bread, must be controlled. But diabetics do not have to eat special food – they eat the same things as anybody else but always as part of a balanced diet. In fact a diabetic diet is super healthy – high in fibre, low in fat and with no sugar.

Young children quickly adapt to both the diet and (something which often surprises parents) to having injections of insulin. Many can do the injections themselves by the time they are about five or six. To check that the level of glucose is staying under control, parents have to test the child's urine and many now check the glucose levels in the blood as well – these are simple procedures which children can soon learn to do for themselves.

WHAT HAPPENS WHEN THE BALANCE BETWEEN INSULIN AND GLUCOSE IS WRONG?

Various things can upset the balance – too little food, too much sugary food, extra exercise which burns up a lot of glucose in the form of energy or just the changing needs of a growing body.

Hypoglycaemia is when the body has too little glucose. This may be because too much insulin has been given for the amount of food to be processed, because too little food has been eaten or because exercise has used up a lot of glucose. It comes on suddenly and the signs are: lack of concentration, sweating, dizziness, vagueness and inability to answer questions, bad temper or weepiness, and sometimes difficulty in speaking.

If untreated, hypoglycaemia can lead to a coma. This is why all diabetics need to carry or have on hand something sweet or sugary to eat at the first warning signs that the blood sugar is falling. A sweet or a sugary biscuit will do and Lucozade is a good idea as well. Once they have begun to recover they should eat something unsugary. If a child does become unconscious call a doctor or get him to the nearest accident and emergency unit immediately – food or fluids should not be given to anyone unconscious because of the real risk of choking.

Hyperglycaemia means there is too much glucose in the body. This is the situation when a child first begins to develop diabetes and before he gets treatment. It is usually slow to develop and, after treatment has begun, may be because too little insulin has been given, an insulin injection is overdue, too many carbohydrate or sugary foods have been eaten, or because the child has an infection such as tonsillitis. The signs are: tiredness, excessive thirst, hunger or passing urine, dry tongue, sweet, fruity smell on the breath, and deep breathing.

Extra injections of insulin are needed, but if the child is dehydrated treatment in hospital may be necessary.

LIFESTYLE FOR DIABETIC CHILDREN

Diabetic children need to eat regularly, need to eat a balanced diet and need to have insulin injections. But these are not restrictions which will prevent them having as full and active a life as any normal child. Parents should not be over-protective or over-indulgent and they should be matter of fact about diet and treatment, which will help the child to accept it as

Diabetic children may need an additional snack during the day

part of life. Obviously parents need to be sure that playgroup organisers and nursery and primary school teachers know and understand about diabetes and how to treat a suspected attack of hypoglycaemia. Food should not be a problem because so many children take packed lunches these days and the child can take an additional snack for playtime. Both parents and children become experts in keeping the balance between insulin and glucose right.

In the beginning parents may well need to talk over both the condition and their own emotions with informed counsellors or a doctor they trust. They may have many confused feelings about the whole subject, but great support and help is available both through other parents and through the British Diabetic Association (see address section, pages 673–6). When the child gets older he too can find valuable support from meeting other diabetic children at specially arranged summer camps.

CYSTIC FIBROSIS (CF)

In this condition all the glands that discharge their secretions directly into the body are affected. The secretions are thick and sticky instead of runny (another name for the condition is mucoviscidosis) so they block up a number of the connecting tubes in the body's system.

The condition occurs in about one in two thousand births, and is an inherited disease caused by the presence of a recessive gene. About one in twenty people are carriers of the CF gene, but it is only when two carriers have a child that there is a one in four chance of that child inheriting both genes and having cystic fibrosis. The chance is the same for each pregnancy, though some couples never have a CF child so never know they are both carriers of the gene. In other families all the children may be affected. The CF gene mainly occurs in Caucasian (white Indo-European) people. Some children are affected less severely than others. CF mainly affects the way the lungs and digestive system work, but it also has an effect in other parts of the body which may at first seem unrelated – what links them is the presence of secretory glands. The problem may be diagnosed at birth when a baby fails to pass meconium – the treacle-like substance present in the gut before birth – or the faeces are unusually dry, bulky and smelly. Sometimes the gut is obstructed, which can be dealt with by an operation. More commonly the problem is discovered in the first few years of life because the child suffers repeated chest infections or does not digest food properly. The diagnosis is confirmed by carrying out a test on the child's sweat, which is abnormal because the sweat glands are affected. The principal symptom of CF is that the mucus or sputum in the lungs is very thick and difficult to remove and can easily become infected. Sometimes this mucus blocks the bronchial tubes, tiny air passages into the lungs, and this can cause lung damage when air can pass through the mucus on breathing in, but cannot pass when breathing out again. Bacteria invading the mucus can also cause lung damage.

In order to clear the mucus, parents of CF children, and later the child himself, must learn physiotherapy which is practised twice a day, or more if the child has a cold, to loosen the mucus. CF children need to learn how to cough up the mucus which their lungs produce and they also need regular antibiotic treatment to prevent germs developing in the mucus. The antibiotics are sometimes taken through a nebuliser, a device which makes mist out of a liquid by blowing air or oxygen through it so the medicine can be delivered directly into the lungs. The final part of the daily treatment routine is taking digestive enzymes to replace the enzymes which would normally be produced by the pancreas to break down and help the body absorb food. Fats are specially difficult for CF sufferers to digest and without drugs they require a very low fat diet. Enzyme capsules now have a special coating, which prevents them being destroyed in the stomach before they reach the gut and enables CF children to eat a more normal diet.

CF children need plenty of high energy food and vitamin supplements to ensure they get the nutrients they need to grow and develop properly. In addition to physiotherapy, exercise is also very important – for the under-fives climbing frames, trampolines, visits to playgrounds, swimming and gym sessions geared to this age are all a good idea. Later learning a sport like tennis or football, athletics, dance and drama are part of an active lifestyle which helps keep the lungs clear and strengthens muscles.

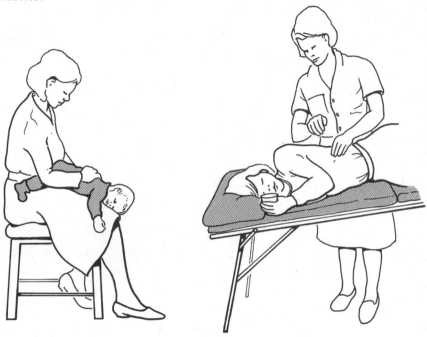

Physiotherapy is needed for babies and older children to loosen lung mucus

Identification in 1989 by geneticists of the CF gene means a test will soon be possible to detect whether a person is a carrier of the faulty gene – this will be by blood analysis or by using a special mouthwash. Research will also soon provide a means of screening for cystic fibrosis in the unborn baby, although to begin with this will only be offered to families known to be at risk.

Sadly, as yet, there is no cure for CF itself, although advances in treatment mean that both the quality of life and the life expectancy for CF children is now vastly improved. When CF was first recognised as a disease in the late 1930s, children died very young from lung infections or digestive problems, but now 75% live to enjoy adult life. Apart from the development of gene therapy in the future, work is also being done with heart–lung transplants when a point is reached when these organs begin to fail. As with all organ transplants though, an insufficient number of donors limits more widespread use of this technique. The Cystic Fibrosis Research Trust can provide further help and information (see address section, pages 673–6).

COELIAC DISEASE

Most children who fail to gain weight properly are not suffering from physical disease: for one reason or another they are just not getting enough to eat, perhaps because they are living in families under stress because of difficult social circumstances. However, there are a small number of conditions in which children fail to thrive even though they are getting a very adequate diet, and coeliac disease is one of these. In this condition the child is unable to tolerate the gluten (a protein) in wheat or rye. Consequently, foods like ordinary bread, cakes and biscuits make him ill. The motions are pale and bulky, and smell offensive. The child not only fails to grow as well as he should, but is often irritable and miserable.

The condition is diagnosed by passing a tube through the mouth into a part of the intestine just beyond the stomach and nipping off a tiny segment (taking a biopsy) of the lining of the gut, so that this can be examined under the microscope. The lining has an abnormal appearance in childen with coeliac disease.

Usually children do very well on a diet free of gluten, but they need to stay on the diet for the rest of their lives. As the diet is quite restrictive, it is important the diagnosis is made properly. The biopsy may be repeated when the child is on a gluten-free diet, in order to make sure the appearance of the lining of the gut has returned to normal.

HEART PROBLEMS

Congenital heart disease is a term used when a baby is born with something wrong with the structure of his heart that affects the way it works. The heart is formed very early in pregnancy, between the sixth and tenth week, after which it grows with the baby. We know that if the mother has *rubella* (German measles) in the first three months of pregnancy it can affect the formation of the baby's heart and it may be that other viruses also have this effect. If the mother has diabetes there is also a slightly increased risk of her child having heart disease, but in the majority of cases we do not know the cause. About eight in every thousand babies born alive have some form of congenital heart disease, but in a third of these children the abnormality is very mild and does not need treatment.

The job of the heart is to receive blood which has already been round the body and given up some of its oxygen (blue blood), pump it to the lungs where it becomes oxygenated again and turns red, and then to pump this red blood back around the body again. It helps to imagine the heart as two pumps, each with its own reservoir, the right side filling with blue blood and sending it to the lungs, the left side filling with red blood from the lungs and pumping it back round the body. The left side of the heart has to be stronger and has more muscle as it has more work to do than the right. These two sides of the heart are separated by partitions or 'septa' so the blue and red blood do not mix. There are four valves which open completely to allow the blood to pass through and then close to prevent the blood flowing backwards. The pumping action followed by a resting period, which allows the heart to fill with blood, is controlled by an electrical circuit directed by nerves.

HEART MURMURS

A murmur is simply the noise made by the blood flowing through the heart and big vessels. It is very common for doctors to discover that a child has a murmur by listening to his heart with a stethoscope during a routine examination – this is not the same as finding the child has heart disease. In most cases such murmurs are what doctors call 'innocent', which means they are not due to heart disease or any other illness. An innocent murmur makes no difference to the way the heart works and will disappear as the child grows. In many cases, even when a heart murmur is found to be due to a heart defect, it quite commonly corrects itself by the time the child reaches school age. In other children the noise comes from an abnormality that will need correcting.

COMMON HEART DISEASE ABNORMALITIES

There may be a hole in the muscular partition which separates the two pumping sides of the heart. This means extra blood from the left side of the heart, where the pressure is higher, enters the right side, consequently more blood is being sent to the lungs and the heart has to work harder. This is commonly known as a hole in the heart. Children with small defects do not show any symptoms and the hole usually becomes smaller and closes of its own accord, although it may take some years and they may have more chest infections than normal children. If the hole is large and causing symptoms, an operation may be necessary. Children can have another abnormality when a narrowing occurs at some point in the arteries so that the heart has to work extra hard to pump the blood through. In some babies the tube between the two arteries, known as the ductus, remains open. This normally closes after birth as the lungs begin to work (see page 127). The effect is that the blood from the main artery going to the body (the aorta) is allowed to flow to the lungs. Again, the lungs receive extra blood and the heart has to work harder. This can be corrected by an operation, which has a very low risk and which will enable the heart to work normally.

Sometimes the veins or arteries are wrongly connected to the heart so blood with a lower amount of oxygen than normal, which is therefore blue in colour, is sent round the body. This will make the skin have a bluish tinge, hence the description 'blue baby'. Procedures are possible to make the condition less severe and allow more oxygenated blood to reach the body, but major surgery will be needed to correct the abnormality. This may be done shortly after birth or deferred till later, depending on the particular problem and baby's progress. More rarely one side of the heart may be weaker than the other.

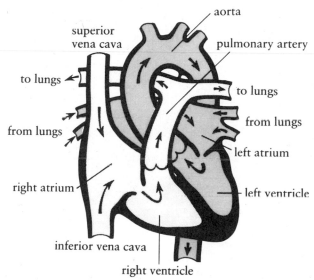

Normal heart circulation

Coarctation of the aorta

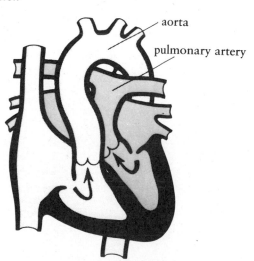

Simple transposition

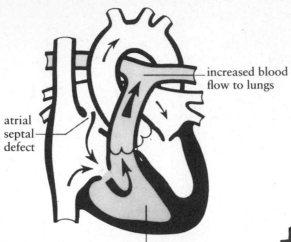

increased blood
flow to lungs

atrial
septal
defect

enlarged
right ventricle

Atrial septal defect

thickened
pulmonary
valve

thick
right ventricle

Pulmonary valve stenosis

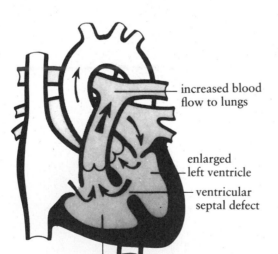

increased blood
flow to lungs

enlarged
left ventricle

ventricular
septal defect

enlarged
right ventricle

Ventricular septal defect

SYMPTOMS

Many babies and children with minor heart problems do not show any symptoms and are not affected. Some become breathless when walking or running or, in the case of a baby, when feeding. This may mean the baby cannot finish the feed and consequently grows more slowly. Some children may have less energy and tire more easily and have more chest infections. In the first instance doctors will carefully examine your child, listen to the heart with a stethoscope and may plan some tests, although many children do not need any.

INVESTIGATIONS AND TESTS

A chest X-ray may be needed and by attaching wires painlessly to chest, arms and legs, doctors can test the electrical activity of the heart (electrocardiogram or ECG) and take a tracing. An ultrasound scan of the child (echocardiogram), similar to the one done in pregnancy, will show a picture of the heart on a television screen. Sometimes doctors need to measure the pressures inside the heart and this test involves a stay of two or three days in hospital. The child is given a sedative and a tube is inserted into a vein and/or artery usually at a point in the groin and steered with the blood flow into the heart chambers. Special dye can be injected through the tube, which shows up on X-ray so a clear outline of the heart and any defects can be seen. The procedure is not painful and the child usually falls asleep while it is being done. Sometimes this test can be used to treat heart problems, for example to stretch narrow valves.

LIFESTYLE

Most children with heart disease can lead ordinary lives and go to ordinary schools. More than half the babies born with heart disease need some kind of investigation in the first year of their lives, and some need an operation at this time. Often doctors prefer to wait until the child is much bigger before undertaking any corrective surgery and treat them in the meantime with medicines. Understandably parents feel anxious about their child and, unless the condition is fully explained, may fear that the condition may suddenly worsen and the child collapse. In fact this is extremely unlikely. If the child's condition does worsen, the only signs will be a gradual slowing down. The most beneficial thing parents can do is to allow their child to enjoy a normal childhood. If there is a real reason for a child not to do too much in the way of games and exercise the heart specialist will explain why. Otherwise it has been shown that children with heart disease are usually very sensible and naturally limit their own activity when necessary. Parents sometimes wonder if crying can harm a baby with heart disease, but this is not the case, although such babies should be comforted in the ordinary way. Children with heart disease should be immunised at the normal time. Just occasionally such children can get a special sort of infection in their hearts from having decayed teeth, significant dental work or other operations. To prevent this they will be given antibiotics by the doctor or dentist when these problems occur.

The majority of children are able to go to normal school. In a few, fatigue, tiredness and blueness may cause lack of concentration and extra help may be necessary. Girls who have heart defects should be able to have children when they grow up, and many thousands of women who have had major defects operated on have had children. However, each case needs to be considered individually. A full range of careers is possible for most heart disease patients, but in a few cases heavy strenuous outdoor work is best avoided and the Services are not willing to take people who have had heart operations even though they may be fit.

AIDS

HIV (Human Immunodeficiency Virus) is a virus which can attack the immune system to produce symptoms of the illness called AIDS (Acquired Immune Deficiency Syndrome). It can lie dormant in the body without causing any symptoms for five or more years, although in some people this period may be shorter. The HIV virus is transmitted from one person to another by an intermingling of blood or sexual contact – it cannot be passed on by touching or in saliva, urine, sweat, or faeces. The number of children in the UK with AIDS is very small and at the start of the 1990s is thought to be in the region of one hundred.

The largest group of these children are haemophiliacs who, tragically, were given a blood product which carried the virus. Haemophiliacs need to be treated with infusions of the clotting factor their bodies lack when they are injured. All blood and blood products are now screened to be sure that they are free of HIV, but in the early 1980s supplies of the clotting factor were largely obtained from the USA and many were contaminated with HIV.

Most of the other infected children in the UK acquired the virus from their mothers before birth in the same way other viruses such as *rubella* may transmit. Almost all the mothers of these children are drug abusers or the sexual partners of drug abusers who contracted the virus by sharing hypodermic needles with an infected person.

Only about one in five of the babies of women carrying the virus are infected. Unfortunately, because all these babies will have antibodies to the virus from their mother's blood, we cannot be sure which children have escaped infection until they are about eighteen months old, by which time the antibody disappears if they are not infected.

Unfortunately most babies who acquire the virus from their mothers do show signs of infection, sometimes serious and occasionally fatal, by the age of 18 months. A minority appear to remain well for at least some years.

TREATMENT

There is no cure for HIV at the time of writing, but children with the virus will be monitored for signs that it may have become active. Any illnesses or injuries that they develop will be treated in the normal way, although obviously special care is needed.

LIFESTYLE

There is no reason why children infected by HIV should not lead normal lives as long as the virus remains dormant and they are therefore in good health. The biggest social problems they face are the fear and prejudice of other parents who mistakenly think they pose a threat to their own children. There is no reason why these children should not go to pram clubs and playgroups and make friends in the ordinary way. The only occasion when care needs to be taken is in the event of an injury where the child with HIV bleeds. Even in these circumstances the risk of infection is extremely low. Provided that the contaminated blood does not come into contact with an open wound, or possibly a mucous membrane, there is no risk of infection. If an infected child does bleed, the area should be thoroughly washed and then cleaned with a hypochlorite-containing disinfectant. Anyone who gets contaminated blood on their hands should wash them immediately and thoroughly.

CLEFT LIP AND PALATE

Seeing a baby who has been born with a cleft lip is one of the most distressing experiences of parenthood. So much attention is focused on a newborn's face; when people say 'What a lovely baby,' they invariably mean 'What an attractive face.' The child born with a cleft lip is really not beautiful.

A cleft is a split and a cleft lip is one with a split so that the upper lip is separated just under the nose (sometimes the phrase 'hare lip' is used but this is becoming rare). Clefts can also occur in the palate and in either place they can be single (unilateral) or double (bilateral). It is the most common birth defect in the head and neck region, about 1 in 700 babies being born with the condition. The exact cause is unknown. There is a small hereditary element, in that if there are clefts in the family there is an increased chance of the condition recurring, but this is only part of the story. What is more certain is that it happens during the first three months of pregnancy.

Fortunately the outlook for children born with clefts is generally good. One of the most reassuring experiences the parents can have is to see a set of photographs of other children before and after surgery, when they can begin to answer for themselves what is usually their first question, 'Can anything be done?' Once information has been given and parents have had a chance to express their entirely natural feelings of anxiety and disappointment, the initial shock passes quickly, within a matter of days in many cases, and plans can be made for the future.

The first task is to manage feeding. Usually there is no real problem, but when the palate is cleft it has a gap in it and milk taken into the mouth returns down the nose (nasal regurgitation). A feed can take up to two hours. There are now several specially designed teats and feeding bottles; midwives and health visitors should be able to give advice.

Next, generally, come plans for surgery. The timing of each stage will depend partly on the nature of the cleft, partly on the surgeon's practice; many think it best to operate for the first time at about three months, but others now begin surgery within the first week. This first-stage operation brings together the edges of the gap in the lip, leaving only a slight scar in most cases. Any gap in the palate is usually left until after the first birthday. By now parents will have met most members of the cleft lip and palate team: plastic surgeon, orthodontist, speech therapist and audiologist.

Audiology is of the utmost importance since hearing loss is frequently associated with clefts and it is essential that full hearing tests are given to all children with them. A full test is one given in a specially equipped clinic; no one should be satisfied with a crude assessment in an ordinary consulting room.

Speech therapists play a key part in the treatment of children with cleft palates and contact should be made early, well before children start to talk, since parents will be the main teachers and if helped can get off to a flying start.

Nursery school and meeting other children come next. At this point parents and children meet a big hurdle, the difficulty of explaining to others the nature of the cleft. The simplest explanation is the best: 'I was born like that. Some people are born short or tall with blue eyes or brown; I was born with something wrong with my mouth.' Parents often worry about the emotional adjustment of children with clefts, but there is no need for concern for they have no more behaviour problems than are expected in any group. Nor is there any particular personality pattern in cleft-lipped children, although there is a slight tendency towards shyness in school.

There is no reason either to anticipate any greater than normal difficulties in school work later on, providing there is no hearing loss, although there is one point that should be guarded against: teachers often underestimate the intelligence of children with a cleft.

Later surgery may be necessary, sometimes not until the teens are reached and the child has stopped growing, sometimes before. The childhood of children with clefts is not all roses, but providing there are no other complications present the outlook is firmly optimistic.

The Cleft Lip and Palate Association has branches all over Britain (see address section, pages 673–6).

GENITAL PROBLEMS

HYPOSPADIAS

When a baby boy is born, it may be obvious that the opening that is normally at the tip of the penis is situated further back. This is one of the commonest types of failure of development, and surgery can usually correct the problem. Most surgeons carry out the operation in two or three stages when the boy is between two and four years old, but it may also be performed in one stage earlier in life.

As children with this problem get older, it is particularly important they are given a good explanation of how they are different from other boys, and what the operation will do. Until the operation is performed, unlike other boys, they will have to urinate sitting down, and they need to know why this is. The outlook is usually good, and there is no reason why sexual function should be affected later on.

UNDESCENDED TESTICLES

The testes begin to develop in the abdomen during pregnancy, and, before the baby is born, normally go down into the scrotum or bag behind the penis. Sometimes the descent does not occur properly and they stay in the abdomen or fail to complete the entire journey or take a wrong turning and finish up in the groin.

The problem should be detected at birth when the doctor carrying out the examination notices that he cannot feel two testicles in the scrotum. If the condition is not noticed immediately after birth, parents may notice it later, or a check-up at a child health clinic may reveal the situation. Children with this condition need an operation because testes left undescended may develop complications at puberty or in adult life. A surgical operation can usually remedy the problem quite easily, and this is usually carried out when the boy is between three to eight years of age.

Again it is very important to explain to boys who are affected in this way what the problem is, why they need an operation, and what is going to happen during the operation and afterwards. Parents are often embarrassed themselves about giving explanations and this, of course, makes an affected boy even more anxious. So if you are worried about what to say to your three- or four-year-old, ask your family doctor or the surgeon who is going to carry out the operation to explain the problem to your child simply.

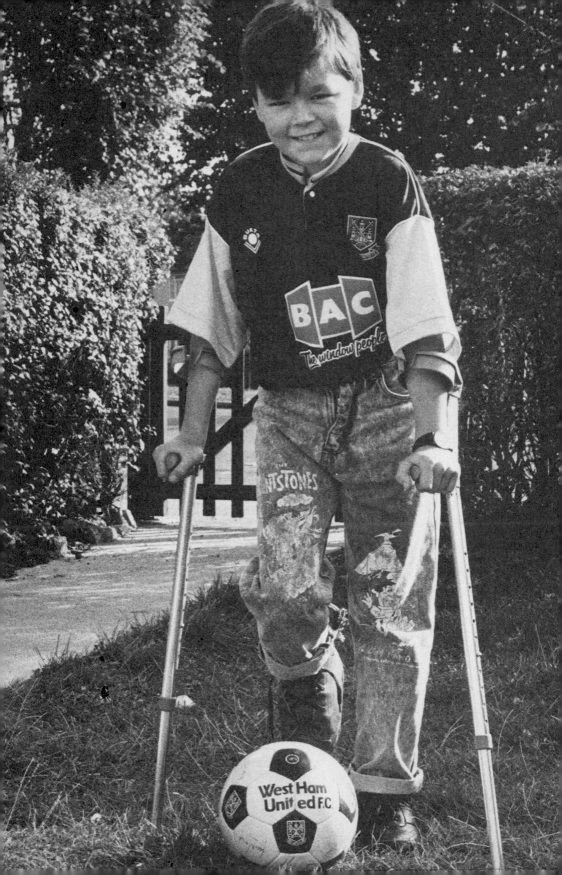

Chapter 19

HANDICAP

Handicap – why do handicaps happen?, types of handicap, how are handicaps discovered?, living with handicap   Deafness and other severe hearing problems   Visual impairment   Cerebral palsy   Spina bifida   Muscular dystrophy   Severe learning difficulties – mental handicap, Down's syndrome, autism

Unfortunately, some children suffer from conditions which, at the present time, cannot be completely successfully treated, and they may be affected all through their childhood and into adulthood. It is not possible to draw a clear line between these chronic long-lasting conditions and short-lived ones. For example, many children have just one or two attacks of asthma, or eczema, but occasionally these conditions can become chronic problems, lasting throughout childhood.

Of course, a long-lasting illness does not necessarily lead to children being handicapped in their everyday lives. It is perhaps surprising to realise that quite mild defects can be more profoundly handicapping than conditions some people regard as really severe. For example, a boy with bat ears, who is also a little overweight, might be teased at school because of his appearance and refuse to go there, missing weeks or months of schooling. A child with diabetes or a heart defect could go regularly to school and not be nearly so handicapped. Yet most people would think that bat ears were pretty unimportant compared to diabetes or a heart condition. If children cannot be cured, and that is sometimes the case, their parents need help to make sure that their children are as little handicapped as possible.

WHY DO HANDICAPS HAPPEN?

Genetic (inherited) causes Either the sperm or the egg involved in fertilisation may contain genetic material that is imperfect. Sometimes both sperm and egg are affected. If there is some serious imperfection, then usually the mother has a miscarriage – nature's way of making sure that, as far as possible, children are not born handicapped. Genetic conditions may not always be obvious at birth. Some conditions, like cystic fibrosis (see page 619), may be obvious at birth or they may only show up when the child is a few months or years old.

Children with spina bifida *can be helped to be as mobile as possible*

Congenital disorders This means the child has been born with the condition. Not all congenital disorders are inherited. If the child has, in some way, been damaged in the womb or at the time of birth, then the problem may be congenital, but not inherited.

Other causes Many chronic handicaps are inherited, but some chronic problems or disorders are caused by events after birth. Injuries due to accidents and infections (especially those affecting the brain) are the most common. Sometimes, as with conditions like asthma, a tendency to develop them may be inherited, but the problem may only occur if children are in contact with particular 'germs', substances or foods to which they have become sensitive, or if they are unusually stressed. Sometimes, too, the causes of chronic conditions are just not known. No one really has any very clear idea about the causes, for example, of some of the rare forms of cancer that occur in childhood.

TYPES OF HANDICAP

Children may be handicapped by physical disorders affecting the body. They may also be handicapped by learning disorders or by emotional or behavioural difficulties. Unfortunately some children are multiply handicapped and show not only physical disorders, but also learning and emotional difficulties as well. Although one often thinks of physical problems as the most disabling, in many multiply handicapped children it is the learning difficulties which handicap the child most.

HOW ARE HANDICAPS DISCOVERED?

If there is a particular reason to think your child has a handicap, then sometimes it can be discovered while the child is still in the womb, by methods of antenatal detection (see page 19). Down's syndrome is an example of a condition that can be detected antenatally, but, of course, this will only occur if there is some special reason to think your child is at risk.

Immediately after birth, your child will be examined by a paediatrician to make sure he has no condition that is detectable by examination. Some problems, like heart defects, undescended testicles or Down's syndrome may be discovered in this way.

A few days later, your child will have a heel prick to take a drop or two of blood. This will be examined to see if your child has a lack of thyroid hormone or a disorder of body chemicals (phenylketonuria). If either of these is detected, your child can be treated and handicap prevented.

The way a handicap is detected after birth will depend almost entirely on what the problem is. An illness such as diabetes may come on quite suddenly over a few days, but then need treatment over a lifetime. Some conditions, like some forms of learning difficulty, may be suspected in the first or second year, but there may be a period of uncertainty lasting months or years before it is clear that there really is a problem or, more happily, that development in this respect is going to be normal.

LIVING WITH HANDICAP

How parents feel when they know their child is going to have a handicap depends a good deal on how mild or serious the problem is, on how quickly they learn about it, on how well or badly they are told about it, and on their own personalities and the way they react to the other stresses of life. If the problem is a severe one and parents hear about it suddenly, they often experience a whole range of feelings in more or less the following order:

Numbness	A kind of blanking out, as if the shock is so great they cannot take in exactly what is being said. This is why explanations of a child's handicap need to be given more than once, so that parents are able to take them in fully, to think and to ask questions.
Disbelief	A feeling that the bad news simply cannot be true, and parents may search desperately for another explanation. Perhaps the doctors are mistaken. Perhaps the test results have been muddled with those of another child. This stage can pass very quickly or last for months.
Anger	This can be directed at themselves, each other, or at doctors. If only, parents may say to themselves, they had noticed something earlier, if only their GP had sent them to a hospital sooner, if only the hospital doctors had acted differently . . .
Despair	A feeling of bleakness without hope. It seems as though the future can only be blackness and misery.
Acceptance	Parents begin to feel less out of control. They understand that an awful event has occurred, and can accept the reasons and the fact that it may not be possible to provide a full explanation. They begin to be able to plan for the future.

Sometimes, especially if the problem is less severe, or parents only understand that there is a problem slowly over a period of months or years, reactions may be very different, and may be mingled with relief at the prospect of finally getting help. One mother says:

'I began to suspect she couldn't hear properly when she was only about five months old. As she got older I kept noticing other signs, but both my health visitor and GP said there was nothing to worry about. They clearly thought I was just over-anxious because I had problems at home and my marriage had broken up. It wasn't until Claire was nearly two years old that my doctor agreed she wasn't learning to talk and sent us to a specialist who found she was practically deaf.'

With problems that are not immediately obvious, parents are often the first to notice or suspect a child's handicap. If they have tried for years to get doctors to take notice, it may come as a tremendous relief to have their fears finally acknowledged and know that help can now be offered.

Most parents, when they realise their child is suffering from a handicap, experience a mixture of feelings towards the child himself. Part of them feels that he needs extra love, care and protection, so that they want to keep closer to the child than they normally would, and may worry about letting him develop independence. Part of them may feel a sense of dislike for a child that is not normal. Fortunately, although this is quite common, the feeling does not usually last very long. Part of them will feel a continuing sense of sadness, but also a determination to make sure he is brought up as normally as possible. Which of these feelings is predominant will often change over time, but traces of each of them may persist over years.

Parents of handicapped children may also have a harder time, not just emotionally, but financially and in their social lives. Fares to hospital may be expensive. A mother who would have gone back to work when her child was two or three years old may find that this is impossible because of the extra demands her handicapped child makes. Chances of promotion may have to be passed up so that the family can live near a particular hospital or school. There may be extra problems finding a babysitter, so parents may feel cooped up and irritable. Sometimes too, differences between parents about how a child with a handicap should be treated may lead to arguments that might not have occurred otherwise, or perhaps might have happened, but around some other less painful topic. Brothers and sisters of the child with a handicap may feel left out and neglected, or perhaps upset because they do not understand what is wrong with the affected child.

With all these possible problems, it should be good news to know that most families with a handicapped child cope remarkably well. Parents usually come to accept the nature of their child's disability and make realistic plans for the future. It is sometimes not easy to explain to relatives (grandparents, for example) and friends about a child's handicap, but if parents can they often find they get more help that way. Neighbours, friends and relatives may, of course, sometimes not believe parents when they say that the child has a problem doctors cannot cure. This can be exasperating, but in time other people usually come to accept the situation too and can be helpful.

If parents are able to be open and frank with their other children about a handicapped child's problems, most brothers and sisters will not develop emotional disturbance. They will perhaps experience at least occasional feelings of resentment against the child who needs extra attention, but they may also grow up to be more caring people than they otherwise might have been.

Coping with a handicapped child is not just a matter of luck. The people who seem to do best are those who follow certain rules. They deal with problems one at a time rather than allowing themselves to be overwhelmed by a whole mass of difficulties. They use a number of different people to give them information and provide help and support, rather than relying entirely on one person. They are encouraged by small improvements, even when they know that, if the child was without a handicap, progress might be very much faster. They prepare themselves for disappointment as well as success, working out beforehand what they will do, for example, if a particular treatment does not work.

Coping parents of children with handicaps are usually able to talk freely to each other about their feelings and sort out differences of opinion about the best thing to do for their child in a friendly fashion. Divorce rates are *not* higher in parents of handicapped children, though when parents of a handicapped child have marital problems they may argue about the right way to bring him up, just as parents of the non-handicapped may. Having a handicapped child certainly changes your marriage, but it does not need to make it worse, and it may make it better.

Single parents bringing up handicapped children on their own have an especially hard time, and, for them, it is particularly important to be able to use outside help from relatives, friends and professionals.

For all handicaps, except the very rare ones, parent organisations exist, and many of these have local branches. If you have a child with a handicap, you should join one if it is at all possible. You may find it extremely helpful and, if you are one of those really successful copers, you will have a lot to contribute to the organisation and others in it who are less fortunate than you are. A list of addresses is given on pages 673–6.

DEAFNESS AND OTHER SEVERE HEARING PROBLEMS

Deafness is better described as 'hearing loss' or 'hearing impairment'. Only about three in a thousand children in the whole population need a hearing aid because of their moderate or severe hearing loss, but between five and ten in every hundred cannot hear properly at times. This large group of children cannot be described as deaf, but their mild hearing loss may be very important because it may prevent language and communication developing as well as they should.

Mild hearing difficulties are usually caused by 'conductive' loss due to chronic infection or other causes of blockage in the ear. More severe hearing difficulties are usually, but not always, caused by 'sensorineural dysfunction' – the organ of hearing or auditory nerves are damaged or fail to develop properly. Some children just have a hearing loss for high-pitched tones, but even this can be handicapping.

Your child should have regular tests for hearing (see page 342), but even if he has recently passed the test, if you suspect a hearing loss has been present for more than a few days you should seek advice straight away. Hearing losses can come and go, and the child may have developed a hearing loss since the testing was done. Remember that by six months your child should be turning immediately to a voice across the room or to a quiet noise made on either side and, by a year, should be responding to hearing his or her name and to other familiar words. Older children may be noticed to be inattentive or not to respond to requests. Of course this is much more likely to be due to hearing loss if they fail to respond to all requests, rather than just to those you think they might not want to hear!

In some centres, newborn babies' hearing can now be tested with special techniques, for example the 'acoustic cradle', but most routine testing is first carried out at seven to eight months old. If your child is suspected to be deaf after routine testing, then further tests may need to be carried out. Tympanometry, for example, involves putting a tube into the ear and changing the air pressure in the ear canal. The air pressures are measured to give an idea of whether there is a fluid blockage – it is quite painless. This gives a good indication how well the ear itself is working. Older children are tested by formal 'audiometry' with headphones in each ear, but this test is usually too difficult for under-threes.

TREATMENT

Most mild deafness is 'conductive' and due to a problem in the ear itself. It usually settles down on its own but can be successfully treated with medicines or minor surgery (see page 571–2).

Children with more severe hearing losses need a good deal of extra help with their communication from the time their problem is first detected. These children will be helped by hearing aids (see page 344). Parents should make sure they have immediate help from a peripatetic teacher of the deaf, however young the child may be. All local authorities have such teachers. It is important that the deaf child can see the parents' lips and face when they are talking, so that the child can use his eyes as well as what limited hearing he has to help understanding. It is important to remember that in deaf children as in normal children understanding of speech comes before expression.

In more seriously affected children, the teacher will explain about the use of sign languages. There are a number of these available, but the most common are Signed English and Makaton. At one time it was thought that use of sign language might prevent spoken language developing, but most experts now agree that deaf children should be encouraged to communicate in every way possible, including signing. Of course it is important that as many children as possible, not just parents, know what the signs mean. (The child may be helped with a hearing aid: the ear moulds need to be regularly changed as the ear gets bigger – see page 344.)

Frustration at not being able to understand people and express needs can be a major problem in the child with a hearing loss, but parents can do

Communicating by signing

a great deal to reduce this by being aware of the sorts of situation in which the child becomes upset, and paying special attention to the child's needs at those times.

EDUCATION

Children with a permanent hearing loss will be able to go to an ordinary school, a special unit attached to an ordinary school or a special school. The right choice will depend on the seriousness of the child's problem and on what is available locally. Obviously if the child is in an ordinary school, teachers will need to make special arrangements, such as sitting the child in the front of the class. Unless the cause of the hearing loss has also affected the brain, the intelligence of the deaf child is likely to be normal, but difficulties in communication will sometimes result in slow educational progress. Information and reading matter about deaf children can be obtained from the National Deaf Children's Society, or the Royal National Institute for the Deaf (see address section, pages 673–6).

Although the combination of deafness and blindness is not common, there are about 10,000 children and adults in the UK who are deaf and blind. Parents needing advice about this problem can obtain it from the National Deaf-Blind and Rubella Association (Sense) (see address section, pages 673–6).

VISUAL IMPAIRMENT

Total blindness is rare. Of all those registered blind, about 90% have some sort of vision and we should be careful to distinguish between degrees of impairment. A very rough rule of thumb is the distinction between blindness and partial sight: the partially sighted person has a significant visual loss, sufficient to get in the way of some activities, but has enough vision to read normal print, sometimes with the help of magnifying devices. The blind person must use Braille to read.

The causes of visual loss are varied. Sometimes it is inherited, sometimes the result of an illness while the mother is pregnant (*rubella* was the most likely illness to cause this in the UK, but in many countries toxoplasmosis is more common), sometimes there is damage at birth and sometimes the child suffers an accident. There is frequently an associated problem: about half the children registered as blind have an additional disability, one-third being mentally handicapped. One-quarter of all people with partial sight have additional disabilities.

The outlook for the baby born with a visual loss then will depend partly on the extent of the loss and partly on the presence or absence of other problems. With good educational opportunities and a supportive family, the blind child who has no other disabilities can reach the highest levels, both personally and professionally.

Babies born blind or with severe visual impairment will need careful handling, and their parents need support and guidance. In Britain this is available from organisations such as the Royal National Institute for the Blind (see address section, pages 673–6) and their advice should be sought as soon as severe visual loss is detected.

An example of the problems that can arise is the behaviour of very young children when a familiar adult enters the room. Sighted babies may wave arms and legs in all directions, gaze at the adult and be generally rewardingly responsive. Blind babies lie still, presumably so that they can use their hearing to its full effect. This lying still can appear to be 'aloofness' and can put parents off, unless they understand that it is an indication that the baby is trying to find out what is going on.

Other areas of difficulty for the severely visually handicapped include feeding problems (solid, chewy food is often resisted) and sleeping difficulties (a bedtime routine is hard to establish when day and night are not seen as different). All children with loss of sight tend to have a reduced vocabulary – how do you explain the word 'ceiling' to someone who has never seen one?

EDUCATION

Even children who are totally blind will be able to go to school. Educational provision is changing in Britain, especially since the recent movement away from segregated special education. There are schools for the blind and for the partially sighted, but the general trend is to educate children both at home and in normal schools as much as possible.

Much of this section has highlighted problems, yet even total blindness is conquerable. Despite inevitable strains and stresses, many downs as well as ups, blind people without associated problems can hold their own in open employment, they can go on from school to higher education, and can and frequently do lead full, happy lives, with excellent jobs and happy marriages. The world of even the severely visually handicapped may be tough, but it is not necessarily one of devastation.

CEREBRAL PALSY

Cerebral palsy is the name given to conditions in which children have a disorder of movement or posture because the brain has failed to develop properly during the pregnancy or been damaged during pregnancy or at birth. It is 'non-progressive', which means that it does not get worse as the child gets older, though obviously as he grows older and bigger the problems will change. It occurs about twice in every thousand babies.

Children with cerebral palsy may suffer anything from a very mild handicap with slight weakness of one hand to much more severe disability with paralysis of both arms and legs. Although the affected muscles are often floppy in the first year or two of life, they often become 'spastic' or 'stiff'. If just one limb is affected, this is called 'monoplegia'. Children with an arm and a leg affected on the same side are 'hemiplegic'; if both legs are more affected than the arms, this is 'diplegia'; and a child with all four limbs equally affected has 'quadriplegia'.

The condition may be suspected early on because of the presence of abnormalities the paediatrician may discover in examining the newborn baby. More often, however, the baby is slow to hold his head up, or sit and stand, and is thought to be rather more floppy than is usual. As the child gets older, it becomes more obvious that there is something wrong, and, except in mildly affected children, other problems may be revealed.

The fact that the brain is damaged may lead to difficulties in addition to the disorder of movement. There may be mild or severe learning problems. The child may have impairment of vision or hearing, or may develop epilepsy. Despite these problems, there are many positive points about children with cerebral palsy. Although they often have learning difficulties, they may well be brighter than they appear. The difficulties in movement may make it hard for them to communicate their feelings and ideas, but there are now many mechanical and electronic aids to improve not only mobility but also communication, so that frustration can be reduced. This is particularly likely in athetoid cerebral palsy in which the movement problem is one of mobile spasms.

TREATMENT

When a child is diagnosed as having cerebral palsy, it is always important for a full assessment of the child's physical state and abilities to be carried

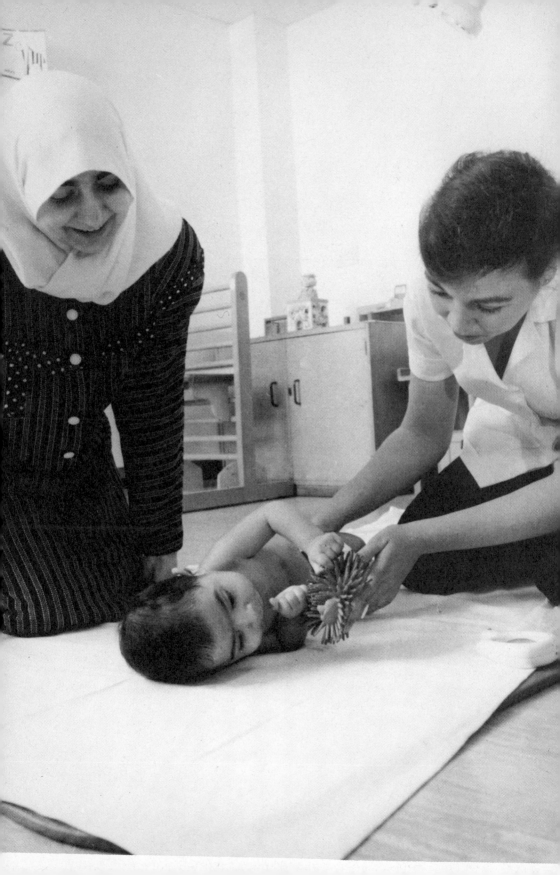

out. This may be done in the paediatric department of a hospital or at a child development centre, often attached to a hospital or part of the Community Child Health Service of the Health District. A number of different specialists, as well as paediatricians, may be involved. Audiologists, physiotherapists, speech therapists, occupational therapists and psychologists are all likely to be able to contribute to an assessment and to advise about the best ways of helping the child to develop as well as possible. It is often difficult for parents to think of ways of helping a child who cannot crawl or walk easily to learn about the world, and these professionals will have experience of how to tackle the problem.

The cerebral palsied child is quite likely to need regular physiotherapy and this should be available locally and will help to make the child more mobile, but, of course, it cannot cure the problem.

Many different methods of treating cerebral palsy have been developed and some are highly intensive. There is no conclusive evidence that the outcome is better in the intensive rather than the traditional regimes that are used in most UK services for children.

EDUCATION

Children with cerebral palsy often have associated learning difficulties, and these may be severe. A number have quite normal ability. Parents, of course, are the people who know the child and his abilities best, but skilled assessment is often helpful to reveal the intelligence present in a severely physically handicapped child.

Whatever their ability, all children are entitled to receive education up to the age of nineteen. For the cerebral palsied child this may begin in a playgroup for normal or handicapped children, in a special unit that may be attached to a child development centre, in a school for the physically handicapped, or in a school for ordinary children. In a good unit, there is ready contact with professionals like physiotherapists and speech therapists, who may work in the school or visit it regularly.

For further information about cerebral palsy you can contact the Spastics Society (see address section, pages 673–6).

SPINA BIFIDA

'When I first knew Caro had spina bifida, I prayed for her to die. But she hung on and now she's three, and I just can't imagine our family without her.'

When a baby has *spina bifida*, it is obvious at birth. There is a swelling in the centre of the back: this may be quite large, and the skin over it may be broken.

The baby's brain and spinal cord grow rapidly during pregnancy. The

Physiotherapy for a baby with cerebral palsy

641

cord is encased in the spinal column or backbone. If the vertebrae making up the backbone do not close completely at the back when they are developing, the child is said to have *spina bifida*. If the defect at the back is large, the covering of the spinal cord or even the spinal cord itself may protrude through the defect. If it is just the sac or bag that protrudes through, and it contains spinal cord lining, this is called a meningocoele. If the cord itself is contained in the sac, then this is a myelomeningocoele. The defect may occur at any level of the spinal column. Wherever it occurs, the cord and nerves below it will be affected, so, broadly speaking, the lower the defect the less the child will be handicapped. In the most common form the defect occurs at a level which affects the nerve supply to the legs, bladder and bowel, producing weakness of the legs and inability to gain control of bowel or bladder.

Another defect that may occur, either alone or with *spina bifida*, arises from obstruction to the circulation of the fluid (cerebrospinal fluid) which fills the brain cavities and drains down into and around the spinal cord. As a result of this blockage, the brain cavities may become enlarged with fluid (hydrocephalus) and the brain tissue may be damaged or destroyed by increased fluid pressure. It may be necessary to put a tube with a valve into the brain to allow the fluid to drain away.

The cause of *spina bifida* is unknown. There is a tendency for it to run in families, and this may be because there is a genetic or inherited factor, or it may be because family members tend to share the same environment.

It is likely, though not absolutely certain, that vitamin deficiency may be one cause. If a mother has had a baby with *spina bifida*, and wishes to become pregnant again, she should consult a doctor about the risk of a recurrence. If she decides to become pregnant, she may be advised to begin a course of specially prescribed vitamins as soon as she stops using birth control methods.

About five in every 2,000 children are born with *spina bifida*, but figures are falling partly because of the increased use of screening. *Spina bifida* can be diagnosed early in pregnancy by an ultrasound scan or by amniocentesis (see chapter 2) by finding raised levels of a chemical substance (alpha-foetoprotein) in samples of blood and the amniotic liquor around the foetus. Knowledge of an affected foetus may lead to discussions about termination of pregnancy.

Children with *spina bifida* will nearly always need special help, for example from physiotherapists, paediatricians, orthopaedic surgeons and urologists, to help them to be as mobile as possible. Depending on where the defect is, some will need wheelchairs, others will be able to get around with callipers or even without any special aids. Development of control of the bowel and bladder may well present problems, but there are a number of techniques that can be used to try and help with this.

TREATMENT

There is no cure for *spina bifida*, but surgery is possible to cover the spine and prevent infection and this means that children can live longer.

Hydrocephalus, however, can be treated by an operation to insert a tube into the brain to drain the fluid – the name for the whole apparatus is a 'shunt', while a valve is part of the apparatus.

EDUCATION

One London survey showed 40% of children with *spina bifida* were at ordinary schools, only needing help with toileting provided the layout of the school was suitable for them to get around. *Spina bifida* children tend to have uneven educational ability so they often learn to read without trouble but find maths very difficult. Like other children with neurological damage they tend to be easily distracted and have poor handwriting. Much depends on the severity of the condition, but some pre-school children need to be seen by a psychologist for assessment and advice about stimulation and further education. Children with hydrocephalus often have a lower IQ, while in those with *spina bifida* but not hydrocephalus the range of intelligence is closer to normal.

LIFESTYLE

This depends on the extent of the impairment – some children have normal intelligence, can walk, although with difficulty, and have less of a problem with incontinence which can usually be greatly helped by modern management. Others are far more profoundly affected in every way.

MUSCULAR DYSTROPHY

This rare condition usually becomes noticeable between the ages of two and five years. The child will usually not learn to run and will have difficulty climbing. The muscles become steadily weaker, and the child's walking is affected, so that he may begin to stumble, fall, or have difficulty with stairs. The most common type, Duchenne muscular dystrophy, which affects only boys, is rapidly progressive, so that, by the age of ten years, most affected boys are in wheelchairs and have a limited life span.

The Duchenne type is inherited, and is a sex-linked recessive condition caused by a defective gene. This means the affected gene may be carried by the mother on one of her two X chromosomes, and only boys are affected (see page 16). If a couple have a boy with the condition, the mother may carry the gene, in which case there is a 50% chance of any subsequent boys being affected, but no girls will be affected. In some cases the abnormal gene may arise in the boy alone as a 'mutation', in which case the risk is different. Genetic counselling in this situation involves discovering if the mother is a carrier, and if so, offering intra-uterine detection and possibly termination of an affected pregnancy.

Another sex-linked form of muscular dystrophy which is milder and rarer than Duchenne is known as Becker dystrophy. Limb-girdle and facio-scapulo-humeral muscular dystrophies are also milder, and are inherited in a different manner.

If increasing difficulty in walking is occurring, the family doctor will probably refer the child to a paediatrician or neurologist who will examine him. A blood test will be carried out to check whether there is an excess of a chemical substance that circulates when muscle tissue is being destroyed.

TREATMENT

Sadly, there is no known cure for muscular dystrophy, but the course that the disease takes is well known and from the time of diagnosis parents have to plan for the future, which will eventually include a wheelchair and the need for special education. Management, as with all handicaps, splits into the physical and the psychological problems – both of which need advice and sympathetic help from specialists in contact with the family. A reasonably controlled diet is important so that obesity does not become an added burden.

EDUCATION

Most young children with the condition will be able to attend normal playgroup, nursery and infant school. A special school becomes necessary once the muscles waste so that movement is severely affected, and in addition there is an overall reduction of intelligence by about twenty IQ points.

LIFESTYLE

> 'When we were told our son had muscular dystrophy, we really had no idea what it meant. The consultant was very sympathetic, but very frank. At the time it seemed cruel because what he had to tell us was so horrifying to take in, but as time went on I was glad he had been honest from the start.'

Parents of a child with progressive muscular dystrophy do have a hard time, as indeed do their children. All the same, there is much that can be done. One couple with two sons with the condition were plunged initially into a state of severe shock and grief. After a couple of years they began to accept the situation, and from that point some positive action was possible. Neither had ever travelled abroad, but when the mother took a cleaning job at the boys' school this enabled them to save for holidays abroad, which all four have enjoyed to the full. Their father put it like this: 'As their lives will be limited, we want to pack in as much as we can, so that when we look back we will never say "If only", but rather "Didn't we have good times." ' Parents may often find it easier to cope with their own distressed feelings if they can share them with each other, as well as with relatives, friends and sometimes professionals. As with parents of children with other physical handicaps, it will often be helpful to learn more about the condition and perhaps, at some stage, meet other parents of affected children. For further information, contact the Muscular Dystrophy Group of Great Britain and Northern Ireland (see address section, pages 673–6).

SEVERE LEARNING DIFFICULTIES – MENTAL HANDICAP

Inevitably, some babies and toddlers will develop faster than others. This will be true not just of the speed with which their bodies grow, but also of the rate at which they develop in their language and in the co-ordination of their movements. Some will be quick to speak and understand, others will be slow. Some will be quick to walk and able to undress and dress themselves; for others this will take longer. The speed of development of a baby or toddler does not allow us to predict how intelligent he will be when he grows into a schoolchild, and gives no indication at all of how bright he will be as an adult. But if a child is very slow to develop in the early years, there may be something wrong with the way his brain is working and, of course, this will mean that he is likely, perhaps in some cases certain, to have learning difficulties later on. This is particularly true for language development. While children who are slow, even sometimes very slow, to walk often do well later unless they have some reason (such as cerebral palsy, see page 639) to explain their slowness, a high proportion of children who are slow to understand and talk, who are not, for example, speaking in little two- or three-word sentences by the age of three years, will have definite learning difficulties in school, and some of them will have severe learning problems or be mentally handicapped.

CAUSES OF MENTAL HANDICAP

About three in every thousand children have severe learning difficulties or mental handicap. There are numerous causes, but nearly always there is something wrong with the way the brain has developed, and some degree of brain malfunction (dysfunction) or even brain damage is present. Usually this has occurred because of an inherited condition, a problem that has been present from the time the egg was fertilised. The most common of these by far is Down's syndrome (mongolism, see page 647), which alone accounts for about one in three of all children with mental handicap. Other, less common, genetic causes account for a further one in seven, so altogether over half of mental handicap is caused in this way. About one in ten mentally handicapped children have had damage to the brain at birth, and another one in ten have had an illness or injury to the brain after birth. Then, in quite a high proportion, about one in four, the cause is unknown.

HOW DOES MENTAL HANDICAP FIRST SHOW ITSELF?

Sometimes it is obvious at birth that a child is probably going to have some degree of mental handicap. This is true of Down's syndrome and children born with very small heads (microcephaly). Sometimes, however, the baby will appear normal at birth, and only gradually, perhaps not until the age of two or three years, will it become obvious that the child is developing very slowly. Often it is the child being very slow to speak that suggests there is a real problem, but the child with mental handicap is also likely to be slow to respond socially with smiles, gurgles and babbling in the first year of life. If the birth has been very difficult, it may have resulted in brain damage, but it is important to remember that most children who have difficult births grow up to be perfectly normal later on.

WHAT CAN BE DONE ABOUT MENTAL HANDICAP?

If your child is one of those thought to be normal after birth, but suspected possibly of having mental handicap because of very slow development, it will first be necessary to check on the actual stage of development of your child in a number of different areas. Your health visitor or family doctor will be able to work out with you whether your child is just a bit slow to develop, which presents no great problem, or whether there is a real cause for worry. Asking you questions about what your baby can do, and checking progress out for themselves as far as possible will be the way they do this. If your child is definitely slow, you will be referred to a paediatrician who will repeat the process and, if he confirms that your child is indeed slow to develop, he will probably carry out blood and urine tests as well as X-rays to see if it is possible to establish a cause. Unfortunately it is most unusual to find a definite cause that is treatable, but all the same it is important to find one if possible, because there may be genetic implications – a risk that you may have further affected children, for example.

All this sounds very clear-cut, but often the process of diagnosis is much more blurred. There may well be a period of one or two years when mental handicap is suspected, but no one can be sure. Some children are very slow to develop in the first two or three years, but then pick up, while in others the presence of mental handicap becomes much more obvious.

Inevitably this realisation will be a time of great sadness and disappointment, and you will need to share your feelings with your partner, with other members of your family, with friends and with the professionals who are trying to help you. You may well have angry feelings as well as being sad and worried. These feelings may stay with you for weeks or months, and may keep coming back over the years, but you should try to make sure they do not prevent you from getting on with the business of helping your mentally handicapped child to develop as best he or she can.

Children with severe learning difficulties or mental handicap *can* learn – but they take longer and need a good deal more help. Almost certainly, a child with mental handicap will be doing more on his fourth birthday than on his third, more on his fifth than on his fourth and so on. Progress may be slow, but it does occur. If possible it is better to check on progress by comparing your child with how he was a year or so ago than by comparing him with other children of the same age who do not have mental handicap.

If your child has mental handicap, the paediatrician will refer you to other professionals, such as a psychologist and a speech therapist, who will work in partnership with you to promote the development of your child. In these early years, they may arrange for you to work with someone who uses the Portage system – a way of promoting development by setting targets within the child's reach. If your child has particular communication difficulties, he may be helped by using a system of communication by signs, such as Makaton. There may be a special assessment or child development unit you can attend locally where you can meet other parents with children with similar problems and be given more intensive help.

It is especially important that your child gets regular checks of vision and hearing, because children with mental handicap are particularly prone to have sensory difficulties.

As time goes on, and certainly before the age of five years, if it is clear your child is mentally handicapped and has severe learning difficulties, there will need to be a plan to meet his special educational needs. In the UK, this involves a number of professionals co-ordinated by the educational psychologist pooling their opinions and, with your help, making a 'statement' to describe the schooling your child requires. You can get further information from MENCAP (Royal Society for Mentally Handicapped Children and Adults – see address section, pages 673–6).

DOWN'S SYNDROME

Down's syndrome is the largest single cause of mental handicap and is due to a chromosomal disorder. Normally we have 23 pairs of chromosomes (see chapter 1), but Down's children have an extra chromosome – in the great majority of cases this is a third chromosome alongside at position 21. The medical name for this condition is trisomy 21, meaning there are three number 21 chromosomes at the 21 position. In the remaining Down's children there is an abnormal rearrangement of chromosomes. Trisomy may be present but only in some cells, a condition which is called mosaicism. This mistake in cell division is more likely in older women, though we do not understand why this is. One child in 700 is a Down's baby, but the risk begins to rise with a mother who is over the age of 35 years, so that by 38 years the figure is more likely to be one in 200.

Down's syndrome is named after the Victorian doctor, John Langdon Down, who first identified the condition. For a long time it was known as

647

mongolism, though this term has fallen into disrepute now and is no longer used. Down's babies are nearly always identified at birth because although they may be very attractive there are distinct physical characteristics: slanting eyes with folds of skin along the lids to the inner corner (epicanthic folds), a wide bridge to the nose, as well as short, stubby toes and fingers, distinctive creases on palms and soles and a large tongue. Down's babies tend to be rather floppy and to grow slowly, so they tend to be short in height. Some Down's babies have heart or intestinal abnormalities which need correcting with surgery. They tend to suffer from infections, especially bronchitis, more than other children.

If your child is diagnosed as having Down's syndrome at birth or shortly afterwards, the paediatrician will see both parents together to break the news as soon as possible. He will also tell you if your baby has been found to have any other problems. Inevitably, the news will be extremely upsetting and, as with parents of other children with mental handicap, you will probably find it helpful to share your feelings with others.

In fact, the range of ability shown by Down's syndrome babies is quite wide. All will have learning difficulties, but while with some this will mean that they are only able to express themselves poorly with a few words in simple sentences, with others it will be possible for education to occur in an ordinary school when the child will fit in with other children of lesser ability. Progress in the first year or two of life is often very encouraging, and after this it gradually becomes clearer to what degree the baby with Down's syndrome will be limited in ability. For further information on promoting ability in the handicapped, see pages 646–7.

Many children with Down's syndrome are placid and lovable – a very few are noisy and boisterous. As he gets older it will gradually become clear to you what sort of personality your Down's syndrome child has – as with other children, you will probably find characteristics you love, and others of which you are less fond!

You can get further information from the Down's Children's Association (see address section, pages 673–6).

AUTISM

Although autism is not a form of mental handicap, quite a high proportion of children with autism do show mental handicap in addition, so the problem is described here.

Autism was first described by an American child psychiatrist, Leo Kanner, in 1943. Children who develop the condition may have it from birth, or it may occur after a period of normal or near-normal development for up to the first two or three years. Boys are affected about four times as commonly as girls.

If the baby has the problem from birth, he will usually be born after a normal pregnancy and delivery. He may be rather unresponsive in the first

A Down's syndrome child can fit happily into family life

few months of life, not showing much interest in you or his surroundings, but being quite happy to be fed and looked after. Towards the end of his first year, it will become more obvious that things are not going well. He may babble a little or not at all. He may dislike being cuddled and seem to prefer to lie in his cot. When you try to look at him he may, as if deliberately, turn his face away (gaze avoidance). He may spend a lot of time looking at his hands. In the second and third year of life, his language delay may become more obvious. He will probably be very slow to understand and to speak, so that it is quite likely he will not be speaking even in single words by the age of three years. In contrast, he is likely to have walked at an early age, and he may be quite good at doing puzzles, like table jigsaws, or posting shapes. By this point he will often have developed fixed patterns of behaviour he hates to have disturbed, getting very upset if his routines are put out.

His way of relating to other people, including his parents, may be odd and unusual. If he wants something, rather than asking or pointing, he may, for example, just take the adult by the hand and lead to where he wants to go. If language does develop, it may be rather slow and mechanical. The child may also echo back things said to him. Normal children do this too, but usually only for brief periods while they are learning to speak. The child with autism is likely to have 'mannerisms' – particular habits like jumping up and down and flapping his hands when excited, putting his hands in front of his eyes and waving them repeatedly, or gazing at his hands while he moves them in front of his face.

A child with autism is likely to be referred by the family doctor to a paediatrician who will check to see if there is a known physical cause and then probably refer him on to a psychologist or psychiatrist. In fact, in most cases, a cause is not detectable, but there is good evidence that the problem is not caused by anything the parents have done but by a dysfunction in the brain. In many cases this is likely to be caused by one of a number of faulty genes (see page 13), but it is unusual to be able to pinpoint exactly the nature of the error in the genes.

Children with autism are, not surprisingly in view of their problems, very difficult to make a relationship with, and parents often find it helpful to talk to a psychologist or psychiatrist to work out ways they can deal best with their child. There may be an associated degree of mental handicap, but, in any case, attendance at a child development centre or child assessment centre where there are a number of children with severe learning difficulties present is very likely to be useful. Parents of children with autism are likely to benefit from the sort of help provided for the mentally handicapped, but they will need extra help with their child's behaviour problems.

Education As with other children with learning difficulties, as the child nears school age, it will be necessary to work out a 'statement' of his educational needs with local professionals and the local education authority. This will almost certainly involve the need for a good deal of individual attention and for teachers experienced in educating children with communication difficulties and severe behaviour problems.

The outlook for children with autism depends on the severity of the condition and on whether some degree of mental handicap is also present. Unfortunately, quite a high proportion of children with autism will persist in having serious difficulties in communication and problems in their social relationships. Autistic children change but do not 'grow out of' their condition. Sadly, many will need extra care, and will find it difficult to cope independently even after they leave school.

Further information is available from the National Autistic Society (see address section, pages 673–6).

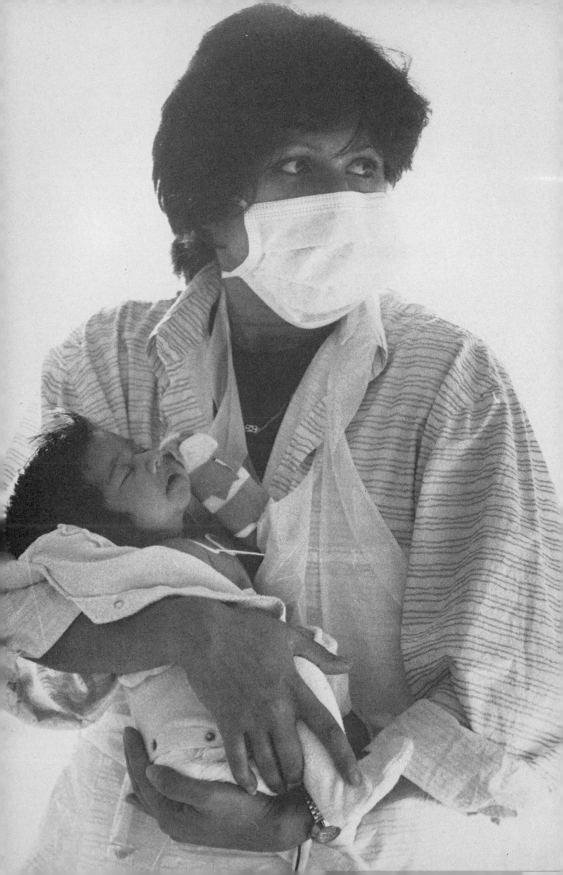

Chapter 20

CHILDREN IN HOSPITAL

Preparing children for a hospital stay   Operations   Who's who in
hospital   Common hospital procedures   Staying or visiting?
Breastfed babies   How parents can help   Looking after
yourself   Coming home

Every year one in four children under five years old goes into hospital, and
more than two million children are seen in accident and emergency units.
So the chances that you will have to take a child to hospital are,
unfortunately, quite high — especially if you have more than one child.
Obviously we would all prefer our children not to be frightened by a
hospital visit. It is encouraging to know that many children cope with
hospital with a sort of casual aplomb we only wish we could manage
ourselves, and some of them actually enjoy the experience.

How your child reacts to a hospital visit will depend especially on his
age, personality, the reason he is in hospital, the way he is admitted, his
previous experience of hospitals, the investigations and treatment he
needs, the attitude and manner of medical and nursing staff, the atmosphere in the hospital and on the ward, and, of course, on your own
anxieties and how well you are able to cope with what is often a very
worrying situation.

It is easy to see how these features can combine to make a hospital visit
less likely or more likely to be upsetting. The first six you cannot change
but you can learn to allow for them. The last three you can sometimes
change for the better. Every child will react differently, but usually
children between one and four years old are most vulnerable when it
comes to hospital visits. This is because they are aware of what is
happening yet not able to understand it all. They are also less likely to have
stayed away from home before or been separated from their parents.

It is more difficult to know how babies under a year old react to
hospitals, but this is an important time when the bond between mother
and baby is still being formed. We do know that babies often behave
differently when their routine is changed; staying with your baby and
keeping as much as possible of his life the same will help. Looking after
very young babies in special care units presents different problems, which
we have talked about in chapter 5.

If your child has already visited or stayed in hospital, what he felt about it will colour the way he handles another visit. If it was distressing or frightening, then think why that was and do what you can to change things – if your child is old enough tell him how and why it can be better.

Do not forget young children pick up all sorts of ideas about what happens in hospitals without ever having been a patient. Visiting mummy after the birth of a new baby is a very common experience for children under five. If all they know about hospital is the inside of a maternity unit full of little babies in plastic boxes on wheels, and if they have been told that is where they were born too, then hearing they have to go to hospital can fill them with mixed ideas. Visiting sick adults in hospital can also leave misleading or worrying impressions, or simply hearing that someone they knew died in hospital can have the same effect. As one mother recalled:

> '*My mother died in hospital when Lucy was just two. She did come with me once to see her granny and I suppose she realised I was very upset when we got the news of her death soon afterwards. Then a year later she had to go into hospital herself to have her tonsils out. I don't know if it was the hospital smell or the sight of the nurses, but when we got there she got very quiet and clingy and eventually said, "I won't have to go to heaven, will I?"*'

Your own attitude to hospital and medical treatment will certainly affect your child's attitude. Parents have a vital role in helping children through what is bound to be an unusual experience for them. You can only carry out that job by staying with your child as much as possible and by giving him the right kind of preparation.

PREPARING CHILDREN FOR A HOSPITAL STAY

Ask most two- to four-year-olds in hospital why they are there and they may well say they feel fine, and there is nothing wrong with them. From their point of view there is no need to be there at all. Small children may find it very difficult to make the connection between a series of sore throats in the past and an operation to have their tonsils out now. Many conditions do not make children feel bad at all – like squints or middle ear problems which may cause loss of hearing. So do not assume your child understands why he is going to hospital from past trips to the doctor – spell it out in simple terms.

WHEN TO TELL YOUR CHILD

It is probably best to mention the subject first after visiting the doctor or hospital where the decision was made. It is less likely at that point to seem like something you have decided out of the blue. Small children have little idea of the passage of time, so tell them at the same time that going into hospital will not happen for a long time and that you will tell them all about it when the hospital writes to you telling you when they have a bed free.

WHILE YOU WAIT

In the intervening time get hold of a few books about hospital visits which will mean something to your child at his age and read them with him once or twice – without necessarily talking directly about his visit, but just about hospitals as places where children go to be made better. If your child asks specifically about his visit then answer questions honestly, but do not burden him with too much information. Most common questions tend to be 'Will you stay with me?' and 'Will it hurt?' If you cannot stay with him or do not know yet whether you will be able to, do not lie. Say something on the lines that you do not know yet, but if they haven't a bed you will stay with him until he is asleep – only you can decide exactly what is best to say to your own child. On the question of pain, again, do not lie and say something will not hurt if you know it will. It is better to tell him that it may hurt for a little but then it will be over. Try to say in very simple terms why it needs to be done to stress the positive side so he does not feel it is just being done for the purpose of hurting him.

BE WELL INFORMED

Find out for yourself as much as you can about what will happen to your child so that you know in advance about anything which might upset him. Nearer the time of the visit you can tell him in a bit more detail what will happen – but again in very simple terms. Like adults, children vary in how much they want to know. If they are old enough to understand, tell them a day or so before they go into hospital some of the simple things which will happen, especially details of the admission procedures (see page 663). Often children can be put out by little things like having to pass urine into a special sort of bottle or pot to give a urine sample or sit on scales with a chair to be weighed. This is usually because they are generally confused, bewildered and anxious, and think almost everything is potentially hurtful. Procedures like blood tests which might worry a child are best not described in detail until shortly before you have to deal with them.

Before you go into hospital, describe to your child, with the help of picture books, what the hospital will be like. Most children find the idea of having their own locker beside their bed rather attractive – talk about what you can put in there. Talk about the doctors, nurses and other people. Even very small children can understand that some of them are also mummies and daddies with children at home and the hospital is where they come to work rather like their own daddy or mummy or other relatives they know who go off to work. This is often a very reassuring

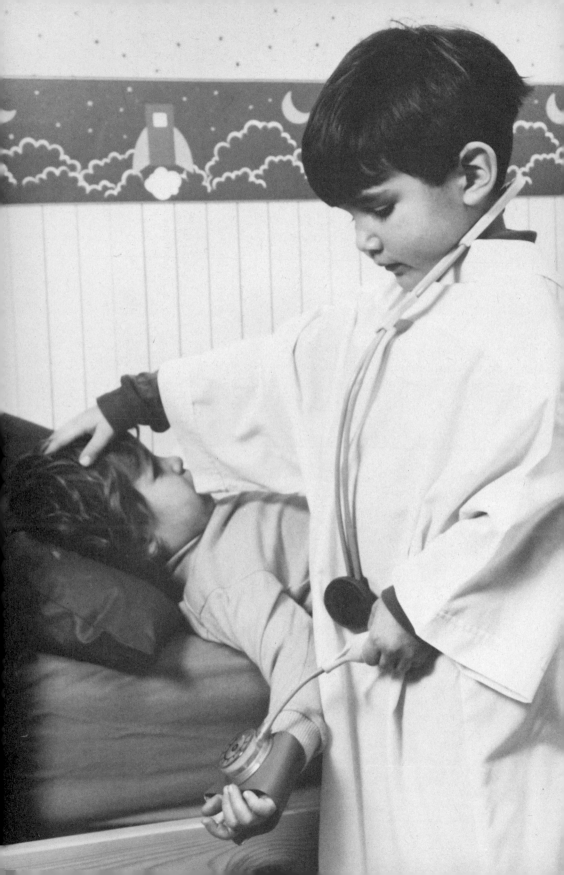

idea. Explain that hospitals have to stay open all the time so nurses and doctors have to take turns working all night as well as all day. Tell them that lights stay on all night in the wards and there is always someone there to look after them.

How much very little children — say from one- to two-and-a-half years old — can understand in advance is very variable. But do not forget their understanding of language is far in advance of what they can actually say. Good, realistic pictures of hospital wards and nurses are invaluable in helping them understand something of where they are going. Most libraries have a selection, or you can look in your local bookshop if you want to invest in one or two.

PACKING

Most children enjoy packing a little suitcase or bag to take to hospital. Children usually regress when they are feeling ill or in unusual surroundings, so choose toys and books that are on the young side and not too taxing. Steer them away from very precious toys which might easily be broken, because one of the enjoyments of life on the ward is showing other children what they have brought with them. Make sure favourite comforters, like blankets, bits of special clothing, toys, dummies or whatever, are taken along, plus a spare if possible. This is definitely not the time to start thinking that your child is far too old to have a dummy, bottle, cup with a lid or to be in nappies. Do not be embarrassed and think it will reflect badly on you because they are too old and should be beyond this stage. All children have habits which parents think perhaps they should have grown out of, but this is a time to put your child's security before your own feelings so make sure you take everything he could want if he was at home.

Playing at being in hospital can help older children — especially three- to five-year-olds. Use play to bring in some of the facts about the operation, like the face mask and hats that theatre staff have to wear. Blue J-cloths are the best material from which to manufacture some realistic theatre headgear for dressing up. Old pyjama tops, stripy shirts and plain white shirts can be used for 'uniforms'. Children very often hate putting on the theatre gown. If you can get the idea across in play that the patient puts on a back-to-front white gown to keep clean too — maybe by dressing teddy up — it might help.

Do not spend a fortune on an expensive doctor's set. You will be annoyed if your child is not interested! For young children a cardboard box with a big red cross and a string handle packed with things like bandages, a syringe (cake-icer), medicine (plastic bottle with label stuck on), plastic scissors and perhaps your eyebrow tweezers will provide as much fun. Even a 'stethoscope' can be made out of a length of plastic clothes line with a cotton reel. Friends and toy libraries can also be a source of doctor's equipment. Your child might like to take his medical kit in to show off to the nurses as well.

OPERATIONS

If your child is going into hospital for an operation give him some realistic idea what to expect, regardless of his age. For most children the essential facts are that they put on a special gown like the doctors' white coats to keep them clean, have something to make them sleepy and are taken on a trolley to the operating room where nurses and doctors wear specially clean clothes (often green or white), hats and masks. Then they will be given something to make them go right to sleep until it is all over. When they wake up they will be back in the ward with you. They may feel a bit sore, but they will soon begin to get better. The younger the child the simpler this version becomes. Obviously you have to be the best judge of exactly what to say, but do not deliberately mislead your child and do make sure you prepare your child however young he may be. It may seem silly to talk to babies, but many mothers find it reassuring themselves when they tell a baby what is going to happen. The precise details of what happens on the day of the operation depend on the consultant, the anaesthetist, the type of operation, the age of the child and hospital practice.

Some hospitals allow parents to cross the red line which marks the beginning of the sterile area in the operating theatre and go with their child into the anaesthetic room. This will mean putting on theatre clothes yourself. Other hospitals do not let parents go with their child to the theatre so you need to say goodbye to them on the ward. Generally hospitals have set rules about this, but if you want to go into the anaesthetic room with your child, the senior nurse on the ward and the anaesthetist are the people to ask.

Before the operation an anaesthetist – if possible the one who will be giving the anaesthetic – will come round and see your child. Tell your child that this is the person who is going to send him to sleep so he does not know anything about the operation, but warn him that when they meet in the theatre again the anaesthetist will look different because he/she will be dressed in special theatre clothes with a hat and a mask hanging round the neck. Most children who are old enough to understand find it reassuring to have 'met' the anaesthetist in more normal circumstances and discover she is just an ordinary-looking person outside the theatre. You can ask the anaesthetist how the pre-med and the anaesthetic will be given and this will help you to prepare your child for what to expect and to answer his questions.

The pre-med is an important part of the operating procedure since your child is fully awake and aware, and it is often what is remembered most about the whole event. One six-year-old, confident of her facts, gave this description of her operation to her fellow patients: 'Do you know what having an operation means? It means having a pin in your bum, that's what.' The pre-med can be given by an injection or as medicine to be swallowed. What is prescribed for your child depends on the child's weight, age and the type of operation he is to undergo, as well as the practice of the particular anaesthetist. Exactly how the anaesthetic is given down in the anaesthetic room also depends on the individual circumstances for that child and on the practice of the anaesthetist. Generally children are sent to sleep with gas initially. Many anaesthetists do not put a mask over the child's face but hold the end of the pipe in their hand, cupped in front of the child's face. If you think your child would cope better with an injection, it is reasonable to ask the anaesthetist if this is possible. Again, you must accept their judgement – if your child does not have very prominent veins for example, repeated attempts to insert the needle could cause more distress.

Before your child has his operation he will see other children putting on operating gowns and being wheeled off on trolleys so he will have some idea of what to expect. Hopefully he will not have seen other children crying because such upset can be highly contagious. If he does and he is old enough, you might try to counter this by telling him the other child is crying because he does not understand what is happening – unlike your own child, of course! A number of children hate taking their own things off and putting the operating gown on – some hospitals insist on paper knickers too. Other hospitals are changing this routine and allow children to wear their own pyjama trousers or loose-fitting nightdresses, and parents or nurses to carry them to the theatre instead of using a trolley. You can ask the consultant about this. If your child does have to wear a gown but objects, try suggesting it is like the doctor's white coat, or like the ones the bigger children on the ward wear, or is like putting a sheet on, or whatever you think might win him over. Children probably get upset at this point because it signals the start of events leading to the operation, and because they feel vulnerable and worried out of their own clothes and in something so strange. It may help if you can have an enticing book to offer to read him once he has changed – it can distract him and reassure him that he is not about to be whisked away.

While waiting for the pre-med to take effect, do whatever you can to help him settle down and relax – this may mean reading him something soothing and familiar, singing to him (if you have the confidence in a busy ward!), or stroking his hair. If he does begin to doze off, do not leave until you have seen him safely on to the trolley. If your child does get upset, only you can decide whether it is better for you to let the nursing staff take over or to stay. One mother described such a scene:

'I was dreading the moment when they came to take my son to the theatre. He was dozing lightly but opened his eyes if I let go of his hand. When the trolley did arrive he fulfilled all my worst fears by springing up and wrapping his arms in a tight grip round my neck and crying. The nurses said I'd better go and as I honestly didn't have a hope of calming him, I went into the sister's office where I watched through the window. The minute I left he lay down on the trolley and stopped crying. I think he was just panicking over the moment of parting. He was wheeled past

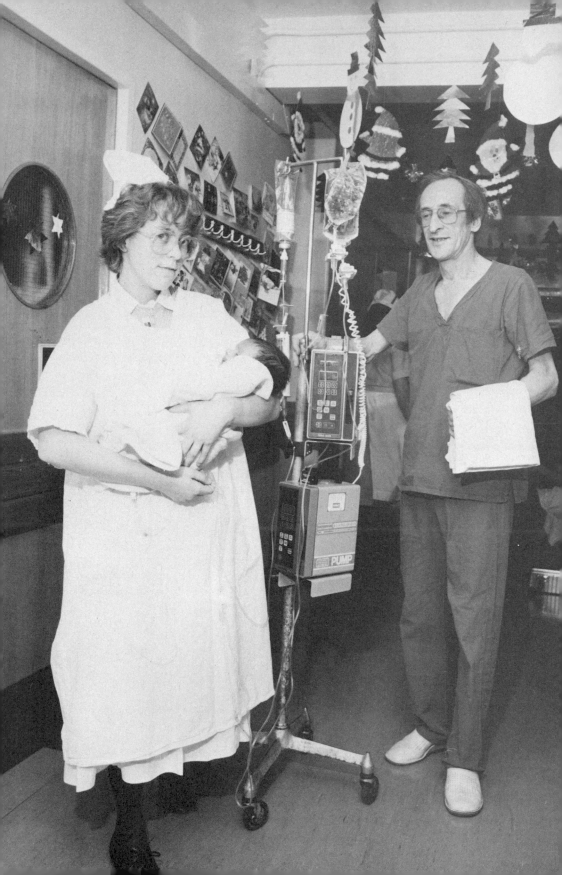

me sucking his thumb with his eyes closed and clutching his blanket.'

It is usually a good idea to send a favoured teddy, blanket or other comforter down on the trolley – if possible labelled. Some theatre staff send toys back with the appropriate bandages to match the owners'!

WHILE YOUR CHILD IS IN THEATRE

The nurses will be able to tell you roughly how long your child will be in the theatre. Afterwards the child will also spend some time in the recovery room where his condition is carefully monitored. It is a good idea to get away from the ward for a coffee or a walk even if you find it hard to think of anything else, because there will be many hours ahead when you need to sit by your child's bedside. When your child comes back to the ward hold his hand and tell him it is over and you are staying with him. He may be in pain or feeling sick, and the nurses will tell you how to help. Often just soothing and reassuring him that it will get better, stroking or holding his hand is the most important job and the kind that only a parent can do.

WHO'S WHO IN HOSPITAL

DOCTORS

Consultant	Will be addressed as Mr if he is a surgeon and Dr if a physician. Each consultant has his own team of doctors working under him and generally sets the practice and tone of that team.
Senior Registrar	Next in seniority and can also carry the title of Mr or Dr.
Registrar	Very likely to see your child on the ward and either he, the senior registrar or consultant will carry out the operation.
Houseman	Does most of the routine work on the ward. These are doctors who are usually attached to a team for about six months at a time before they specialise in hospital work or train to be family doctors.
Medical Students	Will be found on the wards in a teaching hospital.

You will probably be dealing with the houseman and possibly the registrar on the ward, but if you are worried about your child's progress, condition or treatment you can ask the ward sister to arrange an appointment to see

A baby being carried to the operating theatre

the consultant. Do not be shy to ask if you do not understand exactly what your child is having done and why. Often nursing staff who may have more time and appear less intimidating, can help. When doctors or nurses ask your child questions, do not butt in and answer for them. This is actually their way of making friends with your child as well as of getting information.

NURSES

District Nursing Officer	Responsible for a group of hospitals.
Director of Nursing Services	In charge of all nurses in one particular hospital — used to be known as 'Matron'. This is the person to write to if you want to enlist nursing support to get a practice changed.
Nursing Officer	Responsible for a number of units or wards.
Ward Sister or Charge Nurse	In charge of that particular ward.
Staff Nurse	Next in line.
Student Nurse Nursery Nurse Auxiliary Nurse Health Care Assistant	Involved in a variety of routine day-to-day nursing duties under supervision.

Nurses can be of tremendous help and support to families who have children in hospital. and very many do well beyond what might be expected. If you want information go to the most senior nurse on duty — usually the ward sister, charge nurse or staff nurse. If something is wrong and you want to speak to one of the doctors, tell her first as well. Although this is not yet the case, all nurses working with children should have had specialist training, and at least the sister heading a children's ward should be a trained children's nurse. Nurses especially trained to look after children are called Registered Sick Children's Nurses.

These days, most children's wards have a playleader or play specialist who will work with you to keep your child occupied, as well as to help with understanding and overcoming his or her anxieties. Make sure you meet them, and tell them what your child likes doing, and if you have any worries about how he is going to settle in hospital. For older children who are well enough to benefit, the hospital school teacher will provide further stimulation.

There are a number of other people who may play a very important part in diagnosing what is wrong with your child and helping him to get better. These include speech therapists, physiotherapists and psychologists. Do try and be present when they come to see your child at least for the first time, so that you can answer questions and help them with their investigations and treatment.

COMMON HOSPITAL PROCEDURES

Admission The admission procedure usually involves a doctor taking a history of your child's health plus details about family history. Your child will get a name tag with a hospital number and the name of his consultant, be weighed and perhaps measured and asked for a urine sample. Children having operations usually, but not always, have a blood test. Pulse and temperature taking happen regularly – this is usually done by holding the thermometer under their armpit.

X-rays Parents are usually allowed into the X-ray rooms of hospitals, but women who think they may be pregnant should not stay because of the risk that X-rays may harm the foetus. If you are asked to hold your child in a particular position then hold him firmly. When the radiographer moves the X-ray tube into position you can reassure your child that it will not come near him because X-rays are taken at not less than three feet distant except for teeth X-rays. There is no radiation in the room except at the moment the exposure button is pressed. X-ray rooms can often look a bit intimidating with all their equipment, but tell your child this is just to take a special kind of photograph and will not hurt.

Painful procedures Having dressings changed or applied, stitches, injections and blood tests are all examples of things which happen commonly on wards or in accident units. Young children usually have to be held but there is no reason why the holder should not be the parent unless he or she would be made upset. A small child who is already hurt who is taken away from his parents is likely to get upset even before anything more happens. You can cuddle and speak to him at the same time as keeping a firm grip. Parents should also realise that if a child cannot be calmed or something needs doing urgently, it is better to get it over with quickly rather than prolong the agony. Often to make sure children keep still they are wrapped in a blanket to hold their limbs still, but again you can ask to be the one who holds them.

Plaster of Paris This is nearly always put on under anaesthetic when the fractured limb is fixed in position, but children can be frightened of the tiny saw which is used to take the plaster off when the limb is healed.

STAYING OR VISITING?

STAYING WITH YOUR CHILD IN HOSPITAL

Try imagining a stay or a visit to hospital through the eyes of a young child. Being left with people he does not know in unfamiliar surroundings is

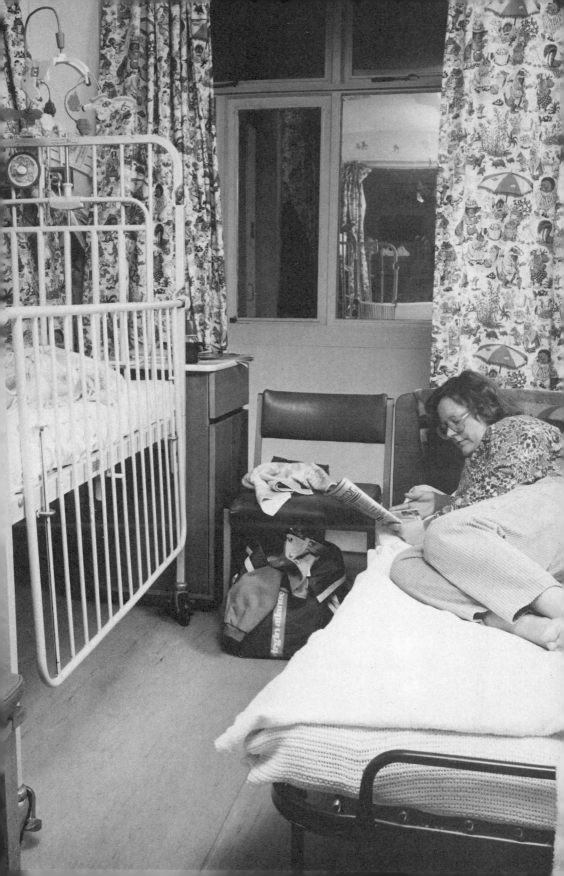

quite a test for a child who may even never have stayed at playgroup or spent a day at school. Then add the occurrence of a routine hospital procedure like temperature taking; even this can be alarming to a child too young to understand what is happening. He needs mum or dad on hand to comfort, explain and reassure.

Unfortunately, some hospitals still have restrictions about parents staying or visiting. This may take the form of difficulties about staying the night, set visiting hours or parents not allowed to help with mealtimes. Sometimes parents are still excluded from wards during doctors' rounds. But in very many cases parents only have to ask to be allowed to stay with their children. Knowing you can ask, making your request in the right way, being confident that your request is reasonable and going on to show medical staff that as a parent you can help and make their job easier, will not only make your child's stay better but also pave the way for other parents. If your child's visit to hospital is planned, then ask the consultant who makes the decision about hospital treatment at the time of the consultation. Check again with the booking office when details come through that they are expecting you to stay. If a consultant is adamant that you cannot stay or visit as much as you feel you need to, or the hospital restricts parental access in a way you think you would find difficult, you can ask to be referred to another hospital. However, this may mean waiting longer for a bed. Your GP is the person to refer you and he, or possibly your local branch of the National Association for the Welfare of Children in Hospital (see address section, pages 673–6), can give advice about hospitals with a different policy.

If your child is admitted through an accident and emergency unit then obviously there is no opportunity to pick a hospital. If you want to stay, tell the doctor who makes the decision to admit your child – in general it is best to make such requests to the most senior member of staff involved. As with most requests you will be more likely to succeed if you can be polite and reasonable while remaining confident and determined – not necessarily easy if you are feeling shaken and anxious because your child has been injured or taken ill suddenly. But if you are in a very emotional state it may sometimes appear to the hospital staff they will have two patients to deal with, instead of one.

Some hospitals try to arrange beds for parents to stay or even mattresses on the floor, otherwise they may be happy for you to stay in a chair beside your child's bed. Some hospitals again have space for parents but away from their child's ward – in other wards, flats, houses and so on. This can be very valuable for the families of children who are staying in hospital for some time or have travelled from far away. It is important to realise that the sort of help you get and the kind of relationship your child enjoys with hospital staff depends not only on the policy of the hospital or a ward, but very much on individual staff themselves. There is no such thing as a typical children's ward. In hospitals not renowned for their relaxed attitude, parents have met doctors and nurses who go out of their way to help. And unfortunately it is sometimes possible to meet a less than sympathetic attitude in hospitals which have a name for welcoming parents.

Sometimes children may be nursed on adult wards and this is more likely if they are in specialist wards like ear, nose and throat units. It is important that the children have proper provision to allow them to play, and free access for parents. If this is not the case, remember that you can ask for your child to be moved to a general children's ward instead.

IF YOU CANNOT STAY WITH YOUR CHILD

Quite apart from the hospital's policy, there may be many reasons why parents find it hard to stay with their child in hospital all the time. They often feel torn between the child in hospital and the demands of other young children at home. Generally, your priority should be for the child in hospital at least for the first few days; children at home may miss you but their life is continuing along reasonably familiar lines and they are not having to cope with medical procedures or feeling ill. A child in hospital has a great deal to cope with and separation from you should be kept to a minimum. If you do not have a partner who can take time off to look after children at home, would a relative or friend help? The local social services department or the social worker at the hospital may be able to help with back-up services or details of home helps, family care workers, day nurseries, child minders and after school centres. If you really cannot stay or visit very much, can you ask a relative or a friend who knows your child well to do so instead? Many hospitals can offer help with the cost of fares or lifts to the hospital if your child is to be in for some time – the ward sister, hospital social worker, or local group of the National Association for the Welfare of Children in Hospital (see address section, pages 673–6) may be able to advise.

VISITING

Be honest about when you are next coming to see your child. You may dread him crying if you cannot come as soon as you would like, but it is far worse for him to wait all day and be disappointed and upset when you do not arrive when expected. If you may be held up or do not know exactly what time you will come, then do not promise a precise time – for example, to be there before tea, or by the time a certain TV programme comes on. Tell the ward sister when you are next coming so they can answer your child's questions, and if your plans change or you are held up, then ring and tell her. If you are going to be at work or out of touch, leave the number of a friend or relative, who would come up if your child is upset – explain to your child that you have arranged for this person to be called until you can get there if they need someone.

When it is time for you to leave after a visit, do not try to sneak out without your child noticing in an attempt to avoid upset. He may then spend the whole of your next visit worrying that you are suddenly going to disappear. Tell one of the nurses when you have to go and, if necessary, hand the child over to her saying when you will be back. This is better than leaving a wailing child alone in a cot, and the nurse can comfort and distract him.

Parents can be upset themselves if they get a mixed reaction when they visit – instead of seeming pleased to see them, children can often burst into tears. This just shows that your child has probably been making an effort not to cry, and breaks down with the relief of seeing you. It is better for him to be able to show his feelings, so comfort and reassure him and do not get overcome with guilt or feel that your visit is making things worse. It is also quite common for children to ignore their parents when they first arrive. This is their way of showing they are angry or hurt that you have been away. Even if you feel rebuffed, continue to be loving and come as often as you possibly can so he does not feel forgotten or abandoned.

BREASTFED BABIES

It is not always easy to carry on feeding a baby in hospital with the lack of privacy and difficulties imposed by the child's illness, but you will be giving him the best sort of comfort as well as food if you do. Mothers have even been able to feed small babies who are immobilised in traction because of fractures or bones that need to be corrected, by lying down on the bed beside them. You need to enlist the help and support of the ward sister, but when you cannot pick your baby up this physical reassurance will be very important to him.

If you have an older child in hospital and are breastfeeding a baby it is sometimes possible to bring the baby in as well. If that is not possible, would a friend visit with you during the day so she can look after the baby in the day room while you give the sick child your attention? Alternatively you could express your milk for your baby to be fed at home – your local branch of the National Childbirth Trust will have a breastfeeding adviser who can help you (see address section, pages 673–6).

Sometimes mothers of breastfed babies have to go into hospital themselves – do not stop feeding unless you plan to or are too sick to continue. Instead you can ask your hospital to arrange for your baby to come in with you, though individual arrangements within hospitals will vary regarding this.

HOW PARENTS CAN HELP

DO look after and entertain your child, freeing nurses for more skilled work.

DO NOT let your child or your visiting children run riot unchecked all over the ward and expect nurses to exercise disciplinary control.

DO continue to exercise authority and discipline over your child or visiting children.

DO NOT give your child sweets, food and drinks when he is not allowed them and without checking with staff or leave sweets, food and drinks in lockers for your child to help himself or to hand round.

DO check with staff whether it is all right to give anything to eat or drink, and keep foodstuffs including sweets out of young children's access.

DO NOT wind your own child, and any others on hand, into a state of anxiety by being emotionally out of control, talking loudly about medical disasters you have known, or being quite obviously panicked by every medical procedure.

DO stay calm, positive and optimistic and put this across to your child.

DO NOT walk away from cots and beds leaving the side down for your child to fall or roll on to the floor.

DO find out about your child's condition and how best you can care for him, as well as about routine rules on the ward.

DO NOT bring valuables on to the ward and raise the alarm regularly because they appear to have gone missing.

DO understand that if your child cannot be pacified or something needs doing urgently, it is better to hold the child or let the nurses hold him and get whatever it is over as quickly as possible. Often the anticipation can be worse than the actual procedure for a child.

DO NOT disappear from the ward without warning the nurses that they need to look after your child or without telling them when you are planning to return.

DO look after your own needs so staff do not have to end up looking after you.

DO NOT ignore your child and spend all your time chatting to other parents.

HOW MUCH CAN PARENTS DO FOR THEIR CHILD?

In some circles the view is that the job of nursing children is changing very rapidly. Instead of carrying out medical and nursing procedures themselves, nurses are often teaching and supervising parents to do things for their own children – for example, giving medicine. In training there is more emphasis on the psychological aspect of nursing in work with children. But obviously these are relatively new ideas and not everyone in the nursing profession agrees with them – when it comes to nursing care parents need to accept the practices of the ward.

However much you are able to do in practical terms for your child, there is an additional unseen way in which you can help to minimise the stress of a hospital visit – and that is in your own attitude towards hospitals, illness and medical staff. Calmness and optimism are the key words and it cannot be over-stressed how much you can encourage your child to make light of illness and treatment and to be confident he will recover by putting across a positive attitude. Children are very sensitive to emotional messages. Of course the more seriously ill your child is, the harder it is for parents to be optimistic. Parents of children likely to be left disabled, seriously sick children and those that are known to be dying need very special support and counselling. But all children unconsciously look to their parents to set the right note – so help them by making sure it is a positive one.

LONG-STAY PATIENTS

The longer your child is in hospital, the greater the strain it places on the family and the harder it is for a parent to stay all the time. Ask friends and relatives to share visiting. Many children who spend several weeks in hospital are in plaster or traction because of fractures. The playleader and, for older children, the hospital school teacher will both try to make sure your child is well stimulated, but they will not always be around. Amusing a young child who cannot move around is very hard indeed. There have been cases of children in traction being nursed at home, so it is worth asking, though you need to be sure you could cope. Older children (aged 3 to 5) can usually be entertained for at least some of the time by stories, television and story tapes and cassettes. For all ages, mirrors fixed at different angles give different views to look at and vary the scene, and so does moving their bed around if possible. For young children, many parents are endlessly inventive, making intriguing things to hang around the cot. Mobiles which make noises, glitter, or can be touched, can be made out of all sorts of junk.

An organisation called STEPS – specifically for families with children who have congenital abnormalities of the lower limbs are happy to offer help and advice to anyone coping with an immobilised child (see address section, pages 673–6).

ISOLATION

A child with an illness which is catching may be barrier-nursed in an infectious diseases unit so others will not get the disease. A child without much resistance to infection, perhaps because he is being treated with drugs which make the immune system less effective, may be protected by reverse barrier nursing. In this case families have to wear gowns and masks. Items cannot be freely taken in or out.

Children in isolation need a parent to stay with them even more than those on an open ward because they are more likely to get lonely or bored. But staying with them is also more stressful than life on an ordinary ward. It is unnatural for parent and child to spend such a lot of time alone together in confined circumstances and both are likely to get irritable, so you need other relatives or friends to give you both a break. Because nurses

need to be able to watch children, the room or cubicle will have windows at least along one side so there is no privacy, which is another strain. Parents need to come in armed to the hilt with amusements, diversions and supplies for themselves and their child because they cannot just wander in and out. The best support for parents in this position tends to be other parents who understand. A parents' room where they can go to have a cup of tea and let off steam is usually a great help.

LOOKING AFTER YOURSELF

All through this chapter we have stressed the importance of staying with your child, whether during a relatively short procedure in an accident and emergency unit, or for a longer period if your child has to stay in hospital for several weeks. But actually staying with children in hospital is emotionally draining, physically exhausting and very demanding. Being marooned by a bedside and cut off from the outside world can be a disorientating experience. It is very important that you try and arrange for other people to visit so that you can get a break, if possible to leave the hospital and go home for a while, and this will help you to be more support to your child in the long run. Do not try to attempt the impossible and manage without sleep for so long you end up being a liability yourself.

It may be difficult for you to leave your child for the first day or so while he is in hospital or during the period after an operation when he will need you by him most of all. This means being well prepared with supplies for yourself because hospital canteens can be a long way away and food and drinks brought round are intended for the patients, not their visitors. Taking a Thermos flask of tea or coffee and some food for yourself, plus a good supply of undemanding reading material is a wise precaution. Even if you are not planning to stay the night a change of clothes is often a good idea in case you end up being there longer than you imagined or your child spills something over you or is sick. Supplies of change for phone calls are also very useful.

Having a child in hospital can be a costly business for a family. If you think you might be entitled to any financial help, do ask the ward sister if you can see the social worker, who will advise you. Do not be afraid to do this – you will be able to give more attention to your child's feelings if you yourself are less worried about making ends meet, and you should claim any benefits to which you may be entitled. You should also ask to see a social worker if you feel it would be helpful to talk about family problems or your own feelings with someone other than family friends and nursing staff. Social workers are trained to help in these situations, and may be able to provide counselling themselves or put you in touch with someone else who can do this. If your child has a long-standing problem they may also be able to put you in touch with an organisation for parents of children with similar conditions.

COMING HOME

However many friends you have made, however nice the nursing staff are, and however short your stay, you will still both be counting the hours until your release. Anyone who has ever been a patient themselves or has stayed with a child knows just how disorientating being in hospital, even for a short time, can become. The real world seems to retreat. Children need time to readjust just like adults do and at first may find ordinary life extra tiring. Even if you stayed with your child in hospital all the time it is very common to find that his behaviour is different to begin with when he first comes home. He may be extra clingy, wakeful at night, regress to more babyish habits, or just be generally unsettled. Just being able to potter around in your own home with so many more things to amuse your child, and able to make cups of tea and food for them when and as you like seems wonderfully relaxing, so take life at the right pace for you and your child to begin with.

Of course some children will still need considerable nursing when they come out of hospital. It is important that you understand just what you need to do, which may mean writing down times to give medicine and amounts to give. There is more about giving medicine on pages 524–5. The good news is that even long hospital stays are unlikely permanently to affect children emotionally. By being honest and explaining things, staying as much as possible, and giving them extra love and comfort, parents can make sure that whatever the reason for a child's hospital stay, the only scars he collects are physical.

ADDRESSES

Amateur Swimming Association,
Harold Fern House,
Derby Square,
Loughborough,
Leicestershire LE11 0AL

ASH (Action on Smoking and
    Health),
5/11 Mortimer Street,
London W1N 7RH

Association for All Speech
    Impaired Children (AFASIC),
347 Central Markets,
Smithfield,
London EC1A 9NH

Association of Breastfeeding
    Mothers,
26 Holmshaw Close,
Sydenham Green,
London SE26 4TH

Association for Improvements in
    Maternity Services (AIMS),
Goose Green Barn,
Much Hoole,
Preston, Lancs
PR4 4TD

Association of Parents of Vaccine
    Damaged Children,
2 Church Street,
Shipston-on-Stour,
Warwickshire CV36 4AP

Association for Post-Natal Illness,
7 Gowan Avenue,
London SW6 6RH

Association of Radical Midwives
    (ARM),
62 Greetby Hill,
Ormskirk,
Lancashire L39 2DT

Association for Spina Bifida and
    Hydrocephalus,
ASBAH House,
42 Park Road,
Peterborough PE1 2UQ

Asthma Society,
300 Upper Street,
London N1 2XX

Baby Life Support Systems (BLISS),
44–5 Museum Street,
London WC1A 1LY

Birthright,
27 Sussex Place,
Regent's Park,
London NW1 4SP

British Diabetic Association,
10 Queen Anne Street,
London W1M 0BD

British Epilepsy Association,
Anstey House,
40 Hanover Square,
Leeds LS3 1BE

British Kidney Patients'
    Association,
c/o Mrs Elizabeth Ward,
Bordon,
Hants GU35 9JS

British Pregnancy Advisory
  Service,
Austy Manor,
Wootton Wawen,
Solihull,
West Midlands B95 6BX

British Standards Institution,
2 Park Street,
London W1A 2BS

Brook Advisory Centres,
233 Tottenham Court Road,
London W1 9AE

Caesarean Support Group,
81 Elizabeth Way,
Cambridge CB4 1BQ

Child Growth Foundation,
2 Mayfield Avenue,
Chiswick,
London W4 1PW

Cleft Lip and Palate Association
  (CLAPA),
1 Eastwood Gardens,
Kenton,
Newcastle upon Tyne NE3 3DQ

Cry-sis,
BM Cry-sis,
London WC1N 3XX

Cystic Fibrosis Research Trust,
Alexandra House,
5 Blyth Road,
Bromley,
Kent BR1 3RS

Down's Syndrome Association,
155 Mitcham Road,
Tooting,
London SW17 9PG

Foresight, the Association for the
  Promotion of Preconceptual
  Care,
The Old Vicarage,
Church Lane,
Witley,
Surrey GU8 5PN

Foundation for Conductive
  Education,
University of Birmingham,
PO Box 363,
Birmingham B15 2TT

Foundation for the Study of
  Infant Deaths – Cot Death
  Research and Support,
15 Belgrave Square,
London SW1X 8PS

Gingerbread Association for One
  Parent Families,
35 Wellington Street,
London WC2E 7BN

Haemophilia Society,
123 Westminster Bridge Road,
London SE1 7HR

Herpes Association,
Omnibus Workspace,
41 North Road,
London N7 9DP

Independent Midwives
  Association,
94 Oakland Road,
London SE19 2DB

International Centre for Active
  Birth,
55 Dartmouth Park Road,
London NW5 1SL

Kids' Clubs Network,
279–81 Whitechapel Road,
London E1 1BY

La Lèche League of Great Britain,
PO Box BM 3424,
London WC1N 3XX

Leukaemia Care Society,
PO Box 82,
Exeter EX2 5DP

Maternity Alliance,
15 Britannia Street,
London WC1X 9JP

Meet-a-Mum Association
  (MAMA),
58 Malden Avenue,
South Norwood,
London SE25 4H6

MENCAP (Royal Society for
  Mentally Handicapped
  Children and Adults),
123 Golden Lane,
London EC1Y 0RT

Miscarriage Association,
18 Stoneybrook Close,
West Bretton,
Wakefield,
West Yorkshire WF4 4TP

Muscular Dystrophy Group of
  Great Britain and Northern
  Ireland,
Nattrass House,
35 Macaulay Road,
London SW4 0QP

Naevus Support Group,
58 Necton Road,
Wheathampstead,
St Albans AL4 8AU

National Association for Maternal
  and Child Welfare (NAMCW),
Stroud House,
46–8 Osnaburgh Street,
London NW1 3NP

National Association for the
  Welfare of Children in Hospital
  (NAWCH),
Argyle House,
29–31 Euston Road,
London NW1 2SD

National Autistic Society,
276 Willesden Lane,
London NW2 5RB

National Campaign for Nursery
  Education (NCNE),
23 Albert Street,
London NW1 7LU

National Childbirth Trust (NCT),
Alexandra House,
Oldham Terrace,
London W3 6NH

National Childcare Campaign Ltd,
Wesley House,
4 Wild Court,
London WC2B 5AU
(9am–5pm)

National Childminding
  Association (NCMA),
8 Masons Hill,
Bromley,
Kent BR2 9EY

National Council for the
  Divorced and Separated,
13 High Street,
Little Shelford,
Cambridge CB2 5ES

National Council for One-Parent
  Families,
255 Kentish Town Road,
London NW5 2LX

National Deaf Blind League
(NDBL),
18 Rainbow Court,
Paston Ridings,
Peterborough PE4 6UP

National Deaf-Blind and Rubella
Association (Sense),
311 Gray's Inn Road,
London WC1X 8PT

National Deaf Children's Society
(NDCS)
45 Hereford Road,
London W2 5AH

National Eczema Society,
Tavistock House North,
Tavistock Square,
London WC1 9SR

Pre-Eclampsia Group,
17 South Avenue,
Hullbridge,
Essex SS5 6HA

Pre-School Playgroups
Association,
61–3 King's Cross Road,
London WC1X 9LL

Relate,
Herbert Gray College,
Little Church Street,
Rugby,
Warwicks CV21 2AP

Royal National Institute for the
Blind,
224 Great Portland Street,
London W1N 6AA

Royal National Institute for the
Deaf,
105 Gower Street,
London WC1E 6AH

Sense: *see* National Deaf-Blind
and Rubella Association

Spastics Society,
12 Park Crescent,
London W1N 4EQ

STEPS,
15 Statham Close,
Lymm,
Cheshire WA13 9NN

Stillbirth and Neonatal Death
Society (SANDS),
28 Portland Place,
London W1N 4DE

Twins Club Association (Twins
and Multiple Births
Association),
59 Sunnyside,
Worksop,
Notts S81 7LN

Vegan Society,
33–5 George Street,
Oxford OX1 2AY

Vegetarian Society UK Ltd,
Parkdale,
Durham Road,
Altrincham,
Cheshire WA14 4QG

Working Mothers Association,
77 Holloway Road,
London N7 8JZ

Working for Childcare,
77 Holloway Road,
London N7 8JZ

INDEX

abdomen of newborn baby, 143
abortion: 'missed', 58; spontaneous,
    55
abruptio placentae, 116, 121
abscesses, breast, 208, 210, 225
accelerated labour, 107
accidents to children, 477–96, 519,
    522; bites and stings, 502–3;
    bleeding, 498–9; broken bones,
    500; chemicals, 499; convulsions,
    503–4; cuts and other accidents
    through play, 491; drowning,
    479, 489–90, 499; electric
    shocks/electrocution, 492, 500;
    emergency first aid, 496–504;
    eyes, 502; falls, 479, 495–6, 498;
    fire, 479, 483–4; foreign bodies,
    501; from toys, 492; head
    injuries, 501, 519, 522; how to
    protect child from, 480–96;
    poisoning, 495, 499; scalds and
    burns, 477, 479, 482–4, 498,
    519; shock, 502, splinters, 501–
    2; sprains, 502; suffocation and
    choking, 477, 479, 480–1, 496–
    7; traffic and road, 479, 484–9
acne, 346
acoustic cradle, 342–3, 636
Active Birth Movement, 34–6, 90,
    95, 98
acupuncture, 97

Acyclovir, 10, 567
adders, 503, 563
adenoids, 554–5; and glue ear, 572
AFP: *see* alpha-foetoprotein
aggression, 453, 454–6
AIDS (HIV), 9, 39, 194, 610, 626–
    7; 'ELISA test', 39
allergic rhinitis, 575
allergy, 246, 252–3; asthma, 590–5;
    bites and stings, 502–3; breast
    feeding's protection from, 206;
    and crying, 300; eye problems,
    575; medicine, 526; *see also* food
    intolerance
alpha-foetoprotein (AFP), levels of,
    40–1, 43, 642
Amateur Swimming Association,
    490
ambulance, 79
amniocentesis, 19, 40, 43, 44, 60,
    642
amniotic fluid, 19, 43, 82, 127,
    135, 138, 188, 504; breaking of
    waters, 81, 82, 84, 103, 106, 114
anaemia, 39, 60, 113, 193, 195,
    198
anaesthetic: epidural, 33, 53, 88,
    90, 95, 96, 101, 107, 108, 110,
    113, 114, 118, 225; general, 90,
    96, 108–9, 110, 113
anencephaly, screening for, 40

antenatal care/clinics, 32, 512; at
end of pregnancy, 40; 'booking
in', 38; clinical tests, 38–9;
medical examination, 39–40;
middle months, novice's guide to,
37–40; other tests, 40–5
antenatal classes, 32, 33–6, 89;
Active Birth Movement, 34–6,
95, 98; hospital, 33–4, 95, 98;
NCT, 34, 90, 98; yoga classes, 36
antibiotics, 193, 521, 525–6, 571,
578, 593, 598; systemic, 525;
topical, 526
antihistamines, 295, 599
anti-wind teats and bottles, 244
anus of newborn baby, 143
Apgar score, 129–30
apnoea, 188, 193
apnoea mattresses, 285
appendix, burst, 29
appetite, loss of, 520
articulation problems, 375
artificial respiration, 497
ASH (Action on Smoking and
Health), 4
Association of Breastfeeding
Mothers, 248
asthma, 541, 553, 575, 589–95,
603, 631, 632; causes of, 590–1;
drugs for, 591–3; growing out of,
594–5; living with children with,
593; treatment, 591–3; what to
do if your child has attack, 593
Asthma Society, 593
astigmatism, 338
audiometry, 636
au pairs, 465–8
autism, 649–51

baby alarm systems and mattresses,
285–6
baby clothes, 73–4
baby nests, 480
baby-sitting, 66
baby walkers, 76
baby wipes, 74
backache, 47, 90, 96

bacteria, bacterial infection, 504,
505, 525–6, 527, 555, 559, 581,
583, 596, 606
balanced diet, 257–61
baths, bathing, 161–3, 508; playing
in, 397; too hot water, 482–3
BCG injection, 150
Becker dystrophy, 644
bed: choking and suffocating in,
480; for baby, 284–5; moving
from cot to, 288–9; position of
baby in, 285; *see also* sleep
bedtime: a book at, 289–91;
routine, 282–4
bed wetting, 416
bee stings, 502, 563
behaviour, 309; discipline, 459–60;
and food intolerance, 275–7;
good, 457–61; handling young
children, 457–9; learning to wait,
460–1
Beta test, 31
bicycles and tricycles, 484–6
binocular vision, 575
birth chairs, 33, 93, 94
birth of baby, 125; at home, 31–2;
bleeding after, 120; checklist for
a better, 98–100; domino
delivery, 32, 33, 39; first
moments of life, 103–5; in
hospital, 32–3, 79, 83–4; minor
problems after, 137; more serious
problems after, 138–40; multiple,
63–5, 108, 118; post-mature
baby in womb, 105–6;
psychoprophylaxis (natural birth),
94–5; restitution, 86; role of
father, 89; small-for-date babies,
114–15, 177, 178, 310, 312;
where to have, 31–3; *see also*
Caesarean section; labour and
delivery; pregnancy; premature
babies; special care babies
birth positions of baby, 54–5, 83,
86, 88, 101, 107; abnormal,
116–17; breech, 54–5, 101, 108,
116, 118, 144, 175; compound,

118; deep transverse arrest, 118; different head presentations and positions, 117; engaged, 54; face presentation, 117; head down, 101; occipito-lateral, 109; occipito-posterior, 101, 109, 117; posterior, 55; rotation of baby's head, 101, 102, 109; shoulder presentation, 117; transverse, 55, 110, 116, 118; unengaged, 54; unstable lie, 55, 117

birth position of mother, 92–4; kneeling on all fours, 92; lithotomy, 92, 109, 110, 119; lying down, 90, 92; and movement, 90; squatting, 94; supported squatting, 92, 94

birth stools, 33, 84, 92, 94

birthing beds, 33, 84, 94

birthing pools, 94

birthmarks, 146, 560–1; port-wine stains, 146, 561; stork marks, 141, 146, 561; strawberry marks, 146, 561

birthweight, 130, 181, 210, 309, 311; low, 2, 130, 177, 181

bites and stings, 562–3; allergic reaction to, 503; first aid, 502–3

biting, 455–6

bladder: *see* toilet training; urine

bleeding, 521; in brain, 178, 195; first aid for, 498–9; gums during pregnancy, 48; and miscarriage, 58; post-partum haemorrhage, 87, 105, 120; in pregnancy, 52–3, 115–16; and premature labour, 113; at start of labour, 115

blindness and visual impairment, 638–9; combined with deafness, 637; education, 638–9; *see also* eyesight

blood, blood tests, 39, 41; anaemia, 39, 60, 113, 193; jaundice, 193; rhesus factor, 39, 61–2; septicaemia, 193

blood banks, 193

blood groups, 39, 61

blood pressure: epidural's lowering of, 96, 101; high, 53, 60, 101, 108, 113; in pregnancy, 38, 83

blue baby, 623

blushing, 346

body waste, 415–16

boils, 560

bonding, 126, 437

bones of children, 315–16; fontanelles, 140, 180, 316

books and stories, 289–91, 367–8

Borning bed, 94

bottle-feeding, 151–2, 203–5, 207–11, 229–39, 359; vs breastfeeding, 203–5, 207–8; changing from breastfeeding to, 227; combined tube and, 186; complementary bottles and breastfeeding, 217; equipment, 232; establishing, 230–2; giving a bottle, 236–7; and hygiene, 505, 507; making up feeds, 232–6; other people feeding your baby, 239; sterilising bottles and equipment, 238, 505, 507; and vitamin supplements, 239

bow legs, 584

bowels, bowel movements, 83–4, 154, 316, 580, 642; of breast-fed babies, 426, 580, 581; constipation, 420–1, 580; infections of the, 581–3; meconium, 103, 119, 138, 140, 143, 154, 426, 580, 619; and toilet training, 415–23 *passim*; in the wrong place, 421–2; *see also* diarrhoea

BPD (broncho-pulmonary dysplasia), 191

bradycardia, 193

brain of child, 316–17; dysfunction (malfunction), 645; and eyes, 331, 332

brain cancer, 611

brain damage, 195, 530, 550, 639, 642, 645

Braxton Hicks contractions, 79, 82

bread and cereals, 259
breast milk, 505, 527; changes
    during feed, 205–6, 212–13, 229;
    differences between cow's milk
    and, 204–5; expressing and
    storing, 186–7, 219–22; not
    having enough, 218; as protection
    from infection, 205, 206, 425,
    505
breast pumps, 186–7, 209, 220–1;
    electric, 221; hand, 220
breast relievers, 220
breastfeeding, 78, 131–3, 151–2,
    166, 187, 193, 203–29, 442–3,
    505; advantages of, 205–7; after
    a Caesarean, 225; at night,
    293–4; baby in special care, 186–
    7, 209; vs bottle-feeding, 203–5;
    changing to bottle-feeding, 227;
    colic, 243–5; combined tube and,
    185; and drugs, 209; and eating
    out, 252; food requirements of
    mothers, 218; giving up, 227;
    going back to work, 222–3, 462;
    handicapped babies, 209–10;
    home truths about, 207–8; in
    hospital, 667; and illness, 208–9,
    425; and immunity, 527; not
    having enough milk, 218; partial,
    223; problems for babies, 227–9;
    problems for mothers, 223–7;
    second and subsequent babies,
    241–2; sicky babies, 242–3;
    triplets, 226–7; twins, 225–6;
    and vitamin supplements, 239–
    41; weaning, 245–50; wind, 242;
    women who cannot breastfeed,
    208–10; women who do not
    want to breastfeed, 210–11
breastfeeding counsellors, 34
breasts, 211–17; abscesses, 208,
    210, 225; after pains, 215; babies
    who will not suck, 215; blocked
    ducts, 224; changes during
    pregnancy of, 30, 212; and
    complementary bottles, 217;
    cracked nipples, 210, 224;

engorgement of, 167, 216, 224;
    expressing milk from, 186–7,
    219; let-down reflex, 214, 216–
    17; mastitis, 208, 210, 224; of
    newborn baby, 143; putting the
    baby to the, 213–14; sore
    nipples, 223–4; taking the baby
    off the, 215; when milk comes in,
    216; which side first?, 215
breathing, 194, 337; BPD, 191;
    CPAP, 189; difficulties, 188, 518,
    519, 521; how babies are helped
    in, 188–90, 191; of newborn
    baby, 127–8, 137; rapid, 518;
    respiratory distress syndrome
    (RDS), 187, 188, 189; of special
    care babies, 175, 176, 177, 185,
    187–91; ventilators, 176, 179–
    80, 182, 189, 190, 191; wet lung,
    188; *see also* asthma; oxygen
breech babies/delivery, 54, 101,
    108, 116, 118, 144, 175
British Diabetic Association, 618
British Electrotechnical Approvals
    Board (BEAB), 479
British Epilepsy Association, 603
British Standards (BS), 479–80,
    494; kite mark, 480; safety mark,
    480
broken bones, first aid for, 500
bronchitis and wheezing, 553
bronchodilators, 591
broncho-pulmonary dysplasia: *see*
    BPD
brothers and sisters: aggression
    between, 456; baby's
    relationships with, 445–7; of
    special care babies, 183
bruising, 521
buggies, 75–6
burn accidents: *see* scalds and burns
buying goods: BEAB, 479; British
    Standards (BS), 479–80; lion
    mark (BTHMA), 480

Caesarean section, 10, 33, 53, 54,
    55, 62, 64, 95, 107, 109, 110–

13, 114, 115, 116, 117, 119, 120, 131, 166, 175, 213, 312; breastfeeding after, 225; epidural, 95; planned or elective, 110; pre-op procedures, 112; twins, 118
caffeine, 522
calcium deficiency, 178
calories, 257
cancer, childhood, 610–12
candida albicans, 567, 579
cannabis, 6
car passengers, child, 486–9; babies, 486, 489; older children, 487; in other people's cars, 489; toddlers and young children, 487
car seat for baby, 75
carbohydrates, 204, 205, 318
Cardiff count-to-ten foetal activity chart, 44
cardiotography (CTG), 44
carry-cots, 74–5, 284
castor oil for inducing labour, 106
CAT (computerised axial tomography) scan, 195
cat nap, 280, 294, 295
centile growth curve, 314
cerebellar tumours, 611
cerebral palsy, 375, 530, 585, 586, 639–41; diplegia, 639; education, 641, hemiplegia, 639; monoplegia, 639; quadriplegia, 639; treatment, 639–41
cervical smear, 40
cervix: dilation of, 82, 83, 84, 85, 89, 90, 106, 110, 116, 119; incompetent, 52–3; tumour in, 117
chalking, 396
changing mat, 74
chemicals: in the eye, 502; first aid for, 499
chest infections, 553
chicken-pox, 547
child/baby minders, 403, 438, 439, 440, 462–9
Child Growth Foundation, 615
choking, 496

chorion villus biopsy, 19, 43–4
Christmas tree lights, safety of, 492
chromosomes, 10–13, 15, 19, 310, 647; karyotype, 12; mistakes in, 13, 14, 15; sex, 12–13; trisomy, 647
circumcised babies, ulcers on tip of penis of, 579
circumcision, 579
cleaning your baby, 160–3; bathing, 161–3, 508; topping and tailing, 160–1
cleft lip (hare lip), 19, 175, 209, 627–8
Cleft Lip and Palate Association, 628
cleft palate, 175, 209, 375, 627–8
clinical tests in pregnancy, 38–9; blood pressure, 38; blood tests, 39; height, 38; urine, 38–9; weight, 38
Clomiphene, 64
clothes: baby, 73–4; mother's, 79; school, 412
club foot, 584
clumsiness, 585–7
cochlea echo, 343
coeliac disease, 621
cold sores, 567
colds, 550–2; babies over six months and older children, 551–2; babies under six months, 550–1
colic, 242, 243–5, 299, 304; drugs for, 244
colostrum, 131, 151, 206, 212, 505; expressed during last months of pregnancy, 78
comfort habits, comforters, 286–8, 293–4, 304–5
communicating with children, 469–75; crying, 359; death, illness and handicap, 472–3; language, 353–77; marriage difficulties, 471; religion, 473; separation and divorce, 471–2; sex, 473–5

community health care/service, 531–
3, 641; development check-ups,
533–4; screening programmes,
343–4
congenital defects/abnormalities, 10,
18, 19, 121, 426–7, 589, 619–26,
631–2; cleft lip and palate, 19,
175, 209, 375, 627–8; club foot,
584; coeliac disease, 621; cystic
fibrosis, 15, 19, 44, 426, 619–21;
genitals, 629; heart disease, 142–
3, 177, 621–6; *see also* genetic
factors; handicaps
conjunctivitis, 193, 574; viral, 574
constipation, 48, 420–1, 580
consultants, 661, 662
continuous positive airway pressure:
see CPAP
contraception: barrier methods, 3;
the coil (IUD), 3, 57–8; the Pill, 3
contractions (during labour), 82–3,
84, 85, 86, 87, 89, 90, 92, 96,
97, 101, 106, 107; Braxton
Hicks, 79, 82; effect of epidural
on, 96
convenience foods, 263
convulsions/fits/seizures, 503–4,
518–19, 521, 530, 550; feverish,
545–7; first aid for, 503–4; long-
term treatment, 546–7; in
newborn babies, 196; signs of,
545; when emergency action is
needed, 546; *see also* epilepsy
cookers, safety of, 482
cortisone injections for premature
babies, 114
cot, 75, 284–5; moving to bed
from, 288–9
cot death, 200–1, 285; lower
incidence with breast-fed babies,
206
coughs, coughing, 552–3; croup,
555–7; persistent, 518, 519;
short, hacking, 553; types and
causes of, 552–3; *see also*
whooping cough
cousins, marriage of, 19

cow's milk, 229–30, 247–8;
bacteria in, 507; food allergy
caused by, 253, 254–5; vs breast
milk, 204–5, 229; *see also*
bottle-feeding
CPAP (continuous positive airway
pressure), 189
'cradle-cap', 145
cramp in pregnancy, 48
crawling, baby's, 336–7
creative play, 379–80
crèches, 465
cribs, 74–5, 284
croup, 555–7
crying, 128, 164, 182, 279, 286,
342; babies who won't stop,
300–6; causes of, 299–300, 359;
and colic, 243–5, 293, 304;
communicating through, 359;
nearing the end of your tether,
306–7; ways of stopping, 301–6;
in young babies, 299–307
Cry-sis, 245, 307
cuts, 491–2, 498–9
cystic fibrosis (CF), 15, 19, 44, 427,
619–21
cytomegalovirus (MCV), 8

D & C (dilatation and curettage),
58, 120
dancing schools, 327
dandruff, 574
deafness, 344, 635–7; blindness
combined with, 637; conductive,
635, 636; education, 637; high
tone, 343–4, 635; and language,
374, 635, 636; overcoming, 345;
sensorineural dysfunction, 635;
special schools, 345; temporary,
344; *see also* hearing
death: of babies, 179, 184, 199–
200; cot, 200–1, 206, 285;
talking about, 469, 472; *see also*
accidents
dehydration, 518, 521, 582
delivery: *see* labour
delivery room, 84

dentist, going to the, 538–9; *see also* teeth
developmental check-ups, 533–4
diabetes, 6, 59, 62–3, 106, 113, 177, 312, 512, 615–18, 621, 632; imbalance between insulin and glucose, 618; lifestyle, 617–18; treatment, 616–17
dialysis, 607–8; haemodialysis, 607–8; peritoneal, 607
diaphragm, contraceptive, 3
diarrhoea, 300, 423, 424, 518, 519, 521, 581, 582, 583
diazepam (Valium), 546
diet/eating: additive-free, 276–7; balanced, 257–61; before and during pregnancy, 5, 45–6, 78; convenience foods, 263; elimination diets in treating eczema, 599; fat children, 272–5; feeding babies, 203–55; feeding under fives, 257–77; food groups, 258–61; food hygiene, 509; fruit and vegetables, 259, 262–3; sweets, 257, 258, 265–6; vegetarian, 259; *see also* feeding
dieting before pregnancy, 6
digestion, breast milk's easier, 206, 212
dimethicone, 244
diphtheria, 527, 529, 530, 605–6
discipline, 459–60
disproportion, 120
divorce and separation, 471–2
DNA (deoxyribonucleic acid), 11, 14
doctors in hospital, 661–2; *see also* GPs; medicines
Domino scheme/delivery, 32, 33, 39
Down's Children's Association, 649
Down's syndrome (mongolism), 13, 41, 60, 175, 585, 632, 645, 647–9
drawing, 373
dreams, 68
dressing a baby, 163–4
dribbling, 521
drinking/alcohol, 4–5, 522
drinks for children, 265

driving to calm crying babies, 305
drowning, 479, 489–90; first aid, 499–500; teaching baby to swim, 489–90
drugs: anti-convulsant, 602; anti-spasmodic, 244; for asthma, 591, 593; and breastfeeding, 208, 209; for colic, 244; and gut problems, 583; for sleepless children 295–6; taken during pregnancy, 6–7; your attitude to, 522–3; *see also* medicines
Duchenne muscular dystrophy, 17, 19, 44, 643
dummies, babies', 244, 288, 304, 507, 538
dysentery, 581

ear(s), 568–73; cross section of, 570; foreign body in, 571; glue, 571–3; middle, 568, 570; of newborn baby, 141–2; outer, 568; wax in, 141; *see also* hearing
ear drum, 568, 571, 572; burst/perforated, 570–1; grommets fitted into, 572–3
ear infections, 344, 374, 521, 568–71, 581; middle (*otitis media*), 344, 568, 570, 571; outer ear canal, 571
earache, 521, 568, 570, 571
eating out with babies and children, 252; *see also* diet; feeding
EBM (expressed breast milk), 186–7
echocardiogram, 625
eclampsia, 53–4
ectopic pregnancy, 24, 41–3, 52
eczema, 296, 346, 541, 558–9, 575, 595–600, 631; atopic, 558–9, 595; elimination diet to treat, 599; hallmarks and effects of, 596–7; helping child cope with, 600; treatment, 597–9; use of antihistamines, 599; use of steroids, 598–9; 'weeping', 596, 598

education, 404, 410–13; autism, 650–1; blind children, 638–9; cerebral palsy, 641; deaf children, 637; epilepsy, 603–4; handicaps, 628, 631; muscular dystrophy, 644; nursery, 403–4, 408, 411–12; and short stature, 615; *spina bifida*, 643; *see also* play; playschools; schools

electrocardiogram (ECG), 625

electrocution/electric shocks, 479, 492; first aid for, 500

electronic monitoring, 101, 102–3

'ELISA test' for AIDS, 39

emotions and anxieties, 65–70; adjusting to parenthood, 65–7; and asthma, 590; benefits of breastfeeding, 207; dreams, 68; effect on skin of, 346; fantasy feelings, 70; morbid feelings, 68; of parents of handicapped children, 633–5; in pregnancy, 67–8; sex, 69; single parents, 69–70; work, 70

employment: entitlements of pregnant women, 36–7; jobs dangerous in pregnancy, 37; *see also* working women

encephalitis, 606

endometriosis, 29

Entonox (laughing gas), 95

environmental factors affecting pregnancy, 2, 3–10

epidurals, epidural anaesthetic, 33, 53, 88, 90, 95, 96, 101, 107, 108, 110, 113, 114, 118, 225

epilepsy, 6, 512, 530, 531, 547, 600–4; and education, 603–4; *grand mal*, 601–2; lifestyle for children with, 603; *petit mal*, 601; treatment, 602–3; what to do during a fit, 602; *see also* convulsions

episiotomy, 33, 54, 85, 105, 107–8, 114, 120, 135, 166

equipment: baby, 74–6; bottle-feeding, 232, 238

Ergometrine, 87, 120

eustachian tubes, 568, 570, 571, 573

exercise and asthma, 591

expressed breast milk: *see* EBM

eye drops, giving, 574

eye reflexes, 148

eye tests, 338, 575, 577

eyelids, 575; crusty, 574; swelling and redness of, 573

eyes/eyesight, 331–9, 573–7; allergy, 575; astigmatic, 338, 577; bloodshot, or sore, 573–4; cataracts, 338; conjunctivitis, 193, 574; continually watering, 573; cross section of, 573; curable conditions, 338; foreign bodies in, 502; glasses for children, 338–9, 577; injuries to, 502; longsighted (hypermetropic), 338, 575, 577; naming and playing, 335–6; of newborn baby, 136, 141, 331–2; on the move, 336–7; perception, 331; problems, 337–8, 573–7; recognising and remembering, 332–5; red eye, 574; shortsighted (myopic), 338, 577; squints, 332, 338, 575–7; sticky eye, 141, 573; sties, 575; visual impairment, 638–9

faintness and palpitations in pregnancy, 48–9

falls and knocks, 479, 495–6; first aid for, 498

family eating habits, 266–8

fantasy feelings, 70

fantasy play, 380

fat children, 272–5, 309

fathers, 65, 66, 133–4; feeding baby, 239; feeling left out, 442–3; labour and birth, 89, 133–4, 441; relationship with baby, 441–5; sharing workload, 443–5; special care babies, 183–4; *see also* parents fats and oils, 261

fear, 461–2; of the dark, 461; of doctors and dentists, 461–2

feeding: and communication, 359; and growth, 317–18; taste, 350

feeding babies, 203–55, 317; bottle-feeding, 151–2, 186, 203–5, 229–39; breastfeeding, 78, 131–3, 151–2, 166, 187–8, 203–29; combined tube and breast or bottle, 185; eating out, 252; expressed breast milk (EBM), 186–7; food groups, 258–61; food intolerance, 252–5; intravenous (TPN), 180, 185; newborn baby, 151–2; problems with early, 242–5; second and subsequent babies, 241–2; special care babies, 184–7; tube, 185; vitamin supplement, 239; weaning, 245–50; *see also* diet

feeding the under fives, 257–77, 317–18; balanced diet, 257–61; behaviour problems and food intolerance, 275–7; children who want food all the time, 270–1; children who won't eat, 268–9; convenience foods, 263; drinks, 265; eating problems, 268–71; family eating habits, 266–71; fat children, 272–5; food used as punishment or reward, 271; fruit and vegetables, 259, 262–3; good eating habits, 261–2; sandwiches, 263–4; sweets, 265–6; weightwatching, 263; *see also* diet

feet: *see* orthopaedic problems

fennel, 244, 305

fertilisation, 23–4; *in vitro* (IVF), 64

fertility, 27–9; pinpointing ovulation, 27–8; problems, 28–9

fertility chart, 27, 28

fertility treatment, test tube, 64; multiple births resulting from, 64

fever and raised temperature, 518, 519–20, 521, 527, 530, 542–50;

anti-convulsant medication, 546; diazepam given rectally, 546; feverish convulsions, 545–7; infectious diseases causing, 547–50; nursing children with, 544–5; taking your child's temperature, 543; tepid sponging to lower, 543–4

fibroids, fibroid cysts or tumours, 43

finger foods, 250

fire accidents, 479, 483

fire blanket, 483

fireworks, 483

first aid, emergency, 496–503; bites and stings, 502–3; bleeding, 498–9; broken bones, 500; chemicals, 499; choking, 496–7; convulsions, 503–4; drowning, 499–500; electrocution, 500; eyes, 502; falls and knocks, 498; foreign bodies, 501; head injuries, 501; poisoning, 499; scalds and burns, 498; shock, 502; splinters, 501–2; sprains, 502; suffocation, 497

fits: *see* convulsions

flat feet, 584–5

fleas, 508, 563–4

fluoride, 537

foetal blood sampling, 44

foetal distress, 119–20

foetoscopy, 19, 44

foetus (unborn baby from nine weeks), 25; Cardiff count-to-ten activity chart, 44; miscarriage, 55–9

folic acid, 5, 46

fontanelles, 140, 180, 316

food hygiene, 508–9; *see also* diet; feeding

food intolerance, 244, 252–5; 300; and behaviour problems, 275–7; *see also* allergy

forceps delivery, 92, 108–9, 114, 115, 117, 120, 175

foreign bodies, 501; in ear, 501, 571; in eye, 502; swallowing, 501

foremilk, 216
Foundation for the Study of Infant
  Deaths, 201
fragile X syndrome, 17
friends, 438, 450–3; difficulties in
  making, 453–4; playing with,
  380, 400, 450–3
fruit and vegetables, 259, 262–3
funeral and burial of baby, 122,
  200
fungus, 505, 560; *Candida albicans*,
  505
furniture, inflammable, 484

games, 380, 453; peekaboo, 334,
  380
gas and air, 95, 119
gastric infections, 424–5, 581–3
gastro-enteritis, 581
gavage feeding, 185
genes, 11; mistakes in individual,
  13–14, 15–17; shared by cousins,
  19
genetic counselling, 10, 18–21, 643
genetic factors/abnormalities, 10–
  17; cystic fibrosis, 619–21;
  Down's syndrome, 13, 41, 60,
  175, 585, 632, 645, 647–9; fresh
  mutation, 11; marriage of
  cousins, 19; muscular dystrophy,
  17, 19, 44, 643–5; patterns of
  inheritance, 14–17; pre-natal
  diagnosis, 19–20; risk of passing
  on, 18–19; *see also* handicaps
genital herpes, 9, 10, 57
genitals, 143, 629; hypospadias,
  629; undescended testicles, 629
German measles (*rubella*), 8–9, 39,
  57, 142, 337, 342, 344, 530,
  547–8, 606, 621, 638
germs, 504–9; caught from pets,
  508; in food, 509; fungi, 505;
  passive immunity, 505; virulent,
  505; *see also* bacteria; viruses
Gingerbread, 70, 469
glasses for children, 338–9
glucose, 178, 616, 618

glue ear, 571–3
glue sniffing, 522
gluing and sticking, 397
gonorrhoea, 9–10
GP units, 32
GPs, 32, 511–22, 531, 541;
  antenatal care by, 32, 39, 40;
  calling at night, 515; changing,
  512–13; choosing, 511–12;
  development check-ups by, 533,
  534; how to get your best from
  your, 513–17; referrals, 517;
  when to call, 517–22; *see also*
  hospital; medicines
grand mal: *see* epilepsy
grandparents, 65, 67, 437, 438,
  472; baby's relationships with,
  447–50
grasp reflex, baby's, 148
Green Cross Code, 484
gripe water, 244
griseofulvin, 560
groin of newborn baby, 144; hernia
  in, 144
growth, 309–18; baby's, 309–15;
  birthweight, 2, 130, 177, 181,
  210, 309, 311; bones, 315–16;
  boys' and girls', 327–9; brain and
  nervous system, 316–17; centile
  growth curve, 314; and feeding,
  317–18; how your doctor
  measures baby's, 314; individual
  variations in, 314–15; large-for-
  dates, 312; measuring, 312–14;
  muscles, 310; pre-term babies,
  311–12; in toddler and pre-
  school child, 315–17; in the
  womb, 310–11; *see also*
  movement; premature babies
growth hormone deficiency, 615
gut, gut problems, 424–5, 580–3;
  blockages, 580, 619; and drugs,
  583; hospital treatment, 582;
  infections, 581; treatment for
  babies, 582; treatment for older
  children, 583
Guthrie test, 150

gymnastics, 327

habituation, 342
haemodialysis, 607–8
haemoglobin, 39, 147
haemophilia, 17, 19, 44, 609–10;
  and AIDS, 626
Haemophilia Society, 610
handicaps, 296, 631–51; autism,
  649–51; breastfeeding, 208, 209–
  10; causes, 631–2; cerebral palsy,
  375, 530, 585, 586, 639–41;
  congenital, 632; deafness, 635–7;
  Down's syndrome, 13, 41, 60,
  175, 585, 632, 645, 647–9;
  genetic, 631; how to discover,
  632; living with, 633–5; mental
  (learning difficulties), 632, 641,
  645–51; muscular dystrophy, 17,
  19, 44, 643–5; *spina bifida*, 19,
  40, 43, 46, 56, 177, 530, 631,
  641–3; types of, 632; visual
  impairment, 638–9; *see also*
  special care babies; congenital
  defects
hay fever, 575, 595
HCG (human chorionic
  gonadotrophin), 30–1, 41
head injuries, 519, 522; first aid,
  501
head lice, 564
head of newborn baby, 140–1;
  circumference, 131; *see also* birth
  position of baby
headaches in pregnancy, 49
headbanging, 297
health clinics/centres, 32, 531–3;
  community screening
  programmes, 343–4; hearing
  tests, 342–3
Health Education Council, 4
health problems, 541–87; *see also*
  drugs; GPs; infection; medicines;
  teeth
health visitors (SRNs), 512, 531–3,
  541; developmental check-ups by,
  533–4

hearing, 339–45, 533, 534; child
  with less, 342; and cleft lips and
  palates, 628; deafness and other
  severe problems, 635–7; language
  and loss of, 343–4, 374; of
  newborn baby, 340; overcoming
  deafness, 345; partial, 345; sound
  play, 342; *see also* deafness;
  ear(s)
hearing aids, 344–5, 635, 636
hearing tests, 342–4, 533, 635–6;
  acoustic cradle, 342–3, 636;
  audiometric, 636; cochlea echo,
  343; tympanometry, 572, 636
heart, heart problems and disease,
  6, 19, 108, 113, 142–3, 177,
  193, 194, 512, 622–6, 632;
  bradycardia, 193; common
  abnormalities, 622–5; congenital,
  142–3, 177, 621–6; heart
  murmur, 142, 194, 622; hole in
  the heart, 142, 622; investigations
  and tests, 625; lifestyle, 625–6;
  PDA, 194; in pregnancy, 60–1,
  106; symptoms, 625
heartburn and indigestion, 49
heat rash, 558, 562
heat shield, 191–2
height in pregnancy, 38
hepatitis, infectious, 39, 608–9
herbs, 305
heroin, 6, 522
herpes, genital, 9, 10, 57
herpes simplex, 567
Herpid, 10
hindmilk, 216
hips of newborn baby, 144–5;
  'clicking', 145; congenital
  dislocation of, 144–5, 175
hitting, 455, 459
HIV: *see* AIDS
home: after the baby, coming, 168–
  71; children coming, after
  hospital, 672; having your baby
  at, 31–2, 533; hygiene, 509;
  premature babies at, 198
hormone therapy, 56–7

hormones, 151; miscarriage caused by deficiency in, 56–7; pessaries or drips used for stimulating labour, 106–7, 117; steroids, 591, 593

horror movies, 370–1

hospital: admission procedure, 83, 663; antenatal classes, 33–4, 95; arrival in, 83–4; babies needing special care, 175–201; breastfeeding babies, 667; children in, 653–72; coming home from, 672; common procedures, 663; funeral arrangements for stillborn baby, 122; GPs' referrals to, 517; having your baby in, 32–3, 79, 83–7, 133, 167; how parents can help, 667–71; if you cannot stay with your child in, 666; isolation, 669–71; long-stay patients, 669; looking after yourself, 671; neonatal intensive care unit, 176, 181; operations, 658–61; play in, 402; post-natal classes/exercises, 166, 400; preparing children for, 654–7; SCBUs, 175, 176; and separation, 437; staying with your child in, 663–6; treatment for asthmatic children, 593; treatment for small babies with diarrhoea, 582; visiting your child in, 666–7; who's who in, 661–3; *see also* antenatal care; birth of baby; labour and delivery

housemen, 661

human chorionic gonadotrophin: *see* HCG

Huntington's chorea, 16

hyaline membrane disease: *see* RDS

hydrocephalus, 19, 43, 642, 643

hygiene, 504–9; in first six months, 505–8; germ know-how, 504–5; at home, 509; keeping your baby clean, 508; older children, 508; pets, 508; preparing food, 509

hyperactivity, 275–6

hyperemesis gravidarum, 51

hyperglycaemia, 617

hypnosis, 98

hypocalcaemia, 195

hypoglycaemia, 178, 195, 617, 618

hypospadias, 629

immune system, 504–5, 507, 526–7, 595, 626

immunisation, 526–31, 605, 606; active, 527; against rare diseases, 529; how is it done?, 529; MMR vaccine, 530; of newborn baby, 150, 527; passive, 527; of premature babies, 196; reactions to, 530–1; triple vaccine, 530, 550, 605; when is it done?, 529; whooping cough, 530–1

impetigo, 559

incontinence, 49, 545

incubators, babies in, 176, 181–2, 184, 189, 191–2, 349; infant care centres, 191

induction of labour, 105–7, 121, 312

infection, 504–5; AIDS, 9, 39, 193, 610, 626–7; bowel, 581–3; breast milk as protection from, 205, 206, 425, 505; causing asthma, 590, 594; chest, 553; ear, 344, 374, 521, 568–71, 581; eye, 573, 574; from food, 509; fungus, 505; gastric, 424–5, 581; gut, 581–3; hepatitis, 608–9; immune system against, 504–5, 507, 526–7, 595, 626; nail, 568; from pets, 508; of premature babies, 178, 193, 196; skin, 596, 598; throat, 568; urinary and kidney, 113, 423–4, 425, 426, 578–80; vaccination against, 507, 527, 529, 530, 605, 606

infection screen, 193

infectious diseases: chicken-pox, 547; diphtheria, 527, 529, 530, 605–6; fever caused by, 547–50; immunisation against, 526–7,

529; measles, 530, 548; miscarriage caused by, 57; mumps, 344, 530, 548–9; polio, 527, 529, 530, 605; risk to pregnant women of, 8–9, 547–8; *rubella*, 8–9, 39, 57, 142, 337, 342, 344, 547–8; scarlet fever, 549; serious, 605–7; tetanus, 527, 530, 605; whooping cough, 196, 527, 530–1, 549–50

infertility, 28–9

influenza, 57, 527

inheritance, 14–17; dominant, 15–16; recessive, 15; X-linked recessive, 16–17

in-laws, relationship with, 65, 67

insomnia in pregnancy, 49–50

Institute of Child Health, xi

insulin, 62–3, 616–17, 618

Intal (sodium cromoglycate), 591

intellectual development, 309

intensive care units, neo-natal, 176, 177, 179, 181, 193, 195

in-toeing, 583–4

intravenous feeding: *see* TPN

in utero surgery, 44–5

iron, 5, 46, 193, 198, 246, 259

irons, danger of burns from, 482

IUD (coil), 3, 57–8

IVH (intra-ventricular haemorrhage), 195

jaundice, 146–8, 175, 178, 193, 608–9

jelly-fish, 563

Kanner, Leo, 649

ketones, 38–9, 62

kidney (renal) disease, 425, 607–8; chronic renal failure, 608; dialysis, 607–8; transplant, 607

kidney infection, 579–80; *see also* urine, urinating

knitted baby clothes, 73–4

knock knees, 584

La Lèche League, 248

labour and delivery, 81–123; abnormal positions of baby, 116–18; accelerated, 107; acupuncture, 97; arrival in hospital, 79, 83–4; basic signs of beginning of, 82–3; bleeding, 115–16, 120; breech delivery, 54–5, 101, 108, 116, 118, 144, 175; checking on you and your baby, 100–3; cord round the neck, 119; crowning of baby's head, 86, 108; different birth positions, 92; disproportion, 120; epidurals, 33, 53, 88, 90, 95, 96, 101, 107, 108, 110, 113, 114, 118; episiotomy, 33, 54, 85, 105, 107–8, 114; false alarms, 82; father's role, 89; first moments of life, 103–5; first stage, 84, 85, 99–100; foetal distress, 119–20; forceps delivery, 92, 108–9, 114, 115, 117, 120, 175; gas and air, 95, 119; how it feels, 87–9; hypnosis, 98; induced, 105–7, 121; intermittent monitoring, 32; large babies, 312; massage during, 90–1; medical intervention, 105–13; monitoring baby's heartbeat, 101–3; pain relief, 33, 88, 90–8; Pethidine, 95; position of baby, 83, 86, 88, 101; problems, 113–23; prolapsed cord, 119; psycho-prophylaxis, 94–5; relaxation and breathing exercises, 89, 95; restitution, 86; rotation of baby's head during delivery, 101, 102, 109; second stage, 85–6, 100; show, 82; small-for-date babies, 114–15; start of, 81–3, 99; stillbirth, 120–3; stitching, 105, 166; third stage, 87, 100; TNS, 96–7; twins and more, 118; underwater delivery, 94; by vacuum, 110, 120; *see also* birth of baby; Caesarean section; contractions; premature babies

labour ward, 83–4
Lact-Aid, 209
language, 342, 345, 353–77; articulation problems, 375; and crying, 359; development of, 354–8, 469; first communications, 358–61; first sounds, 359–60; first words, 361–4; and hearing loss, 345, 374, 636; listening and understanding, 360–1; problems, 374–7; reading and writing, 371–3, 404; sign, 345, 636; slowness to understand or speak, 374–5; stories, books, TV, 367–71; voice and fluency problems, 375–7; what is?, 354
lanugo, 26, 135, 180–1
large-for-date babies, 312
laryngoscope, 190
larynx infection: *see* croup
lavatory: *see* toilet training
learning difficulties: *see* mental handicap
leaving your baby, 438–40
Lee, Laurie: 'The Firstborn', 134
leukaemia, 611
Leukaemia Society, 612
lice, head, 564
lichenification of skin, 596
lip reading, 345
lips and tongue, blue coloration of, 518
lithotomy position, 92, 109, 110, 119
liver: *see* jaundice
lochia, 120
lockjaw: *see* tetanus
longsightedness (hypermetropic), 338, 575, 577
loose joints, 585
lullabies, 340
lumbar puncture, 193, 606–7
lungs of newborn babies, 143, 147, 176, 182, 183, 189, 190–1, 194; pneumonia, 138, 193; pneumothorax, 140, 191; surfactant in, 187–8; *see also*

breathing; oxygen
luteinising hormone (LH), 28

massage: during labour, 90–1; to relax babies, 305–6
mastitis, 208, 210, 224
maternal serum screening test, 41
mattresses, 480
measles, 530, 548, 606
mebendazole, 566
meconium, 103, 119, 143, 154, 426, 580, 619; inhalation, 138, 140
medical examination in pregnancy, 39–40
medical interventions (birth of baby), 105–13; accelerated labour, 107; Caesarean section, 10, 33, 53, 54, 55, 62, 64, 95, 107, 109, 110–13, 114, 115, 116, 117, 119, 120, 131, 166, 175, 213, 312; episiotomy, 33, 54, 85, 105, 107–8, 114, 120, 135, 166; forceps, 92, 108–9, 114, 115, 117, 120, 175; induction, 105–7, 121, 312; vacuum delivery, 110
medicines, 516, 522–31; allergic reactions, 526; antibiotics, 193, 525–6; anti-convulsant, 546; giving, 523–4; immunisations, 150, 196, 526–31; over-the-counter, 526; pharmacist, 526; storing, 523; taking, without tears, 524–5; your attitude to drugs, 522–3; *see also* drugs; GPs; health clinics/centres; health problems; health visitors
memory, baby's, 334
MENCAP (Royal Society for Mentally Handicapped Children and Adults), 647
meningitis, 344, 581, 606; bacterial, 606; mumps, 549; viral, 606
mental handicap (learning difficulties), 632, 641, 645–51;

and autism, 649–51; and breastfeeding, 209–10; causes, 645–6; Down's Syndrome, 13, 41, 60, 175, 585, 632, 645, 647–9; how it first shows itself, 646; what can be done about, 646–7

microcephaly, 646

midwives, 83, 88, 94, 100, 101, 105, 106, 531; antenatal care, 37, 40, 45; community, 32, 33

migraine, 603

milk: *see* breast milk; cow's milk

minerals, 5, 204–5, 229, 257, 318

miscarriage, 3, 9, 29, 31, 40, 43, 55–9, 69, 113, 121, 122; and age, 57; causes of, 56–7; and the coil, 57–8; coping with, 59; hormone deficiency, 56–7; immunological causes of, 57, 59; and infection, 57, 59; recurrent, 56, 59; signs of, 58–9

molar pregnancy, 52

moles, 146, 560

molluscum contagiosum, 560

Mongolian blue spot, 146

mongolism: *see* Down's syndrome

Montgomery's tubercles, 211

Moro reflex, baby's, 148

mosaicism, 647

Moses basket, 75

mosquito bites, 563

mothers: adjusting to motherhood, 435–7; baby's relationship with, 429–40; bond between babies and, 126; breastfeeding problems, 223–7; coming home, 168–71; effect of cutting breastfeeds, 247; eye-to-eye contact with baby, 331; father's share of workload, 443–5; first contact with baby, 126–7; food requirements of breastfeeding, 218; and good behaviour of children, 457–61; leaving your baby, 438–40; looking after your new baby, 150–65; making friends, 400; making love again, 172–3; not

having enough milk, 218; older first-time, 60; organising your life, 171–2; piles and varicose veins, 52, 166–7; post-natal depression, 167–8; post-natal exercises, 166; problems of brothers and sisters, 445–7; reactions to premature birth, 197–8; regaining figure by breastfeeding, 206; separation from baby, 437–8; skin-to-skin contact with baby, 346–7; social life, 454; time in hospital after the baby, 167; your body, after the birth, 165–7; *see also* birth of baby; breastfeeding; labour and delivery; parents; pregnancy

mouth of baby, 141, 567; cold sores, 567; thrush, 505, 567; ulcers, 567

mouth to mouth resuscitation, 497

movement, 318–27; boys and girls, 327–9; development of, 320–6; helping your child, 326–7; how child learns, 318–19; *see also* growth

multiple pregnancies/births, 41, 63–5, 108, 118, 195

mumps, 344, 530, 548–9; meningitis, 549

muscles, 316

muscular dystrophy, 643–5; Becker, 644; Duchenne, 17, 19, 44, 643; education, 644; facio-scapulo-humeral, 644; lifestyle, 644–5; limb-girdle, 644; treatment, 644

mycoplasma, 57

myelinisation of nervous system, 317

myringotomy, 572

nail clippers, 74

nail infections, 568

Naloxone, 137

naming and playing, baby's, 335–6

nannies, 465–6

nappies, 71–3, 74, 154–60, 415, 417; care of, and folding terry towelling, 159–60; changing, 152, 154–5, 156–8, 299, 505; dry, 518; equipment for changing, 155; safety pins, 71; terry towelling vs disposable, 71, 79, 155–6; *see also* toilet training

nappy bag, 74

nappy liners, 71, 155

nappy rash, 558

naso-gastric feeding, 185

National Autistic Society, 651

National Childbirth Trust (NCT), 32, 34, 187, 301, 304, 469; ante-natal classes, 34, 36, 95, 98; Breastfeeding Promotion Group, 248; Post-Natal Support System, 307

National Council for One-Parent Families, 70, 469

National Deaf Children's Society, 637

National Deaf-Blind and Rubella Association, 637

navels, 144

nebuliser, 591, 593

nerves, nervous system, 316–17

newborn baby, 125–73; affected by Pethidine, 137; anus, 143; Apgar score, 128–30; appearance, 134–5; asleep and awake, 152; bathing, 161–3; birthweight, 130; body waste, 416; bowel movements, 154, 416; cleaning, 160–3; clearing airways, 128, 137; crying and comforting, 128, 164; developmental check-ups, 533; dislocated hips, 144–5; dressing, 163–4; ears, 141–2; eyes, 141; fathers, 65, 66, 89, 133–4; feeding, 151–2; first breathing, 127–8, 137; first check-up, 140–50; first reactions, 125–33; genitals, 143; gut problems, 580; handling, 152–4; head, 140–1; head circumference, 130, 131; hearing, 340, 636; heart, 142–3; hygiene, 505–6; immune system, 504–5; jaundice, 146–8; language development, 355; looking after, 150–65; lungs, 143, 147; meconium inhalation, 138, 140; mother's skin-to-skin contact with, 346–7; naming and playing, 335–6; nappies and nappy changing, 154–60; nose and mouth, 141; oxygen, lack of, 121, 137, 138; passive immunity, 505; play, 383; pneumonia, 138; pneumothorax, 140; recognising and remembering, 332–5; reflex actions, 148–50, 151; sensations of birth experienced by, 135–6; senses, 136–7; sight, 331–2; skin problems, 145–8, 558, 560–1; sleep patterns, 280–1; suckling, 131–3, 151, 185, 186, 207, 209, 213–15, 216, 244; taste and smell, 136–7, 350; tests and immunisation, 150; topping and tailing, 160–1; umbilical cord, 143–4; warmth, 164–5; *see also* birth; labour and delivery; special care babies

night drinks, 293

nightclothes and dressing gowns, flame resistant, 483

nightmares/night terrors, 297

nipples, 208–9, 211, 213–14, 215, 293, 294; cracked, 210, 224; inverted, 40; 'rooting for', 131; sore, 223–4; *see also* breasts

noise, 342

nose, 141; inflammation of (allergic rhinitis), 575

nosebleeds in pregnancy, 50

nursery schools, 403–4, 408, 465, 628; parent helpers, 403; private, 404; state (day), 403–4; *see also* playgroups

nurses in hospital, 662; *see also* midwives

obesity, 206, 309
oral reflexes, baby's, 148
orthopaedic problems, 583–5; bow legs, 584; club foot, 584; flat feet, 584–5; in-toeing, 583–4; knock knees, 584; loose joints, 585
outdoors, playing, 395–6
ovulation, 23, 27–8, 64
oximeters, 189
oxygen, 121, 127, 138, 140, 147, 188–9, 190, 191; BPD, 191; measuring levels of, 189; *see also* breathing
oxytocin, 82, 106–7, 112, 215, 216, 217

pain relief during labour, 33, 88, 90–8; different birth positions, 92–4; epidural anaesthetic, 96; gas and air, 95; Pethidine, 95; position and movement, 90–1; psychoprophylaxis, 94–5
painting for young children, 395
parasites, 563–7; fleas, 508, 563–4; headlice, 564; roundworms, 566; scabies, 566–7; threadworms, 559, 565–6, 579
parent helpers, 403, 413
Parent Teacher Association, 413
parents, parenthood, 65–6, 89, 133–4; adoptive, 441; communicating with children, 467–75; discipline, 459–60; good behaviour of children, 457–9; handling young children, 458–60; helping children in hospital, 667–71; hygiene, 503–9; marriage difficulties, 471; protecting your child, 477–509; reaction to premature birth, 197–8; separated and divorced, 469, 471–2; single, 69–70, 442, 468–9; talking about death, illness and handicap, 472–3; talking about religion, 473; talking about sex, 473–5; *see also* fathers; mothers
passive immunity, 505

PDA (patent ductus arteriosus), 194
peanuts, danger to small children of, 481
pedestrian accidents, 484–6
peekaboo games, 334, 380
pelvic infections, 29
perception, 331
perineum, 85, 92, 101, 107, 108, 120
periods: increasingly painful, 29; infrequent, 29; missed, 2, 30
pertussis: *see* whooping cough
Pethidine, 95, 137, 188
petit mal: *see* epilepsy
petrol or paraffin, 483, 484
pets, 508
pharmacist, 526
Phenergan, 295
phenylketonuria (PKU), 150, 632
phosopholipids, 57
phototherapy, 147–8, 175
physically handicapped babies, breastfeeding, 208, 209–10
piles (haemorrhoids), 52, 166–7
Pill, 3, 53
pillows, 480
pimples, 560
piperazine, 566
placenta or afterbirth, 52, 53, 87, 100, 105, 106, 115, 118, 120; *abruptio placentae*, 115–16; position in pregnancy, 43; retained, 120
placenta praevia, 43, 53, 110, 115
plaque, 536
plaster of Paris, 663
plastic bags, danger of, 481
plastic pants, baby's, 73, 155–6
play, 335, 379–408; creative, 379–80; cuts and other accidents through, 491–2; different types of, 379–80; experimental, 379; fantasy, 380; freedom, 391–2; with friends, 380; in hospital, 402; indoors, 396–7; making friends, 400, 451–4; messy, 380, 393–7; and order, 392–3;

play – *cont.*
   organising, 391–3; outdoors, 395–6; parents' help in, 380–2; physical, energetic, 379; routine, 399–400; safety, 382, 391; for sick children, 400–2; sound, 342; stages of, 383–9; storage of toys, 392–3; water, 395, 397; *see also* education
playdough, 396
playgrounds, safety of, 492
playgroups, 403, 404–8, 411, 465; boys vs girls, 407; choosing, 404–7; preparing your child to start, 407–8; singing and storytelling, 407; *see also* nursery schools
playpen, 76, 491
pneumonia, 138, 193, 530
pneumothorax (puncture of the lung), 140, 192
poisoning, 479, 494–5; first aid for, 499
poliomyelitis (polio), 527, 529, 530, 605
pollutants, 6
polycythaemia, 195
polytube feeding, 185
Portuguese man-of-war sting, 563
port wine stains, 146, 561
post-natal classes, 33, 34, 400
post-natal depression (the blues), 167–8
post-natal exercises, 166
post-partum haemorrhage, 87, 105
potty training: *see* toilet training
prams, 75–6
pre-conceptual (antenatal) care, 1–21; environmental factors, 3–10; genetic counselling, 18–21; genetic factors, 10–17
pre-eclampsia/pre-eclamptic toxaemia, 38, 40, 53, 106, 113
pregnancy, 23–79; age and other risks, 57, 59–60; antenatal classes, 32, 33–6; avoiding X-rays in early, 46–7; becoming pregnant, 27–8; bleeding, 52–3; changes in breasts during, 30, 212; clinical tests, 38–9; dangers of *rubella*, 8–9, 547–8; diabetes, 62–3; dreams, 68; dropping of baby's head in last weeks, 78; early days of life, 24–7; eating sensibly and weight gain, 45–6; ectopic, 24, 41; emotions during, 67–8; expressing colostrum in last months, 78; fantasy feelings, 70; fertilisation, 23–4; fertility, 27–9; first twelve weeks, 2; growth of baby in womb, 310–11; heart disease, 60–1; high blood pressure and pre-eclampsia, 38, 40, 53, 60; how you feel during, 65–70; *in utero* surgery, 44–5; making decisions, 31–7; medical examination, 39–40; minor physical problems, 47–52; miscarriage, 55–9; molar, 52; morbid feelings during, 68; more serious problems, 52–9; multiple, 41, 63–5; novice's guide to antenatal care, 37–40; older first-time mothers, 60; packing a bag, 79; pre-conceptual care, 1–21; rhesus factor, 39, 61–2; second and third, 60; sex during, 69; shopping for baby, 71–6; sickness and nausea during, 30, 50–1; signs of, 29–31; single parents, 69–70; towards the end of, 78–9; travel arrangements, 79; unusual birth positions, 54–5; vaginal discharge, 51; *see also* birth of baby; labour and delivery
pregnancy tests, 30–1
premature babies/labour, 9, 60, 69, 107, 110, 113–14, 121, 177–200; apnoeic attacks, 188; blood and heart problems, 193–4; brain damage, 195; breastfeeding, 186–7, 209, 217; breathing, 187–91; death, 179, 183, 199–200; development, 196; and growth, 311–12; immunisation, 196;

infection, 193; keeping them warm, 191–2, 285; multiple births, 64, 118, 195; parents' reactions to, 197–8; twins and more, 195; weight, 181, 311–12; what they look like, 180–1; *see also* birth of baby; labour and delivery; special care babies
pre-med, 658–9
Preschool Playgroups Association, 404
projectile vomiting, 243
prolactin, 212
prolapse, 107
prolapsed cord, 110, 119, 121
prostaglandin pessaries to induce labour, 106
prostaglandins, 82, 243
protecting your child, 477–509; buying goods, 479–80; emergency first aid, 496–504; hygiene, 503–9; parents' checklist of accidents, 480–96; safety, 477–80
protein, 257, 258–9, 318; AFP levels, 40–1; in breast milk, 204; in cow's milk, 205, 229; in urine, 38, 53
psoriasis, 346
psychoprophylaxis (natural childbirth), 94–5
pubic shave, 83–4, 112
pudental block, 108
punishment, 460–1
pyloric stenosis, 243

Queen Elizabeth Hospital, xi
quins, 64, 195

radiant heater/warmer, 192, 193
radio-immunoassay test, 31
rapid eye movement sleep: *see* REM sleep
RDS (respiratory distress syndrome), 187, 188, 189; CPAP to relieve, 189
reading and writing, 371–3, 404

recognising and remembering, baby's, 332–5, 337
red eye, 574
referrals, GP's, 517
reflex actions, baby's, 148–50, 151, 209
Regional Health Authority, Family Practitioner Committee, 512, 513
registrar, 661
relationships, 429–75; adjusting to motherhood, 435–7; aggression, 454–6; and baby's social development, 430–4; bonding, 126, 437, 442; breastfeeding, 435, 442–3; brothers and sisters, 445–7; communicating with children, 469–75; fathers, 441–5; fears, 461–2; friends, 450–4; good behaviour, 457–61; grandparents, 447–50; leaving your baby, 438–40; separation, 437–8; sharing, 456–7; sharing the workload, 443–5; single parenthood, 468–9; social problems, 453–4; working mothers and child minders, 438–9, 462–9; your baby, 429–30; your baby and other people, 441–53
relaxation and breathing exercises, 33, 34, 47, 89, 95
religion, talking about, 473
REM (rapid eye movement) sleep, 280
renal failure: *see* kidney disease
reproductive organs, female, 24
respiratory distress syndrome, *see* RDS
restitution, 86
retinoscopy, 577
rhesus factor, 39, 61–2
'ringworm', 560
rotavirus, 583
roundworms, 508, 566; from dogs and cats, 566
Royal National Institute for the Deaf, 637, 638

Royal Society for the Prevention of Accidents, 484; 'Tufty' clubs, 484
rubella: *see* German measles

safety, 477–80, 508; buying goods, 479–80; in play, 382, 391; *see also* accidents to children; first aid
safety-gate, 495
safety harnesses, 486–9, 495
safety-pins, nappy, 71
salbutamol (Ventolin), 591, 593
sandpit, 395
SANDS (Stillbirth and Neonatal Death Society), 122
sandwiches, 263–4
sauna baths, 6
scabies, 559, 566–7
scalds and burns, 477, 479, 482–4, 519; baths, 482–3; cookers, 482; fireworks, 483; first aid for, 498; irons, 482; matches and lighters, 483; night clothes and dressing gowns, 483; petrol or paraffin, 483
scarlet fever, 549
school(s), 410–13; choosing, 410–11; clothes, 412; deaf, 345; infants', 403; nursery, 403–4, 408, 411, 465, 628; opting out, 410; parent helpers, 413; prep, 404; primary, 404, 410–11; private, 411; special, 179; starting, 411–13; *see also* education; playgroups
screaming, 519
senses, 331–51; hearing, 339–45; taste and smell, 350–1; touch, 345–9; vision, 331–9
sentences, first, 362–3
separation and divorce, 469, 471–2
separation of mother from baby, 437–40
septicaemia, 193
sex: during pregnancy, 69; making love again after birth, 172–3; talking about, 473–5

sexual abuse, 474–5
sextuplets, 64
sexually transmitted diseases, in pregnancy, 9–10; *see also* AIDS
sharing, 456–7
sheath (contraceptive), 3
shingles, 547
shock, first aid for, 502
shopping for baby, 71–6; clothes, 73–4, 79; equipment, 74–8; incidentals, 74; nappies, 71–3, 79
short-sightedness (myopia), 338, 577
short stature, 614–15
sickle cell disease, 39, 44, 612–13
sickness and nausea in pregnancy, 30, 50–1; *see also* vomiting
sign language, 345, 636
single parents, 442, 468–9; of handicapped children, 635; pregnancy, 69–70
sleep, sleeping, 279–99; baby alarm systems and mattresses, 285–6; bed for baby, 284–5; bedtime routine, 282–4; a book at bedtime, 289–91; cat naps, 280; changing bad sleeping habits, 293–4; children who won't go to bed, 294–5; comforters and comfort habits, 286–8, 293–4; drugs for, 295–6; early wakers, 296–7; encouraging different pattern between day and night, 281; fear of the dark, 297; four stages of, 280; head banging, 297; moving from cot to bed, 288–9; nightmares and night terrors, 297; older children, 294, 296; patterns in newborn baby, 280–1; position of baby, 285; problems, 291–9; REM, 280; twins, 295; types of, 280; ways of settling children at night, 293–4; which room?, 286; why we need, 280; *see also* crying
skin, 557–62; birthmarks, 146, 560–1; control of temperature

through, 345–6, 557, 589; diseases, 346; dry, 558; eczema, 296, 346, 541, 558–9, 575, 595–600; effect of emotions on, 346; heat rash and sweat rash, 558; impetigo, 559–60; infants' and older children's problems, 558–61; infection, 596, 598–9; learning through, 345–6; moles, 560; *molluscum contagiosum*, 560; nappy rash, 558; newborn and young babies' problems, 145–8, 558; pimples and boils, 560; in pregnancy, 51; 'ringworm', 560; and state of health, 346; sunburn and heatstroke, 561–2; warts, 560–1
skin-to-skin contact, 346–7
sleepwalking and sleeptalking, 297
slings, baby, 302, 332
small babies, 177–81; temperature/warmth of, 192–3; *see also* premature babies; special care babies
small-for-date babies, 114–15, 177, 178, 310, 312
smallpox, 527
smell, baby's sense of, 136, 350
smoke detector, 484
smoking, 522, 523; and asthma, 590; in bed, 483; in pregnancy, 3–4, 53, 310
snake bites, 503, 563
sneezing of newborn baby, 141
social problems of children: aggression, 454–6; difficulties in making friends, 453–4; sharing, 456–7
sodium cromoglycate (Intal), 591
sore throat, 521, 545, 553
sound(s): first, 359–60; habituation, 342; linking meaning with, 340; newborn baby's reaction to, 136, 341–2; play, 342; to soothe babies, 303, 340; *see also* hearing
Spastics Society, 641
special care babies, 175–201; blood and heart problems, 193–4; brain damage, 195; breathing, 187–91; death of, 179, 183, 199–201; development, 196; feeding, 184–7; fits, 195; immunisation, 196; infection, 193; intensive care units, 176; parents' reactions, 197–8; problems, 184–95; separation of mothers, 437; small babies, 177–81; surgery for, 177; temperature-warmth, 177, 180, 191–2; twins and more, 195; weight, 177, 181; what it means for the family, 181–4; *see also* premature babies
Special Care Baby Units (SCBU), 175, 176
speech: and cleft lips and palates, 375, 627–8; and hearing, 342, 344; problems, 374–7; *see also* language
spina bifida, 19, 40, 43, 46, 56, 177, 530, 641–3; education, 643; lifestyle, 643; treatment, 642
spinhaler, 591
splinters, first aid for, 501–2
sports and games, 326–7
spots: harmless, 145; septic, 146
sprains, first aid for, 502
squatting during labour, 92; supported, 92, 94
squint, 332, 338, 517, 575–7
startle reflex, baby's, 148–9
steroids, 591, 593, 598–9
sticky eye, 141, 573
sties, 575
stillbirth, 9, 120–3; the birth, 121; practicalities, 122; reactions after, 122–3
stings: *see* bites and stings
stitches after childbirth, 105, 166
stomach infections/upsets, 424–5, 580–3
stork marks, 141, 146, 561
strawberry marks, 146, 561
stretch marks, 51, 166
stretch-suits, 73, 79

suckling, sucking, 131–3, 151, 184, 186, 207, 209, 213–15, 216, 244; for comfort, 288, 304–5, 349; *see also* breastfeeding
suffocation and choking, 477, 479, 480–1; first aid for, 496–7
sugar, 350; as cause of tooth decay, 537–8; in urine, 38
sunburn, 561–2
surfactant, 114, 127, 188–9
surgery/operations, 658–61; babies needing, 177; for cleft lips and palates, 627–8; *in utero*, 44–5; *see also* medical interventions
swaddling, 245, 303–4
sweat rash, 558
sweating, 346; in pregnancy, 51
sweets, 257, 258, 265–6
swelling (oedema), in pregnancy, 40, 51, 53
swimming, 326, 489, 490
swings and slides, safety of, 492
Syntocinon, 87
syphilis, 9, 39

table manners, 266
taste, 137, 350; *see also* diet; feeding
teeth, 534–9; food for healthy, 537–8; going to the dentist, 538–9; looking after, 536–7; milk, 534, 536; order of appearance, 534, 536; plaque, 536; when to start cleaning, 536–7
teething, 534
telemetric equipment, 103
television, 336, 367, 368, 370–1
temperature: raised, 542–5; skin's control of, 345–6, 557; of small babies, 191–2; taking your child's, 543; tepid sponging to lower, 543–4; *see also* fever and raised temperature
TENS: *see* transcutaneous nerve stimulation
terry towelling nappies, 71, 79, 154–60; care of, 159; changing,

156–8; folding, 159–60; vs disposable nappies, 155–6
testicles, 143; undescended, 629, 632
test-tube treatments, 64
tetanus (lockjaw), 527, 530, 605
thalassaemia, 39, 44, 614
thermal blanket, 192
thermometer, 543
threadworms, 559, 565–6, 579
throat: infections, 553; sore, 521, 545, 553; tonsillitis, 554–5
thrush, 505, 567, 579
thumb sucking, 286–7, 304–5
thyroid glands, 150
TNS: *see* transcutaneous nerve stimulation
toilet training, 317, 415–27, 449; accidental wetting, 423–4; body waste, 415–16; common problems, 420–7; early setbacks, 419; illness and infection, 424–7; potty or lavatory, 419–20; when to start, 416–18
tonsils, tonsillitis, 554–5
toothpastes, 537
topping and tailing, 160–1, 508
total parental nutrition: *see* TPN
touch, 345–9; feeling through skin, 345–6; importance of contact, 346–7; individual differences, 347–9; and sight, 332, 334–5
toxocara, 508
toxocariasis, 566
toxoplasmosis, 8, 57, 508, 638
toys and playthings, 383–400; accidents from, 492; hygiene, 507; storage, 392–3
TPN (total parental nutrition), 184, 186
traffic/road accidents, 479, 484–9; children as car passengers, 486–8; Green Cross Code, 484; pedestrians, 484–6; travelling in other people's cars, 488
transcutaneous nerve stimulation (TNS or TENS), 96–7

transcutaneous oxygen electrode, 189
transverse arrest, 109
triplets, 63, 64, 195, 226–7
trisomy, 647
tube-feeding, 185
tuberculosis (TB), 150
Turner's syndrome, 13
twins, 63–4; breastfeeding, 225–6; fraternal, 63, 64, 118; identical, 63, 64, 118; labour and delivery, 118; premature, 118; sleeping, 295; in special care, 195
Twins Club, 65, 225
tympanometer, 572, 636

uE₃ (unconjugated oestriol), 41
ulcers: mouth, 567; on tip of penis, 579
ultrasound scans, 19, 26, 31, 41, 43, 44, 45, 53, 58, 64, 115, 178, 196, 578, 625, 642
umbilical cord, 87, 100, 103, 105, 115, 127, 135, 212; after being cut, 143–4; infection of, 144; prolapsed, 117, 119; round the neck, 119
umbilical hernia, 144
underwater delivery, 94
urine, urinating, 38–9, 53; accidental wetting, 423–4; and congenital disorders, 426–7; foreskin infections, 579; infection, 113, 423–5, 426, 521, 578–9, 581; kidney disease/infection, 425, 578, 579–80, 607–8; mid-stream urine sample, 38, 83, 578; not passing as much, 521; pain passing, 521; in pregnancy, 30, 38–9, 49; problems, 521; smelling, 521, 578; and vaginal discharge, 579; *see also* toilet training
urticaria, neonatal, 146
uterus, 120; contraction of muscles, 84, 85, 87

vaccinations, 507, 527, 529, 530, 605; MMR vaccine, 530; triple vaccine, 530, 550, 605, 606; reactions to, 530, *see also* immunisation
vacuum delivery, 110
vacuum extractor (or ventouse), 110, 120
vagina: and birth of baby, 85–6, 87, 92, 103, 105, 108, 109, 120, 567; discharge, 51, 579; infection, 579
Vallergan, 295
varicose veins, 40, 52, 166–7
VDUs (visual display units), 6
vegetarian and vegan diets, before pregnancy, 5
ventilators, babies on, 176, 179–80, 182, 190, 191
Ventolin (salbutamol), 591, 593
vernix (greasy protective film), 26, 135
verrucas, 560
vesico-ureteric reflux, 425, 426
vests, baby, 73, 79
videos, 370–1
viruses, viral infections, 504–5, 525–6, 526, 547–8, 560, 567, 574, 581, 606, 608–9, 626–7
visual display units: *see* VDUs
visual impairment: *see* eyesight
vitamins, 5, 46, 150, 204–5, 239–41, 257, 318
voice problems, 375, 377
vomiting, 518, 519, 521, 522, 581, 582, 583; projectile, 243

wakefulness, 279, 286, 291; *see also* crying; sleep
walking reflex, baby's, 150
warmth, 164–5; of small babies, 178, 180, 191–2, 346
warts, 560
washing machine, 71
washing up, playing at, 397
wasp stings, 562–3
water play, 395, 397

waters, breaking of amniotic, 81, 82, 84, 103, 106; prematurely, 114

weaning, 245–50, 293; cow's milk, 247; cutting breastfeeds, 248; cutting down on milk, 247; finger food, 250; first tastes – what to expect, 246; learning about lumps, 248; learning to feed themselves, 250; vitamin supplements, 239–41; what to feed, 246

weather, asthma triggered by, 591

weight: birthweight, 2, 130, 177, 181, 210, 311; and growth, 312–14; overweight children, 263, 272–5, 309; during pregnancy, 38, 45

wet lung (transient tachypnoea), 189

wetting, 416, 423–4

wheezing, 553; asthmatic, 590–1, 593, 594, 595

whooping cough (pertussis), 549–50, 555, 581; immunisation, 527, 530–1

wind, bringing up, 216, 237, 242, 243

witches' milk, 143

womb, growth of baby in, 310–11; *see also* pregnancy

working women, 171; and breastfeeding, 222–3, 462; child minders, 438, 463–8; entitlements, 36–7; pregnant, 36–7, 65, 70; separation from baby, 437; single parents, 468–9

worry, *see* emotions and anxieties

X-rays, 8, 46–7, 625, 663

yoga classes, 36